Cambodia

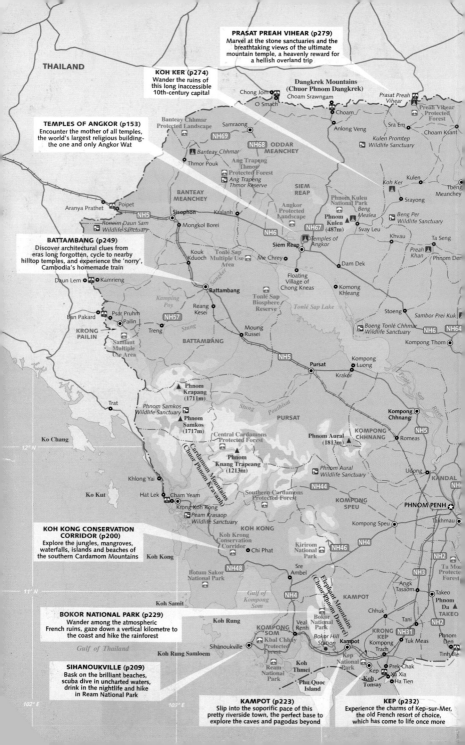

THAILAND

PRASAT PREAH VIHEAR (p279)
Marvel at the stone sanctuaries and the
breathtaking views of the ultimate
mountain temple, a heavenly reward for
a hellish overland trip

KOH KER (p274)
Wander the ruins of
this long inaccessible
10th-century capital

TEMPLES OF ANGKOR (p153)
Encounter the mother of all temples,
the world's largest religious building-
the one and only Angkor Wat

BATTAMBANG (p249)
Discover architectural clues from
eras long forgotten, cycle to nearby
hilltop temples, and experience the 'norry',
Cambodia's homemade train

**KOH KONG CONSERVATION
CORRIDOR (p200)**
Explore the jungles, mangroves,
waterfalls, islands and beaches of
the southern Cardamom Mountains

BOKOR NATIONAL PARK (p229)
Wander among the atmospheric
French ruins, gaze down a vertical kilometre to
the coast and hike the rainforest

SIHANOUKVILLE (p209)
Bask on the brilliant beaches,
scuba dive in uncharted waters,
drink in the nightlife and hike
in Ream National Park

KAMPOT (p223)
Slip into the soporific pace of this
pretty riverside town, the perfect base to
explore the caves and pagodas beyond

KEP (p232)
Experience the charms of Kep-sur-Mer,
the old French resort of choice,
which has come to life once more

Dangkrek Mountains
(Chuor Phnom Dangkrek)

Chong Jom
O Smach
Choam Srawngam
Choam
Prasat Preah
Vihear
Preah Vihear
Protected
Forest

Banteay Chhmar
Protected Landscape
Samraong
NH69
ODDAR
MEANCHEY
Sra Em
Choam Ksant

Thmor Pouk
Banteay Chhmar
Ang Trapeng
Thmor
Protected Forest
NH68
Anlong Veng
Kulen Promtep
Wildlife Sanctuary

BANTEAY
MEANCHEY
Ang Trapeng
Thmor Reserve
SIEM
REAP
Koh Ker
Kulen
Tbeng
Meanchey

Aranya Prathet
Poipet
Sisophon
Kralanh
Phnom Kulen
National Park
Phnom
Kulen
(487m)
Beng
Mealea
Beng Per
Wildlife Sanctuary
Srayong

NH5
Roneim Daun Sam
Wildlife Sanctuary
Mongkol Borei
Angkor
Protected
Landscape
NH6
NH67
Temples of
Angkor
Svay Leu
Khvau
Preah
Khan
Ta Seng
Phnom Der

Kouk
Kduoch
Tonlé Sap
Multiple Use
Area
Siem Reap
Me Chrey
Dam Dek

Daun Lem
Kamrieng
Battambang
Reang
Kesei
Floating
Village of
Chong Kneas
Komong
Khleang

Ban Pakard
Psar Pruhm
Pailin
NH57
Treng
Kamping
Poy
Tonlé Sap
Biosphere
Reserve
Tonlé Sap Lake
Stoeng
Sambor Prei Kuk
NH6
NH64

KRONG
PAILIN
Samlaut
Multiple
Use Area
Stung
BATTAMBANG
Moung
Russei
Boeng Tonlé Chhmar
Wildlife Sanctuary
Kompong Thom

Trat
Phnom
Krapang
(1711m)
NH5
Pursat
Kompong
Luong
Krakor
Kompong
Chhnang

Phnom Samkos
Wildlife Sanctuary
Phnom
Samkos
(1717m)
PURSAT
Stung
Pouthisat
KOMPONG
CHHNANG
NH5
Romeas

Ko Chang
Central Cardamons
Protected Forest
Phnom Aural
(1813m)

12° N
Phnom
Knang Trapeang
(1213m)
Phnom Aural
Wildlife Sanctuary
Udong
KANDAL
NH

Khlong Yai
Southern Cardamons
Protected Forest
NH44
KOMPONG
SPEU
PHNOM PENH

Ko Kut
Hat Lek
Cham Yeam
Krong Koh Kong
Peam Krasaop
Wildlife Sanctuary
Kompong Speu
Takhmau

Koh Kong
Koh Kong
Conservation
Corridor
Chi Phat
KOH KONG
Kirirom
National
Park
NH4
NH46
NH2
Ta Mor
Protected
Forest

Koh Samit
Botum Sakor
National Park
NH48
Sre Ambel
NH3
Angk
Tasaom
Takeo
Phnom
Du
TAKEO

11° N
Koh Rung
NH4
Veal
Renh
Bokor
National
Park
KAMPOT
Chhuk
Tani
NH31
Phnom Den

Gulf of
Kompong
Som
KOMPONG
SOM
Kbal Chhay
Protected
Forest
Bokor Hill
Station
KRONG
KEP
Kompong
Trach
Tuk Meas
Tinh Bie

Sihanoukville
Ream
National
Park
Koh
Thmei
Kampot
Kep
National
Park
Prek-Chak
Xa Xia

Gulf of Thailand
Koh Rung Samloem
Phu Quoc
Island
Kep
Koh
Tonsay
Ha Tien

102° E
103° E

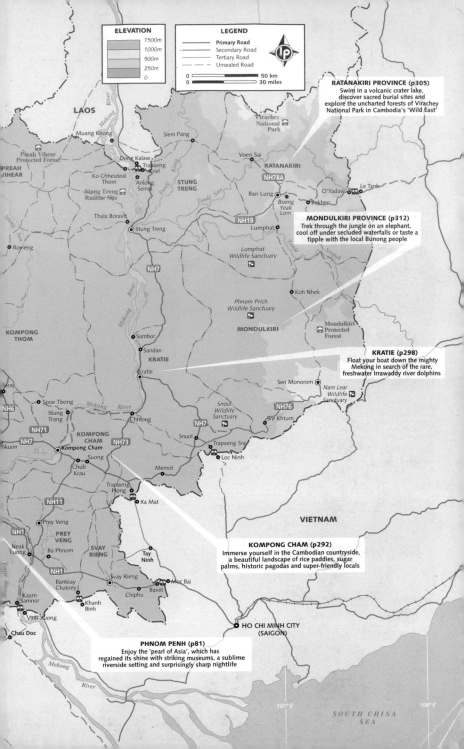

ELEVATION

1500m
1000m
500m
250m
0

LEGEND

Primary Road
Secondary Road
Tertiary Road
Unsealed Road

0 ——— 50 km
0 ——— 30 miles

RATANAKIRI PROVINCE (p305)
Swim in a volcanic crater lake,
discover sacred burial sites and
explore the uncharted forests of Virachey
National Park in Cambodia's 'Wild East'

MONDULKIRI PROVINCE (p312)
Trek through the jungle on an elephant,
cool off under secluded waterfalls or taste a
tipple with the local Bunong people

KRATIE (p298)
Float your boat down the mighty
Mekong in search of the rare,
freshwater Irrawaddy river dolphins

KOMPONG CHAM (p292)
Immerse yourself in the Cambodian countryside,
a beautiful landscape of rice paddies, sugar
palms, historic pagodas and super-friendly locals

PHNOM PENH (p81)
Enjoy the 'pearl of Asia', which has
regained its shine with striking museums, a sublime
riverside setting and surprisingly sharp nightlife

LAOS

PREAH VIHEAR

Preah Vihear
Protected Forest

Muang Khong

Siem Pang

Dong Kalaw
Trapaeng
Kriel
Ko Chheuteal
Thom
Anlong
Seima
Stung Treng
Ramsar Site

Thala Boravit

STUNG
TRENG

Virachey
National
Park

Voen Sai

RATANAKIRI

NH78A

Ban Lung

O'Yadaw

Le Tanh

Bokheo

Boeng
Yeak
Lom

Rovieng

Stung Treng

NH19

Lumphat

Lomphat
Wildlife Sanctuary

KOMPONG
THOM

NH7

Koh Nhek

Sambor

Sandan

KRATIE

Kratie

Phnom Prich
Wildlife Sanctuary

MONDULKIRI

Mondulkiri
Protected
Forest

Jaray

Spoe Tbong

Stung
Trang

Chhlong

Sen Monorom

Nam Lear
Wildlife
Sanctuary

NH6

NH71

KOMPONG
CHAM

NH7

Snoul
Wildlife
Sanctuary

NH76

Sre Khtum

NH7

Skuon

Kompong Cham

NH73

Suong

Snoul

Trapaeng Sre

Loc Ninh

Chub
Krau

Memot

NH11

Trapaeng
Plong

Xa Mat

Prey Veng

PREY
VENG

NH1

SVAY
RIENG

Tay
Ninh

VIETNAM

Neak
Luong

Ba Phnom

Svay Rieng

Moc Bai

NH1

Banteay
Chakrey

Chiphu

Bavet

Kaam
Samnor

Khanh
Binh

Vinh Xuong

HO CHI MINH CITY
(SAIGON)

Chau Doc

Mekong
River

Mekong
River

SOUTH CHINA
SEA

107° E

108° E

On the Road

NICK RAY Coordinating Author
This photo was taken at Prasat Preah Vihear (p279), the king of the mountain temples, and has to be one of my favourite views in Cambodia – the extensive plains of lowland Cambodia melting into the infinite horizon. Border tensions between Thailand and Cambodia means almost no tourists are visiting at this time. A motorcycle adventure from the Cambodian side remains a real adventure, although a risky one with the two armies facing off over barbed wire. Preah Vihear was where the Khmer Rouge made their last stand, so you still need to be careful of land mines, but equally dangerous are the ferocious winds that whip across the ridge. Careful how close you stand to the edge.

DANIEL ROBINSON This enormous jackfruit, for sale on an upturned roadside basket, made my mouth water as I anticipated its sweet, spongy, fragrant flesh. The local kids – this was on the car-less Mekong island of Koh Paen (p293) – were as captivated by me as I was by the monster fruit.

GREG BLOOM The notorious 57km 'road' from Koh Nhek to Lumphat is a convoluted maze of rutted single tracks bisecting the backcountry of Ratanakiri and Mondulkiri. Here I'm standing at the point where the trail empties into the Srepok River in Lumphat (p311), having just survived the four-hour trip on the back of a *moto*. From there, it was on to Ban Lung for a well-deserved frosty beverage.

For full author biographies see p372.

Cambodia Highlights

For a relatively small country, Cambodia packs in the highlights, offering everything from ancient jungle temples to sophisticated designer restaurants, from isolated and windswept national parks to a pristine coastline peppered with tropical islands.

Angkor is a tour de force of temples, but even Phnom Penh is no slouch with its iconic Silver Pagoda. Provincial destinations provide charming escapes, including the chance to ride the bamboo train in Battambang or chow down on crab in Kep.

Wherever you go, the welcome is warm and the smiles are wide, as the Cambodian people are some of the friendliest in the region.

JOHN BANAGAN

1 BAYON, ANGKOR

Ever get the feeling you're being watched? More than 200 carved stone faces, thought to be portraits of the Khmer King Jayavarman VII, gaze down from the lofty towers of Bayon (p172), giving visitors a distinct inferiority complex.

Laurakb, Traveller

JULIET COO

2 THE PEOPLE OF CAMBODIA

Cycling around Cambodia gave us the opportunity to visit the main attractions as well as smaller towns and villages. Wherever we went, one thing remained constant: the Cambodian people love to chat! We were greeted with smiles and a chorus of hellos wherever we went, and the high standard of English among the young enabled more in-depth discussions. Although some were shy at first, we found that stumbling through a sentence in Khmer (p363) soon broke the ice, and before long the conversation was flowing.

Claire Dann and Tabitha Langford, Travellers

ANDERS BLOM

3 TA PROHM

The temple of Ta Prohm (p181), in the middle of the jungle at Angkor, is one of the most awe-inspiring places I have ever been in. Walk through the ruined temples, half devoured by the giant roots of the trees, and pull a Lara Croft if you can!

Crisonthemove, Traveller

ROYAL PALACE & SILVER PAGODA

Angkor Wat is impressive, but head to the Royal Palace (p92) in the nation's capital for a truly rich experience! The Silver Pagoda's temple floor, covered with gleaming silver tiles, seems out of place in the weathered Cambodian landscape. The Royal Palace grounds are equally remarkable. Cambodia is a land of extremes, and this is the lush, royal end of it.

moontorch, Traveller

4

CAROL WILEY

BATTAMBANG

I had an awesome day exploring the country-side around Battambang (p249) on the back of a motorbike. We hired *moto* drivers for the day who took us to visit local villages – we saw the muscle-straining way that rice noodles are made, watched chillies drying in the sun and smelled the unforgettable stench of giant vats of maturing fish paste. Caked in dust by the end of the day, we then climbed aboard the ingenious bamboo train for the ride back to Battambang.

Sasha Baskett, Lonely Planet Staff

DANIEL BOAG

5

ANDREW BURKE

6

BOKOR HILL STATION

Walk among the ruins of the ghostly Bokor Hill Station (p229), an old colonial retreat built by the French in the 1920s and later occupied by Khmer Rouge and Vietnamese forces in the war. The eerie hotel has been likened to the one in *The Shining,* but this one has bullet holes in the walls.

cheryn, Traveller

BAMBOO TRAIN

Take one engine and an axle, place on railway tracks and balance fence panel on top – welcome to Cambodia's bamboo train (p252). Take your seat and hold on tight, relying on your 10-year-old driver to suss whether there's a train coming in the opposite direction. Short prayer optional.

providores, Traveller

NEIL SETCHFIELD / AL.

7

JERRY REDFERN / ONASIA

8

CRAB IN KEP

The seaside town of Kep (p232) is slowly waking up from its post-war slumber and is fast becoming a fresh-seafood mecca. Picking our own sea creatures and having them prepared before our eyes made this a real highlight. We joined the banter and bought crab from the women keeping the crustaceans fresh in floating baskets – the competition is fierce and it's a lot of fun. We were spoilt for choice, but the omnipresent crab with Kampot pepper is surely not to be missed. We left Kep licking our lips.

Annelies Mertens, Lonely Planet Staff

FELIX

9

MASSAGE IN SIEM REAP

After sweltering among the temples, we opted for a soothing massage with Siem Reap's blind masseurs (p136). Have you ever conversed with someone where neither of you spoke the same language and they couldn't interpret your visual clues? Despite comic misunderstandings, we finally donned loose pyjamas and lay down. An elderly woman, with an astonishing amount of strength in her small hands, began pummelling me. It may not have been the soothing experience I was looking for, but I was inspired on so many levels – ability despite disability; determination in spite of circumstance.

Jennifer Garrett, Lonely Planet Staff

Contents

On the Road   4

Cambodia Highlights   5

Destination
Cambodia   12

Getting Started   14

Events Calendar   19

Itineraries   20

History   25

The Culture   44

Food & Drink   57

Environment   66

Colours of Cambodia   73

Phnom Penh   81
History   82
Orientation   83
Information   85
Dangers & Annoyances   91
Sights   92
Activities   98
Walking Tour   100
Phnom Penh for Children   101
Tours   102
Sleeping   102
Eating   106
Drinking   114
Entertainment   116
Shopping   117
Getting There & Away   120
Getting Around   121

AROUND PHNOM PENH   123
Kien Svay   123
Udong   124
Tonlé Bati   125
Phnom Tamao Wildlife
Rescue Centre   126
Phnom Chisor   126
Kirirom National Park   127

Siem Reap   128
History   129
Orientation   129
Information   129
Dangers & Annoyances   131
Sights   132
Activities   136
Siem Reap for Children   137
Tours   137
Sleeping   137
Eating   142
Drinking   146
Entertainment   147
Shopping   147
Getting There & Away   149
Getting Around   150
AROUND SIEM REAP   151
Prek Toal Bird Sanctuary   151
Ang Trapeng Thmor
Reserve   151
Floating Village of
Chong Kneas   151
Flooded Forest of
Kompong Pluk   152
Kompong Khleang   152
Me Chrey   152

Temples of Angkor 153
History   153
Archaeology of Angkor   157
Architectural Styles   157
Orientation   159
Information   159
Itineraries   162
Tours   165
Getting There & Around   165
ANGKOR WAT   167
Symbolism   167
Architectural Layout   168
Bas-Reliefs   169
ANGKOR THOM   172

Bayon	172
Baphuon	176
Royal Enclosure & Phimeanakas	177
Preah Palilay	177
Tep Pranam	177
Preah Pithu	177
Terrace of the Leper King	177
Terrace of Elephants	178
Kleangs & Prasat Suor Prat	178
AROUND ANGKOR THOM	**179**
Baksei Chamkrong	179
Phnom Bakheng	179
Chau Say Tevoda	180
Thommanon	180
Spean Thmor	180
Ta Keo	181
Ta Nei	181
Ta Prohm	181
Banteay Kdei & Sra Srang	182
Prasat Kravan	182
Preah Khan	184
Preah Neak Poan	185
Ta Som	185
Eastern Baray & Eastern Mebon	185
Pre Rup	186
Banteay Samré	186
Western Baray & Western Mebon	186
ROLUOS TEMPLES	**187**
Preah Ko	187
Bakong	187
Lolei	188
AROUND ANGKOR	**188**
Phnom Krom	188
Phnom Bok	188
Chau Srei Vibol	189
Banteay Srei	189
Kbal Spean	190
Phnom Kulen	190
Beng Mealea	191
Remote Angkorian Sites	193

South Coast   194

KOH KONG PROVINCE	**196**
Krong Koh Kong	196
Koh Kong Conservation Corridor	200
KOMPONG SOM PROVINCE	**209**
Sihanoukville	209
Around Sihanoukville	222
KAMPOT PROVINCE	**223**

Kampot	223
Around Kampot	228
Bokor National Park	229
Kompong Trach	231
KRONG KEP	**232**
Kep	232
Around Kep	235
TAKEO PROVINCE	**236**
Takeo	236
Around Takeo	238

Northwestern Cambodia   240

KOMPONG CHHNANG PROVINCE	**242**
Kompong Chhnang	242
PURSAT PROVINCE	**245**
Pursat	245
Kompong Luong	247
Northern Cardamom Mountains	247
BATTAMBANG PROVINCE	**249**
Battambang	249
Around Battambang	256
KRONG PAILIN	**258**
Pailin	258
Samlaut	260
BANTEAY MEANCHEY PROVINCE	**261**
Poipet	261
Sisophon	263
Banteay Chhmar	265
ODDAR MEANCHEY PROVINCE	**266**
Samraong	266
O Smach	267
Anlong Veng	268
PREAH VIHEAR PROVINCE	**272**
Preah Khan	272
Koh Ker	274
Tbeng Meanchey	276
Tmatboey Ibis Project	277
Chhep Vulture-Feeding Station	278
Choam Ksant	278
Prasat Preah Vihear	279
KOMPONG THOM PROVINCE	**280**
Kompong Thom	281
Around Kompong Thom	284

Eastern Cambodia   288

SVAY RIENG PROVINCE	**290**
Svay Rieng	291

PREY VENG PROVINCE	**291**
Prey Veng	291
Neak Luong	291
Ba Phnom	292
KOMPONG CHAM PROVINCE	**292**
Kompong Cham	292
Around Kompong Cham	296
KRATIE PROVINCE	**297**
Kratie	298
Around Kratie	300
Chhlong	301
Snuol	301
STUNG TRENG PROVINCE	**301**
Stung Treng	302
Around Stung Treng	304
RATANAKIRI PROVINCE	**305**
Ban Lung	305
Around Ban Lung	309
MONDULKIRI PROVINCE	**312**
Sen Monorom	312
Around Sen Monorom	316
Seima Protection Forest	317
Mimong	318
Koh Nhek	318

Directory   319

Accommodation	319
Activities	320
Business Hours	321
Children	322
Climate Charts	323
Courses	323
Customs Regulations	323
Dangers & Annoyances	323
Discount Cards	326
Embassies & Consulates	326
Festivals & Events	326
Food	326
Gay & Lesbian Travellers	327
Holidays	327
Insurance	327
Internet Access	327
Legal Matters	328
Maps	328
Money	328
Photography & Video	330
Post	331
Shopping	331
Telephone & Fax	332
Time	333

Toilets 333
Tourist Information 334
Travellers with
Disabilities 334
Visas 334
Volunteering 335
Women Travellers 336
Work 336

Transport 337

GETTING THERE & AWAY 337
Entering the Country 337
Air 337
Land 339
River 345
Tours 345
GETTING AROUND 346
Air 346
Bicycle 346
Boat 347
Bus 347
Car & Motorcycle 348

Hitching 350
Local Transport 350
Share Taxi & Pick-Up
Trucks 352
Train 352

Health 353

BEFORE YOU GO 353
Insurance 353
Recommended
Vaccinations 353
Further Reading 353
Other Preparations 353
IN TRANSIT 355
Deep Vein Thrombosis
(DVT) 355
Jet Lag & Motion
Sickness 355
IN CAMBODIA 356
Availability & Cost of
Health Care 356
Infectious Diseases 356
Traveller's Diarrhoea 359

Environmental Hazards 360
Women's Health 362

Language 363

Glossary 370

The Authors 372

Behind the Scenes 374

Index 383

GreenDex 390

Map Legend 392

Regional Map Contents

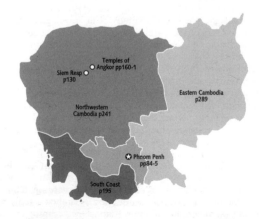

Destination Cambodia

There's a magic about Cambodia that casts a spell on many who visit this charming yet confounding kingdom. Ascend to the realm of the gods at the mother of all temples, Angkor Wat, a spectacular fusion of symbolism, symmetry and spirituality. Descend into the hell of Tuol Sleng and come face to face with the Khmer Rouge and its killing machine. Welcome to the conundrum that is Cambodia: a country with a history both inspiring and depressing, an intoxicating place where the future is waiting to be shaped.

The years of fear and loathing are finally over and Angkor is once more the symbol of the nation, drawing pilgrims from across the globe. Peace has come to this beautiful yet blighted land after three decades of war, and the Cambodian people have opened their arms to the world. Tourism has well and truly taken off, yet a journey here remains an adventure as much as a holiday.

Contemporary Cambodia is the successor state to the mighty Khmer empire, which, during the Angkorian period, ruled much of what is now Laos, Thailand and Vietnam. The remains of this empire can be seen at the fabled temples of Angkor, monuments unrivalled in scale and grandeur in Southeast Asia. The traveller's first glimpse of Angkor Wat, the ultimate expression of Khmer genius, is simply staggering and is matched by only a few select spots on earth, such as Machu Picchu or Petra.

Just as Angkor is more than its wat, so too is Cambodia more than its temples. The chaotic yet charismatic capital of Phnom Penh is a hub of political intrigue, economic vitality and intellectual debate. All too often overlooked by hit-and-run tourists ticking off Angkor on a regional tour, the revitalised city is finally earning plaudits in its own right thanks to a gorgeous riverside location, a cultural renaissance, and a dining and drinking scene to rival the best in the region.

Siem Reap and Phnom Penh may be the heavyweights, but to some extent they are a bubble, a world away from the Cambodia of the countryside. This is the place to experience the rhythm of rural life and timeless landscapes of dazzling rice paddies and swaying sugar palms. Spend some time in the *srok* (provinces), as Cambodians call them, enjoying a *dar leng* (walkabout) to discover the true flavour of the country.

The South Coast is fringed by tropical islands, with just a handful of beach huts in sight. The next Ko Samui or Gili Trawangan awaits discovery and, for now, visitors can play Robinson Crusoe, but probably not for much longer. Inland from the coast lie the Cardamom Mountains, part of a vast tropical wilderness that provides a home to elusive wildlife and is the gateway to emerging ecotourism adventures. The mighty Mekong River cuts through the country and is home to some of the region's last remaining freshwater dolphins; cyclists and dirt bikers can follow the river's length as it meanders through traditional communities. The northeast is a world unto itself, its wild and mountainous landscapes a home for Cambodia's ethnic minorities and an abundance of natural attractions, including thundering waterfalls and pristine crater lakes.

Despite this beautiful backdrop, life is no picnic for the average Cambodian. Cambodia remains one of the poorest countries in Asia and it's a tough existence for much of the population, as they battle it out against the whims of nature and, sometimes, their politicians. According to the UN Development Programme (UNDP; www.undp.org), Cambodia remains in worse shape than Congo and the Solomon Islands, just scraping in ahead of Myanmar,

FAST FACTS

Population: 14.5 million

Life expectancy: 62 years

Infant mortality: 55 per 1000 births

GDP: US$11.25 billion (2008)

Adult literacy rate: 76.3%

Number of tourists per year: 2 million and rising

Number of monks in Cambodia: 60,000

Annual freshwater fish catch: 290,000 to 430,000 tonnes per year

Bombs dropped on Cambodia: 539,000 tonnes

Number of psychiatrists in Cambodia: 26

'Ascend to the realm of the gods at the mother of all temples, Angkor Wat, a spectacular fusion of symbolism, symmetry and spirituality' while Transparency International (www.transparency.org), the anticorruption watchdog, rates the country a lowly 158 out of the 180 countries ranked. Income remains desperately low for many Khmers, with annual salaries in the hundreds rather than thousands of dollars, and public servants, such as teachers, unable to eke out a living on their meagre wages.

Cambodia's pristine environment may be a big draw, but much of it is currently under threat. Ancient forests are being razed to make way for plantations, rivers are being sized up for major hydroelectric power plants and the south coast is being explored by leading oil companies. All this helped add up to an ever-stronger economy, at least until the global financial crisis swept through town, but it's unlikely to encourage the ecotourism that is just starting to develop.

Cambodia is like the teen starlet who has just been discovered by an adoring public: everyone wants something from her but not everyone wants what is in her best interests. The government, long shunned by international big business, is keen to benefit from all these new-found opportunities. Contracts are being signed off like autographs and there are concerns for the long-term development of the country. The Chinese have come to the table to play for big stakes and pledged US$1.1 billion in assistance in late 2009, considerably more than all the other donors put together, and with no burdensome strings attached. Good governance? Beijing preaches a different faith to that of Brussels.

Tourism has brought many benefits to Cambodia: it provides opportunity and employment for a new generation of Khmers, has helped spark a rebirth of the traditional arts, and has given the country a renewed sense of pride and optimism as it recovers from the dark decades of war and genocide. However, not all tourism has been good for the country and there is the dark side of sex tourism, human exploitation and a gambling culture. Cambodia is in a great position to learn from the mistakes of other countries in the region and follow a sustainable road to tourism development. However, it may be that the government is more focused on the short-term gain that megabucks investments can provide. Can Cambodia be all things to all visitors? So far, so good, but a new era is about to begin and the beaches are the next battleground.

There are two faces to Cambodia: one shiny and happy, the other dark and complex. For every illegal eviction of city dwellers or land grab by a general, there will be a new NGO school offering better education, or a new clean-water initiative to improve the lives of the average villager. Such is the yin and yang of Cambodia, a country that inspires and confounds. The more layers you unravel, the more it makes you want to cry, but these are spontaneous tears, sometimes of sorrow, sometimes of joy.

Despite having the eighth wonder of the world in its backyard, Cambodia's greatest treasure is its people. The Khmers have been to hell and back, struggling through years of bloodshed, poverty and political instability. Thanks to an unbreakable spirit and infectious optimism, they have prevailed with their smiles intact. No visitor comes away from Cambodia without a measure of admiration and affection for the inhabitants of this enigmatic kingdom.

Cambodia: beaches as beautiful as Thailand but without the tourist tide; wilds as remote as Laos but even less explored; cuisine as subtle as Vietnam but yet to be discovered; and temples that leave Myanmar (Burma) and Indonesia in the shade. This is the heart of Southeast Asia, with everything the region has to offer packed into one bite-sized country. If you were only planning to spend a week in Cambodia, it's time to think again.

'Despite having the eighth wonder of the world in its backyard, Cambodia's greatest treasure is its people'

Getting Started

A journey to Cambodia offers a window on the soul of Southeast Asia. The magnificent temples of Angkor are unrivalled, and beyond the rich legacy of the ancient Khmer empire lie the buzzing capital of Phnom Penh, countless kilometres of unspoilt tropical beaches, the mighty Mekong River, a vibrant culture and some of the friendliest people in the region. It's not the most 'sophisticated' destination in the world (though for many this makes it all the more charming), so be sure to pack some patience and humour. Cambodia is full of surprises, so gear up for the adventure.

See Climate Charts (p323) for more information.

WHEN TO GO

Cambodia can be visited at any time of the year. The ideal months are December and January, when humidity levels are relatively low, there is little rainfall and a cooling breeze whips across the land, but this is also peak season when the majority of visitors descend on the country.

From early February, temperatures keep rising until the killer month, April, when the mercury often exceeds 40°C (104°F). Some time in May or June, the southwestern monsoon brings rain and high humidity, cooking up a sweat for all but the hardiest of visitors. The wet season, which lasts until October, isn't such a bad time to visit, as the rain tends to come in short, sharp downpours. Angkor is surrounded by lush foliage and the moats are full of water at this time of year. If you are planning to visit remote areas, however, the wet season makes for tough travel.

Some visitors like to coordinate their trip with one of the annual festivals, such as Bon Om Tuk or Khmer New Year (see p19).

COSTS & MONEY

The cost of travelling in Cambodia covers the whole spectrum, from very cheap to outrageously expensive, depending on taste and comfort. Penny-pinchers can survive on as little as US$15 per day, while budget travellers with an eye on enjoyment can live it up on US$30 a day. Midrange travellers can turn on the style with US$75 to US$150 a day, staying in smart places, dining well and travelling in comfort. At the top end, you'll need US$200 a day or more to live a life of luxury.

Accommodation starts from as little as US$2 to US$5 in popular destinations. Spending US$10 to US$20 will add amenities such as air-conditioning, satellite TV, fridge and hot water. Stepping up to US$50, you enter the world of three-star standards and charming boutique resorts. Forking out US$100

DON'T LEAVE HOME WITHOUT...

Actually, bring as little as possible. Cambodia has virtually everything you find at home and it's usually available at lower prices. All the soaps and smellies are plentiful, and clothing, shoes and backpacks are available at a fraction of the price in the West. Tampons are available in all major towns and cities, but not in more remote areas.

A Swiss Army knife or equivalent comes in handy, but you don't need 27 separate functions. A torch (flashlight), compass, a flash drive and extra camera memory are also useful.

Other handy items include earplugs to block the ever-present noise, a universal plug adaptor, a rain cover for your backpack and insect repellent to keep the bugs at bay. Finally, the secret of successful packing: plastic bags. Not only do they keep things separate and clean, but also dry. That means a lot at the end of a long, wet day.

or more brings a five-star fling. Don't be afraid to negotiate for a discount if it is low season or traffic is down.

While Cambodian cuisine may not be as well known as that of neighbouring Thailand and Vietnam, it can certainly compete with the best of them. Snack on the street or chow down in the market, with meals starting at just 2000r or so, or indulge in a banquet for a few bucks. Local Khmer restaurants are a step up in comfort, and a meal will cost around US$2. Next are the sophisticated Khmer, Asian and international restaurants. Meals start from about US$4 at the cheaper places, rising to US$10 and up at the smarter ones, and US$50 or more is possible if you go wild with the wine list.

Domestic flights link Phnom Penh to Siem Reap. Fast boats link several popular destinations in Cambodia and the journey can be more scenic than by road. There is now a healthy selection of bus companies connecting towns and cities throughout Cambodia and prices are rock bottom. On the rougher roads, share taxis and pick-ups take the strain. Train travel is no longer possible, as passenger services have been suspended, but that could be seen as a blessing in disguise given that trains crawl along at an average speed of 20km/h. For ultimate flexibility, rent a car or 4WD and travel with a guide. See the Transport chapter (p337) for more information.

Visitors to Angkor (which is surely everybody coming to Cambodia) will have to factor in the cost of entrance fees, which are US$20 for one day, US$40 for three days and US$60 for one week. An additional expense is transport to get to, from and around the ruins; from US$2 for a bicycle, about US$8 for a *moto* (small motorcycle with driver), US$10 to US$15 for a *remork-moto* (motorcycle with carriage, aka *tuk tuk*) and US$25 to US$50 for a car.

Small budget, big budget, it doesn't really matter; Cambodia is the place to be. Soak it up in the style that suits.

> **HOW MUCH?**
>
> Hotel room with air-con US$10-20
>
> Restaurant meal US$4-15
>
> Internet access per hour US$0.40-2.00
>
> *Cambodia Daily* news-paper 1200r
>
> *Krama* (checked scarf) US$1-2

TRAVELLING RESPONSIBLY

Since our inception in 1973, Lonely Planet has encouraged readers to tread lightly, travel responsibly and experience the magic of independent travel. International travel is growing at a dizzying rate and we still firmly believe in the benefits it can bring but, as always, we encourage you to consider the impact your visit will have on both the global environment and the local economies, cultures and ecosystems.

Cambodia has been to hell and back and there are many ways that you can put a little back into the country. Staying a bit longer, travelling further, and spreading the wealth around (by getting off the beaten path) is obvious advice, but even for those on a short stay, it is possible to engage with locals in markets and spend money in restaurants and outlets that assist disadvantaged Cambodians. See the boxed text, p60, in the Food and Drink chapter, as well as the Eating and Shopping sections in the Phnom Penh and Siem Reap chapters, and other town entries, for more ideas.

The following websites have more information on sustainable tourism and tips on responsible travel:

Cambodia Community-Based Ecotourism Network (www.ccben.org) The official website promoting community-based ecotourism in Cambodia. Browse here for more on projects and initiatives across the country.

ChildSafe (www.childsafe-cambodia.org) Learn about the ChildSafe campaign, which aims to stop child-sex tourism and protect vulnerable children from all forms of exploitation.

ConCERT (www.concertcambodia.org) Siem Reap–based organisation 'connecting communities, environment and responsible tourism'.

Heritage Watch (www.heritagewatch.org) The home of the heritage-friendly tourism campaign to raise interest in remote heritage sites and their protection.

Mekong Discovery Trail (www.mekongdiscoverytrail.org) The official website for the Mekong Discovery Trail, promoting community-based tourism initiatives on the upper Mekong.

Responsible Travel (www.responsible-travel.org) A no-nonsense website with commonsense advice on how to travel with a conscience.

Sam Veasna Center for Wildlife Conservation (www.samveasna.org) The best source of information on sustainable visits to Cambodia's world-class bird sanctuaries.

Stay Another Day (www.stay-another-day.org) A great website dedicated to tempting tourists into staying another day in Cambodia, packed with ideas on day trips, project visits and alternative things to see and do.

TRAVEL LITERATURE

The classic Cambodian read is Norman Lewis' *A Dragon Apparent: Travels in Cambodia, Laos & Vietnam* (1951), an account of his 1950 foray into an Indochina that would soon disappear. In the course of his travels, Lewis circumnavigated Tonlé Sap Lake, with a pause at Angkor. The book has been reissued as part of *The Norman Lewis Omnibus* (1995).

Written by authors who know and love their countries, *To Asia with Love: A Connoisseur's Guide to Cambodia, Laos, Thailand and Vietnam* (2004), an anthology edited by Kim Fay, is a delightful introduction to Cambodia and the Mekong region for those looking for some inspiration and adventure. A new *To Cambodia with Love* is still on the cards and should finally be out some time during the lifetime of this book.

Travels in Siam, Cambodia, Laos and Annam (1864) by Henri Mouhot has been reprinted in English by White Lotus and gives the inside story of the man credited with 'rediscovering' Angkor.

Jon Swain's *River of Time* (1995) takes the reader back to an old Indochina, partly lost to the madness of war, and includes firsthand accounts of the French embassy stand-off in the first days of the Khmer Rouge takeover.

Tim Page's *Derailed in Uncle Ho's Victory Garden* (1995) covers this legendary photographer's quest for the truth behind the disappearance of photojournalist Sean Flynn (son of Errol) in Cambodia in 1970, and his mission to secure a monument to fallen correspondents on all sides of the Indochina conflict.

An excellent account of life on the Mother River is *The River's Tale: A Year on the Mekong* (2001) by Edward Gargan. A war-protester-turned-foreign-correspondent, Gargan sees for himself how Cambodia and its neighbours have brought themselves back from the brink.

The Indochina Chronicles (2005) by Phil Karber is a lively travelogue taking in adventures and misadventures in Cambodia, Laos and Vietnam.

Amit Gilboa's *Off the Rails in Phnom Penh – Guns, Girls and Ganja* (1998) deals with such murky subjects as prostitution and drugs. It feels like he got too close to his subject at times and it's not really a side of Cambodia of which most Khmers are proud.

The ultimate spoof guidebook, *Phaic Tăn: Sunstroke on a Shoestring* (2004) is a pastiche of Southeast Asian countries that pokes fun at all of us. No one is spared: not the locals, not the travellers – not even hallowed guidebook authors.

INTERNET RESOURCES

Andy Brouwer's Cambodia Tales (www.andybrouwer.co.uk) Gateway to all things Cambodian, this site includes comprehensive links to other sites and regular travel articles from veteran Cambodia adventurers. Includes a popular blog.

Angkor Wat Portal (www.angkor.com) When it comes to links, this site has them, spreading its cyber-tentacles into all sorts of interesting areas.

TOP 10

ANCIENT TEMPLES

Cambodia is the temple capital of Asia. The kingdom is littered with the lavish legacy of the god-kings. Choose from majestic mountain-top temples, forbidding and forgotten jungle fortresses, incredible carved riverbeds and pre-Angkorian brick cities.

1 Angkor Wat (p167), the mother of all temples

2 Banteay Chhmar (p265), the forgotten complex of the far northwest

3 Banteay Srei (p189), the jewel in the crown of Angkorian art

4 Bayon (p172), with its 216 enigmatic faces

5 Beng Mealea (p191), Angkor-sized but swallowed by jungle

6 Kbal Spean (p190), the River of a Thousand Lingas

7 Koh Ker (p274), an usurper capital of huge proportions

8 Prasat Preah Vihear (p279), the most spectacular of the mountain temples

9 Sambor Prei Kuk (p284), the first temple city in the region

10 Ta Prohm (p181), left as explorers first saw it – nature run riot

THE CAMBODIAN TRAGEDY IN WORDS

In stark contrast to the glories of the Angkor empire is the dark void into which the country plunged in the 1970s. A brutal civil war raged for five years, delivering the Khmer Rouge to power. This regime turned the clocks to Year Zero in what was to become one of the world's most radical and bloody revolutions. Read your way into these tumultuous events to understand how it all happened.

1 *Sideshow: Kissinger, Nixon and the Destruction of Cambodia* by William Shawcross (1979)

2 *Brother Enemy* by Nayan Chanda (1985)

3 *History of Cambodia* by David Chandler (1994)

4 *Prince of Light, Prince of Darkness* by Milton Osbourne (1994)

5 *The Pol Pot Regime* by Ben Kiernan (1996)

6 *Voices from S-21* by David Chandler (1999)

7 *First They Killed My Father* by Luong Ung (2001)

8 *The Gate* by Francois Bizot (2003)

9 *Pol Pot: The History of a Nightmare* by Phillip Short (2004)

10 *The Lost Executioner* by Nic Dunlop (2005)

ADVENTURES

If you are looking for adventures in Asia, then you have come to the right place. The roads may be rough, but the stories will be smooth and stay with you forever.

1 Make the overland pilgrimage to Prasat Preah Vihear (p279)

2 Beachcomb on the beautiful island of Koh Kong (p203)

3 Disappear for a week into the wildlife-rich forests of Virachey National Park (p311)

4 Paddle a dugout through the flooded forest of Kompong Pluk (p152)

5 Go underground at Kampot Province's cave pagodas (p228 and p231)

6 Ride the bamboo train in Battambang, Cambodia's local express (p252)

7 Camp out in the jungle at the temple of Preah Khan (p272)

8 See some of Asia's rarest large waterbirds at Prek Toal Bird Sanctuary (p151)

9 Mountain bike through traditional villages on the Mekong Discovery Trail (p300)

10 Penetrate the vast rainforests of the remote Cardamoms like an explorer of old (p200)

Biking Southeast Asia with Mr Pumpy (www.mrpumpy.net) The definitive but dated website for cyclists passing through Cambodia is written with candour and humour by Mr Pumpy's best friend Felix Hude.

Expat Advisory (www.expat-advisory.com) News and events site aimed at expats in Asia, with up-to-date information on happenings in Phnom Penh.

Lonely Planet (www.lonelyplanet.com) Offers information on travelling to and within Cambodia, the Thorn Tree travel forum and up-to-date travel news.

Ministry of Tourism (www.mot.gov.kh) The official Cambodian tourism website is dated, but there are some useful links for hotels, restaurants and travel agents.

Tales of Asia (www.talesofasia.com) This popular website has detailed information on overland travel in Cambodia, including the Bangkok–Siem Reap overland run.

Things Asian (www.thingsasian.com) Bubbling with information on the culture of the Mekong region, this site has everything including architecture, literature and fashion.

Events Calendar

Why not plan your trip to coincide with one of Cambodia's major festivals? Holidays and festivals take place according to the lunar calendar, so dates vary from year to year. Check the internet for the exact dates.

JANUARY–APRIL

CHAUL CHNAM CHEN
(CHINESE NEW YEAR)   late Jan–mid-Feb
The Chinese inhabitants of Cambodia celebrate their New Year somewhere between late January and mid-February – for the Vietnamese, this is Tet. As many of Phnom Penh's businesses are run by Chinese, commerce grinds to a halt around this time and there are dragon dances all over town. Many Vietnamese living in Cambodia return to their homeland for a week or more.

CHAUL CHNAM KHMER
(KHMER NEW YEAR)   mid-Apr
This is a three-day celebration of the Khmer New Year, and is like Christmas, New Year and birthdays all rolled into one. Cambodians make offerings at wats, clean out their homes, and exchange gifts. It is a lively time to visit the country as the Khmers go wild with water and talcum powder, leaving a lot of bemused tourists looking like plaster-cast figures. Large crowds congregate at Wat Phnom in the capital, but females should watch out for the over-eager attention of young gangs of males. Throngs of Khmers flock to Angkor, and it's absolute madness at most temples, so avoid the celebration if you want a quiet, reflective Angkor experience. That said, it is nowhere near as excessive as in Thailand or Laos, so it might seem quiet by comparison.

MAY–AUGUST

CHAT PREAH NENGKAL
(ROYAL PLOUGHING CEREMONY)   early May
Led by the royal family, the Royal Ploughing Ceremony is a ritual agricultural festival held to mark the traditional beginning of the rice-growing season. It takes place in front of the National Museum (p93), near the Royal Palace in Phnom Penh, and the royal oxen are said to have a nose for whether it will be a good harvest or a bad one.

VISAKHA PUJA (BUDDHA DAY)   May/Jun
Celebrating Buddha's birth, enlightenment and *parinibbana* (passing away), activities are centred on wats. The festival falls on the eighth day of the fourth moon and is best observed at Angkor Wat, where you can see candle-lit processions of monks.

SEPTEMBER–DECEMBER

P'CHUM BEN
(FESTIVAL OF THE DEAD)   Sep/Oct
This festival is a kind of All Souls' Day, when respects are paid to the dead through offerings made at wats. Offerings include paper money, flowers, candles and incense, as well as food and drink, all passed through the medium of the monks. P'chum Ben lasts for several days and devout Buddhists are expected to visit seven wats during the festival.

BON OM TUK
(WATER FESTIVAL)   Oct/Nov
Celebrating the epic victory of Jayavarman VII over the Chams, who occupied Angkor in 1177, this festival also marks the remarkable natural phenomenon of the reversal of the current of the Tonlé Sap River. It is one of the most important festivals in the Khmer calendar and is a wonderful, if chaotic, time to be in Phnom Penh or Siem Reap. Boat races are held on the Tonlé Sap and Siem Reap Rivers, with each boat colourfully decorated and holding 40 rowers. As many as two million people flood the capital for the fun and frolics – which also include live concerts, food stands, fair rides and fireworks – so be sure to book ahead for accommodation.

Itineraries
CLASSIC ROUTES

CAMBODIA SNAPSHOT   Two Weeks
Whether you start in Siem Reap and travel south, or head north to Angkor, this is the ultimate journey, via temples, beaches and the capital.

Hit **Phnom Penh** (p81) for sights such as the impressive **National Museum** (p93), with its excellent Angkorian sculpture collection, and the stunning **Silver Pagoda** (p92). There is superb shopping at the **Psar Tuol Tom Pong** (p119), and a **night shift** (p114) that never sleeps.

Take a fast boat to **Phnom Da** (p238), then go south to the colonial-era town of **Kampot** (p223). From here, visit **Bokor Hill Station** (p229), the seaside town of **Kep** (p232) and the cave pagodas at **Phnom Chhnork** (p228) and **Phnom Sorsia** (p229).

Go west to **Sihanoukville** (p209), Cambodia's beach capital, to sample the seafood, dive the nearby waters or just soak up the sun. Backtrack via Phnom Penh to **Kompong Thom** (p281) and get a taste of what's to come by visiting the pre-Angkorian brick temples of **Sambor Prei Kuk** (p284).

Finish the trip at Angkor, a mind-blowing experience with which few sights compare. See **Angkor Wat** (p167), perfection in stone; **Bayon** (p172), weirdness in stone; and **Ta Prohm** (p181), nature triumphing over stone – before venturing further afield to **Kbal Spean** (p190) or jungle-clad **Beng Mealea** (p191).

This trip can take two weeks at a steady pace or three weeks at a slow pace. Public transport serves most of this route. Rent a motorbike for side trips to Kep and Sambor Prei Kuk, and try out a *remork-moto (tuk tuk)* at Angkor. More money, less time? Rent a car and set the pace.

THE BIG ONE   One Month

Cambodia is a small country and even though the roads are sometimes bad and travel can be slow, most of the big hitters can be visited in a month.

Setting out from **Phnom Penh** (p81), take in the beauty of the northeast, following the Run to the Hills itinerary (p23). Choose between **Ratanakiri Province** (p305) and **Mondulkiri Province** (p312) to ensure maximum time elsewhere. The gentle hills of Mondulkiri are better for budget travellers as traversing overland is easy, while Ratanakiri makes sense for those planning an overland journey between Cambodia and Laos. Tough choice…can't decide? Flip a coin, if you can find one in this coinless country.

Head to the South Coast, taking the route outlined in the Cambodia Snapshot itinerary (opposite). Take your time and consider a few nights in **Kep** (p232) or on one of the nearby islands, and a boat trip from **Sihanoukville** (p209) to explore the up-and-coming islands off the coast. On your way back to the capital, check out **Kirirom National Park** (p127), home to pine trees, black bears, and some spectacular views of the Cardamom Mountains.

Then it's time to turn northwest and head to charming **Battambang** (p249), one of Cambodia's best preserved colonial-era towns and a base from which to discover rural life and ride the bamboo train. Take the proverbial slow boat to **Siem Reap** (p128), passing through stunning scenery along the snaking Sangker River, and turn your attention to the **temples of Angkor** (p153).

Visit all the greatest hits in and around Angkor, but set aside some extra time to venture further to the rival capital of **Koh Ker** (p274), which is cloaked in thick jungle, or **Prasat Preah Vihear** (p279), where it is all about location, location, location – a mountain temple perched precariously atop a cliff-face on the Thai border.

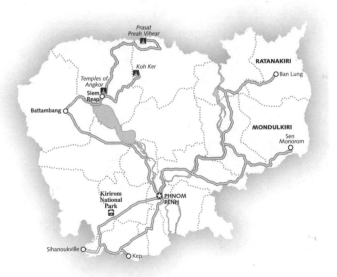

Overlanders can run this route in reverse, setting out from Siem Reap and exiting Cambodia by river into Vietnam or Laos. Entering from Laos, divert east to Ratanakiri before heading south. Getting about is generally easy, as there are buses on the big roads, taxis on the small roads and buzzing boats on the many rivers.

ROADS LESS TRAVELLED

THE LOST TEMPLES OF THE NORTHWEST

The magnificent temples of Angkor are renowned for their splendour, but these represent no more than the capital of what was an unrivalled empire spanning Southeast Asia. In the steaming jungles of Cambodia, forgotten to the world for centuries, lie several stunning religious monuments that make the perfect excuse to extend your adventure.

The beauty of this tough trip on rough roads is that it is the alternative way to link Cambodia's vibrant capital, Phnom Penh, with Siem Reap, gateway to Angkor. Starting in **Phnom Penh** (p81), head north through **Kompong Thom** (p281) and on to the pre-Angkorian capital of **Sambor Prei Kuk** (p284), Asia's first temple city. Bid farewell to civilisation from here and make the tough journey (dry season only) northwest to the vast jungle temple of **Preah Khan** (p272), one of the largest structures from the Angkorian era.

Continue on to **Koh Ker** (p274), an usurper capital from the 10th century, with a wealth of monuments spread throughout the forest.

Most breathtaking of the temples is **Prasat Preah Vihear** (p279). The height of Angkorian architectural audacity, its foundation stones stretch to the edge of a precipitous cliff. Breathe in the views – they are simply astounding. From here, it is an easy run to **Siem Reap** (p128) via the former Khmer Rouge stronghold of **Anlong Veng** (p268), where you can visit Pol Pot's cremation site. In Siem Reap, finish with the compulsory **temples of Angkor** (p153) or continue to the beautiful **Banteay Chhmar** (p265) if you still have the energy reserves.

This is a tough trip with little in the way of public transport. It should not be attempted in the wet season and takes at least a week. Seasoned motorbike riders can do it on a dirt bike. For less pain, a 4WD is the way to go. The trip is possible using a combination of pick-up truck and *moto* (small motor-cycle with driver), but you'll need massage therapy afterwards.

RUN TO THE HILLS

Northeast Cambodia is a world unto itself, a landscape of rolling hills and secret waterfalls, and home to a patchwork of ethnic minorities, a few of whom still use elephants to get around. It's not only the sights and sounds that are different up here – the temperature is also notably cooler.

Leaving the capital **Phnom Penh** (p81), pass through the bustling Mekong town of **Kompong Cham** (p292) before heading east to **Sen Monorom** (p312), the charming capital of Mondulkiri Province. Spend a few days here to bathe at **Bou Sraa Waterfall** (p316), one of Cambodia's biggest; learn about **elephant behaviour** (p316); and explore Bunong villages before heading back to the Mekong at **Kratie** (p298). This attractive little town is the base for an encounter with one of the rarest mammals on earth, the elusive Irrawaddy river dolphin, which lives in ever-dwindling numbers upstream from here.

Push north up the Mekong to **Stung Treng Province** (p302), site of several budding ecotourism excursions and home to another dolphin pool near the Lao border. To the east lies **Ban Lung** (p305), provincial capital of Ratanakiri Province and base for an adventure to remember. From here plunge into Cambodia's most beautiful natural swimming pool at **Boeng Yeak Lom** (p306); visit ethnic minority villages around Voen Sai (p309) and **Andong Meas** (p310); forge a river adventure along the Tonlé San around **Ta Veng** (p310); or trek deep into the forests of **Virachey National Park** (p311).

Adventurers and motorbikers can link Mondulkiri and Ratanakiri Provinces directly via the village of **Koh Nhek** (p318). Sen Monorom to Koh Nhek is a breeze, but the roads all but disappear from there and a *moto* driver as a guide is almost essential.

On main roads, this trip is easy to manage using share taxis or pick-ups, but until the roads are finished it's a frightening prospect in the wet season. Motorbikers can link Mondulkiri and Ratanakiri Provinces on one of Cambodia's more devilish roads – not for amateurs. Finishing up in Ratanakiri, overlanders can carry on into Laos.

TAILORED TRIP

UNTAMED CARDAMOMS & UNEXPLORED COAST

Visitors can get a sense of the diverse ecosystems of the Cardamom Mountains – from the pine-forested highlands down through dense rainforest to the mangrove-fringed shoreline and pristine beaches – along the **Koh Kong Conservation Corridor** (p200) in Cambodia's far southwestern corner. Starting out from the one-time smugglers' port of **Krong Koh Kong** (p196), travel by *moto* or boat to the **Tatai River** (p202), where you can stay in ecologically sustainable accommodation. Drive inland to the **Thma Bang ranger station** (p204), in the Central Cardamoms Protected Forest, to explore the Areng River habitats of the endangered dragonfish (Asian arowana) and Siamese crocodile (p205). Krong Koh Kong is also a good base for an excursion by open skiff through the pristine mangrove forests of **Peam Krasaop Wildlife Sanctuary** (p202) and on to **Koh Kong Island** (p203), the western side of which has seven unspoilt beaches, some with hidden lagoons. The northwest coast of **Botum Sakor National Park** (p205) is just across the channel from the island, but the superb beaches further south are easier to get to from **Koh Sdach** (p205), an island that is accessible on the **Sihanoukville–Koh Sdach ferry** (p220) and is not far from some excellent snorkelling grounds. To visit the park's mangrove-lined east coast – including **Ta Op stream** (p205) and its monkeys – hire a boat in **Andoung Tuek** (p206), where you can also cruise upriver to the village of **Chi Phat** (p206). Once notorious for its poachers, it is now the site of a pioneering community-based ecotourism project. Ecolodges situated around the Koh Kong Conservation Corridor include Rainbow Lodge (p202) and Four Rivers Floating Ecolodge (p202), both on the Tatai River.

History

'The good, the bad and the ugly' is a simple way to sum up Cambodian history. Things were good in the early years, culminating in the vast Angkor empire, unrivalled in the region during four centuries of dominance. Then the bad set in, from the 13th century, as ascendant neighbours steadily chipped away at Cambodian territory. In the 20th century it turned downright ugly, as a brutal civil war culminated in the genocidal rule of the Khmer Rouge (1975–79), from which Cambodia is still recovering.

THE ORIGIN OF THE KHMERS

Cambodia came into being, so the legend says, through the union of a princess and a foreigner. The foreigner was an Indian Brahman named Kaundinya and the princess was the daughter of a naga king who ruled over a watery land. One day, as Kaundinya sailed by, the princess paddled out in a boat to greet him. Kaundinya shot an arrow from his magic bow into her boat, causing the fearful princess to agree to marriage. In need of a dowry, her father drank up the waters of his land and presented them to Kaundinya to rule over. The new kingdom was named Kambuja.

Like many legends, this one is historically opaque, but it does say something about the cultural forces that brought Cambodia into existence, in particular its relationship with its great subcontinental neighbour, India. Cambodia's religious, royal and written traditions stemmed from India and began to coalesce as a cultural entity in their own right between the 1st and 5th centuries AD.

Very little is known about prehistoric Cambodia. Much of the southeast was a vast, shallow gulf that was progressively silted up by the mouths of the Mekong, leaving pancake-flat, mineral-rich land ideal for farming. Evidence of cave-dwellers has been found in the northwest of Cambodia. Carbon dating on ceramic pots found in the area shows that they were made around 4200 BC, but it is hard to say whether there is a direct relationship between these cave-dwelling pot makers and contemporary Khmers. Examinations of bones dating back to around 1500 BC, however, suggest that the people living in Cambodia at that time resembled the Cambodians of today. Early Chinese records report that the Cambodians were 'ugly' and 'dark' and went about naked. A healthy dose of scepticism may be required, however, when reading the reports of imperial China concerning its 'barbarian' neighbours.

For the full flavour of Cambodian history, from the humble beginnings in the prehistoric period through the glories of Angkor and right up to the present day, grab a copy of *The History of Cambodia* by David Chandler (1994).

TIMELINE

4200 BC	AD 100	245
Cave dwellers capable of making pots inhabit caves around Laang Spean; archaeological evidence suggests the vessels made may be similar to those still made in Cambodia today.	The process of Indianisation begins with the arrival of Indian traders and holy men: the religions, language and sculpture of India start to take root in Cambodia.	The Chinese Wei emperor sends a mission to the countries of the Mekong region and is told that a barbarous but rich country called Funan exists in the Delta region.

THE EARLY CAMBODIAN KINGDOMS

Cambodian might didn't begin and end with Angkor. There were a number of powerful kingdoms present in this area before the 9th century.

From the 1st century, the Indianisation of Cambodia occurred through trading settlements that sprang up on the coastline of what is now southern Vietnam, but was then inhabited by the Khmers. These settlements were important ports of call for boats following the trading route from the Bay of Bengal to the southern provinces of China. The largest of these nascent kingdoms was known as Funan by the Chinese, and may have existed across an area between Ba Phnom in Prey Veng Province, a site only worth visiting for the archaeologically obsessed today, and Oc-Eo in Kien Giang Province in southern Vietnam. Funan would have been a contemporary of Champasak in southern Laos (then known as Kuruksetra) and other lesser fiefdoms in the region.

Funan is a Chinese name, and may be a transliteration of the ancient Khmer word *bnam* (mountain). Although very little is known about Funan, much has been made of its importance as an early Southeast Asian centre of power.

It is most likely that between the 1st and 8th centuries Cambodia was a collection of small states, each with its own elites who strategically intermarried and often went to war with one another. Funan was no doubt one of these states, and as a major sea port would have been pivotal in the transmission of Indian culture into the interior of Cambodia.

The little that historians do know about Funan has mostly been gleaned from Chinese sources. These report that Funan-period Cambodia (1st to 6th centuries AD) embraced the worship of the Hindu deities Shiva and Vishnu and, at the same time, Buddhism. The *linga* (phallic totem) appears to have been the focus of ritual and an emblem of kingly might, a feature that was to evolve further in the Angkorian cult of the god-king. The people practised primitive irrigation, which enabled successful cultivation of rice, and traded raw commodities such as spices with China and India.

From the 6th century, Cambodia's population gradually concentrated along the Mekong and Tonlé Sap Rivers, where the majority remains today. The move may have been related to the development of wet-rice agriculture. From the 6th to 8th centuries it was likely that Cambodia was a collection of competing kingdoms, ruled by autocratic kings who legitimised their absolute rule through hierarchical caste concepts borrowed from India.

This era is generally referred to as the Chenla period. Again, like Funan, it is a Chinese term and there is little to support the idea that Chenla was a unified kingdom that held sway over all of Cambodia. Indeed, the Chinese themselves referred to 'water Chenla' and 'land Chenla'. Water Chenla was located around Angkor Borei and the temple mount of Phnom Da, near the present-day provincial capital of Takeo, and land Chenla in the upper reaches of the Mekong River and east of Tonlé Sap Lake, around Sambor Prei Kuk, an essential stop on a chronological jaunt through Cambodia's history.

Margin notes

Cambodia's Funan-period trading port of Oc-Eo, now located in Vietnam's Mekong Delta, was a major commercial crossroads between Asia and Europe, and archaeologists there have unearthed Roman coins and Chinese ceramics.

Founded by King Isanavarman I in the early 7th century, Sambor Prei Kuk was originally known as Isanapura and was the first major temple city to be constructed in Southeast Asia.

The ancient Khmers were like the Romans of Southeast Asia, building a network of long highways across the region to connect their regional cities.

600	802	889
The first inscriptions are committed to stone in Cambodia in ancient Khmer, offering historians the first contemporary accounts of the pre-Angkorian period other than from Chinese sources.	Jayavarman II proclaims independence from Java in a ceremony to anoint himself a *devaraja* (god-king) on the holy mountain of Phnom Kulen, marking the birth of the Khmer Empire of Angkor.	Yasovarman I moves the capital from the ancient city of Hariharalaya (Roluos today) to the Angkor area, 16km to the northwest, and marks the location with three temple mountains.

THE RISE OF THE ANGKOR EMPIRE

Gradually the Cambodian region was becoming more cohesive. Before long the fractured kingdoms of Cambodia would merge to become a sprawling Asian empire.

A popular place of pilgrimage for Khmers today, the sacred mountain of Phnom Kulen (p190), northeast of Angkor, is home to an inscription that tells of Jayavarman II (r 802–50) proclaiming himself a 'universal monarch', or *devaraja* (god-king) in 802. It is believed that he may have resided in the Buddhist Shailendras' court in Java as a young man. Upon his return to Cambodia, he instigated an uprising against Javanese control over the southern lands of Cambodia. Jayavarman II then set out to bring the country under his control through alliances and conquests, becoming the first monarch to rule most of what we call Cambodia today.

Jayavarman II was the first of a long succession of kings who presided over the rise and fall of the greatest empire mainland Southeast Asia has ever see…, one that was to bequeath the stunning legacy of Angkor. The key to the meteoric rise of Angkor was a mastery of water and an elaborate hydraulic system that allowed the ancient Khmers to tame the elements. The first records of the massive irrigation works that supported the population of Angkor date to the reign of Indravarman I (r 877–89) who built the *baray* (reservoir) of Indratataka. His rule also marks the flourishing of Angkorian art, with the building of temples in the Roluos area, notably Bakong (p187).

By the turn of the 11th century, the kingdom of Angkor was losing control of its territories. Suryavarman I (r 1002–49), a usurper, moved into the power vacuum and, like Jayavarman II two centuries before, reunified the kingdom through war and alliances, stretching the frontiers of the empire. A pattern was beginning to emerge, and is repeated throughout the Angkorian period: dislocation and turmoil, followed by reunification and further expansion under a powerful king. Architecturally, the most productive periods occurred after times of turmoil, indicating that newly incumbent monarchs felt the need to celebrate, even legitimise, their rule with massive building projects.

By 1066, Angkor was again riven by conflict, becoming the focus of rival bids for power. It was not until the accession of Suryavarman II (r 1112–52) that the kingdom was again unified. Suryavarman II embarked on another phase of expansion, waging costly wars in Vietnam and the region of central Vietnam known as Champa. Suryavarman II is immortalised as the king who, in his devotion to the Hindu deity Vishnu, commissioned the majestic temple of Angkor Wat (p167). For an insight into events in this epoch, see the bas-reliefs on the southwest corridor of Angkor Wat, which depict the reign of Suryavarman II.

Suryavarman II had brought Champa to heel and reduced it to vassal status, but the Chams struck back in 1177 with a naval expedition up the

India wasn't the only power to have a major cultural impact on Cambodia. The island of Java was also influential, colonising part of 'water Chenla' in the 8th century.

Chinese emissary Chou Ta Kuan lived in Angkor for a year in 1296, and his observations have been republished as *The Customs of Cambodia* (2000), a fascinating insight into life during the height of the empire.

924	1002	1112
Usurper king Jayavarman IV transfers the capital to Koh Ker and begins a mammoth building spree, but the lack of water sees the capital move back to Angkor just 20 years later.	Suryavarman I comes to power and expands the extent of the kingdom by annexing the Buddhist kingdom of Louvo, known as Lopburi in modern-day Thailand, and increases trade links with the outside world.	Suryavarman II commences the construction of Angkor Wat, the mother of all temples, dedicated to Vishnu and designed as his funerary temple.

Mekong and into Tonlé Sap Lake. They took the city of Angkor by surprise and put King Dharanindravarman II to death. The following year a cousin of Suryavarman II rallied the Khmer troops and defeated the Chams in yet another naval battle. The new leader was crowned Jayavarman VII in 1181.

A devout follower of Mahayana Buddhism, Jayavarman VII (r 1181–1219) built the city of Angkor Thom (p172) and many other massive monuments. Indeed, many of the temples visited around Angkor today were constructed during Jayavarman VII's reign. However, Jayavarman VII is a figure of many contradictions. The bas-reliefs of the Bayon (p172) depict him presiding over battles of terrible ferocity, while statues of the king depict a meditative, otherworldly aspect. His program of temple construction and other public works was carried out in great haste, no doubt bringing enormous hardship to the labourers who provided the muscle, and thus accelerating the decline of the empire. He was partly driven by a desire to legitimise his rule, as there may have been other contenders closer to the royal bloodline, and partly by the need to introduce a new religion to a population predominantly Hindu in faith. However, in many ways he was also Cambodia's first progressive leader, proclaiming the population equal, abolishing castes and embarking on a program of school, hospital and road building.

For more on the Angkorian period, see p153.

One of the definitive guides to Angkor is *A Guide to the Angkor Monuments* by Maurice Glaize, first published in the 1940s and now out of print. Download it free at www.theangkorguide.com.

DECLINE & FALL OF ANGKOR

Angkor was the epicentre of an incredible empire that held sway over much of the Mekong region, but, like all empires, the sun was to eventually set.

A number of scholars have argued that decline was already on the horizon at the time Angkor Wat was built, when the Angkorian empire was at the height of its remarkable productivity. There are indications that the irrigation network was overworked and slowly starting to silt up due to the massive deforestation that had taken place in the heavily populated areas to the north and east of Angkor. Massive construction projects such as Angkor Wat and Angkor Thom no doubt put an enormous strain on the royal coffers and on thousands of slaves and common people who subsidised them in hard labour and taxes. Following the reign of Jayavarman VII, temple construction effectively ground to a halt, in large part because Jayavarman VII's public works quarried local sandstone into oblivion and had left the population exhausted.

Another challenge for the later kings was religious conflict and internecine rivalries. The state religion changed back and forth several times during the twilight years of the empire, and kings spent more time engaged in iconoclasm, defacing the temples of their predecessors, than building monuments to their own achievements. From time to time this activity boiled over into civil war.

Recent analysis of fossilised tree remains in the Mekong region suggests that Angkor was affected by severe droughts and floods in the 14th and 15th centuries during an earlier period of global warming and this probably contributed to the failure of the complex irrigation system.

1152	1177	1181
Suryavarman II is killed in a disastrous campaign against the Dai Viet (Vietnamese), provoking this rising northern neighbour and sparking centuries of conflict between the two countries.	The Chams launch a surprise attack on Angkor by sailing up the Tonlé Sap, defeat the powerful Khmers and occupy the capital for four years.	The Chams are vanquished as Jayavarman VII, the greatest king of Angkor and builder of Angkor Thom, takes the throne, changing the state religion to Mahayana Buddhism.

Angkor was losing control over the peripheries of its empire. At the same time, the Thais were ascendant, having migrated south from Yunnan to escape Kublai Khan and his Mongol hordes. The Thais, first from Sukothai, later Ayuthaya, grew in strength and made repeated incursions into Angkor before finally sacking the city in 1431 and making off with thousands of intellectuals, artisans and dancers from the royal court. During this period, perhaps drawn by the opportunities for sea trade with China and fearful of the increasingly bellicose Thais, the Khmer elite began to migrate to the Phnom Penh area. The capital shifted several times over the centuries but eventually settled in present-day Phnom Penh.

The commercial metropolis that is now Ho Chi Minh City (Saigon) in Vietnam was, in 1600, a small Cambodian village called Prey Nokor.

From 1600 until the arrival of the French in 1863, Cambodia was ruled by a series of weak kings beset by dynastic rivalries. In the face of such intrigue, they sought the protection – granted, of course, at a price – of either Thailand or Vietnam. In the 17th century, the Nguyen lords of southern Vietnam came to the rescue of the Cambodian king in return for settlement rights in the Mekong Delta region. The Khmers still refer to this region as Kampuchea Krom (Lower Cambodia), even though it is well and truly populated by the Vietnamese today.

In the west, the Thais controlled the provinces of Battambang and Siem Reap from 1794 and held much influence over the Cambodian royal family. Indeed, one king was crowned in Bangkok and placed on the throne at Udong (p124) with the help of the Thai army. That Cambodia survived through the 18th century as a distinct entity is due to the preoccupations of its neighbours: while the Thais were expending their energy and resources in fighting the Burmese, the Vietnamese were wholly absorbed by internal strife. The pattern continued for more than two centuries, the carcass of Cambodia pulled back and forth between two powerful tigers.

Cambodia's turbulent past is uncovered in a series of articles, oral histories and photos in an excellent website called *Beauty and Darkness: Cambodia, the Odyssey of the Khmer People.* Find it at www.mekong.net/cambodia.

THE FRENCH IN CAMBODIA

The era of yo-yoing between Thai and Vietnamese masters came to a close in 1863, when French gunboats intimidated King Norodom I (r 1860–1904) into signing a treaty of protectorate. Ironically, it really was a protectorate, as Cambodia was in danger of going the way of Champa and vanishing from the map. French control of Cambodia developed as a sideshow to their interests in Vietnam, uncannily similar to the American experience a century later, and initially involved little direct interference in Cambodia's affairs. The French presence also helped keep Norodom on the throne despite the ambitions of his rebellious half-brothers.

The French did very little to encourage education in Cambodia and, by the end of WWII, after 70 years of colonial rule, there were no universities and only one high school in the whole country.

By the 1870s French officials in Cambodia began pressing for greater control over internal affairs. In 1884 Norodom was forced into signing a treaty that turned his country into a virtual colony, sparking a two-year rebellion that constituted the only major uprising in Cambodia before WWII. The rebellion only ended when the king was persuaded to call

1219	**1253**	**1296**
Jayavarman VII dies aged in his 90s and the empire of Angkor slowly declines due to a choking irrigation network, religious conflict and the rise of powerful neighbours.	The Mongols of Kublai Khan sack the Thai kingdom of Nanchao in Yunnan, sparking an exodus southwards which brings them into direct conflict with the weakening Khmer empire.	Chinese emissary Chou Ta Kuan spends one year living at Angkor and publishes *The Customs of Cambodia,* the only contemporary account of life at the great Khmer capital.

upon the rebel fighters to lay down their weapons in exchange for a return to the status quo.

During the following decades, senior Cambodian officials opened the door to direct French control over the day-to-day administration of the country, as they saw certain advantages in acquiescing to French power. The French maintained Norodom's court in a splendour unseen since the heyday of Angkor, helping to enhance the symbolic position of the monarchy. In 1907 the French were able to pressure Thailand into returning the northwest provinces of Battambang, Siem Reap and Sisophon in return for concessions of Lao territory to the Thais. This meant Angkor came under Cambodian control for the first time in more than a century.

King Norodom I was succeeded by King Sisowath (r 1904–27), who was succeeded by King Monivong (r 1927–41). Upon King Monivong's death, the French governor-general of Japanese-occupied Indochina, Admiral Jean Decoux, placed 19-year-old Prince Norodom Sihanouk on the Cambodian throne. The French authorities assumed young Sihanouk would prove pliable, but this eventually proved to be a major miscalculation (see the boxed text, opposite).

During WWII, Japanese forces occupied much of Asia, and Cambodia was no exception. However, with many in France collaborating with the occupying Germans, the Japanese were happy to let their new Vichy France allies control affairs in Cambodia. The price was conceding to Thailand (a Japanese ally of sorts) much of Battambang and Siem Reap Provinces once again, areas that weren't returned until 1947. However, with the fall of Paris in 1944 and French policy in disarray, the Japanese were forced to take direct control of the territory by early 1945. After WWII, the French returned, making Cambodia an autonomous state within the French Union, but retaining de facto control. The immediate postwar years were marked by strife among the country's various political factions, a situation made more unstable by the Franco-Vietminh War then raging in Vietnam and Laos, which spilled over into Cambodia. The Vietnamese, as they were also to do 20 years later in the war against Lon Nol and the Americans, trained and fought with bands of Khmer Issarak (Free Khmer) against the French authorities.

During the 1960s, Cambodia was an oasis of peace while wars raged in neighbouring Vietnam and Laos. By 1970 that had all changed. For the full story, read *Sideshow: Kissinger, Nixon and the Destruction of Cambodia* by William Shawcross (1979).

THE SIHANOUK YEARS

The post-independence period was one of peace and great prosperity. It was Cambodia's golden time, a time of creativity and optimism. Phnom Penh grew in size and stature, the temples of Angkor were the leading tourist destination in Southeast Asia and Sihanouk played host to a succession of influential leaders from across the globe. However, dark clouds were circling, as the American war in Vietnam became a black hole, sucking in neighbouring countries.

1353	1431	1594
Lao prince Chao Fa Ngum ends his exile at Angkor and is sponsored by his Khmer father-in-law on an expedition to conquer the new Thai kingdoms, declaring himself leader of Lan Xang (Land of a Million Elephants).	The Thais sack Angkor definitively, carting off most of the royal court to Ayuthaya, including nobles, priests, dancers and artisans.	The temporary Cambodian capital of Lovek falls when, according to legend, the Siamese fire a cannon of silver coins into the capital's bamboo defences. The soldiers cut down the protective bamboo to retrieve the silver, leaving the city exposed.

In late 1952 King Sihanouk dissolved the fledgling parliament, declared martial law and embarked on his 'royal crusade': his travelling campaign to drum up international support for his country's independence. Independence was proclaimed on 9 November 1953 and recognised by the Geneva Conference

SIHANOUK: THE LAST OF THE GOD-KINGS

Norodom Sihanouk has been a towering presence in the topsy-turvy world of Cambodian politics. A larger-than-life character of many enthusiasms and shifting political positions, his amatory exploits dominated his early life. Later he became the prince who stage-managed the close of French colonialism, led Cambodia during its golden years, was imprisoned by the Khmer Rouge and, from privileged exile, finally returned triumphant as king. He is many things to many people, a political chameleon, but whatever else he may be, he has proved himself a survivor.

Sihanouk, born in 1922, was not an obvious contender for the throne, as he was from the Norodom branch of the royal family. He was crowned in 1941, at just 19, with his education incomplete. In 1955 Sihanouk abdicated and turned his attention to politics, his party winning every seat in parliament that year. By the mid-1960s Sihanouk had been calling the shots in Cambodia for a decade. During this period, after innumerable love affairs, he finally settled on Monique Izzi, the daughter of a Franco-Italian father and a Cambodian mother, as his consort.

The conventional wisdom was that 'Sihanouk is Cambodia', his leadership the key to national success. However, as the country was inexorably drawn into the American war in Vietnam and government troops battled with a leftist insurgency in the countryside, Sihanouk was increasingly seen as a liability. With the economy in tatters, his obsessive involvement in the Cambodian film industry (p56) and his public announcements proclaiming Cambodia 'an oasis of peace' suggested a man who had not only abdicated from the throne but also from reality.

On 18 March 1970 the National Assembly voted to remove Sihanouk from office. Sihanouk went into exile in Beijing and joined the communists. Following the Khmer Rouge victory on 17 April 1975, Sihanouk returned to Cambodia as head of the new state of Democratic Kampuchea. He resigned after less than a year and was confined to the Royal Palace as a prisoner of the Khmer Rouge. He remained there until early 1979 when, on the eve of the Vietnamese invasion, he was flown back to Beijing. It was to be more than a decade before Sihanouk finally returned to Cambodia.

Sihanouk never quite gave up wanting to be everything for Cambodia: international statesman, general, president, film director, and man of the people. On 24 September 1993, after 38 years in politics, he settled once more for the role of king. His second stint as king was a frustrating time; reigning rather than ruling, he had to take a back seat to the politicians. He pulled Cambodia through a political impasse on several occasions, but eventually enough was enough and he abdicated on 7 October 2004. Many reasons for his abdication were cited (old age, failing health), but most observers agree it was a calculated political decision to ensure the future of the monarchy, as the politicians were stalling on choosing a successor. His son King Sihamoni ascended to the throne and Cambodia came through another crisis. However, Sihanouk's place in history is assured, the last in a long line of Angkor's god-kings.

1772	1834	1863
Cambodia is caught between the powerful Vietnamese and Siamese, and the latter burn Phnom Penh to the ground, another chapter in the story of inflamed tensions that persists today.	The Vietnamese take control of much of Cambodia during the reign of Emperor Minh Mang and begin a slow revolution to 'teach the barbarians their customs'.	The French force King Norodom I into signing a treaty of protectorate, which prevents Cambodia being wiped off the map and thus begins 90 years of French rule.

of May 1954, which ended French control of Indochina. In 1955, Sihanouk abdicated, afraid of being marginalised amid the pomp of royal ceremony. The 'royal crusader' became 'citizen Sihanouk'. He vowed never again to return to the throne. Meanwhile his father became king. It was a masterstroke that offered Sihanouk both royal authority and supreme political power. His newly established party, Sangkum Reastr Niyum (People's Socialist Community), won every seat in parliament in the September 1955 elections and Sihanouk was to dominate Cambodian politics for the next 15 years.

Although he feared the Vietnamese communists, Sihanouk considered South Vietnam and Thailand, both allies of the mistrusted USA, the greatest threats to Cambodia's security, even survival. In an attempt to fend off these many dangers, he declared Cambodia neutral and refused to accept further US aid, which had accounted for a substantial chunk of the country's military budget. He also nationalised many industries, including the rice trade. In 1965 Sihanouk, convinced that the USA had been plotting against him and his family, broke diplomatic relations with Washington and veered towards the North Vietnamese and China. In addition, he agreed to let the communists use Cambodian territory in their battle against South Vietnam and the USA. Sihanouk was taking sides, a dangerous position in a volatile region.

These moves and his socialist economic policies alienated conservative elements in Cambodian society, including the army brass and the urban elite. At the same time, left-wing Cambodians, many of them educated abroad, deeply resented his domestic policies, which stifled political debate. Compounding Sihanouk's problems was the fact that all classes were fed up with the pervasive corruption in government ranks, some of it uncomfortably close to the royal family. Although most peasants revered Sihanouk as a semi-divine figure, in 1967 a rural-based rebellion broke out in Samlot, Battambang, leading him to conclude that the greatest threat to his regime came from the left. Bowing to pressure from the army, he implemented a policy of harsh repression against left-wingers.

By 1969 the conflict between the army and leftist rebels had become more serious, as the Vietnamese sought sanctuary deeper in Cambodia. Sihanouk's political position had also decidedly deteriorated – due in no small part to his obsession with film-making, which was leading him to neglect affairs of state. In March 1970, while Sihanouk was on a trip to France, General Lon Nol and Prince Sisowath Sirik Matak, Sihanouk's cousin, deposed him as chief of state, apparently with tacit US consent. Sihanouk took up residence in Beijing, where he set up a government-in-exile in alliance with an indigenous Cambodian revolutionary movement that Sihanouk had nicknamed the Khmer Rouge. This was a definitive moment in contemporary Cambodian history, as the Khmer Rouge exploited its partnership with Sihanouk to draw new recruits into their small organisation. Talk to many former Khmer Rouge fighters and they all say that they 'went to the hills'

Pol Pot travelled up the Ho Chi Minh trail to visit Beijing in 1966 at the height of the Cultural Revolution there. He was obviously inspired by what he saw, as the Khmer Rouge went even further than the Red Guards in severing links with the past.

Lon Nol's military press attaché was known for his colourful, even imaginative media briefings that painted a rosy picture of the increasingly desperate situation on the ground. With a name like Major Am Rong, few could take him seriously.

1885

Rebellion against French rule in Cambodia breaks out in response to a new treaty giving the French administrators wide-ranging powers. The treaty is signed under the watch of French gunboats in the Mekong River.

1907

French authorities successfully negotiate the return of the northwest provinces of Siem Reap, Battambang and Preah Vihear, which have been under Thai control since 1794.

1942

Japanese forces occupy Cambodia, leaving the administration in the hands of Vichy France officials, but fan the flames of independence as the war draws to a close.

(a euphemism for joining the Khmer Rouge) to fight for their king and knew nothing of Mao or Marxism.

DESCENT INTO CIVIL WAR

The lines were drawn for a bloody era of civil war. Sihanouk was condemned to death *in absentia*, an excessive move on the part of the new government that effectively ruled out any hint of compromise for the next five years. Lon Nol gave communist Vietnamese forces an ultimatum to withdraw their forces within one week, which amounted to a virtual declaration of war, as no Vietnamese fighters wanted to return to the homeland to face the Americans.

On 30 April 1970, US and South Vietnamese forces invaded Cambodia in an effort to flush out thousands of Viet Cong and North Vietnamese troops who were using Cambodian bases in their war to overthrow the South Vietnamese government. As a result of the invasion, the Vietnamese communists withdrew deeper into Cambodia, further destabilising the Lon Nol government. Cambodia's tiny army never stood a chance and within the space of a few months, Vietnamese forces and their Khmer Rouge allies overran almost half the country. The ultimate humiliation came in July 1970 when the Vietnamese occupied the temples of Angkor.

In 1969 the USA had begun a secret program of bombing suspected communist base camps in Cambodia. For the next four years, until bombing was halted by the US Congress in August 1973, huge areas of the eastern half of the country were carpet-bombed by US B-52s, killing what is believed to be many thousands of civilians and turning hundreds of thousands more into refugees. Undoubtedly, the bombing campaign helped the Khmer Rouge in their recruitment drive, as more and more peasants were losing family members to the aerial assaults. While the final, heaviest bombing in the first half of 1973 may have saved Phnom Penh from a premature fall, its ferocity also helped to harden the attitude of many Khmer Rouge cadres and may have contributed to the later brutality that characterised their rule.

Savage fighting engulfed the country, bringing misery to millions of Cambodians; many fled rural areas for the relative safety of Phnom Penh and provincial capitals. Between 1970 and 1975, several hundred thousand people died in the fighting. During these years, the Khmer Rouge came to play a dominant role in trying to overthrow the Lon Nol regime, strengthened by the support of the Vietnamese, although the Khmer Rouge leadership would vehemently deny this from 1975 onwards.

The leadership of the Khmer Rouge, including Paris-educated Pol Pot and Ieng Sary, had fled into the countryside in the 1960s to escape the summary justice then being meted out to suspected leftists by Sihanouk's security forces. They consolidated control over the movement and began to move against opponents before they took Phnom Penh. Many of the Vietnamese-trained

In Francis Ford Coppola's *Apocalypse Now* (1979), a renegade colonel, played by Marlon Brando, goes AWOL in Cambodia. Martin Sheen plays a young soldier sent to bring him back, and the ensuing encounter makes for one of the most powerful indictments of war ever made.

During the US bombing campaign, more bombs were dropped on Cambodia than were used by all sides during WWII.

The Killing Fields (1985) is the definitive film on the Khmer Rouge period in Cambodia. It tells the story of American journalist Sidney Schanberg and his Cambodian assistant Dith Pran during and after the war.

1947

The provinces of Battambang, Siem Reap and Sisophon, seized by the Thais during the Japanese occupation, are returned to Cambodia.

1953

Sihanouk's royal crusade for independence succeeds and Cambodia goes it alone without the French on 9 November, ushering in a new era of optimism.

1955

King Sihanouk abdicates from the throne to enter a career in politics; he founds the Sangkum Reastr Niyum (People's Socialist Community) party and wins the election with ease.

Cambodian communists who had been based in Hanoi since the 1954 Geneva Accords returned down the Ho Chi Minh trail to join their 'allies' in the Khmer Rouge in 1973. Many were dead by 1975, executed on orders of the anti-Vietnamese Pol Pot faction. Likewise, many moderate Sihanouk supporters who had joined the Khmer Rouge as a show of loyalty to their fallen leader rather than a show of ideology to the radicals were victims of purges before the regime took power. This set a precedent for internal purges and mass executions that were to eventually bring the downfall of the Khmer Rouge.

It didn't take long for the Lon Nol government to become very unpopular as a result of unprecedented greed and corruption in its ranks. As the USA bankrolled the war, government and military personnel found lucrative means to make a fortune, such as inventing 'phantom soldiers' and pocketing their pay, or selling weapons to the enemy. Lon Nol was widely perceived as an ineffectual leader, obsessed by superstition, fortune tellers and mystical crusades. This perception increased with his stroke in March 1971 and for the next four years his grip on reality seemed to weaken as his brother Lon Non's power grew.

Despite massive US military and economic aid, Lon Nol never succeeded in gaining the initiative against the Khmer Rouge. Large parts of the countryside fell to the rebels and many provincial capitals were cut off from Phnom Penh. Lon Nol fled the country in early April 1975, leaving Sirik Matak in charge, who refused evacuation to the end. 'I cannot alas leave in such a cowardly fashion… I have committed only one mistake, that of believing in you, the Americans' were the words Sirik Matak poignantly penned to US ambassador John Gunther Dean. On 17 April 1975 – two weeks before the fall of Saigon (now Ho Chi Minh City) – Phnom Penh surrendered to the Khmer Rouge.

THE KHMER ROUGE REVOLUTION

Upon taking Phnom Penh, the Khmer Rouge implemented one of the most radical and brutal restructurings of a society ever attempted; its goal was a pure revolution, untainted by those that had gone before, to transform Cambodia into a peasant-dominated agrarian cooperative. Within days of the Khmer Rouge coming to power, the entire population of Phnom Penh and provincial towns, including the sick, elderly and infirm, was forced to march into the countryside and work as slaves for 12 to 15 hours a day. Disobedience of any sort often brought immediate execution. The advent of Khmer Rouge rule was proclaimed Year Zero. Currency was abolished and postal services were halted. The country cut itself off from the outside world.

In the eyes of Pol Pot, the Khmer Rouge was not a unified movement, but a series of factions that needed to be cleansed. This process had already begun with attacks on Vietnamese-trained Khmer Rouge and Sihanouk's supporters, but Pol Pot's initial fury upon seizing power was directed against the former regime. All of the senior government and military figures who

1962	1963	1964
The International Court rules in favour of Cambodia in the long-running dispute over the dramatic mountain temple of Preah Vihear, perched on the Dangkrek Mountains, but it remains a divisive issue today.	Pol Pot and Ieng Sary flee from Phnom Penh to the jungles of Ratanakiri to launch a guerrilla war against Sihanouk's government with training from the Vietnamese.	Following the US-sponsored coup against President Diem in South Vietnam in 1963, Sihanouk veers to the left, breaking diplomatic ties with the USA and nationalising the rice trade, antagonising the ethnic Chinese business community.

had been associated with Lon Nol were executed within days of the takeover. Then the centre shifted its attention to the outer regions, which had been separated into geographic zones. The loyalist Southwestern Zone forces, under the control of one-legged general Ta Mok, were sent into region after region to purify the population, and thousands perished.

BLOOD BROTHER NO 1

Pol Pot, Brother No 1 in the Khmer Rouge regime, is a name that sends shivers down the spines of Cambodians and foreigners alike. It is Pol Pot who is most associated with the bloody madness of the regime he led between 1975 and 1979, and his policies heaped misery, suffering and death on millions of Cambodians.

Pol Pot was born Saloth Sar in a small village near Kompong Thom in 1925. As a young man he won a scholarship to study in Paris, and it is here that he is believed to have developed his radical Marxist thought, later to transform into the politics of extreme Maoism.

In 1963 Sihanouk's repressive policies sent Saloth Sar and comrades fleeing to the jungles of Ratanakiri. It was from this moment that he began to call himself Pol Pot. Once the Khmer Rouge was allied with Sihanouk, following his overthrow by Lon Nol in 1970 and subsequent exile in Beijing, its support soared and the faces of the leadership became familiar. However, Pol Pot remained a shadowy figure, leaving public duties to Khieu Samphan and Ieng Sary.

When the Khmer Rouge marched into Phnom Penh on 17 April 1975, few people could have anticipated the hell that was to follow. Pol Pot and his clique were the architects of one of the most radical and brutal revolutions in the history of mankind. Year Zero was 1975 and Cambodia was on a self-destructive course to sever all ties with the past.

Pol Pot was not to emerge as the public face of the revolution until the end of 1976, after returning from a trip to his mentors in Beijing. He granted almost no interviews to foreign media and was seen only on propaganda movies produced by government TV. Such was his aura and reputation that, by the last year of the regime, a cult of personality was developing around him and stone busts were produced.

When the Vietnamese invaded Cambodia on 25 December 1978, Pol Pot and his supporters fled into the jungle near the Thai border, from where they spent the next decade launching attacks on government positions in Cambodia.

Pol Pot spent much of the 1980s living in Thailand and was able to rebuild his shattered forces and once again threaten Cambodia. His enigma increased as the international media speculated as to the real fate of Pol Pot. His demise was reported so often that when he finally passed away on 15 April 1998, many Cambodians refused to believe it until they had seen his body on TV or in newspapers. Even then, many were sceptical and rumours continue to circulate about exactly how he met his end. Officially, he was said to have died from a heart attack, but the full autopsy was not carried out before his body was cremated on a pyre of burning tyres.

For more on the life and times of Pol Pot, pick up one of the excellent biographies written about him: *Brother Number One* by David Chandler or *Pol Pot: The History of a Nightmare* by Phillip Short.

1969

US President Nixon authorises the secret bombing of Cambodia, which starts with the carpet bombing of border zones, but eventually spreads to the whole country, continuing until 1973 and killing as many as 250,000 Cambodians.

1970

Sihanouk throws in his lot with the Khmer Rouge after being overthrown by military commander Lon Nol and his cousin Prince Sirik Matak, and sentenced to death *in absentia*, marking the start of a five-year civil war.

1971

Lon Nol, leader of the Khmer Republic, launches the Chenla offensive against Vietnamese communists and their Khmer Rouge allies in Cambodia, but it turns out to be a disaster. He also suffers a stroke, but struggles on as leader until 1975.

The cleansing reached grotesque heights in the final and bloodiest purge against the powerful and independent Eastern Zone. Generally considered more moderate than other Khmer Rouge factions, the Eastern Zone was ideologically, as well as geographically, closer to Vietnam. The Pol Pot faction consolidated the rest of the country before moving against the east from 1977 onwards. Hundreds of leaders were executed before open rebellion broke out, sparking a civil war in the east. Many Eastern Zone leaders fled to Vietnam, forming the nucleus of the government installed by the Vietnamese in January 1979. The people were defenceless and distrusted – 'Cambodian bodies with Vietnamese minds' or 'duck's arses with chicken's heads' – and were deported to the northwest with new, blue *kramas* (scarves). Had it not been for the Vietnamese invasion, all would have perished, as the blue *krama* was a secret party sign indicating an eastern enemy of the revolution.

It is still not known exactly how many Cambodians died at the hands of the Khmer Rouge during the three years, eight months and 20 days of their rule. The Vietnamese claimed three million deaths, while foreign experts long considered the number closer to one million. Yale University researchers undertaking ongoing investigations estimated that the figure was close to two million.

Hundreds of thousands of people were executed by the Khmer Rouge leadership, while hundreds of thousands more died of famine and disease. Meals consisted of little more than watery rice porridge twice a day, but were meant to sustain men, women and children through a back-breaking day in the fields. Disease stalked the work camps, malaria and dysentery striking down whole families; death was a relief for many from the horrors of life. Some zones were better than others, some leaders fairer than others, but life for the majority was one of unending misery and suffering in this 'prison without walls'.

As the centre eliminated more and more moderates, Angkar (the organisation) became the only family people needed and those who did not agree were sought out and destroyed. The Khmer Rouge detached the Cambodian people from all they held dear: their families, their food, their fields and their faith. Even the peasants who had supported the revolution could no longer blindly follow such madness. Nobody cared for the Khmer Rouge by 1978, but nobody had an ounce of strength to do anything about it…except the Vietnamese.

ENTER THE VIETNAMESE

Relations between Cambodia and Vietnam have historically been tense, as the Vietnamese have slowly but steadily expanded southwards, encroaching on Cambodian territory. Despite the fact the two communist parties had fought together as brothers in arms, old tensions soon came to the fore.

From 1976 to 1978, the Khmer Rouge instigated a series of border clashes with Vietnam, and claimed the Mekong Delta, once part of the Khmer empire.

1973	1975	1977
Sihanouk and his wife Monique travel down the Ho Chi Minh trail to visit Khmer Rouge allies at the holy mountain of Phnom Kulen near Angkor, a propaganda victory for Pol Pot.	The Khmer Rouge march into Phnom Penh on 17 April and turn the clocks back to Year Zero, evacuating the capital and turning the whole nation into a prison without walls.	The Pol Pot faction of the Khmer Rouge launch their bloodiest purge against the Eastern Zone of the country, sparking a civil war along the banks of the Mekong and drawing the Vietnamese into the battle.

THE POLITICS OF DISASTER RELIEF

The Cambodian famine became a new front in the Cold War, as Washington and Moscow jostled for influence from afar. As hundreds of thousands of Cambodians fled to Thailand, a massive international famine relief effort, sponsored by the UN, was launched. The international community wanted to deliver aid across a land bridge at Poipet, while the new Vietnamese-backed Phnom Penh government wanted all supplies to come through the capital via Kompong Som (Sihanoukville) or the Mekong River. Both sides had their reasons – the new government did not want aid to fall into the hands of its Khmer Rouge enemies, while the international community didn't believe the new government had the infrastructure to distribute the aid – and both were right.

Some agencies distributed aid the slow way through Phnom Penh, and others set up camps in Thailand. The camps became a magnet for half of Cambodia, as many Khmers still feared the return of the Khmer Rouge or were seeking a new life overseas. The Thai military convinced the international community to distribute all aid through their channels and used this as a cloak to rebuild the shattered Khmer Rouge forces as an effective resistance against the Vietnamese. Thailand demanded that, as a condition for allowing international food aid for Cambodia to pass through its territory, food had to be supplied to the Khmer Rouge forces encamped in the Thai border region as well. Along with weaponry supplied by China, this international assistance was essential in enabling the Khmer Rouge to rebuild its military strength and fight on for another two decades.

Incursions into Vietnamese border provinces left hundreds of Vietnamese civilians dead. On 25 December 1978 Vietnam launched a full-scale invasion of Cambodia, toppling the Pol Pot government two weeks later. As Vietnamese tanks neared Phnom Penh, the Khmer Rouge fled westward with as many civilians as it could seize, taking refuge in the jungles and mountains along the Thai border. The Vietnamese installed a new government led by several former Khmer Rouge officers, including current Prime Minister Hun Sen, who had defected to Vietnam in 1977. The Khmer Rouge's patrons, the Chinese communists, launched a massive reprisal raid across Vietnam's northernmost border in early 1979 in an attempt to buy their allies time. It failed and after 17 days the Chinese withdrew, their fingers badly burnt by their Vietnamese enemies. The Vietnamese then staged a show trial in which Pol Pot and Ieng Sary were condemned to death for their genocidal acts.

A traumatised population took to the road in search of surviving family members. Millions had been uprooted and had to walk hundreds of kilometres across the country. Rice stocks were destroyed, the harvest left to wither and little rice planted, sowing the seeds for a widespread famine in 1979 and 1980.

As the conflict in Cambodia raged, Sihanouk agreed, under pressure from China, to head a military and political front opposed to the Phnom Penh government. The Sihanouk-led resistance coalition brought together – on paper, at least – Funcinpec (the French acronym for the National United Front for an

Learn more about politics and life in Cambodia during the 1980s by picking up *Cambodia After the Khmer Rouge* by Evan Gottesman, which sheds new light on a little-known period.

Journalist Henry Kamm spent many years filing reports from Cambodia and his book *Cambodia: Report from a Stricken Land* is a fascinating insight into recent events.

1979	1980	1982
Vietnamese forces liberate Cambodia from Khmer Rouge rule on 7 January 1979, just two weeks after launching the invasion, and install a friendly regime in Phnom Penh.	Cambodia is gripped by a terrible famine, as the dislocation of the previous few years means that no rice has been planted or harvested, and worldwide 'Save Kampuchea' appeals are launched.	Sihanouk is pressured to join forces with the Khmer Rouge as head of the Coalition Government of Democratic Kampuchea (CGDK), a new military front against the Vietnamese-backed government in Phnom Penh.

Independent, Neutral, Peaceful and Cooperative Cambodia), which comprised a royalist group loyal to Sihanouk; the Khmer People's National Liberation Front, a non-communist grouping under former prime minister Son Sann; and the Khmer Rouge, officially known as the Party of Democratic Kampuchea and by far the most powerful of the three. The crimes of the Khmer Rouge were swept aside to ensure a compromise that suited the realpolitik of the day.

During the mid-1980s the British government dispatched the Special Air Service (SAS) to a Malaysian jungle camp to train guerrilla fighters in land-mine-laying techniques. Although the SAS was officially assisting the smaller factions, it is certain the Khmer Rouge benefited from this experience. It then used these new-found skills to intimidate and terrorise the Cambodian people. The USA gave more than US$15 million a year in aid to the non-communist factions of the Khmer Rouge–dominated coalition.

Between four and six million land mines dot the Cambodian countryside. Lifetime rehabilitation of the country's estimated 40,000 victims costs US$120 million.

For much of the 1980s Cambodia remained closed to the Western world, save for the presence of some humanitarian aid groups. Government policy was effectively under the control of the Vietnamese, so Cambodia found itself very much in the Eastern-bloc camp. The economy was in tatters for much of this period, as Cambodia, like Vietnam, suffered from the effects of a US-sponsored embargo.

In 1984 the Vietnamese overran all the major rebel camps inside Cambodia, forcing the Khmer Rouge and its allies to retreat into Thailand. From this time the Khmer Rouge and its allies engaged in guerrilla warfare aimed at demoralising their opponents. Tactics used by the Khmer Rouge included shelling government-controlled garrison towns, planting thousands of mines in rural areas, attacking road transport, blowing up bridges, kidnapping village chiefs and targeting civilians. The Khmer Rouge also forced thousands of men, women and children living in the refugee camps it controlled to work as porters, ferrying ammunition and other supplies into Cambodia across heavily mined sections of the border.

Western powers, including the USA and UK, ensured the Khmer Rouge retained its seat at the UN general assembly in New York until 1991, a scenario that saw those responsible for the genocide representing their victims on the international stage.

The Vietnamese, for their part, laid the world's longest minefield, known as K-5 and stretching from the Gulf of Thailand to the Lao border, in an attempt to seal out the guerrillas. They also sent Cambodians into the forests to cut down trees on remote sections of road to prevent ambushes. Thousands died of disease and from injuries sustained from land mines. The Khmer Rouge was no longer in power, but for many the 1980s were almost as tough as the 1970s: one long struggle to survive.

THE UN COMES TO TOWN

As the Cold War came to a close, peace began to break out all over the globe, and Cambodia was not immune to the new spirit of reconciliation. In September 1989, Vietnam, with a devastated economy and eager to end its international isolation, announced the withdrawal of all of its troops from Cambodia. With the Vietnamese gone, the opposition coalition, still

1984	1985	1989
The Vietnamese embark on a major offensive in the west of Cambodia and the Khmer Rouge and its allies are forced to retreat to refugee camps and bases inside Thailand.	There is a changing of the guard at the top and Hun Sen becomes Prime Minister of Cambodia, a title he still holds today with the Cambodian People's Party.	As the effects of President Gorbachev's perestroika (restructuring) begin to impact on communist allies, Vietnam feels the pinch and announces the withdrawal of its forces from Cambodia.

THE NAME GAME

Cambodia has changed its name so many times over the last few decades that there are understandable grounds for confusion. To the Cambodians, their country is Kampuchea. The name is derived from the word Kambuja, meaning 'those born of Kambu', the mythical founder of the country. It dates back as far as the 10th century. The Portuguese 'Camboxa' and the French 'Cambodge', from which the English name 'Cambodia' is derived, are adaptations of 'Kambuja'.

Since gaining independence in 1953, the country has been known in English by various names before coming full circle:

- The Kingdom of Cambodia
- The Khmer Republic (under Lon Nol, who reigned from 1970 to 1975)
- Democratic Kampuchea (under the Khmer Rouge, which controlled the country from 1975 to 1979)
- The People's Republic of Kampuchea (under the Vietnamese-backed government from 1979 to 1989)
- The State of Cambodia (from mid-1989)
- The Kingdom of Cambodia (from May 1993)

It was the Khmer Rouge that insisted the outside world use the name Kampuchea. Changing the country's official English name back to Cambodia was intended as a symbolic move to distance the present government in Phnom Penh from the bitter connotations of the name Kampuchea, which Westerners associate with the murderous Khmer Rouge regime.

---

dominated by the Khmer Rouge, launched a series of offensives, forcing the now-vulnerable government to the negotiating table.

Diplomatic efforts to end the civil war began to bear fruit in September 1990, when a peace plan was accepted by both the Phnom Penh government and the three factions of the resistance coalition. According to the plan, the Supreme National Council (SNC), a coalition of all factions, would be formed under the presidency of Sihanouk. Meanwhile, the UN Transitional Authority in Cambodia (Untac) would supervise the administration of the country for two years, with the goal of free and fair elections.

Untac undoubtedly achieved some successes, but for all of these, it is the failures that were to cost Cambodia dearly in the 'democratic' era. Untac was successful in pushing through many international human-rights covenants; it opened the door to a significant number of non-governmental organisations (NGOs); and, most importantly, on 25 May 1993, elections were held with an 89.6% turnout. However, the results were far from decisive. Funcinpec, led by Prince Norodom Ranariddh, took 58 seats in the National Assembly, while the Cambodian People's Party (CPP), which represented the previous communist government, took 51 seats. The CPP had lost the election, but senior leaders

The Documentation Center of Cambodia is an organisation established to document the crimes of the Khmer Rouge as a record for future generations. Its excellent website is a mine of information about Cambodia's darkest hour. Take your time to visit www.dccam.org.

1991	**1993**	**1994**
The Paris Peace Accords are signed, in which all parties, including the Khmer Rouge, agree to participate in free and fair elections supervised by the UN.	The pro-Sihanouk royalist party Funcinpec under the leadership of Prince Ranariddh wins the popular vote, but the CPP threaten secession in the east to muscle their way into government.	The Khmer Rouge target foreign tourists in Cambodia, kidnapping and killing groups travelling by taxi and train to the south coast, reinforcing Cambodia's overseas image as a dangerous country.

threatened a secession of the eastern provinces of the country. As a result, Cambodia ended up with two prime ministers: Norodom Ranariddh as first prime minister, and Hun Sen as second prime minister.

Even today, Untac is heralded as one of the UN's success stories. The other perspective is that it was an ill-conceived and poorly executed peace because so many of the powers involved in brokering the deal had their own agendas to advance. To many Cambodians who had survived the 1970s, it was unthinkable that the Khmer Rouge would be allowed to play a part in the electoral process after presiding over a genocide.

The UN's disarmament program took weapons away from rural militias who for so long provided the backbone of the government's provincial defence network against the Khmer Rouge. This left communities throughout the country vulnerable to attack, while the Khmer Rouge used the veil of legitimacy conferred upon it by the peace process to re-establish a guerrilla network throughout Cambodia. By 1994, when it was finally outlawed by the government, the Khmer Rouge was probably a greater threat to the stability of Cambodia than at any time since 1979.

Untac's main goals had been to 'restore and maintain peace' and 'promote national reconciliation' and in the short term it achieved neither. It did oversee free and fair elections, but these were later annulled by the actions of Cambodia's politicians. Little was done during the UN period to try to dismantle the communist apparatus of state set up by the CPP, a well-oiled machine that continues to ensure that former communists control the civil service, judiciary, army and police today.

For the latest on political gossip in Cambodia, visit http://ki-media.blogspot.com.

THE SLOW BIRTH OF PEACE

When the Vietnamese toppled the Pol Pot government in 1979, the Khmer Rouge disappeared into the jungle. The guerrillas eventually boycotted the 1993 elections and later rejected peace talks aimed at establishing a ceasefire. The defection of some 2000 troops from the Khmer Rouge army in the months after the elections offered some hope that the long-running insurrection would fizzle out. However, government-sponsored amnesty programs initially turned out to be ill conceived: the policy of re-conscripting Khmer Rouge troops and forcing them to fight their former comrades provided little incentive to desert.

To stay on top of recent events in Cambodia, check out the Phnom Penh Post website at www.phnompenhpost.com.

In 1994 the Khmer Rouge resorted to a new tactic of targeting tourists, with horrendous results for a number of foreigners in Cambodia. During 1994 three people were taken from a taxi on the road to Sihanoukville and subsequently shot. A few months later another three foreigners were seized from a train bound for Sihanoukville and in the ransom drama that followed they were executed as the army closed in.

The government changed course during the mid-1990s, opting for more carrot and less stick in a bid to end the war. The breakthrough came in 1996 when Ieng Sary, Brother No 3 in the Khmer Rouge hierarchy and foreign

1995	1997	1998
Prince Norodom Sirivudh is arrested and exiled for allegedly plotting to kill Prime Minister Hun Sen, removing another potential rival from the scene.	Second Prime Minister Hun Sen overthrows First Prime Minister Norodom Ranariddh in a military coup, referred to as 'the events of 1997' in Cambodia.	Pol Pot passes away on 15 April 1998 as Anlong Veng falls to government forces, and many observers ponder whether the timing is coincidental.

minister during its rule, was denounced by Pol Pot for corruption. He subsequently led a mass defection of fighters and their dependants from the Pailin area, and this effectively sealed the fate of the remaining Khmer Rouge. Pailin, rich in gems and timber, had long been the economic crutch that kept the Khmer Rouge hobbling along. The severing of this income, coupled with the fact that government forces now had only one front on which to concentrate their resources, suggested the days of civil war were numbered.

By 1997 cracks were appearing in the coalition and the fledgling democracy once again found itself under siege. But it was the Khmer Rouge that again grabbed the headlines. Pol Pot ordered the execution of Son Sen, defence minister during the Khmer Rouge regime, and many of his family members. This provoked a putsch within the Khmer Rouge leadership, and the one-legged hardliner general Ta Mok seized control, putting Pol Pot on 'trial'. Rumours flew about Phnom Penh that Pol Pot would be brought there to face international justice, but events dramatically shifted back to the capital.

A lengthy courting period ensued in which both Funcinpec and the CPP attempted to win the trust of the remaining Khmer Rouge hardliners in northern Cambodia. Ranariddh was close to forging a deal with the jungle fighters and was keen to get it sewn up before Cambodia's accession to Asean, as nothing would provide a better entry fanfare than the ending of Cambodia's long civil war. He was outflanked and subsequently outgunned by Second Prime Minister Hun Sen. On 5 July 1997, fighting again erupted on the streets of Phnom Penh as troops loyal to the CPP clashed with those loyal to Funcinpec. The heaviest exchanges were around the airport and key government buildings, but before long the dust had settled and the CPP once again controlled Cambodia.

Following the coup, the remnants of Funcinpec forces on the Thai border around O Smach formed an alliance with the last of the Khmer Rouge under Ta Mok's control. The fighting may have ended, but the deaths did not stop there: several prominent Funcinpec politicians and military leaders were victims of extrajudicial executions, and even today no one has been brought to justice for these crimes. Many of Funcinpec's leading politicians fled abroad, while the senior generals led the resistance struggle on the ground.

As 1998 began, the CPP announced an all-out offensive against its enemies in the north. By April it was closing in on the Khmer Rouge strongholds of Anlong Veng and Preah Vihear, and amid this heavy fighting Pol Pot evaded justice by dying a sorry death on 15 April in the captivity of the Khmer Rouge. The fall of Anlong Veng in April was followed by the fall of Preah Vihear in May, and the big three, Ta Mok, Khieu Samphan and Nuon Chea, were forced to flee into the jungle near the Thai border with their remaining troops.

The 1998 election result reinforced the reality that the CPP was now dominant force in the Cambodian political system and on 25 December Hun Sen received the Christmas present he had been waiting for: Khieu Samphan

On 31 March 1997 a grenade was thrown into a group of Sam Rainsy supporters demonstrating outside the National Assembly. Sam Rainsy blamed Hun Sen and the CPP for the attack and even the FBI got involved in the investigation.

The Khmer Rouge period is politically sensitive in Cambodia, due in part to the connections the current leadership have with the communist movement – so much so that the history of the genocide was not taught in high schools until 2009.

When Pol Pot passed away on 15 April 1998, his body was hastily cremated on a pyre of burning tyres without an autopsy, leading many Cambodians to speculate that he was actually murdered.

1999	**2002**	**2003**
Cambodia finally joins Asean after a two-year delay, taking its place among the family of Southeast Asian nations, welcoming the country back to the world stage.	Cambodia holds its first ever local elections at commune level, a tentative step in dismantling the old communist system of control and bringing grass-roots democracy to the country.	The CPP wins the election, but political infighting prevents the formation of the new government for almost a year until the old coalition with Funcinpec is revived.

and Nuon Chea were defecting to the government side. The international community began to pile on the pressure for the establishment of some sort of war-crimes tribunal to try the remaining Khmer Rouge leadership. After lengthy negotiations, agreement was finally reached on the composition of a court to try the surviving leaders of the Khmer Rouge. The CPP was suspicious of a UN-administered trial as the UN had sided with the Khmer Rouge–dominated coalition against the government in Phnom Penh and the ruling party wanted a major say in who was to be tried for what. The UN for its part doubted that the judiciary in Cambodia was sophisticated or impartial enough to fairly oversee such a major trial. A compromise solution – a mixed tribunal of three international and four Cambodian judges requiring a super majority of two plus three for a verdict – was eventually agreed upon.

Early 2002 saw Cambodia's first ever local elections to select village and commune level representatives, an important step in bringing grassroots democracy to the country. Despite national elections since 1993, the CPP continued to monopolise political power at local and regional levels and only with commune elections would this grip be loosened. The national elections of July 2003 saw a shift in the balance of power, as the CPP consolidated their grip on Cambodia and the Sam Rainsy Party overhauled Funcinpec as the second party. After nearly a year of negotiating, Funcinpec ditched the Sam Rainsy Party once again and joined a coalition with the CPP for another term.

CONTEMPORARY CAMBODIA

Cambodia is at a crossroads in its road to recovery from the brutal years of Khmer Rouge rule. Compare Cambodia today with the dark abyss into which it plunged under the Khmer Rouge and the picture looks pretty optimistic, but look to its more successful neighbours and it's easy to be pessimistic. Cambodia must choose its path: pluralism, progress and prosperity or intimidation, impunity and injustice. The jury is still very much out on which way things will go.

Another jury still out is that of the Khmer Rouge trial, sidelined by the politics of the Cold War for two decades, and then delayed by bureaucratic bickering at home and abroad. The Extraordinary Chambers in the Courts of Cambodia (ECCC) trial is finally underway after many a dispute between the Cambodian authorities and the international community, but it is by no means certain that the wheels of justice will turn fast enough to keep up with the ageing of the surviving Khmer Rouge leaders. Military commander Ta Mok died in custody in 2006 and both Ieng Sary and Nuon Chea are suffering health issues. However, the trial of Kaing Guek Eav, aka Comrade Duch, dominated headlines for much of 2009 and at the time of writing a verdict was anticipated in early 2010. The prosecution has asked for a 40-year sentence, although some victims are calling this too lenient given the magnitude of his crimes and the mountain of evidence. Trials were also underway for former Khmer Rouge foreign minister Ieng Sary and former head of state Khieu Samphan.

When Jemaah Islamiyah (affiliated with Al Qaeda) bomber Hambali was arrested in Thailand in August 2003, it later surfaced that he had been living in a backpacker hostel on Boeng Kak Lake for about six months.

2004	2005	2006
In a move that catches observers by surprise, King Sihanouk abdicates from the throne and is succeeded by his son King Sihamoni, a popular choice as Sihamoni has steered clear of politics.	Cambodia joins the WTO, opening its markets to free trade, but many commentators feel it could be counterproductive as the economy is so small and there is no more protection for domestic producers.	Lawsuits and counter lawsuits see political leaders moving from conflict to the courtroom in the new Cambodia and the revolving doors end with opposition leader Sam Rainsy back in the country and Prince Ranariddh out.

In the meantime, the budget for the trial just keeps on rising, reaching the US$150 million mark, amid allegations of corruption and political interference on the Cambodian side. Some Cambodians feel the trial will send an important political message about accountability that may resonate with some in power in Cambodia today. However, others argue that the trial is a major waste of money given the overwhelming evidence against surviving senior leaders and that a truth and reconciliation commission may have provided more reaching answers for Cambodians wanting to understand what motivated the average Khmer Rouge cadre.

The royal family has been a constant in contemporary Cambodian history and no one more so than the mercurial monarch King Sihanouk, who once again surprised the world with his abdication in 2004. His relatively unknown son King Sihamoni assumed the throne and has brought renewed credibility to the monarchy, untainted as he is by the partisan politics of the past. Meanwhile, the political arm of the royal family, Funcinpec, has continued to haemorrhage. Prince Ranariddh was ousted as leader of the party he founded, and launched his own Norodom Ranariddh Party. Some democrats jumped ship to join Sam Rainsy, while others defected to join the CPP. Meanwhile Ranariddh was forced into exile on charges of 'breach of trust' for adultery and selling the Funcinpec party headquarters. The end result of all the machinations is two parties claiming the royalist mantle, their cause weaker and more divided than ever before.

But there's a new royal family in town, the CPP, and they are making plans for the future with dynastic alliances between their offspring. Just look at the roll call of marriages in the past decade and it soon becomes apparent that senior leaders have their eyes firmly on the future and a possible handover of power to the children of the CPP. At the head of this elite is Prime Minister Hun Sen, who has proved himself a survivor, personally as well as politically, for he lost an eye during the battle for Phnom Penh in 1975. It would appear that for the time being at least, with a poorly educated electorate and a divided opposition, 'in the country of the blind, the one-eyed man is king'.

Opposition leader Sam Rainsy continues to berate the country's rulers for their lack of leadership and has made real inroads in urban areas, setting the stage for some showdowns with the CPP in the coming years. Sometimes they get a little too spicy and Sam Rainsy and several of his fellow parliamentarians have been regularly stripped of their immunity from prosecution and charged with defamation.

The more Cambodia integrates into the regional economy and the more investment continues to flow, the harder it will be for politicians to go back to old ways. One way or the other, it looks like the royalists are on a one-way ticket out of the political scene and future contests will be between the entrenched CPP and the populist Sam Rainsy Party.

Several of the current crop of Cambodian leaders were previously members of the Khmer Rouge, including Prime Minister Hun Sen and Head of the Senate Chea Sim, although there is no evidence to implicate them in mass killings.

For a no-holds-barred look at contemporary Cambodia through the eyes of its diverse population, look out for a copy of *Cambodia Now* by Karen Coates.

Keep up to date with the latest developments in the Khmer Rouge trial by visiting the official website of the Cambodian Tribunal Monitor at www.cambodiatribunal monitor.org.

2007

Royalist party Funcinpec continues to implode in the face of conflict, intrigue and defections, with democrats joining Sam Rainsy, loyalists joining the new Norodom Ranariddh Party and others joining the CPP.

2008

Elections are held and the CPP increases its share of the vote to 58%, while the opposition vote is split across several parties.

2009

Cambodia's economy takes a battering from the global economic storm, with investments down, house and land prices tumbling and visitor numbers reduced.

The Culture

THE NATIONAL PSYCHE

Since the glory days of the Angkorian empire of old, the Cambodian people have been on the losing side of many a historical battle, their country all too often a minnow amid the circling sharks. Popular attitudes have been shaped by this history, and the relationship between Cambodia and its neighbours Thailand and Vietnam is marked by a cocktail of fear, admiration and animosity.

Cambodian attitudes towards the Thais and Vietnamese are complex. The Thais aren't always popular, as some Cambodians feel the Thais fail to acknowledge their cultural debt to Cambodia and generally look down on their poorer neighbour. Cambodian attitudes towards the Vietnamese are more ambivalent. There is a certain level of mistrust, as many feel the Vietnamese are out to colonise their country. Many Khmers still call the lost Mekong Delta 'Kampuchea Krom', meaning 'Lower Cambodia'. However, it is balanced with a grudging respect for their 'liberation' from the Khmer Rouge in 1979 (see p36). But when liberation became occupation in the 1980s, the relationship soured once more.

At first glance, Cambodia appears to be a nation of shiny, happy people, but look deeper and it is a country of contradictions. Light and dark, rich and poor, love and hate, life and death – all are visible on a journey through the kingdom. Most telling of all is the evidence of the nation's glorious past set against its tragic present.

Angkor is everywhere: on the flag, the national beer, cigarettes, hotels and guesthouses – anything and everything. It's a symbol of nationhood and fierce pride, a two-fingered salute to the world – no matter how ugly things got in the bad old days, the Cambodians built Angkor Wat and it doesn't come bigger than that.

Jayavarman VII, Angkor's greatest king, is nearly as omnipresent as his temples. The man that vanquished the occupying Chams and took the empire to its greatest glories is a national hero.

Contrast this with the abyss into which the nation was sucked during the years of the Khmer Rouge. Pol Pot is a dirty word in Cambodia due to the death and suffering he inflicted on the country. Whenever you hear his name, it will be connected with stories of endless personal tragedy, of dead brothers, mothers and babies, from which most Cambodians have never had the chance to recover. As the Khmer Rouge trial edges forward, no one has tasted justice, the whys and hows remain unanswered and the older generation must live in the shadow of this trauma.

If Jayavarman VII and Angkor are loved and Pol Pot and the Khmer Rouge despised, then the mercurial Sihanouk, the last of the god-kings who has ultimately shown his human side, is somewhere in between. Many Cambodians love him as the 'father of the nation', but to others he is the man who failed the nation by his association with the Khmer Rouge. In many ways, his contradictions match those of contemporary Cambodia. Understand Sihanouk and what he has had to survive and you will understand much of Cambodia.

LIFESTYLE

For many older Cambodians, life is centred on family, faith and food, a timeless existence that has stayed the same for centuries. Family is more than the nuclear family we now know in the West: it's the extended family

The Cambodian and Lao people share a close bond, as Fa Ngum, the founder of the original Lao kingdom of Lan Xang (Land of a Million Elephants), was sponsored by his Khmer father-in-law.

Jayavarman VII was a Mahayana Buddhist and directed his faith towards improving the lot of his people, with the construction of hospitals, universities, roads and shelters.

of third cousins and obscure aunts – as long as there is a bloodline, there is a bond. Families stick together, solve problems collectively, listen to the wisdom of the elders and pool resources. The extended family comes together during times of trouble and times of joy, celebrating festivals and successes, mourning deaths and disappointments. Whether the Cambodian house is big or small, there will be a lot of people living inside.

For the majority of the population still living in the countryside, these constants carry on as they always have: several generations sharing the same roof, the same rice and the same religion. But during the dark decades of the 1970s and 1980s, this routine was ripped apart by war and ideology, as the peasants were dragged from all they held dear to fight a bloody civil war and later forced into slavery. Angkar, the Khmer Rouge organisation, took over as the moral and social beacon in the lives of the people. Families were forced apart, children turned against parents, brother against sister. The bond of trust was broken and is only slowly being rebuilt today.

Faith is another rock in the lives of many older Cambodians, and Buddhism (mixed with a dash of Hinduism and animism for good measure) has helped them to rebuild their lives after the Khmer Rouge. Most Cambodian houses contain a small shrine to pray for luck and, come Buddha Day, the wats are thronging with the faithful.

Food is more important to Cambodians than to most, as they have tasted what it is like to be without. Famine stalked the country in the late 1970s and, even today, malnutrition and food shortages are common during times of drought. For country folk (still the majority of the Cambodian population), their livelihood is their fields. Farmers are attached to their land, their very survival dependent on it, and the harvest cycle dictates the rhythm of rural life.

For the young generation, brought up in a post-conflict, post-communist period of relative freedom, it's a different story – arguably thanks to their steady diet of MTV and steamy soaps. Cambodia is experiencing its very own '60s swing, as the younger generation stands ready for a different lifestyle to the one their parents had to swallow. This creates plenty of feisty friction in the cities, as rebellious teens dress as they like, date who they want and hit the town until all hours. But few actually live on their own: they still come home to ma and pa at the end of the day (and the arguments start again).

Cambodia is a country undergoing rapid change, but for now the traditionalists are just about holding their own, although the onslaught of karaoke is proving hard to resist. Cambodia is set for major demographic changes in the next couple of decades. Currently, just 20% of the population lives in urban areas, which contrasts starkly with the country's more-developed neighbours, such as Malaysia and Thailand. Increasing numbers of young people are likely to migrate to the cities in search of opportunity, forever changing the face of contemporary Cambodian society. However, for now at least, Cambodian society remains much more traditional than in Thailand and Vietnam, and visitors need to keep this in mind.

Even the destructive Khmer Rouge paid homage to the mighty Angkor Wat on its flag, with three towers of the temple in yellow, set against a blood-red background.

For more on the incredible life and times of Norodom Sihanouk, read the biography *Prince of Light, Prince of Darkness* (1994) by Milton Osborne.

Greetings

Cambodians traditionally greet each other with the *sompiah*, which involves pressing the hands together in prayer and bowing, similar to the *wai* in Thailand. The higher the hands and the lower the bow, the more respect is conveyed – important to remember when meeting officials or the elderly. In recent times this custom has been partially replaced by the handshake but, although men tend to shake hands with each other, women usually use the traditional greeting with both men and women.

TOP 10 TIPS TO EARN THE RESPECT OF THE LOCALS

Take your time to learn a little about the local culture in Cambodia. Not only will this ensure that you don't inadvertently cause offence or, worse, spark an international incident, but it will also ingratiate you to your hosts. Here are a few top tips to help you go native.

Dress Code

Respect local dress standards, particularly at religious sites. Covering the upper arms and upper legs is appropriate, although some monks will be too polite to enforce this. Always remove your shoes before entering a temple, as well as any hat or head covering. Nude sunbathing is considered *totally* inappropriate, even on beaches.

Making a Contribution

Since most temples are maintained from the donations received, remember to make a contribution when visiting a temple. When visiting a Khmer home, a small token of gratitude in the form of a gift is always appreciated.

Meet & Greet

Learn the Cambodian greeting, the *sompiah* (see p45), and use it when introducing yourself to new friends. When beckoning someone over, always wave towards yourself with the palm down, as palm up with fingers raised can be suggestive, even offensive.

A Woman's Touch

Monks are not supposed to touch or be touched by women. If a woman wants to hand something to a monk, the object should be placed within reach of the monk or on the monk's 'receiving cloth'.

Keep Your Cool

No matter how high your blood pressure rises, do not raise your voice or show signs of aggression. This will lead to a 'loss of face' and cause embarrassment to the locals, ensuring the situation gets worse rather than better.

It's on the Cards

Exchanging business cards is an important part of even the smallest transaction or business contact in Cambodia. Get some printed before you arrive and hand them out like confetti. Always present them with two hands.

Deadly Chopsticks

Leaving a pair of chopsticks sitting vertically in a rice bowl looks very much like the incense sticks that are burned for the dead. This is a powerful sign and is not appreciated anywhere in Asia.

Mean Feet

Cambodians like to keep a clean house and it's usual to remove shoes when entering somebody's home. It's rude to point the bottom of your feet towards other people. Never, ever point your feet towards anything sacred, such as an image of Buddha.

Hats off to Them

As a form of respect to the elderly or other esteemed people, such as monks, take off your hat and bow your head politely when addressing them. Never pat or touch an adult on the head – in Asia, the head is considered the most sacred part of the body.

Toothpicks

While digging out those stubborn morsels from between your teeth, it is polite to use one hand to perform the extraction and the other hand to cover your mouth so others can't see you do it.

It is considered acceptable (or perhaps excusable) for foreigners to shake hands with Cambodians of both sexes.

Dress

Both men and women often wear cotton or silk sarongs, especially at home. Most urban Khmer men dress in trousers and these days many urban women dress in Western-style clothing.

On formal occasions, such as religious festivals and family celebrations, women often wear a *hol* (a type of shirt) during the day. At night they change into single-colour silk dresses called *phamuong*, which are decorated along the hems. If the celebration is a wedding, the colours of such garments are dictated by the day of the week on which the wedding falls. The women of Cambodia are generally modest in their dress, although this is fast changing in the bigger towns and cities.

ECONOMY

Badly traumatised by decades of conflict, Cambodia's economy was long a gecko amid the neighbouring dragons. This has slowly started to change, as the economy has been liberalised and investors are circling to take advantage of the new opportunities. Asian investors are flocking to Phnom Penh, led by the South Koreans who have inked deals for skyscrapers all over the low-rise city. Westerners are starting to realise that they are on to something and investment funds and venture capitalists are sniffing around. However, the 2009 global economic crisis put the brakes on things, with a number of projects mothballed for a year or two.

Cambodia today is a far cry from the days of civil war, genocide and famine. However, it's a fairly exclusive boom, limited to foreign investors, wealthy Cambodians and a small number of city dwellers. Some say that to ensure a stable future, the government needs to expand the opportunities to the people of the countryside.

Before the civil war, rubber was the leading industry and it's bouncing back with new plantations. Other plantation industries taking off include palm oil and paper pulp. Virgin forest is being cut down on the pretext of replanting, but often the ecosystem fails to recover.

The garment sector is important to the economy, with factories ringing the Cambodian capital. Cambodia is trying to carve a niche for itself as an ethical producer, with good labour relations and air-conditioned factories. It's no picnic in the factories, but the alternative is often the rice fields or the shadowy fringes of the entertainment industry, often a one-way ticket into prostitution. When it comes to the garment industry's future, it remains to be seen if profit or purpose will triumph in the international marketplace. The global economic crisis saw a huge number of job losses in this sector, running close to 100,000 young women, and it may take a few years to recover.

Tourism is a big deal in Cambodia, with more than two million visitors arriving in 2008, a doubling of numbers in just a few years. Thousands of jobs are being created every year and this is proving to be a great way to integrate the huge number of young people into the economy. Wages are low by regional standards, but tips can add up to a princely sum that might support an extended family. Once again, tourism was dented by the global situation in 2009, but seems to be recovering faster than other sectors.

Foreign aid was long the mainstay of the Cambodian economy, supporting half the government's budget, and NGOs have done a lot to force important sociopolitical issues onto the agenda. However, with multi-billion-dollar investments stacking up and the Chinese government loaning vast sums with no

Travellers crossing the border from liberal Thai islands such as Ko Pha Ngan or Ko Chang should remember they have crossed back in time as far as traditions are concerned, and that wandering around the temples of Angkor barechested (men) or scantily clad (women) will not be appreciated.

Cambodia's economy was among the fastest growing in the world from 2006 to 2008, hitting the magic 10%-a-year target in 2007. However, growth slowed considerably in 2009 due to the global economic crisis.

strings attached, it looks like the NGOs' days in the sun could be numbered, and the government may no longer be influenced by their lobbying.

For many Cambodians, economy seems too grand a word for their lives, which are about subsistence survival. Subject to the vagaries of burning sun and drowning rains, the best they can hope for is a stable crop and the chance to sell a little at the end of the season.

A PENNY MORE, NOT A PENNY LESS Nick Ray

Cambodians have a proverb for every walk of life and the rampant problem of corruption is no exception. The saying goes, 'Small people take small bribes, big people take big bribes' and this aptly sums up the situation in Cambodia today. *Puk roluy* is Khmer for 'corruption' and translates literally as 'something that is rotten and should be thrown away'.

According to anti-corruption watchdog Transparency International and its annual Corruption Perceptions Index (CPI), Cambodia ranks 158 out of 180 countries on the league table for corrupt nations, tied with Central African Republic, Tajikistan and Laos. At an anti-corruption awareness concert in Phnom Penh in May 2009, US ambassador Carol Rodley said that corruption costs the Cambodian government an estimated US$500 million per year.

Corruption is by no means a new trend in Cambodia – by the 19th century the problem was so widespread that many Cambodians had virtually enslaved themselves to their protectors. Yet another proverb summed up the situation succinctly: 'The rich must protect the poor, just as clothing protects the body'.

Following Cambodia's independence, the word 'government' became synonymous with corruption. The situation worsened when the USA moved in to prop up the Lon Nol government; nonexistent soldiers were added to the payroll and deaths and desertions went unreported. It is thought that by 1972 the military was pocketing the pay of about 100,000 of these phantom fighters.

Corruption faded during the Pol Pot era, but for many Cambodians the stakes were much higher, as often they were buying their lives in gold or jewellery. Following the overthrow of the Khmer Rouge by the Vietnamese, survival was often the daily challenge and there was little or no scope for widespread corruption. However, in the Thai border camps, small-scale corruption was rampant as unscrupulous characters bartered and sold aid supplies.

It was the arrival of the free market and, later, the UN that really sent corruption spiralling out of control. When then World Bank head James Wolfensohn visited Cambodia in 2005, he was asked to sum up Cambodia's problems in three words. In front of a who's who of the Cambodian government, he responded 'Corruption, corruption and corruption'. The saddest part of the saga is that the majority of Cambodians are extremely honest and their struggle to survive is already hard enough without having to contend with widespread corruption.

The average Cambodian encounters corruption from an early age – some doctors and nurses are known to demand money before administering treatment, even when it should be entirely free of charge. It is not uncommon for students to bribe teachers to see exam papers in advance or for well-connected pupils to buy someone else's results after the test, thus depriving an able student of the chance for a scholarship. Although education is officially free, in order to supplement their own meagre incomes many teachers levy a charge for pupils to attend class, preventing poor families from sending their children to school.

Jobs in the police force and the army can also be particularly lucrative, and for the tourist this is usually the only time you will encounter corruption. Traffic police are visible all over Phnom Penh, but certain areas of the city are considered more desirable than others because they offer the opportunity for a shakedown or two.

Corruption needs to be eradicated in Cambodia before the country can realistically travel the road to development. However, with low salaries and little action, it would appear the country is set for many more years of *puk roluy*. If you are a tourist, you'll probably part with only a few thousand riel due to corruption during your visit, but, if you're on business, you'd better come with a briefcase stuffed full of cash – that's dollars, not riel.

Corruption remains a way of life in Cambodia. It is a major element of the Cambodian economy and exists to some extent at all levels of government. Sometimes it is overt, but increasingly it is covert, with private companies often securing very favourable business deals on the basis of their connections. It seems everything has a price, including ancient temples, national parks and even genocide sites. For more on this, see the boxed text, opposite.

POPULATION

Cambodia's second postwar population census was carried out in 2008 and put the country's population at about 13.5 million. With a rapid growth rate of about 2% per year, the population is predicted to reach 20 million by 2025.

Phnom Penh is the largest city, with a population of almost two million. Other major population centres include the boom towns of Siem Reap, Sihanoukville, Battambang and Poipet. The most populous province is Kompong Cham, where more than 10% of Cambodians live.

The much-discussed imbalance of men to women due to years of conflict is not as serious as it was in 1980, but it is still significant: there are about 95 males to every 100 females, up from 86.1 to 100 in 1980. There is, however, a marked imbalance in age groups: more than 40% of the population is under the age of 16.

> Among Cambodia's 24 provinces, Kandal has the densest population with more than 300 people per square kilometre; Mondulkiri has the sparsest population with just two people per square kilometre.

SPORT

The national sport of Cambodia is *pradal serey* (Cambodian kickboxing). It's similar to kickboxing in Thailand (don't make the mistake of calling it Thai boxing over here, though) and there are regular weekend bouts on CTN and TV5. It is also possible to go to the TV arenas and watch the fights live.

Football is another national obsession, although the Cambodian team is a real minnow, even by Asian standards. Many Cambodians follow the Premier League in England religiously and regularly bet on games.

The French game of *pétanque,* also called boules, is also very popular here and the Cambodian team has won several medals in regional games.

> Cambodia is one of the leading lights in disabled volleyball and came third in the world championships, held in Phnom Penh in 2007.

MULTICULTURALISM

Ethnic Khmers

According to official statistics, over 90% of the people who live in Cambodia are ethnic Khmers, making the country the most ethnically homogeneous in Southeast Asia. Ethnic minorities include Vietnamese, Chinese, Cham, Lao and indigenous peoples of the rural highlands.

The Khmers have inhabited Cambodia since the beginning of recorded history (around the 2nd century), many centuries before Thais and Vietnamese migrated to the region. Over the centuries, the Khmers have mixed with other groups residing in Cambodia, including Javanese and Malays (8th century), Thais (10th to 15th centuries), Vietnamese (from the early 17th century) and Chinese (since the 18th century).

> In 2009 Cambodia was ranked a lowly 176 in the FIFA rankings of national teams.

Ethnic Vietnamese

Vietnamese are one of the largest non-Khmer ethnic groups in Cambodia. According to government figures, Cambodia is host to around 100,000 Vietnamese. Unofficial observers claim that the real figure may be somewhere between half a million and two million. They play a big part in the fishing and construction industries in Cambodia. However, there is still some distrust between the Cambodians and the Vietnamese, even among those who have been living in Cambodia for generations.

KHMER KROM

The Khmer Krom people of southern Vietnam are ethnic Khmers separated from Cambodia by historical deals and Vietnamese encroachment on what was once Cambodian territory. Nobody is sure just how many of them there are and estimates vary from one million to seven million, depending on who is doing the counting.

The history of Vietnamese expansion into Khmer territory has long been a staple of Khmer textbooks. King Chey Chetha II of Cambodia, in keeping with the wishes of his Vietnamese queen, first allowed Vietnamese to settle in the Cambodian town of Prey Nokor in 1623. It was obviously the thin edge of the wedge – Prey Nokor is now better known as Ho Chi Minh City (Saigon).

The Vietnamese government has pursued a policy of forced assimilation since independence, which has involved ethnic Khmers taking Vietnamese names and studying in Vietnamese. According to the Khmer Kampuchea Federation (KKF), the Khmer Krom continue to suffer persecution, including a lack of access to health services, religious discrimination and outright racism. Several monks have been defrocked for nonviolent protests in recent years and the Cambodian government has even assisted in deporting some agitators, according to Human Rights Watch.

Many Khmer Krom would like to see Cambodia act as a mediator in the quest for greater autonomy and ethnic representation in Vietnam. The Cambodian government, for its part, turns a blind eye to the vast numbers of illegal Vietnamese inside its borders, as well as reports of Vietnamese encroachments on the eastern borders of Cambodia. The Cambodian government takes a softly, softly approach towards its more powerful neighbour, perhaps borne of the historic ties between the two political dynasties.

For more about the ongoing struggles of the Khmer Krom, visit www.khmerkrom.org.

Ethnic Chinese

The government claims that there are around 50,000 ethnic Chinese in Cambodia. Informed observers say there are more likely to be as many as half a million to one million in urban areas. Many Chinese Cambodians have lived in Cambodia for generations and have adopted the Khmer culture, language and identity. Until 1975, ethnic Chinese controlled the economic life of Cambodia. In recent years the group has re-emerged as a powerful economic force, mainly due to increased investment by overseas Chinese.

Look out for Chinese and Vietnamese cemeteries dotting the rice fields of provinces to the south and east of Phnom Penh. Khmers do not bury their dead, but practise cremation and the ashes may be interred in a stupa in the grounds of a wat.

Ethnic Cham

Cambodia's Cham Muslims (known locally as the Khmer Islam) officially number around 200,000. Unofficial counts put the figure higher at around 400,000. The Chams live in villages on the banks of the Mekong and Tonlé Sap Rivers, mostly in the provinces of Kompong Cham, Kompong Speu and Kompong Chhnang. They suffered vicious persecution between 1975 and 1979, when a large part of their community was exterminated. Many Cham mosques that were destroyed under the Khmer Rouge have been rebuilt.

Ethno-Linguistic Minorities

Cambodia's diverse Khmer Leu (Upper Khmer) or *chunchiet* (ethnic minorities), who live in the country's mountainous regions, probably number between 75,000 and 100,000.

Not all Cham are actually descended from the kingdom of Champa, as some are descended from Malay traders who settled from the 18th century and intermarried with the Cham people.

The majority of these groups live in the northeast of Cambodia, in the provinces of Ratanakiri, Mondulkiri, Stung Treng and Kratie. The largest group is the Tompuon (many other spellings are also used), who number nearly 20,000. Other groups include the Bunong, Kreung, Kavet, Brau and Jarai.

The hill tribes of Cambodia have long been isolated from mainstream Khmer society, and there is little in the way of mutual understanding. They practise shifting cultivation, rarely staying in one place for long. Finding a new location for a village requires a village elder to mediate with the spirit world. Very few of the minorities retain the sort of colourful traditional costumes found in Thailand, Laos and Vietnam.

MEDIA

Cambodia's media scene looks to be in good shape on paper, with freedom of the press enshrined in the constitution, but the everyday reality is a different story. Opposition parties have far less access to the media than the dominant Cambodian People's Party (CPP), with many more pro-government newspapers and radio and TV stations. Corruption exists in the local journalism ranks, and it's not unheard of for money to change hands in return for positive stories or to help prevent the publication of negative stories.

Khmer TV is mostly in the hands of the CPP, including state-run TVK and private channels like Bayon, but even the 'independent' channels like CTN aren't that autonomous. **Reporters Without Borders** (www.rsf.org/cambodia) sums up the issue, stating 'Cambodia boasts 11 TV stations, but none of them is genuinely independent'.

Most urban Cambodians look to cable TV news channels, like the BBC and CNN, for their news, or tune their radios in to BBC World Service or Voice of America.

RELIGION
Buddhism

Buddhism came to Cambodia with Hinduism, but only became the official religion from the 13th and 14th centuries. Most Cambodians today practise Theravada Buddhism. Between 1975 and 1979 the majority of Cambodia's Buddhist monks were murdered by the Khmer Rouge and nearly all of the country's wats (more than 3000) were damaged or destroyed. In the late 1980s, Buddhism once again became the state religion and today young monks are a common sight throughout the country. Many wats have been rebuilt or rehabilitated and money-raising drives for this work can be seen on roadsides across the country.

The ultimate goal of Theravada Buddhism is nirvana – 'extinction' of all desire and suffering to reach the final stage of reincarnation. By feeding monks, giving donations to temples and performing regular worship at the local wat, Buddhists hope to improve their lot, acquiring enough merit to reduce their number of rebirths.

Every Buddhist male is expected to become a monk for a short period in his life, optimally between the time he finishes school and starts a career or marries. Men or boys under 20 years of age may enter the sangha (monastic order) as novices. Nowadays men may spend as little as one week or 15 days to accrue merit as monks.

Hinduism

Hinduism flourished alongside Buddhism from the 1st century AD until the 14th century. During the pre-Angkorian period, Hinduism was represented by the worship of Harihara (Shiva and Vishnu embodied in a single deity). During the time of Angkor, Shiva was the deity most in favour with the royal family, although in the 12th century he was superseded by Vishnu. Today some elements of Hinduism are still incorporated into important ceremonies involving birth, marriage and death.

Animism

Both Hinduism and Buddhism were gradually absorbed from beyond the borders of Cambodia, fusing with the animist beliefs already present among

Lowland Khmers are being encouraged to migrate to Cambodia's northeast where there is plenty of available land. But this is home to the country's minority peoples, who have no indigenous concepts of property rights or land ownership; this may see their culture marginalised in coming years.

Cambodia was ranked 117 out of 175 countries in the *Press Freedom Index 2009* report prepared by Reporters Without Borders, 13 places above Thailand, which came in at 130.

Buddhism in Cambodia draws heavily on its predecessors, incorporating many cultural traditions from Hinduism for ceremonies, such as those relating to birth, marriage and death, as well as genies and spirits, such as Neak Ta, which link back to a pre-Indian animist past.

the Khmers before Indianisation. Local beliefs didn't disappear, but were incorporated into the new religions to form something uniquely Cambodian. The concept of Neak Ta has its foundations in animist beliefs regarding sacred soil and the sacred spirit around us. Neak Ta can be viewed as a mother-earth concept, an energy force uniting a community with its earth and water. It can be represented in many forms, from stone or wood to termite hills – anything that symbolises both a link between the people and the fertility of their land.

Islam

Cambodia's Muslims are descendants of Chams, who migrated from what is now central Vietnam after the final defeat of the kingdom of Champa by the Vietnamese in 1471. Like their Buddhist neighbours, the Cham Muslims call the faithful to prayer by banging a drum, rather than with the call of the muezzin, as in most Muslim lands.

Christianity

Christianity made limited headway into Cambodia compared with neighbouring Vietnam. There were a number of churches in Cambodia before the war, but many of these were systematically destroyed by the Khmer Rouge, including Notre Dame Cathedral in Phnom Penh. Christianity made a comeback of sorts throughout the refugee camps on the Thai border in the 1980s, as a number of food-for-faith-type charities set up shop dispensing religion with every meal. Many Cambodians changed their public faith for survival, before converting back to Buddhism on their departure from the camps, earning the moniker 'rice Christians'.

WOMEN IN CAMBODIA

The position of women in Cambodia is in a state of transition, as the old generation yields to the new generation, the conservative to the challenging. Traditionally the woman's role has been in the home. While this trend continues among the older generation, there are signs that women of the younger generation won't be limited in the same way.

While something like 20% of women head the household, and in many families women are the sole breadwinners, men have a monopoly on the most important positions of power at a governmental level and have a dominant social role at a domestic level.

Cambodian political and religious policies do not directly discriminate against women, but females are rarely afforded the same opportunities as males. In the 1990s, laws were passed on abortion, domestic violence and human trafficking; these have improved the legal position of women but have had little effect on the bigger picture.

As young children, females are treated fairly equally, but as they get older their access to education has traditionally become more restricted. This is particularly so in rural areas, where girls cannot live and study in wats like the boys.

Many women set up simple businesses in their towns or villages, but it is not an easy path should they want to progress further. Women currently make up just over 15% of legislators in parliament, even though they make up 56% of the voters. Only 15% of administrative and management positions and 35% of professional positions are held by women nationally. It remains a man's world in the sociopolitical jungle that is Cambodia.

Other issues of concern for women in Cambodia are domestic violence, prostitution and the spread of sexually transmitted infections (STIs). Domestic violence is quite widespread but, because of fear and shame, it's not known exactly how serious a problem it is. There is a high incidence of child prostitution and illegal trafficking of prostitutes in Cambodia. See the boxed text, p90, for more on the scourge of child prostitution in Cambodia.

During the 1990s, Cambodia had the highest rate of HIV infection in the whole of Southeast Asia. Many families in Cambodia ended up infected due to the actions of an errant husband. However, infection rates are now well under control thanks to the impact of powerful public awareness programs.

ARTS

The Khmer Rouge's assault on the arts was a terrible blow to Cambodian culture. Indeed, for a number of years the common consensus among Khmers was that their culture had been irrevocably lost. The Khmer Rouge not only did away with living bearers of Khmer culture, it also destroyed cultural artefacts, statues, musical instruments, books and anything else that served as a reminder of a past it was trying to efface. The temples of Angkor were spared as a symbol of Khmer glory and empire, but little else survived. Despite this, Cambodia is witnessing a resurgence of traditional arts and a growing interest in experimentation in modern arts and cross-cultural fusion.

> The famous Hindu epic the *Ramayana* is known as the *Reamker* in Cambodia; Reyum Publishing has issued a beautifully illustrated book telling the story: *The Reamker* (1999).

Dance

More than any of the other traditional arts, Cambodia's royal ballet is a tangible link with the glory of Angkor. Its traditions stretch long into the past, when the art of the *apsara* (nymph) resounded to the glory of the divine king. Early in his reign, King Sihanouk released the traditional harem of royal *apsara* that went with the crown.

Dance fared particularly badly during the Pol Pot years. Very few dancers and teachers survived. In 1981, with a handful of teachers, the University of Fine Arts was reopened and the training of dance students resumed.

Much of Cambodian royal dance resembles that of India and Thailand (the same stylised hand movements, the same sequined, lamé costumes and the same opulent stupa-like headwear), as the Thais incorporated techniques from the Khmers after sacking Angkor in the 15th century. Although royal dance was traditionally an all-female affair (with the exception of the role of the monkey), there are now more male dancers featured.

> Amrita Performing Arts (www.amritaperforming arts.org) has collaborated on a number of ground-breaking dance and theatre projects in Cambodia, including collaborations with French and Japanese performers.

Music

The bas-reliefs on some of the monuments in the Angkor region depict musicians and *apsara* holding instruments similar to the traditional Khmer instruments of today, demonstrating that Cambodia has a long musical tradition all of its own.

Customarily, music was an accompaniment to a ritual or performance that had religious significance. Musicologists have identified six types of Cambodian musical ensemble, each used in different settings. The most traditional of these is the *areak ka,* an ensemble that performs at weddings. The instruments of the *areak ka* include a *tro khmae* (three-stringed fiddle), a *khsae muoy* (single-stringed bowed instrument) and *skor areak* (drums), among others.

Much of Cambodia's golden-era music from the pre-war period was lost during the Pol Pot years. The Khmer Rouge targeted famous singers and the great Sin Sisamuth and female diva Ros Sereysothea, Cambodia's most famous songwriters and performers, both disappeared in the early days of the regime.

After the war, many Khmers settled in the USA, where a lively Khmer pop industry developed. Influenced by US music and later exported back to Cambodia, it has been enormously popular.

> Cambodia's great musical tradition was almost lost during the Khmer Rouge years, but the Cambodian Master Performers Program is dedicated to reviving the country's musical tradition. Visit its website at www.cambodianmasters.org.

A new generation of overseas Khmers growing up with influences from the West is producing its own sound. Cambodian Americans are now returning to the homeland raised on a diet of rap, and lots of new artists are breaking through, such as the ClapYaHandz collective started by Sok 'Cream' Visal.

There's also a burgeoning pop industry, many of whose famous stars perform at outdoor concerts in Phnom Penh. It is easy to join in the fun by visiting one of the innumerable karaoke bars around the country. Preap Sovath is the Robbie Williams of Cambodia and, if you flick through the Cambodian channels for more than five minutes, chances are he will be performing. Soun Chantha is one of the more popular young female singers with a big voice, but it's a changeling industry and new stars are waiting in the wings.

Dengue Fever is the ultimate fusion band, rapidly gaining a name for itself beyond the USA and Cambodia. Cambodian singer Chhom Nimol fronts five American prog rockers who dabble in psychedelic sounds.

One form of music unique to Cambodia is *chapaye*, a sort of Cambodian blues sung to the accompaniment of a two-stringed wooden instrument similar in sound to a bass guitar without the amplifier. There are few old masters, such as Kong Nai (the Ray Charles of Cambodia), left alive, but *chapaye* is still often shown on late-night Cambodian TV before transmission ends.

One of the greatest '70s legends to seek out is Nuon Sarath, the Jimi Hendrix of Cambodia, with his screaming vocals and wah-wah pedals. His most famous song, 'Chi Cyclo', is an absolute classic.

Check out www. tinytoones.org for more on a hip-hop cooperative seeking to empower the youth of Cambodia to a healthier lifestyle free of drugs and exposure to HIV. Keep an eye out for their performances around Phnom Penh.

Literature

Cambodia's literary tradition is limited and very much tied in with Buddhism, and myth and legend. Sanskrit, and later Pali, came to Cambodia with Hinduism and Buddhism and much of Cambodia's religious scripture exists only in these ancient languages. Legend has been used to expound the core Cambodian values of family and faith, as well as obedience to authority.

Architecture

Khmer architecture reached its peak during the Angkorian era (9th to 14th centuries). Some of the finest examples of architecture from this period are Angkor Wat and the structures of Angkor Thom. See p157 for more information on the architectural styles of the Angkorian era.

Today, most rural Cambodian houses are built on high wood pilings (if the family can afford it) and have thatch roofs, walls made of palm mats and floors of woven bamboo strips resting on bamboo joists. The shady space underneath is used for storage and for people to relax at midday. Wealthier families have houses with wooden walls and tiled roofs, but the basic design remains the same.

The French left their mark in Cambodia in the form of some handsome villas and government buildings built in neoclassical style – Romanesque pillars and all. Some of the best architectural examples are in Phnom Penh, but most of the provincial capitals have at least one or two examples of architecture from the colonial period.

Cambodian architect Vann Molyvann helped shape modern Phnom Penh; some of his best-known buildings include the Olympic Stadium (p97) and the Chatomuk Theatre (p117).

Sculpture

Even in the pre-Angkorian era, the periods generally referred to as Funan and Chenla, the people of Cambodia were producing masterfully sensuous sculpture that was more than just a copy of the Indian forms on which it was modelled. Some scholars maintain that the Cambodian forms are unrivalled, even in India itself.

The earliest surviving Cambodian sculpture dates from the 6th century AD. Most of it depicts Vishnu with four or eight arms. A large eight-armed Vishnu from this period is displayed at the National Museum (p93) in Phnom Penh.

Also on display at the National Museum is a statue of Harihara from the end of the 7th century, a divinity who combines aspects of both Vishnu and Shiva, but looks more than a little Egyptian – a reminder that Indian sculpture drew from the Greeks, who in turn were influenced by the Pharaohs.

Innovations of the early Angkorian era include free-standing sculpture that dispenses with the stone aureole that in earlier works supported the multiple arms of Hindu deities. The faces assume an air of tranquillity, and the overall effect is less animated.

The Banteay Srei style of the late 10th century is commonly regarded as a high point in the evolution of Southeast Asian art. The National Museum has a splendid piece from this period: a sandstone statue of Shiva holding Uma, his wife, on his knee. The Baphuon style of the 11th century was inspired to a certain extent by the sculpture of Banteay Srei, producing some of the finest works to have survived today.

The statuary of the Angkor Wat period is felt to be conservative and stilted, lacking the grace of earlier work. The genius of this period manifests itself more clearly in the immense architecture and incredible bas-reliefs of Angkor Wat itself.

The final high point in Angkorian sculpture is the Bayon period from the end of the 12th century to the beginning of the 13th century. In the National Museum, look for the superb representation of Jayavarman VII, an image that simultaneously projects great power and sublime tranquillity.

Cambodian sculptors are rediscovering their skills now that there is a ready market among visitors for reproduction stone carvings of famous statues and busts from the time of Angkor.

> For details on the religious, cultural and social context of Angkorian-era sculpture, seek out a copy of *Sculpture of Angkor and Ancient Cambodia: Millennium of Glory* by Helen Jessup (1997).

Painting

There is a new contemporary art scene emerging in Cambodia, which is pushing the boundaries of traditional culture and form. Young artists are emerging unshackled by the baggage of the past to define a new future for Khmer painting. This has been given extra momentum by new galleries and art venues in Phnom Penh and Siem Reap that are promoting these artists to the wider world. Check out places like the Art Café (p118), Java Café (p118) and Meta House (p118) in Phnom Penh or Alliance Café (p145) and the Arts Lounge in Hotel de la Paix (p141) in Siem Reap.

Leading lights on the art scene include Tuol Sleng survivor Vann Nath, spiritually inspired artist Chhim Sothy and challenging young Battambang artist Oeur Sokuntevy.

> Reyum (p119) is an exhibition space in Phnom Penh established to promote Khmer arts and culture and has given support and encouragement to young artists and writers. Its website is www.reyum.org.

Handicrafts

With a tradition of craftsmanship that produced the temples of Angkor, it is hardly surprising to find that even today Khmers produce exquisitely carved silver, wood and stone. Many of the designs hark back to those of the Angkorian period and are tasteful objects of art.

Pottery is also an industry with a long history in Cambodia, and there are many ancient kiln sites scattered throughout the country. Designs range from the extremely simple to much more intricate: drinking cups carved in the image of elephants, teapots carved in the image of birds, and jars carved in the image of gods.

> Check out the rockumentary *Don't Think I've Forgotten* on Cambodia's lost rock 'n' roll from the 1960s at http://cambodianrock.com.

Cinema

The film industry in Cambodia was given a new lease of life in 2000 with the release of *Pos Keng Kong* (The Giant Snake). A remake of a 1950s Cambodian classic, it tells the story of a powerful young girl born from a rural relationship between a woman and a snake king. It is an interesting

SIHANOUK & THE SILVER SCREEN

Between 1965 and 1969 Sihanouk (former king and head of state of Cambodia) wrote, directed and produced nine feature films, a figure that would put the average workaholic Hollywood director to shame. Sihanouk took the business of making films very seriously, and family and officials were called upon to do their bit: the minister of foreign affairs played the male lead in Sihanouk's first feature, *Apsara* (Heavenly Nymph; 1965), and his daughter Princess Bopha Devi, the female lead. When, in the same movie, a show of military hardware was required, the air force was brought into action, as was the army's fleet of helicopters.

Sihanouk often took on the leading role himself. Notable performances saw him as a spirit of the forest and as a victorious general. Perhaps it was no surprise, given the king's apparent addiction to the world of celluloid dreams, that Cambodia should challenge Cannes with its Phnom Penh International Film Festival. The festival was held twice, in 1968 and 1969. Sihanouk won the grand prize on both occasions. He continued to make movies in later life and it is believed he has made around 30 films during his remarkable career. For more on the films of Sihanouk, visit the website www.norodomsihanouk.org.

Rithy Panh's 1996 film *Bophana* tells the true story of Hout Bophana, a beautiful young woman, and Ly Sitha, a regional Khmer Rouge leader, who fall in love and are executed for their 'crime'.

The first major international feature film to be shot in Cambodia was *Lord Jim* (1964), starring Peter O'Toole.

love story, albeit with dodgy special effects, and achieved massive box-office success around the region.

The success of *Pos Keng Kong* heralded a mini revival in the Cambodian film industry and local directors are now turning out a few films a year. However, most of these new films are amateurish horror films and are of dubious artistic value.

At least one overseas Cambodian director has had huge success in recent years: Rithy Panh's *People of the Rice Fields* was nominated for the Palme d'Or at the Cannes Film Festival in 1995. The film touches only fleetingly on the Khmer Rouge, depicting the lives of a family eking out an arduous existence in the rice fields. His other films include *One Night after the War* (1997), the story of a young Khmer kickboxer falling for a bar girl in Phnom Penh; and the award-winning *S-21: The Khmer Rouge Killing Machine* (2003), a powerful documentary in which survivors from Tuol Sleng are brought back to confront their guards.

The definitive film about Cambodia is *The Killing Fields* (1985), which tells the story of American journalist Sydney Schanberg and his Cambodian assistant Dith Pran. Most of the footage was actually shot in Thailand, as it was filmed in 1984 when Cambodia was effectively closed to the West.

Quite a number of international films have been shot in Cambodia in recent years, including *Tomb Raider* (2001), *City of Ghosts* (2002) and *Two Brothers* (2004), all worth seeking out for their beautiful Cambodian backdrops.

Food & Drink

It's no secret that the dining tables of Thailand and Vietnam are home to some of the finest food in the world, so it should come as no surprise to discover that Cambodian cuisine is also rather special. Unlike the culinary colossuses that are its neighbours, the cuisine of Cambodia is not that well known in international circles, but all that looks set to change. Just as Angkor has put Cambodia on the tourist map, so too *amoc* (baked fish with coconut, lemon grass and chilli in banana leaf) could put the country on the culinary map.

Cambodia has a great variety of national dishes, some similar to the cuisine of neighbouring Thailand and Laos, others closer to Chinese and Vietnamese cooking, but all come with that unique Cambodian twist.

Freshwater fish forms a huge part of the Cambodian diet thanks to the natural phenomenon that is Tonlé Sap Lake. The fish come in every shape and size, from the giant Mekong catfish to teeny, tiny whitebait, which are great beer snacks when deep-fried. The French left their mark, too, with baguettes becoming the national bread and Cambodian cooks showing a healthy reverence for tender meats.

Cambodia is a crossroads in Asia, the meeting point of the great civilisations of India and China, and, just as its culture has drawn on both, so too has its cuisine. Whether it's spring rolls or curry that takes your fancy, you will find it in Cambodian cooking. Add to this a world of dips and sauces to complement the cooking and a culinary journey through Cambodia becomes as rich a feast as any in Asia.

The closest thing Cambodia has to a national dish is *amoc* (baked fish wrapped in banana leaf with coconut, lemon grass and chilli). Sometimes it arrives more like a soup, served in the shell of a young coconut.

STAPLES & SPECIALITIES

Cambodia's lush fields provide the rice and its abundant waterways the fish that is fermented into *prahoc* (fermented fish paste), which forms the backbone of Khmer cuisine. Built around this is the flavours that give the cuisine its kick: the secret roots, the welcome herbs and the aromatic tubers. Together they give the salads, snacks, soups and stews a unique aroma and taste that smacks of Cambodia.

Rice is the principal staple, enshrined in the Khmer word for 'eating' or 'to eat', *nam bai* – literally 'eat rice'. Many a Cambodian, particularly drivers, will run out of steam if they run out of rice. It doesn't matter that the same carbohydrates are available in other foods, it is rice and rice alone that counts. Battambang Province is Cambodia's rice bowl and produces the country's finest yield.

For the taste of Cambodia in a bowl, try the local *kyteow,* a rice-noodle soup that will keep you going all day. This full, balanced meal will cost you just 4000r in markets and about US$1.50 in local restaurants. Don't like noodles? Then try the *bobor* (rice porridge), a national institution, for breakfast, lunch and dinner, and best sampled with some fresh fish and a splash of ginger.

A Cambodian meal almost always includes a *samlor* (traditional soup), which will appear at the same time as the other courses. *Samlor machou bunlay* (hot and sour fish soup with pineapple and spices) is popular. Other popular soups include *samlor chapek* (ginger-flavoured pork soup), *samlor machou bawng kawng* (prawn soup similar to the popular Thai *tom yam*) and *samlor ktis* (fish soup with coconut and pineapple).

Much of the fish eaten in Cambodia is freshwater, from the Tonlé Sap Lake or the Mekong River. *Trey ahng* (grilled fish) is a Cambodian speciality (*ahng* means 'grilled' and can be applied to many dishes). Traditionally, the fish is eaten as pieces wrapped in lettuce or spinach leaves and then dipped

Friends (p107) is one of the best-known restaurants in Phnom Penh, turning out a fine array of tapas, shakes and specials to help street children in the capital. Its cookbook *The Best of Friends* is a visual feast showcasing its best recipes.

For the scoop on countryside cooking in Cambodia, pick up *From Spiders to Waterlilies*, a cookbook produced by Romdeng restaurant (p107) in Phnom Penh.

into *teuk trey*, a fish sauce that is a close relative to Vietnam's *nuoc mam*, but with the addition of ground peanuts.

Cambodian salad dishes are also popular and delicious, although quite different from the Western idea of a cold salad. *Phlea sait kow* is a beef and vegetable salad, flavoured with coriander, mint and lemon grass. These three herbs find their way into many Cambodian dishes.

Desserts can be sampled cheaply at night markets around the country. One sweet snack to look out for is the ice-cream sandwich. No kidding – it's popular with the kids and involves putting a slab of homemade ice cream in a piece of sponge or bread. It actually doesn't taste too bad.

Cambodia is blessed with many tropical fruits and sampling these is an integral part of a visit to the country. All the common fruits can be found in abundance, including *chek* (banana), *menoa* (pineapple) and *duong* (coconut). Among the larger fruit, *khnau* (jackfruit) is very common, often weighing more than 20kg. Beneath the green skin are bright yellow segments with a distinctive taste and rubbery texture. The *tourain* (durian) usually needs no introduction, as you can smell it from a mile off. The exterior is green with sharp spines, while inside is a milky, soft interior regarded by the Chinese as an aphrodisiac. It stinks, although some maintain it is an acquired taste – best acquired with a nose peg.

The fruits most popular with visitors include the *mongkut* (mangosteen) and *sao mao* (rambutan). The small mangosteen has a purple skin that contains white segments with a divine flavour. Queen Victoria is said to have offered a reward to anyone able to transport an edible mangosteen back to England. Similarly popular is the rambutan, the interior like a lychee, but the exterior covered in soft red and green spines.

Best of all, although common throughout the world, is the *svay* (mango). The Cambodian mango season is from March to May. Other varieties of mango are available year round, but it's the hot-season ones that are a taste sensation.

DRINKS

Cambodia has a lively local drinking culture, and the heat and humidity will ensure that you hunt out anything on offer to quench your thirst. Coffee, tea, beer, wine, soft drinks, fresh fruit juices or some of the more exotic 'firewaters' are all widely available. Tea is the national drink, but these days it is just as likely to be beer in the glass.

Beer

It's never a challenge to find a beer in Cambodia and even the most remote village usually has a stall selling a few cans. Angkor is the national beer, produced in vast quantities in a big brewery down in Sihanoukville. It costs around US$1.50 to US$3 for a 660ml bottle in most restaurants and bars. Draught Angkor is available for around US$1 in the main tourist centres.

Teuk trey (fish sauce), one of the most popular condiments in Cambodian cooking, cannot be taken on international flights in line with regulations on carrying strong-smelling or corrosive substances.

The local brew for country folk is sugar-palm wine, distilled daily direct from the trees and fairly potent after it has settled. Sold in bamboo containers off the back of bicycles, it's tasty and cheap, although only suitable for those with a cast-iron stomach.

TRAVEL YOUR TASTEBUDS

No matter what part of the world you come from, if you travel much in Cambodia, you are going to encounter food that is unusual, strange, maybe even immoral, or just plain weird. The fiercely omnivorous Cambodians find nothing strange in eating insects, algae, offal or fish bladders. They will dine on a duck foetus, brew up some brains or snack on some spiders. They will peel live frogs to grill on a barbecue or down the wine infused with cobra to increase their virility.

To the Khmers there is nothing 'strange' about anything that will sustain the body. To them a food is either wholesome or it isn't; it's nutritious or it isn't; it tastes good or it doesn't. And that's all they worry about. They'll try anything once, even a burger.

BOTTOMS UP

When Cambodian men propose a toast, they usually stipulate what percentage must be downed. If they are feeling generous, it might be just *ha-sip pea-roi* (50%), but more often than not it is *moi roi pea-roi* (100%). This is why they love ice in their beer, as they can pace themselves over the course of the night. Many a *barang* (foreigner) has ended up face down on the table at a Cambodian wedding when trying to outdrink the Khmer boys without the aid of ice.

A beer brand from neighbouring Laos, Beer Lao, is very drinkable and is also one of the cheapest ales you can get. Tiger Beer is produced locally and is a popular draught in the capital. Some Khmer restaurants have a bevy of 'beer girls', each promoting a particular beer brand. They are always friendly and will leave you alone if you prefer not to drink.

A word of caution for beer seekers in Cambodia. While the country is awash with good brews, there is a shortage of refrigeration in the countryside. Go native: learn how to say '*Som teuk koh*' (Ice, please).

Wine & Spirits

Local wine in Cambodia generally means rice wine; it is popular with the minority peoples of the northeast. Some rice wines are fermented for months and are super strong, while other brews are fresher and taste more like a demented cocktail. Either way, if you are invited to join a session in a minority village, it's rude to decline. Other local wines include light sugar-palm wine and ginger wine.

In Phnom Penh and Siem Reap, foreign wines and spirits are sold in supermarkets at bargain prices, given how far they have to travel. Wines from Europe and Australia start at about US$4, while the famous names of the spirit world cost between US$4 and US$10. Yes, a bottle of Stoli vodka is just US$4.

Most of the locally produced spirits are best avoided, although some expats contend that Sra Special (around US$2), a local whisky-like concoction, is not bad. There has also been a surge in the popularity of 'muscle wines' (something like Red Bull meets absinthe), with enticing pictures of strongmen on the labels and names like Hercules, Commando Bear and Brace of Loma. They contain enough unknown substances to contravene the Geneva Chemical Weapons Convention and should be approached with caution.

Tea & Coffee

Chinese-style *tai* (tea) is a bit of a national institution, and in most Khmer and Chinese restaurants a pot will automatically appear for no extra charge as soon as you sit down. *Kaa fey* (coffee) is sold in most restaurants. It is either black or *café au lait* – served with dollops of condensed milk.

Water & Soft Drinks

Drinking tap water *must* be avoided, especially in the provinces, as it is rarely purified and may lead to stomach complications (p362). Locally produced mineral water starts at 500r per bottle at shops and stalls, though some locals and expats alike doubt the purity of the cheapest stuff. Those with a weak constitution might want to opt for one of the international brands, such as Evian.

Although tap water should be avoided, it is generally OK to have ice in your drinks. Throughout Cambodia, *teuk koh* (ice) is produced with treated water at local ice factories, a legacy of the French.

All the well-known soft drinks are available in Cambodia. Bottled drinks are about 1000r, while canned drinks cost about 2000r and more again in restaurants or bars.

Some Cambodian nightclubs allow guests to rent premium bottles of spirits, like Johnnie Walker Blue Label, to display on the table – a way of maintaining face despite the fact it's actually Johnnie Walker Red Label in the glass.

The best food blog on Cambodia can be found at www.phnomenon. com, which covers Khmer food, surfing the streets and the up-and-coming dining scene. Originally authored by Phil Lees, it remains to be seen if someone will take up the gauntlet in his absence.

Fruit Shakes

Teuk kalohk are popular throughout Cambodia. They are a little like fruit smoothies and are a great way to wash down a meal. Stalls are set up around local night markets sometime before dark and the drinks cost around 2000r. Watch out for how much sugar goes in if you don't like sweet drinks, and pass on the offer of an egg if you don't want it super frothy.

CELEBRATIONS

Cambodians enjoy celebrating, be it a wedding, a festival or a football match. For a festival, the family coffers are broken open and no matter how much they hold, it is deemed insufficient. The money is splurged on those treats that the family may not be able to afford at other times, such as duck, shrimp or crab. Guests are welcomed and will be seated at large round tables, then the food is paraded out course after course. Everyone eats until they can eat no more and drinks beyond their limit. Glasses are raised, toasts are given, and everyone downs in one.

WHERE TO EAT & DRINK

Whatever your taste, some eatery in Cambodia is sure to help out, be it the humble peddler, a market stall, a local diner or a slick restaurant.

It is easy to sample inexpensive Khmer cuisine throughout the country, mostly at local markets and cheap restaurants. For more refined Khmer dining, the best restaurants are in Phnom Penh and Siem Reap, where there is also the choice of excellent Thai, Vietnamese, Chinese, Indian, French and Mediterranean cooking. Chinese, and to a lesser extent Vietnamese, food is available in towns across the country due to the large urban populations of both of these ethnic groups.

There are few Western fast-food chains in Phnom Penh as yet, with the exception of KFC, but there are a few local copycats. The most successful has been Lucky Burger, with lots of branches in the capital.

There are often no set hours for places to eat but, as a general rule of thumb, street stalls are open from very early in the morning until early evening, although some stalls specialise in the night shift. Most restaurants are open all day, while some of the fancier places are only open for lunch (usually 11am to 2.30pm) and dinner (usually 5pm to 10pm).

Quick Eats

Because so much of life is lived outside the home, street food is an important part of everyday Cambodian life. Like many Southeast Asian people,

---

Before becoming a member of the WTO, copyright protection was almost unknown in Cambodia and that spawned a host of copycat fast-food restaurants including KFC (Khmer Fried Chicken?), Pizza Hot and Burger Queen, all now sadly closed.

Longteine De Monteiro runs several Cambodian restaurants on the east coast of the USA and she has put together her favourite traditional Khmer recipes at www.elephantwalk.com.

TOP FIVE REGIONAL RESTAURANTS HELPING CAMBODIA

There are lots of NGOs attempting to assist Cambodia as it walks the road to recovery. Some of these have established restaurants and eateries to raise funds and give young disadvantaged Cambodians some experience in the hospitality sector. There are also several recommended restaurants in Phnom Penh (p107) and Siem Reap (p144) supporting good causes.

Epic Arts Café (p227) A lively little cafe in Kampot assisting the deaf community and promoting arts education for the disabled.

Fresh Eats Café (p254) A cosy place in Battambang that helps children from families affected by HIV/AIDS.

Gelato Italiano (p220) A modern *gelateria* staffed by students from Sihanoukville's Don Bosco Hotel School.

Smile Restaurant (p295) A new non-profit restaurant in Kompong Cham, it has big breakfasts, a healthy menu and free wi-fi.

Starfish Bakery & Café (p219) A homely cafe in Sihanoukville offering delectable cakes and light lunches, with all proceeds going to community projects.

LUU MENG Nick Ray

Renowned Cambodian celebrity chef and restaurateur Luu Meng is the face behind a handful of Phnom Penh's best-known restaurants and cafes.

Luu Meng's love of cooking started at a young age, as his Chinese-Cambodian family ran a restaurant on Sothearos Blvd in the late 1960s. 'My family had a typical Chinese restaurant, so I grew up around food and we always ate well', Luu explains. He joined the Sofitel Cambodiana Hotel (now Hotel Cambodiana, p106) as the country opened its doors to the world once more and soon became one of the country's rising culinary stars. 'I travelled the region, working in Thailand and at the famous Sofitel Metropole in Hanoi', Meng continues, an experience which brought him into contact with new flavours and regional specialities. Returning to Cambodia, he eventually formed Man Co, the group behind such popular Phnom Penh restaurants as Malis (p109) and Topaz (p110).

We discuss Cambodian cuisine and what differentiates it from its neighbours. 'Thai food is hot, spicy and sweet, while Vietnamese is more Chinese influenced', explains Meng. 'Khmer cuisine is all about fresh spices. There are influences from India, but always with fresh ingredients, not powders. Our cuisine is not as spicy as Thai and we don't use as much fish sauce as Vietnam, although we do love prahoc [fish paste].' He pauses to reflect. 'It's all about freshness.'

On the subject of Cambodian tastes and a Cambodian national dish, he is animated, and naturally amoc (mild baked fish curry) leads the discussions. 'Amoc is typically Cambodian and takes advantage of our abundance of fresh fish from the Tonlé Sap', Meng points out. 'Cambodian cuisine also has some superb salads, which often surprises people. Sait ko plear [raw beef salad] can be prepared carpaccio style with fresh, finely grated lemon grass and is a symphony of subtle flavours.'

Travelling widely and cooking for a diverse audience, Meng has taken on many influences, but is quite a traditionalist at heart. 'For me, the most important thing about cooking is quality. Quality of the ingredients, quality of the kitchen, quality of the service', he continues. 'If a chef knows and understands this, it can be applied to different cuisines.' However, he prefers to concentrate on his strengths and promote local ingredients and traditional dishes. 'If we plan to promote another cuisine, then we bring in a specialist chef from that culinary culture', he explains. 'That way, we always guarantee the authentic flavour.'

Naturally, we end up discussing the best restaurants in Phnom Penh for traditional Cambodian food. 'For me, you have to go over the bridge [Chruoy Changvar Bridge] for the real taste of Cambodia', he enthuses. 'Many of the places in town serve a bit of everything from the region, but over the bridge are the real Cambodian restaurants.' A favourite? He laughs. 'It has to be Rum Chang, as they offer very traditional recipes and a peaceful setting.'

Luu Meng is the managing director of Man Co (Management Company),
which runs several hotels and restaurants in Cambodia.

Cambodians are inveterate snackers. They can be found at impromptu stalls at any time of the day or night, delving into a range of unidentified frying objects. Drop into the markets for an even greater range of dishes and the chance of a comfortable seat. It's a cheap, cheerful and cool way to get up close and personal with Khmer cuisine. Some of the new shopping malls, such as Sorya Shopping Centre (p108) in Phnom Penh, have food courts where it is possible to sample the street food in hygienic air-conditioned comfort.

VEGETARIANS & VEGANS

Few Cambodians understand the concept of strict vegetarianism and many will say something is vegetarian to please the customer when in fact it is not. If you are not a strict vegetarian and can deal with fish sauces and the like, you should have few problems ordering meals, and those who eat fish can sample Khmer cooking at its best. In the major tourist centres, many of the international restaurants feature vegetarian meals, although

One of the most popular street snacks in Cambodia is the unborn duck foetus. The white duck eggs contain a little duckling, feathers and all. Don't order kaun pong tear if you want to avoid this.

these are not budget options. In Khmer and Chinese restaurants, stir-fried vegetable dishes are readily available, as are vegetarian fried rice dishes, but it is unlikely these 'vegetarian' dishes have been cooked in separate woks from other fish- and meat-based dishes. Indian restaurants in the popular tourist centres can cook up genuine vegetarian food, as they usually understand the vegetarian principle better than the *prahoc*-loving Khmers. Siem Reap has several excellent vegetarian restaurants.

EATING WITH KIDS

Family is at the heart of life in Cambodia, so it is hardly surprising that family-oriented restaurants are found throughout the country. Most local restaurants will welcome children with open arms, particularly foreign kiddies, as staff don't get a chance to see them up close that often. Sometimes the welcome will be too much, with pinches and pats coming left, right and centre, but such is the way in Cambodia.

Ironically, it is often the upmarket Western restaurants where the reception may be terse if the children are playing up, as some stiff expats seem to have forgotten that they started out life that small. That said, there are plenty of excellent, child-friendly cafes and restaurants in Phnom Penh and Siem Reap serving dishes from home. There are rarely children's menus anywhere, but with food so affordable, there is little room to quibble.

Most of the snacks children are accustomed to back home are available in Cambodia…and so much more. It is a great country for fruit, and the sweetness of mangosteens or the weirdness of dragon fruit or rambutan is a sure way to get them interested.

There is sometimes monosodium glutamate (MSG) in local Cambodian food. If your child has problems digesting it or you prefer to avoid it, stick to restaurants with an English-language menu that are used to dealing with tourists.

For more information on travelling with children in Cambodia, see p322.

HABITS & CUSTOMS

Enter the Cambodian kitchen and you will learn that fine food comes from simplicity. Essentials consist of a strong flame, clean water, basic cutting utensils, a mortar and pestle, and a well-blackened pot or two.

Cambodians eat three meals a day. Breakfast is either *kyteow* or *bobor*. Baguettes are available at any time of day or night, and go down well with a cup of coffee.

Lunch starts early, around 11am. Traditionally lunch is taken with the family, but in towns and cities many workers now eat at local restaurants or markets.

Dinner is the time for family bonding. Dishes are arranged around the central rice bowl and diners each have a small eating bowl. The procedure is uncomplicated: spoon some rice into your bowl, and lay 'something else' on top of it.

When ordering multiple courses from a restaurant menu don't worry – don't even think – about the proper succession of courses. All dishes are placed in the centre of the table as soon as they are ready. Diners then help themselves to whatever appeals to them, regardless of who ordered what.

Table Etiquette

Sit at the table with your bowl on a small plate, chopsticks or fork and spoon at the ready. Some Cambodians prefer chopsticks, some prefer fork and spoon, but both are usually available. Each place setting will include a small bowl, usually located at the top right-hand side for the dipping sauces.

Both Phnom Penh and Siem Reap have child-friendly eateries. Check out Le Jardin (p113) or Living Room (p114) in Phnom Penh or Singing Tree (p144) in Siem Reap and sit back and relax. Some of the fast-food places in the capital also have children's adventure playgrounds.

Cambodia exports a lot of unprocessed rice to Thailand and Vietnam, from where it is exported to the West or re-imported by Cambodia.

As well as eating the notorious tarantulas of Skuon (p293), Cambodians also like to eat crickets, beetles, larvae and ants. Some scientists have suggested insect farms as a way to solve food problems of the future. For once, Cambodia may be ahead of the curve.

DOS & DON'TS

- *Do* wait for your host to sit first.
- *Don't* turn down food placed in your bowl by your host.
- *Do* learn to use chopsticks.
- *Don't* leave chopsticks in a V-shape in the bowl, a symbol of death.
- *Do* tip about 5% to 10% in restaurants, as wages are low.
- *Don't* tip if there is already a service charge on the bill.
- *Do* drink every time someone offers a toast.
- *Don't* pass out face down on the table if the toasting goes on all night.

When serving yourself from the central bowls, use the communal serving spoon so as not to dip your chopsticks or spoon into the food. To begin eating, just pick up your bowl with the left hand, bring it close to your mouth, and spoon in the rice and food.

It is polite for the host to offer more food than the guests can eat, and it is polite for the guests not to eat everything in sight.

COOKING COURSES

If you are really taken with Cambodian cuisine, it is possible to learn some tricks of the trade by signing up for a cooking course. It's a great way to introduce your Cambodian experience to your friends; no one wants to sit through the slide show of photos, but offer them a mouth-watering meal and they will all come running.

There are courses available in Phnom Penh, Siem Reap, Battambang and Sihanoukville, and more are popping up all the time. In Phnom Penh, Frizz Restaurant (p98) offers courses, as do some of the hotels. In Siem Reap, Le Tigre de Papier (p136) offers daily courses in conjunction with the Sala Bai Training School, plus more and more hotels are getting into the game. In Battambang, the Smokin' Pot (p252) is a cracking little kitchen restaurant offering a cheap introduction to the secrets of Cambodian cooking.

EAT YOUR WORDS
Food Glossary
BREAKFAST

bread	*nohm paang*	នំបុ័ង
butter	*bœ*	បឺរ
fried eggs	*pohng moan jien*	ពងមាន់ចៀន
rice porridge	*bobor*	បបរ
vegetable noodle soup	*kyteow dak buhn lai*	គុយទាវដាក់បន្លែ

LUNCH & DINNER

beef	*sait kow*	សាច់គោ
chicken	*sait moan*	សាច់មាន់
crab	*k'daam*	ក្ដាម
curry	*karii*	ការី
eel	*ahntohng*	អន្ទង់
fish	*trey*	ត្រី
fried	*jien, chaa*	ចៀន, ឆា
frog	*kawng kaip*	កង្កែប

grilled	*ahng*	អាំង
lobster	*bawng kawng*	បង្កង
noodles	*mii* (egg)	មី
	kyteow (rice)	គុយទាវ
pork	*sait j'ruuk*	សាច់ជ្រូក
rice	*bai*	បាយ
shrimp	*bawngkia*	បង្គា
snail	*kh'jawng*	ខ្យង
soup	*sup*	ស៊ុប
spring rolls	*naim* (fresh)	ណែម
	chaa yaw (fried)	ឆាយ៉
squid	*meuk*	មឹក
steamed	*jamhoi*	ចំហុយ
vegetables	*buhn lai*	បន្លែ

FRUITS

apple	*phla i powm*	ផ្លែប៉ោម
banana	*chek*	ចេក
coconut	*duong*	ដូង
custard apple	*tiep*	ទៀប
dragon fruit	*phlai srakaa neak*	ផ្លែស្រកានាគ
durian	*tourain*	ធូរេន
grapes	*tompeang baai juu*	ទំពាំងបាយជូរ
guava	*trawbaik*	ត្របែក
jackfruit	*khnau*	ខ្នុរ
lemon	*krow-it ch'maa*	ក្រូចឆ្មារ
longan	*mien*	មៀន
lychee	*phlai kuulain*	ផ្លែគូលេន
mandarin	*krow-it khwait*	ក្រូចខ្វិច
mango	*svay*	ស្វាយ
mangosteen	*mongkut*	មង្ឃុត
orange	*krow-it pow saat*	ក្រូចពោធិសាត់
papaya	*l'howng*	ល្ហុង
pineapple	*menoa*	ម្នាស់
pomelo	*krow-it th'lohng*	ក្រូចថ្លុង
rambutan	*sao mao*	សាវម៉ាវ
star fruit (carambola)	*speu*	ស្ពឺ
watermelon	*euv luhk*	ឪឡឹក

CONDIMENTS

chilli	*m'teh*	ម្ទេស
fish sauce	*teuk trey*	ទឹកត្រី
garlic	*kh'tuhm saw*	ខ្ទឹមស
ginger	*kh'nyei*	ខ្ញី
ice	*teuk koh*	ទឹកកក
lemon grass	*sluhk kray*	ស្លឹកគ្រៃ
pepper	*m'rait*	ម្រេច
salt	*uhmbuhl*	អំបិល
soy sauce	*teuk sii iw*	ទឹកស៊ីអ៊ីវ
sugar	*skaw*	ស្ករ

DRINKS

banana shake	*teuk kralohk*	ទឹកក្រឡុកចេក
beer	*bii-yœ*	បៀរ
black coffee	*kaa fey kh'mav*	កាហ្វេខ្មៅ
coffee	*kaa fey*	កាហ្វេ
iced coffee	*kaa fey teuk koh*	កាហ្វេទឹកកក
lemon juice	*teuk krow-it ch'maa*	ទឹកក្រូចឆ្មារ
mixed fruit shake	*teuk kralohk chek*	ទឹកក្រឡុកផ្លែឈើ
orange juice	*teuk krow-it pow sat*	ទឹកក្រូចពោធិ៍សាត់
tea	*tai*	តែ
tea with milk	*tai teuk dawh kow*	តែទឹកដោះគោ
water	*teuk*	ទឹក
white coffee	*kaa fey ohlay* (ie *café au lait*)	កាហ្វេអូឡេ

Environment

THE LAND

Cambodia's borders, as we know them today, are the result of a classic historical squeeze. As the Vietnamese moved south into the Mekong Delta and the Thais pushed west towards Angkor, Cambodia's territory – which in Angkorian times stretched from southern Burma to Saigon and north into Laos – began shrinking. Only the arrival of the French prevented Cambodia from going the way of the Chams, who became a people without a state. In that sense, French colonialism created a protectorate that actually protected.

Modern-day Cambodia covers 181,035 sq km, making it a little more than half the size of Vietnam (about the same size as the US state of Washington, or England and Wales combined). The country is a bit wider (about 580km) east–west than it is north–south (about 450km). To the west and northwest it borders Thailand, to the northeast Laos, and to the east and southeast Vietnam; to the south is the Gulf of Thailand.

Cambodia's two dominant geographical features are the mighty Mekong River and a vast lake, the Tonlé Sap – see opposite for more on this natural miracle.

At Phnom Penh the Mekong splits into three channels: the Tonlé Sap River, which flows into, and out of, the Tonlé Sap Lake; the Upper River (usually called simply the Mekong or, in Vietnamese, Tien Giang); and the Lower River (the Tonlé Bassac, or Hau Giang in Vietnamese). The rich sediment deposited during the Mekong's annual wet-season flooding has made central Cambodia incredibly fertile. This low-lying alluvial plain is where the vast majority of Cambodians live, fishing and farming in time with the rhythms of the monsoon.

> The volume of water in the Tonlé Sap can expand by up to a factor of 70 during the wet season.

In Cambodia's southwest quadrant, much of the landmass is covered by mountains up to 1813m high: the Cardamom Mountains (Chuor Phnom Kravanh), covering parts of the provinces of Koh Kong, Battambang, Pursat and Krong Pailin, which are now opening up to ecotourism; and, southeast of there, the Elephant Mountains (Chuor Phnom Damrei), situated in the provinces of Kompong Speu, Koh Kong and Kampot.

Cambodia's 435km coastline is a big draw for visitors on the lookout for isolated tropical beaches. There are islands aplenty off the coast of Sihanoukville (p214), Kep (p235) and the Koh Kong Conservation Corridor (p203).

> The Tonlé Sap provides a huge percentage of Cambodians' protein intake, 70% of which comes from fish.

Along Cambodia's northern border with Thailand, the plains collide with a striking sandstone escarpment more than 300km long that towers up to 550m above the lowlands: the Dangkrek Mountains (Chuor Phnom Dangkrek). One of the best places to get a sense of this area is Prasat Preah Vihear (p279).

In the northeastern corner of the country, the plains give way to the Eastern Highlands, a remote region of densely forested mountains and high plateaux that extends east into Vietnam's Central Highlands and north into Laos. The wild provinces of Ratanakiri (p305) and Mondulkiri (p312) provide a home to many minority (hill tribe) peoples and are taking off as an ecotourism hot spot.

WILDLIFE

Cambodia's forest ecosystems were in excellent shape until the 1990s and, compared with its neighbours, its habitats are still relatively intact. The years of war took their toll on some species, but others thrived in the remote jungles of the southwest and northeast. Ironically, peace brought increased threats as loggers felled huge areas of primary forest and the illicit trade in

---

TONLÉ SAP: HEARTBEAT OF CAMBODIA

The Tonlé Sap, the largest freshwater lake in Southeast Asia, is an incredible natural phenomenon that provides fish and irrigation water for half the population of Cambodia – and a home for 90,000 people, many of them ethnic Vietnamese, who live in 170 floating villages.

Linking the lake with the Mekong, at Phnom Penh, is a 100km-long channel known as the Tonlé Sap River. From June to early October, wet-season rains rapidly raise the level of the Mekong, backing up the Tonlé Sap River and causing it to flow northwestward into the Tonlé Sap Lake. During this period, the lake surface increases in size by a factor of four or five, from 2500 sq km to 3000 sq km up to 10,000 sq km to 16,000 sq km, and its depth increases from an average of about 2m to more than 10m. An unbelievable 20% of the Mekong's wet-season flow is absorbed by the Tonlé Sap. In October, as the water level of the Mekong begins to fall, the Tonlé Sap River reverses direction, draining the waters of the lake back into the Mekong.

This extraordinary process makes the Tonlé Sap an ideal habitat for birds, snakes and turtles, as well as one of the world's richest sources of freshwater fish: the flooded forests make for fertile spawning grounds, while the dry season creates ideal conditions for fishing. Experts believe that fish migrations from the lake help to restock fisheries as far north as China.

This unique ecosystem was declared a Unesco Biosphere Reserve (www.tsbr-ed.org) in 2001, but this may not be enough to protect it from the twin threats of upstream dams (see p71) and rampant deforestation.

You can learn more about the Tonlé Sap and its unique ecosystem at the Gecko Centre (p152) near Siem Reap.

---

wildlife targeted endangered species. Because of years of inaccessibility, scientists are only just beginning to research and catalogue the country's plant and animal life.

Animals

Cambodia is home to an estimated 212 species of mammal, including tigers, elephants, bears, leopards and wild oxen. Some of the biggest characters, however, are the smaller creatures, including the binturong (nicknamed the bear cat), the pileated gibbon (the world's largest population lives in the Cardamoms) and the slow loris, which hangs out in trees all day. The country also has a great variety of butterflies.

Most of Cambodia's fauna is extremely hard to get a look at in the wild. The easiest way to see a healthy selection is to visit the Phnom Tamao Wildlife Rescue Centre (p126) near Phnom Penh, which provides a home for rescued animals and includes all the major species.

A whopping 720 bird species find Cambodia a congenial home, thanks in large part to its year-round water resources, first and foremost the marshes around the Tonlé Sap. Relatively common birds include ducks, rails, cranes, herons, egrets, cormorants, pelicans, storks and parakeets, with migratory shorebirds, such as waders, plovers and terns, around the south coast estuaries. Serious twitchers should consider a visit to Prek Toal Bird Sanctuary (p151); Ang Trapeng Thmor Reserve (p151), home to the extremely rare sarus crane, depicted on the bas-reliefs at Angkor; the Tmatboey Ibis Project (p277), where the critically endangered giant ibis, Cambodia's national bird, can be seen; and – for the truly adventurous – the Chhep Vulture Feeding Station (p278). For details on birdwatching in Cambodia, check out the Siem Reap–based Sam Veasna Center (see p346).

Cambodia is home to about 240 species of reptile, including nine species of snake whose venom can be fatal. The mere whisper of their names sends a shiver down the spine: the king cobra, monocellata cobra, Indo-Chinese spitting cobra, banded krait, Malayan krait, red-headed krait, Russel's viper,

For a close encounter with tigers at the temples of Angkor, watch Jean-Jacques Annaud's 2004 film *Two Brothers*, the story of two orphan tiger cubs during the colonial period.

The *khting vor* (spiral-horned ox), so rare that no one had ever seen a live specimen, was considered critically endangered until DNA analysis of its distinctive horns showed that the creature had never existed – the 'horns' belonged to ordinary cattle and buffalos!

Malayan pit viper and white-lipped pit viper. The Sihanoukville NGO Hand of Help (p212) produces antivenenes.

Snake bites are responsible for more amputations in Cambodia than land mines these days. Many villagers go to the medicine man for treatment and end up with infection, gangrene and/or a funeral.

ENDANGERED SPECIES

Unfortunately it is getting mighty close to checkout time for a number of species in Cambodia.

The kouprey (wild ox), declared Cambodia's national animal by King Sihanouk back in the 1960s, and the Wroughton's free-tailed bat, previously thought to exist in only one part of India, but recently discovered in Preah Vihear Province, are the only Cambodian mammals on the 'Globally Threatened: Critical' list, the last stop before extinction.

Other animals under serious threat in Cambodia include the Asian elephant, tiger, banteng (another kind of wild ox), gaur, Asian golden cat, Asiatic wild dog, black gibbon, clouded leopard, fishing cat, marbled cat, sun bear, wild water buffalo, pangolin (p204), giant ibis and, in the wild, the dragonfish (Asian arowana) and Siamese crocodile (p205).

Researchers estimate that about 50 to 100 wild elephants live in Mondulkiri Province. A similar number live in the Cardamom Mountains, including Botum Sakor National Park.

Cambodia has some of the last remaining freshwater Irrawaddy dolphins (*trey pisaut* in Khmer), instantly identifiable thanks to their bulging forehead and short beak. At the time of writing it is estimated that there may be as few as 64 left (down from 80 to 100 in 2006), inhabiting stretches of the Mekong between Kratie and the Lao border. Viewing them at Kampi (p300) is a popular activity. More Irrawaddy dolphins inhabit the saline estuaries and mangrove swamps of Koh Kong Province and can be viewed around Peam Krasaop Wildlife Sanctuary (p202) and Ream National Park (p222). For details, check out the website of the WWF at www.panda.org.

In terms of fish biodiversity, the Mekong is second only to the Amazon, but dam projects threaten migratory species. The Mekong giant catfish, which can weigh up to 300kg, is critically endangered due to habitat loss and overfishing.

Plants

No one knows how many plant species are present in Cambodia because no comprehensive survey has ever been conducted, but it's estimated that the country is home to 15,000 species (including 2300 vascular plants), at least a third of them endemic.

In the southwest, rainforests grow to heights of 50m or more on the rainy southern slopes of the mountains, with montane (pine) forests in cooler climes above 800m and mangrove forests fringing the coast. In the northern mountains there are broadleaved evergreen forests, with trees soaring 30m above a thick undergrowth of vines, bamboos, palms and assorted woody and herbaceous ground plants. The northern plains support dry dipterocarp forests,

---

NGOS ON THE ENVIRONMENTAL FRONTLINE

The following environmental groups – staffed in Cambodia mainly by Khmers – are playing leading roles in protecting Cambodia's wildlife:

- Conservation International (www.conservation.org)
- Flora & Fauna International (www.fauna-flora.org)
- Maddox Jolie-Pitt Foundation (www.mjpasia.org)
- Wildlife Alliance (formerly WildAid; www.wildlifealliance.org)
- Wildlife Conservation Society (www.wcs.org)
- WWF (www.worldwildlife.org)

TIGER, TIGER, BURNING OUT?

In the mid-1990s, somewhere between 100 and 200 Cambodian tigers were being killed every year, their carcasses bringing huge sums around Asia (especially China) because of their supposed aphrodisiacal powers. By 1998 annual incidents of tiger poaching had dropped to 85 and in 2005 just two tigers were killed. Sadly, it's more likely that these estimates reflect a crash in tiger numbers rather than increased community awareness or more effective law enforcement.

Experts fear there may be only 50 of the big cats left in the wild in Cambodia. Numbers are so low that, despite repeated efforts, camera traps set by researchers in recent years have failed to photograph a single tiger, though footprints and other signs of the felines' presence have been recorded. As far as anyone can tell, the surviving tigers live in very low densities in very remote areas, making it difficult for both poachers and scientists to find them – and hard for environmentalists to protect them.

A significant poaching threat comes from police and military units stationed in remote jungle locations. Encouragingly, some former poachers are now employed as rangers, making it easier to educate other hunters about the ecological impact of 'wildlife crimes'.

At present, tigers are known to inhabit two areas: the central part of the Cardamom Mountains and Mondulkiri Province. In addition, they are thought to be present in small numbers in Ratanakiri, Preah Vihear and Oddar Meanchey Provinces and perhaps even in Bokor National Park (p229).

For insights, stories and links about tigers in Cambodia and what's being done to protect them, visit the website of the Cat Action Treasury at www.felidae.org.

---

while around the Tonlé Sap there are flooded (seasonally inundated) forests. The Eastern Highlands are covered with deciduous forests and grassland. Forested upland areas support many varieties of orchid.

The sugar palm, often seen towering over rice fields, provides fronds to make roofs and walls for houses, and fruit that's used to produce medicine, wine and vinegar. Sugar palms grow taller over the years, but the barkless trunk doesn't get any thicker, hence retaining shrapnel marks from every battle that has ever raged around them.

NATIONAL PARKS

In the late 1960s Cambodia had six national parks, together covering 22,000 sq km (around 12% of the country). The long civil war effectively destroyed this system and it wasn't reintroduced until 1993, when a royal decree designated 23 areas as national parks, wildlife sanctuaries, protected landscapes and multiple-use areas. Several more protected forests were recently added to the list, bringing the area of protected land in Cambodia to over 43,000 sq km, or around 25% of the country.

Cambodia became the first Southeast Asian country to establish a national park when it created a protected area in 1925 to preserve the forests around the temples of Angkor.

This is fantastic news in principle, but in practice the authorities don't always protect these areas in any way other than drawing a line on a map. The government has enough trouble finding funds to pay the rangers who patrol the most popular parks, let alone to recruit staff for the remote sanctuaries, though in recent years a number of international NGOs have been helping to train and fund teams of enforcement rangers (see the boxed text, opposite).

The Mondulkiri Protected Forest (p317), at 4294 sq km, is now the largest protected area in Cambodia and is contiguous with Yok Don National Park in Vietnam. The Central Cardamoms Protected Forest (see p204 and p247), at 4013 sq km, borders the Phnom Samkos Wildlife Sanctuary (p248) to the west and the Phnom Aural Wildlife Sanctuary (p248) to the east, creating almost 10,000 sq km of designated protected land. The noncontiguous Southern Cardamoms Protected Forest (1443 sq km; p206) is along the Koh Kong Conservation Corridor (p200), whose ecotourism potential is as vast as its jungles are impenetrable.

Cambodia's highest mountain, at 1813m, is Phnom Aural in Pursat Province (see p248).

CAMBODIA'S MOST IMPORTANT NATIONAL PARKS

Park	Size	Features	Activities	Best Time to Visit
Bokor (p229)	1581 sq km	ghost town, views, waterfalls, orange lichen	trekking, biking, wildlife watching	Dec-May
Botum Sakor (p205)	1834 sq km	mangroves, beaches, monkeys, dolphins, elephants	boat rides, swimming, hiking	Dec-May
Kirirom (p127)	350 sq km	waterfalls, vistas, pine forests	hiking, wildlife watching	Nov-Jun
Ream (p222)	150 sq km	beaches, islands, mangroves, dolphins, monkeys	boating, swimming, hiking, wildlife watching	Dec-May
Virachey (p311)	3325 sq km	unexplored jungle, waterfalls	trekking, adventure, wildlife watching	Dec-Apr

ENVIRONMENTAL ISSUES
Land mines
Farmland and forests in some parts of Cambodia (eg along the Thai frontier) conceal highly dangerous anti-personnel mines planted during the civil war. For more information, see p269.

Logging
The greatest threat to Cambodia's globally important ecosystems is logging for charcoal and timber and to clear land for cash-crop plantations. During the Vietnamese occupation, troops stripped away swaths of forest to prevent Khmer Rouge ambushes along highways. The devastation increased in the 1990s, when the shift to a capitalist market economy led to an asset-stripping bonanza by well-connected businessmen.

International demand for timber is huge, and, as neighbouring countries such as Thailand and Vietnam began to enforce much tougher logging regulations, foreign logging companies flocked to Cambodia. At the height of the country's logging epidemic (at the end of 1997), just under 70,000 sq km of the country's land area – about 35% of its total surface area – had been allocated as concessions, amounting to almost all of Cambodia's forest land except national parks and protected areas. However, even in these supposed havens, illegal logging continued. According to environmental watchdog **Global Witness** (www.globalwitness.org), the Royal Cambodian Armed Forces (RCAF) is the driving force behind much of the recent logging in remote border regions.

In the short term, deforestation is contributing to worsening floods along the Mekong, but the long-term implications of logging are hard to assess. Without trees to cloak the hills, rains will inevitably carry away large amounts of topsoil during future monsoons and in time this will have a serious effect on Tonlé Sap. Will the shallow waters recede as a result of siltation, creating an environmental crisis similar to that marking the fall of the Angkorian empire? Combined with overfishing, pollution and dams, these problems may lead to the eventual destruction of the lake – a catastrophe for future generations.

Since about 2002, things have been looking up. Under pressure from donors and international institutions, all logging contracts were effectively frozen pending further negotiations with the government. Industrial-scale logging ceased and the huge trucks thundering up and down the country's dirt highways disappeared. However, small-scale illegal logging

In the mid-1960s Cambodia was reckoned to have around 90% of its original forest cover intact. Estimates today vary, but 30% is a common estimate.

continued, including cutting for charcoal production and slash-and-burn for settlement.

The latest threat to Cambodia's forests comes from 'economic concessions' granted to establish plantations of cash crops such as rubber, mango, cashew and jackfruit, or agro-forestry groves of acacia and eucalyptus to supply wood chips for the paper industry. There are legal limits – land grants for plantations cannot be larger than 100 sq km, but even this generous allocation is often flouted. Worse still, there have been cases where concessionaires chop down all the trees to prepare the ground – and then fail to plant anything at all.

According to the 'Conservation of Tropical Forests and Biological Diversity in Cambodia', *US Foreign Assistance Act 118/119 Analysis* (April 2005): 'Management of [Cambodia's] rich natural resources, especially forests and the Tonlé Sap Lake, is hampered by corruption, extreme inequality of access rights, insufficient or nonexistent right of tenure, a weak civil society, ethnic divisions and growing population pressures.'

Banned in Cambodia, the damning 2007 report *Cambodia's Family Trees* (www.globalwitness.org /media_library_detail .php/546/en/cambodias _family_trees), by the UK-based environmental watchdog Global Witness, exposes Cambodia's most powerful illegal logging syndicates.

Pollution

Phnom Penh's air isn't anywhere near as bad as Bangkok's, but as vehicles multiply it's getting worse. In provincial towns and villages, the smoke from garbage fires can ruin your dinner or worse. Some hotel rooms have such poor ventilation that mould and mildew can leave you gasping for air.

Cambodia has extremely primitive sanitation systems in urban areas, and nonexistent sanitary facilities in rural areas – only a tiny percentage of the population has access to proper facilities. These conditions breed and spread disease: epidemics of diarrhoea are not uncommon and it is the number-one killer of young children in Cambodia.

Detritus of all sorts, especially plastic bags and bottles, can be seen in distressing quantities on beaches, around waterfalls, along roads and carpeting towns, villages and hamlets.

A new challenge is oil, which has been discovered off Sihanoukville. Sloppy extraction could devastate Cambodia's lovely coast, including pristine mangrove forests.

In September 2005, three enforcement rangers working with the NGO Flora & Fauna International to prevent illegal hunting and logging in the Cardamom Mountains were murdered in two separate incidents, apparently by poachers.

Mekong Be Dammed

The Mekong rises in Tibet and flows for 4800km – including almost 500km in Cambodia, where it can be up to 5km wide – before continuing through southern Vietnam into the South China Sea. With energy needs spiralling ever upwards across Southeast Asia, it is very tempting for poor countries like Cambodia – in which only 20% of households have electricity, most of them in Phnom Penh – and its upstream neighbours, including China, to built hydroelectric dams on the Mekong and its tributaries.

Environmentalists fear that damming the mainstream Mekong may be nothing short of catastrophic for the flow patterns of the Mekong, the migratory patterns of fish, the survival of the freshwater Irrawaddy dolphin (p300) and the very life of the Tonlé Sap (p67). Plans now under consideration include the Sambor Dam, a massive 3300MW project 35km north of Kratie, and the Don Sahong (Siphandone) Dam just north of the Cambodia–Laos border.

Also of concern is the potential impact of dams on the annual monsoon flooding of the Mekong, which deposits nutrient-rich silt across vast tracts of land used for agriculture. A drop of just 1m in wet-season water levels on the Tonlé Sap would result in around 2000 sq km less flood area, with potentially disastrous consequences for Cambodia's farmers.

DOING YOUR BIT

Every visitor to Cambodia can make at least a small contribution to the country's ecological sustainability.

- Lead by example and dispose of your rubbish responsibly.
- Drink fresh coconuts, in their natural packaging, rather than soft drinks in throwaway cans and bottles.
- Choose trekking guides who respect both the ecosystem and the people who live in it.
- Avoid eating wild meat, such as bat, deer and shark fin.
- Don't touch live coral when snorkelling or diving – and don't buy coral souvenirs.
- If you see wild animals being killed, traded or eaten, take down details of what and where and contact the Wildlife Alliance, an NGO that helps manage the government's **Wildlife Rapid Rescue Team** (☎ 012 500094; nickmarx@online.com.kh, wildlifealliance@online.com.kh). Rescued animals are either released or taken to the Phnom Tamao Wildlife Rescue Centre (p126).
- Try some of the places listed in this book's GreenDex (p390).

Overseeing development plans for the river is the **Mekong River Commission** (MRC; www.mrcmekong.org). Formed by the UNDP and comprising Cambodia, Thailand, Laos and Vietnam, it is ostensibly committed to sustainable development.

Sand Extraction

Sand dredging in the estuaries of Koh Kong Province, including inside the protected Peam Krasaop Wildlife Sanctuary, threatens delicate mangrove ecosystems and the sea life that depends on them. According to a 2009 investigation by the *Phnom Penh Post*, local fishermen in Krong Koh Kong have reported reduced catches and changes in the behaviour of sea life, including crabs, since the arrival of the dredging barges, which churn up riverbed silt. Much of the sand is destined for Singapore. For details, see Global Witness' 2009 report *Country for Sale* (www.globalwitness.org /media_library_detail.php/713/en/country_for_sale).

Back in the early 1990s, Cambodia had such extensive forest cover compared with its neighbours that some environmentalists were calling for the whole country to be made a protected area.

MICK ELMORE

COLOURS OF CAMBODIA

Travelling through Cambodia reveals a vivid palette of colour: rural rice fields glimmer like emeralds; Buddhist monks' saffron robes shimmer in the sunlight. Cambodia's ancient temples are hewn from sandstone, but are cloaked in green moss or drip with dappled shadows. Khmer food is as striking in colour as it is in flavour. Even the arts are bright, with exquisite dance costumes. But the people of Cambodia bring the most colour of all, their beautiful smiles and warm welcome an enduring memory of any visit.

Temple-Hopping

Cambodia is the undisputed temple capital of Asia and we are not just talking about the awesome Angkor Wat, the mother of all temples. Angkor is heaven on earth – the home of the gods, cast in stone – but all over the country, hidden away in the jungle, lie monuments that attest to the glories of the Khmer empire.

❶ Angkor Wat

Follow in the footsteps of pilgrims of old along the immense causeway of the 'temple that is a city', the holiest of holies, the one and only, Angkor Wat (p167).

❷ Jungle Temples

Iconic Ta Prohm (pictured left, p181) is the original jungle temple, with serpentine root systems slowly strangling the stones. Further afield lies Beng Mealea (pictured right, p191), smothered then swallowed by the voracious jungle.

❸ Preah Khan

Experience spiritual harmony in the ultimate fusion-temple, Preah Khan (p184), which is dedicated to the Hindu trinity of Shiva, Vishnu and Brahma, as well as the Buddha.

❹ Koh Ker

Discover the rival capital of Koh Ker (p274), carved out of the jungle in the 10th century and home to some of the most epic sculptures from the Angkorian era.

❺ Banteay Chhmar

Venture off the trail to the 'narrow fortress' of Banteay Chhmar (p265), one of the monumental creations of Jayavarman VII, complete with the signature faces of Avalokiteshvara, the Bodhisattva of Compassion.

❻ Life Before Angkor

Cambodia didn't begin and end with Angkor. There are relics of the powerful pre-Angkorian kingdoms of Funan and Chenla all over the country, including Sambor Prei Kuk (p284), the first temple-city in Southeast Asia.

People & Culture

The Khmer people have opened their arms to the world and make any visit to the kingdom a humbling lesson in the endurance of the human spirit. The past is not forgotten in devotion to their ancestors and pilgrimages to pagodas, but the future is embraced, as youngsters seize the day. Share the adventure with a local meal, a traditional performance or a meeting with the minorities.

❸ Country Life
The majority of Cambodians still live in the countryside, eking out a living from farming or fishing, while an incredible 50% of the population is under the age of 16 (p49).

❹ The Living Arts
The royal ballet (p53), folk dance and shadow puppetry are a tangible link with the glorious days of Angkor, recounting myths and legends from an earlier, Hindu past.

❶ Buddhist Monks
Witness the rebirth of the Buddhist faith (p51), so nearly destroyed during the Khmer Rouge regime, as saffron-clad monks wander the streets of towns and cities across Cambodia.

❷ A Culinary Adventure
Cambodia is not only a feast for the senses. An epicurean journey into a little-known cuisine (p57), it is on the culinary crossroads of Asia, combining the best of Thailand, Vietnam, India and China.

❺ Multiculturalism
Sitting in the heart of Asia, it's no surprise to discover that Cambodia is home to a diverse array of peoples (p49), including the majority Khmers, ethnic Chinese, Vietnamese and Chams, and minority hill tribes in the remote northeast.

❻ Handicrafts
The ancient artisans of Angkor were incredibly skilled carvers and the tradition is alive and well today (p331), with a range of stone sculpture, woodcarving and intricate silver available, as well as exquisite silk and delicate lacquerware.

Natural Wonders

Wiped off the map for more than three decades by war and revolution, there are plenty of unexplored wilds in Cambodia that are now beginning to draw visitors. Explore the meandering Mekong, penetrate the vast wilderness of the Cardamoms, trek in nascent national parks, take the plunge in the waterfalls of the northeast, or beachcomb like Robinson Crusoe.

❶ Tonlé Sap Lake
Take to the waters of the largest lake in Southeast Asia to explore floating villages and flooded forests. Tonlé Sap (p67) acts as a natural flood barrier for the Mekong River.

❷ The Caves of Kampot
Go underground around Kampot (p228) to discover the many caves that pepper this region of limestone karst, some containing ancient Hindu temples that look like they were built yesterday.

❸ The Wild East
Head to the hills of Mondulkiri (p312) or Ratanakiri (p305), where elephants are still a regular means of transport, to explore a different Cambodia of dense jungle, hidden waterfalls and shy minority peoples.

❹ Deserted Beaches
Comb the coast of Cambodia to discover pristine tropical beaches and deserted paradise hideaways, including the islands off Sihanoukville (p214) and Kep (p235), and the national parks of Koh Kong Province (p196).

❺ The Mekong
Go with the flow and follow the mighty Mekong, the mother river, on its journey through the heart of Cambodia, with the chance to see rare freshwater Irrawaddy dolphins (p300) along the way.

❻ Cardamom Mountains
Venture into one of Asia's last great wildernesses, the untamed Cardamom Mountains (p200), where dense jungle tumbles down from mountain peaks to the crystal-clear waters of the Gulf of Thailand.

Phnom Penh
ភ្នំពេញ

Phnom Penh: the name can't help but conjure up an image of the exotic. The glimmering spires of the Royal Palace, the fluttering saffron of the monks' robes and the luscious location on the banks of the mighty Mekong – this is one of Asia's oft-overlooked gems. But it's also a city on the rise, as a new wave of investors move in, perhaps forever changing the character, and skyline, of this classic capital. Phnom Penh sits at the crossroads of Asia's past and present: it's a city of extremes of poverty and excess, of charm and chaos, a city that never fails to captivate.

Phnom Penh can be an assault on the senses. Motorbikes whiz through the laneways without a thought for pedestrians; stalls and markets exude pungent scents; and all the while the sounds of life, of commerce, of survival, reverberate through the streets. But this is all part of the attraction. This is not just another metropolis, an identikit image of a modern capital, it is an older Asia that many dreamed of when first imagining their adventures overseas.

Once the 'Pearl of Asia', Phnom Penh's shine was tarnished by the impact of war and revolution. But the city has since risen from the ashes to take its place among the hip capitals of the region. Delve into the ancient past at the National Museum or struggle to make sense of the recent trauma at Tuol Sleng Museum. Browse the city's markets for a bargain or linger in the beautiful boutiques that are putting Phnom Penh on the style map. Street-surf local stalls for a snack or enjoy the refined surrounds of a designer restaurant. Whatever your flavour, no matter your taste, it's all here in Phnom Penh.

HIGHLIGHTS

- Be dazzled by the 5000 silver floor tiles of the **Silver Pagoda** (p92), part of the Royal Palace

- Discover the world's finest collection of Khmer sculpture at the stunning **National Museum** (p93)

- Check out the huge dome of **Psar Thmei** (p119), the art-deco masterpiece that is Phnom Penh's central market

- Delve into the dark side of Cambodian history with a visit to **Tuol Sleng Museum** (p94), essential to understanding the pain of the past

- Experience Phnom Penh's legendary nightlife with a happy-hour cocktail, a local meal and a crawl through the city's **lively bars** (p114)

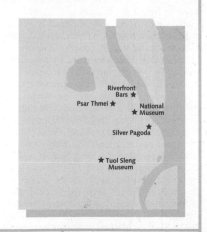

Riverfront Bars ★

Psar Thmei ★

National ★ Museum

Silver Pagoda ★

★ Tuol Sleng Museum

| ■ TELEPHONE CODE: 023 | ■ POPULATION: 2 MILLION | ■ AREA: 290 SQ KM |

HISTORY

Legend has it that the city of Phnom Penh was founded when an old woman named Penh found four Buddha images that had come to rest on the banks of the Mekong River. She housed them on a nearby hill, and the town that grew up here came to be known as Phnom Penh (Hill of Penh).

The story gives no hint as to why, in the 1430s, Angkor was abandoned and Phnom Penh chosen as the site of the new Cambodian capital. The move has been much lamented as evidence of cultural decline and the fall of an empire, but it made a good deal of practical sense. Angkor was poorly situated for trade and subject to attacks from the Siamese (Thai) kingdom of Ayuthaya. Phnom Penh commanded a more central position in the Khmer territories and was perfectly located for riverine trade with Laos and China, via the Mekong Delta. The Tonlé Sap River provided access to the rich fishing grounds of Tonlé Sap Lake.

By the mid-16th century, trade had turned Phnom Penh into a regional power. Indonesian and Chinese traders were drawn to the city in large numbers. A century later, however, Vietnamese incursions into Khmer territory had robbed the city of access to sea lanes, and Chinese merchants driven south by the Manchu (Qing) dynasty began to monopolise trade. The landlocked and increasingly isolated kingdom became a buffer between ascendant Thais and Vietnamese. In 1772, the Thais burnt Phnom Penh to the ground. Although the city was rebuilt, Phnom Penh was buffeted by the rival intrigues of the Thai and Vietnamese courts, until the French took over in 1863. Its population is thought not to have risen much above 25,000 during this period.

The French protectorate in Cambodia gave Phnom Penh the layout we know today. The city was divided into districts or *quartiers:* the French administrators and European traders inhabited the area north of Wat Phnom between Monivong Blvd and the Tonlé Sap River; the Chinese merchants occupied the riverfront area south of Wat Phnom to the Royal Palace and west as far as Norodom Blvd; and the Cambodians and Vietnamese lived around and to the south of the palace. By the time the French departed in 1953, they had left many important landmarks, including the Royal Palace, National Museum, Psar Thmei (Central Market) and many impressive government ministries.

The city grew fast in the post-independence peacetime years of Sihanouk's rule. By the time he was overthrown in 1970, the population of Phnom Penh was approximately 500,000. As the Vietnam War spread into Cambodian territory, the city's population swelled with refugees and reached nearly three million in early 1975. The Khmer Rouge took the city on 17 April 1975 and, as part of its radical revolution, immediately forced the entire population into the countryside. Different factions of the Khmer Rouge were responsible for evacuating different zones of the city; civilians to the east of Norodom Blvd were sent east, those south of the palace to the south, and so on. Whole families were split up on those first fateful days of 'liberation' and, for many thousands of Cambodians, their experience of the Khmer Rouge rule depended on which area of the city they had been in that day.

During the time of Democratic Kampuchea, many tens of thousands of former Phnom Penhois – including the vast majority of the capital's educated residents – were killed. The population of Phnom Penh during the Khmer Rouge regime was never more than about 50,000, a figure made up of senior party members, factory workers and trusted military leaders.

Repopulation of the city began when the Vietnamese arrived in 1979, although at first it was strictly controlled by the new government. During much of the 1980s, cows were more common than cars on the streets of the capital, and it was not until the government dispensed with its communist baggage at the end of the decade that Phnom Penh began to develop. The 1990s were boom years for some: along with the arrival of the UN Transitional Authority in Cambodia (Untac) came US$2 billion, much of it in salaries for expats. Well-connected residents were only too happy to help foreigners part with their money through high rents and hefty price-hikes. Businesses followed hot on the heels of Untac and commercial buildings began to spring up.

Phnom Penh has really begun to change in the last decade, with roads being repaired, sewage pipes laid, parks inaugurated and riverbanks reclaimed. Business is booming in many parts of the city with skyscrapers under development, investors rubbing their hands with the sort of glee once reserved for Bangkok or Hanoi and swanky new restaurants opening up. Phnom Penh is finally on the move as a new middle class emerges to re-place the thousands eliminated by the Khmer Rouge, and the elite invest their dollars at home rather than taking the risk of hiding them abroad. Phnom Penh is back, and bigger changes are set to come.

ORIENTATION

Phnom Penh is a fairly easy city in which to navigate as it is laid out in a numbered grid, a little like New York City. The major boul-evards of Phnom Penh run north–south, par-allel to the banks of the Tonlé Sap and Tonlé Bassac Rivers. Monivong Blvd cuts north–south through the centre of town, passing just west of Psar Thmei. Its northern sector is a busy shopping strip and home to some of the oldest (read least-appealing) hotels in town. Norodom Blvd runs north–south from Wat Phnom, and is largely lined with administrative buildings; the northern end contains banks, while further south are government ministries and embassies. Samdech Sothearos Blvd runs north–south near the riverfront, past the Royal Palace and Silver Pagoda. Sisowath Quay hugs the river and is where many of the city's most popular restau-rants and bars are located. The major east–west boulevards are Russian Blvd in the north of town; Sihanouk Blvd, which runs from Olympic Stadium past the Independence Monument and ends near the National Assembly; and Mao Tse Toung Blvd, a ring road of sorts that also runs north–south in the west of the city.

Intersecting the main boulevards is a network of hundreds of numbered smaller streets. As a rule of thumb, streets running east–west have even numbers that increase as you head south from the Chruoy Changvar Bridge, while streets that run north–south have odd numbers that increase as you head west away from the river.

Most buildings around town have signs with both their building number and street number. Finding a building purely by its ad-dress, however, is not always easy, as num-bers are rarely sequential. See the boxed text, below, and pity the postman.

Most buses, taxis and pick-ups arrive in the centre of town around Psar Thmei and it is just a short *moto* (small motorcycle with driver), *remork-moto (tuk tuk)* or taxi ride to most guesthouses and hotels. Some buses arrive at the north end of the riverfront near St 104 and there are persistent rumours the government will eventually develop out-of-town bus stations to ease traffic congestion. The train station is a couple of blocks north-west of Psar Thmei, but there are currently no passenger services. Boats from Siem Reap and Chau Doc (Vietnam) arrive at the tourist boat dock on the Tonlé Sap River at the eastern end of St 104. Hundreds of *motos* await in ambush. This area has been touted for redevelopment as a marina, but it is unlikely to happen in the very near future.

Phnom Penh International Airport is 7km west of central Phnom Penh.

Maps

For a handy pocket-size map, look out for a free copy of the *Phnom Penh 3-D Map*, which is distributed at the airport and

KNOWING WHEN YOUR NUMBER'S UP

Navigating the streets of Phnom Penh should be pretty straightforward thanks to the grid system put in place by the French. The total and utter lack of an effective house-numbering system, however, makes some guesthouses, restaurants and offices that bit harder to track down. The long years of war, abandonment and reoccupation destroyed the old system and as residents began to repopulate the city they seem to have picked numbers out of the air. It is not uncommon to drive past a row of houses numbered 13A, 34, 7, 26. Make sense of that and you might get a job as a code cracker. Worse still, several different houses might use the same number on the same street. The long and the short of it is that when you get to a guesthouse or restaurant recom-mended in this chapter only to discover it appears to have turned into a *prahoc* (fermented fish paste) shop, don't curse us for the bad smell. Just down the road will be another place with the same number – the guesthouse or restaurant you were looking for…unless, of course, it really has gone into the *prahoc* business.

When getting directions, ask for a cross-reference for an address, such as 'close to the inter-section of St 110 and Norodom Blvd'. The letters 'EO' after a street address stand for *étage zéro* (ground floor).

PHNOM PENH

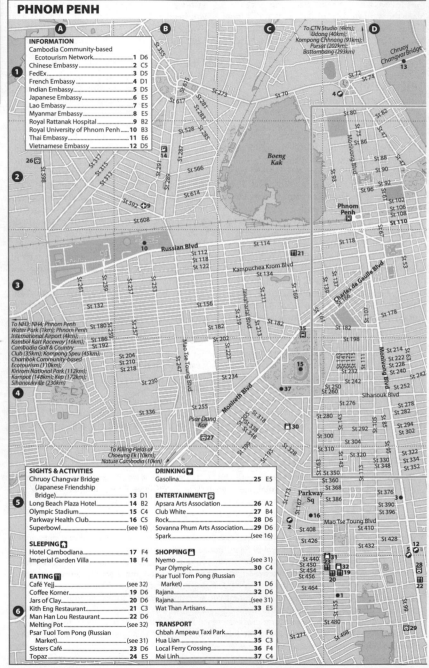

INFORMATION
Cambodia Community-based Ecotourism Network	**1** D6
Chinese Embassy	**2** C5
FedEx	**3** D5
French Embassy	**4** D1
Indian Embassy	**5** D5
Japanese Embassy	**6** E5
Lao Embassy	**7** E5
Myanmar Embassy	**8** E5
Royal Rattanak Hospital	**9** B2
Royal University of Phnom Penh	**10** B3
Thai Embassy	**11** E6
Vietnamese Embassy	**12** D5

SIGHTS & ACTIVITIES
Chruoy Changvar Bridge (Japanese Friendship Bridge)	**13** D1
Long Beach Plaza Hotel	**14** B2
Olympic Stadium	**15** C4
Parkway Health Club	**16** C5
Superbowl	(see 16)

SLEEPING
Hotel Cambodiana	**17** F4
Imperial Garden Villa	**18** F4

EATING
Café Yejj	(see 32)
Coffee Korner	**19** D6
Jars of Clay	**20** D6
Kith Eng Restaurant	**21** C3
Man Han Lou Restaurant	**22** D6
Melting Pot	(see 32)
Psar Tuol Tom Pong (Russian Market)	(see 31)
Sisters Café	**23** D6
Topaz	**24** E5

DRINKING
Gasolina	**25** E5

ENTERTAINMENT
Apsara Arts Association	**26** A2
Club White	**27** B4
Rock	**28** D6
Sovanna Phum Arts Association	**29** D6
Spark	(see 16)

SHOPPING
Nyemo	(see 31)
Psar Olympic	**30** C4
Psar Tuol Tom Pong (Russian Market)	**31** D6
Rajana	**32** D6
Rajana	(see 31)
Wat Than Artisans	**33** E5

TRANSPORT
Chbah Ampeau Taxi Park	**34** F6
Hua Lian	**35** C3
Local Ferry Crossing	**36** F4
Mai Linh	**37** C4

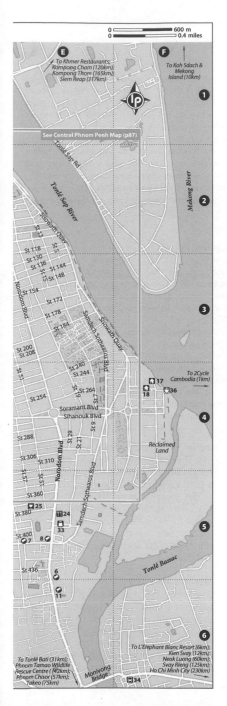

See Central Phnom Penh Map (p87)

selected bars and restaurants around the city. Both the *Phnom Penh Visitors' Guide* and the *Phnom Penh Pocket Guides*, freely available in the capital, have up-to-date maps.

INFORMATION

For up-to-date contact information on businesses in Phnom Penh, visit the **Yellow Pages** (www.yellowpages.com.kh). Check out *Drinking and Dining* for the low-down on bars and restaurants, or *Out and About* for shops and services, both produced by **Pocket Guide Cambodia** (www.cambodiapocketguide.com). The **Phnom Penh Visitors' Guide** (www.canbypublications .com) is brimming with useful information on the capital and beyond, while **AsiaLife Phnom Penh** (www.asialifecambodia.com) is a reliable read.

Bookshops

Bohr's Books (Map p87; 5 Samdech Sotheáros Blvd) A locally owned secondhand bookshop near the riverfront.
D's Books (Map p87; www.ds-books.com; off Norodom Blvd 79 St 240; Riverfront area 7 St 178) The largest chain of secondhand bookshops in the capital, with a good range of titles, plus a third branch in the Boeng Kak backpacker area.
Monument Books (Map p87; ☎ 217617; 111 Norodom Blvd) The best-stocked bookshop in town, with almost every Cambodia-related book currently in print available. There's also a small branch of Java Café (p113) here. Plus an airport branch.

Emergency

Ambulance (☎ 119)
Fire (☎ 118)
Police (☎ 117)

There are 24-hour emergency numbers for the English-speaking **tourist police** (☎ 724793 or 097-7780002) or the Khmer-speaking **police** (☎ 012 999999) in Phnom Penh. There is also an emergency number with English-speaking operators for Phnom Penh's **ambulance service** (☎ 724891).

In the event of a medical emergency it may be necessary to be evacuated to Bangkok. See p86 for details of medical services in Phnom Penh.

Internet Access

Phnom Penh is now well and truly wired, with prices dropping to less than US$0.50 per hour. There are internet cafes all over the city.

Many guesthouses also offer some sort of internet access, and in the main backpacker

PHNOM PENH IN...

One Day

With just a day in town, start early with a riverfront stroll to see the mass t'ai chi and aerobics sessions taking place in front of the **Royal Palace** (p92), although it seems to be mainly aerobics these days. Grab breakfast at one of the riverfront cafes before venturing into the Royal Palace compound to see the dazzling treasures of the **Silver Pagoda** (p92). Next is the **National Museum** (p93) and the world's most wondrous collection of Khmer sculpture. Have lunch at nearby **Friends** (p107) restaurant, giving street children a helping hand into tourism. After lunch, check out the funky architecture of **Psar Thmei** (p119), but save the shopping for the treasure trove that is **Psar Tuol Tom Pong** (p119), more commonly known as the Russian Market. Take a deep breath and continue to **Tuol Sleng Museum** (p94), a savage reminder of Cambodia's tragic past. Sobering indeed – it may be time for a happy-hour drink to reflect on the highs and lows of the day. Enjoy dinner in one of the many good **Khmer restaurants** (p106) in town, before joining the nightshift at some of the rockin' **bars** (p114).

Two Days

With two days, it is easy to get to grips with Cambodia's capital. Start the first day as per the one-day itinerary with a visit to the cultural splendours that are the **National Museum** (p93) and **Royal Palace** (p92). In the afternoon, visit the harrowing **Tuol Sleng Museum** (p94) before continuing on to the **Killing Fields of Choeung Ek** (p95), where prisoners from Security Prison 21 were taken for execution. It is a grim afternoon, but essential for understanding just how far Cambodia has come in the intervening years. Wind up with a sunset cruise on the **Mekong River** (p98) offering a beautiful view over the Royal Palace.

On the second day, it is time to get serious about shopping. Browse through art-deco **Psar Thmei** (p119) and then **Psar Tuol Tom Pong** (p119), a maze of stalls selling everything from textiles and handicrafts to DVDs and cut-price clothing. Keep some cash for the excellent **shops** (p118) that support good causes, all of which stock a solid selection of silk.

In the afternoon, take a look at the **Independence Monument** (p97), modelled on Angkor Wat's central tower, and wander up the riverfront to **Wat Phnom** (p96), where Khmers prefer to pray for luck. From here it is a short stroll to hit the riverfront bars (p114) with their happy-hour cocktails, the perfect warm-up for a final fling in Phnom Penh.

---

areas there are several internet cafes. Anyone staying in more expensive hotels should venture out to find an online fix, as in-house business centres are overpriced.

Several of the midrange and top-end hotels now offer wi-fi access at a price, while many of the more popular cafes, restaurants and bars offer a free service.

Laundry

Most guesthouses around town offer reasonably priced laundry services and there are cheap local laundries scattered across the city. Tourists staying in high-end hotels can save a small fortune by using a local laundry while in town.

Libraries

The National Library (p98) has a pretty limited selection of reading material for foreign visitors, but is set in a lovely building. French speakers should call into the **French Cultural Centre** (Map p87; St 184), which has a good range of reading material.

The **Bophana Centre** (Map p87; ☎ 992174; 64 St 200), established by Cambodian-French filmmaker Rithy Panh, is an audiovisual resource for filmmakers and researchers, and visitors can explore its archive of old photographs and films.

Medical Services

It is important to be aware of the difference between a clinic and a hospital in Phnom Penh. Clinics are good for most situations, but in a genuine emergency it is best to make for one of the hospitals.

Calmette Hospital (Map p87; ☎ 426948; 3 Monivong Blvd; ⊗ 24hr) French-administered and the best of the local hospitals.

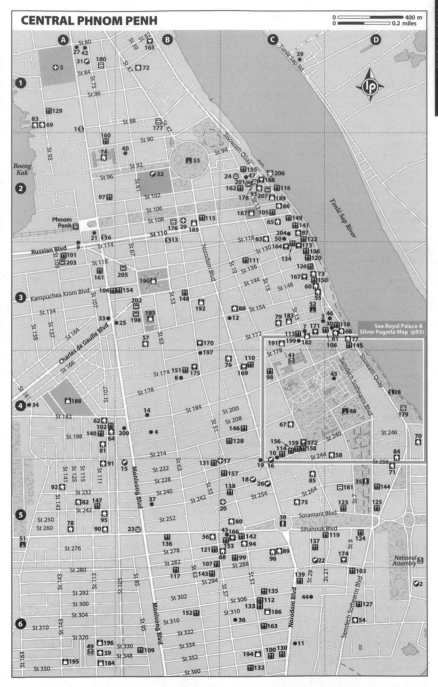

CENTRAL PHNOM PENH

See Royal Palace & Silver Pagoda Map (p93)

PHNOM PENH

INFORMATION
Acleda Bank..**1** A1
ANZ Royal Bank......................(see 73)
Australian Embassy........................**2** D6
Bohr's Books.....................................**3** C3
Bophana Centre...............................**4** B4
Calmette Hospital............................**5** A1
Canadia Bank....................................**6** A2
ChildSafe..**7** C3
Cooperation Committee
  for Cambodia................................**8** B4
DHL...**9** A3
D's Books..**10** C4
D's Books....................................(see 61)
EMS...(see 24)
European Dental Clinic................**11** C6
Exotissimo......................................**12** C3
Foreign Trade Bank......................**13** B2
French Cultural Centre................**14** B4
German Embassy............................**15** B5
Hanuman Tourism....................(see 186)
Indonesian Embassy....................**16** C5
International SOS Medical
  Centre..**17** C5
Malaysian Embassy.......................**18** C5
Monument Books...........................**19** C5
Naga Clinic......................................**20** C5
Pharmacie de la Gare...................**21** A2
Philippines Embassy.....................**22** C5
Post Office.......................................**23** B5
Post Office (Main).........................**24** C2
PTM Travel & Tours.......................**25** B3
SBC BANK....................................(see 118)
Singapore Embassy.......................**26** C5
TNT...**27** A1
Tourism Office................................**28** D4
Tropical & Travellers
  Medical Clinic............................**29** B2
U-Care Pharmacy...........................**30** D3
UK Embassy.....................................**31** A1
US Embassy......................................**32** B2
VLK Tourism.....................................**33** A3

SIGHTS & ACTIVITIES
Cambodian Boxkator
  Academy......................................**34** A4
Cambodian Cooking Class....(see 114)
Cambodia-Vietnam
  Friendship Monument.............**35** D5
Champei Spa....................................**36** C6
In Style...**37** B5
Independence Monument...........**38** C5
Kidz Cool..**39** C1

Nail Bar......................................(see 113)
National Library.............................**40** B2
National Museum...........................**41** C4
O Spa...**42** A1
Place Gym..**43** C5
Prayuvong Buddha
  Factories......................................**44** C6
Royal Palace....................................**45** D4
Scan Shuffleboard Lounge.......(see 89)
Scuba Nation...................................**46** D3
Seeing Hands Massage.................**47** C2
Silver Pagoda..................................**48** D4
Spa Bliss...................................(see 159)
Tuol Sleng Museum.......................**49** A6
Vicious Cycle...................................**50** C2
Wat Moha Montrei........................**51** A5
Wat Ounalom..................................**52** C3
Wat Phnom......................................**53** B2

SLEEPING 🏠
Almond Hotel..................................**54** D6
Amanjaya Pancam Hotel..............**55** C3
Amber Villa......................................**56** B5
Billabong..**57** B3
Blue Lime...................................(see 98)
Boddhi Tree Aram.........................**58** D4
Boddhi Tree Umma........................**59** A6
Bougainvillier Hotel......................**60** C3
Bright Lotus Guesthouse.............**61** D3
Capitol Guesthouse.......................**62** A4
Dara Reang Sey Hotel...................**63** C2
Dragon Guesthouse.......................**64** A4
Eye of the Mekong.........................**65** C2
Fairyland Guesthouse...............(see 92)
Foreign Correspondents'
  Club...**66** D3
Golden Mekong Hotel...................**67** C4
Goldie Boutique
  Guesthouse.................................**68** C5
Grand View Guesthouse..............**69** A1
Himawari..**70** D4
Home...**71** D5
Hotel Cara.......................................**72** B1
Hotel Castle...............................(see 150)
Hotel Indochine.............................**73** C3
Hotel Le Royal................................**74** A2
Kabiki..**75** C5
Kambuja Inn....................................**76** C4
Khmer Royal Hotel........................**77** D3
King Angkor.....................................**78** A5
Last Home..**79** C3
Manor House...................................**80** C5
Narin 2 Guesthouse......................**81** A4

Narin Guesthouse..........................**82** A5
Number 10 Lakeside
  Guesthouse.................................**83** A1
Okay Guesthouse...........................**84** D4
Paragon Hotel...........................(see 106)
Pavilion...**85** C5
Quay..(see 60)
River 108..**86** C2
River Star Hotel..............................**87** C2
Royal Guesthouse..........................**88** C3
Scan Hotel.......................................**89** C5
Sky Park Guesthouse.....................**90** A5
Spring Guesthouse.........................**91** A5
Sunday Guesthouse.......................**92** A5
Tat Guesthouse.........................(see 82)
Tonle Sap Guesthouse..................**93** C2
Top Banana Guesthouse...............**94** C5
Town View Hotel............................**95** A5
Villa Langka.....................................**96** C5

EATING 🍴
112 Restaurant...............................**97** A2
Alley Cat Café.................................**98** C4
Anjali's.......................................(see 150)
Annam...**99** C5
Baitong...**100** C6
Bayon Supermarket....................**101** A3
BB World....................................(see 193)
Bites..**102** A4
Boat Noodle Restaurant.............**103** D6
Boddhi Tree Umma
  Restaurant.............................(see 59)
Bopha Phnom Penh
  Restaurant...........................(see 116)
Café Sentiment.............................**104** A3
Cantina......................................(see 118)
Chi Cha..**105** C2
Chiang Mai Riverside...................**106** C3
Chill...(see 106)
Chocolate Shop.......................(see 156)
Comme a la Maison......................**107** B5
Corner 33..**108** D3
Del Gusto Café..............................**109** B6
Dosa Corner.............................(see 142)
Ebony Apsara Café.......................**110** C4
El Mundo...................................(see 106)
Eye of the Mekong...................(see 65)
Fatboy Sub & Sandwich
  Shop...**111** C3
Fish...(see 86)
Foreign Correspondents'
  Club..(see 66)
Freebird....................................(see 114)

European Dental Clinic (Map p87; ☎ 211363; 160A Norodom Blvd; ⏲ 7.30am-12.30pm & 1.30-7.30pm Mon-Sat) With international dental services and a good reputation.

International SOS Medical Centre (Map p87; ☎ 216911; www.internationalsos.com; 161 St 51; ⏲ 8am-5.30pm Mon-Fri, 8am-noon Sat) One of the best medical services around town, but with prices to match. Also has a resident foreign dentist.

Naga Clinic (Map p87; ☎ 211300; www.nagaclinic.com; 11 St 254; ⏲ 24hr) A French-run clinic for reliable consultations.

Pharmacie de la Gare (Map p87; ☎ 430205; 81 Monivong Blvd; ⏲ 7am-7pm Mon-Sat, 8am-noon Sun) A pharmacy with English- and French-speaking consultants.

Royal Rattanak Hospital (Map pp84-5; ☎ 365555; www.royalrattanakhospital.com; 11 St 592; ⏲ 24hr) International hospital affiliated with Bangkok Hospital and boasting top facilities, but prone to promote expensive fixes.

Tropical & Travellers Medical Clinic (Map p87; ☎ 366802; www.travellersmedicalclinic.com; 88 St 108) Well-regarded British-run clinic.

Fresco **112** C6
Friends **113** C3
Frizz Restaurant **114** C4
Garden Center Café **115** B2
Goldfish River Restaurant **116** C2
Green Pepper ......(see 46)
Hagar **117** B6
Happy Herb's Pizza **118** D3
Java Café **119** D5
Kandal House **120** C3
Khmer Borane Restaurant ......(see 145)
Khmer Surin **121** B5
Kiwi Bakery **122** C2
K'nyay **123** D5
Ko Ko Ro **124** D5
Kravanh **125** D5
La Croisette **126** C3
La Marmite ......(see 176)
La Patate 2 ......**127** D6
La Residence **128** C4
Lazy Gecko Café **129** A1
Le Cedre **130** C6
Le Duo **131** B5
Le Jardin **132** C6
Le Lotus Blanc **133** C6
Le Safran ......(see 112)
Le Wok ......(see 171)
Lemongrass **134** C3
Living Room **135** C6
Lucky Burger ......(see 136)
Lucky Supermarket **136** B5
Luna D'Autunno **137** C5
Magnolia **138** C5
Malis **139** C6
Mama Restaurant **140** A4
Master Suki Soup ......(see 193)
Mekong River Restaurant **141** C2
Metro ......(see 73)
Mount Everest ......(see 43)
Nature & Sea **142** C5
Ocean **143** B6
Oh My Buddha! ......(see 129)
Origami **144** D5
Pacharan **145** D3
Pencil Supermarket **146** C4
Penny Lane **147** A5
Pho Fortune ......(see 30)
Pop Café ......(see 66)
Psar O Russei ......(see 188)
Psar Ta Pang **148** B3
Psar Thmei ......(see 190)
Riverhouse Asian Bistro **149** C2
Riverside Bistro **150** C3

Romdeng **151** B4
Rorg Damrei **152** B6
Saffron **153** C5
Sam Doo Restaurant **154** B3
Seven Bright Restaurant **155** C2
Sher-e-Punjab ......(see 134)
Shop **156** C4
Slek Chak **157** C5
Sorya Shopping Centre
  Food Court ......(see 193)
Sugar Palm **158** C4
Tamarind Bar **159** C4
Tell Restaurant **160** A2
Thai Huot Supermarket **161** A3
Van's Restaurant **162** C2
Veijo Tonlé ......(see 120)
VIP Minimart **163** C6
Yi Sang ......(see 54)

DRINKING
Blue Chilli ......(see 110)
Brauhaus **164** C3
Chinese House **165** B1
Chiva's Shack ......(see 134)
Dodo Rhum House ......(see 110)
Elephant Bar ......(see 74)
Elsewhere Bar ......(see 94)
Equinox Bar **166** C5
Flavour ......(see 94)
Fly Lounge **167** C3
Green Vespa **168** C2
Gym Bar **169** C4
Heart of Darkness **170** B3
Howie's Bar ......(see 170)
Pickled Parrot ......(see 93)
Pink Elephant ......(see 118)
Quay ......(see 60)
Rising Sun ......(see 61)
Riverhouse Lounge ......(see 149)
Rory's Pub **171** C3
Rubies **172** C4
Salt Lounge **173** C3
Talkin to a Stranger **174** D5
Zeppelin Café **175** B4

ENTERTAINMENT
Art Café **176** B2
Casa **177** B1
Cavern **178** C2
Chatomuk Theatre **179** D4
Manhattan Club **180** A1
Memphis Pub ......(see 141)
Meta House **181** D5

SHOPPING
Ambre ......(see 8)
Art Café ......(see 176)
Asasax Art Gallery **182** C3
Aw-kun Shop **183** C3
Bliss Boutique ......(see 159)
Cambodian Handicraft
  Association **184** A6
Colours of Cambodia ......(see 66)
Couleurs d'Asie ......(see 159)
Friends & Stuff ......(see 113)
Jasmine ......(see 114)
Java Café ......(see 119)
Kambuja ......(see 185)
Mekong Quilts ......(see 114)
Meta House ......(see 181)
NCDP Handicrafts **185** B2
Nyemo **186** C6
Psar Chaa **187** C2
Psar O Russei **188** A4
Psar Reatrey **189** C2
Psar Thmei **190** B3
Reyum **191** C3
Sobbhana **192** B3
Sorya Shopping Centre **193** B3
Subtyl ......(see 156)
Tabitha **194** C6
Tuol Sleng Shoes **195** A6
Villageworks **196** A6
Water Lily ......(see 156)

TRANSPORT
Angkor Motorcycles! **197** B4
Betelnut Jeep Tours ......(see 129)
Blue Cruiser ......(see 206)
Capitol Tour ......(see 62)
GST **198** B3
Hang Chau ......(see 206)
Harley Tours Cambodia ......(see 174)
Little Bikes **199** C3
Lucky! Lucky! **200** B4
Mekong Express ......(see 168)
Neak Krorhorm ......(see 86)
New! New! ......(see 200)
Paramount Angkor
  Express **201** C2
Phnom Penh Sorya **202** B3
Rith Mony **203** A3
Riverside Moto **204** C2
Sok Sokha ......(see 207)
Taxi Park **205** B3
Tourist Boat Dock **206** C2
Virak Buntham **207** C2

U-Care Pharmacy (Map p87; ☎ 222399; 26 Samdech Sothearos Blvd; ☉ 8am-9pm) International-style pharmacy with a convenient location near the river.

Money

Those looking to change cash into riel need look no further than jewellery stalls around the markets of Phnom Penh. Psar Thmei (p119) and Psar Tuol Tom Pong (p119) are the most convenient.

A number of upmarket hotels offer money-changing services, although this is usually reserved for their guests. Most banks in Phnom Penh are open from roughly 8am to 3.30pm weekdays, plus Saturday mornings.

The main cluster of banks is found along the avenue formed by Sts 110 and 114, Cambodia's very own answer to Wall St.

ANZ Royal Bank (Map p87; ☎ 726900; 265 Sisowath Quay) ATMs galore all over town, including at supermarkets and petrol stations, but there is a US$4 charge per transaction.

CHILD PROSTITUTION

The sexual abuse of children by foreign paedophiles is a serious problem in Cambodia. Paedophilia is a crime in Cambodia and several foreigners have served or are serving jail sentences. There is no such thing as an isolation unit for sex offenders in Cambodia. Countries such as Australia, France, Germany, the UK and the USA have also introduced much-needed legislation that sees nationals prosecuted in their home country for having under-age sex abroad.

This child abuse is slowly but surely being combated, although in a country as poor as Cambodia, money can tempt people into selling babies for adoption and children for sex. The trafficking of innocent children has many shapes and forms, and the sex trade is just the thin end of the wedge. Poor parents have been known to rent out their children as beggars, labourers or sellers; many child prostitutes in Cambodia are Vietnamese and have been sold into the business by family back in Vietnam. Once in the trade, it is difficult to escape a life of violence and abuse. Drugs are also being used to keep children dependent on their pimps, with bosses giving out *yama* (a dirty meta-amphetamine) or heroin to dull their senses.

Paedophilia is not unique to Western societies and it is a big problem with Asian tourists as well. The problem is that some of the home governments don't treat it as seriously as some of their Western counterparts. Even more problematic is the domestic industry of virgin-buying in Cambodia, founded on the superstition that taking a virgin will enhance one's power. Even if NGOs succeed in putting off Western paedophiles, confronting local traditions may be a greater challenge.

Visitors can do their bit by keeping an eye out for any suspicious behaviour on the part of foreigners. Don't ignore it – pass on any relevant information such as the name and nationality of the individual to the embassy concerned. There is also a **Cambodian hotline** (☎ 023-997919) and a confidential **ChildSafe Hotline** (☎ 012 311112; www.childsafe-cambodia.org). When booking into a hotel or jumping on transport, look out for the ChildSafe logo, as each establishment or driver who earns this logo supports an end to child sex tourism and has undergone child-protection training. **End Child Prostitution and Trafficking** (Ecpat; www.ecpat.org) is a global network aimed at stopping child prostitution, child pornography and the trafficking of children for sexual purposes, and has affiliates in most Western countries.

Canadia Bank (Map p87; ☎ 215286; cnr St 110 & Monivong Blvd) Spiffy new HQ that changes travellers cheques of several currencies for a 2% commission, plus free cash advances on MasterCard and Visa. Canadia Bank ATMs around town incur no transaction charges.

Foreign Trade Bank (Map p87; ☎ 723466; 3 St 114; ☼ 7am-3.45pm Mon-Fri) Lowest commission in town on US dollar travellers cheques at 1%.

SBC Bank (Map p87; ☎ 990688; 315 Sisowath Quay; ☼ 8am-8pm) Convenient hours and location, ATMs with no charge, plus represents Western Union.

Those needing to organise an international money transfer can use the Foreign Trade Bank. It may be quicker (and more expensive) to use an international company such as MoneyGram or Western Union. MoneyGram is represented by Canadia Bank, while Western Union can be found at SBC or **Acleda Bank** (Map p87; ☎ 998777; 61 Monivong Blvd).

Post

The main **post office** (Map p87; St 13; ☼ 7am-7pm) is in a charming building just east of Wat Phnom.

It offers postal services as well as telephone and fax links. There is another post office on Monivong Blvd, near the corner of Sihanouk Blvd. For average postal rates, see p331.

If you need to get valuables or belongings home in a hurry, there are several international courier companies (p331) represented in Phnom Penh.

Telephone & Fax

The cheapest local and domestic calls in Phnom Penh are available from private booths found throughout the city. Whatever the number you are dialling, private booths will have a selection of telephones to make sure you get the best rate. Local calls start at 300r a minute.

Many internet cafes in Phnom Penh offer telephone services at reasonable prices, including internet phone calls, which are much cheaper than normal international calls. Most places have Skype services or similar available for those with an account.

For further information on phone and fax services, see p332.

Tourist Information

Phnom Penh finally has a **tourism office** (Sisowath Quay) located on the riverfront near the Chatomuk Theatre, and while it doesn't carry a whole lot of information for now, it does offer clean bathrooms. Armed with this guidebook, the recommended free guides under Information (p85) and with tips from your guesthouse or fellow travellers, you should be in good shape.

Cambodia Community-Based Ecotourism Network (Map pp84-5; ☎ 355272; www.ccben.org; 10A St 468; ⏱ 8am-noon, 1.30-5.30pm Mon-Fri) Information on ecotourism and community-based activities all over Cambodia.

ChildSafe (Map p87; www.childsafe-cambodia.org; 186 St 13) Located opposite the popular Friends restaurant, this drop-in office for the ChildSafe campaign aims to raise awareness among visitors about the problems of child begging, sex tourism and more.

Travel Agencies

There are plenty of travel agents around town, including some long-running places near Psar Thmei. Try the following:

Exotissimo (Map p87; ☎ 218948; www.exotissimo.com; Norodom Blvd)

Hanuman Tourism (Map p87; ☎ 218356; www.hanumantourism.com; 12 St 310)

PTM Travel & Tours (Map p87; ☎ 364768; www.ptm-travel.com; 200 Monivong Blvd)

VLK Tourism (Map p87; ☎ 723331; www.vlktravel.com; 195 Monivong Blvd)

DANGERS & ANNOYANCES

Phnom Penh is not as dangerous as people imagine, but it is important to take care. Armed robberies do sometimes occur, but statistically you would be very unlucky to be a victim.

Should you become the victim of a robbery, do not panic and do not, under any circumstances, struggle. Calmly raise your hands and let your attacker take what they want. *Do not* reach for your pockets as the assailant may think you are reaching for a gun. Do not carry a bag at night, as it is more likely to make you a target.

It pays to be cautious in crowded bars or nightclubs that are frequented by the Khmer elite. Many pampered children hang out in popular places, bringing their bodyguards along for good luck. This is fine until a drunk foreigner treads on their toes or they decide they want to hit on a Western girl. Then the problems start and if they have bodyguards with them, it will only end in tears, big tears.

If you ride your own motorbike during the day, some police may try to fine you for the most trivial of offences, such as turning left in violation of a no-left-turn sign. At their most audacious, they may try to get you for riding with your headlights on during the day although, worryingly, it does not seem to be illegal for Cambodians to travel without their headlights on at night. The police will most likely demand US$5 from you and threaten to take you to the police station for an official US$20 fine if you do not pay. If you are patient with them and smile, you can usually get away with handing over US$1. The trick is not to stop in the first place by not catching their eye.

The riverfront area of Phnom Penh, particularly places with outdoor seating, attracts many beggars, as do Psar Thmei and Psar Tuol Tom Pong markets. Generally, however, there is little in the way of push and shove. For more thoughts on how to handle beggar fatigue, see p323.

Flooding is a major problem during heavy downpours in the wet season (June to October). Phnom Penh's drainage system is notoriously unreliable and when the big rains kick off, some streets turn into canals for a few hours. The Japanese government has just finished rebuilding the drains and sewers along the riverfront, which may well ease things.

BAG SNATCHING

Bag snatching has become a real problem in Phnom Penh and foreigners are often targeted. Hot spots include the riverfront and busy areas around popular markets, but there is no real pattern and the speeding motorbike thieves can strike any time, any place. In 2007, this ended in tragedy for a young French woman who was dragged from a speeding *moto* into the path of a vehicle. Try to wear close-fitting bags such as backpacks that don't dangle from the body temptingly. Don't hang expensive cameras around the neck and keep things close to the body and out of sight, particularly when walking in the road, crossing the road or travelling by *moto*, *remork* or *cyclo*. These guys are real pros and only need one chance.

SIGHTS

Phnom Penh is a relatively small city and most of the major sights are fairly central. The most important cultural sights can be visited on foot and are located near the riverfront in the most beautiful part of the city.

Royal Palace & Silver Pagoda

ព្រះបរមរាជវាំង/និង វត្តព្រះកែវ

With its classic Khmer roofs and ornate gilding, the **Royal Palace** (Map p87; Samdech Sothearos Blvd; admission incl camera/video 25,000r; ◷ 8-11am & 2-5pm) dominates the diminutive skyline of Phnom Penh. It is a striking structure near the riverfront, bearing a remarkable likeness to its counterpart in Bangkok. Hidden away behind protective walls and beneath shadows of soaring ceremonial buildings, it's an oasis of calm with lush gardens and leafy havens.

Being the official residence of King Sihamoni, parts of the massive compound are closed to the public. Visitors are only allowed to visit the palace's Silver Pagoda and its surrounding compound. However, photography is not permitted inside the pagoda itself. Visitors need to wear shorts that reach to the knee, and T-shirts or blouses that reach to the elbow; otherwise they will have to rent an appropriate covering. The palace gets very busy on Sundays when countryside Khmers come to pay their respects, but this can be a fun way to experience the place, thronging with locals.

CHAN CHAYA PAVILION

Performances of classical Cambodian dance were once staged in the Chan Chaya Pavilion, through which guests enter the grounds of the Royal Palace. This pavilion is sometimes lit up at night to commemorate festivals or anniversaries.

THRONE HALL

The Throne Hall, topped by a 59m-high tower inspired by the Bayon at Angkor, was inaugurated in 1919 by King Sisowath; the present cement building replaced a vast wooden structure that was built on this site in 1869. The Throne Hall is used for coronations and ceremonies such as the presentation of credentials by diplomats. Many of the items once displayed here were destroyed by the Khmer Rouge. In the courtyard is a curious iron house given to King Norodom by Napoleon III of France, hardly designed with the Cambodian climate in mind.

SILVER PAGODA

The Silver Pagoda is named in honour of the floor, which is covered with more than 5000 silver tiles weighing 1kg each, adding up to five tonnes of gleaming silver. You can sneak a peek at some of the 5000 tiles near the entrance – most are covered for their protection. It is also known as Wat Preah Keo (Pagoda of the Emerald Buddha). It was originally constructed of wood in 1892 during the rule of King Norodom, who was apparently inspired by Bangkok's Wat Phra Keo, and was rebuilt in 1962.

The Silver Pagoda was preserved by the Khmer Rouge to demonstrate its concern for the conservation of Cambodia's cultural riches to the outside world. Although more than half of the pagoda's contents were lost, stolen or destroyed in the turmoil that followed the Vietnamese invasion, what remains is spectacular. This is one of the few places in Cambodia where bejewelled objects embodying some of the brilliance and richness of Khmer civilisation can still be seen.

The staircase leading to the Silver Pagoda is made of Italian marble. Inside, the Emerald Buddha, believed to be made of Baccarat crystal, sits on a gilded pedestal high atop the dais. In front of the dais stands a life-size gold Buddha decorated with 9584 diamonds, the largest of which, set in the crown, is a whopping 25 carats. Created in the palace workshops around 1907, the gold Buddha weighs in at 90kg. Directly in front of it is a miniature silver-and-gold stupa containing a relic of Buddha brought from Sri Lanka. To the left is an 80kg bronze Buddha, and to the right a silver Buddha. On the far right, figurines of solid gold tell of the life of the Buddha.

Behind the shrine is a standing marble Buddha from Myanmar (Burma). Nearby is a bed once used by the king on his coronation day and designed to be carried by 12 men; the gold-work alone weighs 23kg.

Along the walls of the pagoda are examples of extraordinary Khmer artisanship, including intricate masks used in classical dance and dozens of gold Buddhas. The many precious gifts given to Cambodia's monarchs by foreign heads of state appear rather spiritless

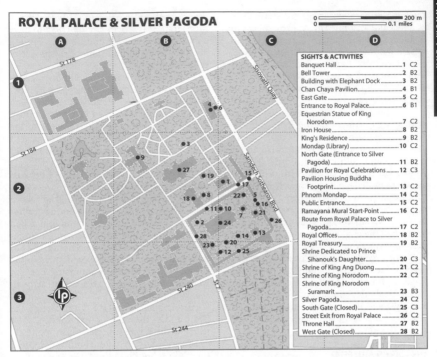

ROYAL PALACE & SILVER PAGODA

0   200 m
0   0.1 miles

SIGHTS & ACTIVITIES

Banquet Hall	1 C2
Bell Tower	2 B2
Building with Elephant Dock	3 B2
Chan Chaya Pavilion	4 B1
East Gate	5 C2
Entrance to Royal Palace	6 B1
Equestrian Statue of King Norodom	7 C2
Iron House	8 B2
King's Residence	9 B2
Mondap (Library)	10 C2
North Gate (Entrance to Silver Pagoda)	11 B2
Pavilion for Royal Celebrations	12 C3
Pavilion Housing Buddha Footprint	13 C2
Phnom Mondap	14 C2
Public Entrance	15 C2
Ramayana Mural Start-Point	16 C2
Route from Royal Palace to Silver Pagoda	17 C2
Royal Offices	18 B2
Royal Treasury	19 B2
Shrine Dedicated to Prince Sihanouk's Daughter	20 C3
Shrine of King Ang Duong	21 C2
Shrine of King Norodom	22 C2
Shrine of King Norodom Suramarit	23 B3
Silver Pagoda	24 C2
South Gate (Closed)	25 C3
Street Exit from Royal Palace	26 C2
Throne Hall	27 B2
West Gate (Closed)	28 B2

when displayed next to such diverse and exuberant Khmer art.

The classic Indian epic of the *Ramayana* (known as the *Reamker* in Cambodia) is depicted on a beautiful and extensive mural enclosing the pagoda compound, created around 1900; the story begins just south of the east gate and includes vivid images of the battle of Lanka.

Other structures to be found in the complex (listed clockwise from the north gate) include the *mondap* (library), which once housed richly decorated sacred texts written on palm leaves (now moved to the safety of air-conditioned storage); the shrine of King Norodom (r 1860–1904); an equestrian statue of King Norodom; the shrine of King Ang Duong (r 1845–59); a pavilion housing a huge footprint of Buddha; Phnom Mondap, an artificial hill with a structure containing a bronze footprint of the Buddha from Sri Lanka; a shrine dedicated to one of Prince Sihanouk's daughters; a pavilion for celebrations held by the royal family; the shrine of Prince Sihanouk's father, King Norodom Suramarit (r 1955–60); and a bell tower, whose bell is rung to order the gates to be opened or closed.

National Museum

សារមន្ទីរជាតិ

Located just north of the Royal Palace, the **National Museum of Cambodia** (Map p87; www.cambodiamuseum.info; cnr St 13 & St 178; admission US$3, camera/video US$1/3; 🕗 8am-5pm) is housed in a graceful terracotta structure of traditional design (built 1917–20), with an inviting courtyard garden. The museum is home to the world's finest collection of Khmer sculpture – a millennia's worth and more of masterful Khmer design.

The museum comprises four pavilions, facing the pretty garden. The most significant displays of sculpture are in the courtyards to the left and directly ahead of the entrance, but most visitors approach the collection in a clockwise chronological direction. The pre-Angkorian collection visualises the journey from the human form of Indian sculpture to the more divine form of Khmer sculpture from the 5th to 8th centuries. Highlights include an imposing eight-armed statue of Vishnu from the 6th or 7th century and a staring Harihara, combining the attributes of Shiva and Vishnu. The Angkor collection includes a striking statue of Shiva (c AD 870), a giant pair of wrestling monkeys, an exquisite frieze from Banteay Srei, and the sublime statue of a seated Jayavarman VII (r 1181–1219), his head bowed slightly in a meditative pose.

The museum also contains displays of pottery and bronzes dating from the pre-Angkorian periods of Funan and Chenla (4th to 9th centuries), the Indravarman period (9th and 10th centuries), the classical Angkorian period (10th to 14th centuries), as well as more recent works such as a beautiful wooden royal barge. There is a permanent collection of post-Angkorian Buddhas, many of which were rescued from Angkor Wat when the civil war erupted. See p54 for more information.

Unfortunately, it is not possible to photograph the collection – only the courtyard. English-, French-, Japanese-speaking guides (from US$5, depending on group size) are available, and there is also a useful booklet, *The New Guide to the National Museum*, available at the front desk.

Tuol Sleng Museum
សារមន្ទីរទួលស្លែង

In 1975, Tuol Svay Prey High School was taken over by Pol Pot's security forces and turned into a prison known as Security Prison 21 (S-21). This soon became the largest centre of detention and torture in the country. Between 1975 and 1978 more than 17,000 people held at S-21 were taken to the killing fields of Choeung Ek (opposite).

S-21 has been turned into the **Tuol Sleng Museum** (Map p87; St 113; admission US$2, video US$5; 😌 8am-5.30pm), which serves as a testament to the crimes of the Khmer Rouge. Entry is on the western side of St 113.

Like the Nazis, the Khmer Rouge leaders were meticulous in keeping records of their barbarism. Each prisoner who passed through S-21 was photographed, sometimes before and after torture. The museum displays include room after room of harrowing black-and-white photographs; virtually all of the men, women and children pictured were later killed. You can tell which year a picture was taken by the style of number-board that appears on the prisoner's chest. Several foreigners from Australia, New Zealand and the USA were also held at S-21 before being murdered. It is worth paying US$2 to have a guide show you around, as they can tell you the stories behind some of the people in the photographs.

As the Khmer Rouge 'revolution' reached ever greater heights of insanity, it began devouring its own. Generations of torturers and executioners who worked here in turn killed by those who took their places. During early 1977, when the party purges of Eastern Zone cadres were getting underway, S-21 claimed an average of 100 victims a day.

When the Vietnamese army liberated Phnom Penh in early 1979, there were only seven prisoners alive at S-21, all of whom had used their skills, such as painting or photography, to stay alive. Fourteen others had been tortured to death as Vietnamese forces were closing in on the city. Photographs of their gruesome deaths are on display in the rooms where their decomposing corpses were found. Their graves are nearby in the courtyard.

Altogether, a visit to Tuol Sleng is a profoundly depressing experience. The sheer ordinariness of the place makes it even more horrific: the suburban setting, the plain school buildings, the grassy playing area where children kick around balls; rusted beds, instruments of torture and wall after wall of disturbing portraits conjure up images of humanity at its worst. It demonstrates the darkest side of the human spirit that lurks within us all. Tuol Sleng is not for the squeamish.

Behind many of the displays at Tuol Sleng is the **Documentation Center of Cambodia** (DC-Cam; www.dccam.org). DC-Cam was established in 1995 through Yale University's **Cambodian Genocide Program** (www.yale.edu/cgp) to research and document the crimes of the Khmer Rouge. It became an independent organisation in 1997 and researchers have spent years translating confessions and paperwork from Tuol Sleng, mapping mass graves, and preserving evidence of Khmer Rouge crimes.

French-Cambodian director Rithy Panh's 1996 film *Bophana* tells the true story of Hout Bophana, a beautiful young woman, and Ly Sitha, a regional Khmer Rouge leader, who fall in love but are made to pay for this 'crime' with imprisonment and execution at S-21 prison. It is well worth investing an hour to watch this powerful documentary, which is screened here at 10am and 3pm daily.

Killing Fields of Choeung Ek
កំលពិឃាតជើងឯក

Between 1975 and 1978 about 17,000 men, women, children and infants who had been detained and tortured at S-21 were transported to the extermination camp of **Choeung Ek** (off Map pp84-5; admission US$3; ⏲ 8am-5.30pm). They were often bludgeoned to death to avoid wasting precious bullets.

The remains of 8985 people, many of whom were bound and blindfolded, were exhumed in 1980 from mass graves in this one-time longan orchard; 43 of the 129 communal graves here have been left untouched. Fragments of human bone and bits of cloth are scattered around the disinterred pits. More than 8000 skulls, arranged by sex and age, are visible behind the clear glass panels of the Memorial Stupa, which was erected in 1988. It is a peaceful place today, masking the horrors that unfolded here less than three decades ago. There is a new museum here, which has some interesting information on the Khmer Rouge leadership and the ongoing trial.

VANN NATH: PORTRAIT OF THE ARTIST Nick Ray

Cambodian artist Vann Nath is famous the world over for his depictions of Khmer Rouge torture scenes at S-21 Security Prison in Phnom Penh. He was one of only seven survivors to emerge from the experience alive and, together with fellow prisoners Chum Mey and Bou Meng, there are just three men alive today to tell their tale.

Vann Nath was born in Battambang in 1946 and took up painting as a teenager, finding work as a sign painter and artist for cinema posters. Like many Cambodians, his life was turned upside down by the Khmer Rouge takeover and he found himself evacuated to the countryside along with other urban Cambodians. On 7 January 1978, he was taken to S-21 prison, aged 32 years, and spent the next year living in hellish surrounds, as thousands perished around him.

As one of the only survivors of the notorious prison, the Vietnamese brought him back to S-21 from 1980 to 1982 to paint the famous images we see today. He spent much of the subsequent decade enlisted in the Cambodian army, battling his former tormentors along the Thai border region.

'I only started to paint again after the 1993 election, as I felt more free to speak openly,' he says. 'This is when I was discovered by the world and became famous for my museum paintings.'

I ask what it feels like to see Tuol Sleng as a tourist attraction today. 'We must think of the souls of those who died there,' he laments. 'These souls died without hope, without light, without a future. They had no life,' he continues, 'so I paint my scenes to tell the world the stories of those who did not survive.'

He remembers a pledge he made back in 1978 when first incarcerated: 'We were taken up to a holding room on the first floor,' he tells me. 'We agreed that whoever survives would need to tell the families of the victims how they met their fate.' As one of the only survivors he is duty-bound to tell the world what happened.

So how does it feel to return to the scene of such personal horrors? 'The first time I went back was a real struggle, as everything looked the same as before,' he recalls. 'I could hardly speak or move.'

We finish by talking about the Khmer Rouge tribunal for surviving leaders. Vann Nath has learnt about human rights in the years since his imprisonment, but it's hard to accept as a victim. 'As a person who represents thousands of dead prisoners, I am not sure the tribunal will deliver enough justice for the dead,' he muses. 'Based on human rights it may be fair, but the Khmer Rouge was about human wrongs as well,' he says with an ironic smile.

'If we talk about human feeling, then we want more than this, but we must ask ourselves what is fair?' he considers. 'If we demand too much justice then it becomes revenge. I just hope the court will deliver justice fairly,' he says with dignity.

Vann Nath painted the scenes of torture and brutality of the Khmer Rouge regime, which are on display at Tuol Sleng Genocide Museum (opposite). He runs the Kith Eng Restaurant (p109), which includes a small gallery of his famous works. He is also the author of 'A Cambodian Prison Portrait: One Year in the Khmer Rouge's S-21', available in Cambodia.

The Killing Fields of Choeung Ek are 15km from central Phnom Penh and well signposted in English. Most people arrive by bicycle, *moto, remork* or taxi – it's too far to walk. To get here, take Monireth Blvd southwest out of the city. The site is 13km from the bridge near St 271 and the road is now paved the whole way. A memorial ceremony is held annually at Choeung Ek on 9 May.

The Killing Fields site was 'privatised' in 2005. Many Khmers and foreign observers alike remain disturbed that a private company has been permitted to exploit Cambodia's tragedy.

Wat Phnom
វត្តភ្នំ

Set on top of a 27m-high tree-covered knoll, **Wat Phnom** (Map p87; admission US$1) is on the only 'hill' in town. According to legend, the first pagoda on this site was erected in 1373 to house four statues of Buddha deposited here by the waters of the Mekong River and discovered by Madame Penh. The main entrance to Wat Phnom is via the grand eastern staircase, which is guarded by lions and *naga* (mythical serpent) balustrades.

Today, many people come here to pray for good luck and success in school exams or business affairs. When a wish is granted, the faithful return to deliver on the offering promised, such as a garland of jasmine flowers or a bunch of bananas, of which the spirits are said to be especially fond.

The *vihara* (temple sanctuary) was rebuilt in 1434, 1806, 1894 and 1926. West of the *vihara* is a huge stupa containing the ashes of King Ponhea Yat (r 1405–67). In a pavilion on the southern side of the passage between the *vihara* and the stupa is a statue of a smiling and rather plump Madame Penh.

A bit to the north of and below the *vihara* is an eclectic shrine dedicated to

---

WARNING: MONKEY BUSINESS AROUND WAT PHNOM

There are large troupes of macaques living around Wat Phnom and they can be aggressive when they see people with food. They have been known to bite children on occasion, so keep a good distance even if your children want to see the 'cute' monkeys.

---

the genie Preah Chau, who is especially revered by the Vietnamese. On either side of the entrance to the chamber containing a statue of Preah Chau are guardian spirits bearing iron bats. On the tiled table in front of the two guardian spirits are drawings of Confucius, as well as two Chinese-style figures of the sages Thang Cheng (on the right) and Thang Thay (on the left). To the left of the central altar is an eight-armed statue of Vishnu.

Wat Phnom can be a bit of a circus. Beggars, street urchins, women selling drinks and children selling birds in cages (you pay to set the bird free, but the birds are trained to return to their cage afterwards) pester everyone who turns up to climb the 27m to the summit. Fortunately it's all high-spirited stuff, and it's difficult to be annoyed by the vendors, who, after all, are only trying to eke out a living. You can also have a short elephant ride around the base of the hill, perfect for those elephant-trekking photos, but without the accompanying sore backside.

Anyone travelling with children should note that the best public playground in Phnom Penh is located just to the southeast side of Wat Phnom, complete with a nearby multicoloured fountain that kicks off around dusk each day.

Wat Ounalom
វត្តឧណ្ណាលោម

This **wat** (Map p87; Samdech Sothearos Blvd; admission free; ☯ 6am-6pm) is the headquarters of Cambodian Buddhism. It was founded in 1443 and comprises 44 structures. It received a battering during the Pol Pot era, but today the wat has come back to life. The head of the country's Buddhist brotherhood lives here, along with a large number of monks.

On the 2nd floor of the main building, to the left of the dais, is a statue of Samdech Huot Tat, fourth patriarch of Cambodian Buddhism, who was killed by Pol Pot. The statue, made in 1971 when the patriarch was 80 years old, was thrown in the Mekong by the Khmer Rouge to show that Buddhism was no longer the driving force in Cambodia. It was retrieved after 1979. To the right of the dais is a statue of a former patriarch of the Thummayuth sect, to which the royal family belongs.

On the 3rd floor of the building is a marble Buddha of Burmese origin that was broken into pieces by the Khmer Rouge and later re-assembled. In front of the dais, to either side, are two glass cases containing flags – each 20m long – used during Buddhist festivals and celebrations. The walls are decorated with scenes from the life of Buddha and were painted when the building was constructed in 1952.

Behind the main building is a stupa containing an eyebrow hair of Buddha with an inscription in Pali (an ancient Indian language) over the entrance.

Wat Moha Montrei
វត្តមហាមន្ត្រី

Situated close to the Olympic Stadium, **Wat Moha Montrei** (Map p87; Sihanouk Blvd; admission free; ⏱ 6am-6pm) was named in honour of one of King Monivong's ministers, Chakrue Ponn, who initiated the founding of the pagoda (*moha montrei* means 'the great minister'). The cement *vihara,* topped with a 35m-high tower, was completed in 1970. Between 1975 and 1979, it was used by the Khmer Rouge to store rice and corn.

Check out the assorted Cambodian touches incorporated into the wall murals of the *vihara,* which tell the story of Buddha. The angels accompanying Buddha to heaven are dressed as classical Khmer dancers and the assembled officials wear the white military uniforms of the Sihanouk period. Along the wall to the left of the dais is a painted wooden lion throne from which religious lessons are preached four times a month. The golden wooden throne nearby is used for the same purpose. All the statues of Buddha were made after 1979.

Independence Monument
វិមានឯករាជ្យ

Modelled on the central tower of Angkor Wat, the **Independence Monument** (Map p87; cnr Norodom & Sihanouk Blvds) was built in 1958 to commemorate the country's independence from France in 1953. It also serves as a memorial to Cambodia's war dead (at least those that the current government chooses to remember) and is sometimes referred to as the Victory Monument. Wreaths are laid here on national holidays. Nearby, beside Samdech Sothearos Blvd, is the optimistically named **Cambodia-Vietnam Friendship Monument**, built to a Vietnamese (and rather communist) design in 1979.

Other Sights

The 700m **Chruoy Changvar Bridge** (Map pp84–5), which spans the Tonlé Sap River, is often referred to by visitors as the Japanese Friendship Bridge. It was blown up during fighting in 1975. Long a symbol of the devastation visited upon Cambodia, it was repaired in 1993 with Japanese funding. Those who have seen the film *The Killing Fields* may be interested to note that it was near here on the afternoon of 17 April 1975 – the day Phnom Penh fell – that Khmer Rouge fighters imprisoned and threatened to kill *New York Times* correspondent Sydney Schanberg and his companions.

Located at the northern end of Monivong Blvd, the **French embassy** (Map pp84-5; ☎ 430020; 1 Monivong Blvd) played a significant role in the dramas that unfolded after the fall of Phnom Penh on 17 April 1975. About 800 foreigners and 600 Cambodians took refuge in the embassy. Within 48 hours, the Khmer Rouge informed the French vice-consul that the new government did not recognise diplomatic privileges and that if all the Cambodians in the compound were not handed over, the lives of the foreigners inside would also be forfeited. Cambodian women married to foreigners could stay; Cambodian men married to foreign women could not. Foreigners wept as servants, colleagues, friends, lovers and husbands were escorted out of the embassy gates. At the end of the month the foreigners were expelled from Cambodia by truck. Many of the Cambodians were never seen again. Today a high whitewashed wall surrounds the massive complex and the French have returned to Cambodia in a big way, promoting French language and culture in their former colony.

Known collectively as the National Sports Complex, the **Olympic Stadium** (Map pp84-5; near cnr Sihanouk & Monireth Blvds) is a striking example of 1960s Khmer architecture and includes a sports arena and facilities for boxing, gymnastics, volleyball and other sports. Turn up after 5pm to see countless football matches, *pétanque* duels or badminton games.

In order to replace the countless Buddhas and ritual objects smashed by the Khmer Rouge, a whole neighbourhood of private workshops making cement Buddhas, *naga* and small stupas has grown up on the grounds of Wat Prayuvong. While the graceless cement figures painted in gaudy colours are hardly works of art, they are an effort by the Cambodian people to restore

Buddhism to a place of honour in their culture. The **Prayuvong Buddha factories** (Map p87; btw St 308 & St 310) are about 300m south of the Independence Monument.

The **National Library** (Bibliothèque Nationale; Map p87; St 92; 8-11am & 2-5pm Tue-Sun) is in a graceful old building constructed in 1924, near Wat Phnom. During its rule, the Khmer Rouge turned the building into a stable and destroyed most of the books. Many were thrown out into the streets, where they were picked up by people, some of whom donated them back to the library after 1979; others used them as food wrappings.

ACTIVITIES

Boat Cruises

Boat trips on the Tonlé Sap or Mekong Rivers are very popular with visitors. Sunset cruises are ideal, the burning sun sinking slowly behind the glistening spires of the Royal Palace. It is also possible to charter them further afield for a visit to **Koh Sdach** and **Mekong Island**, neighbouring islands connected by bridge, where there is a cottage industry of silk weavers. Consider renting a bicycle to bring out to these islands for a little pedal-powered exploring.

Local **tourist boats** are available for hire on the riverfront in Phnom Penh and can usually be arranged on the spot for between US$10 and US$20 an hour, depending on negotiations and numbers.

Bowling

There is only one bowling alley in town, the **Superbowl** (Map pp84-5; Mao Tse Toung Blvd; per hr US$9, shoe hire US$1) at Parkway Sq. Hourly rates are per lane, with any number of bowlers.

Cooking Courses

To learn more about the art of Cambodian cooking, sign up for the **Cambodian Cooking Class** (Map p87; ☎ 012 524801; www.cambodian-cooking-class.com; 67 St 240), based at Frizz Restaurant. The cooking class costs US$20/12.50 per full day/half day, includes a booklet of recipes, and operates Monday to Saturday from 9am.

Cycling Trips

Decent imported bikes (Trek and Giant) are available for rent through the **Vicious Cycle** (Map p87; ☎ 012 462165; www.grasshopperadventures.com; 29 St 130; per day US$8), which represents Grasshopper Adventures here. There are even a couple of family bikes available with kiddie seats for US$10. Tours include the Mekong River islands (US$29) or Udong (US$44), both including lunch.

Venture across the Mekong River on a local ferry in front of the Imperial Garden Villa Hotel and you'll find bikes for hire just a short stroll from the ferry pier. **2Cycle Cambodia** (off Map pp84-5; ☎ 015 696376; www.2cyclecambodia.com) rents out local-ish mountain bikes from US$2 per hour to US$6 for the day and have smaller bikes available for children. Book the day before you plan to ride. This is a great way to

---

THE SHOOTING RANGES

Shooting ranges have long been a popular activity for gung-ho travellers visiting Cambodia. Cambodia's lack of law enforcement and culture of impunity allowed visitors to do pretty much anything they wanted in the bad old days. The Cambodian military wasn't blind to the market opportunities this presented, and with a hefty surplus of weapons from 25 years of civil war, it began to offer its own ammunition reduction scheme involving feisty foreigners wanting to do the Rambo thing. A number of military bases near Phnom Penh were transformed into shooting ranges and rapidly became popular with tourists wanting to try their luck with an AK-47, M-60 or B-40 grenade launcher. The government periodically launched crackdowns, but the business continued largely unabated.

And so the show goes on. There is a rather incongruous range near the Killing Fields of Choeung Ek, while another popular one is located just beyond the go-cart track (opposite) in Kambol district off NH4. Visitors can try out a range of weapons, but most of the machine guns work out at about US$1 a bullet. Handguns are available at the lower end, while at the other extreme it is possible to try shooting a B-40 rocket-propelled grenade launcher (US$350).

There have been rumours that it is possible to shoot live animals at these places, such as a chicken or cow. Naturally, we in no way endorse such behaviour. Does it ever happen? It is a possibility, as Cambodia is an impoverished country where money talks.

CAMBODIAN FIGHT CLUB

The whole world knows about *muay Thai* (Thai boxing) and the sport of kickboxing, but what is not so well known is that this contact sport probably originated in Cambodia. *Pradal serey* (literally 'free fighting') is Cambodia's very own version of kickboxing and it is possible to see some fights in Phnom Penh. Popular Cambodian TV channel CTN hosts live bouts at 2pm on Saturday and Sunday out at their main studio on National Hwy 5. It is about 4km north of the Chruoy Changvar Bridge. Entry is free and there is usually a rowdy local crowd surreptitiously betting on the fights. Most bouts are ended by a violent elbow move and there is a lot more ducking and diving than with other kickboxing genres.

An even older martial art is *bokator*, or *labokatao*, which some say dates back to the time of Angkor. It translates as 'pounding a lion' and was originally conceived for battlefield confrontations. Weapons include bamboo staffs and short sticks, as well as the *krama* in certain situations. Grand Master San Kim Sean operates the **Cambodian Boxkator Academy** (Map p87; ☎ 012 651845; www.khmerboxkatorempire.com; 169 St 161) in Phnom Penh and offers hourly lessons from 5.30pm to 7.30pm daily for US$5.

escape the city without pedalling through the traffic and the countryside is very beautiful.

Diving

No, we're not recommending the Mekong or the Tonlé Sap Rivers. **Scuba Nation** (Map pp84-5; ☎ 012 604680; www.divecambodia.com; 18 Samdech Sothearos Blvd) is one of the leading dive companies operating in Sihanoukville and has an office in the capital for advance bookings or pool-based courses for expats.

Go-carting

Kambol Kart Raceway (off Map pp84-5; ☎ 012 232332; www.kkraceway.com; per 10min US$12) is a professional circuit located about 12km beyond the airport, and 2km off the road to Sihanoukville. It organises races on Sundays, so if you fancy yourself as the new Michael Schumacher, turn up then. Prices include helmets and racing suits.

Golf

A round of golf is expensive by Cambodian standards, but pretty cheap for the region. If you can't survive without a swing, contact **Royal Cambodia Phnom Penh Golf Club** (off Map pp84-5; ☎ 011 290552; NH4; per round Mon-Fri US$40, shoe/club hire US$5/10), on the road to Sihanoukville, or **Cambodia Golf & Country Club** (off Map pp84-5; ☎ 363666; www.cambodia-golf.com; NH4; per round US$43, shoe/club hire US$5/10).

Gymnasiums

There are plenty of backstreet local gyms in Phnom Penh that charge about US$1 per hour and have very basic weights.

The smartest gym in town is the **Place Gym** (Map p87; ☎ 726999; The Place, 90 Sihanouk Blvd; per day US$10, 10 sessions US$55). Set over three floors, this is absolutely state of the art with views over Independence Monument and free internet after a workout.

Massage & Spas

There are plenty of massage parlours in Phnom Penh, but some are purveying 'naughty' massages. However, there are also now a lot of legitimate massage centres and a number of superb spas for that pampering palace experience.

Most of the more upmarket hotels offer traditional massage services, but one of the best value options in town is the long-running **Seeing Hands Massage** (Map p87; ☎ 012 680 934; 12 St 13; fan/air-con room per hr US$5/7). The blind masseurs here have been in the business for many years and can sort out those niggling aches and pains, offering shiatsu or foot massages. There are several other similar cooperatives around town.

When it comes to spas, there is now an enticing selection of places. Some of the leading addresses for massage, facials, manicures and the full spa menu:

Champei Spa (Map p87; ☎ 222846; www.champeispa.net; 38 St 57) Khmer, Swedish and other massages, plus beauty care and hairdresser.

In Style (Map p87; ☎ 986747; www.instylespa-cambodia.com; 63 St 242) Garden spa and wellness centre with massage, facials and spa treatments.

Nail Bar (Map pp84-5; Mith Samlanh Training Centre behind Friends Restaurant, 215 St 13; ⏰ noon-4pm) Cheap manicures, pedicures, foot massages, hand massages and nail painting, all to help Mith Samlanh train street children in a new vocation.

O Spa (Map p87; ☎ 992405; www.ospacambodia.com; 4B St 75) An oasis of calm with rejuvenating hot-stone massage, plus Balinese and Thai treatments.

Spa Bliss (Map p87; ☎ 215754; 29 St 240) One of the most established spas in town, set in a lovely old French house on popular 240.

Quad Biking

Nature Cambodia (off Map pp84-5; ☎ 012 676381; www. nature-cambodia.com; near Choeung Ek) offers quad biking (ATV trips) in the countryside around Phnom Penh. The quads are automatic, so easy to handle for beginners, and prices are pretty affordable at US$15 for one and a half hours or US$35 for a half day. Despite its proximity to the capital, this is rural Cambodia and very beautiful. Longer trips and jeep tours are also available. Follow signs to Choeung Ek and it is about 300m before the entrance. Call ahead as numbers are limited.

Running

A good opportunity to meet local expatriates is via the Hash House Harriers, usually referred to simply as 'the Hash'. A weekly run/walk takes place every Sunday. Participants meet in front of Phnom Penh train station (Map p87) at 2.15pm. The fee of US$5 includes refreshments (mainly a lot of beer) at the end.

Shuffleboard

Unlikely though it may be, Phnom Penh is home to Southeast Asia's only dedicated shuffleboard lounge, the **Scan Shuffleboard Lounge** (Map p87; ☎ 092-791449; www.shufflelounge.com; 4 St 282; per hr US$3). For the uninitiated, it is like tabletop curling and a lot of fun over a cold beer or two. It's located on the rooftop of the Scan Hotel.

Swimming

Many of the midrange and top-end hotels have swimming pools in which to cool off on a hot day. Most open their pools to the public for a fee. The Hotel Cambodiana (p106) charges just US$7 during the week, while Hotel Le Royal demands US$20 per day for use of the pool and gym. Part of the same hotel group, the Blue Lime (p105) – no families – and the Kabiki (p105) – families welcome – both allow non-guests to swim for US$5 per day. There is also a small

swimming pool at popular bar-restaurant Elsewhere (p115); a dip is free.

Other options include the hotel **Himawari** (Map p87; ☎ 214555; 313 Sisowath Quay), which charges US$10 including access to the gym; **Parkway Health Club** (Map pp84-5; ☎ 982928; 113 Mao Tse Toung Blvd; US$6), which has an indoor pool, steam bath, sauna and gym; and **Long Beach Plaza Hotel** (Map pp84-5; ☎ 998007; St 289; US$1), a bargain for a lap-sized pool.

There is also a beautiful swimming pool at L'Elephant Blanc Resort (p106) about 7km out of town on the road to Neak Luong. It costs US$4/2 per adult/child, half again when it is quiet during the week, and there is a restaurant-bar here.

WALKING TOUR

What better place to kick off a walking tour of the city (Map p101) than the landmark temple of **Wat Phnom** (1; p96), perched atop the only hill in town? Pray for luck like the locals, or at least pray that you won't fall into one of Phnom Penh's open drains on your wanderings. Take a look southwest at the fortress that is the **US embassy (2)**.

Head west along St 92 and pause at the **National Library** (3; p98), a classic example of French colonial–era architecture. Just along the road is the striking facade of **Hotel Le Royal** (4; p106), now owned by the Raffles group. Bookmark it for a happy-hour cocktail some time between 4pm and 8pm. Turn left onto Monivong Blvd, the capital's main commercial thoroughfare. Fast approaching on the right is Phnom Penh's **train station (5)**, a grand old building, home to not-so-grand old trains.

Swing southeast towards the dominant dome of **Psar Thmei** (6; p119). This is a market to remember, packed to the rafters with everything and anything you can imagine and some things you can't, such as deep-fried insects and peeled frogs. Browse awhile and take in the natural air-conditioning of the immense centre. Don't get liberal with your wallet, however, as sellers here are known to overcharge. That said, the food stalls are a great place for cheap local bites.

Continue south on St 63 and take a peek at the modern equivalent of the Central Market, aka **Sorya Shopping Centre** (7; p117). The food court here is bigger and cleaner than at the market and offers the advantage of air-conditioning, plus you can get some great

PHNOM PENH

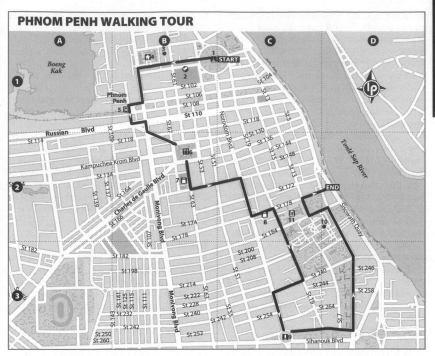

PHNOM PENH WALKING TOUR

WALK FACTS

Start Wat Phnom
Finish Sisowath Quay
Distance 6km
Duration 8 hours (including plenty of sightseeing time)

aerial shots of Psar Thmei from the top floor balcony (level 8 by lift).

Snake east on St 154 and then turn south on to Norodom Blvd, before taking a left on to St 178, a lively strip to browse the many **art shops** (**8**; p117). Turn right onto St 19 before swinging west again, along St 240, one of the more fashionable stretches in the capital. Take your pick from one of the many bustling cafes, restaurants or bars along here to recharge the batteries for the second half of the walk.

Head southwards on to Norodom Blvd again and make for the **Independence Monument** (**9**; p97), which was modelled on the central tower of Angkor Wat and built to commemorate freedom from the French.

From here make a loop east and then take Samdech Sothearos Blvd north.

Take an hour or more to experience the treasures of the **Royal Palace and Silver Pagoda complex** (**10**; p92) before delving into the world's finest collection of Khmer sculpture from the Angkor period at the stunning **National Museum** (**11**; p93). After an hour or so exploring this magnificent old building, wander east towards the riverfront. Stroll riverside along the Tonlé Sap or duck into a bar or restaurant for a well-earned drink.

PHNOM PENH FOR CHILDREN

With its chaotic traffic, lack of public parks, and open sewers, at first glance Phnom Penh is not the most child-friendly city in Asia. However, there are a few little gems that help to pass the time in the capital.

Most sights will be overwhelming for younger children, but the Royal Palace (p92) is an interesting place to explore and Wat Phnom (p96) has the option of an elephant ride around the base.

Many of the leading hotels have swimming pools (opposite) that are open to the public for a fee, and the go-cart track (p99) might prove popular if you have the next Lewis Hamilton in tow. **Phnom Penh Water Park** (off Map pp84-5; ☎ 881008; Russian Blvd; admission weekends/weekdays US$3/2; ☽ 8am-6pm), with its slides and wave pool, is a definite hit with the young-uns and a world away from bustling downtown Phnom Penh, but it's pretty dirty compared with the hotel pools. There is also a small fairground here. Sorya Shopping Centre (p117) includes a roller-skating rink on the upper floor, while there is ten-pin bowling at Superbowl (p98). There are also lots of children's playgrounds with ball ponds, trampolines and walkways, including one at Pencil Supermarket (p114) and a great outdoor one at Wat Phnom (p96).

One playground that is particularly worth the diversion is the new **Kidz Cool** (Map p87; ☎ 432100; www.kidzcoolcambodia.com; Tonlé Sap Rd; admission weekends/weekdays US$10/5, adults free; ☽ 8am-6.30pm), which offers a huge playground, a climbing wall, bouncy castles and a swimming pool in a big complex across the river. Affordable food is available on site and it's about 500m south of the Chruoy Changvar Bridge.

Many of the restaurants and cafes are child friendly, but there are a few specifically aimed at families, including Le Jardin (p113) and Living Room (p114), while Fresco (p113) has a kiddies corner complete with PlayStation (big kids, hands off!). Gasolina (p115) is another good option thanks to its huge garden, plus most of the riverfront places draw a breeze.

The most interesting attractions are beyond the city limits and would make good day trips to give the children a break from the hustle and bustle of the city. Phnom Tamao Wildlife Rescue Centre (p126) is a rescue centre for Cambodia's incredible wildlife and the huge enclosures here include tigers, elephants and bears. Further afield is Kirirom National Park (p127), with gentle waterfalls and cooler temperatures, plus the fun Kirirom Hillside Resort (p127), which offers fresh air, pine trees, giant dinosaurs and activities such as horse riding and kayaking.

TOURS

Travelling independently, Phnom Penh is a city best enjoyed at your own pace, without the timetable of a tour. If you really want to have an organised city tour, most of the leading guesthouses organise tours including the sights listed earlier for around US$6 per person. Prices quoted do not include entrance fees.

Those interested in the new-wave Khmer architecture from the Sangkum era (1953–70) should sign up with **Khmer Architecture Tours** (www.ka-tours.org). These introductory tours take in some of the most prominent buildings in the city and take place on foot or by *cyclo*, usually starting at 8.30am every other weekend. The website also includes a DIY map of the most popular walking tour. For more on this landmark architecture, pick up a copy of *Cultures of Independence* (2001) or *Building Cambodia: New Khmer Architecture 1953–70* (2006).

SLEEPING

Phnom Penh offers a world-class selection of places to stay. There is an excellent range of guesthouses, hotels and luxury palaces to suit all wallets passing through the capital. With the surge in visitors, new hotels are also under development.

Affordable guesthouses are springing up all over the city. Some places charge as little as US$2 a room; US$5 will guarantee a small room with a fan and there are some smart new pads with air-con rooms from US$10. The best hotel deals in Phnom Penh fall in the midrange category and for around US$25 it is possible to get hooked up with air-con, satellite TV and a smart bathroom. Spend a little more cash and there are places that have a swimming pool for around US$50. Top-end travellers will find a selection of properties, including the grand, the bland and the boutique.

Budget

There are two popular backpacker strips, one along the eastern shore of Boeng Kak Lake and the other around the long-running Capitol Guesthouse along St 182 and St 111, just west of Monivong Blvd. The area around Boeng Kak is a bit rough and likely to be swallowed by hungry developers during the lifetime of this book.

MONIVONG WEST AREA

The most popular budget accommodation area starts near Psar O Russei and heads south towards Sihanouk Blvd along a network of backstreets.

our pick **Narin Guesthouse** (Map p87; ☎ 982554; touchnarrin@hotmail.com; 50 St 125; r US$3-10; ✖ 🖳) We first stayed here back in 1995 and it remains a popular place thanks to a family atmosphere and some budget beds. Rooms are quite basic, but there is a relaxed terrace for taking some time out.

Narin 2 Guesthouse (Map p87; ☎ 350411; 20 St 111; r US$6-15; ✖ 🖳) More like a hotel than its sister property, Narin 2 is located just a few blocks away. Includes a smart restaurant.

King Angkor (Map p87; ☎ 220512; www.theking angkor.com; 74 St 141; r US$6-25; ✖ 🖳 ⚅) The range of rooms is as wide as the king's girth (that's Elvis, not Sihamoni!) and there is a huge restaurant and travel centre downstairs. Recently refurbished, so it's in good shape.

Dragon Guesthouse (Map p87; ☎ 012 239066; 238 St 107; r US$7-12; ✖ 🖳 ⚅) A likeable little guesthouse, all rooms here include cable TV and bathroom. There is also a lively balcony restaurant with an international menu.

Spring Guesthouse (Map p87; ☎ 222155; spring _guesthouse@yahoo.com; 34 St 111; r US$7-12; ✖ 🖳) This was the first of a new generation of smart guesthouses in this area. It offers bright, spotless rooms, complete with cable TV. Long-term discounts also available.

Sunday Guesthouse (Map p87; ☎ 211623; 97 St 141; r US$8-16; ✖ 🖳 ⚅) A friendly, family-run spot on any day of the week, the rooms here are in fine shape, making them good value for money. The English-speaking staff can help with travel arrangements.

Sky Park Guesthouse (Map p87; ☎ 992718; sky parkguesthouseepp@gmail.com; 78 St 111; r US$8-20; ✖ 🖳 ⚅) One of the tallest guesthouses in this part of town, the Sky Park is a real deal for such cleanliness and comfort. Air-con starts at US$12 and all rooms have cable TV and hot water, plus there's a lift.

Fairyland Guesthouse (Map p87; ☎ 092-538834; fairylandhotel@yahoo.com; 99 St 141; r US$13-15; ✖ 🖳) Brand new in late 2009, this towering guesthouse looks very promising with large, bright rooms, decent linen and smart bathrooms. The more expensive rooms include a double and single bed.

Other good spots in this area:

Tat Guesthouse (Map p87; ☎ 099-801000; tatguest house@hotmail.com; 52 St 125; r US$3-15; ✖) A friendly, family-run place with cheap and cheerful rooms, plus a breezy rooftop restaurant.

Capitol Guesthouse (Map p87; ☎ 724104; www. capitolkh.com; 14 St 182; r US$3-18; ✖ 🖳) The original

guesthouse in town has several annexes with good-value rooms and a bustling cafe with travel info. A reliable place to book city tours.

AROUND THE CITY

Other guesthouses are spread evenly across the city.

Okay Guesthouse (Map p87; ☎ 986534; 3B St 258; r US$3-15; ✖ 🖳 ⚅) Okay is more than just OK thanks to a popular restaurant, an appealing garden, cheap rooms and a friendly vibe. Budget rooms start with shared bathroom, and top whack brings air-con, TV and hot water.

Last Home (Map p87; ☎ 012 831702; www.lasthome cambodia.com; 21 St 172; r US$5-15; ✖ 🖳) Tucked away discreetly behind Wat Ounalom along up-and-coming St 172, Last Home has a loyal following among regular visitors. Added extras include cable TV and smartish bathrooms.

Home (Map p87; ☎ 077-663221; www.home-cam bodia.com; 8 St 258; r US$6-12; ✖ 🖳) A brand new place in 2010, Home has a fun vibe with just a handful of rooms and a lively bar-restaurant out front.

Top Banana Guesthouse (Map p87; ☎ 012 885572; www.topbanana.biz; cnr Sts 51 & 278; r US$6-15; ✖ 🖳 ⚅) Boasting a great location on a popular corner opposite Wat Langka, this place has a rooftop chill-out area above the dust. Cheap rooms don't come with hot water, but the more expensive ones include brisk air-con.

Royal Guesthouse (Map p87; ☎ 218026; 91 St 154; r US$8-15; ✖ 🖳) This old-timer has some smarter rooms that verge on the flashpacker side, with sparkling bathrooms and tasteful decoration.

Dara Reang Sey Hotel (Map p87; ☎ 428181; www. darareangsey.com; 45 St 13; r US$8-35; ✖ 🖳 ⚅) This long-running place has good-value rooms, and the family here really look after the staff, bringing a feel-good factor to the whole place.

Hotel Indochine (Map p87; ☎ 724239; indochinehtl@ camnet.com.kh; 251 Sisowath Quay; r US$10-25; ✖) One of the oldies on the riverfront, but the price is right. Aim for a balcony river-view, but all rooms include TV, fridge and hot water.

Boddhi Tree Umma (Map p87; www.boddhitree. com; 50 St 113; r US$12-32; ✖ 🖳 ⚅) Some might be unnerved by the location opposite Tuol Sleng Museum, but for those who don't get nightmares this is a wonderfully atmospheric place to stay. The old wooden house includes air-con options and there is a divine restaurant in the verdant garden.

Bright Lotus Guesthouse (Map p87; ☎ 990446; 22 St 178; r US$16-22; ✖ 🖵 🛜 👪) Occupying a strategic corner with grand views of the National Museum, Royal Palace and, if you have a neck like Mr Fantastic, the riverfront, this guesthouse is one place where it is worth climbing the stairs. Wi-fi available for a fee.

BOENG KAK AREA

Most of the lakeside guesthouses are built on wooden platforms over Boeng Kak, a seriously polluted body of water that no one should swim in, however much they have drunk or smoked. For some it's like experiencing Ko Pha Ngan in the city, only Boeng Kak isn't quite the Gulf of Thailand. Valuables should be kept in lockers, as most rooms aren't very secure. Unfortunately, this whole area is slated for redevelopment and the lake is fast disappearing, replaced by sand dunes and floating rubbish in the small pockets of water that remain.

Number 10 Lakeside Guesthouse (Map p87; ☎ 012 725032; 10 St 93; r US$3-10) This stalwart on the lake has some bargain rooms with share bathroom or bigger rooms with hot water and cable TV. The drinking and dining area (smoking and joking for others) is a mellow place to hang out. Next door are several similar guesthouses with a relaxed vibe.

Grand View Guesthouse (Map p87; ☎ 430766; www.grandview.netfirms.com; St 93; r US$4-10; ✖ 🖵 👪) Thailand meets Vietnam, with boxy rooms *à la* Bangkok housed in a tall, skinny structure *à la* Saigon. Upper floors involve a real hike, but the views of the lake are unrivalled.

Midrange

For those looking to spend between US$20 and US$80 for a room, there are some excellent deals to be had around town. Some of the fancier midrange places with a swimming pool are not that far behind the top-range hotels in comfort.

As with the budget guesthouses, there is no single midrange hotel area. Probably the best choice, and definitely the best location, is along the riverfront on Sisowath Quay. The area to the southwest of the Independence Monument also has a concentration of midrange deals.

RIVERFRONT AREA

Paragon Hotel (Map p87; ☎ 222607; 219 Sisowath Quay; r US$17-38; ✖ 🖵) A 40-room property on a lively stretch of the riverfront, this hotel represents good value. All rooms have TV and minibar, plus the pricier options have smart showers.

River Star Hotel (Map p87; ☎ 990501; www.riverstarhotel.com; 185 Sisowath Quay; r US$18-35; ✖ 🖵 👪) The reliable rooms here include the usual cable TV, fridge and air-con, and are quite spacious. Downstairs is a popular bar-restaurant and there's even a lift.

Bougainvillier Hotel (Map p87; ☎ 220528; www.bougainvillierhotel.com; 277 Sisowath Quay; r US$58-100; ✖ 🖵 👪) One of the most impressive hotels in this range, the rooms are lavishly decorated with Chinese-Khmer furniture and elegant silk. The suites are a worthy investment with acres of space and an unobstructed view of the Tonlé Sap. There is also a highly regarded French restaurant where the complimentary breakfast is served.

Hotel Castle (Map p87; ☎ 211425; www.hotelcastle.com.kh; 4 St 148; r from US$65; ✖ 🖵 🛜 🐾 👪) This modern hotel is not quite on the riverfront, but more than makes up for it with smart business-like rooms, a swimming pool and free wi-fi.

Imperial Garden Villa (Map pp84-5; ☎ 219991; www.imperialgarden-hotel.com; 315 Sisowath Quay; s/d US$65/70; ✖ 🖵 🛜 🐾 👪) Rooms here are a pretty good deal for the three-star standard and include a buffet breakfast and free wi-fi. There's a large pool and a tennis court, plus Mekong views.

Foreign Correspondents' Club (Map p87; ☎ 210142; www.fcccambodia.com; 363 Sisowath Quay; r US$80-155; ✖ 🖵 👪) This landmark location is a fine place to recapture the heady days of the war correspondents. The rooms are delightfully finished in wood and include DVD players. All include a minibar clearly aimed at the journalists who pass through town – the spirits come in 1L bottles rather than miniatures. The restaurant-bar (p111) always draws a crowd.

And there are more:

Tonle Sap Guesthouse (Map p87; ☎ 986722; www.tonlesapguesthouse.com; 4 St 104; r US$18-40; ✖ 🖵 👪) Located above the Pickled Parrot (p115), this is a good choice for the 24-hour party people.

Eye of the Mekong (Map p87; ☎ 092-880240; eyeofthemekong@gmail.com; 30 St 110; r US$20-40; ✖ 🖵) Just four rooms here, but the two larger rooms are a great deal, with original furnishings and a rain shower.

Khmer Royal Hotel (Map p87; ☎ 223824; www.khmerroyalhotel.com; Sisowath Quay; r US$45-55; ❇ 🖳) The brash exterior conceals some smart rooms. Request a river view if available.

CENTRAL PHNOM PENH

One area that is worth seeking out for those wanting good value is the so-called 'Golden Mile', a strip of hotels on St 278 that all feature 'Golden' in their name. There is little to choose between them, as all offer air-con, cable TV, fridge, hot water and free laundry for around US$15.

Town View Hotel (Map p87; ☎ 992939; 30 St 111; www.townviewhotel.com; r from US$20; ❇ 🖳 ♿) A smart hotel in a popular budget district, rooms here remain good value. All include cable TV, minibar and sparkling bathrooms, plus there's a lift.

Goldie Boutique Guesthouse (Map p87; ☎ 996670; 6B-D St 57; r US$23-30; ❇ 🖳 ♿) As the address suggests, this place has been patched together from three houses, but the results are pretty impressive. Most rooms come with a balcony and the decor is stylish throughout. The family rooms at US$30 include a second bedroom.

Kambuja Inn (Map p87; ☎ 223377; kambujainn@camnet.com.kh; 10 St 174; r US$25-40; ❇ ♿) Attractively set in a cluster of old French shophouses near Norodom Blvd, the 10 rooms here offer a degree of charm and comfort. All have a wood and silk finish and the more expensive are almost suites.

Scan Hotel (Map p87; ☎ 214498; www.hotel-scandinavia-cambodia.com; 4 St 282; r US$30-55; ❇ 🖳 🖳 ♿) Long popular with Phnom Penh aficionados, rooms here include a DVD player and minibar, plus there is a swimming pool in the garden, a restaurant, an art gallery *and* rooftop shuffleboard. Internet available for a fee.

Hotel Cara (Map p87; ☎ 430066; www.hotelcara.com; 18 St 47; s/d from US$34/39; ❇ 🖳 ♿) This hotel exudes real style at an affordable price. Rooms are finished in contemporary Khmer materials with original furnishings, and most include a balcony.

our pick Amber Villa (Map p87; ☎ 216303; www.amber-kh.com; 1A St 57; r US$35-40; ❇ 🖳 ♿) A homely little place with the feel of a bed and breakfast, the rooms are a good size with a tidy trim. Prices include free internet and laundry.

Billabong (Map p87; ☎ 223703; www.thebillabonghotel.com; 5 St 158; r US$36-62; ❇ 🖳 🖳 ♿) Near Psar Thmei but an oasis of calm by comparison, this boutique hotel has 15 rooms set around a large swimming pool. Standard rooms are smallish, so it's better to invest in the pool-view rooms for space and style.

Manor House (Map p87; ☎ 992566; www.manorhousecambodia.com; 21 St 262; s/d from US$38/43; ❇ 🖳 🖳 ♿) Set in a small villa in the backstreets, this gay-friendly guesthouse offers artfully decorated rooms and a small swimming pool. Deluxe rooms have a DVD player, but children are not accepted.

our pick Pavilion (Map p87; ☎ 222280; www.thepavilion.asia; 227 St 19; r US$40-90; ❇ 🖳 🛜 🖳 ♿) Housed in one of the most elegant French villas in town, this is an atmospheric place to stay. Furnishings show a Chinese-Khmer touch and some rooms have commanding pool views. Expanded into a second contemporary building next door, some of the newer rooms include a private plunge pool. There's free wi-fi and a gorgeous garden to while away the days, but no children allowed.

Villa Langka (Map p87; ☎ 726771; www.villalangka.com; 14 St 282; r US$40-110; ❇ 🖳 🖳 ♿) A popular boutique hotel near Wat Langka, the 27 rooms here face a tempting swimming pool and garden cafe. Cheaper rooms are smaller and the decor gets more expressive with the price, rising to US$100 suites. Add 10% to rates for tax.

Kabiki (Map p87; ☎ 222290; www.thekabiki.com; 22 St 264; r US$50-75; ❇ 🖳 🖳 ♿) The most family-friendly place in town, the Kabiki offers an extensive garden and an inviting swimming pool with a little kiddies pool for the small ones. Family rooms include bunks and most rooms have a private garden terrace.

Other places in the mix:

Golden Mekong Hotel (Map p87; ☎ 211721; www.goldenmekonghotel.com; 205 St 19; r US$20-30; ❇ 🖳 ♿) Atmospheric hotel behind the Royal Palace offering a good deal for the standard and comfort.

Blue Lime (Map p87; ☎ 222260; www.bluelime.asia; 42 St 19; r US$40-60; ❇ 🖳 🖳 ♿) Hip hotel from the team behind the Pavilion, rooms are minimalist in style and many overlook the lovely swimming pool.

Boddhi Tree Aram (Map p87; www.boddhitree.com; 70 St 244; r US$58-68; ❇ 🖳 ♿) Those on a bigger budget than Boddhi Tree Umma (p103) might consider this elegant place with stylish rooms, located near the Royal Palace.

Almond Hotel (Map p87; ☎ 220822; www.almondhotel.com.kh; 128F Samdech Sothearos Blvd; r US$58-86; ❇ 🖳 ♿) A boutique business hotel is probably the best way to sum up this popular place.

BEYOND THE CITY

L'Elephant Blanc Resort (off Map pp84-5; ☎ 222988; NH1; r US$25-30; 🍴 ☐ 🐾 ♿) A lovely little resort beyond the city limits, this is a peaceful retreat for those who have tired of the city life. Rooms are large and comfortable and the pool is a real treat. It tends to be much quieter during the week, as expats descend at the weekend.

Top End

Walk-in rates at many of Phnom Penh's luxury hotels are on the high side, so consider booking via the internet or through a travel agent for a better deal, which can be as little as half the published rate.

River 108 (Map p87; ☎ 218785; www.river108.com; 2 St 108; ste from US$78; 🍴 ☐ ♿) This hip new boutique hotel near the riverfront has a chic chintz look to it. Rooms include flat-screen TVs and ample bathrooms, plus some have river-view terraces.

Hotel Cambodiana (Map pp84-5; ☎ 426288; www.hotelcambodiana.com; 313 Sisowath Quay; s/d US$100; 🍴 ☐ 🐾 ♿) A real Phnom Penh landmark, the Cambodiana is steadily being upgraded to keep up with the newer hotels. Facilities include decent tennis courts, a swimming pool and mouth-watering bakery. The unfinished hotel was used as a military base by the Lon Nol government, and by 1975 thousands of refugees from the countryside sheltered under its concrete roof.

Quay (Map p87; www.thequayhotel.com; Sisowath Quay; r from US$100; 🍴 ☐ ♿) Cambodia's first carbon-neutral hotel, this is a stylish riverfront property with a touch of the Philippe Starck about it. The river-view panoramic suites (from US$140) are the beds of choice, as they are far more spacious than the windowless rooms at the rear. The property includes fusion restaurant Chow, a great rooftop bar and a rooftop jacuzzi to unwind.

Himawari (Map p87; ☎ 214555; www.himawarihotel.com; 313 Sisowath Quay; apt US$128; 🍴 ☐ 🐾 ♿) Another residential-style property offering rooms, suites and apartments, Himawari has a great location on the banks of the Mekong. Facilities include a pool and a gym, plus riverside dining. Definitely request a nonsmoking room, as smokers have left their stamp on some rooms.

Amanjaya Pancam Hotel (Map p87; ☎ 219579; www.amanjaya.com; 1 St 154; ste US$155-250; 🍴 ☐ ♿) Occupying a superb location near the riverfront, with panoramic views over the Tonlé Sap and Wat Ounalom, Amanjaya was the original boutique hotel in Phnom Penh. All rooms are suites, and are spacious and stylish, with elegant Khmer drapes and tropical furnishings.

our pick **Hotel Le Royal** (Map p87; ☎ 981888; www.raffles.com; cnr Monivong Blvd & St 92; r from US$200; 🍴 ☐ 🐾 ♿) From the golden age of travel, this is one of Asia's grand old palaces, in the illustrious company of the Oriental in Bangkok and Raffles in Singapore. This classic colonial-era property is Phnom Penh's leading address, with a heritage to match its service and style. Indulgent diversions include two swimming pools, a gym, a spa, and bars and restaurants with lavish food and drink. Between 1970 and 1975 many famous journalists working in Phnom Penh stayed here.

EATING

For foodies, Phnom Penh is a real delight, boasting a superb selection of restaurants that showcase the best in Khmer cooking, as well as the greatest hits from world cuisine such as Chinese, Vietnamese, Thai, Indian, French, Italian, Spanish, Mexican and more. Visitors to Phnom Penh are quite literally spoilt for choice these days. Most local restaurants open around 6.30am and serve food until 9pm or so. International restaurants stay open until about 10pm, but some close between breakfast and lunch or between lunch and dinner.

The best bet for budget dining in Phnom Penh is to head to one of the city's many markets. The dining areas may not be the most sophisticated in the world, but the food is tasty and cheap. If the markets are just too hot or claustrophobic for your taste, then look out for the mobile street sellers carrying their wares on their shoulders or wheeling it around in small carts.

Local hole-in-the-wall restaurants are slightly more civilised but still very cheap. Many of the international restaurants around town are expensive by local standards, but compared with dining in the West, the prices are very reasonable.

Some travellers get into the habit of hunkering down on their guesthouse balcony, encouraged by proprietors talking up the dangers of Phnom Penh. Don't do it, as a culinary adventure awaits…

Khmer

After dark, Khmer eateries scattered across town illuminate their Angkor Beer signs, hailing locals in for fine fare and generous jugs of draught beer. Don't be shy, and heed the call – the food is great and the atmosphere lively. A typical dish will cost just US$2 to US$4 and a jug of beer is only about US$2.

Soup chhnang dei (cook-your-own soup) restaurants are very popular with Khmers and are great fun if you go in a group. Other diners will often help with protocol, as it is important to cook things in the right order so as not to overcook half the ingredients and eat the rest raw. These places also offer *phnom pleung* (hill of fire), which amounts to cook-your-own

beef, shrimp or squid (or anything else that takes your fancy) over a personal barbecue.

The best markets for breakfast and lunch are Psar Thmei (Central Market; Map p87), Psar Tuol Tom Pong (Russian Market; Map pp84–5) and Psar O Russei (Map p87), which is handy given these are also great shopping venues. Most dishes cost a reasonable 3000r to 6000r. There are also several areas around the city with open-air food stalls during the early evening – try **Psar Ta Pang** (Map p87; cnr Sts 51 & 136) for excellent *bobor* (rice porridge) and tasty desserts.

GOOD CAUSE DINING

There are several restaurants around town that are run by aid organisations to help fund their social programs in Cambodia. These are worth seeking out, as the proceeds of a hearty meal go towards helping Cambodia's recovery and allow restaurant staff to gain valuable work experience.

Café Yejj (Map pp84-5; 170 St 450; mains US$3-6; 🕙 7am-5pm Mon-Sat, 9.30am-2pm Sun) An air-con escape from Psar Tuol Tom Pong (aka Russian Market), this bistro-style cafe specialises in pastas and salads. Or indulge in a frappucino and chocolate brownie. Promoting fair trade and responsible employment.

Ebony Apsara Café (Map p87; 42 St 178; mains US$2-5; 🕙 11am-midnight, until 2am weekends) A stylish little cafe near Norodom Blvd serving health shakes, vegetarian treats, Khmer food and international favourites. A good spot for late-night fixes as 40% of profits go to the Apsara Arts Association (p117).

our pick **Friends** (Map p87; ☎ 426748; www.friends-international.org; 215 St 13; dishes US$2-8; 🕙 11am-9pm) One of Phnom Penh's most loved restaurants, this place offers tasty tapas, heavenly smoothies and creative cocktails. With a prime location near the National Museum, this place is a must and offers former street children a helping hand into the hospitality industry.

Hagar (Map p87; ☎ 012 306075; www.hagarcambodia.com; 23 St 288; 🕙 7am-4pm) The lunch buffet is a tempting deal at US$4.50 and all proceeds go towards assisting destitute or abused women. The menu includes Asian and Western dishes from US$3 to US$12.

Lazy Gecko Café (Map p87; ☎ 017 912935; 23B St 93; mains US$1.50-4.50; 🕙 8am-11pm) Boasting 'homemade hummus just like when mum was dating that chap from Cyprus', this fun place serves international dishes and supports a local orphanage. Thursday is quiz night, while Saturday involves an orphanage visit with dinner and a performance by the children.

Le Lotus Blanc (Map p87; ☎ 995660; 152 St 51; mains US$6, set menu US$12; breakfast & lunch Mon-Fri) This swish new restaurant is a training centre for youths who previously survived by scouring the city dump. Run by French NGO, Pour un Sourire d'Enfant (For the Smile of a Child), it serves classy Western and Khmer cuisine. The original restaurant is still operating at the PSE compound in Stung Meanchey.

Le Rit's (Map p87; ☎ 213160; 71 St 240; mains US$3-5; 🕙 7am-5pm Mon-Sat) Recently relocated to St 240, the main menu includes Khmer and Thai dishes, and good value three-course lunches (US$6). Proceeds assist disadvantaged women to re-enter the workplace.

our pick **Romdeng** (Map p87; ☎ 092-219565; 74 St 174; mains US$4-7; 🕙 11am-10pm Mon-Sat) Also part of the Friends' extended family, the elegant Romdeng specialises in Cambodian country fare and offers a staggering choice of traditional Khmer recipes, including the legendary deep-fried spiders. It's located in a stunning French-era villa, with a swimming pool as the centrepiece of a lush garden.

Veijo Tonlé (Map p87; ☎ 012 847419; 237 St Sisowath Quay; mains US$3-6; 🕙 7am-late) A little restaurant on the breezy riverfront, the menu here includes pizzas, international favourites, Khmer cuisine and Thai tastes. Some proceeds go towards helping a local orphanage.

If the market stalls look a little raw, and street-surfing doesn't appeal, then consider the air-conditioned alternative in the shape of the **Sorya Shopping Centre Food Court** (Map p87; 4th fl, cnr Sts 63 & 154). Run on the coupon system like in Thailand, there are more than 20 outlets serving Khmer, Chinese, Thai, Vietnamese and more, plus desserts and fruit shakes. It's always full of locals and most dishes are just 4000r to 8000r. A few floors up is **Master Suki Soup** (7th fl; soup from US$5), which may be a Japanese concept but has a very Khmer touch and is a great way to try *soup chhnang dei*, with photos to help choose the ingredients. There are superb views over Psar Thmei from the top floor.

K'nyay (Map p87; ☎ 225225; 25K Soramarit Blvd; mains US$2-5; ☯ noon-9pm Tue-Fri, 7am-9pm Sat, closed Sun) A stylish little Cambodian restaurant that is hidden away from the main road in a leafy villa. The menu includes a generous selection of vegetarian and vegan options and original health shakes. Plus homemade ice cream such as ginger and honey.

Goldfish River Restaurant (Map p87; Sisowath Quay; mains US$2-8; ☯ 7am-10pm) Sitting on stilts over the Tonlé Sap, this restaurant may not be designed to impress, but the menu offers authentic Cambodian food with a generous breeze for free. Crab with black pepper, squid with fresh peppercorns; the selection is dizzying with more than 300 dishes available.

Seven Bright Restaurant (Map p87; ☎ 012 833555; St 13; mains US$2-8; ☯ 5.30am-10.30pm) This was Gerard Depardieu's hotel lobby in the movie *City of Ghosts*. The lunch buffet is a deal at just US$3, plus there is occasional live music. Sunrise opening makes it a good place for breakfast before an early bus ride.

Bopha Phnom Penh Restaurant (Map p87; ☎ 992800; Sisowath Quay; mains US$2-10; ☯ 6am-11pm) Right next door to Goldfish, this place *is* designed to impress, complete with Angkorian-style carvings, heavy furniture and an attractive riverside terrace. The menu includes Khmer, Asian and Western dishes, plus cheaper lunchtime sets are available.

Frizz Restaurant (Map p87; ☎ 220953; 67 St 240; mains US$3-7; ☯ 7am-10pm) True, the name doesn't sound that Khmer, but the aromatic Cambodian cuisine here is some of the most delicious in town, plus there are international offerings like steak and Guinness pie. The restaurant also operates cooking classes (p98).

Kravanh (Map p87; ☎ 012 792088; 112 Samdech Sothearos Blvd; mains US$3-8; ☯ 11.30am-10pm) A stylish new Khmer restaurant under the stewardship of a Franco-Khmer, the linen and decor set this place apart from its neighbours.

DINING OUT 'OVER THE BRIDGE'

The reconstruction of the Chruoy Changvar Bridge (Japanese Friendship Bridge) spanning the Tonlé Sap River created a restaurant boom on the river's east bank. There are dozens of restaurants lining the highway – from the decidedly downmarket to the obviously over-the-top – but most are interesting places for a very Cambodian night out. These are restaurants frequented by well-to-do Khmers, and on the weekend they are packed with literally thousands of people on a big night out. Most charge about US$3 to US$10 a dish (with around 300 dishes to choose from). Heading north, the restaurants start to appear about 1km from the bridge on the east bank. Many of the larger places include a resident band and the amps are often cranked up to 11 – remember to sit a fair distance from the stage.

Places come in and out of favour, but following are some of the consistently popular. All are signposted from the main road. A *moto* should cost about US$1 or so each way from the city centre.

- **Boeng Bopha Restaurant** – the food here is similar to elsewhere, but this is a popular place for a younger crowd out drinking.

- **Rum Chang Restaurant** – long one of the best places for authentic Khmer food, there is no band here and the location overlooking the Mekong is very breezy. Recommended by Luu Meng (p61).

- **Ta Oeu Restaurant** – this simple place is popular for its value-for-money food, which has a reputation as being authentic and tasty.

- **Tata Restaurant** – one of the newer breed of smart and sophisticated places, it hosts leading comedians at the weekend and is popular.

The menu includes traditional salads, scented soups and regional specialities.

Khmer Surin (Map p87; ☎ 363050; 9 St 57; mains US$3-8; ☺ 11am-10pm) Popular with tour groups thanks to the atmospheric ambience with floor cushions, flowering plants and antique furnishings, this restaurant serves reliable Cambodian and Thai food. Set over three levels, it is still possible to find a quiet corner.

ourpick Slek Chak (Map p87; ☎ 012 979199; 165D St 51; mains US$3-10; ☺ 11.30am-10.30pm) Owned by the legendary Preap Sovath, pretty much the Robbie Williams of Cambodia, this place doesn't look much from the street, but venture inside for a dining experience that includes a zesty frogs legs and quails eggs in a sugar palm and black pepper clay pot or a fish egg soup. The lunch buffet is just US$3.

Sugar Palm (Map p87; ☎ 220956; 19 St 240; mains US$4-9; ☺ 11.30am-late) A homely restaurant-bar on lively St 240, this delivers the traditional taste of Cambodia in cool, contemporary surrounds. Have a cocktail downstairs, then head up to the balcony for an intimate dinner.

ourpick Malis (Map p87; ☎ 221022; 136 Norodom Blvd; mains US$5-15; ☺ 6am-11pm) The leading Khmer restaurant in the capital, Malis is a chic place to see and be seen. The garden is the most atmospheric, but air-conditioned dining is available in the maze-like building. The original menu includes beef in bamboo strips, sand goby with ginger and traditional soups and salads. Popular for a boutique breakfast, as the menu is a good deal at US$1.50 to US$3.

It's Cambodia – of course there are more:
Khmer Borane Restaurant (Map p87; ☎ 012 290092; 389 Sisowath Quay; mains US$2-5; ☺ 11am-11pm) Traditional Khmer recipes in a riverfront setting near the Royal Palace.
Rorg Damrei (Map pp84-5; ☎ 017 236069; 41 St 310; mains US$2-5) Al fresco Cambodian dining in the heart of NGOsville, the food here is wholesome and good value.
Green Pepper (Map pp84-5; ☎ 017 417776; Samdech Sothearos Blvd; mains US$2.50-4) Hole-in-the-wall spot near the riverfront serving up great value Khmer and Thai dishes, plus has an inviting mezzanine with floor seating.
Kith Eng Restaurant (Map pp84-5; ☎ 012 853845; 336 St 169; mains US$3-5) Another celebrity-owned restaurant, this time under the stewardship of Tuol Sleng artist Vann Nath (see p95), with traditional Khmer food and an attached art gallery featuring his famous paintings.
Le Safran (Map pp84-5; ☎ 217646; 18 St 306; mains US$3-9) Sophisticated Cambodian-French restaurant with stylish decor and an original menu of classic Cambodian dishes and some fusion dishes with a French accent.

Thai

ourpick Boat Noodle Restaurant (Map p87; ☎ 012 200426; St 294; mains 3000r-10,000r; ☺ 10am-10pm) This old wooden house, in a leafy garden brimming with water features, offers some of the best-value Thai and Cambodian food in town. With tasty noodle soups for breakfast and special set lunches each day, it's worth a visit.

Baitong (Map p87; ☎ 092-500400; 7 St 360; mains US$2-5; ☺ 7am-11pm; ♿) Promoting itself as a Thai restaurant, it offers a range of Mekong flavours, including Khmer, Lao and Vietnamese. The prices are very reasonable and options include a buffet lunch for around US$3. It acts as a bit of a hub for the NGO community with a resource library and meeting rooms.

Chiang Mai Riverside (Map p87; ☎ 012 832369; 227 Sisowath Quay; mains US$2-5; ☺ 10am-10pm) One of the original riverfront restaurants, it's still going strong thanks to the taste of Thailand at an affordable price. The fish cakes are good, plus there are some authentic curries to spice up your life.

Lemongrass (Map p87; ☎ 211054; 14 St 130; mains US$4-8; ☺ 10am-10pm) A higher class Thai restaurant with a fair selection of Khmer classics, the prices are pretty reasonable given the look of the place. Plus a good vegetarian selection.

Vietnamese

VIP Minimart (Map p87; 156 St 51; pho US$2) An expanding chain of minimarts has won praise for its huge, steaming bowls of *pho bo* (Vietnamese beef noodle soup). It comes with a veritable jungle of herbs.

Pho Fortune (Map p87; ☎ 012 871753; 11 St 178; mains from US$2-4; ☺ 8am-9pm) Great location near the riverfront for good *pho*, the noodle soup that keeps Vietnam moving forward, plus a smattering of dishes from other regions of the world.

Magnolia (Map p87; ☎ 012 529977; 55 St 51; mains US$3-6; ☺ 6am-10pm) Set in a gracefully restored old house, this place offers an affordable lunchtime buffet, wafer-thin *ban xeo* (Vietnamese savoury pancakes) and an array of classics from Hanoi to Saigon.

Chinese

There are numerous Chinese restaurants around Phnom Penh, many offering an authentic taste of the Middle Kingdom.

There are several real-deal Chinese restaurants along St 136, opposite the bus station, with names like Peking and Shanghai. These are the perfect place for a budget meal before or after a long bus ride and most also do good dim sum.

Sam Doo Restaurant (Map p87; ☎ 218773; 56 Kampuchea Krom Blvd; mains US$2-10; ☯ 7am-2am) Many Chinese Khmers swear this has the best food in town. Choose from spicy morning glory, signature 'Sam Doo fried rice', *trey chamhoy* (steamed fish with soy sauce and ginger), and fresh seafood. It's open late and has delicious dim sum.

Man Han Lou Restaurant (Map pp84-5; ☎ 721966; 456 Monivong Blvd; mains US$5-10; ☯ 10am-11pm) Chinese, Khmer, Thai, Vietnamese, this restaurant covers all bases, but the real draw here is the microbrewery turning out beer in golden (lager), red (bitter), black (stout) and 'green' (not sure) shades.

Yi Sang (Map pp84-5; ☎ 220822; 128 Samdech Sothearos Blvd; mains US$5-20; ☯ 6.30am-10pm) Located in the Almond Hotel, this is all about contemporary Chinese cuisine with a kitchen overseen by Guangzhou natives. The menu includes live seafood, or at least recently alive, plus authentic dim sum.

Japanese

Ko Ko Ro (Map p87; ☎ 012 601095; 18 Sihanouk Blvd; dishes US$2-7; ☯ 11.30am-2pm & 5.30-9pm) This tiny little Japanese restaurant, aka Mr Sushi, has a big personality thanks to the friendly and attentive owner who will advise on selection. The walls are plastered with photos of his creations and the fish is very fresh.

our pick **Origami** (Map p87; ☎ 012 968095; 88 Samdech Sothearos Blvd; set menus US$8-30; ☯ 11.30am-2pm & 5.30-9.30pm) This elegant Japanese eatery takes the art of Japanese food to another level. Set menus include beautifully presented sushi, sashimi and tempura sets, plus affordable business lunches for those in a hurry. The *Kobe* set is a personal favourite.

Indian Subcontinent

Dosa Corner (Map p87; 5E St 51; mains US$2-4; ☯ 7.30am-10pm) Fans of Indian dosas will be pleased to discover this place does just what it says on the label, namely a generous variety of savoury pancakes from the south. Great value.

Chi Cha (Map p87; ☎ 366065; 27 St 110; set menus US$3; ☯ 7.30am-12.30am) Actually Bangladeshi, this established curry house offers some of the cheapest subcontinental selections in town. The thalis (set meals) are a bargain and the menu is 100% halal.

our pick **Saffron** (Map p87; ☎ 012 247832; 11 St 278; curries US$4-8; ☯ 11am-11pm) Home to some of the best curries in town, Saffron specialises in Pakistani, Afghani and Middle Eastern cuisine. The Lahori fish curry is *lahore na* (very good in Khmer) and it doubles as a wine bar by night.

Annam (Map p87; ☎ 726661; 1C St 282; mains US$4-8; ☯ 11.30am-2.30pm & 6-10.30pm) Attractive garden restaurant that offers excellent Indian recipes in refined surrounds, including Chettinad specialities and cheaper set lunches.

More spots for a curry fix:

Mount Everest (Map p87; ☎ 213821; 98 Sihanouk Blvd; curries US$2-5) One of the oldest curry houses in town, the menu includes popular Indian and Nepalese dishes, which are great value.

Sher-e-Punjab (Map p87; ☎ 992901; 16 St 130; mains US$2-10) One of the most reliable Indian restaurants in town; the tandoori dishes are particularly good.

French

Comme a la Maison (Map p87; ☎ 360801; 13 St 57; mains US$3-8; ☯ 6am-10.30pm) Just like at home, at least if you are lucky enough to live with a first-class French chef, this place offers succulent steaks and a tour of provincial France, plus Italian aplenty.

La Marmite (Map p87; ☎ 012 391746; 80 St 108; mains US$5-10; ☯ 11am-2.30pm & 6-10.30pm) It may not be the most traditional French name, but the menu at La Marmite is a traditional French bistro with classic Gallic flavours. Choose from daily specials such as scallops or go with the regular menu that includes tender tournedos and herb-infused lamb.

Eye of the Mekong (Map p87; ☎ 092-165469; 30 St 110; mains US$5-10; ☯ 7am-midnight) Hip French diner showcasing some striking photographs on the walls. The menu includes some superb cuts of beef, drizzled in a Kampot pepper sauce.

Topaz (Map pp84-5; ☎ 221622; 182 Norodom Blvd; dishes US$5-20; ☯ 11am-2pm & 6-11pm) One of Phnom Penh's first designer restaurants, Topaz is housed in an elegant villa with reflective pools and a walk-in wine cellar. The menu is classic Paris, including delicate Bourgogne snails drizzled in garlic and steak tartare for those with rare tastes.

our pick **Van's Restaurant** (Map p87; ☎ 722067; 5 St 13; dishes US$5-25; ☯ 11.30am-2.30pm & 5-10.30pm)

Located in one of the grandest buildings in the city, the former Banque Indochine, you can still see the old vault doors as you make your way to the refined dining room upstairs. Dishes are beautifully presented with a decorative flourish, and menu highlights include sea perch carpaccio, tender veal and Grand Marnier soufflé. Cheaper set lunches available.

La Residence (Map p87; ☎ 224582; 22 St 214; mains US$7-25; 🕑 lunch & dinner) Part of Princess Marie's family home has been converted into this classy contemporary restaurant. Pass through the immense wooden doors and enjoy fine French food, including a foie gras speciality menu and superb seafood, plus a great Café de Paris steak.

112 Restaurant (Map p87; ☎ 990880; 1A St 102; mains US$15-40; 🕑 11.30am-2.30pm & 6.30-10pm) One of the most salubrious French restaurants in town near Hotel Le Royal, it offers a great value US$10 buffet at lunchtime, accompanied by cheap free-flow drinks. Or indulge by night.

Italian

Happy Herb's Pizza (Map p87; ☎ 362349; 345 Sisowath Quay; pizzas US$4-8; 🕑 8am-11pm) No, happy doesn't mean it comes with free toppings, it means pizza *à la* ganja. The non-marijuana pizzas are also pretty good, but don't involve the free trip. Good place to sip a cheap beer as well.

our pick **Pop Café** (Map p87; ☎ 012 562892; 371 Sisowath Quay; 🕑 11am-3pm & 6-10pm; pizzas US$4-10) Owner Giorgio welcomes diners as if you are coming to his own home for dinner, making this a popular spot for authentic Italian cooking. Thin-crust pizzas, homemade pastas and tasty gnocchi, it could be Roma.

Le Duo (Map p87; 17 St 228; mains US$5-15; 🕑 lunch & dinner) A classy Italian restaurant set in a garden villa, with fresh pasta and authentic pizzas. Try ravioli with ceps, thin-crust pizzas, or delicious meats and fish.

Luna D'Autunno (Map p87; ☎ 220895; 6C St 29; mains US$5-15; 🕑 11am-2.30pm & 5.30-10.30pm) This elegant garden restaurant has an open kitchen firing up delicious pizzas from US$6 to US$10. Inside is a sophisticated restaurant with a walk-in wine cellar with bottles from the homeland. The menu includes some fresh seafood and traditional Italian favourites.

International
RIVERFRONT AREA

The number of international restaurants in Phnom Penh is ever-expanding and between them they offer a tantalising array of tastes. Many of the most popular are found along the riverfront.

Kandal House (Map p87; ☎ 012 525612; 239B Sisowath Quay; mains US$2-5) Blink and you'll miss it, this riverfront restaurant turns out some delicious homemade pastas, salads and soups, plus a smattering of Asian favourites. Anchor draught available in pints.

Cantina (Map p87; ☎ 222502; 347 Sisowath Quay; mains US$3-6; 🕑 3-11pm, closed Sat) This is the spot for tostadas, fajitas and other Mexican favourites, all freshly prepared. It's also a 'refuge for media analysts, lords of poverty and screen icons' with professional margaritas and tequilas.

Pacharan (Map p87; ☎ 224394; 389 Sisowath Quay; dishes US$3-15; 🕑 11am-midnight) A Spanish taverna and tapas restaurant, it occupies one of the finest French-era buildings in town. Tapas bites include a vegetarian selection and plenty of seafood, plus there is the popular paella. Spanish wines feature strongly.

our pick **Fish** (Map p87; ☎ 218785; 2 St 108; mains US$4-12; 🕑 10am-1am; 🛗) No prizes for guessing the speciality of the house. This new restaurant serves some of the best fish and chips in town, as well as sophisticated seafood creations, such as the superb antipasti and a bouillabaisse. Stylish and fun.

Riverside Bistro (Map p87; ☎ 213898; 273 Sisowath Quay; mains US$4-15; 🕑 7am-midnight; 🖳 🛗) This popular corner restaurant has a menu with Cambodian favourites like grilled pork on lemon-grass skewers and a strong showing from Mitteleuropa. It doubles as a popular bar later in the night and there are two pool tables here, plus regular live music.

our pick **Metro** (Map p87; ☎ 222275; cnr Sisowath Quay & St 148; mains US$4-18; 🛗) Metro is one of the leading spots on the riverfront strip thanks to a striking design and an adventurous menu. Small plates are for sampling and include rare-pepper tuna and tequila black-pepper prawns, while large plates include twice-cooked duck with lychee. It also pulls a well-heeled Khmer crowd.

Foreign Correspondents' Club (FCC; Map p87; ☎ 724014; 363 Sisowath Quay; mains US$5-15; 🕑 7am-midnight; 🛗) One of those must-see places in Cambodia, almost everyone swings by for a drink during a visit to Phnom Penh. Set in a colonial-era gem with high ceilings, the 'F', as expats call it, has voluptuous views over the Tonlé Sap River and the National Museum. Hit the happy hour between 5pm and 7pm and linger over dinner to soak up the atmosphere, as the menu includes a tempting selection of Asian and international dishes.

Riverhouse Asian Bistro (Map p87; ☎ 212302; cnr St 110 & Sisowath Quay; mains US$5-15; ⏰ 10.30am-11pm; &) Remodelled as a contemporary dining space, the new menu here veers towards Asian fusion, with light bites and hearty mains, including a superb value beef tournedos or a tasty mix of skewers. It gets very busy at the weekend when diners warm up for a night at the upstairs lounge (p116).

More riverfront area options:

La Croisette (Map p87; ☎ 220554; 241 Sisowath Quay; mains US$3-8; ⏰ 7am-late; &) The stylish Croisette is a popular riverfront spot with a good range of Western and Asian favourites.

Mekong River Restaurant (Map p87; ☎ 991150; cnr St 118 & Sisowath Quay; mains US$3-9; ⏰ 10am-11pm) Good value set menus with a generous selection of Asian and international choices, plus tapas.

AROUND THE CITY

It's worth steering a course away from the river for some more great places.

ourpick Boddhi Tree Umma Restaurant (Map p87; ☎ 211397; 50 St 113; mains US$2-7; ⏰ 7am-9pm; &) This is heaven compared to the hell of Tuol Sleng across the road. The lush garden is the perfect place to seek solace and silence after the torture museum. The impressive menu includes fusion flavours, Asian dishes, sandwiches and salads, innovative shakes and tempting desserts.

Del Gusto Café (Map p87; ☎ 211396; 43 St 95; mains US$3-7; ⏰ 7am-9pm; &) This elegant art-deco-style villa is buried beneath a tumble of tropical plants. The menu here is predominantly Mediterranean, with breads and dips, salads and wraps, all consumed to a soundtrack of jazz and classical music. Rooms are also available.

Nature & Sea (Map p87; ☎ 017 953810; 78 St 51; mains US$3-8; ⏰ 8am-10pm) Perched on a rooftop above the lively 278 strip and with views over Wat Langka, Nature & Sea has excellent fruit shakes including passionfruit and honey blends. The specialities are savoury whole-wheat pancakes and fresh fish in English, Australian, French or Italian styles.

Tamarind Bar (Map p87; ☎ 012 830139; 31 St 240; mains US$3-9; ⏰ 10am-midnight) Very Moorish you might say, as this place brings the magic of the Maghreb to Phnom Penh with some classic Moroccan tajines and a small selection of tapas, plus some French influences. Downstairs is an inviting bar with high ceilings, while the rooftop offers al-fresco dining.

Ocean (Map p87; ☎ 017 766690; 11 St 288; mains US$4-15; ⏰ noon-2pm & 6-10pm, closed Sun lunch) Another seafood speciality restaurant, Ocean's menu is predominantly Mediterranean and includes a tempting selection of fish and crustaceans.

Le Wok (Map p87; ☎ 092-821857; 33 St 178; mains US$5-15; ⏰ 9am-11pm) One of the better fusion restaurants in town, the name says it all – French flair with an Asian flavour. Choose from a tempting menu of regular meals, plus some daring specials like snail cassoulet or scallop salad.

Tell Restaurant (Map p87; ☎ 430650; 13 St 90; mains US$5-15; ⏰ 11.30am-2pm & 5-11pm) With fondues and *raclettes* (melted cheese with vegetables), this restaurant brings a Swiss touch to the Wat Phnom area. Portions are generous and dishes include a selection of tenderised meats. There's also a remodelled garden and German beers.

More international bites:

Alley Cat Café (Map p87; ☎ 012 306845; near cnr Sts 178 & 19; mains US$2-5; ⏰ 11am-11pm) Friendly little restaurant-bar turning out tasty tacos, burritos and enchiladas. Large portions, plus plenty of booze at the bar.

Le Cedre (Map p87; ☎ 997965; St 360; mains US$3-10; ⏰ 10am-2pm & 5pm-late, closed Sun) Phnom Penh's original Lebanese restaurant boasts an atmospheric setting and a chef from Beirut, plus superb set lunches.

La Patate 2 (Map p87; ☎ 012 840522; 128D Samdech Sothearos Blvd; mains US$4-12; ⏰ 10am-11pm) New in 2009, this classy Belgian restaurant turns out some of the best *frites* in town, as well as filling sandwiches.

Fast Food & Bar Food

The first fast-food chain only recently arrived in Phnom Penh in the shape of KFC. A few years ago, that would have meant Khmer Fried Chicken, but these days it's the Kentucky variety. Among the local outlets, **Lucky Burger** (Map p87; 160 Sihanouk Blvd; ⏰ 7am-9pm) is one of the most established. BB World in Sorya Shopping Centre (Map p87) also has a children's playground for those seeking a diversion over lunch. Don't expect McDonalds, but at least the ingredients are fresh. The Pizza Company is the most popular fast food pizza place, with branches all over the city, including one in the aforementioned Sorya Shopping Centre.

Many of the recommended bars (p114) have great food, including Green Vespa, Rising Sun, Gym Bar, Talkin to a Stranger and Equinox.

One place that has particularly excellent bar food and could equally be at home under Eating or Drinking is **Freebird** (Map p87; ☎ 224712; 69 St 240; mains US$3-7; ⏰ 7am–midnight; &), an American-style bar-diner with a great selection of burgers, salads, wraps and Tex-Mex.

Fatboy Sub & Sandwich Shop (Map p87; ☎ 991430; 124 St 130; subs from US$3.75; ⏰ 11am-11pm) Check out this new place for the best in huge subs, including foot-long specials like beef tenderloin or Cajun chicken.

Cafes

Le Jardin (Map p87; ☎ 011 723399; 16 St 360; mains US$2-5; ⏰ 7am-6pm, closed Mon) Taking full advantage of the garden, this is a family-oriented cafe with a giant sandpit, a playhouse and toys. Snacks and salads for adults, pastas and titbits for kids, and everyone loves the ice cream.

our pick Shop (Map p87; ☎ 986964; 39 St 240; mains US$2-5; ⏰ 7am-7pm) If you are craving the local deli back home, then make for this haven, which has a changing selection of sandwich and salad specials. The pastries and cakes are delectable and worth the indulgence. Almost next door and under the same management is the Chocolate Shop (Map p87; 35 St 240), a highly dangerous spot for recovering chocoholics open from 8am to 8pm.

El Mundo (Map p87; ☎ 012 520775; 219 Sisowath Quay; mains US$2-6; ⏰ 6.30am-10.30pm; &) A mellow riverfront establishment, which grinds up great coffee. The menu includes a range of global food and pastries, plus there's an upstairs lounge for movies. Newly opened next door is Chill (Map p87), the capital's first dedicated ice-cream lounge, with original homemade flavours. It is open from 8am until midnight.

Java Café (Map p87; ☎ 987420; 56 Sihanouk Blvd; mains US$2-7; ⏰ 7am-10pm; &) One of the most popular cafe-restaurants in the city, thanks to a breezy balcony and air-conditioned interior. The creative menu includes crisp salads, homemade sandwiches, towering burgers and daily specials, plus health drinks, fruit shakes and coffee from several continents. It has recently expanded downstairs with some comfy couches and more great cakes.

Fresco (Map p87; ☎ 224891; cnr Sts 51 & 306; mains US$3-10; ⏰ 7am-7pm; 🛜 &) A chic cafe in the popular NGO district, there is an air-con interior, a breezy rooftop, plus a kiddies' play area. Sandwiches and salads dominate, plus some good value lunch combos. Wi-fi is free from 3pm to 5pm. There is a second smaller branch beneath FCC (p111).

Garden Center Café (Map p87; ☎ 997850; 60 St 108; mains US$4-15; ⏰ 7am-10pm, closed Mon) Relocated to the Wat Phnom area, there is less garden, but it is more central than before. It remains an expat favourite thanks to the big breakfasts and huge portions of home-cooked food. Most mains come with a side salad, plus there are Sunday roasts and tasty desserts.

Cafe culture doesn't stop there:

Café Sentiment (Map p87; ☎ 221922; 64 Monivong Blvd; mains US$1-4; ⏰ 7am-11pm; &) Popular cafe

---

RUSSIAN MARKET RETREATS

There is nothing better than an ice coffee or fresh fruit shake after surviving the scrum that is the Russian Market. Make for the following boltholes after a successful shopping trip. All are in spitting distance of the market, but don't try it, as you won't be popular with the locals.

Coffee Korner (Map pp84-5; ☎ 012 867667; 174 St 155; mains US$2-6; ⏰ 7am-10pm) Lively corner cafe with a huge menu of international and Asian food, good for people-watching.

Jars of Clay (Map pp84-5; ☎ 300281; 39 St 155; cakes US$1, mains US$2-4; ⏰ 9am-5.30pm Tue-Sat) Thirst-quenching drinks, light bites and home-baked cakes, plus air-conditioning on a hot day.

Melting Pot (Map pp84-5; ☎ 092-453247; 168A St 155; mains US$2-5; ⏰ 8am-5.30pm Tue-Sat) French-influenced cafe with a healthy range of salads and savoury crepes, plus some tempting desserts.

Sisters Café (Map pp84-5; ☎ 092-918244; 98 St 450; cakes US$1, mains US$2-4; ⏰ 6.30am-6pm) Tiny little place that punches above its weight with excellent homemade cakes, including a zesty lemon meringue pie.

set over several floors on a busy Monivong junction. Great value pastries, snacks and coffees.

Living Room (Map p87; ☎ 726139; 9 St 306; mains US$2-5; 7am-6.30pm Tue-Thu, to 9.30pm Fri-Sun, closed Mon;) Family-friendly place with garden and playroom, plus a healthy menu and organic coffee. Free wi-fi.

Corner 33 (Map p87; ☎ 092-998850; 33 Samdech Sothearos Blvd; mains US$2-6; 7am-late;) A smart cafe near the riverfront, the classy interior makes for a relaxing place. Cakes, coffees and shakes, free wi-fi, plus free internet for those without a laptop.

Penny Lane (Map p87; ☎ 218970; 23A St 111; mains US$2-7; 6.30am-11pm, to 3.30pm Sun;) Popular new cafe in a backpacker-friendly part of town. Fresh coffee, Italian flavours and free wi-fi.

Backpacker Cafes

There are few backpacker cafes of the sort so popular in nearby Vietnam, unless you include all the restaurants in the more popular guesthouses. Or try the Lazy Gecko Café (p107), which has a great vibe.

Mama Restaurant (Map p87; 10C St 111; mains US$1.50-4; 7am-9.30pm) This long-running little place turns out cheap specials, including a succulent beef ragout. The menu includes a bit of Khmer, Thai, French and even African.

Bites (Map p87; 240 St 107; mains US$1.50-4; 7.30am-10pm) Mixing Malaysian, Padang and some international options, this is a clean little restaurant in a popular budget area of town.

Oh My Buddha! (Map p87; St 93; mains US$1.50-4) Located in the heart of the backpacker lakeside area, this is a welcoming place with cheap food and big breakfasts.

Anjali (Map p87; ☎ 012 457901; 273 Sisowath Quay; mains US$2.50-6) A new spot on the riverfront. Calling it a backpacker cafe might be misleading, but the prices are more than reasonable for this part of town, with good pub grub and some Asian highlights.

Bakeries

Kiwi Bakery (Map p87; ☎ 215784; Sisowath Quay) The Kiwi Bakery offers fresh bread, cakes and pies. Owned by a Khmer family who ran a bakery in New Zealand, it has everything from Eccles cakes to éclairs.

Among the aforementioned restaurants and cafes, the Shop (p113) has a great selection of breads and pastries, as does Fresco (p113).

Most of the city's finest hotels also operate bakery outlets with extravagant pastries, but prices are higher than in cafes or restaurants. Drop in after 6pm when they offer a 50% discount, and gorge away. Hotel Cambodiana (p106) has the best selection. The larger supermarkets also stock their own range of breads and cakes, freshly baked on the premises.

Self-Catering

Self-catering is easy enough in Phnom Penh, but it often works out considerably more expensive than eating like the locals. The markets are well stocked with fruit and vegetables, fish and meat, all at reasonable prices if you are prepared to bargain a little. Local baguettes are widely available, and start from 500r. Phnom Penh's supermarkets are remarkably well stocked. Imported items are plentiful, including German meats, French cheeses and American snacks.

Popular supermarkets:

Bayon Market (Map p87; 33 St 114) Recently relocated to a bigger premises, Bayon Market has a good range of products, including some nice surprises that don't turn up elsewhere in the city.

Lucky Supermarket (Map p87; 160 Sihanouk Blvd; 7am-9pm) This is the biggest supermarket chain in town with a serious range of products, including one of the best delicatessens for meats and cheeses in town.

Pencil Supermarket (Map p87; St 214; 7am-9pm) This popular Thai-run place is one of the largest supermarkets in town and is well stocked.

Thai Huot Supermarket (Map p87; 103 Monivong Blvd) This is the place for French travellers who are missing home, as it stocks many French products, including Bonne Maman jam and creamy chocolate.

Many petrol stations include shops with a good selection of imported products; most Starmart shops at Caltex petrol stations on major junctions in the city are now open until midnight or later. There has also been an explosion of minimarts in recent years and many of these are now open 24 hours.

DRINKING

Phnom Penh has some great bars and it's definitely worth at least one big night on the town. Many popular venues are clustered along the riverfront, but one or two of the best are tucked away in the backstreets. Most bars are open until midnight and beyond.

Should it survive the developer's wrecking ball, the lakeside is a great place for sunset drinks. Laze in a hammock and watch the sun burn red – this is a must. Two of the more popular backpacker bars up here are

---

FLOWER POWER

Anyone who spends a night or two on the town in Phnom Penh will soon be familiar with young girls and boys hovering around popular bars and restaurants to sell decorative flowers. The kids are incredibly sweet and most people succumb to their charms and buy a flower or two. All these late nights for young children might not be so bad if they were benefiting from their hard-earned cash, but usually they are not. Look down the road and there will be a *moto* driver with an ice bucket full of these flowers waiting to ferry the children to another popular spot. Yet again, the charms of children are exploited for the benefit of adults who should know better but are too poor to worry about it. Think twice before buying from them, as the child probably won't reap the reward.

---

the Magic Sponge and the Drunken Frog, but neither is on the water.

Keep an eye out for happy hours around town as these include two-for-one offers and the like that can save quite a bit of cash. The happy hours at FCC (p111) from 5pm to 7pm are particularly popular thanks to superb views over the riverfront and a welcoming breeze.

Several of the leading hotels have affordable happy hours that are worth the diversion. **Elephant Bar** (Map p87; St 92; ☾ 2pm-midnight) has been drawing journalists, politicos, and the rich and famous for 80 years. This sophisticated spot at Hotel Le Royal offers half-price happy hours between 4pm and 8pm, plus there are accompanying snacks and a pool table. Or head up to the rooftop of **Quay** (Map p87; 277 Sisowath Quay; ☾ 7am-11pm) for big views, cooling breezes and happy hours (half price) from 4pm to 8pm. The cocktail list here is arguably the most creative in town, including zesty infusions like ginger and lemon grass.

Talkin to a Stranger (Map p87; ☎ 012 798530; 21B St 294; ☾ 5pm-late, closed Sat) An enduringly popular garden bar, the congenial hosts have earned the place a loyal following with their killer cocktails and dinner specials. Regular events include quiz nights and live bands.

Green Vespa (Map p87; 95 Sisowath Quay; ☾ 6.30am-late) A favourite watering hole for local expats, the Vespa has a huge drinks collections, including some serious single malts. It's become a dining destination in its own right thanks to its original hearty pub fare and great selection of sophisticated specials.

Chinese House (Map p87; Sisowath Quay; ☾ 11.30am-late) Located in one of the most atmospheric colonial-era properties in the city, there is an art gallery below and a refined bar above that hosts regular bands. Happy hours run from 4pm to 8pm daily and they serve up monster mojitos, as well as tasty Chinese bites.

Brauhaus (Map p87; 34 St 130; ☾ 11am-midnight) This German bar, pork knuckles and all, is a cosy place boasting the largest beer selection in Phnom Penh, including fancy flavours from Belgium and Germany and cheaper local brews. Live music most nights.

Flavour (Map p87; 21B St 278; ☾ 7am-late) Located on the corner of the 'Golden Mile', this place was always destined to be popular and is a darling of the NGO crowd, with cheap beer on tap, cocktails and a menu that travels the world.

Gym Bar (Map p87; 42 St 178; ☾ 11am-late) The only workout going on here is raising glasses, as this is the number one sports bar in town. You won't find a better selection of big – no, make that giant – screens in this part of the world. Cold beer, pub grub and a rowdy crowd for the big ball games.

Pickled Parrot (Map p87; 4 St 104; ☾ 24hr) One of the few bars in town where you can wash up any time of the day and find a fellow drinker supping a beer, this is a friendly air-con spot with big screens, a pool table and cheap drinks. Not a hostess bar, unlike many others in this strip.

Rubies (Map p87; cnr Sts 240 & 19; ☾ 5.30pm-late, closed Mon) If you prefer the grape to the grain, then make for this small wine bar with a big personality. The bar is lined with wood and spills out onto the pavement, while the lengthy wine list includes the best of the new-world wines.

Elsewhere Bar (Map p87; 2 St 278; ☾ 10am-late, closed Tue) It recently moved elsewhere, but the new location is right in the heart of the action on St 278. Ambient vibes, a great drinks menu, and two plunge pools for punters, it's sedate by day but sexy by night. Hit the happy hours from 4pm to 8pm and forget your worries over an 'amnesia' cocktail.

Gasolina (Map pp84-5; 56-58 St 57; ☾ 6pm-late, closed Mon) This stylish garden bar specialises in the sensual sounds of South America and even offers salsa lessons (Tuesday and Thursday nights). Rum punches, cheap beers and a tasty bar menu round things off. Check out the weekend brunches.

Salt Lounge (Map p87; 217 St 136; ⊙ 6pm-late) Sleek, modern and minimalist, this cool cocktail bar is one of the most gay-friendly in town. The original interior draws a mixed crowd, making for a great spot.

Fly Lounge (Map p87; 21 St 148; ⊙ 5pm-2am) A newish bar that is turning heads. Enter the cocktail lounge, chill out amid cushions and drapes in the middle and then take a swim in the indoor pool, part of the small nightclub out back.

Riverhouse Lounge (Map p87; cnr St 110 & Sisowath Quay; ⊙ 4pm-2am) Almost a club as much as a pub, this atmospheric lounge bar has DJs and live music through the week. It's chic and cool, adding up to the place where the hip young Khmers hang out.

Heart of Darkness (Map p87; 26 St 51; ⊙ 8pm-late) More like the Heart of Business these days, it's evolved into a nightclub more than a bar, but remains a place to see and be seen thanks to the alluring Angkorian theme.

Other admired establishments with liquid menus:

Blue Chilli (Map p87; 36 St 178; ⊙ 6pm-late) Another leading gay bar that draws all-comers; the original interior design includes tropical aquariums and some quiet corners.

Chiva's Shack (Map p87; 42C St 130) Washed up from the shores of Sihanoukville, this bar has the cheapest draught beer in town at US$0.50 a pop.

Dodo Rhum House (Map p87; 42C St 178; ⊙ 5pm-late) Specialising in homemade flavoured rums, this friendly bar also offers excellent fish dishes.

Equinox Bar (Map p87; ☎ 012 586139; 3A St 278) Popular place with a welcoming outdoor bar downstairs, plus a pool table and an intimate lounge upstairs. Cheap drinks, good food and happy hours from 5pm to 8pm.

Howie's Bar (Map p87; 32 St 51; ⊙ 7pm-6am) Friendly and fun place that is the perfect spillover when the Heart of Darkness is packed.

Pink Elephant (Map p87; 343 Sisowath Quay; ⊙ 11am-midnight) A long-running riverfront bar, it merges into neighbouring Happy Herb's Pizza (p111).

Rising Sun (Map p87; 20 St 178; ⊙ 7am-11pm) English pub meets backpacker bar with affordable drinks and top pub grub, including slap-up breakfasts.

Rory's Pub (Map p87; 33 St 178; ⊙ 7am-midnight, later at weekends) A very popular Irish pub in an inviting central location.

Zeppelin Café (Map p87; St 51; ⊙ 4pm-late) Who says vinyl is dead? It lives on here in the Cambodian capital, thanks to the owner of this old-school rock bar manning the turntables every night.

ENTERTAINMENT

For news on what's happening here while you are in town, grab a copy of *AsiaLife Phnom Penh*, or check the Friday issue of the *Phnom Penh Post*, which includes the *7 Days* magazine supplement.

Nightclubs

There aren't many out-and-out nightclubs in Phnom Penh and the few that there are tend to be playgrounds of the privileged, attracting children of the country's political elite who aren't always the best-behaved people to hang out with. The volume is normally cranked up to 11 and drinks are pretty expensive. Most places open around 7pm, but don't expect a crowd until well after 10pm. Among the many bars listed earlier, the best dance spots are Heart of Darkness (left) on any night of the week or the classy Riverhouse Lounge (left) on weekends.

The latest spot to open in Phnom Penh is **Club White** (Map pp84-5; 305C Mao Tse Toung Blvd; admission depends on event; ⊙ 8pm-late), which is the closest thing to a full-on nightclub in London or New York. Guest DJs regularly fly in from around the region and there are plenty of hip-hop or house nights.

Other clubbing options where you can see Cambodians at play:

Casa (Map p87; St 47; admission depends on event; ⊙ until late) Casa has guest DJs, themed nights and local celebs.

Manhattan Club (Map p87; St 84; admission free; ⊙ until daylight) Cambodia's longest running full-on club with banging techno and a big crowd.

Rock (Map pp84-5; Monivong Blvd; admission depends on event; ⊙ until late) Looks like a gigantic Home Depot, but Khmers go crazy for the place, complete with karaoke rooms and all.

Spark (Map pp84-5; Mao Tse Toung Blvd; admission depends on event; ⊙ until late) Owned by the daughter of Prime Minister Hun Sen, security should be tight.

Cinemas

There has been a renaissance of the cinema scene in Phnom Penh, following an appeal for the reopening of certain historic cinemas by King Sihanouk in 2001. There are almost no English-language films on offer, just a steady diet of low-budget Khmer films about zombies, vampires and ghosts.

Many lakeside guesthouses show movies every night, particularly those with a Cambodian connection such as the heartwrenching *The Killing Fields*.

The Mekong River Restaurant (p112) screens two original films in English, one covering the Khmer Rouge and the other on the subject of land mines. Showings are hourly from 11am to 9pm and cost US$3.

Meta House (Map p87; www.meta-house.com; 6 St 264; 🕙 6pm-midnight, closed Mon) is a night gallery that has a great program of films, documentaries and shorts about Cambodia (usually with English subtitles), including presentations by some of those involved.

The French Cultural Centre (p86) has frequent movie screenings in French during the week, usually kicking off at 6.30pm. Check at the centre, where a monthly program is available.

Classical Dance & Arts

Apsara Arts Association (Map pp84-5; ☎ 990621; www. apsara-art.org; 71 St 598) Alternate performances of classical dance and folk dance (US$5) are held every Saturday at 7.30pm. Visitors are also welcome from 7.30am to 10.30am and from 2pm to 5pm Monday to Saturday to watch the students in training (donations accepted). However, it is important to remember that this is a training school – noise and flash photography should be kept to a minimum.

Sovanna Phum Arts Association (Map pp84-5; ☎ 987564; www.shadow-puppets.org; 4 St 99) Impressive traditional shadow puppet performances and classical dance shows are held here at 7.30pm on Saturday nights. Tickets are usually US$5/3 per adult/child. Classes are available here in the art of shadow puppetry, puppet making, classical and folk dance, and traditional Khmer musical instruments.

Check the latest information on performances at the **Chatomuk Theatre** (Map p87; Sisowath Quay), just north of the Hotel Cambodiana. Officially, it has been turned into a government conference centre, but it regularly plays host to cultural performances.

Live Music

Live music used to be in short supply in Phnom Penh compared with the bigger Asian capitals, but things are finally starting to move as bands make a diversion to visit this cool little capital. FCC (p111) is hosting more live bands these days, either in the main bar or on the rooftop. Riverhouse Lounge (opposite) and Club White (opposite) have hosted some pretty big DJs in recent times, including Cash Money in 2009.

Memphis Pub (Map p87; 3 St 118; 🕙 5pm-1am) It's not closed, it just has soundproof doors. This is the leading live-music venue in Phnom Penh, with live rock 'n' roll from Tuesday to Saturday, including a Wednesday jam session.

Cavern (Map pp84-5; 19 St 104; 🕙 11.30am-2am) Bang in the middle of infamous St 104, this place hosts regular live music on Fridays and plays decent rock anthems at other times.

Art Café (Map p87; www.artcafe-phnom-penh.com; 84 St 108; 🕙 11am-11pm) This cultured cafe and art space, offering German and Central European fare, promotes live music and plays host to blues, classical and traditional Khmer musicians on Friday and Saturday nights. See the website for performances.

Several of the larger hotels have lobby bands from the Philippines, including the Hotel Cambodiana (p106), but it can be more muzak than music.

SHOPPING

There is some great shopping to be had in Phnom Penh, but don't forget to bargain in the markets or you'll have your 'head shaved', local-speak for being ripped off. Most markets are open from around 6.30am to 5.30pm. Some shops keep shorter hours by opening later, while tourist-oriented stores often stay open into the evening.

As well as the markets, there are now some shopping malls in Phnom Penh. While these may not be as glamorous as the likes of the Siam Paragon in Bangkok, they are good places to browse thanks to the air-conditioning. **Sorya Shopping Centre** (Map p87; cnr Sts 63 & 154) is currently pick of the crop with a good range of shops and superb views over the more traditional Psar Thmei.

Art Galleries

There are plenty of shops selling locally produced paintings along St 178, opposite the National Museum. It used to be a pretty sorry selection of the amateurish Angkorian paintings seen all over the country, but now with a new generation of artists coming up, the selection is much stronger. It is necessary to bargain. There are also lots of reproduction busts of famous Angkorian sculptures available along this stretch – great for the mantelpiece back home.

Many of the leading hotels and restaurants dedicate some space to art or photographic exhibitions. There are several galleries and art spaces of note to seek out around the city:

Art Café (Map p87; 84 St 108; 🕙 11am-11pm) Cafe and gallery with changing exhibitions of local and international artists.

Asasax Art Gallery (Map p87; 192 St 178; 🕙 9am-8pm) High-end gallery featuring the striking work of artist Asasax.

Java Café (Map p87; 56 Sihanouk Blvd; 🕙 7am-10pm) Strong supporter of the art scene in Cambodia with challenging exhibitions.

Meta House (Map p87; www.meta-house.com; 6 St 264; 🕙 2pm-midnight, closed Mon) Contemporary art space

---

SHOPPING TO HELP CAMBODIA

There are a host of tasteful shops selling handicrafts and textiles to raise money for projects to assist disadvantaged Cambodians. These are a good place to spend some dollars, as it helps to put a little bit back into the country.

Aw-kun Shop (Map p87; ☎ 990250; 19D St 172; 🕙 8.30am-9.30pm) Not-for-profit shop selling a range of fair-trade handicrafts and knick-knacks.

Cambodian Handicraft Association (Map p87; ☎ 012 913861; 54 St 113; 🕙 8am-6pm) This well-stocked showroom and workshop sells fine handmade clothing, scarves, toys, bags and photo albums.

Colours of Cambodia (Map p87; ☎ 217974; 373 Sisowath Quay; 🕙 9am-6pm) Tucked away underneath FCC, this is a popular fair-trade gift shop supporting NGO craft projects. Lines include silk, woodcarvings, T-shirts and jewellery.

Friends & Stuff (Map p87; ☎ 426748; 215 St 13; 🕙 11am-9pm Mon-Sat) The closest thing to a charity shop or thrift store in Phnom Penh, with a good range of new and secondhand products sold to generate money to help street children.

Mekong Blue (Map p87; ☎ 012 609730; www.mekongblue.com; 9 St 130; 🕙 9am-6pm) Phnom Penh boutique for Stung Treng's best known silk cooperative to empower women, producing beautiful scarves and shawls.

Mekong Quilts (Map p87; ☎ 219607; www.mekong-quilts.com; 49 St 240; 🕙 9am-7pm) The place to come for delightful handmade quilts and throws, helping women in remote rural villages.

NCDP Handicrafts (Map p87; ☎ 213734; 3 Norodom Blvd; 🕙 8am-6pm) This shop was set up by the National Centre for Disabled Persons (NCDP). The collection includes exquisite silk scarves, throws, bags and cushions. Other items include *kramas* (scarves), shirts, wallets and purses, notebooks and greeting cards.

Nyemo Main store (Map p87; ☎ 213160; www.nyemo.com; 71 St 240; 🕙 7.30am-4.30pm); Outlet store (Map pp84-5; Psar Tuol Tom Pong) Helping disadvantaged women return to work, Nyemo's focus is on quality silk. It has a convenient outlet in Psar Tuol Tom Pong.

Rajana Main store (Map pp84-5; ☎ 364795; 170 St 450; 🕙 8am-6pm); Market store (Map pp84-5; Psar Tuol Tom Pong) There are two convenient branches of Rajana, both aimed at promoting fair wages and training. They have a beautiful selection of cards, some quirky metalware products, quality jewellery, bamboo crafts and a range of condiments from Cambodia.

Sobbhana (Map p87; ☎ 219455; www.sobbhana.org; 23 St 144; 🕙 9am-noon & 2.30-6pm) Established by Princess Marie, the Sobbhana Foundation is a not-for-profit organisation training women in traditional weaving. Beautiful silks in a stylish boutique.

Tabitha (Map p87; ☎ 721038; www.tabitha.ca; St 51; 🕙 7am-6pm) This is another NGO shop with a good collection of silk bags, tableware, bedroom decorations and children's toys. Proceeds go towards rural community development, such as well drilling.

Villageworks (Map p87; ☎ 215732; 118 St 113; 🕙 8am-5pm) Opposite Tuol Sleng Museum, this shop has the inevitable silk, as well as some delightful handmade cards and coconut-shell utensils.

Wat Than Artisans (Map pp84-5; ☎ 216321; 180 Norodom Blvd; 🕙 8am-5pm) Located in the grounds of Wat Than, this handicrafts shop is similar to NCDP, with an emphasis on products made from Khmer silk. Proceeds go to help land-mine and polio victims.

and night gallery with local exhibitions, international collections and photography.

Reyum (Map p87; ☎ 217149; www.reyum.org; 47 St 178) If you happen to be browsing St 178, drop in on Reyum, a nonprofit institute of arts and culture that hosts regular exhibitions on all aspects of Cambodian culture.

Designer Boutiques

There are several boutiques specialising in silk furnishings and stylish clothing, as well as glam accessories. Many are conveniently located on St 240, Cambodia's answer to London's King's Rd.

Ambre (Map p87; ☎ 217935; 37 St 178) Leading Cambodian fashion designer Romyda Keth has turned this striking French-era mansion into an ideal showcase for her stunning silk collection.

Bliss Boutique (Map p87; ☎ 215754; 29 St 240) Attractive home decoration and interior design in silk and textiles, plus some casual clothing.

Couleurs d'Asie (Map p87; ☎ 221075; 33 St 240) Specialising in sumptuous silks for the home, this is the place for hangings, bedspreads and throws.

Jasmine (Map p87; ☎ 223103; 73 St 240) Popular boutique specialising in elegant evening wear and sartorial silk; there are some bold creations here.

Kambuja (Map p87; ☎ 986209; 165 St 110) Blending the best of Cambodian materials with innovative international designs, the Cambodian and American designers have made a name for themselves.

Subtyl (Map p87; ☎ 992710; 43 St 240) French-run boutique offering stylish accessories and clothes, plus the new Chilli Kids line for hip youngsters.

Tuol Sleng Shoes (Map p87; ☎ 012 739358; 144 St 143) Scary name, but there's nothing scary about the price of these handmade shoes.

Water Lily (Map p87; ☎ 986241; 37 St 240) Popular jewellery and accessory shop with strikingly original designs.

Markets

Bargains, and bargaining sessions await in Phnom Penh's lively markets – put on your haggling hat and enter the fray.

PSAR THMEI
ផ្សារធ្មី

A landmark building in the capital, the artdeco **Psar Thmei** (Central Market; Map p87; St 53) is often called the Central Market, a reference to its location and size. The huge domed hall resembles a Babylonian ziggurat and some claim it ranks as one of the 10 largest domes in the world. The design allows for maximum ventilation, and even on a sweltering day the central hall is cool and airy. The market has four wings filled with stalls selling gold and silver jewellery, antique coins, dodgy watches, clothing and other such items. For photographers, the fresh food section affords many opportunities. For a local lunch, there are a host of food stalls located on the western side, which faces Monivong Blvd.

Psar Thmei is undoubtedly the best market for browsing. However, it has a reputation among Cambodians for overcharging on most products. The French government is currently assisting with renovations to restore it to its former glory. Parts of the market have already reopened and are looking much improved.

PSAR TUOL TOM PONG
ផ្សារទួលទំពូង

More commonly referred to by foreigners as the Russian Market (Russians shopped here during the 1980s), **Psar Tuol Tom Pong** (Map pp84–5; south of Mao Tse Toung Blvd) is the best place in town for souvenir and clothes shopping. It has a large range of handicrafts and antiquities (many fake), including miniature Buddhas, woodcarvings, betel-nut boxes, silks, silver jewellery, musical instruments and so on. Bargain hard, as thousands of tourists pass through here each month.

This is also the market where all the Western clothing made in garment factories around Phnom Penh turns up, all at just 10% of the price back home. Popular brands include Banana Republic, Billabong, Calvin Klein, Colombia, Gap, Gant and Next, but other names are contracting to Cambodia as time goes on. There are also fakes floating around, so be suspicious of labels like Kevin Clein.

This is the one market all visitors should come to at least once during a trip to Phnom Penh.

PSAR O RUSSEI
ផ្សារអូរុស្សី

Not to be confused with the Russian Market, **Psar O Russei** (Map p87; St 182) sells foodstuffs, costume jewellery, imported toiletries, secondhand clothes and everything else you can imagine from hundreds of stalls. The market is housed in a huge labyrinth of a building that looks like a shopping mall from the outside.

OTHER MARKETS

Psar Reatrey (Phnom Penh Night Market; Map p87; St 108 & Sisowath Quay; ☿ 4pm-midnight) A cooler al-fresco version of Psar Tuol Tom Pong, this night market takes place every Friday, Saturday and Sunday evening, if rain doesn't stop play. Bargain vigorously, as prices can be on the high side. Interestingly, it's probably more popular with Khmers than foreigners.

Psar Chaa (Map p87; St 108) This is a scruffy place that deals in household goods, clothes and jewellery. There are small restaurants, food vendors and jewellery stalls, as well as some good fresh-fruit stalls outside.

Psar Olympic (Map p84-5; St 310) Items for sale include bicycle parts, clothes, electronics and assorted edibles. This is quite a modern market set in a covered location.

GETTING THERE & AWAY
Air

For information on international and domestic air services to/from Phnom Penh, see p337.

Boat

There are numerous fast-boat companies that operate from the **tourist boat dock** (Map p87; Sisowath Quay) at the eastern end of St 104. Boats go to Siem Reap up the Tonlé Sap River and then Tonlé Sap Lake, but there are no longer services up the Mekong from Phnom Penh. For details on the international boat services connecting Phnom Penh with Chau Doc and the Mekong Delta in Vietnam, see p345.

The fast boats to Siem Reap (US$35, five to six hours) aren't as popular as they used to be. When it costs just US$6 for an air-conditioned bus or US$35 to be bundled on the roof of a boat, it is not hard to see why. It is better to save your boat experience for elsewhere in Cambodia.

Several companies have daily services departing at 7am and usually take it in turns to make the run. The first stretch of the journey along the river is scenic, but once the boat hits the lake, the fun is over as it is a vast inland sea with not a village in sight. Most tourists prefer to sit on the roof of the express boats, but don't forget a head covering and sunscreen as thick as paint. In the dry season, the boats are very small and sometimes overcrowded.

Bus

Bus services have improved dramatically with the advent of revitalised roads in Cambodia, and most major towns are now accessible by air-conditioned bus from Phnom Penh. Most buses leave from company offices, which are generally clustered around Psar Thmei or located near the northern end of Sisowath Quay.

Leading bus companies:

Capitol Tour (Map p87; ☎ 217627; 14 St 182) Services to Battambang, Ho Chi Minh City, Poipet, Siem Reap and Sihanoukville.

GST (Map p87; ☎ 218114; Psar Thmei area) Services to Ban Lung, Battambang, Ho Chi Minh City, Kratie, Pakse, Poipet, Siem Reap, Stung Treng, Sihanoukville and Tbeng Meanchey.

Hua Lian (Map pp84-5; ☎ 223025; Monireth Blvd & Olympic Stadium) Far-flung services include Ban Lung & Sen Monorom in the northeast, plus Kampot, Kratie, Sihanoukville and Stung Treng.

Mai Linh (Map pp84-5; ☎ 211888; 391 Sihanouk Blvd) Vietnamese company with buses to Siem Reap, plus Ho Chi Minh City.

Mekong Express (Map p87; ☎ 427518; 87 Sisowath Quay) Upmarket services to Siem Reap (US$11) and Sihanoukville (US$7) complete with in-drive hostesses. Plus Ho Chi Minh City (US$12).

Neak Krorhorm (Map p87; ☎ 219497; 4 St 108) Services to Battambang, Poipet, Siem Reap and Sisophon.

Paramount Angkor Express (Map p87; ☎ 427567; 24 St 102) Double-decker buses to Battambang, Koh Kong, Kompong Cham, Kratie, Pailin, Pakse, Poipet, Siem Reap, Sihanoukville and Stung Treng.

Phnom Penh Sorya (Map p87; ☎ 210359; Psar Thmei area) Most established company serving Ban Lung, Battambang, Ho Chi Minh City, Kampot, Kep, Koh Kong, Kompong Cham, Kompong Chhnang, Kratie, Neak Luong, Pakse, Poipet, Siem Reap, Sihanoukville, Stung Treng and Takeo.

Rith Mony (Map p87; ☎ 012 878919; 137 St 118) Buses to Ban Lung, Battambang, Ho Chi Minh City, Koh Kong, Kompong Cham, Kratie, Pakse, Siem Reap, Sihanoukville and Stung Treng.

Sok Sokha (Map p87; ☎ 991414; 121 Sisowath Blvd) Upmarket buses to Siem Reap, with free hotel pick-up.

Virak Buntham (Map p87; ☎ 016 786270; St 106) Buses to Bangkok, Koh Kong and Sihanoukville, plus the first sleeper bus (11pm) to Siem Reap (US$9).

Most buses charge a similar price, with the exception of premium services. The following list of destinations includes price, duration and frequency: Ban Lung (from US$10, 12 hours, several early departures), Battambang (from US$5, five hours, frequent until lunchtime), Kampot (from US$4, three to four hours, several per day), Kep (from

US$4, four hours, several per day), Kompong Cham (from US$3, two hours, frequent until 4pm), Kompong Chhnang (from US$2.50, two hours, frequent), Koh Kong (from US$10, six hours, several in the morning), Kratie (from 25,000r, five hours, several in the morning), Poipet (from US$7.50, eight hours, several early departures), Sen Monorom (from US$10, 10 hours, one daily), Siem Reap (from US$5, six hours, frequent until lunchtime), Sihanoukville (from US$3.50, four hours, frequent until lunchtime), Stung Treng (from US$9.50, seven hours, several in the morning) and Takeo (from US$2.50, two hours, frequent).

Most of the long-distance buses drop off and pick up in major towns along the way, such as Kompong Thom en route to Siem Reap or Pursat on the way to Battambang. However, it is necessary to buy tickets in advance to ensure a seat, plus full fare is usually charged anyway.

For more details on bus services between Phnom Penh and Ho Chi Minh City in Vietnam, see p343.

Share Taxi, Minibus & Pick-up

Share taxis, pick-ups and minibuses leave Phnom Penh for destinations all over the country, but have lost a lot of ground to cheaper and more comfortable buses as the road network continues to improve. Vehicles for Svay Rieng and Vietnam leave from Chbah Ampeau taxi park (Map pp84–5) on the eastern side of Monivong Bridge in the south of town, while those for most other destinations leave from around Psar Thmei. Different vehicles run different routes depending on the quality of the road, but the fast share taxis are more popular than the bumpy pick-ups and overcrowded minibuses. The following prices are those quoted for the most commonly used vehicle on that particular route, but are indicative rather than definitive, as even Khmers have to bargain a bit.

Share taxis run to Sihanoukville (25,000r, 2½ hours), Kampot (20,000r, two hours), Kompong Thom (20,000r, 2½ hours), Siem Reap (40,000r, five hours), Battambang (30,000r, four hours), Pursat (20,000r, three hours), Kompong Cham (15,000r, two hours) and Kratie (35,000r, five hours).

It is also possible to hire share taxis by the day. Rates start at US$25 to US$50 for Phnom Penh and nearby destinations, and then go up according to distance and the language skills of the driver.

Pick-ups are almost a thing of the past, but still take on some of the long-distance runs to places such as Mondulkiri (US$15, nine hours), but it is better to cover the good roads by bus and then switch to pick-ups for the shorter bumpy legs.

Minibuses aren't much fun and are best avoided when there are larger air-con buses or faster share taxis available, which is pretty much everywhere. See the individual entries in the Eastern Cambodia chapter for details of 'express minibuses' connecting Ban Lung and Stung Treng with Phnom Penh.

Train

There are currently no passenger services operating on the Cambodian rail network, but this should be seen as a blessing in disguise, given that the trains are extremely slow, travelling at about 20km/h. Yes, for a few minutes at least, you can outrun the train!

Just for reference, Phnom Penh's train station (Map p87) is located at the western end of St 106 and St 108, in a grand old colonial-era building that is a shambles inside. The railway is due to be overhauled in the next few years, so there may be the option of passenger services by 2012 or so.

GETTING AROUND

Being such a small city, Phnom Penh is quite easy to get around, although traffic is getting worse by the year and traffic jams are common around the morning and evening rush hour, particularly around Monivong and Norodom Blvds.

To/From the Airport

Phnom Penh International Airport (off Map pp84–5) is 7km west of central Phnom Penh, via Russian Blvd. Official taxis from the airport to the city centre cost US$9. Taxi drivers will take you to only one destination for this price, so make sure that they take you to where you want to go, not where they want you to go. A *remork* will cost about US$7 to the downtown area, perhaps half that if you walk outside. Official *motos* into town have been fixed at US$2. The journey usually takes about 30 minutes.

Heading to the airport from central Phnom Penh, a taxi should cost no more than US$6 to US$7 and a *moto* about US$1.50. *Remarks* can be had for about US$4.

Bicycle

It is possible to hire bicycles at some of the guesthouses around town for about US$1 to US$2 a day, but take a look at the chaotic traffic conditions before venturing forth. Once you get used to the anarchy, it can be a fun way to get around, if a little dusty. See Cycling (p98) for some day-tripping options around Phnom Penh.

Bus

Local buses don't exist in Phnom Penh. Most Cambodians use *motos* or *cyclos* to get around the city. With the long, straight boulevards crisscrossing the city, it would be perfect for trams or trolley buses, but developments like these are still some years away.

Car & Motorcycle

Car hire is available through travel agencies, guesthouses and hotels in Phnom Penh. Everything from cars (from US$25) to 4WDs (from US$60) are available for travelling around the city, but prices rise if you venture beyond.

There are numerous motorbike hire places around town. Bear in mind that motorbike theft is a problem in Phnom Penh, and if the bike gets stolen you will be liable. Ask for a lock and use it, plus only leave the bike in guarded parking areas where available, such as outside popular markets (300r). A 100cc Honda costs from US$4 to US$6 per day and 250cc dirt bikes run from US$10 to US$20 per day. The following are some popular motorcycle rental shops:

Angkor Motorcycles! (Map p87; ☎ 012 722098; 92 St 51)

Little Bikes (Map p87; ☎ 017 329338; 178 St 13)

Lucky! Lucky! (Map p87; ☎ 212788; 413 Monivong Blvd)

New! New! (Map p87; 417 Monivong Blvd)

Serious off-roaders may want to talk to one of the specialists. See p349 for details on dirt bike touring companies. The following companies are based in Phnom Penh:

Riverside Moto (Map p87; ☎ 223588; www.riverside motorcycletours.com; 30 St 118) This place specialises in upcountry touring, has well-serviced bikes and can provide a tool kit and spares.

Two Wheels Only (Map pp84–5; ☎ 012 200513; www. twocambodia.com; 34 St 368) Two specialises in repairs and imported accessories, but also has well-maintained bikes available to rent for touring.

Harley Tours Cambodia (Map p87; ☎ 012 948529; www.harleycambodia.com; 21 St 294) For those looking for a little more muscle on the road, Harley Tours organise Harley rides around Phnom Penh, including overnighters to places like Kompong Cham or Kep. Day rental is available, but prices are similar to luxury car rental back home.

Cyclo

They are still common on the streets of Phnom Penh, but *cyclos* have lost a lot of ground to the *moto*. Travelling by *cyclo* is a more relaxing way to see the sights in the centre of town, but they are just too slow for going from one end of the city to another. For a day of sightseeing, expect to pay around US$8 to US$10 depending on exactly where you go and how many hours of pedalling it includes. Late at night, *cyclos* would have to be considered a security hazard for all but the shortest of journeys, but

---

WE'RE ON A ROAD TO NOWHERE

Taking a ride on a *remork-moto, moto* or *cyclo* is not as easy as it looks. Drivers who loiter around guesthouses, hotels, restaurants and bars may speak streetwise English and know the city well, but elsewhere the knowledge and understanding required to get you to your destination dries up fast. Flag one down on the street or grab one from outside the market, and you could end up pretty much anywhere in the city. You name your destination, and they nod confidently, eager for the extra money a foreigner may bring, but not having the first clue of where you want to go. They start driving or pedalling furiously down the road and await your instructions. You don't give them any instructions, as you think they know where they are going. Before you realise it, you are halfway to Sihanoukville or Siem Reap. The moral of the story is always carry a map of Phnom Penh and keep a close eye on the driver unless he speaks enough English to understand where on earth you want to go.

most drivers are asleep in their *cyclos* at this time anyway. Costs are generally similar to *moto* fares, although negotiate if picking one up at popular spots around town.

It's also possible to arrange a *cyclo* tour through the **Cyclo Centre** (☎ 991178; www.cyclo. org.uk), dedicated to supporting cyclo drivers in Phnom Penh. This is a good cause, and themed trips are available such as pub crawls or cultural tours. Prices run from US$2.50 an hour to US$10 for a full day.

Moto

In areas frequented by foreigners, *moto* drivers generally speak English and sometimes a little French. Elsewhere around town it can be difficult to find anyone who understands where you want to go – see the boxed text, opposite. Most short trips are about 1000r to 2000r and more again at night, although if you want to get from one end of the city to the other, you have to pay up to US$1. Prices were once rarely negotiated in advance when taking rides, but with so many tourists paying over the odds, it may be sensible to discuss the price first. For those staying in a luxury hotel, negotiation is essential. Likewise, night owls taking a *moto* home from popular drinking holes should definitely negotiate to avoid an expensive surprise.

Many of the *moto* drivers who wait outside the popular guesthouses and hotels have good English and are able to act as guides for a daily rate of about US$8 to US$10 depending on the destinations.

Remork-moto

Also commonly known as *tuk tuks, remorks* are motorbikes with carriages and are now pretty popular around Phnom Penh. They come in every shape and size from China, India and Thailand, plus the home-grown variety such as those pioneered in Siem Reap. Average fares are about double those of *motos,* and increase if you pack on the passengers.

Taxi

Phnom Penh now has metered taxis and they are cheap at just US$1 per kilometre. Try **Global Meter Taxi** (☎ 011 311888) or **Choice Taxi** (☎ 888023) but call ahead. **Taxi Vantha** (☎ 012 855000; www.taxivantha.com) is an older company offering taxis 24 hours a day, but has a limited number of cars.

Private taxis tend to wait outside popular nightspots, but it is important to agree on a price in advance.

AROUND PHNOM PENH

There are several attractions around Phnom Penh that make good day trips, although they are kind of low key when compared with what's on offer in other parts of the country. The Angkorian temple of Tonlé Bati and hilltop pagoda of Phnom Chisor are best visited in one trip, and can be built into a journey south to either Takeo (p236) or Kampot (p223). Udong, once the capital of Cambodia, is also a potential day trip and can be combined with a visit to Kompong Chhnang (p242), known for being a 'genuine' Cambodian town.

There is a clean, comfortable and cheap bus network operated by Phnom Penh Sorya Transport (p120) covering most of the following places. For experienced riders, motorcycles (opposite) are another interesting way to visit these attractions, as there are plenty of small villages along the way. If time is more important than money, you can rent a taxi to whisk you around for between US$40 and US$60 a day, depending on the destination. Some of the more popular guesthouses offer inexpensive tours, with or without a guide, to most of the places covered here.

KIEN SVAY
កៀនស្វាយ

Kien Svay is a very popular picnic area on a small tributary of the Mekong. Hundreds of bamboo huts have been built over the water and Khmers love to come here on the weekend and sit around gossiping and munching.

Kien Svay is a peculiarly Cambodian institution, mixing the universal love of picnicking by the water with the unique Khmer fondness for lounging about on mats. It works like this: for 5000r an hour, picnickers rent an area on a raised open hut covered with reed mats. Be sure to agree on the price *before* you rent a space.

All sorts of food is sold at Kien Svay, although it is necessary to bargain to ensure a fair price. Prices generally seem reasonable thanks to the massive competition – there are perhaps 50 or more sellers here. Popular dishes include grilled chicken and fish, river lobster and fresh fruit. The area is pretty deserted during the week, but this can make it a calmer time to picnic.

Getting There & Away

Kien Svay is a district in Kandal Province, and the actual picnic spot is just before the small town of Koki, about 15km east of Phnom Penh. To get here from Phnom Penh, turn left off NH1, which links Phnom Penh with Ho Chi Minh City, through a wat-style gate at a point 15km east of the Monivong Bridge. You will know you are on the right track if you see plenty of beggars and hundreds of cars. Buses regularly depart for Kien Svay from Psar Thmei and cost just 4000r. A round-trip *moto* should cost about US$5.

UDONG

ភ្នំឧដុង្គ

Udong (the Victorious) served as the capital of Cambodia under several sovereigns between 1618 and 1866, suggesting 'victorious' was an optimistic epithet, as Cambodia was in terminal decline at this time. A number of kings, including King Norodom, were crowned here. The main attractions today are the two small humps of Phnom Udong, which have several stupas on them. Both ends of the ridge have good views of the Cambodian countryside dotted with innumerable sugar palm trees. Udong is not a leading attraction, but for those with the time it's worth the visit.

The smaller ridge has two structures and several stupas on top. **Ta San Mosque** faces westward towards Mecca. Across the plains to the south of the mosque you can see **Phnom Vihear Leu**, a small hill on which a *vihara* (temple sanctuary) stands between two white poles. To the right of the *vihara* is a building used as a prison under Pol Pot's rule. To the left of the *vihara* and below it is a pagoda known as **Arey Ka Sap**.

The larger ridge, Phnom Preah Reach Throap (Hill of the Royal Fortune), is so named because a 16th-century Khmer king is said to have hidden the national treasury here during a war with the Thais. The most impressive structure on Phnom Preah Reach Throap is **Vihear Preah Ath Roes**. The *vihara* and the statue of Buddha, dedicated in 1911 by King Sisowath, were blown up by the Khmer Rouge in 1977; only sections of the walls, the bases of eight enormous columns and the

right arm and part of the right side of the original Buddha statue remain. The Buddha has been reconstructed and the roof has now been rebuilt.

About 120m northwest of Vihear Preah Ath Roes is a line of small *viharas*. The first is **Vihear Preah Ko**, a brick-roofed structure that contains a statue of Preah Ko, the sacred bull; the original statue was carried away by the Thais long ago. The second structure, which has a seated Buddha inside, is **Vihear Preah Keo**. The third is **Vihear Prak Neak**, its cracked walls topped with a thatched roof. Inside this *vihara* is a seated Buddha who is guarded by a *naga* (*prak neak* means 'protected by a *naga*').

At the northwestern extremity of the ridge stand four large stupas. The first is the **Chet Dey Mak Proum**, the final resting place of King Monivong (r 1927–41). Decorated with *garudas* (mythical half-man, half-bird creatures), floral designs and elephants, it has four faces on top. The middle stupa, **Tray Troeng**, is decorated with coloured tiles; it was built in 1891 by King Norodom to house the ashes of his father, King Ang Duong (r 1845–59), but some say King Ang Duong was in fact buried next to the Silver Pagoda in Phnom Penh. The third stupa, **Damrei Sam Poan**, was built by King Chey Chetha II (r 1618–26) for the ashes of his predecessor, King Soriyopor. The fourth stupa contains a relic of the Buddha, believed to be an eyebrow hair, which was relocated from the blue stupa in front of Phnom Penh railway station in 2002.

An east-facing staircase leads down the hillside from the stupa of King Monivong. Just north of its base is a **pavilion** decorated with graphic murals depicting Khmer Rouge atrocities.

At the base of the ridge, close to the road, is a **memorial** to the victims of Pol Pot, which contains the bones of some of the people who were buried in approximately 100 mass graves, each containing about a dozen bodies. Instruments of torture were unearthed along with the bones when a number of the pits were disinterred in 1981 and 1982.

Sleeping & Eating

There is a **Cambodia Vipassana Dhura Buddhist Meditation Centre** (contact Mrs Kim Simoeun ☎ 012 221505; www.cambodiavipassanacenter.com) at Udong and it is possible for foreigners to stay here and practise meditation with experienced monks or nuns. The rooms are fairly comfortable by monastic standards, but not always kept that clean. There is no fixed price for a meditative retreat here, but a figure of US$20 for a day, including lunch, or US$30 with an overnight stay is what one of the French-speaking nuns suggested in the past. The electricity usually stops at 8pm, but you may be able to request the generator is turned on for an extra donation.

There are plenty of food stalls around the base of Udong or several more substantial restaurants, with views across to Udong's twin peaks, near the Prek Kdam bridge over the Tonlé Sap River.

Getting There & Away

Udong is 41km from the capital. Head north out of Phnom Penh on NH5 and turn left (south) at the signposted archway. Udong is 3.5km south of the turn-off; the access road goes through the village of Psar Dek Krom, and passes by a memorial to Pol Pot's victims, before arriving at a short staircase.

A cheap and convenient way to get to Udong is by air-con local bus (10,000r, one hour) from Phnom Penh. Buses depart from near Psar Thmei and run regularly throughout the day. The bus drivers can drop you at the access road to Udong, from where you can arrange a *moto* to the base of the hill for US$1. Buses to/from Kompong Chhnang (p242) also stop here, so you can combine your visit to the temples with a visit to a Cambodian town that sees few tourists.

A taxi for the day trip from Phnom Penh will cost around US$40. *Moto* drivers also run people to Udong for about US$10 or so for the day, but compared with the bus this isn't the most pleasant way to go, as the road is pretty busy and very dusty.

TONLÉ BATI
ទន្លេបាទី

Tonlé Bati (admission incl a drink US$3) is the collective name for a pair of old Angkorian-era temples and a popular lakeside picnic area. Anyone who has already experienced the mighty temples of Angkor can probably survive without a visit, but if Angkor is yet to come, these attractive temples are worth the detour.

TA PROHM
តាព្រហ្ម
The laterite temple of Ta Prohm was built by King Jayavarman VII (r 1181–1219) on the site of an ancient 6th-century Khmer shrine. Today the ruined temple is surrounded by colourful flowers and plants, affording some great photo opportunities.

The main sanctuary consists of five chambers; in each is a *linga* (phallic symbol) and all show signs of the destruction wrought by the Khmer Rouge.

Entering the sanctuary from the east gate, 15m ahead on the right is a bas-relief depicting a woman, and a man who is bowing to another, larger woman. The smaller woman has just given birth and failed to show proper respect for the midwife (the larger woman). The new mother has been condemned to carry the afterbirth on her head in a box for the rest of her life. The husband is asking that his wife be forgiven.

YEAY PEAU
យាយពៅ
Yeay Peau temple, named after King Prohm's mother, is 150m north of Ta Prohm in the grounds of a modern pagoda. Legend has it that Peau gave birth to a son, Prohm. When Prohm discovered his father was King Preah Ket Mealea, he set off to live with the king. After a few years, he returned to his mother but did not recognise her and, taken by her beauty, asked her to become his wife. He refused to believe Peau's protests that she was his mother. To put off his advances she suggested a contest…for the outcome of this legend, see p296.

LAKEFRONT
About 300m northwest of Ta Prohm, a long, narrow peninsula juts into Tonlé Bati. It used to be packed at weekends with vendors selling food and drink, but high prices meant many Phnom Penh residents stayed away. However, fixed food and drink prices are now printed on the reverse of the entry ticket, so it should start to take off again as the word spreads. The views (and breezes) across the lake are pretty inviting.

Getting There & Away
The access road heading to Tonlé Bati is signposted on the right on NH2 at a point 31km south of Phnom Penh. The temples and picnic area are 2.5km from the highway.

Buses leave for Takeo at fairly regular intervals throughout the day and can drop passengers at the access road. The fare is 6000r. The first bus from Phnom Penh leaves at 7am

PHNOM PENH

and there are hourly services until 4pm. Buses returning from Takeo pass the turn-off regularly throughout the day. If you are heading to the wildlife sanctuary at Phnom Tamao, these services also apply.

PHNOM TAMAO WILDLIFE RESCUE CENTRE
ភ្នំតាម៉ៅ

Cambodia's foremost wildlife sanctuary, the **Phnom Tamao Wildlife Rescue Centre** (adult/child US$5/2) is a home for animals confiscated from traffickers or saved from poachers' traps. It occupies a vast site south of the capital and its animals are kept in varying conditions that are rapidly improving with help from international wildlife NGOs. Spread out as it is, it feels like a zoo crossed with a safari park. The way things are moving, Phnom Tamao is set to become one of the region's best-run animal sanctuaries in the coming years.

Popular enclosures include huge areas for the large tiger population, and there are elephants that sometimes take part in activities such as painting. There is also a walk-through area with macaques and deer, and a huge aviary.

The centre is home to the world's largest captive collections of pileated gibbons and Malayan sun bears, as well as other rarities such as Siamese crocodiles and greater adjutant storks. Wherever possible animals are released back into the wild once they have recovered and the centre operates breeding programs for a number of globally threatened species.

Cambodia's wildlife is usually very difficult to spot, as larger mammals inhabit remote areas of the country. Phnom Tamao is the perfect place to discover more about the incredible variety of animals in Cambodia.

If you don't like zoos, you probably won't like this wildlife sanctuary, but remember that these animals have been rescued from traffickers and poachers and need a home. Visitors that come here will be doing their own small bit to help in the protection and survival of Cambodia's varied and wonderful wildlife.

Free the Bears (www.freethebears.org.au; volunteer asianbears@freethebears.org.au) operates a 'volunteer bear keeper' initiative (for a small fee) to allow those with a genuine interest in wildlife a better understanding of the Asian black bear and Malayan sun bear. Placements are available for between one week and six weeks and the experience includes feeding and washing the

young bears in their care. There are currently nearly 90 bears being looked after here.

Betelnut Jeep Tours (Map p87; ☎ 012 619924; www.betelnuttours.com; per person US$30), based at the Lazy Gecko Café, offers day trips here departing at 10am on Tuesday, Thursday and Saturday, including entry, a guided tour, lunch and a chance to meet some of the residents.

Getting There & Away
Phnom Tamao is about 44km from Phnom Penh, down NH2. Take a right turn after the sign for the zoo (37km), and it is 6km further down a sandy track. On weekends, you can combine an air-con bus ride with a *moto*, but on weekdays it may be easier to rent a motorbike or charter a taxi. See p125 for details on bus times and prices.

PHNOM CHISOR
ភ្នំជីស

A temple from the Angkorian era, **Phnom Chisor** (admission US$3, levied at the summit) is set upon a solitary hill in Takeo Province (p236), offering some superb views of the countryside. Try to get to Phnom Chisor early in the morning or late in the afternoon, as it is a very uncomfortable climb in the heat of the midday sun.

The main temple stands on the eastern side of the hilltop. Constructed of laterite and brick with carved lintels of sandstone, the complex is surrounded by the partially ruined walls of a 2.5m-wide gallery with windows.

Inscriptions found here date from the 11th century, when this site was known as Suryagiri. The wooden doors to the sanctuary in the centre of the complex, which open to the east, are decorated with carvings of figures standing on pigs. Inside the sanctuary are statues of Buddha.

On the plain to the west of Phnom Chisor are the sanctuaries of **Sen Thmol**, just below Phnom Chisor, **Sen Ravang** and the former sacred pond of **Tonlé Om**. All three of these features form a straight line from Phnom Chisor in the direction of Angkor. During rituals held here 900 years ago, the king, his Brahmans and their entourage would climb a monumental 400 steps to Suryagiri from this direction.

There is a spectacular view of the temples and plains from the roofless gallery opposite the wooden doors to the central shrine. If you haven't got the stamina for an overland adventure to Preah Vihear (p279), this is the next best thing for a temple with a view. Near the main temple is a modern Buddhist *vihara* that is used by resident monks.

Getting There & Away

The eastward-bound access road to Phnom Chisor is signposted on the left about 52km south of central Phnom Penh. It's about 5km from the highway to the base of the hill.

The cheapest way to get to Phnom Chisor is to take a Takeo-bound bus from Phnom Penh and ask to be let off at the turn-off from NH2. This costs 8500r and from here you can take a *moto* to the bottom of the hill for US$1. Alternatively, from Phnom Penh you can charter a taxi for about US$50 to visit both Phnom Chisor and Tonlé Bati.

KIRIROM NATIONAL PARK
ឧទ្យានជាតិគីរីរម្យ

The hill station of **Kirirom National Park** (admission US$5), set amid lush forest and pine groves, has been established as a national park. It is popular with Khmers at weekends as it is 675m above sea level with a climate notably cooler than Phnom Penh. There are several small **waterfalls** in the park, which are popular picnic spots for Khmers, and a number of basic walking trails. For a more substantial walk, consider hooking up with a ranger (about US$5) for a two-hour hike up to **Phnom Dat Chivit** (End of the Life Mountain) where an abrupt cliff face offers an unbroken view of the **Elephant Mountains** and **Cardamom Mountains** to the west. It is often possible to see wildlife on this trail, including black bears scavenging the pine trees for honey.

Kirirom is one of the few national parks to have a nearby community tourism program. Set just beyond the park boundaries, about 10km beyond the Kirirom Hillside Resort, **Chambok Community-Based Ecotourism** (admission adult/child US$3/1) program is based in Chambok commune, where nearby attractions include a 40m-high waterfall, traditional ox-cart rides (Cambodia's original 4WDs) and nature walks. It is also possible to sample traditional Cambodian country fare at the small restaurant or arrange a local homestay with a bit of notice. The program was originally established by local NGO **Mlup Baitong** (☎ 023-214409; www.mlup.org), and a percentage of the proceeds is pumped back into the local community.

The trek to the waterfall takes about one hour, with about 1.7km of uphill climbing,

but the reward is a stunning cascade pouring over a jungle-clad cliff face. Few refreshments are available once you leave the flat trail, so carry water. The first two falls signposted are less spectacular than the main waterfall, so keep on trekking.

Sleeping & Eating

There are two options for staying at Kirirom and they are worlds apart. The very basic **Kirirom Guesthouse** (☎ 012 957700; r US$20) is pretty rundown for such a stunning location, but the rooms have clean sheets, a fan and attached bathroom. The restaurant (mains US$2.50 to US$7.50) here is more memorable with outdoor pavilions offering superb views.

Kirirom Hillside Resort (☎ 016 590999; www.kiriromresort.com; camping incl tent US$17, r from US$50, bungalow from US$65; ✕ 🖳 ⚗) is located just beneath the entrance to the national park. At first glance this is a kitsch place aimed at local tourists wanting a taste of country life. The castle-like entrance and plastic dinosaurs put off most Westerners, but for families with children it offers plenty of activities such as biking, horse-riding and kayaking. Hidden away at the back in the spacious grounds are some Scandinavian-style bungalows in various shapes and sizes, with TV, minibar and hot showers. Facilities include a swimming pool, sauna and several restaurants. The pool has a lovely setting with the hills of Kirirom as a backdrop and is open to non-guests for US$5 per day.

The **Paradise Restaurant** (mains US$3-6) has a pretty good selection of Khmer, Asian and Western dishes at reasonable prices, including a steamed snapper at US$4.75.

Getting There & Away

Kirirom National Park is 112km southwest of Phnom Penh, located about 24km to the west of NH4. Unless you have your own transport, it is not that easy to get here. One possibility is to catch a bus going to Sihanoukville and ask to be let off at Kirirom or Preah Suramarit Kossomak National Park (the full name in Khmer). However, it still requires a *moto* to get around the park itself. The best way to visit is to hire a motorcycle in Phnom Penh or get a group together and charter a taxi for about US$60. Coming under your own steam, the turn-off for the park is about 87km from Phnom Penh, and is marked by a large sign on the right of the highway.

Siem Reap
សៀមរាប

Back in the 1960s, Siem Reap (*see*-em ree-*ep*) was the place to be in Southeast Asia and saw a steady stream of the rich and famous. After three decades of slumber, it's well and truly back and is one of the most popular destinations on the planet right now. The life-support system for the temples of Angkor, Cambodia's eighth wonder of the world, Siem Reap was always destined for great things, but few people saw them coming this thick and this fast. It has reinvented itself as the epicentre of the new Cambodia, with more guesthouses and hotels than temples, as well as world-class wining and dining and sumptuous spas.

At its heart, Siem Reap is still a little charmer, with old French shop-houses, shady tree-lined boulevards and a slow-flowing river. But it is expanding at breakneck speed, with new houses and apartments, hotels and resorts sprouting like mushrooms in the surrounding countryside. The tourist tide has arrived and locals are riding the wave. Not only is this great news for the long-suffering Khmers, but it has transformed the town into a pulsating place for visitors. Forget the naysayers who mutter into their beers about Siem Reap in the 'old days'; now is the time to be here, although you may curse your luck when stuck behind a jam of tour buses on the way back from the temples.

Angkor is a place to be savoured, not rushed, and this is the base to plan your adventures. Still think three days at the temples is enough? Think again, with Siem Reap on the doorstep.

HIGHLIGHTS

- Encounter some of the world's rarest large water birds at **Prek Toal Bird Sanctuary** (p151)
- Explore the flooded forest of **Kompong Pluk** (p152), an incredible village of bamboo skyscrapers
- Discover the quiet temples of Angkor hidden away in the modern pagodas of **Wat Athvea** and **Wat Preah Inkosei** (p132)
- Dive into **Pub St** (p146), the drinking capital of Siem Reap, and discover nearby restaurants and bars
- Learn the secrets of Khmer cuisine with a **cooking course** (p136), the perfect way to impress friends back home

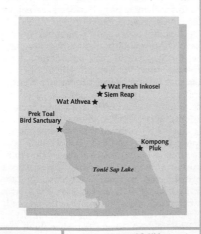

- TELEPHONE CODE: 063
- POPULATION: 120,000 (TOWN)
- AREA: 10,299 SQ KM

HISTORY
The name Siem Reap means 'Siamese Defeated', hardly the most tactful name for a major city near Thailand. Imagine Birmingham with the name 'Germany Defeated'? The empire of Angkor once included much of modern-day Thailand, but there's a touch of irony about the name, given that Thailand ultimately defeated Cambodia and controlled Siem Reap and Angkor from 1794 to 1907.

Siem Reap was little more than a village when French explorers discovered Angkor in the 19th century. With the return of Angkor to Cambodian – or should that be French – control in 1907, Siem Reap began to grow, absorbing the first wave of tourists. The Grand Hotel d'Angkor (p141) opened its doors in 1929 and the temples of Angkor remained one of Asia's leading draws until the late 1960s, luring luminaries such as Charlie Chaplin and Jackie Kennedy. With the advent of war and the Khmer Rouge, Siem Reap entered a long slumber from which it only began to awake in the mid-1990s.

Tourism is the lifeblood of Siem Reap and, without careful management, it could become Siem Reapolinos, the not so Costa-del-Culture of Southeast Asia. However, there are promising signs that developers are learning from the mistakes that have blighted other regional hot spots, with restrictions on the height of hotels and bus sizes. Either way, Angkor is centre stage on the world travel map right now and there is no going back for its supply line, Siem Reap.

ORIENTATION
Siem Reap is still a small town at heart and is easy enough to navigate. The centre is around Psar Chaa (Old Market; p148); the administrative district is along the western bank of the river; and accommodation is spread throughout town. National Hwy 6 (NH6) cuts across the northern part of town, passing Psar Leu (Main Market) in the east of town and the Royal Residence and the Grand Hotel d'Angkor (p141) in the centre, and then heads to the airport and beyond to the Thai border. Siem Reap River (Stung Siem Reap) flows north–south through the centre of town, and has enough bridges that you won't have to worry too much about being on the wrong side. Like Phnom Penh, however, street numbering is haphazard to say the least, so take care when hunting down specific addresses.

Angkor Wat and Angkor Thom are only 6km and 8km north of town respectively – see Map pp160–1 for the location of all the leading temples.

Buses and share taxis usually drop passengers off at the bus station/taxi park about 3km east of the town centre, from where it is a short *moto* or *remork-moto (tuk tuk)* ride to nearby guesthouses and hotels. Fast boats from Phnom Penh and Battambang arrive at Phnom Krom, about 11km south of town, and most places to stay include a free transfer by *moto* or minibus. Siem Reap International Airport is 7km west of town and there are plenty of taxis and *motos* available for transfers to the town centre. For more details, see p150.

INFORMATION
Pick up a copy of the *Siem Reap Angkor Visitors Guide* (www.canbypublications.com), which is packed with listings and comes out quarterly. Check out *Drinking and Dining* for the low-down on bars and restaurants, or *Out and About* for shops and services, both produced by **Pocket Guide Cambodia** (www.cambodiapocketguide.com) and widely available.

Bookshops
Cheap books on Angkor and Cambodia are hawked by kids around the temples, and by amputees trying to make a clean start in Siem Reap. Be aware that many are illegal photocopies and the print quality is poor.

Blue Apsara (Map p134; ☎ 012 601483; Psar Chaa area) Longest-running secondhand bookstore in town, with a good selection of English, French and German titles.

D's Books (Map p134; Pithnou St; ☉ 9am-10pm) The largest chain of secondhand bookshops in Cambodia, this is conveniently located for night browsing.

Monument Books (Map p134; FCC Angkor) Well-stocked new bookstore, with an additional branch at the airport.

Siem Reap Book Center (Map p134; Pithnou St) Large selection of new titles on Angkor and beyond.

Emergency
Tourist police (Map p130; ☎ 097-7780013) Located at the main ticket checkpoint for the Angkor area, this is the place to come and lodge a complaint if you encounter any serious problems while in Siem Reap.

Internet Access
Internet shops have spread through town like wildfire and your nearest online fix will never be far away. Prices are US$0.50 to US$1 per hour

SIEM REAP

SIEM REAP

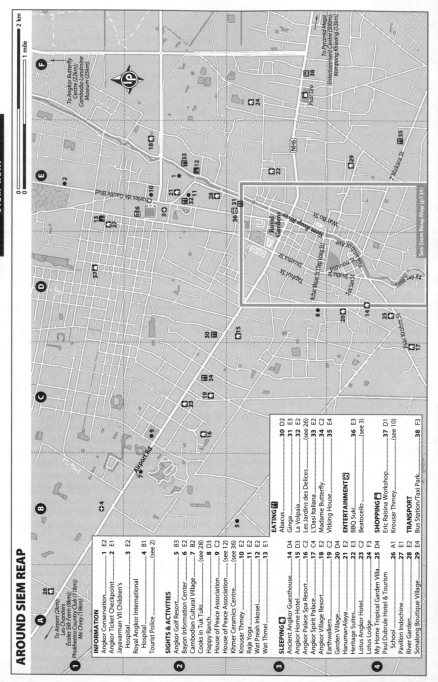

AROUND SIEM REAP

To Airport (2km);
Les Chantiers;
Écoles Silk Farm (9km);
Phokheetra Country Club (11km);
Me Chrey (19km)

To Angkor Butterfly
Centre (22km);
Cambodia Landmine
Museum (25km)

To Pyramid Mega
Entertainment Centre (500m);
Kompong Khleang (55km)

Charles de Gaulle Blvd

Airport Rd

NH6

Royal
Gardens

Siem Reap River

Wat Bo St

Achar Mean St (Tep Vong) St
Sivatha St
Sivatha St
Phum Daun
Pok Senchai Ave
Taphul St
Taphul St
Pok Ski St
Psar Krom St
Tonle Sap Rd

See Siem Reap Map (p134)

INFORMATION
Angkor Conservation	1 E2
Angkor Ticket Checkpoint	2 E1
Jayavarman VII Children's Hospital	3 E2
Royal Angkor International Hospital	4 B1
Tourist Police	(see 2)

SIGHTS & ACTIVITIES
Angkor Golf Resort	5 B3
Bayon Information Center	6 E2
Cambodian Cultural Village	7 B2
Cooks in Tuk Tuks	(see 28)
Happy Ranch	8 D3
House of Peace Association	9 C2
House of Peace Association	(see 12)
Khmer Ceramics Centre	(see 36)
Krousar Thmey	10 E2
Raja Yoga	11 E2
Wat Preah Inkosei	12 E2
Wat Thmei	13 E1

SLEEPING
Ancient Angkor Guesthouse	14 D4
Angkor Home Hotel	15 D3
Angkor Palace Spa Resort	16 C2
Angkor Spirit Palace	17 C4
Angkor Village Resort	18 E2
Earthwalkers	19 C2
Garden Village	20 D4
HanumanAlaya	21 E2
Heritage Suites	22 E3
Lotus Angkor Hotel	23 C2
Lotus Lodge	24 F3
My Home Tropical Garden Villa	25 D4
Paul Dubrule Hotel & Tourism School	26 A1
Pavillon Indochine	27 E1
River Garden	28 E2
Sonalong Boutique Village	29 E4

EATING
Abacus	30 D2
Ginga	31 E3
La Volpaia	32 E2
Les Jardins des Delices	(see 26)
L'Oasi Italiana	33 E2
Madame Butterfly	34 C2
Viking House	35 E4

ENTERTAINMENT
BBQ Suki	36 E3
Beatocello	(see 3)

SHOPPING
Eric Raisina Workshop	37 D1
Krousar Thmey	(see 10)

TRANSPORT
Bus Station/Taxi Park	38 F3

and most places also offer cheap internet-based telephone calls. The greatest concentration is along Sivatha St and around the Psar Chaa area. Many guesthouses and hotels also offer affordable access or free services for guests. Many of the leading restaurants and bars, as well as many midrange hotels, offer free wi-fi.

Medical Services

Siem Reap now has an international-standard hospital for emergencies. However, any serious complications will still require relocation to Bangkok.

Angkor Children's Hospital (Map p134; ☎ 963409; ⊙ 24hr) This international-standard paediatric hospital is the place to take your children if they fall sick. Will also assist adults in an emergency for up to 24 hours (after which time a transfer elsewhere would be expected). Donations accepted.

Royal Angkor International Hospital (Map p130; ☎ 761888; www.royalangkorhospital.com; Airport Rd) A new international facility, affiliated with the Bangkok Hospital, so very expensive.

U-Care Pharmacy (Map p134; ☎ 965396; Pithnou St; ⊙ 8am-9pm) Smart pharmacy and shop like Boots in Thailand (and the UK). English spoken.

Money

For cash exchanges, markets (usually at jewellery stalls or dedicated money-changing stalls) are faster and less bureaucratic than the banks.

ANZ Royal Bank (Map p134; ☎ 023 726900; Achar Mean St) Provides free credit-card advances and can change travellers cheques in most major currencies. Several branches and plenty of international ATMs (US$4 per withdrawal) around town.

Canadia Bank (Map p134; ☎ 964808; Sivatha St) Offers free credit-card cash advances and changes travellers cheques in most major currencies at a 2% commission. International ATM with no transaction fees.

Union Commercial Bank (Map p134; ☎ 964703; Psar Chaa) Charges 2% commission for travellers cheques and offers free Visa advances.

Post

DHL (Map p134; ☎ 964949; Central Market) Courier.

EMS (Map p134; ☎ 760000) Courier inside the main post office.

Main post office (Map p134; ⊙ 7am-5.30pm) Services are more reliable these days, but it doesn't hurt to see your stamps franked.

Telephone & Fax

Making international calls is straightforward. The cheapest way is to use the major internet cafes, with calls starting at about US$0.10 per minute, but there can be some delay. The cheapest 'unblemished' calls can be arranged with one of the many private booths advertising these telephone services. Hotels impose hefty surcharges on calls, so check the rates before you dial.

Tourist Information

The tourism office in Siem Reap is in a white building opposite the Grand Hotel d'Angkor (p141). There's a sign saying 'Tourist Information', but this is a little optimistic from experience. Guesthouses and hotels are often a more reliable source of information, as are fellow travellers who have been in town for a few days.

Many travellers passing through Siem Reap are interested in contributing something to the communities they visit as they explore the temples and surrounding areas. **ConCERT** (Map p134; ☎ 963511; www.concertcambodia.org; 560 Phum Stoeung Thmey; ⊙ 9am-5pm Mon-Fri) is a Siem Reap–based organisation that is working to build bridges between tourists and good-cause projects in the Siem Reap–Angkor area. It offers information on anything from ecotourism initiatives to volunteering opportunities.

DANGERS & ANNOYANCES

Siem Reap is a pretty safe city, even at night. However, if you rent a bike, don't keep your bag in the basket, as it will be easy pickings for a drive-by snatch. Likewise, lone females should try to walk home with travelling companions when leaving late-night spots, particularly if heading through poorly lit areas.

There are a lot of commission scams in Siem Reap that involve certain guesthouses and small hotels paying *moto* and taxi drivers to deliver guests. Ways to avoid these scams include booking ahead via the internet and arranging a pick-up, or sticking with a partner guesthouse if you are coming from Phnom Penh. Alternatively, just go with the flow and negotiate with the hotel or guesthouse on arrival.

For more on the commission scams facing those travelling to Siem Reap by land from Bangkok, see the boxed text on p342.

There are a lot of beggars around town and some visitors quickly develop beggar fatigue. However, try to remember that with no social security network and no government support, life is pretty tough for the poorest of the poor in Cambodia. In the case of children, it is often better not to encourage begging, but, if you are compelled to help, then offer food, as money usually ends up being passed on to someone else. These days the problem is less serious, as many have been retrained to sell books or postcards to tourists instead of simply begging.

Out at the remote temple sites beyond Angkor, stick to clearly marked trails. There are still land mines at locations such as Phnom Kulen and Kbal Spean. For more information about Cambodia's land mines, see p326.

SIGHTS

Visitors come to Siem Reap to see the temples of Angkor. The sights in and around the town pale in comparison, but they are a good diversion for those who find themselves templed out after a few days. That said, some of the best sights are…yet more temples.

Pagodas

Modern pagodas around Siem Reap offer an interesting contrast to the ancient sandstone structures of Angkor. **Wat Bo** (Map p134; 6am-6pm) is one of the town's oldest temples and has a collection of well-preserved wall paintings from the late 19th century depicting the *Reamker,* Cambodia's interpretation of the *Ramayana.* Another wat to consider is **Wat Preah Inkosei** (Map p130; 6am-6pm), built on the site of an early Angkorian brick temple north of town, which still stands today at the rear of the compound.

South of the city centre, **Wat Athvea** (off Map p134; 6am-6pm) is an attractive pagoda on the site of an ancient temple. The old temple is still in very good condition and sees far fewer visitors than the main temples in the Angkor area, making it a peaceful spot in the late afternoon.

On the left fork of the road to Angkor Wat, **Wat Thmei** (Map p130; 6am-6pm) has a small memorial stupa containing the skulls and bones of victims of the Khmer Rouge. It also has plenty of young monks wanting to practise their English.

Wat Dam Nak (Map p134; 6am-6pm) was formerly a royal palace during the reign of King Sisowath, hence the name *dam nak* (palace). Today it is home to the **Centre for Khmer Studies** (www.khmerstudies.org), an independent institution promoting a greater understanding of Khmer culture with a drop-in research library on site.

Les Chantiers Écoles

Siem Reap is the epicentre of the drive to revitalise Cambodian traditional culture, which was dealt such a harsh blow by the Khmer Rouge and the years of instability that followed its rule.

Les Chantiers Écoles (Map p134) is a school specialising in teaching wood- and stone-carving techniques to impoverished youngsters. On the premises the school has a beautiful shop called Artisans d'Angkor (p148), which sells everything from stone and wood reproductions

---

ANGKOR NATIONAL MUSEUM

Looming large on the road to Angkor is the **Angkor National Museum** (Map p134; ☎ 966601; www. angkornationalmuseum.com; 968 Charles de Gaulle Blvd; admission adult/child under 1.2m US$12/6; 8.30am-6.30pm), a state-of-the-art showpiece on the Khmer civilisation and the majesty of Angkor. Displays are themed by era, religion and royalty as visitors move through the impressive galleries. After a short presentation, visitors enter the Zen-like 'Gallery of a Thousand Buddhas', which has a fine collection of images. Other collections include the pre-Angkorian periods of Funan and Chenla, the great Khmer kings, Angkor Wat, Angkor Thom and the inscriptions.

Presentations include touch-screen video, epic commentary and the chance to experience a panoramic sunrise at Angkor Wat, but for all the technology there seems to be a scarcity of sculpture compared with the National Museum (p93) in Phnom Penh. That said, it remains a very useful experience for first-time visitors to put the story of Angkor and the Khmer empire in context before exploring the temples. The downside is the price, which at US$12 is simply too high, given that US$20 buys admission to all the temples at Angkor. Visitors also have to pay a US$2 camera fee, but can't snap everywhere, and an audio tour is available for US$3. Attached to the museum is a 'Cultural Mall', lined with shops, galleries and cafes, but this hasn't really taken off and sees few visitors.

of Angkorian-era statues to household furnishings. Tours are available daily from 7.30am to 5.30pm to learn more about traditional techniques. Tucked down a side road, the school is well signposted from Sivatha St.

There is also a second shop opposite Angkor Wat in the Angkor Café building and outlets at Phnom Penh and Siem Reap international airports. Profits from sales go back into funding the school and bringing more teenagers into the training program.

Les Chantiers Écoles also maintains a **silk farm** (off Map p130), which produces some of the best work in the country, including clothing, interior design products and accessories. All stages of the production process can be seen here, from the cultivation of mulberry trees through the nurturing of silk worms to the dyeing and weaving of silk. Free tours are available daily between 7am and 5pm and there is a free shuttle bus departing from Les Chantiers Écoles at 9.30am and 1.30pm. The farm is about 16km west of Siem Reap, just off the road to Sisophon in the village of Puok.

Khmer Ceramics Centre

This **ceramics centre** (Map p130; ☎ 092-476689; www.khmerceramics.com; Charles de Gaulle Blvd; ☾ 8am-6pm) is dedicated to reviving the Khmer tradition of pottery, which was an intricate art during the time of Angkor. The centre has recently relocated to the road to Angkor, but it is still possible to visit and try your hand at the potter's wheel. Courses in traditional techniques are available from US$15 to US$30 per day. There are plenty of elegant items on sale here and the centre is working with **Heritage Watch** (www.heritagewatch.org) to offer a sustainable livelihood to remote villagers.

Shadow Puppets

The creation of leather *sbei tuoi* (shadow puppets) is a traditional Khmer art form, and the figures make a memorable souvenir. Characters include gods and demons from the *Reamker*, as well as exquisite elephants with intricate armour. These are a very Cambodian keepsake. The **House of Peace Association** (Map p130), about 4km down NH6 on the way to the airport, makes these puppets, and small puppets start from US$15 while larger pieces can be as much as US$150. A second workshop is located at Wat Preah Inkosei (opposite). It is possible to watch a shadow puppet show at La Noria Restaurant (p147).

Miniature Replicas of Angkor's Temples

One of the more quirky places in town is the **garden** (Map p134; admission US$1.50) of a local master sculptor, which houses miniature replicas of Angkor Wat, the Bayon, Banteay Srei and other temples. It is a bluffer's way to get that aerial shot of Angkor without chartering a helicopter, although the astute might question the presence of oversized insects in the shot.

Cambodian Cultural Village

It may be kitsch, it may be kooky, but it is very popular with Cambodians, and provides a diversion for families travelling with children. This is the **Cambodian Cultural Village** (Map p130; ☎ 963836; www.cambodianculturalvillage.com; Airport Rd; admission adult/child under 1.1m US$9/free; ☾ 8am-7pm), which tries to represent all of Cambodia in a whirlwind tour of recreated houses and villages. The visit begins with a wax museum and includes homes of the Cham, Chinese, Kreung and Khmer people, as well as miniature replicas of landmark buildings in Cambodia. There are dance shows and performances throughout the day, but it still doesn't add up to a turn-on for most foreign visitors, unless they have the kiddies in tow. It is located about midway between Siem Reap and the airport.

Cambodia Landmine Museum

Established by DIY de-miner Aki Ra, the **Cambodia Landmine Museum** (off Map p130; ☎ 012 598951; www.cambodialandminemuseum.org; admission US$2; ☾ 7.30am-5.30pm) is very popular with travellers thanks to its informative displays on the curse of land mines in Cambodia. The museum includes an extensive collection of mines, mortars, guns and weaponry used during the civil war. The site includes a mock minefield so that visitors can attempt to spot the deactivated mines. Not only a weapon of war, land mines are a weapon against peace and proceeds from the museum are ploughed into mine awareness campaigns and support an on-site orphanage, rehabilitation centre and training facility. The museum is about 25km from Siem Reap in Banteay Srei and is easily combined with a visit to Banteay Srei temple, about 6km beyond.

For those wanting to learn more about the after-effects of an amputation, it is possible to visit the **Physical Rehabilitation Centre** (Map p134; ☾ 8am-noon & 2-5pm Mon-Fri), run by **Handicap International** (www.handicapinternational.be). There are informative displays including a variety

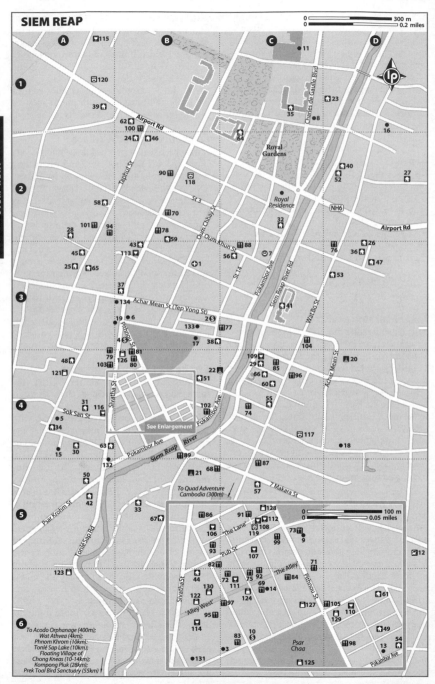

SIEM REAP

SIEM REAP

INFORMATION
Angkor Children's Hospital................**1** B3
ANZ Royal Bank...................................**2** B3
Blue Apsara...**3** C6
Canadia Bank.....................................**4** B3
ConCERT...**5** A4
DHL...**6** B3
D's Books.....................................(see 128)
EMS...(see 7)
Main Post Office.................................**7** C3
Monument Books.........................(see 32)
Siem Reap Book Center................(see 9)
Tourism Office....................................**8** C1
U-Care Pharmacy...............................**9** C5
Union Commercial Bank...................**10** C6

SIGHTS & ACTIVITIES
Angkor National Museum................**11** C1
Angkor Palm...............................(see 71)
Aqua...**12** D5
Bodia Spa.....................................(see 9)
Bodytune..**13** D6
Frangipani...**14** C6
Kong Kea Spa.............................(see 41)
Le Tigre de Papier....................(see 107)
Les Chantiers Écoles.........................**15** A4
Miniature Replicas of
    Angkor's Temples........................**16** D1
Physical Rehabilitation
    Centre..**17** B3
Sam Veasna Center...........................**18** D4
Sanctuary Spa..............................(see 56)
Seeing Hands Massage 4...................**19** B3
Visaya Spa..................................(see 32)
Wat Bo..**20** D4
Wat Dam Nak....................................**21** B5
Wat Preah Prohm Roth......................**22** B4

SLEEPING
Amansara...**23** D1
Angkorland Hotel.............................**24** B2
Auberge Mont Royal.........................**25** A3
Babel Guesthouse.............................**26** D3
Borann L'Auberge des
    Temples.......................................**27** D2
Central Boutique Angkor
    Hotel..**28** A2
City River Hotel.................................**29** C4
EI8HT Rooms.....................................**30** A4
Encore Angkor Guesthouse..............**31** A4
FCC Angkor.......................................**32** C2
Golden Banana..................................**33** B5
Golden Temple Villa..........................**34** A4
Grand Hotel d'Angkor.......................**35** C1
Happy Guesthouse............................**36** D3
Hotel de la Paix................................**37** B3
Ivy Guesthouse 2..............................**38** B3
Jasmine Lodge...................................**39** A1
La Noria Guesthouse.........................**40** D2
La Résidence d'Angkor......................**41** C3
Mandalay Inn....................................**42** A5
Mekong Angkor Palace......................**43** B3
Molly Malone's
    Guesthouse..................................**44** B6
Mommy's Guesthouse........................**45** A3

Mon Papa Guesthouse......................**46** B2
MotherHome Guesthouse..................**47** D3
Native Khmer....................................**48** A4
Neth Socheata
    Guesthouse..................................**49** D6
Popular Guesthouse..........................**50** A5
Prohm Roth Guesthouse...................**51** B4
Rosy Guesthouse...............................**52** D2
Sala Bai Hotel &
    Restaurant School...................(see 94)
Seven Candles Guesthouse...............**53** D3
Shadow of Angkor
    Guesthouse..................................**54** D6
Shadow of Angkor II
    Guesthouse..................................**55** C4
Shinta Mani.......................................**56** C3
Siem Reap Hostel..............................**57** C5
Smiley Guesthouse............................**58** A2
Somadevi Angkor Hotel.....................**59** B2
Soria Moria Hotel.............................**60** C4
Steung Siem Reap Hotel....................**61** D6
Ta Som Guesthouse...........................**62** B1
Terrasse des Elephants......................**63** A4
Victoria Angkor Hotel.......................**64** C2
Villa Siem Reap.................................**65** A3
Viroth's Hotel....................................**66** C4
Wat's Up Guesthouse........................**67** B5

EATING
AHA..(see 124)
Alliance Cafe....................................**68** B5
Amok..**69** C6
Angkor Market..................................**70** B2
Angkor Palm.....................................**71** C5
Blackwheat Creperie.........................**72** C6
Blue Pumpkin....................................**73** C5
Butterflies Garden
    Restaurant...................................**74** C4
Café de la Paix.............................(see 37)
Café Indochine............................(see 43)
Cambodian BBQ................................**75** C6
Chamkar.....................................(see 75)
Chivit Thai..**76** D3
Common Grounds..............................**77** C3
Curry Walla.......................................**78** B2
Dead Fish Tower...............................**79** A4
FCC Angkor..................................(see 32)
Happy Herb's Pizza..........................**80** B4
Hong Kong Restaurant......................**81** B4
In Touch...**82** B5
Joe-to-Go...**83** C6
Khmer Kitchen Restaurant................**84** C6
Le Café...**85** C4
Le Malraux..**86** B5
Le Tigre de Papier.....................(see 107)
Les Orientalistes...............................**87** C5
L'Escale des Arts & des
    Sens...**88** C3
Local Food Stalls..............................**89** B4
Lucky Market.....................................**90** B2
Maharajah...**91** C5
Moloppor Café.............................(see 29)
n.y.d.c...**92** C6
Psar Chaa....................................(see 125)
Red Piano..**93** B5

Sala Bai Hotel & Restaurant
    School..**94** A2
Samot..**95** B6
Selantra..**96** C4
Singing Tree Café..............................**97** C6
Socheata II Restaurant......................**98** D6
Soup Dragon.....................................**99** C5
Starmart..**100** B1
Sugar Palm......................................**101** A2
Swensen's Ice Cream.......................**102** B4
Tell Restaurant................................**103** A4
Viroth's Restaurant.........................**104** C3
Viva..**105** D6

DRINKING
4 Faces..**106** B5
Angkor What?.................................**107** C5
Banana Leaf.....................................**108** C5
Central..(see 83)
Chilli Si-Dang..................................**109** C4
Island Bar...................................(see 121)
Laundry Bar....................................**110** D6
Linga Bar...**111** C6
Miss Wong.......................................**112** C5
Nest...**113** B3
Sports Bar.......................................**114** B6
Temple Club................................(see 119)
Trey Kon..**115** A1
Warehouse..................................(see 129)
X Bar..**116** A4

ENTERTAINMENT
Apsara Theatre................................**117** C4
Dining Room................................(see 41)
Koulen II Restaurant........................**118** B2
La Noria Restaurant....................(see 40)
Temple Club....................................**119** C5
Tonlé Sap Restaurant......................**120** A1

SHOPPING
Angkor Night Market.......................**121** A4
Artisans d'Angkor.......................(see 15)
Bambou Indochine..........................**122** B6
Bloom...(see 110)
Garden of Desire.........................(see 69)
Hagar Design...............................(see 14)
IKTT...**123** A6
Jasmine..(see 32)
McDermott Gallery..........................**124** C6
Nyemo...(see 121)
Psar Chaa..**125** C6
Rajana...**126** B4
Rehab Craft.................................(see 54)
Rogue..**127** C5
Samatoa...**128** C5
Senteurs d'Angkor...........................**129** D6
Tabitha Cambodia........................(see 70)
Wanderlust......................................**130** B6

TRANSPORT
Capitol Tour....................................**131** B6
GST...**132** A5
Helicopters Cambodia.....................**133** B3
Helistar...**134** B3
Mekong Express...........................(see 6)

of homemade prosthetics that it has replaced with international-standard artificial limbs, plus it is possible to meet some of the locals receiving assistance here.

Angkor Butterfly Centre

New in 2009, the **Angkor Butterfly Centre** (off Map p130; ☎ 011 348460; www.angkorbutterfly.com; entry adult/child US$4/2; ☺ 9am-5pm daily) is a worthwhile place to include on a trip to Banteay Srei and the Cambodia Landmine Museum. The largest fully enclosed butterfly centre in Southeast Asia, there are more than 30 species of Cambodian butterflies fluttering about. It is a good experience for children, as they can see the whole process from egg to caterpillar to cocoon to butterfly. The centre is trying to provide a sustainable living for the rural poor and most of the butterflies are farmed around Phnom Kulen. It is located about 7km before Banteay Srei on the right-hand side of the road: finding it is as easy as ABC.

ACTIVITIES
Cooking Courses

Cooking classes have really taken off in Siem Reap with a number of restaurants and hotels now offering an introduction to the secrets of Cambodian cooking, including many of the top-end places. Some classes with a good reputation:

Angkor Palm (p142) Informal cooking classes at just US$10/15/20 for 1/2/3 dishes, held from 8am to 5pm.

Cooks in Tuk Tuks (Map p130; ☎ 963400; www.the rivergarden.info; per person US$25) Starts at 10am daily with a visit to Psar Leu market, then returns to the River Garden (p140) for a professional class.

Le Tigre de Papier (p144) Starts at 10am daily and includes a visit to the market for US$12. Proceeds go to supporting Sala Bai Hotel and Restaurant School (p144), making it great value and a good cause.

Golf

Siem Reap has several international-standard golf courses. **Phokheetra Country Club** (off Map p130; ☎ 964600; www.sofitel.com) hosts a tournament on the Asian tour annually and includes an ancient Angkor bridge amid its manicured fairways and greens. The **Angkor Golf Resort** (Map p130; ☎ 761139; www.angkor-golf.com) was designed by legendary British golfer Nick Faldo and is world class.

Greens fees for both are around US$100, plus more for a caddy, clubs and carts.

Horse Riding

The **Happy Ranch** (Map p130; ☎ 012 920002; www. thehappyranch.com; 1hr–half-day ride US$17-80) offers the chance to explore Siem Reap on horseback, taking in surrounding villages and secluded temples. This is a calm way to experience the countryside, far from the traffic and crowds elsewhere. Popular rides take in Wat Athvea (p132), a modern pagoda with an ancient temple on its grounds, and Wat Chedi, a temple set on a flood plain near the Tonlé Sap Lake. Riding lessons are also available for children and beginners. Book directly for the best prices.

Massage & Spa

You may well need a massage if you have been exploring the roller-coaster roads of Preah Vihear Province. Deserving of support is **Seeing Hands Massage 4** (Map p134; ☎ 012 836487; 324 Sivatha St; per hr fan/air-con US$5/7), which trains blind people in the art of massage. Watch out for copycats, as some of these are just exploiting the blind for profit. **Krousar Thmey** (Map p130; massage US$7) also has massage by the blind in the same location as its free Tonlé Sap Exhibition.

Foot massage is a big hit in Siem Reap – not surprising given all those steep stairways at the temples. There are half a dozen or more places offering a massage for about US$6 or US$7 an hour on the strip running northwest of Psar Chaa. Some are more authentic than others, so dip your toe in first before selling your sole.

For an alternative foot massage, brave the waters of **Dr Fish**. Basically a paddling pool full of cleaner fish, they nibble away at your dead skin. Heaven for some, tickly as hell for others. Originally housed in the Angkor Night Market, copycats have sprung up all over town, including about 10 outlets around Pub St and Psar Chaa.

There are also some indulgent spas to pamper your inner princess:

Bodia Spa (Map p134; ☎ 761593; www.bodia-spa.com; Pithnou St; ☺ 10am-midnight) Sophisticated spa near Psar Chaa offering a full range of scrubs and natural remedies, including its own line of herbal products.

Bodytune (Map p134; ☎ 764141; www.bodytune.co.th; 293 Pokambor Ave; massages US$12-37; ☺ 10am-10pm) A lavish outpost of a popular Thai spa, this is a fine place to relax and unwind on the riverfront.

Frangipani (Map p134; ☎ 964391; www.frangipanisiem reap.com; The Alley; ☺ 10am-10pm) Located down an

SIEM REAP

alley between Psar Chaa and Bar St, this delightful little place offers massage and a whole range of spa treatments.

Many top-end hotels have in-house spas that are open to all. Those with the best reputation include **Sanctuary Spa** (Map p134) at Shinta Mani (p141), voted second best in Asia by readers of the *Spa Asia* magazine; and **Visaya Spa** (Map p134) at FCC Angkor (p141). **Kong Kea Spa** (Map p134) at La Residence d'Angkor (p141) is worthy of a special mention, as it is a stunning new place with superb facilities.

Quad Biking
Quad biking has finally come to Siem Reap thanks to **Quad Adventure Cambodia** (off Map p134; ☎ 092-787216; www.q-adventure-cambodia.com; rides US$25-195). For those who haven't tried it, all-terrain biking is serious fun and all rides include a short introductory lesson. Rides around Siem Reap involve rice fields at sunset, pretty temples and back roads through traditional villages where children wave and shout. Quad Adventure Cambodia is well signposted in the Wat Dam Nak area.

Swimming
It's hot work clambering about the temples and there is no better way to wind down than a dip in a swimming pool. Pay by the day at most hotels for use of the swimming pool and/or gym, ranging from just US$5 at some of the midrange hotels to US$20 at the five-star palaces. More and more of the cheaper hotels and resorts are putting in pools and this can be a worthwhile splash for weary travellers.

Or head to **Aqua** (Map p134; www.aquacambodia. com; 7 Makara St; swimming US$2), where there is a large pool and a lively little bar-restaurant. Locals like to swim in the waters of the Western Baray (p186) at the weekend.

Yoga
If the temples of Angkor put you in a spiritual frame of mind, try some 'ancient wisdom for modern times' with **Raja Yoga** (Map p130; ☎ 761712; www.bkrajayoga.org; near HanumanAlaya hotel). Free sessions are available daily and longer retreats by appointment.

SIEM REAP FOR CHILDREN
Siem Reap is a great city for children these days thanks to a range of activities beyond the temples. Many of the temples themselves will appeal to older children, particularly the Indiana Jones atmosphere of Ta Prohm (p181) and Beng Mealea (p191), the sheer size and scale of Angkor Wat (p167) or the weird faces at the Bayon (p172).

Other activities that might be popular include boat trips on the Tonlé Sap to visit the other-worldly villages (p151); swimming at a hotel or resort (left); pottery classes at the Khmer Ceramics Centre (p133); exploring the countryside on horseback (opposite) or quad bike (left); goofing around at the Cambodian Cultural Village (p133); exploring the Angkor Butterfly Centre (opposite); or just enjoying the cafes and restaurants of Siem Reap at a leisurely pace. Ice-cream shops might be popular if a little naughty, while the local barbecue restaurants are always well liked by older children.

TOURS
Most visitors are in Siem Reap to tour the temples of Angkor. See p165 for more on temple tours and p345 for a list of recommended Cambodian tour operators.

SLEEPING
Siem Reap has the best range of accommodation in Cambodia. A vast number of family-run guesthouses charging US$3 to US$20 a room cater for budget travellers, while those looking for midrange accommodation can choose upmarket guesthouses from US$20, or small hotels from US$25 per room.

There are plenty of midrange to top-end hotels around town, and, as the construction boom continues unabated, these will be supplemented by further arrivals. In the low season (April to September), it may be possible to negotiate discounts at some of these places. Top-end hotels usually publish high-and low-season rates.

The places listed below are just a selection of our favourites. There are many more good places around town that we simply don't have the room to cover, so the lack of a listing here doesn't mean it's not a decent place to stay.

Commission scams abound in Siem Reap, so keep your antennae up. See Dangers & Annoyances (p131) for more details.

Budget
Touts for budget guesthouses wait at the taxi park, Phnom Krom (where the fast boat from

SIEM REAP

Phnom Penh docks) and at the airport. Even if you have not yet decided where to stay in Siem Reap, do not be surprised to see a noticeboard displaying your name, as most guesthouses in Phnom Penh either have partners up here or sell your name on to another guesthouse. This system usually involves a free ride into town. There is no obligation to stay at their guesthouse if you don't like the look of it, but the 'free lift' might suddenly cost US$1 or more.

PSAR CHAA AREA

Popular Guesthouse (Map p134; ☎ 963578; chom@cam net.com.kh; r US$3-18; ☒ ☐) Popular by name, popular by nature, this extensive guesthouse has more than 70 well-tended rooms. There's a rooftop restaurant with great food.

Prohm Roth Guesthouse (Map p134; ☎ 012 466495; www.prohmroth-guesthouse.com; r US$7-18; ☒ ☐ ☜ ☝) Very central, yet tucked away down a side street which runs parallel to Wat Preah Prohm Roth, this is a friendly place to stay. Air-con rooms start from US$11 and the wi-fi is free.

Mandalay Inn (Map p134; ☎ 761662; www.mandalay inn.com; 148 Sivatha St; r US$8-20; ☒ ☐ ☜ ☝) This smart guesthouse promises Burmese hospitality meets Khmer smiles, offering spotless rooms plus free wi-fi and a rooftop 'gym'.

Shadow of Angkor Guesthouse (Map p134; ☎ 964774; www.shadowofangkor.com; 353 Pokambor Ave; r US$8-25; ☒ ☐ ☝) Boasting a choice setting in a grand old French-era building overlooking the river, this friendly place offers budget fan rooms, affordable air-con and free internet.

our pick **Neth Socheata Guesthouse** (Map p134; ☎ 963294; www.angkorguesthousenethsocheata.com; r US$15-18; ☒ ☐ ☜ ☝) One of the newest guesthouses around Psar Chaa, this has a likeable location in the warren of alleys to the northeast of the market. Tasteful furnishings, sparkling bathrooms and free internet/wi-fi add up to a tempting deal.

Other options near the market:

Ivy Guesthouse 2 (Map p134; ☎ 012 602930; r US$6-12; ☒ ☐) An inviting guesthouse with a chill-out area and bar, the Ivy is a lively place to stay.

EI8HT Rooms (Map p134; ☎ 969788; www.ei8htrooms. com; r US$14-16; ☒ ☐ ☜ ☝) Smart little boutique guesthouse with bright silks, a DVD player and free internet and wi-fi. So popular, there are 16 rooms now.

SIVATHA ST AREA

Garden Village (Map p130; ☎ 012 217373; www.garden villageguesthouse.com; dm US$1, r US$3-15; ☒ ☐ ☝)

This sprawling place offers some of the cheapest beds in town; choose from eight-bed dorms or US$3 cubicles with shared bathroom.

our pick **My Home Tropical Garden Villa** (Map p130; ☎ 760035; www.myhomecambodia.com; r US$8-18; ☒ ☐ ☜ ☝) Offering hotel standards at guesthouse prices, this is a fine place to rest your head. The decor includes some subtle silks and the furnishings are tasteful. There's free internet in the lobby and free wi-fi in the rooms; air-con starts at US$15.

Native Khmer (Map p134; ☎ 965935; r US$8-20; ☒ ☐ ☝) More like Native Woodstock, this place near the Angkor Night Market pays homage to the likes of Bob Marley and Jerry Garcia. If you can survive the cheeky banter, then the rooms here are a reasonable deal.

Golden Temple Villa (Map p134; ☎ 012 943459; www. goldentemplevilla.com; r US$8-30; ☒ ☐ ☝) This place remains popular thanks to its funky decor and fun outlook. Rooms are painted in vivid colours and include cable TV. There is a bar-restaurant downstairs, plus free internet.

Ancient Angkor Guesthouse (Map p130; ☎ 012 772862; www.ancient-angkor.com; r US$12-30; ☒ ☐ ☜ ☒ ☝) Now expanded into two buildings, this place offers real value for money, with smart rooms and a small swimming pool. Free internet and wi-fi.

Sala Bai Hotel & Restaurant School (Map p134; ☎ 963329; www.salabai.com; Taphul St; r US$15-30; ☒ ☝) Immerse yourself in the intimate surrounds of this training school hotel, where the super staff are ever helpful. Rooms include silk wall hangings, woven throw pillows and wicker wardrobes.

A few more friendly, family-run options:

Mommy's Guesthouse (Map p134; ☎ 012 941755; r US$4-15; ☒) This homely villa has large rooms with air-con, as well as cheap digs with cold showers. Friendly owners.

Mon Papa Guesthouse (Map p134; ☎ 761923; r US$6-10; ☒ ☐ ☜ ☝) No relation to Mommy's, but a clean, well-run and likeable little guesthouse. Free wi-fi.

Smiley Guesthouse (Map p134; ☎ 012 852955; r US$8-15; ☒) One of the first guesthouses to undergo a hotel-style makeover, this place has more than 70 rooms set around a garden courtyard.

AIRPORT RD

Earthwalkers (Map p130; ☎ 012 967901; www.earthwalk ers.no; off NH6; dm US$5, s/d from US$12/15; ☒ ☐ ☒ ☝) The original backpacker hostel in town, Earthwalkers is popular thanks to the signature 'footprint' swimming pool. Dorms include breakfast and private rooms come with fan or air-con to suit all budgets. Extensive travel information provided.

Ta Som Guesthouse (Map p134; ☎ 964970; www.tasom guesthouse.com; NH6; r US$6-12; ✂ ☐ ♿) Hooked up with the popular Capitol Tour (p149), this guesthouse has affordable fan rooms and the location is more central than most places on this strip.

Jasmine Lodge (Map p134; ☎ 760697; www.jasmine lodge.com; NH6; r US$6-22; ✂ ☐ ♿) Offering a home away from home, this long-running guesthouse has upgraded its rooms in recent years. The elevated bar-restaurant includes a pool table. Unique offerings include free cooking classes and traditional country homestays.

WAT BO AREA

our pick Seven Candles Guesthouse (Map p134; ☎ 963380; www.sevencandlesguesthouse.com; 307 Wat Bo St; r US$7-15; ✂ ☐ ♿) An original guesthouse run by the Ly family, profits help the Ponheary Ly Foundation which seeks to promote education in rural communities. Rooms are meticulously clean thanks to the novel idea of dust covers on the beds and include hot water, TV and fridge.

Shadow of Angkor II Guesthouse (Map p134; ☎ 760363; www.shadowofangkor.com; Wat Bo St; r US$15-35; ✂ ☐ ♿ ♿) New and has smarter rooms than the original (opposite) and the added advantage of a small pool.

There's a whole strip of guesthouses in a backstreet running parallel to the north end of Wat Bo St, including the following:

Happy Guesthouse (Map p134; ☎ 012 960879; www. angkorhotels.com/happy; r US$4-10; ✂ ☐ ♿) Really will make you happy thanks to welcoming owners, good value rooms and free internet.

MotherHome Guesthouse (Map p134; ☎ 760302; www.motherhomeguesthouse.com; r US$9-20; ✂ ☐ ♿) A smart newer place in the same area, offering clean, spacious rooms, plus free use of bicycles and internet.

And the budget beat goes on:

Wat's Up Guesthouse (Map p134; ☎ 012 675881; r US$6-20; ✂ ☐ ♿) A smart guesthouse with a memorable name in a quieter part of town. Family-friendly initiatives include a baby bed, a stroller, a car seat and bike seat.

Rosy Guesthouse (Map p134; ☎ 965059; www. rosyguesthouse.com; Siem Reap River Rd; r US$8-30; ✂ ☐ ♿) Recently renovated, the rooms are a fair deal for the riverside location, plus it's not far to the bustling bar downstairs.

Midrange

Great deals are available thanks to an explosion in Siem Reap's midrange options. Most rates include a free transfer from the airport or boat dock.

PSAR CHAA AREA

Molly Malone's Guesthouse (Map p134; ☎ 963533; www. mollymalonescambodia.com; Pub St; r US$20-35; ✂ ☐ ♿) If you want to be in the heart of the action, this smart B&B above a popular Irish pub (p146) has a small selection of guestrooms, creatively finished with four-poster beds.

Golden Banana (Map p134; ☎ 761259; www.golden -banana.com; r US$25-89; ✂ ☐ ♿ ♿) The Banana just keeps on growing, with the addition of a new colonial-style wing. The original cheaper rooms are set in pagoda-style bungalows, but newer suites are set on two floors with swing chairs and a pool view. Some rooms include a rain shower and alfresco bath-tub. Gay-friendly.

Terrasse des Elephants (Map p134; ☎ 380117; www.terrasse-des-elephants.com; s/d from US$50/55; ✂ ☐ ♿ ♿) This place is very memorable thanks to its kitsch Angkor theme, including bas-reliefs in the bedroom and ornate Bayon-themed bathrooms, complete with four faces. As central as it gets, the rooftop pool and garden are a nice surprise.

Steung Siem Reap Hotel (Map p134; ☎ 965167; www.steungsiemreaphotel.com; s/d from US$70/80; ✂ ☐ ♿) In keeping with the French colonial air around Psar Chaa, this hotel has high ceilings, louvre shutters and wrought-iron balconies. Three-star rooms feature a smart wooden trim. The location is hard to beat.

SIVATHA ST AREA

Villa Siem Reap (Map p134; ☎ 761036; www.thevilla siemreap.com; 153 Taphul St; r US$18-50; ✂ ☐ ♿) Homely service in intimate surrounds make this a popular place. Rooms are nicely finished and include a safe and a minibar. Popular tours are available to some of the far-flung sights.

our pick Encore Angkor Guesthouse (Map p134; ☎ 969400; www.encoreangkor.com; 456 Sok San St; r US$20-50; ✂ ☐ ♿ ♿) The stylish lobby sets the tone for a budget boutique experience. Rooms include all the usual touches, plus oversized beds and an in-room safe. Their motto is 'just don't tell anyone'. Sorry, guys.

Auberge Mont Royal (Map p134; ☎ 964044; www. auberge-mont-royal.com; r US$25-60; ✂ ☐ ♿ ♿) Set

SIEM REAP

in a classic colonial-style villa, the Auberge has smart rooms at a smart price, with the swimming pool and spa making it a cut above other offerings in this price bracket.

The list goes on:

Mekong Angkor Palace (Map p134; ☎ 963636; www.mekongangkorpalace.com; Sivatha St; r US$25-40; ✖ 🖳 🕿 🕭) Set back from the main drag, this hotel offers large, bright rooms and an inviting pool.

Central Boutique Angkor Hotel (Map p134; ☎ 764030; www.centralboutiqueangkorhotel.com; Ta Phul Village; r US$35; ✖ 🖳 🕿 🕭) The main attraction here is the swimming pool, but the rooms include a balcony terrace, soft linens and a safe.

AIRPORT RD

Paul Dubrule Hotel & Tourism School (École d'Hôtellerie et de Tourisme Paul Dubrule; Map p130; ☎ 963673; www.ecolepauldubrule.org; r US$20-35; ✖ 🖳 🕭) Paul Dubrule co-founded the Accor hotel group, so it's no surprise his tourism school hotel offers slick service and smart rooms. Proceeds are ploughed into the training centre. The rooms are a great deal, but there are just four.

WAT BO AREA

Siem Reap Hostel (Map p134; ☎ 964660; www.thesiemreaphostel.com; 10 Makara St; dm US$8, r US$30-45; ✖ 🖳 🕿 🕭) Angkor's first full-on backpacker hostel, it's pretty slick and caters to the budget backpacker and the aspiring 'flashpacker'. The dorms are pricey, but the rooms are fairly smart and include breakfast. There's a lively bar-restaurant and a covered pool.

Green Village Palace (off Map p134; ☎ 760623; www.greenvillagepalace.com; Wat Dam Nak St; r US$15-30; ✖ 🖳 🕿 🕭) It is quite palatial for this sort of money, as the smart rooms include sweeping silks, plus TV and fridge. There's also a small swimming pool and a gym.

our pick Soria Moria Hotel (Map p134; ☎ 964768; www.thesoriamoria.com; Wat Bo St; r US$40-75; ✖ 🖳 🕿 🕭) A hotel with a heart, promoting local causes to help the community, this boutique place has attractive rooms with smart bathroom fittings. Fusion restaurant downstairs, sky hot tub upstairs.

La Noria Guesthouse (Map p134; ☎ 964242; www.lanoriaangkor.com; r US$44; ✖ 🖳 🕿 🕭) Lovely La Noria is set in a lush tropical garden with a pretty swimming pool. Rooms have a traditional trim and include a verandah but no TV or fridge.

Borann L'Auberge des Temples (Map p134; ☎ 964740; www.borann.com; r US$44; ✖ 🖳 🕿 🕭)

Sister hotel to La Noria, Borann is almost identical and is a similarly idyllic retreat.

Other recommendations:

Babel Guesthouse (Map p134; ☎ 965474; babelsiemreap@gmail.com; r US$14-24; ✖ 🖳 🕭) An upmarket guesthouse with a relaxing tropical garden. The service and presentation are better than nearby budget places.

City River Hotel (Map p134; ☎ 763000; www.cityriverhotel.com; r from US$45; ✖ 🖳 🕿 🕭) Smart, modern rooms in a great riverside location, with a rooftop swimming pool.

FURTHER AFIELD

Lotus Lodge (Map p130; ☎ 966140; www.lotuslodgecambodia.com; r US$25-35; ✖ 🖳 🕿 🕭) The Lotus offers a good deal for those wanting a peaceful retreat after a day at the temples. Rooms are clean and comfortable, plus there is a spacious swimming pool with a welcoming restaurant-bar. Free bikes, free evening shuttles.

Pavillon Indochine (Map p130; ☎ 012 849681; www.pavillon-indochine.com; r US$50-55, ste US$70-85; ✖ 🖳 🕿 🕭) The Pavillon offers charming colonial-chic rooms set around a small swimming pool. The trim includes Asian antiques, billowing mosquito nets and a safe.

River Garden (Map p130; ☎ 963400; www.therivergarden.info; r US$55-99; ✖ 🖳 🕿 🕭) Invitingly set amid an enchanting garden, this wooden resort has a small selection of atmospheric rooms, some with large balconies and deep baths. Relax by the pool, indulge in an ice-cream buffet or join its 'cooks in *tuk tuks*' culinary class (p136).

HanumanAlaya (Map p130; ☎ 760582; www.hanumanalaya.com; r US$60-90; ✖ 🖳 🕿 🕭) A blissful boutique retreat, HanumanAlaya is set around a lush garden and pretty swimming pool. Rooms are decorated with antiques and handicrafts, but include modern comforts like cable TV, a minibar and safe. It's also home to the Sita Spa and Reahoo Restaurant, popular for authentic Khmer flavours.

More for the mix:

Angkor Spirit Palace (Map p130; ☎ 760029; www.angkorspiritpalace.com; r US$35-55; ✖ 🖳 🕿 🕭) Invest in the 'Palace' or 'Spirit' rooms for more space and better amenities. Almost in the countryside, the pool is relaxing.

Sonalong Boutique Village (Map p130; ☎ 012 913376; www.sonalongvillage.com; r from US$50; ✖ 🖳 🕿 🕭) A new resort to the west of Wat Bo, rooms here are set around a verdant garden and swimming pool, and include a balcony (upstairs) or verandah (downstairs).

Top End

Most of the hotels in this range levy an additional 10% government tax, 2% tourist tax, and sometimes an extra 10% for service, but breakfast is included. It is essential to book ahead at most places from November through to March, particularly for the glamorous spots. Booking online or through a travel agent can save considerable money on the walk-in rate.

Viroth's Hotel (Map p134; ☎ 761720; www.viroth-hotel.com; r from US$90; ❄ ▯ 🛜 🍽 ⓖ) Minimalist and modern, this small boutique property has seven rooms finished in contemporary chic. Facilities include a pool, a hot tub and free wi-fi.

Shinta Mani (Map p134; ☎ 761998; www.shintamani.com; Oum Khun St; s/d/tr US$90/100/130; ❄ ▯ 🍽 ⓖ) Established as a training institute to give disadvantaged youth a helping hand into the tourism industry, rooms feature designer bathrooms and sleigh beds, as well as a small pool. Shinta Mani has won several international awards for responsible tourism practices and has lots of community programs. It is slated for a major makeover.

FCC Angkor (Map p134; ☎ 760280; www.fcccambodia.com; Pokambor Ave; s/d from US$135/155; ❄ ▯ 🛜 🍽 ⓖ) This funky property is a member of Design Hotels and wouldn't look out of place in any chic European capital. However, there are Khmer touches, and rooms feature large bath-tubs, Cambodian silks and wi-fi throughout. The black-tiled swimming pool and Visaya Spa complete the picture.

Angkor Village Resort (Map p130; ☎ 963561; Phum Traeng St; r US$149; ❄ ▯ 🍽 ⓖ) This lovely resort has a snaking pool that wends its way through the grounds like a river. The rooms are spacious and include elegant bathrooms and mod cons, such as TVs.

Victoria Angkor Hotel (Map p134; ☎ 760428; www.victoriahotels-asia.com; r from US$155; ❄ ▯ 🍽 ⓖ) The Victoria is a popular choice for those craving the French touch in Indochine. The classy lobby is the perfect introduction to one of the most impressive courtyard pools in town. The rooms are well finished and many include a striking pool view.

our pick **La Résidence d'Angkor** (Map p134; ☎ 963390; www.residencedangkor.com; Siem Reap River Rd; r from US$185; ❄ ▯ 🍽 ⓖ) The open-plan, all-wooden rooms are among the most inviting in town, complete with huge jacuzzi-sized tubs. Wander through the subtle reception to a stunning swimming pool, which is perfect for laps. A recent extension has added some contemporary rooms with huge bathrooms and walk-in closets, plus the divine Kong Kea Spa.

Hotel de la Paix (Map p134; ☎ 966000; www.hoteldelapaixangkor.com; Sivatha St; r from US$265; ❄ ▯ 🍽 ⓖ) This place is all about funky, contemporary design, trendy interiors and minimalist style; traditionalists be warned. Rooms include open-plan bathrooms and iPods. On-site Meric restaurant serves up cutting-edge cuisine.

Grand Hotel d'Angkor (Map p134; ☎ 963888; www.raffles.com; r from US$360; ❄ ▯ 🍽 ⓖ) The hotel with history on its side, this place has been welcoming guests since 1929, including Charlie Chaplin, Charles de Gaulle, Jackie Kennedy and Bill Clinton. Ensconced in such opulent surroundings, you can imagine what it was like to be a tourist in colonial days. Rooms include classic colonial-era touches and a dizzying array of bathroom gifts.

TOP FIVE: LOW-SEASON DEALS

A number of hotels offer enticing deals in the low season (mid-April to mid-October). Here are some of the most popular:

Lotus Angkor Hotel (Map p130; ☎ 965555; www.lotusangkor.com; Airport Rd; r from US$50; ❄ ▯ 🍽 ⓖ) Popular with tour groups thanks to smart rooms and a full-sized pool.

Somadevi Angkor Hotel (Map p134; ☎ 967666; www.somadeviangkor.com; Sivatha St; r from US$50; ❄ ▯ 🍽 ⓖ) Huge hotel just off the main drag with smart, spacious rooms and a large T-shaped pool.

Angkorland Hotel (Map p134; ☎ 760544; www.angkorland.com; off Airport Rd; r from US$59; ❄ ▯ 🍽) Big hotel with a heavy wood finish and a large courtyard pool.

Borei Angkor Resort & Spa (Map p130; ☎ 964406; www.boreiangkor.com; NH6 East; r from US$60; ❄ ▯ 🍽 ⓖ) Popular resort within walking distance of the town centre.

Angkor Home Hotel (Map p130; ☎ 969797; www.angkorhomehotel.com; off Airport Rd; r from US$79; ❄ ▯ 🍽 ⓖ) Very swish new hotel with elegant rooms and a large pool.

SIEM REAP

Amansara (Map p134; ☎ 760333; www.amanresorts. com; r from US$750; [icons]) Set in the old guest villa of Norodom Sihanouk, the suites here are among the largest in town and some include a private plunge pool. Rates include tours around the main Angkor temples. Former guests already include a who's who of the rich and famous, such as Sir Mick Jagger and Angelina Jolie (not together; she was with Brad).

Other ideas for indulging:

Angkor Palace Spa Resort (Map p130; ☎ 760511; www.angkorpalaceresort.com; off Airport Rd; r US$155; [icons]) This Balinese-style resort is a huge place with lovely open-plan rooms and a huge swimming pool. Good value.

Heritage Suites (Map p130; ☎ 969100; www. relaischateaux.com/heritage; r from US$235; ste US$345; [icons]) Designed in the colonial style, the suites here are spectacular and open plan.

Sothea (Map p130; ☎ 966788; www.thesothea. com; Airport Rd; r from US$290; [icons]) New exclusive resort with a romantic inclination, part of the Preferred Boutique group.

EATING

The dining scene in Siem Reap is something to savour, offering a superb selection of street dining, Asian eateries and sumptuous restaurants. The range encompasses something from every continent, with new temptations constantly on offer. Sample the subtleties of Khmer cuisine in Siem Reap, or simply indulge in home comforts or gastronomic delights prior to – or after – hitting the remote provinces.

Tourist numbers mean many top restaurants are heaving during high season. But with so many places to choose from, keep walking and you'll find somewhere more tranquil. The restaurants reviewed here represent just a fraction of the food on offer.

Some of the budget guesthouses have good menus offering a selection of local dishes and Western meals; while it's easy to order in-house food, it hardly counts as the full Siem Reap experience. Several of the midrange hotels and all the top-end places have restaurants, some excellent. For details on dinner and a performance of classical dance, as featured at several hotels and restaurants around town, see Entertainment (p147).

For more on the lunch options available in and around Angkor, see the boxed text on p163.

THINGS CHANGE...FAST

Siem Reap has developed at a rapid rate in recent years, so we have grown used to dealing with wholesale change. As we are going to press, many places are once again on the move. Indian restaurant Kama Sutra shut its doors, although it's rumoured to be reopening in the Alley. Vegetarian-friendly V and A has also closed, but Joe-to-Go, a good-cause cafe formerly located on the same site, is reopening nearby. The Roluos Tea Garden may also be on the move due to a dispute with Apsara Authority. Finally, Alley West is continuing its meteoric rise, with lots of small boutiques and socially responsible businesses opening up. You get the message: Siem Reap doesn't stand still.

Khmer

When it comes to cheaper Khmer eats, **Psar Chaa** (Map p134; ☉ 7am-9pm) has plenty of food stalls on the northwest side, all with signs and menus in English. These are atmospheric places for a local meal at local-ish prices. Some dishes are on display, others are freshly flash fried to order, but most dishes are just US$1.50 to US$3. Another good strip of **local food stalls** (Map p134) sits opposite Wat Dam Nak, and you can judge the quality and value by the number of *motos* parked outside.

The Alley is wall-to-wall with good Cambodian restaurants, many of which are family owned. Most have 'Khmer' in the name and offer cheap beers and meal deals. Take a stroll and see what takes your fancy.

Socheata II Restaurant (Map p134; ☎ 761416; Pithnou St; mains US$2-5; ☉ 7am-10pm) A blink-and-you'll-miss-it Khmer restaurant that offers a big range of Cambodian classics, including very tasty salads such as banana leaf, pomelo and watercress.

Khmer Kitchen Restaurant (Map p134; ☎ 964154; The Alley; mains US$2-5; ☉ 11am-10pm) Can't get no (culinary) satisfaction? Then follow in the footsteps of Sir Mick and try this popular place, which offers an affordable selection of Khmer and Thai favourites, including feisty curries.

Angkor Palm (Map p134; ☎ 761436; www.angkor palm.com; Pithnou St; mains US$3-8; ☉ 10am-10pm) This award-winning Cambodian restaurant offers the authentic taste of Cambodia. Even Khmers go crazy for the legendary *amoc* (baked fish in banana leaf) here and they offer a great sampling platter for two. Cooking classes are available.

Viroth's Restaurant (Map p134; ☎ 016 951800; Wat Bo St; mains US$4-8; ☺ lunch & dinner) A sophisticated garden restaurant near Wat Bo, this is where Khmer cuisine meets Balinese design. It is popular with tour groups, but still manages to retain an element of intimacy.

Café Indochine (Map p134; ☎ 012 804952; Sivatha St; mains US$4-8; ☺ 10am-3pm & 5-11pm) One of the few remaining traditional Khmer houses in town, this attractive restaurant offers a blend of Asian and European flavours. Enjoy the ambience by dining later to dodge the crowds.

Amok (Map p134; ☎ 965407; The Alley; mains US$4-9; ☺ 5-11pm) The name pays homage to Cambodia's national dish, *amoc* (or *amok*), and this is indeed a fine place to try baked fish curry in banana leaf or, better still, an *amoc* tasting platter with four varieties. It is in the heart of the Alley.

Madame Butterfly (Map p130; ☎ 016 909607; Airport Rd; mains US$4-10; ☺ 6-11pm) This traditional wooden house has been sumptuously decorated with fine silks and billowing drapes. The menu is Khmer and a fusion of Asian cuisines.

our pick Sugar Palm (Map p134; ☎ 964838; Taphul St; mains US$5-9; ☺ 11am-late) Set in a beautiful wooden house in the west of town, the Sugar Palm is the place to sample traditional flavours infused with herbs and spices, including delicious '*char kroeng*' (curried lemongrass) dishes. It also doubles as a popular cocktail bar to warm up or wind down.

L'Escale des Arts & des Sens (Map p134; ☎ 761442; www.escale-arts-sens.com; Oum Khun St; mains US$5-20; ☺ 6.30am-10pm; ♿) Promoting new Asian cuisine, try the wonderful tapas platters that include a selection of teasing tasters and are washed down with rice wine. Mains include beef cooked seven ways, inspired by a royal recipe for tiger meat, thankfully not on the menu.

Cambodian BBQ (Map p134; ☎ 966052; The Alley; mains US$7-10; ☺ dinner) Another tasty option along the Alley, Cambodian BBQ uses crocodile, snake, ostrich and kangaroo to add a twist to the traditional *phnom pleung* (hill of fire) grills.

Other Asian

Hong Kong Restaurant (Map p134; ☎ 012 966226; Pithnou St; mains US$2-4; ☺ 9am-10pm) A tiny Chinese restaurant specialising in authentic *dim sum*

at a reasonable price. Try the spicy *mopor tofu* (minced pork with tofu).

Curry Walla (Map p134; ☎ 965451; Sivatha St; mains US$2-5; ☺ 10.30am-11pm) For good-value Indian food, this place is hard to beat. The *thalis* (set meals) are a bargain and the owner knows his share of spicy secrets from the subcontinent.

Dead Fish Tower (Map p134; Sivatha St; mains US$2-5; ☺ 7am-late; 🖥 ♿) Looking more like an adventure playground than a restaurant at first glance, this place has floor dining and tree-trunk tables. The restaurant promises 'we don't serve dog, cat, rat or worm', so bad luck if you like any of those. However, it does keep crocodiles on site, which might put off some.

Soup Dragon (Map p134; ☎ 964933; Pub St; Vietnamese mains US$2-6, Western mains US$5-10; ☺ 6am-11pm; ♿) This three-level restaurant has a split personality: the ground floor serves up classic Asian breakfasts like *pho* (Vietnamese rice-noodle soup) for around US$1 – just the recipe for tackling the temples – while upstairs serves a diverse menu of Asian and international dishes, including Italian and Moroccan.

Chivit Thai (Map p134; ☎ 012 830761; 130 Wat Bo St; mains US$3-8; ☺ 7am-10pm) The most atmospheric Thai place in town, this is set in a beautiful wooden villa surrounded by a lush garden. Choose between floor dining on Thai cushions or table dining. The food includes a delicious *laab* (spicy Thai salad with fish or meat).

Ginga (Map p130; ☎ 963366; mains US$6-15; ☺ lunch & dinner) This popular Japanese restaurant draws the Tokyo crowd for traditional Japanese cuisine. The menu includes some affordable sashimi and sushi sets, plus combo boxes at lunchtime.

Other Asian offerings include the following:

Moloppor Café (Map p134; ☎ 966690; Siem Reap River Rd; mains US$1-4; ☺ 10am-11pm) One of the cheapest deals in Siem Reap, it offers Japanese, Asian and Italian dishes at silly prices.

In Touch (Map p134; ☎ 963240; Pub St; mains US$3-6; ☺ 11am-late) Located on a prime corner, In Touch has spectacular lighting to set the mood. The flavours are Thai, but dine early unless you want to be serenaded by the band.

Maharajah (Map p134; ☎ 966221; Psar Chaa area; mains US$3-7; ☺ 10am-11pm) Formerly the popular Taj restaurant near Psar Chaa, the owners continue to turn out authentic and affordable Indian food.

TOP FIVE: DINING FOR A CAUSE

These are some good restaurants that support worthy causes or assist in the training of Cambodia's future hospitality staff with a subsidised ticket into the tourism industry. If you dine at the training places, it gives the trainees a good opportunity to hone their skills with real customers.

Butterflies Garden Restaurant (Map p134; ☎ 761211; www.butterfliesofangkor.com; mains US$3-8; ⊙ 8am-10pm) Set in a blooming garden that provides a backdrop for hundreds of butterflies, this is dining with a difference. The menu includes Khmer flavours, some classics from home and indulgent desserts. Supports good causes, including Cambodian Living Arts and communities affected by HIV/AIDS.

Common Grounds (Map p134; ☎ 965687; 719 St 14; light meals US$3-5; ⊙ 7am-10pm; 🖳 🛜) Sophisticated international cafe akin to Starbucks. Great coffee, homemade cakes, light bites, and free wi-fi *and* internet terminals. Offers free computer classes and English classes for Cambodians, plus supports good causes.

Les Jardins des Delices (Map p130; ☎ 963673; Paul Dubrule Hotel & Tourism School; NH6; set lunch US$12; ⊙ noon-2pm Mon-Fri) Enjoy Sofitel standards at an affordable price, with a three-course meal of Asian and Western food prepared by students training in the culinary arts.

Sala Bai Hotel & Restaurant School (Map p134; ☎ 963329; www.salabai.com; set lunch US$8; ⊙ 7-9am & noon-2pm Mon-Fri) This school trains young Khmers in the art of hospitality and serves an affordable menu of Western and Cambodian cuisine.

our pick **Singing Tree Café** (Map p134; ☎ 965210; www.singingtreecafe.com; mains US$2-5; ⊙ closed Mon) Recently relocated to the up-and-coming Alley West, which saw a host of new openings in early 2010, this is a smaller pavement cafe with scrumptious muffins, creative coffees and original health foods.

International

our pick **Blue Pumpkin** (Map p134; ☎ 963574; Pithnou St; mains US$2-6; ⊙ 6am-10pm; 🍴 🛜 🚼) Downstairs it looks like any old cafe, albeit with a delightful selection of cakes, breads and homemade ice cream. Upstairs is another world of white minimalism, with beds to lounge on and free wi-fi. Light bites, great sandwiches, filling specials and divine shakes – what more can you ask for?

our pick **Le Tigre de Papier** (Map p134; ☎ 760930; Pub St; mains US$2-9; ⊙ 24hr; 🛜 🚼) One of the best all-rounders in Siem Reap, the popular Tigre serves up authentic Khmer food, great Italian dishes and a selection of favourites from most other corners of the globe. Doubles as a popular bar by night, with frontage on both Pub St and the Alley. Free wi-fi.

Tell Restaurant (Map p134; ☎ 963289; Sivatha St; mains US$2-10; ⊙ 10am-10pm; 🍴 🚼) Soak up the air-con on a hot day at this friendly restaurant, which has a huge and great-value menu of Asian dishes, international favourites and Swiss specialities, such as fondue and *raclette*.

Red Piano (Map p134; ☎ 963240; Pub St; mains US$3-6; 🚼) Strikingly set in a restored colonial gem, there is a big balcony for watching the action unfold on the streets below. The menu has a reliable selection of Asian and international food, all at reasonable prices. Former celebrity guest Angelina Jolie has a cocktail named in her honour.

AHA (Map p134; ☎ 965501; The Alley; tapas US$3-10; 🍴 🚼) A trendy little tapas emporium and wine bar, there are a variety of tasting platters here, including cheese, veggie, Khmer, classic and contemporary. Inventive cuisine.

Samot (Map p134; ☎ 092-410400; mains US$5-10; ⊙ 4pm-midnight) Hidden away down the extended 'Alley', this inviting little restaurant's name translates as 'sea' and it offers the bounty of the oceans to diners in the know. Choose from sea bass, king prawns or, sometimes, scallops, plus some meats for landlubbers.

FCC Angkor (Map p134; ☎ 760280; mains US$5-15; ⊙ 7am-midnight; 🚼) This bold building draws people in from the riverside thanks to a reflective pool, torchlit dining and a garden bar. Inside, the colonial chic continues with lounge chairs and an open kitchen turning out a range of Asian and international food. Try the beautifully presented tasting plates.

Other internationally inclined places:

Viva (Map p134; ☎ 012 209154; Pithnou St; mains US$2-6; ⊙ 11.30am-late) Spice up your life with Mexican food and margaritas. Lively location.

Blackwheat Creperie (Map p134; ☎ 092-963213; Psar Chaa area; mains US$3-8; ⊙ 11am-2am) Exotic crepes, including fusion flavours and a wholesome vegetarian selection. Pancakes will never be the same again.

Selantra (Map p134; ☎ 963097; Wat Bo St; mains US$4-10; ⊙ 11.30am-late) New in 2009, established by a former Hotel de la Paix employee, this offers creative international flavours in stylish surrounds.

Les Orientalistes (Map p134; ☎ 760278; 613 Wat Bo St; mains US$4-12; ☻ lunch & dinner) This place conjures up the souks of the Maghreb, with an international mix of Khmer, French and Moroccan cuisine, including tasty tapas.

French

Le Malraux (Map p134; ☎ 966041; mains US$5-12; ☻ 7am-midnight) A good spot for gastronomes, this classy art-deco cafe-restaurant offers fine French food. Try the combination salmon tartare and carpaccio to start, followed by a quality cut from the selection of steaks. Asian dishes also available.

Alliance Cafe (Map p134; ☎ 017 809010; mains US$5-15; ☻ 10am-11pm) Set in an attractive French colonial-era villa, this classy French restaurant also pays homage to its Cambodian context, with some original Asian recipes. Try scallops on a bed of spinach and graduate to duck breast in a passionfruit sauce, but remember to save space for dessert. Doubles as an art venue.

ourpick Abacus (Map p130; ☎ 012 644286; off Airport Rd; mains US$8-20; ☻ 11am-late; ✗) Arguably the finest dining in town, the food here is predominantly French, with steaks in black-truffle sauce, succulent lamb and superb seafood, including tuna *maguro*. Dine in the garden or the cool interior. Also hosts regular events.

Italian

Happy Herb's Pizza (Map p134; ☎ 092-838134; Pithnou St; pizzas US$3-7; ☻ 7am-11pm) The Siem Reap outpost of a Phnom Penh institution, the 'happy' in question is a somewhat illegal herb that leaves diners on a high. Non-happy pizzas also available.

L'Oasi Italiana (Map p130; ☎ 092-418917; meals US$4-10; ☻ 6-10pm Mon, 11am-2pm & 6-10pm Tue-Sun) This really is something of an oasis, hidden away in a forest near Wat Preah Inkosei. Expats swear by the gnocchi and homemade pasta, including ravioli with porcini mushrooms.

La Volpaia (Map p130; ☎ 764184; www.lavolpaia.com; Charles de Gaulle Blvd; pizzas US$5-10; ☻ 11am-11pm; ✗) Set in a verdant garden villa, the Italian dishes here are authentic and delicious, including thin-crust pizza and plenty of expressive *carne* and frutti di mare dishes.

Vegetarian

Vitking House (Map p130; ☎ 012 563673; 7 Makara St; mains US$1-2; ☻ 7am-9pm) Popular with students from the nearby university, this is one of the cheapest veggie spots in town, with sizzling

platters of shitake mushrooms and noodles. Worth the detour.

ourpick Chamkar (Map p134; ☎ 092-733150; The Alley; mains US$3-5; ☻ 11am-11pm, closed Sun lunch; ✗) The name translates as 'farm' and the supplies must be coming from a pretty impressive organic vegetable supplier given the creative dishes on the menu here. Asian flavours primarily, such as stuffed pumpkin or vegetable kebabs in black pepper sauce.

Cafes

Some very good cafes are covered in the 'Top Five: Dining for a Cause' boxed text (opposite).

Swensen's Ice Cream (Map p134; ☎ 966424; Pokambor Ave; cone US$1.25; ☻ 9am-9pm) Located inside the Angkor Trade Center shopping mall, this place turns out some of the best ice cream in town, plus great-value sundaes.

Le Café (Map p134; ☎ 092-271392; Wat Bo area; snacks US$2-4; ☻ 7.30am-9pm; ⚇) Run in partnership with the Paul Dubrule Hotel & Tourism School (p140), this cafe brings five-star sandwiches, salads and shakes to the French Cultural Centre.

Joe-to-Go (Map p134; ☎ 092 532640; www.theglobalchild.org; Psar Chaa area; mains US$2-5; ☻ 7am-9.30pm) Reopened in 2010, gourmet coffee is the main draw here, but the new venue has a more extensive menu and stylish surrounds. Proceeds support education for street children and help to house them in a safer environment.

Café de la Paix (Map p134; Hotel de la Paix, Sivatha St; meals US$3-5; ☻ 6am-10pm; ✗ 🛜 ⚇) Sounds unlikely, but the opulent de la Paix is home to an affordable cafe serving up a superb selection of sandwiches, salads and Lavazza coffees. The ice cream is among the best in town, plus there's free wi-fi.

n.y.d.c. (Map p134; ☎ 965886; The Alley; meals US$3-5; ☻ 6am-10pm; ⚇) NYC-style deli with subs, sandwiches and wraps, plus tall coffees. Twenty per cent of profits goes to support family care around Siem Reap.

Self-Catering

The markets are well stocked with fruit and fresh bread. For more substantial treats, like cheese and chocolate, try the local supermarkets. Eating in the market usually works out cheaper than self-catering, but some folks like to make up a picnic for longer days on the road.

Try these outlets:

Angkor Market (Map p134; Sivatha St) Recently relocated to a bigger premises over the road, this has a steady supply of international treats.

Lucky Market (Map p134; Sivatha St) Part of a big shopping mall on Sivatha St, this is the biggest supermarket in town.

Starmart (Map p134; Caltex Starmart, NH6 West) Has a good selection of imports, including ice creams.

DRINKING

Siem Reap rocks. The transformation from sleepy overgrown village to an international destination for the jet set has been dramatic and Siem Reap is now firmly on the nightlife map of Southeast Asia. The Psar Chaa area is a good hunting ground, with one street even earning the moniker Pub St – dive in, crawl out! Pub St is closed to traffic every evening. However, the floodgates open around midnight.

Great spots running parallel to Pub St include the Alley, to the south, where the volume control is just a little lower, plus a series of smaller lanes to the north. There are plenty more places around town, so make sure you plan at least one big night out.

Most of the bars here have happy hours, but so do some of the fancier hotels, which is a good way to sample the high life even if you are not staying at those places, although the atmosphere can be a little austere.

As well as the storming selection of bars below, some of the aforementioned restaurants double up as lively bars by night, including atmospheric Abacus (p145), Aqua (p137) with its tempting swimming pool, classic FCC Angkor (p144), the popular Red Piano (p144) and the rooftop Soup Dragon (p143), which donates 7% of the take to the Angkor Children's Hospital, so you are helping someone else's liver, if not your own.

Warehouse (Map p134; Psar Chaa area; ☻ 10.30am-3am; 🛜) This popular bar opposite Psar Chaa occupies a strategic corner that draws them in. Top tunes, table football, a pool table, bar food and devilish drinks keep them coming until the early hours.

Laundry Bar (Map p134; Psar Chaa area; ☻ 6pm-late) One of the most alluring bars in town thanks to low lighting and discerning decor, be sure to put on your freshest undies for a trip here. It gets busy on weekends or when guest DJs crank up the volume. Happy hour until 9pm.

Angkor What? (Map p134; Pub St; ☻ 6pm-late) Siem Reap's original bar is still serving up serious hangovers every night. The happy hour (to 9pm) lightens the mood for later when everyone's bouncing along to indie anthems, sometimes on the tables, sometimes under them.

Temple Club (Map p134; Pub St; ☻ 10am-late) The only worshipping going on at this temple is 'all hail the ale'. With a popular restaurant, this place starts moving early and doesn't stop. The loud tunes and some liberally minded locals draw a dance crowd. Insane happy hours from 10am to 10pm.

Molly Malone's (Map p134; Pub St; ☻ 7.30am-midnight) Siem Reap's first Irish pub brings the sparkle of the Emerald Isle to homesick Irish and a whole host of honorary Dubliners. Serves up Powers whiskey, Guinness and excellent pub grub. It also hosts occasional live bands.

Linga Bar (Map p134; The Alley; ☻ 5pm-late) This chic gay bar attracts all comers thanks to a relaxed atmosphere, a cracking cocktail list and some big beats, which draw a dancing crowd later into the night.

Miss Wong (Map p134; The Lane; ☻ 6pm-late) Another gay-friendly bar that's popular with the mixed expat crowd, Miss Wong carries you back to the chic of 1920s Shanghai. The cocktails are a draw here, making it a cool place to while away an evening.

THE CAMBODIAN BEER GARDEN EXPERIENCE

There are dozens of beer gardens around Siem Reap that cater to young Cambodians working in the tourism industry. These can be a great experience for cheap beer, local snacks and getting to know some Cambodians beyond your driver or guide. All serve up ice-cold beer, some served in 3L beer towers complete with chiller. They can be a bit laddish by Cambodian standards, so solo female travellers might want to hook up with a traveller crowd before venturing forth.

The best strip is just north of the Airport Rd from the first set of traffic lights after Sivatha St. **Trey Kon** (Map p134; ☎ 017 999023; ☻ 5pm-late) is one of the best of this lot, with a huge circular bar, regular football on big screens and mighty beer towers. Wander around this area to see where the local are hanging out.

Chilli Si-Dang (Map p134; ☎ 012 723488; Siem Reap River Rd; ⏳ 7am-late; 📶) Boasting a tranquil riverside location and balcony views, this is a relaxed wine bar from which to quaff some vintages or sample some cocktails. Happy hour is from 5pm to 8pm and wi-fi is free.

Nest (Map p134; ☎ 017 925181; Sivatha St; ⏳ 4pm-late) A memorable bar thanks to its sweeping sail-like shelters and stylish seating, this place has one of the most creative cocktail lists in town. Curl up in a sleigh bed and relax for the night. Not quite so chic in the wet season.

X Bar (Map p134; Sivatha St; ⏳ 4pm-sunrise) One of *the* late-night spots in town, X Bar draws revellers for the witching hour when other places are closing up. Early-evening movies on the big screen, pool tables and even a skateboard pipe…if you're not too hammered.

Other places to imbibe:

Banana Leaf (Map p134; Pub St) Spread along the sidewalk, this place is good for people watching.

4 Faces (Map p134; Psar Chaa area; ⏳ 10am-late; 📶) Paying homage to the Bayon, this friendly bar-restaurant doubles as a photo gallery. Big screens for sports fans, plus free wi-fi.

Island Bar (Map p134; Angkor Night Market; ⏳ 4pm-late) Lurking at the back of the night market, this is a great spot to relax after a shopping spree.

Sports Bar (Map p134; The Alley West; ⏳ 4pm-6am) Siem Reap's only dedicated sports bar, with several big screens, a pool table and booze aplenty.

Central (Map p134; Psar Chaa area; ⏳ 4am-late; 📶) Bohemian cafe-bar that plays host to regular live bands. Free wi-fi.

ENTERTAINMENT

Several restaurants and hotels offer cultural performances during the evening, and for many visitors such shows offer the only opportunity to see Cambodian classical dance. While they may be aimed at tourists and are nowhere near as sophisticated as a performance of the Royal Ballet in Phnom Penh, to the untrained eye it is nonetheless graceful and alluring. Prices usually include a buffet meal. Look out for special performances to support cultural organisations and orphanages, as these can be a good way to assist the local community.

Acodo Orphanage (off Map p134; ☎ 012 734306; www. acodo.org; admission free) offers a free traditional dance show every night at 6.30pm. Donations are very welcome and it's signposted on the road to the Tonlé Sap Lake.

Temple Club (Map p134; Pub St) offers a free traditional dance show upstairs from 7.30pm,

providing punters order some food and drink from the very reasonably priced menu.

The most atmospheric show is at **Apsara Theatre** (Map p134; www.angkorvillage.com/theatre.php; admission US$25) at Angkor Village, as the setting is a striking wooden pavilion finished in the style of a wat, but the set menu is less inspiring. There are two shows per night. The Grand Hotel d'Angkor (p141) has an attractive performance stage behind its swimming pool and, while admission is US$32, the buffet is superb.

Better than both of these is the performance at the **Dining Room** (Map p134; free performance Tue, Thu & Sat), the restaurant (mains US$15 to US$50) at La Résidence d'Angkor (p141), as you can dine à la carte in the garden.

Tonlé Sap Restaurant (Map p134; ☎ 963388; NH6 West; show US$12; ⏳ 7.30pm) and **Koulen II Restaurant** (Map p134; ☎ 012 630090; Sivatha St; show US$12; ⏳ 7pm) both offer major shows that pull in the big tour groups who chow down on a wide spread of buffet dishes.

For something a bit different, try the Wednesday and Sunday evening shadow-puppet show with classical dance at **La Noria Restaurant** (Map p134; ☎ 964242; mains US$4-8), which includes a set dinner. Part of the fee is donated to a charity supporting local children.

BBQ Suki (Map p130; ☎ 965650; Charles de Gaulle Blvd; buffet US$5-10) offers a free nightly shadow-puppet show at 7.30pm, although the set dinner is less exciting than the BBQ and buffet downstairs.

Beatocello (Map p130; www.beatocello.com; ⏳ 7.15pm Sat), better known as Dr Beat Richner, performs cello compositions at Jayavarman VII Children's Hospital. Entry is free, but donations are welcome, as they assist the hospital in offering free medical treatment to the children of Cambodia.

One wonder of the world pays homage to another at the glitzy new **Pyramid Mega Entertainment Centre** (off Map p130; ☎ 967778; www. pyramid-megaclub.com; NH6). The **disco** (admission free; ⏳ 7pm-3am or 4am) has a state-of-the-art sound system; outside is a net-enclosed paint-ball field. Situated about 4km southeast of town on the road to Phnom Penh.

SHOPPING

Much of what you see on sale in the markets of Siem Reap can also be purchased from children and vendors throughout the temple area. Some people get fed up with the endless sales pitches as they navigate the ancient wonders, while others enjoy the banter and a chance to interact with Cambodian people. It's often children out selling, and some visitors will argue that they should be at school instead. However, most do attend school at least half of the time, if their families can afford it.

Items touted at the temples include postcards, T-shirts, temple bas-relief rubbings, curious musical instruments, ornamental knives and crossbows – the last may raise a few eyebrows with customs should you try to take one home! Be sure to bargain, as overcharging is pretty common.

When it comes to shopping in town, Psar Chaa (Map p134) is well stocked with anything you may want to buy in Cambodia, and lots you don't. Silverware, silk, wood carvings, stone carvings, Buddhas, paintings, rubbings, notes and coins, T-shirts, table mats…the list goes on. There are bargains to be had if you haggle patiently and humorously. Avoid buying old stone carvings that vendors claim are from Angkor. Whether or not they are real, buying these artefacts serves only to encourage their plunder and they will usually be confiscated by customs. Buy modern replicas instead and bury them in the garden for a few months – they will soon look the same.

Angkor Night Market (Map p134; near Sivatha St; 4pm–midnight) is a popular addition to the Siem Reap shopping scene. It is packed with stalls selling a variety of handicrafts, souvenirs and silks and is well worth a browse to take advantage of cooler temperatures. It's also possible to chill out in the Island Bar (p147), indulge in a Dr Fish massage (p136) or watch a 3-D event movie (US$3) about the Khmer Rouge or the scourge of land mines.

There are now lots of memorable shops in Siem Reap. Some of the standout places include the following:

Bambou Indochine (Map p134; ☎ 966071; Alley West; 10am–10pm) Original clothing designs inspired by Indochina. A cut above the average souvenir T-shirts.

TOP 10: SHOPPING FOR A CAUSE

There are several shops that support Cambodia's disabled and disenfranchised through their production process or their profits. Consider spending some money at one of these worthy places:

Artisans d'Angkor (Map p134; ☎ 963330; www.artisansdangkor.com; 7.30am–6.30pm) High-quality reproduction carvings and exquisite silks are available. Impoverished youngsters are trained in the arts of their ancestors (see p132).

Bloom (Map p134; Psar Chaa area; 10am–10pm) Most of the items here are made from recycled materials, including hip bags made from old Cambodian rice sacks.

Hagar Design (Map p134; The Alley; 9am–9pm) Small boutique specialising in silk scarves and attractive bags and accessories. Helps women who have been abused or mistreated.

IKTT (Map p134; Tonlé Sap Rd; 9am–5pm) A traditional wooden house that is home to the Institute for Khmer Traditional Textiles. Fine *kramas*, scarves, throws and more.

Krousar Thmey (Map p130; Charles de Gaulle Blvd; 8am–5.30pm) Small shop selling shadow puppets, traditional scarves, paintings and postcards, all to assist blind children in Cambodia.

Nyemo (Map p134; Angkor Night Market; 4pm–midnight) Silk products such as cushions, hangings and throws, plus children's toys. Proceeds are used to help HIV/AIDS sufferers and vulnerable women generally. Located in the Angkor Night Market.

Rajana (Map p134; Sivatha St; 9am–9pm, closed Sun) Sells quirky wooden and metalwork objects, well-designed silver jewellery and handmade cards. Rajana promotes fair trade and employment opportunities for Cambodians.

Rehab Craft (Map p134; 353 Pokambor Ave; 9am–9pm) This shop specialises in quality silk products, such as wallets, handbags and the like. Profits train and sustain the disabled community.

Senteurs d'Angkor (Map p134; ☎ 964860; Pithnou St; 8.30am–9.30pm) Opposite Psar Chaa, this shop has an eclectic collection of silk and carvings, as well as a superb range of traditional beauty products and spices, all made locally. It targets rural poor and disadvantaged for jobs and training, and sources local products from farmers. It is also possible to visit their Botanic Garden on Airport Rd – ask the shop staff for more details.

Tabitha Cambodia (Map p134; ☎ 760650; off Sivatha St; 7am–6pm) Attractive range of silk scarves, cushion covers and throws to choose from. Proceeds go towards Tabitha projects, like house building and well drilling.

Eric Raisina Workshop (Map p130; ☎ 965207; Wat Thmei area; ☒ by appointment) Renowned designer Eric Raisina brings a unique cocktail of influences to his couture. Born in Madagascar, raised in France and resident in Cambodia, he offers a striking collection of clothing and accessories.

Garden of Desire (Map p134; ☎ 012 312116; The Alley; ☒ 10am-9.30pm Mon-Sat, from 3pm Sun) Designer jewellery for the discerning dresser. Original creations in silver and semi-precious stones (from northeast Cambodia).

Jasmine (Map p134; ☎ 760610; Pokambor Ave; ☒ 9am-10pm) Located in FCC Angkor, this boutique produces stylish silk clothing for any occasion.

McDermott Gallery (Map p134; ☎ 012 274274; www. mcdermottgallery.com; The Alley; ☒ 10am-10pm) These are the famous images you have seen of Angkor. Calendars, cards and striking sepia images of the temples, plus regular exhibitions.

Rogue (Map p134; Pithnou St; ☒ 10am-10pm) Dedicated to selling iPods, downloads, accessories and T-shirts.

Samatoa (Map p134; ☎ 965310; Pithnou St; ☒ 8am-11pm) Designer clothes finished in silk with the option of a tailored fit in 48 hours. Promotes fair trade.

Wanderlust (Map p134; ☎ 965980; The Alley West; ☒ 8am-10pm) Small designer boutique with fun and funky fashion and accessories, in an old house that looks straight out of Provence.

GETTING THERE & AWAY
Air
There are direct international flights from Siem Reap to Bangkok in Thailand; Vientiane, Luang Prabang and Pakse in Laos; Ho Chi Minh City (Saigon), Hanoi and Danang in Vietnam; Hong Kong; Kuala Lumpur in Malaysia; Kunming in China; Seoul in South Korea; Singapore; and Taipei in Taiwan. For more information on international flights to and from Siem Reap, see the Transport chapter (p337).

Domestic links are currently limited to Phnom Penh, and only Cambodia Angkor Airways currently operates on this route (from US$55/110 one-way/return). Demand for the limited number of flights is high during peak season, so book as far in advance as possible. There are plans to relaunch flights to Sihanoukville some time during the life of this book.

Airline offices around town:

Bangkok Airways (☎ 380191; www.bangkokair.com)
Cambodia Angkor Air (☎ 964488; www.cambodia angkorair.com)
China Eastern Airlines (☎ 965229; www.ce-air.com)
Jetstar Asia (☎ 964388; www.jetstarasia.com)

Lao Airlines (☎ 963283; www.laoairlines.com)
Malaysia Airlines (☎ 964135; www.malaysia -airlines.com)
Siem Reap Airways (☎ 380191; www.siemreap airways.com)
Vietnam Airlines (☎ 964488; www.vietnam airlines.com)

Boat
There are daily express boat services between Siem Reap and Phnom Penh (US$35, five to six hours) or Battambang (US$20, three to eight hours depending on the season). The boat to Phnom Penh is a bit of a rip-off these days, given it is just as fast by road and about a fifth of the price. The Battambang trip is *very* scenic, but breakdowns are *very* common. See the Phnom Penh (p120) and Battambang (p255) listings for more details.

Boats from Siem Reap leave from the floating village of Chong Kneas near Phnom Krom, 11km south of Siem Reap. The boats dock in different places at different times of the year; when the lake recedes in the dry season, both the port and floating village move with it. An all-weather road to improve access is still under construction.

Most of the guesthouses in town sell boat tickets. Buying the ticket from a guesthouse usually includes a *moto* or minibus ride to the port. Otherwise, a *moto* out here costs about US$1 to US$2, a *remork-moto* about US$5. A taxi is more like US$10.

Bus
The road linking Siem Reap to Phnom Penh is in good condition, and air-con buses thunder up and down daily. The road west to Sisophon, Thailand and Battambang has been completely rebuilt and is in great condition.

All buses depart from the bus station/taxi park (Map p130), which is 3km east of town and about 200m south of NH6. Tickets are available at guesthouses, hotels, bus offices, travel agencies and ticket kiosks. Some bus companies send a minibus around to pick up passengers at their place of lodging. Most departures to Phnom Penh are between 7am and 1pm; buses to other destinations generally leave early in the morning. Upon arrival in Siem Reap, be prepared for a rugby scrum of eager *moto* drivers when getting off the bus.

There are a number of bus companies that serve Siem Reap:

Capitol Tour (Map p134; ☎ 963883; Psar Chaa area) Serves Phnom Penh, Poipet, Battambang and Bangkok.

GST (Map p134; ☎ 092-905016; Sivatha St) Serves Phnom Penh and Anlong Veng.

Mekong Express (Map p134; ☎ 963662; 14A Sivatha St) Serves Phnom Penh and Ho Chi Minh City.

Neak Kror Horm (Map p130; ☎ 964924; bus station/ taxi park) Phnom Penh and Poipet.

Paramount Angkor Express (Map p130; ☎ 966469; bus station/taxi park) Serves Phnom Penh, Sisophon and Battambang.

Phnom Penh Sorya (Map p130; ☎ 012 235618; bus station/taxi park) Serves Phnom Penh, Poipet and Battambang.

Rith Mony (Map p130; ☎ 012 344377; bus station/taxi park) Serves Phnom Penh and Stung Treng.

Tickets to Phnom Penh (six hours), via NH6, cost US$5 to US$11, depending on the level of service (air-con, comfy seats, a toilet, a hostess) and whether there's hotel pick-up. Many companies charge the same price to Kompong Thom as they do to Phnom Penh. Several companies offer direct services to Kompong Cham (US$6, five or six hours), Battambang (US$3.75, three hours), Sisophon (US$3.75, two hours) and Poipet (US$3.75, three hours). GST has a bus to Anlong Veng (US$4, two hours). There are even some buses through to Ho Chi Minh City (from US$20).

Car, Share Taxi, Minibus & Pick-up

As well as buses, share taxis and other vehicles operate some of the main routes and these can be a little quicker than buses.

Destinations include Phnom Penh (US$10, five hours), Kompong Thom (US$5, two hours), Sisophon (US$5, two hours) and Poipet (US$7, three hours). To get to the temple of Banteay Chhmar, head to Sisophon and arrange onward transport there. For details on getting to Anlong Veng, see p271.

To get to Prasat Preah Vihear (via either Anlong Veng or Koh Ker), catch a share taxi (US$15, five or six hours) or pick-up (inside/ on the back US$12.50/10) along NH6 about 100m east of the ANZ Royal Bank, 1km west of the bus station turning.

For more on the overland trip between Bangkok and Siem Reap, see the boxed text, p342.

GETTING AROUND

For more on transport around Angkor, see p165. Following are insights on the most common forms of transport used for getting around Siem Reap.

To/From the Airport

Siem Reap International Airport is 7km from the town centre. Many hotels and guesthouses in Siem Reap have a free airport pick-up service if you have booked in advance. Official taxis are available next to the terminal for US$7. A trip to the city centre on the back of a *moto* is US$2. *Remork-motos* are available for about US$5, depending on the hotel or guesthouse location.

Bicycle

Some of the guesthouses around town hire out bicycles, as do a few shops around Psar Chaa, usually for US$1 to US$2 a day. Try to support the **White Bicycles** (www.thewhitebicy cles.org) project to help the local community (see p165).

Car & Motorcycle

Most hotels and guesthouses can organise car hire for the day, with a going rate of US$25 and up. Upmarket hotels may charge more. Foreigners are forbidden to rent motorcycles in and around Siem Reap. If you want to get around on your own motorcycle, you need to hire one in Phnom Penh and ride it to Siem Reap. For details on dirt-bike tours to remote temples, see p349.

Moto

A *moto* with a driver will cost about US$7 to US$9 per day. The average cost for a short trip within town is 1000r to 2000r, more to places strung out along the roads to Angkor or the airport. It is probably best to negotiate in advance these days, as a lot of drivers have got into the habit of overcharging with the tourism boom.

Remork-Moto

Remork-motos are sweet little motorcycles with carriages (commonly called *tuk tuks* around town) and are a nice way for couples to get about Siem Reap, although drivers like to inflate the prices. Try for US$1 on trips around town, although drivers may charge US$2 for a trip to the edges of town at night. Prices rise when you pile in more people.

AROUND SIEM REAP

PREK TOAL BIRD SANCTUARY
ជំរកបក្សីព្រែកទួល

Prek Toal is one of three biospheres on Tonlé Sap Lake, and this stunning bird sanctuary makes Prek Toal the most worthwhile and straightforward of the three to visit. It is an ornithologist's fantasy, with a significant number of rare breeds gathered in one small area, including the huge lesser and greater adjutant storks, the milky stork and the spot-billed pelican. Even the uninitiated will be impressed, as these birds have a huge wingspan and build enormous nests.

Visitors during the dry season (December to April) will find the concentration of birds like something out of a Hitchcock film. It is also possible to visit from September, but the concentrations may be lower. As water starts to dry up elsewhere, the birds congregate here. Serious twitchers know that the best time to see birds is early morning or late afternoon and this means an early start or an overnight at Prek Toal's environment office, where there are basic beds for US$15/20 per single/double.

There are two ecotourism companies that arrange trips out to Prek Toal. **Sam Veasna Center** (Map p134; ☎ 963710; www.samveasna. org; Wat Bo area) offers trips to Prek Toal that contribute to the conservation of the area. Sam Veasna uses ecotourism to provide an income for local communities in return for a ban on hunting and cutting down the forest. The trips cost about US$98 per person if travelling in a group of four to six people. **Osmose** (☎ 012 832812; www.osmosetonlesap.net) also runs organised day trips to Prek Toal. The day trips cost US$95 per person with a minimum group of four.

Tours include transport, entrance fees, guides, breakfast, lunch and water. Binoculars are available on request, plus the Sam Veasna Center has a spotting scope. Both outfits can arrange overnight trips for serious enthusiasts. Some proceeds from the tours go towards educating children and villagers about the importance of the birds and the unique flooded-forest environment, and the trip includes a visit to one of the local communities. Day trips include a hotel pick-up around 6am and a return by nightfall.

Sunscreen and head protection are essential, as it can get very hot in the dry season. The guides are equipped with booklets with the bird names in English, but they speak little English themselves, hence the advantage of travelling with the Sam Veasna Center or Osmose (both of which can provide English-speaking guides).

Getting to the sanctuary under your own steam requires you to take a 20-minute *moto* (US$2 or so) or taxi (US$10 one-way) ride to the floating village of Chong Kneas and then a boat to the environment office (around US$55 return, one hour each way). From here, a small boat (US$30 including a guide) will take you into the sanctuary, which is about one hour further on.

ANG TRAPENG THMOR RESERVE

There is another bird sanctuary, **Ang Trapeng Thmor Reserve** (admission US$10), just across the border in the Phnom Srok region of Banteay Meanchey Province, about 100km from Siem Reap. It's one of only two places in the world where it is possible to see the extremely rare sarus crane, as depicted on bas-reliefs at Bayon. These grey-feathered birds have immensely long legs and striking red heads. The reserve is based around a reservoir created by forced labour during the Khmer Rouge regime, and facilities are very basic, but it is an incredibly beautiful place. Bring your own binoculars, however, as none are available.

To reach here, follow the road to Sisophon for about 72km before turning north at Prey Mon. It's 22km to the site, passing through some famous silk-weaving villages. The Sam Veasna Center (left) arranges birding trips (US$75 per person with a group of four to six) out here, which is probably the easiest way to undertake the trip. It also arranges specialist birding trips to remote parts of northwestern Cambodia in partnership with the **Wildlife Conservation Society** (www.wcs.org): see p278 and p278.

FLOATING VILLAGE OF CHONG KNEAS
ភូមិបណ្តែតចុងឃ្នាស

This famous floating village is now extremely popular with visitors wanting a break from the temples, and is an easy, if somewhat pricey, excursion to arrange yourself. If you want something a bit more peaceful, try venturing to one of the other Tonlé Sap villages further afield. Visitors arriving by boat from Phnom

Penh or Battambang get a sneak preview, as the floating village is near Phnom Krom, where the boat docks. It is very scenic in the warm light of early morning or late afternoon and can be combined with a view of the sunset from the hilltop temple of Phnom Krom (p188). The downside is that tour groups tend to take over, and boats end up chugging up and down the channels in convoy.

Visitors should also check out the **Gecko Centre** (www.tsbr-ed.org; ☙ 8.30am-5.30pm), an informative centre that is located in the floating village and helps to unlock the secrets of the Tonlé Sap. It has displays on flora and fauna of the area, as well as information on communities living around the lake.

The village moves depending on the season and you will need to rent a boat to get around it properly. A joint-venture cooperative called Sou Ching has fixed boat prices at US$11 per person, plus a US$2 entrance fee, to visit the floating village.

Probably the best way to visit for the time being is to hook up with the **Tara Boat** (☎ 092-957765; www.taraboat.com), which offers all-inclusive trips with a meal aboard its converted cargo boat. Prices include transfers, entry fees, local boats, a tour guide and a two-course meal, starting from US$27 for a lunch to US$33 for a sunset dinner.

To get to the floating village from Siem Reap costs US$2 by *moto* each way (more if the driver waits), or US$15 or so by taxi. The trip takes 20 minutes. Or rent a bicycle in town and just pedal out here, as it is a leisurely 11km through pretty villages and rice fields.

FLOODED FOREST OF KOMPONG PLUK
ព្រៃលិចទឹកកំពង់ភ្លុក

More memorable than Chong Kneas, but harder to reach, is the village of **Kompong Pluk** (entry US$2), an other-worldly place built on soaring stilts. Nearby is a flooded forest, inundated every year when the lake rises to take the Mekong's overflow. As the lake drops, the petrified trees are revealed. Exploring this area by wooden dugout in the wet season is very atmospheric. The village itself is a friendly place, where most of the houses are built on stilts of about 6m or 7m high, almost bamboo skyscrapers. It looks like it's straight out of a film set.

There are two ways to get to Kompong Pluk. One is to come via the floating village of Chong Kneas, where a boat (1¼ hours) can be arranged from US$55 round trip, and the other

is to come via the small town of Roluos by a combination of road (about US$5 by *moto*) and boat (US$8). However, an all-weather elevated access road is under construction and will be completed some time during the life of this book. It is rumoured to be another toll road, which means a private company will start levying charges to visit Kompong Pluk. All said, the road/boat route will take up to two hours, but it depends on the season – sometimes it's more by road, sometimes more by boat. The new road may well bring the access time to less than one hour. Tara Boat (left) also offers day trips here for US$60 per person.

KOMPONG KHLEANG
កំពង់ឃ្លាំង

One of the largest communities on the Tonlé Sap, Kompong Khleang is more of a town than the other villages, and comes complete with several ornate pagodas. Like Kompong Pluk, most of the houses here are built on towering stilts to allow for a dramatic change in water level. Few tourists visit here compared with the floating villages closer to Siem Reap, but that might be a reason to visit in itself. There is only a small floating community on the lake itself, but the stilted town is an interesting place to browse for an hour or two. A boat trip around the town and out to the lake is about US$20 for a couple of hours. It is not that difficult to reach from Siem Reap thanks to an all-weather road via the junction town of Dam Dek. It is also possible to get here via Chong Kneas, but it is a long boat ride of about three hours.

ME CHREY
មេជ្រី

One of the more recently 'discovered' floating villages, this community lies midway between Siem Reap and Prek Toal. It is one of the smaller villages in the area, but sees far fewer tourists than busy Chong Kneas. Due to a pricing dispute between tour operators and Sou Ching over access to Chong Kneas, some upmarket operators have been visiting Me Chrey (entry US$1) as an alternative. Like Chong Kneas it moves with the water level and is more pretty during the wet season when houses are anchored around an island pagoda. It is located to the south of Puok district, about 25km from Siem Reap. Arrange transport by road before switching to a boat (US$13 for under 10 people) to explore the area.

Temples of Angkor

Welcome to heaven on earth. Angkor is the earthly representation of Mt Meru, the Mt Olympus of the Hindu faith and the abode of ancient gods. Angkor is the perfect fusion of creative ambition and spiritual devotion. The Cambodian 'god-kings' of old each strove to better their ancestors in the size, scale and symmetry of their temples, culminating in the world's largest religious building, Angkor Wat. The hundreds of temples surviving today are but the sacred skeleton of the vast political, religious and social centre of Cambodia's ancient Khmer empire, a city that, at its zenith, boasted a population of one million when London was a scrawny town of 50,000. The houses, public buildings and palaces of Angkor were constructed of wood – now long decayed – because the right to dwell in structures of brick or stone was reserved for the gods.

For Indian Hindus, the Himalayas represent Mt Meru, the home of the gods, while the Khmer kings of old adopted Phnom Kulen as their symbolic Mt Meru.

This is the heart and soul of Cambodia. The temples of Angkor are a source of inspiration and national pride to all Khmers as they struggle to rebuild their lives after years of terror and trauma. Today, the temples are a point of pilgrimage for all Cambodians, and no traveller to the region will want to miss their extravagant beauty. Angkor is one of the world's foremost ancient sites, with the epic proportions of the Great Wall of China, the detail and intricacy of the Taj Mahal and the symbolism and symmetry of the pyramids, all rolled into one.

Abandoned to the jungles for centuries, the magnificent temples are set amid the region's oldest national park, with towering trees and a refreshing lack of modern development amid the audacious architecture. With such a wealth of temples, it is also possible to plan a peaceful pilgrimage here, far from the madding crowds, which really are madding at some temples at certain times of day.

Some visitors assume they will be templed out within a day or two, but soon discover the sheer diversity in design among the temples that switches dramatically from one god-king to another. Come face to face (quite literally) with Bayon, one of the world's weirdest buildings; experience the excitement of the first European explorers at Ta Prohm, where nature runs riot; or follow the sacred River of a Thousand Lingas like pilgrims of old. The most vexing part of a visit is working out what to see. If any of the 'second string' holy sites were anywhere else in the region they would have top billing. One day at Angkor? Sacrilege! Don't even consider it, as there is no greater concentration of architectural riches anywhere on earth.

HISTORY
Early Years
For more on the pre-Angkorian period, check out the History chapter (p26). The Angkorian period spans more than 600 years from AD 802 to

---

ANGKOR EXPERIENCES

- See the sun rise over the holiest of holies, Angkor Wat (p167), the world's largest religious building.
- Contemplate the serenity and splendour of the Bayon (p172), its 216 enigmatic faces staring out into the jungle.
- Witness nature reclaiming the stones at the mysterious ruin of Ta Prohm (p181), the *Tomb Raider* temple.
- Stare in wonder at the delicate carvings adorning Banteay Srei (p189), the finest seen at Angkor.
- Trek deep into the jungle to discover the River of a Thousand Lingas at Kbal Spean (p190).

1432. This incredible period of history saw the construction of the temples of Angkor and the consolidation of the Khmer empire's position as one of the great powers in Southeast Asia. This era encompasses periods of decline and revival, and wars with rival powers in Vietnam, Thailand and Myanmar. This brief history deals only with the periods that produced the temples that can be seen at Angkor.

The Angkorian period began with the rule of Jayavarman II (r 802–50). He was the first to unify Cambodia's competing kingdoms before the birth of Angkor. His court was situated at various locations, including Phnom Kulen (p190), 40km northeast of Angkor Wat, and Roluos (p187; known then as Hariharalaya), 13km east of Siem Reap.

> Jayavarman II spent his formative years on the island of Java, at the court of the Shailendras Kingdom, and may have been inspired by the Hindu temples of Prambanan and the great Buddhist temple of Borobudur.

Jayavarman II proclaimed himself a *devaraja* (god-king), the earthly representative of the Hindu god Shiva, and built a 'temple-mountain' at Phnom Kulen, symbolising Shiva's dwelling place of Mt Meru, the holy mountain at the centre of the universe. This set a precedent that became a dominant feature of the Angkorian period and accounts for the staggering architectural productivity of the Khmers at this time.

Indravarman I (r 877–89) is believed to have been a usurper, and probably inherited the mantle of *devaraja* through conquest. He built a 6.5 sq km *baray* (reservoir) at Roluos and established Preah Ko (p187). The *baray* was the first stage of an irrigation system that created a hydraulic city, the ancient Khmers mastering the cycle of nature to water their lands; as is often the case, form and function work together in harmony. It also had religious significance as, according to legend, Mt Meru is flanked by lakes. Indravarman's final work was Bakong (p187), a pyramidal representation of Mt Meru.

Indravarman I's son Yasovarman I (r 889–910) looked further afield to celebrate his divinity and glory in a temple-mountain of his own. He first built Lolei (p188) on an artificial island in the *baray* established by his father, before beginning work on the Bakheng. Today this hill is known as Phnom Bakheng (p179), a favoured spot for viewing the sunset over Angkor Wat. A raised highway was constructed to connect Phnom Bakheng with Roluos, 16km to the southeast, and a large *baray* was constructed to the east of Phnom Bakheng. Today it is known as the Eastern Baray (p185), but has entirely silted up. Yasovarman I also established the temple-mountains of Phnom Krom (p188) and Phnom Bok (p188).

After the death of Yasovarman I, power briefly shifted from the Angkor region to Koh Ker (p274), around 80km to the northeast, under another usurper – Jayavarman IV (r 924–42). In AD 944 power returned again to Angkor under the leadership of Rajendravarman II (r 944–68), who built the Eastern Mebon (p185) and Pre Rup (p186). The reign of his son Jayavarman V (r 968–1001) produced the temples Ta Keo (p181) and Banteay Srei (p189), the latter built by a brahman rather than the king.

Classical Age

> Many major cities in the Mekong region were important Khmer settlements in the 11th and 12th centuries, including the Lao capital of Vientiane and the Thai city of Lopburi.

The temples that are now the highlight of a visit to Angkor – Angkor Wat and those in and around the walled city of Angkor Thom – were built during the classical age. The classical appellation conjures up images of a golden age of abundance and leisurely temple construction, but while this period is marked by fits of remarkable productivity, it was also a time of turmoil, conquests and setbacks. The great city of Angkor Thom owes its existence to the fact that the old city of Angkor – which stood on the same site – was destroyed during the Cham invasion of 1177.

Suryavarman I (r 1002–49) was a usurper to the throne who won the day through strategic alliances and military conquests. Although he adopted the

TOP 10 KINGS OF ANGKOR

A mind-numbing array of kings ruled the Khmer empire from the 9th to 14th centuries AD. All of their names include the word *'varman'*, which means 'armour' or 'protector'. Forget the small fry and focus on the big fish in our Top 10:

Jayavarman II (r 802–50) Founder of the Khmer empire in AD 802.

Indravarman I (r 877–89) Builder of the first *baray* (reservoir), Preah Ko (p187) and Bakong (p187).

Yasovarman I (r 889–910) Moved the capital to Angkor and built Lolei (p188) and Phnom Bakheng (p179).

Jayavarman IV (r 924–42) Usurper king who moved the capital to Koh Ker (p274).

Rajendravarman II (r 944–68) Builder of Eastern Mebon (p185), Pre Rup (p186) and Phimeanakas (p177).

Jayavarman V (r 968–1001) Oversaw construction of Ta Keo (p181) and Banteay Srei (p189).

Suryavarman I (r 1002–49) Expanded the empire into much of Laos and Thailand.

Udayadityavarman II (r 1049–65) Builder of the pyramidal Baphuon (p176) and the Western Mebon (p186).

Suryavarman II (r 1112–52) Legendary builder of Angkor Wat (p167) and Beng Mealea (p191).

Jayavarman VII (r 1181–1219) The king of the god-kings, building Angkor Thom (p172), Preah Khan (p184) and Ta Prohm (p181).

Hindu cult of the god-king, he is thought to have come from a Mahayana Buddhist tradition and may even have sponsored the growth of Buddhism in Cambodia. Buddhist sculpture certainly became more commonplace in the Angkor region during his time.

Little physical evidence of Suryavarman I's reign remains at Angkor, but his military exploits brought much of southern Thailand and southern Laos under the control of Angkor. His son Udayadityavarman II (r 1049–65) embarked on further military expeditions, extending the empire once more, and building Baphuon (p176) and the Western Mebon (p186).

From 1066 until the end of the century, Angkor was again divided as rival factions contested the throne. The first important monarch of this new era was Suryavarman II (r 1112–52), who unified Cambodia and extended Khmer influence to Malaya and Burma (Myanmar). He also set himself apart religiously from earlier kings through his devotion to the Hindu deity Vishnu, to whom he consecrated the largest and arguably most magnificent of all the Angkorian temples, Angkor Wat (p167).

The reign of Suryavarman II and the construction of Angkor Wat signifies one of the high-water marks of Khmer civilisation. However, there were signs that decline was waiting in the wings. It is thought that the hydraulic system of reservoirs and canals that supported the agriculture of Angkor had by this time been pushed beyond its limits, and was slowly starting to silt up due to overpopulation and deforestation. The construction of Angkor Wat was a major strain on resources, and, on top of this, Suryavarman II led a disastrous campaign against the Dai Viet (Vietnamese) late in his reign, during the course of which he was killed in battle.

In 1177 the Chams of southern Vietnam, then the Kingdom of Champa and long annexed by the Khmer empire, rose up and sacked Angkor. They burned the wooden city and plundered its wealth. Four years later Jayavarman VII (r 1181–1219) struck back, emphatically driving the Chams out of Cambodia and reclaiming Angkor.

Jayavarman VII's reign has given scholars much to debate. It represents a radical departure from the reigns of his predecessors. For centuries the fount of royal divinity had reposed in the Hindu deity Shiva (and, occasionally, Vishnu). Jayavarman VII adopted Mahayana Buddhism and looked to Avalokiteshvara, the Bodhisattva of Compassion, for patronage during his reign. In doing so he may well have been converting to a religion that already enjoyed wide popular support among his subjects. It may also be that the

While Suryavarman II may have planned Angkor Wat as his funerary temple or mausoleum, he was never buried there and it is believed he may have died while returning from a failed expedition to subdue the Dai Viet (Vietnamese).

When the Chams sacked Angkor in 1177, it caught the Khmers completely by surprise, as they attacked by sea, river and lake rather than the traditional land routes.

destruction of Angkor was such a blow to royal divinity that a new religious foundation was thought to be needed.

The King's Last Song by Geoff Ryman weaves together the story of Jayavarman VII with a contemporary drama involving kidnapping and the Khmer Rouge.

During his reign, Jayavarman VII embarked on a dizzying array of temple projects that centred on Baphuon (p176), which was the site of the capital city destroyed by the Chams. Angkor Thom (p172), Jayavarman VII's new city, was surrounded by walls and a moat, which became another component of Angkor's complex irrigation system. The centrepiece of Angkor Thom was Bayon (p172), the temple-mountain studded with faces that, along with Angkor Wat, is the most famous of Cambodia's temples. Other temples built during his reign include Ta Prohm (p181), Banteay Kdei (p182) and Preah Khan (p184). Further away, he rebuilt vast temple complexes, such as Banteay Chhmar (p265) and Preah Khan (p272), making him by far the most prolific builder of Angkor's many kings.

Jayavarman VII also embarked on a major public-works program, building roads, schools and hospitals across the empire. Remains of many of these roads and their magnificent bridges can be seen across Cambodia. Spean Praptos at Kompong Kdei, 65km southeast of Siem Reap on National Hwy 6 (NH6), is the most famous, but there are many more lost in the forest on the old Angkorian road to the great Preah Khan, including the now accessible Spean Ta Ong, about 28km east of Beng Mealea near the village of Khvau.

After the death of Jayavarman VII around 1219, the Khmer empire went into decline. The state religion reverted to Hinduism for a century or more and outbreaks of iconoclasm saw Buddhist sculpture adorning the Hindu temples vandalised or altered. The Thais sacked Angkor in 1351, and again with devastating efficiency in 1431. The Khmer court moved to Phnom Penh, only to return fleetingly to Angkor in the 16th century; in the meantime, it was abandoned to pilgrims, holy men and the elements.

Angkor Rediscovered

The French 'discovery' of Angkor in the 1860s made an international splash and created a great deal of outside interest in Cambodia. But 'discovery', with all the romance it implied, was something of a misnomer. When French explorer Henri Mouhot first stumbled across Angkor Wat, it included a wealthy, working monastery with monks and slaves. Moreover, Portuguese travellers in the 16th century encountered Angkor, referring to it as the Walled City. Diogo do Couto produced an accurate description of Angkor in 1614, but it was not published until 1958.

The glorious Siamese capital of Ayuthaya, which enjoyed a golden age from the 14th to 18th centuries, was in many ways a recreation of the glories of Angkor from which the Thai conquerors drew inspiration.

Still, it was the publication of *Voyage à Siam et dans le Cambodge* by Mouhot, posthumously released in 1868, that first brought Angkor to the public eye. Although the explorer himself made no such claims, by the 1870s he was being celebrated as the discoverer of the lost temple-city of Cambodia. In fact, a French missionary known as Charles-Emile Bouillevaux had visited Angkor 10 years before Mouhot and had published an account of his own findings. However, the Bouillevaux account was roundly ignored and it was Mouhot's account, with its rich descriptions and tantalising pen-and-ink colour sketches of the temples, that turned the ruins into an international obsession.

Henri Mouhot was French by birth, but was married to an English-woman. His 'journey of discovery' to Angkor was actually funded by the Royal Geographic Society of London.

From the time of Mouhot, Angkor became the target of French-financed expeditions and, in 1901, the **École Française d'Extrême-Orient** (EFEO; www.efeo.fr) began a long association with Angkor by funding an expedition to Bayon. In 1907 Angkor was returned to Cambodia, having been under Thai control for almost 150 years, and the EFEO took responsibility for clearing and restoring the whole site. In the same year, the first foreign tourists arrived in Angkor – an unprecedented 200 of them in three months. Angkor had been 'rescued' from the jungle and was assuming its place in the modern world.

ARCHAEOLOGY OF ANGKOR

With the exception of Angkor Wat, which was restored for use as a Buddhist shrine in the 16th century by the Khmer royalty, the temples of Angkor were left to the jungle for many centuries. The majority of temples are made of sandstone, which tends to dissolve when in prolonged contact with dampness. Bat droppings took their toll, as did sporadic pilfering of sculptures and cut stones. At some monuments, such as Ta Prohm, the jungle had stealthily waged an all-out invasion, and plant-life could only be removed at great risk to the structures it now supported in its web of roots.

Initial attempts to clear Angkor under the aegis of the EFEO were fraught with technical difficulties and theoretical disputes. On a technical front, the jungle tended to grow back as soon as it was cleared; on a theoretical front, scholars debated the extent to which temples should be restored and whether later additions, such as Buddha images in Hindu temples, should be removed.

It was not until the 1920s that a solution came along – anastylosis. This was the method the Dutch had used to restore Borobudur in Java. Put simply, it was a way of reconstructing monuments using the original materials and in keeping with the original form of the structure. New materials were permitted only where the originals could not be found, and were to be used discreetly. An example of this method can be seen on the causeway leading to the entrance of Angkor Wat, as the right-hand side was originally restored by the French.

The first major restoration job was carried out on Banteay Srei in 1930. It was deemed such a success that many more extensive restoration projects were undertaken elsewhere around Angkor, culminating in the massive Angkor Wat restoration in the 1960s. Large cranes and earthmoving machines were brought in, and the operation was backed by a veritable army of surveying equipment.

The Khmer Rouge victory and Cambodia's subsequent slide into an intractable civil war resulted in far less damage to Angkor than many had assumed, as EFEO and Ministry of Culture teams had removed many of the statues from the temple sites for protection. Nevertheless, turmoil in Cambodia resulted in a long interruption of restoration work, allowing the jungle to grow back and once again resume its assault on the monuments. The illegal trade of *objets d'art* on the world art market has also been a major threat to Angkor, although it is the more remote sites that have been targeted recently. Angkor has been under the jurisdiction of the UN Educational Scientific and Cultural Organisation (Unesco) since 1992 as a World Heritage Site, and international and local efforts continue to preserve and reconstruct the monuments. In a sign of real progress, Angkor was removed from Unesco's endangered list in 2003.

Many of Angkor's secrets remain to be discovered, as most of the work at the temples has concentrated on restoration efforts above ground rather than archaeological digs and surveys below. Underground is where the real story of Angkor and its people lies – the inscriptions on the temples give us only a partial picture of the gods to whom each structure was dedicated, and the kings who built them.

ARCHITECTURAL STYLES

From the time of the earliest Angkorian monuments at Roluos, Khmer architecture was continually evolving, often from the rule of one king to the next. Archaeologists therefore divide the monuments of Angkor into nine separate periods, named after the foremost example of each period's architectural style.

A 17th-century Japanese pilgrim drew a detailed plan of Angkor Wat, though he mistakenly recalled that he had seen it in India.

Architect Lucien Fournereau travelled to Angkor in 1887. He produced plans and meticulously executed cross-sections that were to stand as the best available until the 1960s.

Between 1970 and 1973, the front line of fighting between Lon Nol forces and Khmer Rouge/North Vietnamese soldiers was midway between Siem Reap and Angkor Wat. Archaeologists were allowed to cross back and forth to continue their work restoring the temples.

GUIDE TO THE GUIDES

Countless books on Angkor have been written over the years, with more and more new titles coming out, reflecting Angkor's rebirth as one of the world's cultural hot spots. Here are just a few of the best:

- *A Guide to the Angkor Monuments* (Maurice Glaize) – the definitive guide to Angkor, downloadable for free at www.theangkorguide.com.

- *A Passage Through Angkor* (Mark Standen) – one of the best photographic records of the temples of Angkor.

- *A Pilgrimage to Angkor* (Pierre Loti) – one of the most beautifully written books on Angkor, based on the author's 1910 journey.

- *Ancient Angkor* (Claudes Jacques) – written by one of the foremost scholars on Angkor, this is the most readable guide to the temples, with photos by Michael Freeman.

- *Angkor: an Introduction to the Temples* (Dawn Rooney) – probably the most popular contemporary guide available.

- *Angkor: Millennium of Glory* (various authors) – a fascinating introduction to the history, culture, sculpture and religion of the Angkorian period.

- *Angkor – Heart of an Asian Empire* (Bruno Dagens) – the story of the 'discovery' of Angkor, complete with lavish illustrations.

- *Angkor: Splendours of the Khmer Civilisation* (Marilia Albanese) – Beautifully photographed guide to the major temples, including some of the more remote places in northern Cambodia.

- *Khmer Heritage in the Old Siamese Provinces of Cambodia* (Etienne Aymonier) – Aymonier journeyed through Cambodia in 1901 and visited many of the major temples.

- *The Customs of Cambodia* (Chou Ta-Kuan) – the only eyewitness account of Angkor, from a Chinese emissary who spent a year at the Khmer capital in the late 13th century.

To learn more about Unesco's activities at Angkor and the incredible diversity of World Heritage Sites, visit http://whc.unesco.org.

The seven-headed *naga*, a feature at many temples, represents the rainbow, which acts as a bridge between heaven and earth.

The evolution of Khmer architecture was based around a central theme of the temple-mountain, preferably set on a real hill, but artificial if there weren't any mountains to hand. The earlier a temple was constructed, the closer it adheres to this fundamental idea. Essentially, the mountain was represented by a tower mounted on a tiered base. At the summit was the central sanctuary, usually with an open door to the east, and three false doors at the remaining cardinal points of the compass.

By the time of the Bakheng period, this layout was being embellished. The summit of the central tower was crowned with five 'peaks' – four at the points of the compass and one in the centre. Even Angkor Wat features this layout, though on a grandiose scale. Other features that came to be favoured include an entry tower and a causeway lined with *nagas* (mythical serpent) balustrades leading up to the temple.

As the temples grew in ambition, the central tower became a less prominent feature, although it remained the focus of the temple. Later temples saw the central tower flanked by courtyards and richly decorated galleries. Smaller towers were placed on gates and on the corners of walls, their overall number often of religious or astrological significance.

These refinements and additions eventually culminated in Angkor Wat, which effectively showcases the evolution of Angkorian architecture. The architecture of the Bayon period breaks with tradition in temples such as Ta Prohm and Preah Khan. In these temples, the horizontal layout of the galleries, corridors and courtyards seems to completely eclipse the central tower.

The curious narrowness of the corridors and doorways in these structures can be explained by the fact that Angkorian architects never mastered the flying buttress to build a full arch. They engineered arches by laying blocks on top of each other, until they met at a central point; known as false arches, they can only support very short spans.

ORIENTATION

Heading north from Siem Reap, Angkor Wat is the first major temple, followed by the walled city of Angkor Thom. To the east and west of this city are two vast former reservoirs (the eastern reservoir now completely dried up), which once helped to feed the huge population. Further east are temples including Ta Prohm, Banteay Kdei and Pre Rup. North of Angkor Thom is Preah Khan and way beyond in the northeast, Banteay Srei, Kbal Spean, Phnom Kulen and Beng Mealea. To the southeast of Siem Reap is the early Angkorian Roluos Group of Temples.

Maps

There are several free maps covering Angkor, including the *Siem Reap Angkor 3D Map,* available at certain hotels, guesthouses and restaurants in town. River Books of Thailand publishes a fold-out *Angkor Map,* which is one of the more detailed offerings available.

INFORMATION
Admission Fees

While the cost of entry to Angkor is relatively expensive by Cambodian standards, the fees represent excellent value. Visitors have a choice of a one-day pass (US$20), a three-day pass (US$40) or a one-week pass (US$60). A new system was introduced in 2009 that allows three-day passes to run over three non-consecutive days in a one-week period and one-week passes to last for a full month. However, you have to actually request this type of new pass or they will still issue the old consecutive-days pass. Purchase the entry pass from the large official entrance booth on the road to Angkor Wat. The **Angkor ticket checkpoint** (Map p130) is due to move location during the lifetime of this book. Passes include a digital photo snapped at the entrance booth, so queues can be quite long at peak times. Visitors entering after 5pm get a free sunset, as the ticket starts from the following day. The fee includes access to all the monuments

> John Thomson was a Scottish photographer who took the first photographs of the temples in 1866. He was the first Westerner to posit the idea that they were symbolic representations of the mythical Mt Meru.

> Stung Siem Reap, the river that runs from the foothills of Phnom Kulen to Tonlé Sap Lake, was diverted to run through most of the major temples and *barays* of Angkor.

HIDDEN RICHES, POLITICAL HITCHES

Angkor Conservation (Map p130) is a Ministry of Culture compound on the banks of the Siem Reap River, about 400m east of the Sofitel Phokheetra Royal Angkor Hotel. The compound houses more than 5000 statues, *lingas* (phallic symbols) and inscribed stelae, stored here to protect them from the wanton looting that has blighted hundreds of sites around Angkor. The finest statuary is hidden away inside Angkor Conservation's warehouses, meticulously numbered and catalogued. Unfortunately, without the right contacts, trying to get a peek at the statues is a lost cause. Some of the statuary is now on public display in the Angkor National Museum (p132) in Siem Reap, but it is only a fraction of the collection.

Formerly housed at Angkor Conservation, but now going it alone in offices throughout Siem Reap, is **Apsara Authority** (Authority for Protection & Management of Angkor & the Region of Siem Reap; www.autoriteapsara.org). This organisation is responsible for the research, protection and conservation of cultural heritage around Angkor, as well as urban planning in Siem Reap and tourism development in the region. Quite a mandate, quite a challenge – especially now that the government is taking such a keen interest in its work. Angkor is a money-spinner; it remains to be seen whether Apsara will be empowered to put preservation before profits.

TEMPLES OF ANGKOR

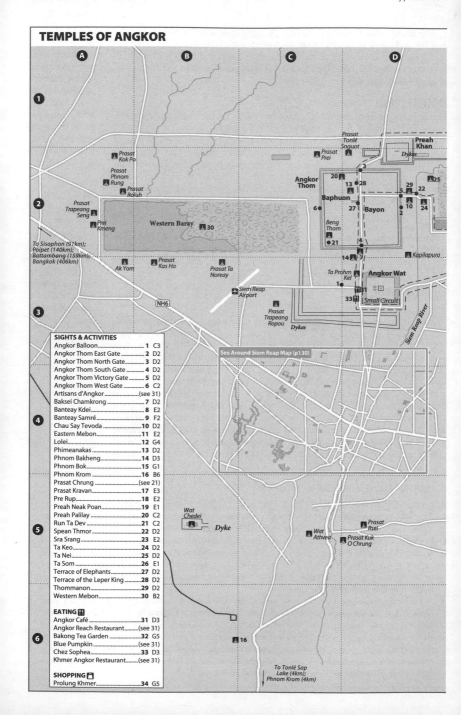

SIGHTS & ACTIVITIES
Angkor Balloon...........................**1** C3
Angkor Thom East Gate...........**2** D2
Angkor Thom North Gate.........**3** D2
Angkor Thom South Gate.........**4** D2
Angkor Thom Victory Gate.......**5** D2
Angkor Thom West Gate...........**6** C2
Artisans d'Angkor...................(see 31)
Baksei Chamkrong....................**7** D2
Banteay Kdei.............................**8** E2
Banteay Samré..........................**9** F2
Chau Say Tevoda.....................**10** D2
Eastern Mebon........................**11** E2
Lolei..**12** G4
Phimeanakas...........................**13** D2
Phnom Bakheng......................**14** D3
Phnom Bok..............................**15** G1
Phnom Krom............................**16** B6
Prasat Chrung.......................(see 21)
Prasat Kravan.........................**17** E3
Pre Rup...................................**18** E2
Preah Neak Poan....................**19** E1
Preah Palilay...........................**20** C2
Run Ta Dev..............................**21** C2
Spean Thmor..........................**22** D2
Sra Srang................................**23** E2
Ta Keo....................................**24** D2
Ta Nei.....................................**25** D2
Ta Som...................................**26** E1
Terrace of Elephants..............**27** D2
Terrace of the Leper King.......**28** D2
Thommanon............................**29** D2
Western Mebon......................**30** B2

EATING 🍴
Angkor Café............................**31** D3
Angkor Reach Restaurant.....(see 31)
Bakong Tea Garden **32** G5
Blue Pumpkin.......................(see 31)
Chez Sophea...........................**33** D3
Khmer Angkor Restaurant.....(see 31)

SHOPPING 🛍
Prolung Khmer.......................**34** G5

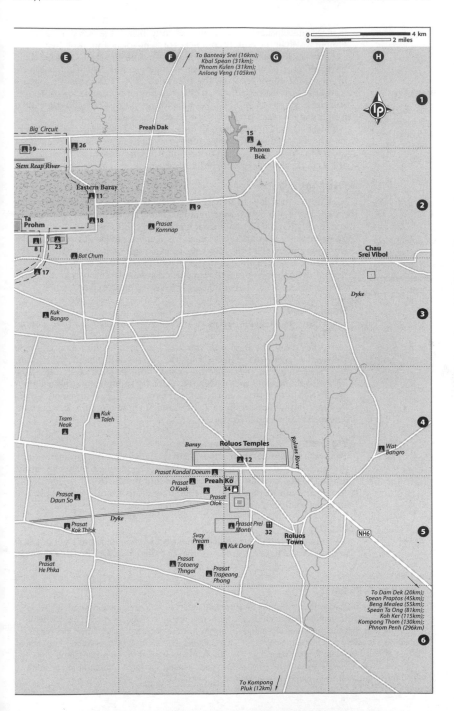

0 ————— 4 km
0 ————— 2 miles

To Banteay Srei (16km);
Kbal Spean (31km);
Phnom Kulen (31km);
Anlong Veng (105km)

E   F   G   H

1

Big Circuit

Preah Dak

🚶 39   🚶 26

15 🚶
Phnom
Bok ▲

Siem Reap River

Eastern Baray

🚶 11   🚶 9

Chau
Srei Vibol

□

2

Ta
Prohm

🚶 18

Prasat
Komnap 🚶

8 🚶   🚶 23

🚶 Bat Chum

🚶 17

Dyke

3

🚶 Kuk
Bangro

Tram
Neak 🚶

🚶 Kuk
Taleh

🚶 Wat
Bangro

4

Baray   **Roluos Temples**

🚶 12

Roluos River

Prasat Kandal Doeum 🚶

Prasat 🚶 **Preah Ko**
Prasat
Daun So 🚶   O Kaek   34 🏠

Prasat
Olok

🚶 Prasat
Kok Thlok   Dyke   Prasat Prei 🏯
Monti   32

🚶 Prasat
He Phka   Svay
Pream 🚶   🚶 Kuk Dong

Roluos
Town

NH6

5

🚶 Prasat
Totoeng
Thngai   Prasat
Trapeang
Phong 🚶

To Dam Dek (20km);
Spean Praptos (45km);
Beng Mealea (55km);
Spean Ta Ong (81km);
Koh Ker (115km);
Kompong Thom (130km);
Phnom Penh (296km)

6

To Kompong
Pluk (12km)

in the Siem Reap area, but does not currently include the sacred mountain of Phnom Kulen or the remote complexes of Beng Mealea and Koh Ker.

Entry tickets to the temples of Angkor are controlled by local hotel chain Sokha Hotels, part of a local petroleum conglomerate called Sokimex, which, in return for administrating the site, takes 17% of the revenue. Apsara Authority (see the boxed text, p159), the body responsible for protecting and conserving the temples, takes 68% for operating costs, if it can extract it from the Finance Ministry, and 15% goes to restoration.

Most of the major temples now have uniformed guards to check the tickets, which has reduced the opportunity for scams. A pass is not required for excursions to villages around or beyond Angkor, but you still have to stop at the checkpoint to explain your movements to the guards.

WARNING!

Visitors found inside any of the main temples without a ticket will be fined a whopping US$100.

ITINERARIES

Back in the early days of tourism, the problem of what to see and in what order came down to two basic temple itineraries: the Small (Petit) Circuit and the Big (Grand) Circuit, both marked on the Temples of Angkor map (Map pp160–1). It's difficult to imagine that anyone follows these to the letter any more, but in their time they were an essential component of the Angkor experience and were often undertaken on the back of an elephant.

For tips on the best times to visit particular temples, the best locations for sunrise and sunset and avoiding the hordes see the boxed text, p164.

Take a virtual tour of Angkor in 360 degrees on the *World Heritage Tour* website at www.world -heritage-tour.org.

Small Circuit

The 17km Small Circuit begins at Angkor Wat and heads north to Phnom Bakheng, Baksei Chamkrong and Angkor Thom, including the city wall and gates, the Bayon, the Baphuon, the Royal Enclosure, Phimeanakas, Preah Palilay, the Terrace of the Leper King, the Terrace of Elephants, the Kleangs and Prasat Suor Prat. It exits from Angkor Thom via the Victory Gate in the eastern wall, and continues to Chau Say Tevoda, Thommanon, Spean Thmor and Ta Keo. It then heads northeast of the road to Ta Nei, turns south to Ta Prohm, continues east to Banteay Kdei and Sra Srang, and finally returns to Angkor Wat via Prasat Kravan.

Big Circuit

The 26km Big Circuit is an extension of the Small Circuit: instead of exiting the walled city of Angkor Thom at the east gate, the Big Circuit exits at the north gate and continues to Preah Khan and Preah Neak Poan, east to Ta Som then south via the Eastern Mebon to Pre Rup. From there it heads west and then southwest on its return to Angkor Wat.

One Day

If you have only one day to visit Angkor, then bad luck, but a good itinerary would be Angkor Wat for sunrise and then stick around to explore the

---

WHEN NATURE CALLS

Angkor is now blessed with some of the finest public toilets in Asia. Designed in wooden chalets and complete with amenities such as electronic flush, they wouldn't be out of place in a fancy hotel. The trouble is that the guardians often choose not to run the generators that power the toilets, meaning it is pretty dark inside the cubicles (but thankfully you can flush manually, too!). Entrance is free if you show your Angkor pass, and they are found near most of the major temples.

Remember, in remote areas, don't stray off the path – being seen in a compromising position is infinitely better than stepping on a landmine.

mighty temple while it is quieter. From there continue to the tree roots of Ta Prohm before breaking for lunch. In the afternoon, explore the temples within the walled city of Angkor Thom and the beauty of the Bayon in the late-afternoon light.

Two Days

A two-day itinerary allows time to include some of the other big hitters around Angkor. Spend the first day visiting petite Banteay Srei, with its fabulous carvings, and stop at Banteay Samré on the return leg. In the afternoon, visit immense Preah Khan, delicate Preah Neak Poan and the tree roots of Ta Som, before taking in a sunset at Pre Rup. Spend the second day following the one-day itinerary to Angkor Wat, Ta Prohm and Angkor Thom.

Three to Five Days

If you have three to five days to explore Angkor, it is possible to see most of the important sites. One approach is to see as much as possible on the first day or two (as covered earlier) and then spend the final days combining visits to other sites such as the Roluos temples and Banteay Kdei. Better still is a gradual build-up to the most spectacular monuments. After all, if you see Angkor Wat on the first day, then a temple like Ta Keo just won't cut it. Another option is a chronological approach, starting with the earliest Angkorian temples and working steadily forwards in time to Angkor Thom, taking stock of the evolution of Khmer architecture and artistry.

> The average stay at Angkor is still just 2½ days, which barely allows enough time to see the major temples, let alone enjoy the action-packed town of Siem Reap.

ANGKORIN' FOR LUNCH

Most of the tour groups buzzing around Angkor head back to Siem Reap for lunch. This is as good a reason as any to stick around the temples, taking advantage of the lack of crowds to explore some popular sites and enjoy a local lunch at one of the many stalls. Almost all the major temples have some sort of nourishment available beyond the walls. Anyone travelling with a *moto* or *remork-moto (tuk tuk)* should ask the driver for tips on cheap eats, as these guys eat around the temples every day. They know the best spots, at the best price, and should be able to sort you out (assuming you are getting along well).

The most extensive selection of restaurants is lined up opposite the entrance to Angkor Wat. It includes several restaurants, such as Khmer Angkor Restaurant (Map pp160–1) and Angkor Reach Restaurant (Map pp160–1), with dishes ranging from US$3 to US$6. There is also now a handy branch of **Blue Pumpkin** (Map pp160-1; dishes US$2-5; 🌐) turning out sandwiches, salads and ice creams, as well as the usual divine fruit shakes, all to take away if required. **Chez Sophea** (Map pp160-1; ☎ 012 858003; meals US$10-20) offers barbecued meats and fish, accompanied by a cracking homemade salad, but prices are at the high end.

There are dozens of local noodle stalls just north of the Bayon, which are a good spot for a quick bite to eat. Other central temples with food available include Ta Prohm, Preah Khan and Ta Keo. There is also a cluster of welcoming Khmer restaurants located along the northern shore of Sra Srang.

Further afield, Banteay Srei has several small restaurants, complete with ornate wood furnishings cut from Cambodia's forests. Further north at Kbal Spean, food stalls at the bottom of the hill can cook up fried rice or a noodle soup, plus there is the inviting **Borey Sovann Restaurant** (meals US$3 to US$6), which is a great place to wind down before or after an ascent. There are also stop-and-dip stalls (dishes US$1 to US$3) near the entrance to Beng Mealea temple.

Water and soft drinks are available throughout the temple area, and many sellers lurk outside the temples, ready to pounce with offers of cold drinks. Sometimes they ask at just the right moment; on other occasions it is the 27th time in an hour that you've been approached and you are ready to scream. Try not to – you'll scare your fellow travellers and lose face with the locals.

It is well worth making the trip to the River of a Thousand Lingas at Kbal Spean for the chance to stretch your legs amid natural and man-made splendour; or the remote, vast and overgrown temple of Beng Mealea. Both can be combined with Banteay Srei in one long day.

One Week

Those with the time to spend a week at Angkor will be richly rewarded. Not only is it possible to fit all the temples of the region into an itinerary, but a longer stay also allows for nontemple activities, such as relaxing by a pool, indulging in a spa treatment or shopping around Siem Reap. Check out the aforementioned itineraries for some ideas on approach, but relax in the knowledge that you'll see it all. You may also want to throw in some of the more remote sites such as Koh Ker (p274), Prasat Preah Vihear (p279) or Banteay Chhmar (p265).

DODGING THE CROWDS

Angkor is on the tourist trail and is getting busier by the year but, with a little planning, it is still possible to escape the hordes. One important thing to remember, particularly when it comes to sunrise and sunset, is that places are popular for a reason, and it is worth going with the flow at least once.

A curious lore of itineraries and times for visiting the monuments developed at Angkor when tourism first began early in the 20th century. It is received wisdom that as Angkor Wat faces west, one should be there for late afternoon, and in the case of the Bayon, which faces east, in the morning. Ta Prohm, most people seem to agree, can be visited in the middle of the day because of its umbrella of foliage. This is all well and good, but if you reverse the order, the temples will still look good – and you can avoid some of the crowds.

The most popular place for sunrise is Angkor Wat. Most tour groups head back to town for breakfast, so stick around and explore the temple while it's cool and quiet. Bayon sees far fewer visitors than Angkor Wat in the early hours. Sra Srang is usually pretty quiet, and sunrise here can be spectacular thanks to reflections in the extensive waters. Phnom Bakheng could be an attractive option, because the sun comes up behind Angkor Wat and you are far from the madding crowd that gathers here at sunset. Ta Prohm is an alternative option, with no sight of sunrise, but a mysterious and magical atmosphere.

The definitive sunset spot is the hilltop temple of Phnom Bakheng, but this has been getting well out of control lately, with as many as 1000 tourists clambering around the small structure. Better to check it out for sunrise or early morning and miss the crowds. Staying within the confines of Angkor Wat for sunset is a rewarding option, as it can be pretty peaceful when most tourists head off to Phnom Bakheng around 4.30pm or so. Pre Rup is popular with some for an authentic rural sunset over the countryside, but this is starting to get busier (although nothing like the circus at Bakheng). Better is the hilltop temple of Phnom Krom, which offers commanding views across Tonlé Sap Lake, but involves a long drive back to town in the dark. The Western Baray takes in the sunset from the eastern end, across its vast waters, or from the Western Mebon island, and is generally a quiet option.

When it comes to the most popular temples, the middle of the day is consistently the quietest time. This is because the majority of the large tour groups head back to Siem Reap for lunch. It is also the hottest part of the day, which makes it tough going around relatively open temples such as Banteay Srei and the Bayon, but fine at well-covered temples such as Ta Prohm, Preah Khan and Beng Mealea, or even the bas-reliefs at Angkor Wat. The busiest times at Angkor Wat are from 6am to 7am and 3pm to 5pm; at the Bayon, from 8am to 10am; and at Banteay Srei, mid-morning and mid-afternoon. However, at other popular temples, such as Ta Prohm and Preah Khan, the crowds are harder to predict, and at most other temples in the Angkor region it's just a case of pot luck. If you pull up outside and see a car park full of tour buses, you may want to move on to somewhere quieter. The wonderful thing about Angkor is that there is always another temple to explore.

TOURS

Most budget and midrange travellers not on package tours prefer to take in the temples at their own pace. However, visitors who have only a day or two at this incredible site may prefer something organised locally.

It is possible to link up with an official tour guide in Siem Reap. The **Khmer Angkor Tour Guides Association** (☎ 063-964347; www.khmerangkortourguide.com) represents some of Angkor's authorised guides. English- or French-speaking guides can be booked from US$20 to US$30 a day; guides speaking other languages, such as Italian, German, Spanish, Japanese and Chinese, are available at a higher rate as there are fewer of them.

For an organised tour around Angkor, check out the recommended Cambodian operators under Tours (p345) in the Transport chapter. Other good Siem Reap–based companies:

Buffalo Trails (☎ 012 297506; www.buffalotrails-cambodia.com) Promotes homestays, walking tours, birdwatching and traditional fishing techniques.

Terre Cambodge (☎ 063-964557; www.terrecambodge.com) Offers trips to a variety of remote sites around Angkor, some by bicycle, plus boat trips on the Tonlé Sap Lake aboard its wooden sampan.

Villa (☎ 063-761036; www.thevillasiemreap.com) Small group trips to the more remote spots, like Beng Mealea temple and Kompong Pluk village, plus lifestyle visits beyond the temples.

GETTING THERE & AROUND

Visitors heading to the temples of Angkor – in other words pretty much everybody coming to Cambodia – need to consider the most suitable way to travel between the temples. Many of the best-known temples are no more than a few kilometres from the walled city of Angkor Thom, which is just 8km from Siem Reap, and can be visited using anything from a car or motorcycle to a sturdy pair of walking boots. For the independent traveller, there is a daunting range of alternatives to consider.

Bicycle

A great way to get around the temples, bicycles are environmentally friendly and are used by most locals living around the area. There are few hills and the roads are good, so there's no need for much cycling experience. Moving about at a slower speed, you soon find that you take in more than from out of a car window or on the back of a speeding *moto*.

White Bicycles (www.thewhitebicycles.org; per day US$2) is supported by some guesthouses around town, with proceeds from the US$2 hire fee going towards community projects. Many guesthouses and hotels in town rent bikes for around US$1 to US$2 per day.

Some places also offer better mountain bikes like Trek or Giant for around US$7 to US$10 per day. Try **Travel Loops** (Map p134; ☎ 063-963776; www.cyclingincambodia.com; Sivatha St, Siem Reap) with Cannondale road bikes for US$5 and mountain bikes with helmet for US$10.

Car & Motorcycle

Cars are a popular choice for getting about the temples. The obvious advantage is protection from the elements, be it rain or the punishing sun. Shared between several travellers, they can also be an economical way to explore. The downside is that visitors are a little more isolated from the sights, sounds and smells as they travel between temples. A car for the day around the central temples is US$25 to US$35 and can be arranged with hotels, guesthouses and agencies in town.

Motorcycle rental in Siem Reap is currently prohibited, but some travellers bring a motorcycle from Phnom Penh. If you manage to get a bike up

Check out the website of Heritage Watch at www.heritagewatch.org to learn about sustainable initiatives to involve the local community in the tourism boom in Angkor.

For the ultimate Angkor experience, try a pick-and-mix approach, with a *moto, remork-moto* or car for one day to cover the remote sites, a bicycle to experience the central temples, and an exploration on foot for a spot of peace and serenity.

The ticketing concession at Angkor is due to be taken over by a South Korean company in 2010 and, as well as relocating the main checkpoint, there are well-founded rumours that electric cars will be introduced for all visitors, so you may not have to worry about how to get around. First mooted in 2000, this may not go down well with local transport drivers.

here, leave it at a guarded parking area or with a stallholder outside each temple, otherwise it could get stolen.

Elephant

People planning adventures further afield to the remote temples in Preah Vihear Province (p272) will need to arrange a 4WD if they don't want to be on a motorcycle for several long days. Think US$80 and up per day.

Travelling by elephant was the traditional way to see the temples way back in the early days of tourism at Angkor, at the start of the 20th century. It is once again possible to take an elephant ride between the south gate of Angkor Thom and the Bayon (US$10) in the morning, or up to the summit of Phnom Bakheng for sunset (US$15). The elephants are owned by the **Angkor Village** (www.angkorvillage.com) resort group, although some tourists have complained about the elephants being poorly treated by handlers.

Helicopter

For those with plenty of spending money, there are tourist flights around Angkor Wat (US$90) and the temples outside Angkor Thom (US$150) with **Helicopters Cambodia** (Map p134; ☎ 012 814500; www.helicopterscambodia.com; 658 Hup Quan St, Siem Reap), which has an office near the Psar Chaa in Siem Reap. The company also offers charters to remote temples such as Prasat Preah Vihear and Preah Khan, with prices starting at around US$1800 per hour plus 10% sales tax. Newcomer **Helistar** (Map p134; ☎ 063-966072; www.helistarcambodia.com; 24 Sivatha St, Siem Reap) is another option.

Minibus

Angkor Balloon (Map pp160-1; ☎ 012 759698; per person US$11) offers a bird's-eye view of Angkor Wat. The balloon carries up to 30 people, is on a fixed line and rises 200m above the landscape.

Minibuses are available from various hotels and travel agents around town. A 12-seat minibus costs from US$50 per day, while a 25- or 30-seat coaster bus is around US$100 per day.

Moto

Many independent travellers end up visiting the temples by *moto*. *Moto* drivers accost visitors from the moment they set foot in Siem Reap, but they often end up being knowledgeable and friendly, and good companions for a tour around the temples. They can drop you off and pick you up at allotted times and places and even tell you a bit of background about the temples as you zip around. Many of the better drivers go on to become official tour guides.

Remork-Moto

Transport will be more expensive to remote temples such as Banteay Srei or Beng Mealea, due to extra fuel costs.

A motorcycle with a twee little hooded carriage towed behind, these are also known as *remorks* or *tuk tuks*. They are a popular way to get around Angkor as fellow travellers can still talk to each other as they explore (unlike on the back of a *moto*). They also offer some protection from the rain. As with *moto* drivers, some *remork* drivers are very good companions for a tour of the temples. Prices run from US$10 to US$20 for the day, depending on the destination and number of passengers.

Walking

Why not forget all these new-fangled methods and simply explore on foot? There are obvious limitations to what can be seen, as some temples are just too far from Siem Reap. However, it is easy enough to walk to Angkor Wat and the temples of Angkor Thom, and this is a great way to meet up with villagers in the area. Those who want to get away from the roads should try the peaceful walk along the walls of Angkor Thom. It is about 13km in total, and offers access to several small, remote temples and some birdlife. Another rewarding walk is from Ta Nei to Ta Keo through the forest.

ANGKOR WAT

អង្គរវត្ត

This is the mother of all temples. Angkor Wat is undoubtedly the most breathtaking of the monuments at Angkor, and is widely believed to be the largest religious building in the world. Hardly surprising given that its name means 'temple that is a city'. Soaring skyward and surrounded by a moat that would make its European castle counterparts blush, Angkor Wat is one of the most inspired and spectacular monuments ever conceived by the human mind.

Simply unique, it is a stunning blend of spirituality and symmetry, an enduring example of man's devotion to his gods. Relish the very first approach, as that spine-tickling moment when you emerge on the inner causeway will rarely be felt again. It is the best-preserved temple at Angkor, as it was never abandoned to the elements, and repeat visits are rewarded with previously unnoticed details. It was probably built as a funerary temple for Suryavarman II to honour Vishnu, the Hindu deity with whom the king identified.

There is much about Angkor Wat that is unique among the temples of Angkor. The most significant fact is that the temple is oriented towards the west. Symbolically, west is the direction of death, which once led a large number of scholars to conclude that Angkor Wat must have existed primarily as a tomb. This idea was supported by the fact that the magnificent bas-reliefs of the temple were designed to be viewed in an anticlockwise direction, a practice that has precedents in ancient Hindu funerary rites. Vishnu, however, is also frequently associated with the west, and it is now commonly accepted that Angkor Wat most likely served both as a temple and a mausoleum for Suryavarman II.

Angkor Wat is famous for its beguiling *apsaras* (heavenly nymphs). Many of these exquisite *apsaras* were damaged during Indian efforts to clean the temples with chemicals during the 1980s, the ultimate bad acid trip, but they are now being restored by the teams with the **German Apsara Conservation Project** (GACP; www.gacp-angkor.de). The organisation operates a small information booth in the northwest corner of Angkor Wat, near the modern wat, where beautiful black-and-white postcards and images of Angkor are available.

SYMBOLISM

Visitors to Angkor Wat are struck by its imposing grandeur and, at close quarters, its fascinating decorative flourishes and extensive bas-reliefs. Holy men at the time of Angkor must have revelled in its multilayered levels of meaning in much the same way a contemporary literary scholar might delight in James Joyce's *Ulysses*.

Eleanor Mannikka explains in her book *Angkor Wat: Time, Space and Kingship* that the spatial dimensions of Angkor Wat parallel the lengths of the four ages (Yuga) of classical Hindu thought. Thus the visitor to Angkor Wat who walks the causeway to the main entrance and through the courtyards to the final main tower, which once contained a statue of Vishnu, is metaphorically travelling back to the first age of the creation of the universe.

Like the other temple-mountains of Angkor, Angkor Wat also replicates the spatial universe in miniature. The central tower is Mt Meru, with its surrounding smaller peaks, bounded in turn by continents (the lower courtyards) and the oceans (the moat). The seven-headed *naga* becomes a symbolic rainbow bridge for man to reach the abode of the gods.

There are more than 3000 *apsaras* (nymphs) carved into the walls of Angkor Wat, each of them unique, and there are 37 different hairstyles for budding stylists to check out.

For the filming of *Tomb Raider*, an elaborate floating village was constructed on the northern pond of Angkor Wat; Angelina Jolie came ashore here before borrowing a mobile phone from a local monk.

TIP

The best times to visit Angkor Wat if you want to avoid the crowds are between 7am and 9am, noon to 2pm, and after 5pm.

MOTIFS, SYMBOLS & CHARACTERS AROUND ANGKOR

The temples of Angkor are intricately carved with myths and legends, symbols and signs, and a cast of characters in the thousands. Deciphering them can be quite a challenge, so here we've highlighted some of the most commonly seen around the majestic temples. For more help unravelling the carvings of Angkor, pick up a copy of *Images of the Gods* by Vittorio Reveda.

Apsaras Heavenly nymphs or goddesses, also known as *devadas;* these beautiful female forms decorate the walls of many temples.

Asuras These devils feature extensively in representations of the Churning of the Ocean of Milk, such as at Angkor Wat.

Devas The 'good gods' in the creation myth of the Churning of the Ocean of Milk.

Flame The flame motif is found flanking steps and doorways and is intended to purify pilgrims as they enter the temple.

Garuda Vehicle of Vishnu; this half-man, half-bird creature features in some temples and was combined with his old enemy *naga* to promote religious unity under Jayavarman VII.

Kala The temple guardian appointed by Shiva; he had such an appetite that he devoured his own body and appears only as a giant head above doorways. Also known as Rehu.

Linga A phallic symbol of fertility, *lingas* would have originally been located within the towers of most Hindu temples.

Lotus Another symbol of purity, the lotus features extensively in the shape of towers, the shape of steps to entrances and in decoration.

Makara A giant sea serpent with a reticulated jaw; features on the corner of pediments, spewing forth a *naga* or some other creature.

Naga The multiheaded serpent, half-brother and enemy of garuda, who controls the rains and, therefore, the prosperity of the kingdom; seen on causeways, doorways and roofs.

Nandi The mount of Shiva; there are several statues of Nandi dotted about the temples, although many have been damaged or stolen by looters.

Rishi A Hindu wise man or ascetic, also known as *essai;* these bearded characters are often seen sitting cross-legged at the base of pillars or flanking walls.

Vine Yet another symbol of purity, the vine graces doorways and lintels and is meant to help cleanse the visitor on their journey to this heaven on earth, the abode of the gods.

Yama God of death who presides over the underworld and passes judgment on whether people continue to heaven or hell.

Yoni Female fertility symbol that is combined with the *linga* to produce holy water infused with fertility.

ARCHITECTURAL LAYOUT

Angkor Wat is surrounded by a 190m-wide moat, which forms a giant rectangle measuring 1.5km by 1.3km. From the west, a sandstone causeway crosses the moat. The sandstone blocks from which Angkor Wat was built were quarried more than 50km away (from the holy mountain of Phnom Kulen) and floated down the Siem Reap River on rafts. The logistics of such an operation are mind-blowing, consuming the labour of thousands – an unbelievable feat given the lack of cranes and trucks that we take for granted in contemporary construction projects.

The rectangular outer wall, which measures 1025m by 800m, has a gate on each side, but the main entrance, a 235m-wide porch richly decorated with carvings and sculptures, is on the western side. There is a statue of Vishnu, 3.25m in height and hewn from a single block of sandstone, located in the right-hand tower. Vishnu's eight arms hold a mace, a spear, a disc, a conch and other items. You may also see locks of hair lying about. These are offerings both from young people preparing to get married and from pilgrims giving thanks for their good fortune.

An avenue, 475m long and 9.5m wide and lined with *naga* balustrades, leads from the main entrance to the central temple, passing between two graceful libraries (the northern one restored by a Japanese team) and then two pools, the northern one a popular spot from which to watch the sun rise.

According to inscriptions, the construction of Angkor Wat involved 300,000 workers and 6000 elephants, yet was still not fully completed.

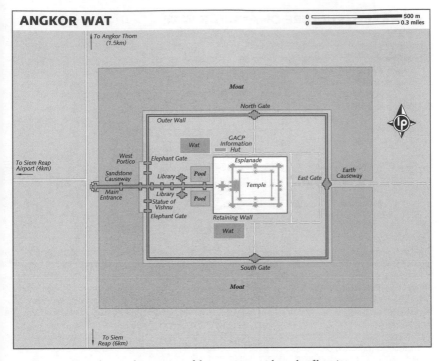

ANGKOR WAT

The central temple complex consists of three storeys, each made of laterite, which enclose a square surrounded by intricately interlinked galleries. The Gallery of a Thousand Buddhas (Preah Poan) used to house hundreds of Buddha images before the war, but many of these were removed or stolen, leaving just the handful we see today.

The corners of the second and third storeys are marked by towers, each topped with symbolic lotus bud towers. Rising 31m above the third level and 55m above the ground is the central tower, which gives the whole grand ensemble its sublime unity. The stairs to the upper level are immensely steep, because reaching the kingdom of the gods was no easy task. Also known as Bakan, access to the upper level of Angkor Wat was not possible from 2007–09, but as we go to press it has just reopened for a limited number of visitors per day with a queuing system. This means it is once again possible to complete the pilgrimage with an ascent to the summit: savour the cooling breeze, take in the extensive views and then find a quiet corner in which to contemplate the symmetry and symbolism of this Everest of temples.

BAS-RELIEFS

Stretching around the outside of the central temple complex is an 800m-long series of intricate and astonishing bas-reliefs. The following is a brief description of the epic events depicted on the panels. They are described in the order in which you'll come to them if you begin on the western side and keep the bas-reliefs to your left. The majority of them were completed in the 12th century, but in the 16th century several new reliefs were added to unfinished panels.

Most of the major sandstone blocks around Angkor include small circular holes. These originally held wooden stakes that were used to lift and position the stones during construction before being sawn off.

Originally, the central sanctuary of Angkor Wat held a gold statue of Vishnu mounted on a garuda (a mythical half-man, half-bird creature) that represented the deified god-king Suryavarman II.

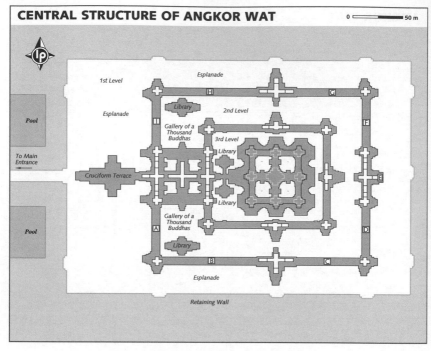

CENTRAL STRUCTURE OF ANGKOR WAT

The bas-reliefs at Angkor Wat were once sheltered by the cloister's wooden roof, which long ago rotted away except for one original beam in the western half of the north gallery. The other roofed sections are reconstructions.

(A) The Battle of Kurukshetra

The southern portion of the west gallery depicts a battle scene from the Hindu *Mahabharata* epic, in which the Kauravas (coming from the north) and the Pandavas (coming from the south) advance upon each other, meeting in furious battle. Infantry are shown on the lowest tier, with officers on elephants, and chiefs on the second and third tiers. Some of the more interesting details (from left to right): a dead chief lying on a pile of arrows, surrounded by his grieving parents and troops; a warrior on an elephant who, by putting down his weapon, has accepted defeat; and a mortally wounded officer, falling from his carriage into the arms of his soldiers. Over the centuries, some sections have been polished (by the millions of hands that fall upon them) to look like black marble. The portico at the southwestern corner is decorated with sculptures representing characters from the *Ramayana*.

(B) The Army of Suryavarman II

The remarkable western section of the south gallery depicts a triumphal battle march of Suryavarman II's army. In the southwestern corner about 2m from the floor is Suryavarman II on an elephant, wearing the royal tiara and armed with a battleaxe; he is shaded by 15 parasols and fanned by legions of servants. Further on is a procession of well-armed soldiers and officers on horseback; among them are bold and warlike chiefs on elephants. Just before the end of this panel is the rather disorderly Siamese mercenary army, with their long headdresses and ragged marching, at that time allied with the Khmers in their conflict with the Chams. The Khmer troops have square breastplates and are armed with spears; the Thais wear skirts and carry tridents.

(C) Heaven & Hell

The eastern half of the south gallery depicts the punishments and rewards of the 37 heavens and 32 hells. On the left, the upper and middle tiers show fine gentlemen and ladies proceeding towards 18-armed Yama (the judge of the dead) seated on a bull; below him are his assistants, Dharma and Sitragupta. On the lower tier, devils drag the wicked along the road to hell. To Yama's right, the tableau is divided into two parts by a horizontal line of garudas: above, the elect dwell in beautiful mansions, served by women and attendants; below, the condemned suffer horrible tortures that might have inspired the Khmer Rouge. The ceiling in this section was restored by the French in the 1930s.

(D) Churning of the Ocean of Milk

The southern section of the east gallery is decorated by the most famous of the bas-relief scenes at Angkor Wat, the Churning of the Ocean of Milk. This brilliantly executed carving depicts 88 *asuras* on the left, and 92 *devas*, with crested helmets, churning up the sea to extract from it the elixir of immortality. The demons hold the head of the serpent Vasuki and the gods hold its tail. At the centre of the sea, Vasuki is coiled around Mt Mandala, which turns and churns up the water in the tug of war between the demons and the gods. Vishnu, incarnated as a huge turtle, lends his shell to serve as the base and pivot of Mt Mandala. Brahma, Shiva, Hanuman (the monkey god) and Lakshmi (the goddess of beauty) all make appearances, while overhead a host of heavenly female spirits sing and dance in encouragement. Luckily for us, the gods won through, as the *apsaras* above were too much for the hot-blooded devils to take. Restoration work on this incredible panel by the **World Monuments Fund** (WMF; www.wmf.org) is due for completion during 2010.

(E) The Elephant Gate

This gate, which has no stairway, was used by the king and others for mounting and dismounting elephants directly from the gallery. North of the gate is a Khmer inscription recording the erection of a nearby stupa in the 18th century.

(F) Vishnu Conquers the Demons

The northern section of the east gallery shows a furious and desperate encounter between Vishnu, riding on a garuda, and innumerable devils. Needless to say, he slays all comers. This gallery was completed at a later date, most likely in the 16th century, and the later carving is notably inferior to the original work from the 12th century.

(G) Krishna & the Demon King

The eastern section of the north gallery shows Vishnu incarnated as Krishna riding a garuda. He confronts a burning walled city, the residence of Bana, the demon king. The garuda puts out the fire and Bana is captured. In the final scene Krishna kneels before Shiva and asks that Bana's life be spared.

(H) Battle of the Gods & the Demons

The western section of the north gallery depicts the battle between the 21 gods of the Brahmanic pantheon and various demons. The gods are featured with their traditional attributes and mounts. Vishnu has four arms and is seated on a garuda, while Shiva rides a sacred goose.

The rectangular holes seen in the Army of Suryavarman II relief were created when, so the story goes, Thai soldiers removed pieces of the scene containing inscriptions that reportedly gave clues to the location of the golden treasures of Suryavarman II, later buried during the reign of Jayavarman VII.

Check out the images of Suryavarman II on the southern gallery and compare him with the image of Rama in the northern gallery and you'll notice an uncanny likeness that helped reinforce the aura of the god-king.

Plans are afoot for night visits to Angkor Wat. A South Korean firm called Sou Ching was granted the concession, but the plans have stalled for now due to controversy over the lighting installations and potential damage to the sandstone structure.

(l) Battle of Lanka

The northern half of the west gallery shows scenes from the *Ramayana*. In the Battle of Lanka, Rama (on the shoulders of Hanuman), along with his army of monkeys, battles 10-headed, 20-armed Ravana, captor of Rama's beautiful wife Sita. Ravana rides a chariot drawn by monsters and commands an army of giants.

ANGKOR THOM

អង្គរធំ

Aptly named, the fortified city of Angkor Thom is indeed a 'Great City' on an epic scale, more than 10 sq km in size. This is the last capital city that took 'monumental' to a whole new level. It was built by Angkor's greatest king, Jayavarman VII, who came to power following the disastrous sacking of the previous Khmer capital by the Chams. At the city's height, it may have supported a population of one million people in the surrounding region. Centred on the Bayon, the mesmerising, if mind-bending, state temple, Angkor Thom is enclosed by a *jayagiri* (square wall) 8m high and 12km in length and encircled by a 100m-wide *jayasindhu* (moat). This architectural layout is yet another monumental expression of Mt Meru surrounded by the oceans.

It's hard to imagine any building bigger or more beautiful than Angkor Wat, but in Angkor Thom the sum of the parts adds up to a greater whole. It is the gates that grab you first: five immense structures, 20m in height, one each in the northern, western and southern walls and two in the eastern wall, topped with the magnanimous faces of the Bodhisattva Avalokiteshvara staring out over the kingdom. They are flanked by a monumental representation of the Churning of the Ocean of Milk, 54 demons and 54 gods engaged in an epic tug of war on the causeway. Imagine being a peasant in the 13th century approaching the forbidding capital for the first time? It would have been an awe inspiring yet unsettling experience to enter such a gateway and come face to face with the divine power of the god-kings.

The causeway at the west gate of Angkor Thom has completely collapsed, leaving a jumble of ancient stones sticking out of the soil, like victims of a terrible historical pile-up.

The south gate is most popular with visitors, as it has been fully restored and many of the heads (mostly copies) remain in place. The gate is on the main road into Angkor Thom from Angkor Wat, and it gets very busy. More peaceful are the east and west gates, found at the end of dirt trails. The east gate was used as a location in *Tomb Raider*, where the bad guys broke into the 'tomb' by pulling down a giant (polystyrene!) *apsara*.

In the centre of the walled enclosure are the city's most important monuments, including the Bayon, the Baphuon, the Royal Enclosure, Phimeanakas and the Terrace of Elephants.

BAYON

បាយ័ន

Unique, even among its cherished contemporaries, Bayon epitomises the creative genius and inflated ego of Cambodia's legendary king, Jayavarman VII. It's a place of stooped corridors, precipitous flights of stairs and, best of all, a collection of 54 Gothic-style towers decorated with 216 coldly smiling, enormous faces of Avalokiteshvara that bear more than a passing resemblance to the great king himself. These huge heads glare down from every angle, exuding power and control with a hint of humanity – this was precisely the blend required to hold sway over such a vast empire, ensuring the disparate and far-flung population yielded to his magnanimous will. As you walk

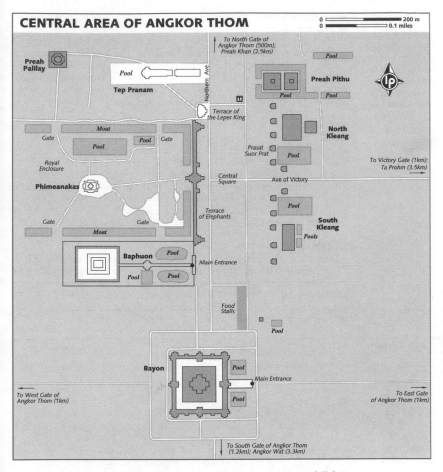

CENTRAL AREA OF ANGKOR THOM

around, a dozen or more of the heads are visible at any one time – full face or in profile, almost level with your eyes or staring down from up high.

Bayon is now known to have been built by Jayavarman VII, though for many years its origins were unknown. Shrouded in dense jungle, it also took researchers some time to realise that it stands in the exact centre of the city of Angkor Thom. There is still much mystery associated with Bayon – such as its exact function and symbolism – and this seems only appropriate for a monument whose signature is an enigmatic smiling face.

The eastward orientation of Bayon leads most people to visit early in the morning, preferably just after sunrise, when the sun inches upwards, lighting face after face. Bayon, however, looks equally good in the late afternoon, and if you stay for the sunset you get the same effect as at sunrise, in reverse. A Japanese team is restoring several outer areas of the temple.

Architectural Layout

Unlike Angkor Wat, which looks impressive from all angles, the Bayon looks rather like a glorified pile of rubble from a distance. It's only when

TIP

The best times to visit Bayon if you want to avoid the crowds are between 6am and 8am, and noon to 2pm.

Some say that the Khmer empire was divided into 54 provinces at the time of Bayon's construction, hence the all-seeing eyes of Avalokiteshvara (or Jayavarman VII) keeping watch on the kingdom's outlying subjects.

you enter the temple and make your way up to the third level that its magic becomes apparent.

The basic structure of the Bayon is a simple three levels, which correspond more or less to three distinct phases of building. This is because Jayavarman VII began construction of this temple at an advanced age, so was never confident it would be completed. Each time one phase was completed, he moved on to the next. The first two levels are square and adorned with bas-reliefs. They lead up to a third, circular level, with the towers and their faces.

Bas-Reliefs

Angkor Wat's bas-reliefs may grab the headlines, but the Bayon's are even more extensive, decorated with 1.2km of extraordinary carvings depicting more than 11,000 figures. The famous carvings on the outer wall of the first level show vivid scenes of everyday life in 12th-century Cambodia. The bas-reliefs on the second level do not have the epic proportions of those on the first level and tend to be fragmented. The reliefs described are those on the first level. The sequence assumes that you enter the Bayon from the east and view the reliefs in a clockwise direction.

(A) CHAMS ON THE RUN

Just south of the east gate is a three-level panorama. On the first tier, Khmer soldiers march off to battle – check out the elephants and the ox carts, which are almost exactly like those still used in Cambodia today. The second tier depicts the coffins being carried back from the battlefield. In the centre of the third tier, Jayavarman VII, shaded by parasols, is shown on horseback followed by legions of concubines (to the left).

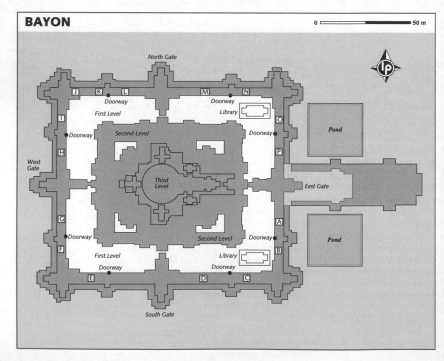

BAYON

BAYON INFORMATION CENTER

New in 2009, the **Bayon Information Center** (Map p130; ☎ 092-165083; www.angkor-jsa.org/bic; entry US$2; ⊗ 8am-4pm Tue, Wed & Fri-Sun) is a well-presented and informative exhibition on the history of the Khmer empire and the restoration projects around Angkor. Set in the beautiful compound of the Japanese government team for Safeguarding Angkor (JSA), it's a big saving on the Angkor National Museum.

(B) LINGA WORSHIP
The first panel north of the southeastern corner shows Hindus praying to a *linga* (phallic symbol). This image was probably originally a Buddha, later modified by a Hindu king.

(C) NAVAL BATTLE
The next panel has some of the best-carved reliefs. The scenes depict a naval battle between the Khmers and the Chams (the latter with head coverings) and everyday life around Tonlé Sap Lake, where the battle was fought. Look for images of people picking lice from each other's hair, of hunters and, towards the western end of the panel, a woman giving birth.

(D) THE CHAMS VANQUISHED
In the next panel, scenes from daily life continue and the battle shifts to the shore where the Chams are soundly thrashed. Scenes include two people playing chess, a cockfight and women selling fish in the market. The scenes of meals being prepared and served are in celebration of the Khmer victory.

(E & F) MILITARY PROCESSION
The last section of the south gallery, depicting a military procession, is unfinished, as is the panel showing elephants being led down from the mountains. Brahmans have been chased up two trees by tigers.

(G) CIVIL WAR
This panel depicts scenes that some scholars maintain is a civil war. Groups of people, some armed, confront each other, and the violence escalates until elephants and warriors join the melee.

(H) THE ALL-SEEING KING
The fighting continues on a smaller scale in the next panel. An antelope is being swallowed by a gargantuan fish; among the smaller fish is a prawn, under which an inscription proclaims that the king will seek out those in hiding.

Before its restoration in the 1930s, some of the Bayon face towers were smothered by immense trees, similar to those seen around Ta Prohm today.

(I) VICTORY PARADE
This panel depicts a procession that includes the king (carrying a bow). Presumably it is a celebration of his victory.

(J) THE CIRCUS COMES TO TOWN
At the western corner of the northern wall is a Khmer circus. A strongman holds three dwarfs, and a man on his back is spinning a wheel with his feet; above is a group of tightrope walkers. To the right of the circus, the royal court watches from a terrace, below which is a procession of animals. Some of the reliefs in this section remain unfinished.

(K) A LAND OF PLENTY
The two rivers, one next to the doorpost and the other a few metres to the right, are teeming with fish.

(L, M & N) THE CHAMS RETREAT
On the lowest level of this unfinished three-tiered scene, the Cham armies are being defeated and expelled from the Khmer kingdom. The next panel depicts the Cham armies advancing, and the badly deteriorated panel shows the Chams (on the left) chasing the Khmers.

(O) THE SACKING OF ANGKOR
This panel shows the war of 1177, when the Khmers were defeated by the Chams, and Angkor was pillaged. The wounded Khmer king is being lowered from the back of an elephant and a wounded Khmer general is being carried on a hammock suspended from a pole. Directly above, despairing Khmers are getting drunk. The Chams (on the right) are in hot pursuit of their vanquished enemy.

(P) THE CHAMS ENTER ANGKOR
This panel depicts another meeting of the two armies. Notice the flag bearers among the Cham troops (on the right). The Chams were defeated in the war, which ended in 1181, as depicted on panel A.

BAPHUON
ប្រាសាទបាពួន

View the striking temples of Angkor Thom in a different light by checking out the sepia, infra-red images of John McDermott at www.mcdermottgallery.com or visit his gallery in Siem Reap (p149).

Sometimes known as the world's largest jigsaw puzzle, Baphuon was the centre of EFEO restoration efforts when the Cambodian civil war erupted and work paused for a quarter of a century. The temple was taken apart piece by piece, in keeping with the anastylosis method of renovation, but all the records were destroyed during the Khmer Rouge years, leaving experts with 300,000 stones to put back into place. The EFEO resumed restoration work in 1995, and continues their efforts today. Baphuon is approached by a 200m elevated walkway made of sandstone, and the central structure is 43m high.

In its heyday, Baphuon would have been one of the most spectacular of Angkor's temples. Located 200m northwest of Bayon, it's a pyramidal representation of mythical Mt Meru. Construction probably began under Suryavarman I and was later completed by Udayadityavarman II. It marked the centre of the capital that existed before the construction of Angkor Thom.

ON LOCATION WITH TOMB RAIDER

Several sequences for *Tomb Raider*, starring Angelina Jolie as Lara Croft, were shot around the temples of Angkor. The Cambodia shoot opened at Phnom Bakheng, with Lara looking through binoculars for the mysterious temple. The baddies were already trying to break in through the east gate of Angkor Thom by pulling down a giant polystyrene *apsara*. Reunited with her custom Land Rover, Lara made a few laps around the Bayon before discovering a back way into the temple from Ta Prohm, where she plucked a sprig of jasmine and fell through into…Pinewood Studios. After battling a living statue and dodging Daniel Craig (aka 007) by diving off the waterfall at Phnom Kulen, she emerged in a floating market in front of Angkor Wat, as you do. She came ashore here before borrowing a mobile phone from a local monk and venturing into the Gallery of a Thousand Buddhas, where she was healed by the abbot.

On the western side of the temple is the retaining wall of the second level. The wall was fashioned – apparently in the 15th or 16th century – into a reclining Buddha 60m in length. The unfinished figure is quite difficult to make out, but the head is on the northern side of the wall and the gate is where the hips should be; to the left of the gate protrudes an arm. When it comes to the legs and feet – the latter are entirely gone – imagination must suffice. This huge project was undertaken by the Buddhist faithful around 500 years ago, which reinforces the fact that Angkor was never entirely abandoned.

ROYAL ENCLOSURE & PHIMEANAKAS
ភិមានអាកាស

Phimeanakas stands close to the centre of a walled area that once housed the royal palace. There's very little left of the palace today except for two sandstone pools near the northern wall. Once the site of royal ablutions, these are now used as swimming holes by local children. It is fronted to the east by the Terrace of Elephants. Construction of the palace began under Rajendravarman II, although it was used by Jayavarman V and Udayadityavarman I. It was later added to and embellished by Jayavarman VII (who else?) and his successors.

Phimeanakas means 'Celestial Palace', and some scholars say that it was once topped by a golden spire. Today it only hints at its former splendour and looks a little worse for wear. The temple is another pyramidal representation of Mt Meru, with three levels. Most of the decorative features are broken or have disappeared. Still, it is worth clambering up to the second and third levels for good views of Baphuon.

PREAH PALILAY
ព្រះបាលីទ្បៃ

Preah Palilay is located about 200m north of the Royal Enclosure's northern wall. It was erected during the rule of Jayavarman VII and originally housed a Buddha, which has long since vanished. Sadly, the immense trees that used to loom large over the temple have been cut down, removing some of the romance of the place in the process.

TEP PRANAM
ទេព្យប្រណាម្យ

Tep Pranam, an 82m by 34m cruciform Buddhist terrace 150m east of Preah Palilay, was once the base of a pagoda of lightweight construction. Nearby is a Buddha that's 4.5m high, but it's a reconstruction of the original. A group of Buddhist nuns lives in a wooden structure close by.

PREAH PITHU
ព្រះពិធូ

Preah Pithu, which is across Northern Ave from Tep Pranam, is a group of 12th-century Hindu and Buddhist temples enclosed by a wall. It includes some beautifully decorated terraces and guardian animals in the form of elephants and lions.

TERRACE OF THE LEPER KING
ទីលានព្រះគម្ងង់

The Terrace of the Leper King is just north of the Terrace of Elephants. It is a 7m-high platform, on top of which stands a nude, though sexless, statue. It is yet another of Angkor's mysteries. The original of the statue is held at Phnom Penh's National Museum (p93), and various theories have been advanced to

TIP

Clamber under the elevated causeway leading to Baphuon for an incredible view of the hundreds of pillars supporting it.

TIP

The northwestern wall of the Royal Enclosure is very atmospheric, with immense trees and jungle vines cloaking the outer side, easily visible on a forest walk from Preah Palilay to Phimeanakas.

VEHICLES OF THE GODS

The great Hindu gods still need transport like the rest of us. Garuda is the vehicle of Vishnu, a half-man, half-bird creature who features in many temples and was later combined with his old enemy *naga* to promote religious unity under Jayavarman VII. Nandi is the mount of Shiva and there are several statues of Nandi dotted about the temples, although many have been damaged or stolen by looters.

---

explain its meaning. Legend has it that at least two of the Angkor kings had leprosy, and the statue may represent one of them. Another theory – a more likely explanation – is that the statue is of Yama, the god of death, and that the Terrace of the Leper King housed the royal crematorium.

The front retaining walls of the terrace are decorated with at least five tiers of meticulously executed carvings of seated *apsaras*; other figures include kings wearing pointed diadems, armed with short double-edged swords and accompanied by the court and princesses, the latter adorned with beautiful rows of pearls. The terrace, built in the late 12th century between the construction of Angkor Wat and the Bayon, once supported a pavilion made of lightweight materials.

TIP

As you follow the inner wall of the Terrace of the Leper King, notice the increasingly rough chisel marks on the figures, an indication that this wall was never completed, like many of the temples at Angkor.

On the southern side of the Terrace of the Leper King (facing the Terrace of Elephants), there is access to the front wall of a hidden terrace that was covered up when the outer structure was built – a terrace within a terrace. The four tiers of *apsaras* and other figures, including *nagas*, look as fresh as if they had been carved yesterday, thanks to being covered up for centuries. Some of the figures carry fearsome expressions.

TERRACE OF ELEPHANTS
ទីលានជល់ដំរី

The 350m-long Terrace of Elephants was used as a giant viewing stand for public ceremonies and served as a base for the king's grand audience hall. As you stand here, try to imagine the pomp and grandeur of the Khmer empire at its height, with infantry, cavalry, horse-drawn chariots and elephants parading across Central Sq in a colourful procession, pennants and standards aloft. Looking on is the god-king, crowned with a gold diadem, shaded by multitiered parasols and attended by mandarins and handmaidens bearing gold and silver utensils.

According to Chinese emissary Chou Ta-Kuan, the towers of Prasat Suor Prat were also used for public trials of sorts – during a dispute the two parties would be made to sit inside two towers, one party eventually succumbing to disease and proven guilty.

The Terrace of Elephants has five piers extending towards the Central Sq – three in the centre and one at each end. The middle section of the retaining wall is decorated with life-size garudas and lions; towards either end are the two parts of the famous parade of elephants, complete with their Khmer mahouts.

KLEANGS & PRASAT SUOR PRAT
ឃ្លាំង/ប្រាសាទសួព្រាត

Along the east side of Central Sq are two groups of buildings, called Kleangs. The North Kleang and the South Kleang may at one time have been palaces. The North Kleang has been dated from the period of Jayavarman V.

Along Central Sq in front of the two Kleangs are 12 laterite towers – 10 in a row and two more at right angles facing the Ave of Victory – known as the Prasat Suor Prat, meaning 'Temple of the Tightrope Dancers'. Archaeologists believe the towers, which form an honour guard along Central Sq, were constructed by Jayavarman VII. It is likely that each one originally contained either a *linga* or a statue. It is said artists performed for the king on tightropes or rope bridges strung between these towers.

AROUND ANGKOR THOM

BAKSEI CHAMKRONG
បក្សីចាំក្រុង

Located southwest of the south gate of Angkor Thom, Baksei Chamkrong is one of the few brick edifices in the immediate vicinity of Angkor. A well-proportioned though petite temple, it was once decorated with a covering of lime mortar. Like virtually all of the structures of Angkor, it opens to the east. In the early 10th century, Harshavarman I erected five statues in this temple: two of Shiva, one of Vishnu and two of Devi.

PHNOM BAKHENG
ភ្នំបាក់ខែង

Located around 400m south of Angkor Thom, the main attraction at Phnom Bakheng is the sunset view over Angkor Wat. Unfortunately, the whole affair has turned into something of a circus, with crowds of tourists ascending the slopes of the hill and jockeying for space once on top. Coming down can be even worse as there is nothing at all in the way of lighting. Some prefer to visit in the early morning when it is cool to climb the hill and the crowds are light. That said, the sunset over the Western Baray is very impressive from here.

Phnom Bakheng also lays claim to being home to the first of the temple-mountains built in the vicinity of Angkor. Yasovarman I chose Phnom Bakheng over the Roluos area, where the earlier capital (and temple-mountains) had been located.

For a great online photographic resource on the temples of Angkor, look no further than www.angkor-ruins.com, a Japanese website with an English translation.

TREKKING AROUND THE TEMPLES

Spread over a vast area of the steamy tropical lowlands of Cambodia, the temples of Angkor aren't the ideal candidates to tackle on foot. However, the area is blanketed in mature forest, offering plenty of shade, and following back roads into temples is the perfect way to leave behind the crowds.

Angkor Thom is the top trekking spot thanks to its manageable size and plenty of rewarding temples within its walls. Starting out at the spectacular south gate of Angkor Thom, admire the immense representation of the Churning of the Ocean of Milk before bidding farewell to the masses and their motorised transport. Ascend the wall of this ancient city and then head west, offering views of the vast moat to the left and the thick jungle to the right. It is often possible to see forest birds along this route, as it is very peaceful. Reaching the southwest corner, admire Prasat Chrung, one of four identical temples marking the corners of the city. Head down below to see the water outlet of Run Ta Dev, as this once powerful city was criss-crossed by canals in its heyday.

Back on the gargantuan wall, continue to the west gate, looking out for a view to the immense Western Baray on your left. Descend at the west gate and admire the artistry of the central tower. Wander east along the path into the heart of Angkor Thom, but don't be diverted by the beauty of Bayon, as this is best saved until last.

Veer north into Baphuon and wander to the back of what some have called the 'world's largest jigsaw puzzle'. Pass through the small temple of Phimeanakas and the former royal palace compound, an area of towering trees, tumbling walls and atmospheric foliage. Continue further north to petite but pretty Preah Palilay.

It's time to make for the mainstream with a walk through the Terrace of the Leper King and along the front of the royal viewing gallery, the Terrace of Elephants. If there is time, you may want to zigzag east to visit the laterite towers of Prasat Suor Prat. Otherwise, continue to the top billing of Bayon: weird yet wonderful, this is one of most enigmatic of the temples at Angkor. Take your time to decipher the bas-reliefs before venturing up to the legendary faces of the upper level.

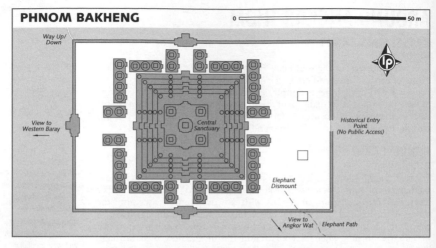

The temple-mountain has five tiers, with seven levels (including the base and the summit). At the base are – or were – 44 towers. Each of the five tiers had 12 towers. The summit of the temple has four towers at the cardinal points of the compass as well as a central sanctuary. All of these numbers are of symbolic significance. The seven levels, for example, represent the seven Hindu heavens, while the total number of towers, excluding the central sanctuary, is 108, a particularly auspicious number and one that correlates to the lunar calendar.

It is possible to arrange an elephant ride up the hill (one-way US$15). Try to book in advance, however, as the rides are very popular with tour groups.

CHAU SAY TEVODA
ចៅសាយទេវតា

Just east of Angkor Thom's east gate is Chau Say Tevoda. It was probably built during the second quarter of the 12th century, under the reign of Suryavarman II, and dedicated to Shiva and Vishnu. It is under renovation by the Chinese to bring it up to the condition of its twin temple, Thommanon.

THOMMANON
ធម្មនន្ត

Thommanon is just north of Chau Say Tevoda. Although unique, the temple complements its neighbour, as it was built to a similar design around the same time. It was also dedicated to Shiva and Vishnu. Thommanon is in good condition thanks to extensive work by the EFEO in the 1960s.

SPEAN THMOR
ស្ពានថ្ម

Spean Thmor (Stone Bridge), of which an arch and several piers remain, is 200m east of Thommanon. Jayavarman VII, the last great builder of Angkor, constructed many roads with these immense stone bridges spanning watercourses. This is the only large bridge remaining in the immediate vicinity of Angkor. The bridge vividly highlights how the water level has changed course over the subsequent centuries and may offer another clue to the collapse of Angkor's extensive irrigation system. Just north of Spean Thmor is a large water wheel.

There are more-spectacular examples of these ancient bridges elsewhere in Siem Reap Province, such as Spean Praptos, with 19 arches, in Kompong

TIP

From the summit of Phnom Bakheng, to get a decent picture of Angkor Wat in the warm glow of the late afternoon sun you will need at least a 300mm lens, as the temple is 1.3km away.

Kdei on NH6 from Phnom Penh; and Spean Ta Ong, a 77m bridge with a beautiful *naga*, forgotten in the forest about 28km east of Beng Mealea.

TA KEO
តាកែវ

Ta Keo is a stark, undecorated temple that undoubtedly would have been one of the finest of Angkor's structures, had it been finished. Built by Jayavarman V, it was dedicated to Shiva and was the first Angkorian monument built entirely of sandstone. The summit of the central tower, which is surrounded by four lower towers, is almost 50m high. This quincuncial arrangement (with four towers at the corners of a square and a fifth tower in the centre) is typical of many Angkorian temple-mountains.

No one is certain why work was never completed, but a likely cause may have been the death of Jayavarman V. Others contend that the hard sandstone was impossible to carve and that explains the lack of decoration.

According to inscriptions, Ta Keo was struck by lightning during construction, which may have been a bad omen and led to its abandonment.

TA NEI
តានី

Ta Nei, 800m north of Ta Keo, was built by Jayavarman VII. There is something of the spirit of Ta Prohm here, albeit on a lesser scale, with moss and tentaclelike roots covering outer areas of this small temple. The number of visitors is also on a lesser scale, making it very atmospheric. It now houses the training unit of Apsara Authority (see the boxed text, p159) and can be accessed by walking across the French-built dam. To get to the dam, take the long track on the left, just after the Victory Gate of Angkor Thom when coming from Siem Reap.

TIP

It is possible to walk from Ta Nei to Ta Keo through the forest, a guaranteed way to leave the crowds behind.

TA PROHM
តាព្រហ្ម

Ta Prohm is undoubtedly the most atmospheric ruin at Angkor and should be high on the hit list of every visitor. Its appeal lies in the fact that, unlike the other monuments of Angkor, it has been swallowed by the jungle, and looks very much the way most of the monuments of Angkor appeared when European explorers first stumbled upon them. Well, that's the theory, but in fact the jungle is pegged back and only the largest trees are left in place, making it manicured rather than raw like Beng Mealea. Still, a visit to Ta Prohm is a unique, other-worldly experience. The temple is cloaked in dappled shadow, its crumbling towers and walls locked in the slow muscular embrace of vast root systems. If Angkor Wat, the Bayon and other temples are testimony to the genius of the ancient Khmers, Ta Prohm reminds us equally of the awesome fecundity and power of the jungle. There is a poetic cycle to this venerable ruin, with humanity first conquering nature to rapidly create, and nature once again conquering humanity to slowly destroy.

Built from 1186 and originally known as Rajavihara (Monastery of the King), Ta Prohm was a Buddhist temple dedicated to the mother of Jayavarman VII. It is one of the few temples in the Angkor region where an inscription provides information about the temple's dependents and inhabitants.

Ta Prohm is a temple of towers, closed courtyards and narrow corridors. Many of the corridors are impassable, clogged with jumbled piles of delicately carved stone blocks dislodged by the roots of long-decayed trees. Bas-reliefs on bulging walls are carpeted with lichen, moss and creeping plants, and shrubs sprout from the roofs of monumental porches. Trees, hundreds of years old – some supported by flying buttresses – tower overhead, their leaves filtering the sunlight and casting a greenish pall over the whole scene. The most popular of the many strangulating root formations is that on the

According to an inscription stela from Ta Prohm, close to 80,000 people were required to maintain or attend at the temple, among them more than 2700 officials and 615 dancers.

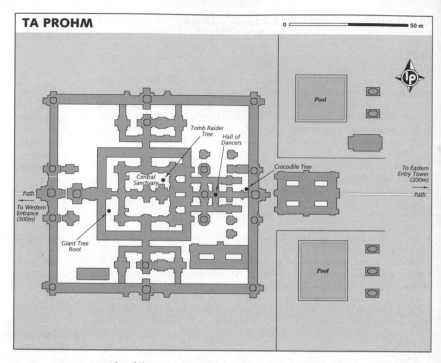

inside of the easternmost *gopura* (entrance pavilion) of the central enclosure, nicknamed the Crocodile Tree. It used to be possible to climb onto the damaged galleries, but this is now prohibited to protect both the temple and visitor. Many of these precariously balanced stones weigh a tonne or more and would do some serious damage if they came down.

BANTEAY KDEI & SRA SRANG
បន្ទាយក្ដី និង ស្រះស្រង់

One of the most famous spots in Ta Prohm is the so-called '*Tomb Raider* tree' where Angelina Jolie's Lara Croft picked a jasmine flower before falling through the earth into... Pinewood Studios.

Banteay Kdei, a massive Buddhist monastery from the latter part of the 12th century, is surrounded by four concentric walls. The outer wall measures 500m by 700m. Each of its four entrances is decorated with garudas, which hold aloft one of Jayavarman VII's favourite themes: the four faces of Avalokiteshvara. The inside of the central tower was never finished and much of the temple is in a ruinous state due to hasty construction. It is considerably less busy than nearby Ta Prohm and this alone can justify a visit.

East of Banteay Kdei is an earlier basin, Sra Srang (Pool of Ablutions), measuring 800m by 400m, reserved for the king and his consorts. A tiny island in the middle once bore a wooden temple, of which only the stone base remains. This is a beautiful body of water from which to take in a quiet sunrise.

PRASAT KRAVAN
ប្រាសាទក្រវ៉ាន់

Uninspiring from the outside, the interior brick carvings concealed within its towers are Prasat Kravan's hidden treasure. The five brick towers here, which are arranged in a north–south line and oriented to the east, were built for Hindu worship in AD 921. The structure is unusual in that it was not constructed by royalty; this accounts for its slightly distant location, away from the centre of the capital. Prasat Kravan is just south of the road between Angkor Wat and Banteay Kdei.

Prasat Kravan was partially restored in 1968, returning the brick carvings to their former glory. The images of Vishnu in the largest central tower show the eight-armed deity on the back wall; taking the three gigantic steps with which he reclaimed the world on the left wall (see p185); and riding a garuda on the right wall. The northernmost tower displays bas-reliefs of Vishnu's consort, Lakshmi.

A EULOGY TO NHIEM CHUN Nick Ray

Nhiem Chun was as much an icon of Angkor as the tangled roots that slowly choke the ancient stones of Ta Prohm. He will forever be remembered as the 'sweeper of Ta Prohm', as Nhiem Chun dedicated his life to stemming the tide of nature, bent double, stooping low over the stones to sweep away the falling leaves each day.

I first met Nhiem back in 1995 when exploring Ta Prohm. He was sprightly then, nimbly gliding over fallen pillars, tumbled stones and moss-clad lintels in search of his quarry, those ever-falling leaves. Nhiem's face was every bit as chiselled and characterful as the beautiful *devadas* that still lined the galleries.

Years later he was immortalised by Lonely Planet when his iconic image was selected as the cover shot for the fourth edition of this Cambodia guidebook. It is a definitive shot, Nhiem standing in front of the 'Tomb Raider tree'. Nhiem soon became an A-list Angkor celebrity and crowds thronged around him wanting a photograph.

Nhiem Chun was born around the same time as King Sihanouk, although their lives could hardly have been more different. He grew up tending buffalo and helping with the harvest, but thanks to a chance meeting with Angkor curator Henri Marchal in 1941 he began work as a labourer, helping with temple restoration at Angkor. It was the start of a lifelong love affair with the temples and Nhiem was destined to spend the next 65 years of his life working amid the sacred stones.

Nhiem's world crumbled around him when the Khmer Rouge came to power. 'In the 1970s, our lives were turned upside down. I could not do my job. I had to work the land', said Nhiem. 'You had no choice. You would be killed.' More precious than his beloved temples, his two sons disappeared during the Khmer Rouge regime. 'When the fighting was over, my two sons were still missing', he recalled. 'I was told they had been killed by the Khmer Rouge, their throats slit with sharpened sugar-palm fronds.'

In 2006 the BBC came to Cambodia to film for the documentary series *Imagine…Who Cares About Art?* and Nhiem Chun, the ever-loyal guardian of Ta Prohm, was our subject. We spent several days with him, learning about his life, his loves, and his loss. 'The older I get, the more I love this place. These temples are the spirit of the Cambodian nation', mused Nhiem, wandering about Ta Prohm. 'I could have built this temple in a past life. If I did not have any connection, I would not be here to take care of it today.'

'I am old now. I can't take care of these temples any more', he opined wistfully. 'But when I am gone, these stones will still be here. These temples are the symbols of our soul. We will not survive if we don't look after our temples.'

Like the ancient stones of Ta Prohm, and like his beloved monarch Sihanouk, Nhiem Chun experienced light and dark. A life lived among beauty and brilliance, he also experienced the ugly side of mankind. But life went on and the leaves continued to fall. 'If I don't sweep, the leaves will cover the temple. I must sweep', he stated. Nhiem Chun was truly a man for all seasons.

Nhiem Chun passed away in April 2009. Ta Prohm has lost its great champion and protector, but let's hope the next generation continues his legacy.

PREAH KHAN

ប្រះខ្ន

The temple of Preah Khan (Sacred Sword) is one of the largest complexes at Angkor – a maze of vaulted corridors, fine carvings and lichen-clad stonework. It is a good counterpoint to Ta Prohm and generally sees slightly fewer visitors. Preah Khan was built by Jayavarman VII and probably served as his temporary residence while Angkor Thom was being built. Like Ta Prohm it is a place of towered enclosures and shoulder-hugging corridors. Unlike Ta Prohm, however, the temple of Preah Khan is in a reasonable state of preservation thanks to the ongoing restoration efforts of the World Monuments Fund.

The central sanctuary of the temple was dedicated in AD 1191 and a large stone stela tells us much about Preah Khan's role as a centre for worship and learning. Originally located within the first eastern enclosure, this stela is now housed safely at Angkor Conservation (see the boxed text, p159). The temple was dedicated to 515 divinities and during the course of a year 18 major festivals took place here, requiring a team of thousands just to maintain the place.

Preah Khan covers a very large area, but the temple itself is within a rectangular enclosing wall of around 700m by 800m. Four processional walkways approach the gates of the temple, and these are bordered by another stunning depiction of the Churning of the Ocean of Milk, as in the approach to Angkor Thom, although most of the heads have disappeared. From the central sanctuary, four long, vaulted galleries extend in the cardinal directions. Many of the interior walls of Preah Khan were once coated with plaster that was held in place by holes in the stone. Today, many delicate reliefs remain, including *rishi* and *apsara* carvings.

Preah Khan is a genuine fusion temple, the eastern entrance dedicated to Mahayana Buddhism with equal-sized doors, and the other cardinal directions dedicated to Shiva, Vishnu and Brahma with successively smaller doors, emphasising the unequal nature of Hinduism.

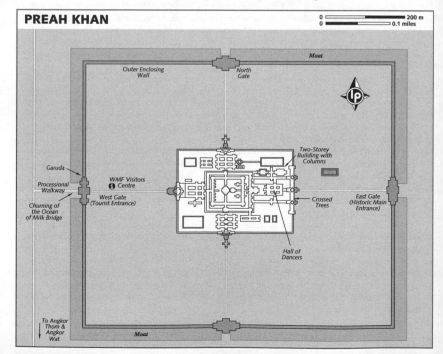

PREAH KHAN

0 — 200 m
0 — 0.1 miles

Moat

Outer Enclosing Wall

North Gate

Garuda

Processional Walkway

Churning of the Ocean of Milk Bridge

WMF Visitors Centre

West Gate (Tourist Entrance)

Two-Storey Building with Columns

Crossed Trees

East Gate (Historic Main Entrance)

Hall of Dancers

To Angkor Thom & Angkor Wat

Moat

THE LONG STRIDER

One of Vishnu's best-loved incarnations was when he appeared as the dwarf Vamana, and proceeded to reclaim the world from the evil demon-king Bali. The dwarf politely asked the demon-king for a comfortable patch of ground upon which to meditate, saying that the patch need only be big enough so that he could easily walk across it in three paces. The demon agreed, only to see the dwarf swell into a mighty giant who strode across the universe in three enormous steps. From this legend, depicted at Prasat Kravan, Vishnu is sometimes known as the 'long strider'.

The main entrance to Preah Khan is in the east but most tourists enter at the west gate near the main road, walk the length of the temple to the east gate before doubling back to the central sanctuary, and exit at the north gate. Approaching from the west, there is little clue to nature's genius, but on the outer retaining wall of the east gate is a pair of trees with monstrous roots embracing, one still reaching for the sky. There is also a curious Grecian-style two-storey structure in the temple grounds, the purpose of which is unknown, but it looks like an exile from Athens. Another option is to enter from the north and exit from the east.

PREAH NEAK POAN
ព្រះនាគពាន់

The Buddhist temple of Preah Neak Poan (Temple of the Intertwined Nagas) is a petite yet perfect temple constructed by – surely, not him again – Jayavarman VII in the late 12th century. It has a large square pool surrounded by four smaller square pools. In the middle of the central pool is a circular 'island' encircled by the two *nagas* whose intertwined tails give the temple its name. It's a safe bet that if an 'Encore Angkor' casino is eventually developed in Las Vegas or Macau, Preah Neak Poan will provide the blueprint for the ultimate swimming complex.

In the pool around the central island there were once four statues, but only one remains, reconstructed from the debris by the French archaeologists who cleared the site. The curious figure has the body of a horse supported by a tangle of human legs. It relates to a legend that Avalokiteshvara once saved a group of shipwrecked followers from an island of ghouls by transforming into a flying horse. A beautiful replica of this statue decorates the main roundabout at Siem Reap International Airport.

Water once flowed from the central pool into the four peripheral pools via ornamental spouts, which can still be seen in the pavilions at each axis of the pool. The spouts are in the form of an elephant's head, a horse's head, a lion's head and a human head. The pool was used for ritual purification rites.

TA SOM
តាសោម

Ta Som, which stands to the east of Preah Neak Peon, is yet another of the late-12th-century Buddhist temples of Jayavarman VII, the Donald Trump of ancient Cambodia. The central area of Ta Som is in a ruinous state, but restoration by the WMF is close to completion.

EASTERN BARAY & EASTERN MEBON
បារាយណ៍ខាងកើត/មេបុណ្យខាងកើត

The enormous one-time reservoir known as the Eastern Baray was excavated by Yasovarman I, who marked its four corners with stelae. This basin, now entirely dried up, was the most important of the public works

---

Preah Neak Poan was once in the centre of a huge 3km-by-900m *baray* serving Preah Khan, known as Jayata-taka, once again partially filled with water due to a new opening in the dyke road. In fact, during the latter half of 2009, access involved walking along a 100m plank bridge.

TIP

The most impressive feature at Ta Som is the huge tree completely overwhelming the eastern *gopura*, providing one of the most popular photo opportunities in the Angkor area.

Eastern Mebon is flanked by earthen ramps, a clue that this temple was never finished and a good visual guide to how the temples were constructed.

of Yasodharapura, Yasovarman I's capital, and is 7km by 1.8km. It was originally fed by the Siem Reap River.

The Hindu temple known as the Eastern Mebon, erected by Rajendravarman II, would have been situated on an islet in the centre of the Eastern Baray reservoir, but is now very much on dry land. This temple is like a smaller version of Pre Rup, which was built 15 to 20 years later and lies to the south. The temple-mountain form is topped off by the now familiar quintet of towers. The elaborate brick shrines are dotted with neatly arranged holes, which attached the original plasterwork. The base of the temple is guarded at its corners by perfectly carved stone figures of elephants, many of which are still in a very good state of preservation.

PRE RUP
ប្រែរូប

TIP

Pre Rup is one of the most popular sunset spots around Angkor, as the view over the surrounding rice fields of the Eastern Baray is beautiful, although some lofty trees are starting to obscure it somewhat.

Pre Rup, built by Rajendravarman II, is about 1km south of the Eastern Mebon. Like its nearby predecessor, the temple consists of a pyramid-shaped temple-mountain with the uppermost of the three tiers carrying five lotus towers. The brick sanctuaries were also once decorated with a plaster coating, fragments of which still remain on the southwestern tower; there are some amazingly detailed lintel carvings here. Several of the outermost eastern towers are perilously close to collapse and are propped up by an army of wooden supports.

Pre Rup means 'Turning the Body' and refers to a traditional method of cremation in which a corpse's outline is traced in the cinders, first in one direction and then in the other; this suggests that the temple may have served as an early royal crematorium.

BANTEAY SAMRÉ
បន្ទាយសំរែ

Banteay Samré dates from the same period as Angkor Wat and was built by Suryavarman II. The temple is in a fairly healthy state of preservation due to some extensive renovation work, although its isolation has resulted in some looting during the past few decades. The area consists of a central temple with four wings, preceded by a hall and also accompanied by two libraries, the southern one remarkably well preserved. The whole ensemble is enclosed by two large concentric walls around what would have been the unique feature of an inner moat, sadly now dry.

Banteay Samré is 400m east of the Eastern Baray, which in practical terms means following the road to Banteay Srei to the village of Preah Dak and continuing straight ahead rather than turning to the left. A visit here can be combined with a trip to Banteay Srei or Phnom Bok.

The Western Baray is the main local swimming pool around Siem Reap. There is a small beach of sorts at the western extreme (complete with picnic huts and inner tubes for rent), which attracts plenty of Khmers at weekends.

WESTERN BARAY & WESTERN MEBON
បារាយណ៍ខាងលិច និងមេបុណ្យខាងលិច

The Western Baray, measuring an incredible 8km by 2.3km, was excavated by hand to provide water for the intensive cultivation of lands around Angkor. Just for the record, these enormous *barays* weren't dug out, rather huge dykes were built up around the edges. In the centre of the Western Baray is the ruin of the Western Mebon temple, where the giant bronze statue of Vishnu now in the National Museum (p93) in Phnom Penh was found. The Western Mebon is accessible by boat (US$10 for the boat) from the dam on the southern shore.

CUNNING LINGAS

Fertility symbols are prominent around the temples of Angkor. The *linga* is a phallic symbol and would have originally been located within the towers of most Hindu temples. It sits inside a *yoni*, the female fertility symbol, combining to produce holy water, charged with the sexual energy of creation. Brahmans poured the water over the *linga* and it drained through the *yoni* and out of the temples through elaborate gutters to anoint the pilgrims outside.

ROLUOS TEMPLES

រលួស

The monuments of Roluos, which served as Indravarman I's capital, Hariharalaya, are among the earliest large, permanent temples built by the Khmers and mark the dawn of Khmer classical art. Before the construction of Roluos, generally only lighter (and less durable) construction materials such as brick were employed.

The temples can be found 13km east of Siem Reap along NH6 near the modern-day town of Roluos.

PREAH KO

ព្រះគោ

Preah Ko was erected by Indravarman I in the late 9th century, and was dedicated to Shiva. The six *prasats* (stone halls), aligned in two rows and decorated with carved sandstone and plaster reliefs, face east; the central tower of the front row is a great deal larger than the other towers. Preah Ko has some of the best surviving examples of plasterwork seen at Angkor and is currently under restoration by a German team. There are elaborate inscriptions in the ancient Hindu language of Sanskrit on the doorposts of each tower.

The towers of Preah Ko (Sacred Ox) feature three *nandis* (sacred oxen), all of whom look like a few steaks have been sliced off them over the years. Preah Ko was dedicated by Indravarman I to his deified ancestors in AD 880. The front towers relate to male ancestors or gods; the rear towers, to female ancestors or goddesses. Lions guard the steps up to the temple.

The sanctuary on the fifth level of Bakong temple was a later addition during the reign of Suryavarman II, in the style of Angkor Wat's central tower.

BAKONG

បាគង

Bakong is the largest and most interesting of the Roluos Group of Temples, and has an active Buddhist monastery just to the north of the east entrance. It was built and dedicated to Shiva by Indravarman I. It's a representation of Mt Meru, and it served as the city's central temple. The east-facing complex consists of a five-tier central pyramid of sandstone, 60m square at the base, flanked by eight towers (or their remains) of brick and sandstone and by other minor sanctuaries. A number of the eight towers below the upper central tower are still partly covered by their original plasterwork.

The complex is enclosed by three concentric walls and a moat. There are well-preserved statues of stone elephants on each corner of the first three levels of the central temple. There are 12 stupas – three to each side – on the third tier.

TIP

Look out for **Prolung Khmer** (www.prolungkhmer.blogspot.com) on the road between Preah Ko and Bakong. It is a weaving centre producing stylish cotton *kramas,* set up as a training collaboration between Cambodia and Japan.

On the grounds of the temple, there is also a very old wat, dating back a century or more, which is currently under restoration.

LOLEI
លលៃ

The four brick towers of Lolei, an almost exact replica of the towers of Preah Ko (although in much worse shape) were built on an islet in the centre of a large reservoir – now rice fields – by Yasovarman I, the founder of the first city at Angkor. The sandstone carvings in the niches of the temples are worth a look and there are Sanskrit inscriptions on the doorposts. According to one of the inscriptions, the four towers were dedicated by Yasovarman I to his mother, his father and his maternal grandparents on 12 July 893.

AROUND ANGKOR

PHNOM KROM
ភ្នំព្រាម

The temple of Phnom Krom, 12km south of Siem Reap on a hill overlooking Tonlé Sap Lake, dates from the reign of Yasovarman I in the late 9th or early 10th century. The name means 'Lower Hill' and is a reference to its geographic location in relation to its sister temples of Phnom Bakheng and Phnom Bok. The three towers, dedicated (from north to south) to Vishnu, Shiva and Brahma, are in a ruined state, but Phnom Krom remains one of the more tranquil spots from which to view the sunset, complete with an active wat. The fast boats from Phnom Penh dock near here, but it is not possible to see the temple from beneath the hill. If coming here by *moto* or car, try to get the driver to take you to the summit, as it is a long, hot climb otherwise.

PHNOM BOK
ភ្នំបុក

Making up the triplet of temple-mountains built by Yasovarman I in the late 9th or early 10th century, this peaceful but remote location sees few visitors. The small temple is in reasonable shape and includes two frangipani trees growing out of a pair of ruinous towers – they look like some sort of extravagant haircut when in full flower. However, it is the views of Phnom Kulen to the north and the plains of Angkor to the south from this 212m hill that make it worth the trip. The remains of a 5m *linga* are also visible at the opposite end of the hill and it's believed there were similar *linga* at Phnom Bakheng and Phnom Krom. Unfortunately, it is not a sensible place for sunrise or sunset, as it would require a long journey in the dark to get here or get back.

Phnom Bok is about 25km from Siem Reap and is clearly visible from the road to Banteay Srei. It is accessible by continuing east on the road to Banteay Samré for another 6km. It is possible to loop back to Siem Reap via the temples of Roluos by heading south instead of west on the return journey, and gain some rewarding glimpses of the countryside.

CHAU SREI VIBOL
ចៅស្រីវិបុល

This petite hilltop temple used to see few visitors, as it was difficult to access, but new roads have put it on the temple map at last. The central sanctuary is in a ruined state, but is nicely complemented by the construction of a modern wat nearby. Surrounding the base of the hill are laterite walls, each with a small entrance hall in reasonable condition. To get here, turn east off the Roluos to Anlong Veng highway at a point about 8km north of NH6, or 5km south of Phnom Bok. There is a small sign (easy to miss) that marks the turn. Locals are friendly and helpful should you find yourself lost.

BANTEAY SREI
បន្ទាយស្រី

The art gallery of Angkor, Banteay Srei is considered by many to be the jewel in the crown of Angkorian artisanship. A Hindu temple dedicated to Shiva, it is cut from stone of a pinkish hue and includes some of the finest stone carving seen anywhere on earth. It is one of the smallest sites at Angkor, but what it lacks in size it makes up for in stature. It is wonderfully well preserved and many of its carvings are three-dimensional.

Construction on Banteay Srei began in AD 967 and it is one of the few temples around Angkor not to be commissioned by a king, but by a brahman, who may have been a tutor to Jayavarman V. The temple is square and has entrances at the east and west, the east approached by a causeway. Of interest are the lavishly decorated libraries and the three central towers, which are decorated with male and female divinities and beautiful filigree relief work.

Classic carvings at Banteay Srei include delicate women with lotus flowers in hand and traditional skirts clearly visible, as well as breathtaking recreations of scenes from the epic *Ramayana* adorning the library pediments (carved inlays above a lintel). However, the sum of the parts is no greater than the whole – almost every inch of these interior buildings is covered in decoration. Standing watch over such perfect creations are the mythical guardians, all of which are copies of originals stored in the National Museum (p93).

Banteay Srei was the first major temple-restoration undertaken by the EFEO in 1930 using the anastylosis method. The project, as evidenced today, was a major success and soon led to other larger projects such as the restoration of the Bayon.

When Banteay Srei was first rediscovered, it was assumed to be from the 13th or 14th centuries, as the refined carving must have come at the end of the Angkor period. It was later dated to AD 967, from inscriptions found at the site. However, some scholars are once again calling for a revision of this date, given that the style of this temple and its carvings are unlike anything else seen in the 10th century. New theories suggest that like the great cathedrals of Europe, some Angkorian temples may have been destroyed and then rebuilt, or altered beyond recognition, and that the inscription stela at Banteay Srei relates to an earlier structure on the site, not the delicate flower of a temple we see today. Either way, it's a beauty.

Banteay Srei is 21km northeast of Bayon or about 32km from Siem Reap. It is well signposted and the road is surfaced all the way – a trip from Siem Reap should take about 45 minutes. *Moto* and *remork-moto* drivers will want a bit of extra cash to come out here, so agree on a sum first. It is possible to combine a visit to Banteay Srei with a trip to the River of a Thousand Lingas at Kbal Spean and Beng Mealea, or to Banteay Samré and Phnom Bok.

In 1923 Frenchman André Malraux was arrested in Phnom Penh for attempting to steal several of Banteay Srei's major statues and pieces of sculpture. Ironically, Malraux was later appointed Minister of Culture under Charles de Gaulle.

Banteay Srei means 'Citadel of the Women' and it is said that it must have been built by a woman, as the elaborate carvings are supposedly too fine for the hand of a man.

Banteay Srei was the first major temple to be restored and it is the first to have been given a full makeover in terms of facilities, with a large car park, a designated dining and shopping area, clear visitor information and a state of the art exhibition on the history of the temple and its restoration.

KBAL SPEAN
ក្បាលស្ពាន

A spectacularly carved riverbed, Kbal Spean is set deep in the jungle to the northeast of Angkor. More commonly referred to in English as the 'River of a Thousand Lingas', the name actually means 'bridgehead', a reference to the natural rock bridge at the site. Lingas have been elaborately carved into the riverbed, and images of Hindu deities are dotted about the area.

It is a 2km uphill walk to the carvings, along a pretty path that winds its way up into the jungle, passing by some interesting boulder formations along the way. Carry plenty of water up the hill, as there is none available beyond the parking area. The path eventually splits to the waterfall or the river carvings. There is an impressive carving of Vishnu on the upper section of the river, followed by a series of carvings at the bridgehead itself, some of which have been tragically hacked off in the past few years. This area is now roped off to protect the carvings from further damage.

Following the river down, there are several more impressive carvings of Vishnu, and Shiva with his consort Uma, and further downstream hundreds of *linga* appear on the riverbed. At the top of the waterfall, there are many animal images, including a cow and a frog, and a path winds around the boulders to a wooden staircase leading down to the base of the falls. Visitors between January and May will be disappointed to see very little water here. The best time to visit is between July and December.

Near the base of the hill is the **Angkor Centre for Conservation of Biodiversity** (www.accb-cambodia.org), committed to rescuing, rehabilitating and reintroducing threatened wildlife. Tours of the centre can be arranged daily at 1pm and species currently under protection here include pileated gibbon, silvered langur, slow loris, civet cat and leopard cat.

Kbal Spean is about 50km northeast of Siem Reap or about 18km beyond the temple of Banteay Srei. The road is now excellent, as it forms part of the new road north from NH6 to Anlong Veng and the Thai border, so it takes just one hour from town.

Moto drivers will no doubt want a bit of extra money to take you here – a few extra dollars should do, or US$12 to US$15 for the day, including a trip to Banteay Srei. Likewise, *remork-moto* drivers will probably up the price to US$20. A surcharge is also levied to come out here by car. Admission to Kbal Spean is included in the general Angkor pass and the last entry to the site is at 3.30pm.

PHNOM KULEN
ភ្នំគូលែន

Considered by Khmers to be the most sacred mountain in Cambodia, Phnom Kulen is a popular place of pilgrimage on weekends and during festivals. It played a significant role in the history of the Khmer empire, as it was from here in AD 802 that Jayavarman II proclaimed himself a *devaraja* (god-king) and announced independence from Java, giving birth to modern-day Cambodia. There is a small wat (Wat Preah Ang Thom) at the summit of the mountain, which houses a large **reclining Buddha** carved into the sandstone boulder upon which it is built. Nearby is a large **waterfall** and above it are smaller bathing areas and a number of carvings in the riverbed, including numerous *lingas*. A private

---

TIP

When exploring Kbal Spean it is best to start with the river carvings and work back down to the waterfall to cool off.

Kbal Spean was 'discovered' in 1969, when EFEO ethnologist Jean Boulbet was shown the area by an *essai;* the area was soon off limits due to the civil war, only becoming safe again in 1998.

LAND-MINE ALERT!

At no point during a visit to Kbal Spean or Phnom Kulen should you leave well-trodden paths, as there may be land mines in the area.

businessman bulldozed a road up here a decade ago and charges a US$20 toll per foreign visitor, an ambitious fee compared with what you get for your money at Angkor. None of the toll goes towards preserving the site.

The road winds its way through some spectacular jungle scenery, emerging on the plateau after a 20km ascent. The road eventually splits: the left fork leads to the picnic spot, waterfalls and ruins of a 9th-century temple; the right fork continues over a bridge and some riverbed carvings to the reclining Buddha. This is the focal point of a pilgrimage here for Khmer people, so it is important to take off your shoes and any head covering before climbing the stairs to the sanctuary. The views from the 487m peak are tremendous, as you can see right across the forested plateau.

The waterfall is an attractive spot, but could be much more beautiful were it not for all the litter left here by families picnicking at the weekend. Near the top of the waterfall is a jungle-clad temple known as **Prasat Krau Romeas**, dating from the 9th century.

There are plenty of other Angkorian sites on Phnom Kulen, including as many as 20 minor temples around the plateau, the most important of which is **Prasat Rong Chen**, the first pyramid or temple-mountain to be constructed in the Angkor area. Most impressive of all are the giant stone animals or guardians of the mountain, known as **Sra Damrei** (Elephant Pond). These are very difficult to get to, with the route passing through mined sections of the mountain (stick to the path!) and the trail impossible in the wet season. The few people who make it, however, are rewarded with a life-size replica of a stone elephant – a full 4m long and 3m tall – and smaller statues of lions, a frog and a cow. These were constructed on the southern face of the mountain and from here there are spectacular views across the plains below. Getting here requires taking a *moto* from Wat Preah Ang Thom for about 12km on very rough trails through thick forest before arriving at a sheer rock face. From here it is a 1km walk to the animals through the forest. Don't try to find it on your own; expect to pay the *moto* driver about US$8 (with some hard negotiating) and carry plenty of water, as none is available.

Before the construction of the private road up Phnom Kulen, visitors had to scale the mountain and then walk across the top of the plateau to the reclining Buddha. It is about a 2km climb and then an hour or more in a westerly direction along the top of the plateau. About 15km east of the new road, the trail winds its way to a small pagoda called Wat Chou, set into the cliff face from which a *tuk chou* (spring) emerges. The water is considered holy and Khmers like to bottle it to take home with them. This water source eventually flows into Tonlé Sap Lake and is thought to bless the waterways of Cambodia.

Phnom Kulen is a huge plateau around 50km from Siem Reap and about 15km from Banteay Srei. To get here on the new toll road, take the well-signposted right fork just before Banteay Srei village and go straight ahead at the crossroads. Just before the road starts to climb the mountain, there is a barrier and it is here that the US$20 charge is levied.

Moto drivers are likely to want about US$15 or more to bring you out here, and rented cars will hit passengers with a surcharge, more than double the going rate for Angkor; forget coming by *remork-moto* as the hill climb is just too tough.

BENG MEALEA
បឹងមាលា

One of the most mysterious temples at Angkor, Beng Mealea is a spectacular sight to behold as nature has well and truly run riot. Built to the same floor plan as Angkor Wat, exploring this titanic of temples is Angkor's ultimate Indiana Jones experience. Built in the 12th century under Suryavarman II,

TIP

It is possible to buy a cheaper entrance ticket to Phnom Kulen for US$12 from the City Angkor Hotel in Siem Reap.

TIP

It is only possible to go up Phnom Kulen before 11am and only possible to come down after midday, to avoid vehicles meeting on the narrow road.

The filming of *Two Brothers* (2004) included some locations in Beng Mealea and the production worked with 20 tigers of all ages for continuity throughout the story.

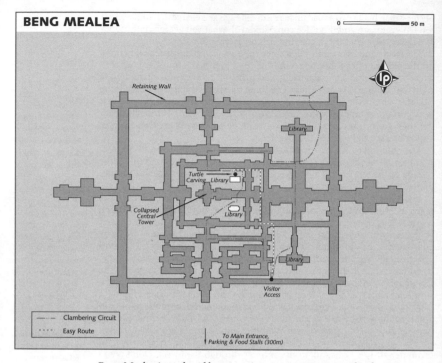

Beng Mealea is enclosed by a massive moat measuring 1.2km by 900m, part of which is now dried up.

The temple used to be utterly consumed by jungle, but some of the dense foliage has been cut back and cleaned up in recent years. Entering from the south, visitors wend their way over piles of finely chiselled sandstone blocks, through long dark chambers and between hanging vines. The central tower has completely collapsed, but hidden away among the rubble and foliage are several impressive carvings, as well as a well-preserved library in the northeastern quadrant. The temple is a special place and it is worth taking the time to explore it thoroughly – Apsara caretakers can show where rock-hopping and climbing is permitted. The large wooden walkway to and around the centre was originally constructed for the filming of Jean-Jacques Annaud's *Two Brothers* (2004), set in 1930s French Indochina and starring two tiger cubs.

There are several very basic, unmarked family homestays a few hundred metres behind the restaurants opposite the temple entrance.

It costs US$5 to visit Beng Mealea and there are additional small charges for transport – make sure you work out in advance with the driver or guide who is paying this.

HARMONY FARM

There is a small orphanage in Beng Mealea village called **Harmony Farm** (www.harmonyfarmcambo dia.org) and staff are able to show visitors around. Volunteers are welcome for English-speaking classes or longer stays.

Beng Mealea is about 40km east of the Bayon (as the crow flies) and 6.5km southeast of Phnom Kulen. By road it is about 68km (one hour by car, longer by *moto* or *remork-moto*) from Siem Reap. For independent travellers, it makes sense to undertake a long day trip combining Beng Mealea, Kbal Spean and Banteay Srei.

The shortest route is via the junction town of Dam Dek, located on NH6 about 37km from Siem Reap in the direction of Phnom Penh. Turn north immediately after the market and continue on this road for 31km. The entrance to the temple lies just beyond the left-hand turn to Koh Ker. Early in the morning, pick-ups link Dam Dek and Beng Mealea. Expect to pay 6000r in the cab, 4000r out back.

Beng Mealea is at the centre of an ancient Angkorian road connecting Angkor Thom and Preah Khan (p272) in Preah Vihear Province. A small Angkorian bridge just west of Chau Srei Vibol temple is the only remaining trace of the old Angkorian road between Beng Mealea and Angkor Thom; between Beng Mealea and Preah Khan there are at least 10 bridges abandoned in the forest. This is a way for extreme adventurers to get to Preah Khan temple (p274); however, don't undertake this journey lightly.

REMOTE ANGKORIAN SITES

Information on the following remote Angkorian sites is found in the Northwestern Cambodia chapter: Banteay Chhmar (p265), Koh Ker (p274), Preah Khan (p272) and Prasat Preah Vihear (p279).

South Coast

Fringed with tropical beaches, pristine mangrove forests and unspoilt islands, Cambodia's South Coast also boasts national parks of global ecological importance and two eerie, partly deserted colonial-era resorts. With a cracking selection of attractions both luxurious and adventurous, the area is now on a convenient, direct overland route from Bangkok.

Kampot, Cambodia's principal seaport until the founding of Sihanoukville in 1959, still retains some of its French-era charm. A great place to chill out, it's also a good base for visiting the misty highlands of Bokor National Park. Kep, once the country's most exclusive beach town, was destroyed during the Khmer Rouge period and the civil war, but is making a slow, stylish comeback. The booming city of Sihanoukville, Cambodia's main beach resort, is a short drive from Ream National Park and a one- to three-hour cruise from the country's best scuba diving.

The western portion of the South Coast, wild and remote, is dominated by the impenetrable jungle of the Cardamom Mountains (Chuor Phnom Kravanh), one of mainland Southeast Asia's largest and best-preserved forest areas. Ecotourism is opening up the Koh Kong Conservation Corridor, home to tigers and elephants, which stretches along NH48 from Krong Koh Kong, near the Thai frontier, to the Gulf of Kompong Som, northwest of Sihanoukville.

Near the Vietnamese border are some fabulous cave-temples and the Takeo–Angkor Borei region, 5th-century birthplace of ancient Cambodian civilisation.

HIGHLIGHTS

- Explore the uninhabited islands, isolated beaches, pristine rainforests, mangrove-lined rivers and remote waterfalls of the **Koh Kong Conservation Corridor** (p200), now opening up to ecotourism
- Soak up the sun in **Sihanoukville** (p209), home to blissful beaches, tropical islands, scuba diving and a lively nightshift
- Journey to fog-enveloped **Bokor National Park** (p229), with its abandoned casino and (sometimes) breathtaking coastal views
- Kick back in quiet **Kampot** (p223), a charming river town with some of Cambodia's best-preserved French architecture
- Explore remote islands and dine on fresh seafood around **Kep** (p232), the midcentury mecca of Cambodia's jet set

| ■ ELEVATION: 0-1800M | ■ POPULATION: 1.8 MILLION | ■ AREA: 27,817 SQ KM |

SOUTH COAST

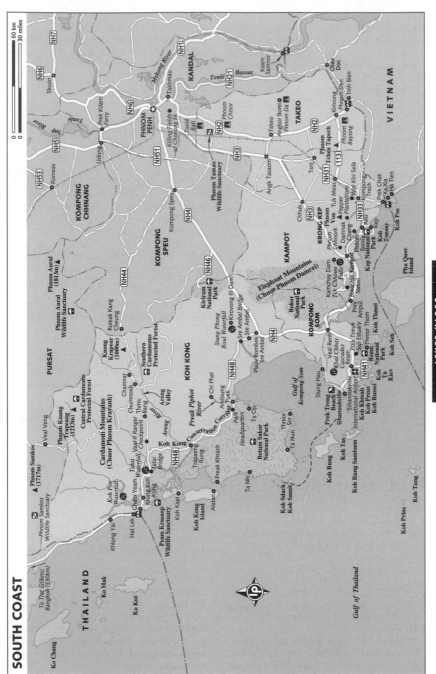

Getting There & Away

Sihanoukville International Airport (p220) may soon have services to Siem Reap, Phnom Penh and a few cities outside Cambodia. There is talk of a ferry service linking Kep with Vietnam's Phu Quoc Island.

The South Coast region has one international crossing with Thailand and two with Vietnam's Mekong Delta:

- Cham Yeam–Hat Lek (p341) 10km west of Krong Koh Kong and 92km southeast of the Thai city of Trat. Cambodia's second-most popular crossing with Thailand (after Poipet), it serves as a gateway to the ecotourism cornucopia of the Koh Kong Conservation Corridor.
- Prek Chak–Xa Xia (p344), 18km south of Kompong Trach, 41km southeast of Kampot and 9km northwest of the Vietnamese town of Ha Tien.
- Phnom Den–Tinh Bien (p344), 58km due south of Takeo. Often used by cycling groups because NH2 has some of Cambodia's finest sealed verges/shoulders.

Phnom Penh is linked with Sihanoukville by NH4, a heavily trafficked toll road; buses are cheap and frequent. NH3 links the capital with Kampot, but buses take the long way around via Angk Tasaom (near Takeo), Kampong Trach and Kep. Nicely paved NH2 links Phnom Penh with Takeo and the Phnom Den–Tinh Bien border crossing. The notorious jungle track from Krong Koh Kong through the Cardamoms to Pursat is slowly improving.

KOH KONG PROVINCE

ខេត្តកោះកុង

Cambodia's far southwestern province, vast and sparsely populated, shelters some of the country's most remarkable and important natural sites. Incredible deserted beaches line the west coast of Botum Sakor National Park and nearby islands – including the largest, Koh Kong Island – while inland are lush rainforests with ecotourism potential as vast as their mountains, streams and hamlets are remote.

The best base for exploring the province's untamed jungle, spread out along the Koh Kong Conservation Corridor, is the riverine town of Krong Koh Kong, 10km from the Thai border. From here, motorboats can whisk you to rushing waterfalls, secluded islands, sandy coves and Venice-like fishers' villages on stilts.

KRONG KOH KONG

ក្រុងកោះកុង

☎ 035 / pop 29,500

Once Cambodia's Wild West, its isolated frontier economy dominated by smuggling, prostitution and gambling, Krong Koh Kong has recently been slouching towards respectability. The city centre is still scruffy but the town now serves as the gateway to some of Southeast Asia's most breathtaking coastal and mountain habitats. The influx of ecotourists has largely scared away the 'sexpat' element.

Koh Kong Conservation Corridor highlights (p200) accessible from here include Peam Krasaop Wildlife Sanctuary, Koh Kong Island, the west coast of Botum Sakor National Park and several waterfalls.

For details on the Cham Yeam–Hat Lek border crossing with Thailand, see p341.

Orientation

Krong Koh Kong's commercial heart is between Psar Leu (the market), bounded on the south by St 2, and the roundabout at the intersection of St 3 and St 8. St 1 runs along Stung Koh Poi, a 2km-wide estuary spanned by a toll bridge. NH48 is known as St 5 as it passes through town.

Information

Guesthouses, hotels and pubs – including the Oasis Bungalow Resort, Bob Bar, Fat Sam's and the Blue Marlin – are the best places to get the local low-down. You can also check out Koh Kong's unofficial website, www.koh-kong.com, and the free, monochrome *Koh Kong Visitors Guide*. Thai mobile phones work here.

INTERNET ACCESS

Asian Hotel (St 1; per hr US$1) Lobby computers are available to non-guests.

Mary Internet (St 2 near St 1; per hr US$1; ☻ 7am or 8am-9pm or 10pm) Has five computers.

Rasmey Buntam (per hr 4000r; ☻ 7am-9pm or later) Has seven computers.

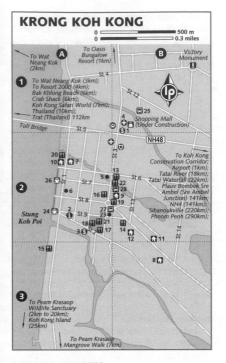

KRONG KOH KONG

INFORMATION	
Acleda Bank	**1** B1
Asian Hotel	(see 7)
Exchange Stalls	(see 17)
Mary Internet	**2** A2
Rasmey Buntam	(see 12)
Ratha Exchange	**3** A2
Sen Sok Clinic	**4** B1

SIGHTS & ACTIVITIES	
Dive Inn	(see 15)
Jungle Cross	**5** A2
Koh Kong Adventure Travel & Tours	**6** A2
Koh Kong Eco Tours	(see 9)

SLEEPING	
Asian Hotel	**7** A2
Blue Moon Guesthouse	**8** B3
Dugout Hotel	**9** B2
Koh Kong City Hotel	**10** B2
Neptune Guesthouse	**11** B2
Rasmey Buntam Guesthouse	**12** B2

EATING	
Baan Peakmai	**13** B2
Blue Marlin	(see 8)
Bob Bar	**14** B2
Café Laurent	(see 10)
Dive Inn	**15** A3
Fat Sam's	**16** A2
Food Stalls	(see 24)
Food Stalls	(see 21)
Fruit Stalls	**17** A2
Fruit Stalls	**18** B2
Night Market	**19** B2
Phou Mint Koh Kong Restaurant	**20** B2
Psar Leu	**21** B2
Pun Pun Supermarket	**22** B2

TRANSPORT	
Bicycle Shops	**23** A2
Boat Dock	**24** A2
Bun Thoun Express	(see 9)
Bus & Taxi Station	**25** B1
Ferry Dock	**26** A2
Phnom Penh Sorya	**27** A2
Rith Mony	**28** B2
Virak-Buntham	(see 9)

SOUTH COAST

MEDICAL SERVICES

In a medical emergency, evacuation to Thailand via the Cham Yeam–Hat Lek border crossing is possible 24 hours a day. In Thailand there's a hospital in Trat, 92km from the border.

Sen Sok Clinic (kkpao@camintel.com; ☎ 012 555060, 012 958788; St 3 cnr St 5; ⏲ 24hr) Has two doctors who speak English and French.

MONEY

Thai baht are in wide use here, though – in part for reasons of national pride – less so than before the ongoing Prasat Preah Vihear crisis.

At the border or in town, *moto* or taxi drivers who offer to 'help' you change money are probably setting you up for a rip-off. Reliable exchange stalls can be found along the southern (St 2) edge of Psar Leu – look for glass counters with little piles of banknotes inside.

It's sometimes possible to use the ATMs on the Thai side of the Cham Yeam–Hat Lek border crossing without visa formalities. To see if Thai officials are in a conciliatory mood, mosey on over to the Thai immigration counter,

explain nicely that you need an ATM and offer to leave them your passport.

Acleda Bank (St 3 cnr St 5) Has an ATM that handles Visa cash advances.

Ratha Exchange (☎ 936300; St 2; ⏲ 7am-5pm) A reliable exchange shop – look for the two gold-painted Chinese lions out front.

Sights & Activities

For information on nearby natural sites, see Koh Kong Conservation Corridor (p200).

Just upriver from the bridge, a rocky promontory on the right (western) bank of the estuary is decorated with life-size statues demonstrating the violent punishments that await sinners in the Buddhist hell. This

SOUTH COAST

graphic tableau belongs to **Wat Neang Kok**, a Buddhist temple that can also be reached by road (turn right a bit towards Thailand from the bridge).

Across the estuary from town and about 2km south of the bridge, **Resort 2000** has a grassy beach area and eating options. Further south, **Bak Khlong Beach** has cheap fish and seafood; the **Crab Shack**, run by a Khmer family, is especially appreciated by local expats.

The relatively shallow waters off Krong Koh Kong often suffer from limited visibility so conditions can be less than ideal for **scuba diving**. Some of the area's best diving sites are three hours from town around **Shark Island** – so named because divers often see blacktip reef sharks (as well as big game fish, or so they say) – but we've heard reports of unpredictable sea conditions and dangerous currents. Koh Kong Island's third beach offers decent **snorkelling**, as does Shark Island. **Koh Kong Adventure Travel & Tours** (☎ 6900073, 017 502784; www.kohkongdivers.com; St 1; ☺ mid-Oct–Jun) runs PADI courses and scuba day trips but prices may be higher than in Sihanoukville. From October to July, the **Dive Inn** (☎ 099-707434; St 1) runs all-day snorkelling trips to Koh Kong Island (US$25 per person, minimum eight participants).

The **pool** at the **Oasis Bungalow Resort** (☎ 092-228342, 016 331556) is open to nonguests for US$3 a day.

Sleeping

Some places pay *moto* drivers a commission and certain bus companies are connected to specific hotels, leading to a whole lot of Sihanoukville-type shenanigans (see p220). Krong Koh Kong is becoming a popular holiday destination for Khmers so hotels fill up – and raise their rates – during Cambodian holidays. The Tatai River, 18km east of town, has a growing number of ecoaccommodation options (p202).

Neptune Guesthouse (☎ 011 984512; r US$3-5) The friendly, German-run Neptune has a beer garden out back and nine very basic rooms with plank beds, mosquito nets, fans, bare neon lights and sinkless cold-water bathrooms. The US$3 rooms have shared bathrooms.

Rasmey Buntam Guesthouse (☎ 016 207771; r with fan/air-con from US$5/8; ✖ ▣) A family-run place with 30 rooms and so many colourful tiles you'll think you're in Tunisia. Of rather old-fashioned design, it has a broad central hallway and small windows.

Blue Moon Guesthouse (bluemoonkohkong@yahoo.com; ☎ 016 575741, 012 575741; r with fan/air-con US$6/10; ✖) Opened in mid-2009, this new place has nine neat, clean rooms with spiffy furnishings and hot water. A great deal. Situated behind Blue Marlin.

Dugout Hotel (☎ 936220, 016 650325; thedugouthotel@yahoo.com; St 3; r with fan/air-con from US$9/12; ✖ ▣) A clean, quiet establishment smack in the centre of town. Five of the seven smallish rooms are arrayed around a 6.5m pool.

Asian Hotel (☎ 936667; www.asiankohkong.com; St 1; d US$15-20; ✖ ▣ ☎) Preferred by many NGO staffers, this professionally run place offers three-star comfort, including proper bathrooms, in its 54 spacious, spotless rooms. Guests get 20 minutes of free internet. Excellent value.

our pick **Oasis Bungalow Resort** (☎ 092-228342, 016 331556; http://oasisresort.netkhmer.com; tr US$20; ✖ ▣) In a quiet rural area 1.5km north of the city centre, this sustainably run oasis of calm has five cheerful, spacious bungalows with all the amenities. To get there from the corner of St 3 and St 4, follow the blue signs north for 1.2km. Call ahead and they'll arrange transport from town or the border.

Koh Kong City Hotel (☎ 012 901902; St 1; http://kkcthotel.netkhmer.com; d/tr US$20/30; ✖ ▣) Worthy competition to the Asian, this riverside establishment has 54 well-lit rooms, some with fine watery views and all with snazzy tub-equipped bathrooms and minibars. Guests receive 15 minutes of free internet.

Eating & Drinking

Cheap daylight **food stalls** (mains US$1) can be found in the southeastern corner of **Psar Leu** (St 2 cnr St 3) and along the alley that leads to the boat dock. For dinner, there's a night market on St 3 north of the roundabout. St 1 has several restaurants that cater to a domestic clientele. Hotels with decent restaurants include the Asian Hotel.

For self-caterers, there are fruit stalls in the southwest and southeast corners of Psar Leu. **Pun Pun Supermarket** (St 3; ☺ 7am-11pm or midnight) carries toiletries, baby supplies and some Western food items.

Phou Mint Koh Kong Restaurant (☎ 011 943497; St 1; mains 50-400B; ☺ 6.30am-10pm) This Thai and Khmer place specialises in reasonably priced soups (120B to 200B), including delicious tom yam, and superfresh seafood. Four breezy pavilions out over the water afford truly romantic sunset views.

KOH KONG SAFARI WORLD

A safari theme park in a country with weak animal rights enforcement sounds like a recipe for horrors, but the Disneyesque gateway to **Koh Kong Safari World** (☎ 016 800811; www.kohkongresort. com; admission for Cambodians/foreigners US$8/12, for children 90-140cm US$4/8; ⏰ 9am-5pm) – in a style that Bavaria's mad King Ludwig II would have found irresistible – doesn't hint at anything sinister, and inside the gardens are neatly landscaped, the outdoor enclosures spacious and the animals happy enough to be having babies.

In addition to Southeast Asian fauna such as the Asiatic black bear, binturong, hornbill, crab-eating macaque, pig-tailed macaque, orang-utan, sambar deer and tiger, most of which are hard to even glimpse in the wild, the park – situated 8km towards the Thai border from Krong Koh Kong – also has exotics, including flamingos (from Singapore) and kangaroos.

More controversial are the live-animal shows. From 9am until about 3pm, dolphins fly through the air, tigers jump through rings, a man puts his head inside a crocodile's toothy, yellow mouth and orang-utans ride bicycles, dance and, dressed up as boxers, throw punches.

Baan Peakmai (☎ 393906; St 6; mains 60-250B; ⏰ 6am-10pm) One of the best restaurants in town, this Thai place, out of doors in a relaxing garden, has a monster menu with two dozen vegetarian choices and a fair spread of seafood.

Fat Sam's (☎ 099-592310; St 3; ⏰ 7am-9pm or later) An informal, South Welsh–run bar with a pool table and a selection of beers and wines. Serves breakfast (US$1 to US$3.75), sandwiches (US$2.75 to US$3.50) and a daily special.

Bob Bar (☎ 016 326455; mains 90-170B; ⏰ 9am-9pm or later, opens 7am mid-Sep–Apr) Breakfast, Western dishes and the best espresso in town are available all day long at this cheery, Aussie-run (at press time) restaurant-bar.

Dive Inn (☎ 099-707434; St 1; mains 100-360B; ⏰ 6.30am-1am or 2am in dry season, to 9pm or later in wet season) Run by a North Welsh master dive instructor, this pub-restaurant has rag-rolled yellow walls and tasty Khmer and Western dishes, including imported T-bone and rib-eye steaks. The latte and cappuccino perfectly complement the homemade scones, cakes and apple pies.

Blue Marlin (☎ 085-508147; mains US$4; ⏰ 9am-9pm or later) Friendly local expats gather round the solid wood tables of this no-frills bar to sip US$1 beers or dine on pizza and/or goulash. Wi-fi is planned for sometime in 2010.

our pick **Café Laurent** (☎ 011 590168; St 1; mains US$4-7; ⏰ 7am-midnight Mon-Sat; 🖳 🛜) Opened in 2009, this chic, French-style cafe and restaurant has an old Citroën Deux Chevaux out front and refined Western pastries and cuisine inside. A great place to start the day with an excellent croissant or *pain au chocolat*, or end

it romantically with a light, crispy personal pizza (from US$5.50).

Getting There & Away

Krong Koh Kong is on NH48 220km northwest of Sihanoukville and 290km west of Phnom Penh. Thanks to four new river bridges along NH48, the town finally has a proper road link with the rest of Cambodia.

Krong Koh Kong is linked to the Thai border by a dual carriageway that some locals treat as if it were two parallel two-lane highways. The 1.9km bridge over Stung Koh Poi, built and run by the Thais, costs 4800r/44B each way for a car and 1200r/11B for a motorbike; cyclists and pedestrians cross for free.

Travel to/from the Cham Yeam–Hat Lek border crossing, a distance of 10km, costs 100B by *moto*, 100B per person in a *remork-moto (tuk tuk)* and 200B by private taxi, not including bridge tolls (44B for a car, 11B for a motorbike).

BOAT

Rumour has it that the ferries to Koh Sdach (p205) and Sihanoukville *may* still run a couple of days a week during the dry season – ask around for the latest information. Note: the boats assigned to this run were designed for river travel, not sailing the open seas, which in these parts can get dangerously rough.

BUS

Buses depart from Krong Koh Kong's **bus and taxi station** (St 12), on the northeast edge of town, which has an unpaved parking lot and a tin-roofed waiting area. Departing passengers can arrange pick-up at guesthouses or hotels, which sell bus tickets, but charge a commission. Arriving passengers are often let off in town – be ready for a rugby scrum of eager, smiling *moto* drivers. Prices fluctuate depending on competition.

The best bus deals are offered by **Phnom Penh Sorya** (☎ 012 429809; www.ppsoryatransport.com; St 3; ✆ 6am-8pm), which has a direct 7.45am bus to Phnom Penh (US$5, five hours) and one-stop service to Sihanoukville (US$7, four hours). **Rith Mony** (☎ 015 404085; St 3; ✆ 6am-8pm) has two early morning buses to Phnom Penh (US$7).

Bun Thoun Express (☎ 085-607727; St 3; ✆ 6.30am-8pm), whose folding-table office is in front of the Dugout Hotel, and **Virak-Buntham** (☎ 089-998760; St 3; ✆ 6am-7.30pm), known for playing hardball with its competitors, have 8am services to Phnom Penh (US$8, five hours) and an overpriced direct bus to Sihanoukville (US$13, four hours). Midday services go to Bangkok (US$20 or 700B, 7½ hours), Ko Chang (US$14 or 500B, 4½ hours), Ko Samet (US$20, five hours) and Pattaya (US$20 or 600B, six hours).

TAXI
Share taxis depart from the bus and taxi station from about 6am to 6pm, though passengers are most numerous in the morning. Destinations include Andoung Tuek (US$5), Sihanoukville (US$10) and Phnom Penh (US$10). Hiring your own taxi costs 200B (plus 44B for the toll) to the Thai border, US$55 to US$60 to Sihanoukville and US$60 to US$65 to Phnom Penh.

Getting Around
BICYCLE
The Dive Inn charges US$2 a day for 21-speed mountain bikes, while Neptune Guesthouse has city/mountain bikes for US$1/2 a day. Two Khmer-run **bicycle shops** (St 3), both without English signs, charge US$2 a day.

BOAT
Krong Koh Kong's **boat dock** (cnr St 1 & St 9) is the best place to hire open-top fibreglass speedboats. Because 40HP outboards really slurp up the petrol, the cost of boat travel is largely a function of the price of fuel and how far you go.

Destinations include Peam Krasaop Wildlife Sanctuary (US$25/40 for up to three/six people), Koh Kong Island via Peam Krasaop

(US$40/60) and Koh Por Waterfall (US$40/60). An all-day trip to Koh Kong Island, via Peam Krasaop, costs about US$60/85, more if you'd like to circumnavigate the island and stop at one of the mainland beaches near Preak Khsach, on the coast of Botum Sakor National Park. Long-tail boats cost a bit less than speedboats, but are much slower.

It's best to set out early in the morning as the sea, often smooth as glass at 7am, tends to get choppy in the afternoon. Make sure your vessel has life jackets on board – and don't count on being able to summon rescuers with your mobile (cell) phone as many offshore areas, including Koh Kong Island's west coast, lack coverage. Bring sunscreen, a hat and plenty of bottled water (for some unknown reason, one local brand is called Porn Marina).

MINIBUS
The Oasis Bungalow Resort can arrange a nine-person minibus (US$45 a day plus fuel) for local touring or travel around the country.

MOTO & MOTORBIKE
Motos are the most popular form of local transport; short hops in town, or out to the Oasis Bungalow Resort, cost 1000r or 20B.

Motorbikes (100cc or 125cc) can be rented from Oasis Bungalow Resort (US$6 for 24 hours for a new bike), the Dive Inn (US$6 a day for a new bike), Blue Marlin (US$4 a day) and Neptune Guesthouse (US$4 a day). Neptune also has 250cc dirt bikes.

KOH KONG CONSERVATION CORRIDOR
Stretching along both sides of NH48 from Krong Koh Kong to the Gulf of Kompong Som (the bay northwest of Sihanoukville), the Koh Kong Conservation Corridor encompasses many of Cambodia's most outstanding natural sites, including the most extensive mangrove forests on mainland Southeast Asia and the southern reaches of the fabled **Cardamom Mountains**, an area of breathtaking beauty and astonishing biodiversity.

The Cardamoms cover 20,000 sq km of southwestern Cambodia. Their remote peaks – up to 1800m high – and 18 major waterways are home to at least 59 globally threatened animal species, including tigers, Asian elephants, bears, Siamese crocodiles (p205), pangolins (p204) and eight species of tortoise and turtle.

Botanically the area is something of an enigma, because basic research has yet to be carried out, but so far more than 100 species of endemic plants have been identified.

The second-largest virgin rainforest on mainland Southeast Asia, the Cardamoms are one of only two sites in the region where unbroken forests still connect mountain summits with the sea (the other is in Myanmar/Burma). Some highland areas receive up to 5m of rain a year. Conservationists hope the Cardamoms will someday be declared a Unesco World Heritage Forest.

While forests and coastlines elsewhere in Southeast Asia were being ravaged by greedy developers and well-connected logging companies, the Cardamom Mountains and the adjacent mangrove forests were protected from the worst ecological outrages by their sheer remoteness and, at least in part, by Cambodia's long civil war. As a result, much of the area is still in pretty good shape, ecologically speaking, so the potential for ecotourism is huge – akin, some say, to that of Kenya's game reserves or Costa Rica's national parks.

The next few years will be critical in determining the future of the Cardamom Mountains. NGOs such as **Conservation International** (CI; www.conservation.org), **Fauna & Flora International** (FFI; www.fauna-flora.org) and the **Wildlife Alliance** (formerly WildAid; www.wildlifealliance. org), and teams of armed enforcement rangers are working night and day to help protect the area's 16 distinct ecosystems from loggers and poachers. But ecotourism, too, can play an important role in generating income for local people and thus giving them sustainable alternatives to logging and poaching.

For information on the northern side of the Cardamom Mountains, accessible from Pursat and Pailin, see p247.

TOURS

The Rainbow Lodge (p202) arranges guided jungle walks and boat excursions. Companies offering Cardamoms treks include Phnom Penh–based **Asia Adventures** (www.asia -adventures.com).

In Krong Koh Kong, a number of establishments organise land and sea trips and overnights along the Koh Kong Conservation Corridor:

Blue Marlin (p199) Runs overnight Cardamoms tours (US$40 per person, including food and transport) to Thma Bang. Has a two-person dinghy (US$25 per person per

day) and a four-person Vietnam War–era jeep (US$40 per person per day).

Blue Moon Guesthouse (p198) Mr Neat, a former park ranger, offers boat trips to Peam Krasaop and Koh Kong Island (dry season only; US$25 per person), island overnights in a tent (US$35 per person) and rainforest overnights in a hammock (US$30 per person).

Jungle Cross (☎ 015 601633; www.junglecross.com; St 3) Based at the old Sauna Garden from October to June, Nick specialises in dirt-bike safaris deep into the Cardamoms, with riverside camping in hammocks. Also does jeep trips and white-water rafting.

Koh Kong Eco Tours (☎ 092-228342, 015 707719; http://oasisresortblog.netkhmer.com; St 3) Jason offers boat trips (eg to Koh Kong Island), birdwatching, fishing and Irrawaddy-dolphin-watching trips (US$50), including overnights. Has an office at the Dugout Hotel.

Neptune Guesthouse (p198) Runs day trips (US$20, including a BBQ lunch), overnights to Koh Kong Island and kayaking excursions.

GETTING THERE & AROUND

All buses, minibuses and share taxis travelling between Krong Koh Kong and points east, including Phnom Penh and Sihanoukville, travel along NH48, with optional stops at the Tatai Bridge (18km southeast of Krong Koh Kong); Andoung Tuek (98km from Krong Koh Kong), gateway to Chi Phat; and Plauv Bombek Sre Ambel (Sre Ambel Junction), where NH48 meets NH4.

Thanks to the efforts of environmental groups, including the Wildlife Alliance, agricultural development and land speculation along NH48 – a common sight, hundreds of metres deep, along new roads almost everywhere else in the country – have been strictly forbidden. The highway is traversed by an elephant corridor, which is why those yellow 'elephant crossing' signs have been put up, though you'll be hard-pressed to find anyone who's had to brake for a pachyderm.

For details on boat, *moto, remork* and taxi hire in Krong Koh Kong, see opposite.

A very rough road goes north through the wild Cardamoms to Pursat, Pailin and Battambang, passing by remote mountain towns such as Veal Veng, O Som (where there's a ranger station) and Promoui (the main town in the Phnom Samkos Wildlife Sanctuary – see p248). It should be attempted only in the dry season by dirt bikers with oodles of off-road experience. Near Krong Koh Kong, the turn-off is on the old road to Phnom Penh past the airport, a few hundred metres beyond the army base. Going south, share taxis link Pursat with Promoui, where it *might* be possible to hire a *moto* for the long trip to Krong Koh Kong.

Motorcycles are loud beasts, scaring off birds and animals and making it impossible for the rider to hear much of anything. In contrast, mountain bikes, which can go anywhere motorcycles can and some places they can't, are silent, letting you hear and feel the jungle – Henry David Thoreau would have said 'commune with' it – as you ride. Bike tours of the Cardamoms are on offer in Chi Phat (p206) and, along with bike-hire options, are sure to sprout up elsewhere in the area.

Koh Por Waterfall

Upriver from Krong Koh Kong, these rapids pour over a stone shelf in a lovely jungle gorge. It's great to clamber around here in the dry season, as there are immense boulders to use as stepping stones. Alas, the site's tranquillity has recently been threatened by a new road.

The best way to get to the waterfall is by speedboat or long-tail boat from Krong Koh Kong (see p200).

Tatai River & Waterfall

When driving east from Krong Koh Kong along NH48, the first bridge you come to – after approximately 18km – spans the Tatai River (Stung Tatai).

Set in a lushly forested gorge a bit upstream from the bridge, Tatai Waterfall is a thundering set of rapids in the wet season, plunging over a 4m rock shelf. In the dry season, when water levels drop, you can walk across much of the ledge and take a dip in the gently flowing river. The water is fairly pure, as it comes down from the high Cardamoms where there are very few human settlements.

SLEEPING

The Tatai River now has four ecoaccommodation options, three of them reminiscent of the Tonlé Sap's floating villages, and more are on the way.

Nature Waterways Resort (☎ 099-211384; www.waterways.thai.li; d US$8) At press time, Andy's Meeting Point (as this Swiss-run establishment is known locally), situated next to a delightful wet-season waterfall, had four en-suite rooms and plans to add four more

rooms and some bungalows. A mini-hydro station supplies electricity. Coming from Krong Koh Kong, it's on the right just before the Tatai Bridge.

Rainbow Lodge (☎ 099-744321, 012 1602585; www.rainbowlodgecambodia.com; s/d US$40/60, f US$80-100) This supremely tranquil ecolodge – built and staffed by locals – has seven frills-free bungalows with bathroom, fan and mosquito net. Solar panels provide electricity; the wash-water arrived as rain. Room rates include three meals a day, prepared with locally sourced ingredients. Activities include kayaking, a sunset river cruise, a day trek and overnight camping. Situated 10 minutes upriver from the Tatai Bridge; call ahead for free pick-up at the bridge.

Four Rivers Floating Ecolodge (☎ 035-6900650, 097-6434032; www.ecolodges.asia; s/d May-Sep US$87/102, Oct-Apr US$102/120; 🛜 🖳) Boasting 'top-of-the-line luxury in harmony with Mother Nature', this ecoresort's South African–made tented villas – 18 are planned, each with 45 sq metres, special septic tanks and partly solar power – float on a branch of the Tatai River estuary 6km downriver from NH48. Access is by boat (20 minutes) from the western (Krong Koh Kong) side of the Tatai Bridge.

River Gypsy Bungalows (☎ 099-317580; hans_loewtatai@yahoo.com; bungalow US$100) Situated 1km upstream from the Tatai Bridge (and 200m downriver from the Rainbow Lodge), this German-run place – not really an ecolodge – has two floating bungalows that can be towed to the overnight site of your choice.

GETTING THERE & AWAY

From Krong Koh Kong, a half-day *moto/remork* excursion to Tatai Waterfall costs US$10/15 return.

Peam Krasaop Wildlife Sanctuary

Anchored to countless alluvial islands, some no larger than a house, millions of magnificent mangroves protect the coast from erosion, serve as a vital breeding and feeding ground for fish, shrimp and shellfish, and provide a home to myriad birds. The area is all the more valuable from an ecological standpoint because similar forests in Thailand have been trashed by short-sighted development.

To get a feel for the delicate mangrove ecosystem – and to understand how mangrove roots can stop a tsunami dead in its tracks – head to the 600m-long **mangrove walk** (admission 5000r; ⊙ 6.30am-6pm), which wends its way above the briny waters to a 15m observation tower. If you're lucky you'll come upon cavorting monkeys with a fondness for fizzy drinks. The walk begins about 7km southeast of Krong Koh Kong; by *moto*, expect to pay US$2.50/5 one-way/return.

The sanctuary, which covers 260 sq km and has been called the 'jewel in the crown' of Cambodia's south coast, is largely uninhabited, though you may come upon **fishing hamlets** whose residents use spindly traps to catch fish, which they keep alive till market time in partly submerged nets attached to floating wooden frames. Further out, on some of the more remote mangrove islands, you pass utterly isolated little **beaches** where you can land and lounge alongside fearless hermit crabs.

On the sanctuary's west coast, along both banks of a channel, is the Venice-like village of **Koh Kapi**. Each of the fishers' houses – held aloft by stilts – has a blue or green wooden boat docked outside. Ask around to find a local family willing to prepare a fresh fish or seafood meal.

Endangered **Irrawaddy dolphins** can sometimes be seen early in the morning (6.30am or 7am) around the entrance to the Stung Koh Poi estuary.

Much of Peam Krasaop is on the prestigious **Ramsar List of Wetlands of International Importance** (www.ramsar.org). The area's habitats and fisheries are threatened by the large-scale dredging of sand for Singapore (p72).

GETTING THERE & AWAY
The best way to see Peam Krasaop is by boat from Krong Koh Kong (p200), perhaps on the way to Koh Kong Island.

Koh Kong Island
កោះកុង

Cambodia's largest island, about 25km south of Krong Koh Kong, towers over seas so crystal clear you can make out individual grains of sand in a couple of metres of water. Its seven pristine **beaches**, all of them along the western coast, get so few visitors that sand crabs scamper obliviously up and down the beach and the shoreline is dotted with colourful shells of the sort you usually see only in souvenir shops.

Several of the beaches – lined with coconut palms and lush vegetation, just as you'd expect in a tropical paradise – are at the mouths of little streams. At the **sixth beach** from the north, a narrow channel leads to a genuine *Gilligan's Island*–style lagoon.

On Koh Kong Island's eastern side, half a dozen forested hills – the highest towering 407m above the sea – drop steeply to the mangrove-lined coast. The fishing village of **Alatan**, the island's only settlement (for now), is on the southeast coast facing the northwest corner of Botum Sakor National Park. The island is not part of any national park or wildlife sanctuary and thus has few protections against mercenary development.

There's a police post near the 20km-long island's northern end, above the second beach you come to, so skippers may be reluctant to stop nearby (though, happily, bribes are no longer demanded of visitors). It's forbidden to explore the thickly forested interior, and there are no guesthouses or bungalows, but camping overnight, long banned, is now possible with a guide (see p201).

GETTING THERE & AWAY
For details on speedboats, day tours and overnights to Koh Kong Island (the northern tip is

SOUTH COAST

'THAT PLACE WAS PARADISE UNTIL LONELY PLANET MENTIONED IT'

If Koh Kong Island is truly such an untouched paradise, why is Lonely Planet recklessly exposing its heretofore hidden charms? Won't publicity hasten the island's ruin?

Cambodia and its people desperately need economic growth, so it's inevitable that natural resources such as Koh Kong Island – hardly a secret either to locals or to Phnom Penh investors – will be developed. The question is: how? Will developers be allowed to construct massive resorts for package tourists interested only in sun, sand and creature comforts, chopping down trees and destroying the island's delicate ecosystem in the process? Or will local residents and the people in charge – in the provincial and national governments – realise that, in the long term, sustainable development that preserves the island's rare natural beauty is the way to go?

Each time you visit an ecotourism site, marvelling at its flora and fauna and unspoilt habitats, you're casting a vote for sustainable development – backed up by cash in local pockets.

about one hour from Krong Koh Kong), see p200 and p201.

Central Cardamoms Protected Forest

The Central Cardamoms Protected Forest (CCPF; 4013 sq km) encompasses three of Southeast Asia's most threatened ecosystems: lowland evergreen forests, riparian forests and wetlands.

The rangers and military policemen who protect this vast area from illegal hunting and logging, with the help of Conservation International, are based at eight strategically sited ranger stations, including one in **Thma Bang**, where they run a **guesthouse** (to coordinate a visit ☎ 012 908560; lly@conservation.org; per person US$5). Opened in 2008, its eight (soon to be 12) double rooms have outside bathrooms and electricity from 6pm to 9pm (there are plans to install solar panels). Meals are US$2. You can also overnight in a nearby homestay. Bring warm clothes as temperatures can drop to as low as 10°C (50°F). Thma Bang now has mobile-phone coverage for numbers beginning with 011, 012, 099 and perhaps 097.

Thma Bang District has the lowest population density (1.35 people per sq km) and the highest levels of poverty in Koh Kong Province. Mostly covered with dense rainforest, it is perfect for birdwatching or hiking – perhaps to a waterfall – with a local guide (rangers can help you find one). The nearby **Areng Valley**, some of whose inhabitants belong to the Khmer Daeum minority community, is home to Asian elephants and the dragonfish (Asian arowana), almost extinct in the wild,

and the world's most important population of critically endangered wild Siamese crocodiles (opposite), toothy critters up to 3.5m long who don't eat people. The valley and its fauna face a grave threat from a huge hydroelectric dam which, if built, will displace 1500 people, flood 90 to 120 sq km of land and inundate an important elephant migration route.

From December to May, the truly intrepid can accompany an armed enforcement ranger patrol on the eight-day trek from Thma Bang north to **Kravanh** (p248), or from **Chamnar** (linked to Thma Bang by road) over the mountains to Kravanh, a five- or six-day affair.

An easier, year-round option is the three- or four-day hike from **Chumnoab**, east of Thma Bang, eastwards to **Roleak Kang Cheung**, linked to Kompong Speu by road. Between the two is **Knong Krapeur** (1000m), set amid high-elevation grassland and pines. Inhabited five centuries ago, the area is known for its giant ceramic funeral jars, still filled with human bones.

For trek information and reservations, contact Conservation International's **La Peng Ly** (☎ 012 908560; lly@conservation.org).

GETTING THERE & AWAY

Few roads of any sort penetrate the Cardamom Mountains, ideal if you're trying to protect the natural habitat – roads, even rudimentary ones, tend to attract loggers, poachers and encroachers – but a bit of a problem if you'd like to visit.

The southern reaches of the CCPF are easiest to reach from the south. It takes about 1½ hours to drive from Krong Koh Kong to Thma Bang (wet-season travel may be difficult). Turn off NH48 about 10km east of the Tatai River bridge; from the Veal II (Veal Pii) ranger checkpoint, it's another hour (longer in the wet).

Thma Bang is linked to Chi Phat (p206) by a difficult trail that can be handled by motorbike, but just barely.

The CCPF's northern sections (see p248) are accessible from Pursat.

Trapaeng Rung

Sometime in 2010, the Wildlife Alliance will inaugurate an ecotourism project similar to the flourishing one in Chi Phat (p206) in the four villages of Trapaeng Rung, situated around the second bridge you come to as you drive southeast along NH48 from Krong Koh Kong. It's slated to include guesthouses, homestays, waterfall hikes and cycling treks.

END OF THE LINE FOR THE PANGOLIN?

In China and Vietnam, the meat of the Malayan (Sunda) pangolin – a kind of nocturnal anteater whose only food is ants and termites – is considered a delicacy, and the creature's blood and scales are believed to have healing powers. As a result, villagers in the Cardamom Mountains, who often hunt with dogs, are paid a whopping US$40 per kilo for live pangolins (the price rises to US$70 in Vietnam and US$100 in China) and pangolin populations have been in freefall. Enforcement rangers are doing their best to crack down on poaching before it's too late.

10 PER CENT

The Siamese crocodile *(Crocodylus siamensis)* was thought to be 'effectively extinct in the wild' until small viable populations were discovered in the Cardamom Mountains in 2000. Today, Cambodia is home to the world's only breeding populations of wild Siamese crocs: three in the Cardamoms and one – possibly – in Mondulkiri Province. Researchers estimate that altogether, they produce just five nests a year.

In 2007, researchers from **Flora & Fauna International** (www.fauna-flora.org/asiapacific_siamese _crocodile.php) found 23 Siamese croc eggs in a nest on the Areng River, in the Central Cardamoms Protected Forest. They took 12 eggs to a protected site where, 45 days later, all hatched; after being blessed by monks, they were released back into the river. Observations confirmed that all 11 eggs left behind also hatched. These 23 hatchlings represented an astounding 10% of the estimated global population of wild Siamese crocodiles, who have disappeared from 99% of their original habitat. In 2008, 34 croc eggs were collected and hatched, but none were found in 2009.

Almost all the critters on Cambodia's 1000-plus croc farms are hybrids, their lineage mixed with that of the larger Australian saltwater crocodiles *(Crocodylus porosus)* – despite their name, also native to Cambodia. Genetic testing carried out in late 2009 determined that 35 of the 69 rescued crocodiles living at the Phnom Tamao Wildlife Rescue Centre (see p126) are pure-bred Siamese. A captive breeding program is set to begin in 2010, with an eye towards eventually releasing the offspring into suitable habitats far from people and dams.

As we go to press, two of the crocs' last Cardamoms habitats – Veal Veng and the Areng Valley – are threatened by massive hydroelectric projects, and the Siamese crocodile is still classified as 'critically endangered' on the **IUCN Red List** (www.iucnredlist.org).

Botum Sakor National Park

Occupying almost the entirety of the 35km-wide peninsula west across the Gulf of Kompong Som from Sihanoukville, this 1834-sq-km national park, encircled by mangroves and beaches, is home to a profusion of wildlife, including elephants (about 20 of them, according to camera-trap evidence), tigers, deer, leopards and sun bears. The highest point is a 402m hill in the park's almost inaccessible interior.

Boats can be taken up into four mangrove-lined streams that are rich with wildlife, including the pileated gibbon, long-tailed macaque and black-shanked douc langur: **Ta Op**, the largest, on the east coast; **Ta Nun** in the middle of the south coast; and **Ta Nhi** and **Preak Khsach** on the east coast.

Although a road was recently forced through the park's eastern side (it will eventually go all the way round the peninsula's coastline), the best way to see Botum Sakor is by boat. To get to the mangrove forests on the east coast and the almost deserted **beaches** on the park's southeastern tip, you can hire a long-tail boat in Andoung Tuek (p206) or Sihanoukville.

The west coast, with its many kilometres of fine beaches, is easiest to reach by boat from Koh Sdach (right).

There are more **beaches** on the west coast, across the strait from Koh Kong Island and

south of the picturesque fishing village of **Preak Khsach**; for these destinations you can hire a boat in Krong Koh Kong (p200).

Grandiose tourist development may soon disfigure the park's wild west coast. A Chinese company has plans to build seven new cities (no, that's not a typo), an airport, golf courses and lots of hotels, though things are on hold while an impact study is carried out. The recent world economic crisis seems to have slowed things up a bit.

Botum Sakor is not yet geared up for tourism, but at the **park headquarters** (☎ 015 374797), on NH48 3.5km west of Andoung Tuek, it should be possible to arrange a hike with a ranger (US$5 a day) or a boat excursion.

The nearest guesthouses are in Andoung Tuek, on the Tatai River and on Koh Sdach. On the south coast, it may be possible to overnight at the **Ta Nun ranger station** or in a basic guesthouse in **Thmor Sor**, an east-coast fishing village. To get there from Sihanoukville's ferry port, take the new road or try to hitch a ride on a fishing boat.

Koh Sdach

កោះស្ដេច

Just off Botum Sakor National Park's southwest tip, this island has a small fishing port, a couple of sandy **beaches**, some modest eateries

SOUTH COAST

and a seaside bungalow outfit called **Mean Chey Guesthouse** (☎ 011 983806; r US$5). There are fine **coral reefs** – excellent for diving or snorkelling – around some of the nearby islands. This is a good place to hire a boat to explore the wonderful, as-yet-undeveloped beaches along the west coast of Botum Sakor National Park (p205).

GETTING THERE & AWAY
The island is linked to Sihanoukville by ferry (p220). In the dry season there *might* be boat services to Krong Koh Kong.

Southern Cardamoms Protected Forest
In an effort to protect the southern Cardamom Mountains from poaching, logging and land-grabbing by turning the rainforest into a source of jobs and income for local people, the **Wildlife Alliance** (www.wildlifealliance.org) has launched a multiphase project to transform the Southern Cardamoms Protected Forest (1443 sq km), whose southern boundary is NH48 between Krong Koh Kong and Andoung Tuek, into a world-class ecotourism destination.

In the next few years, the thriving ecotourism project in Chi Phat (right) will be joined by a similar initiative in Trapaeng Rung (p204), and **visitors centres** are planned for Chi Phat and the Tatai River (p202).

Andoung Tuek
អណ្តូងទឹក
On the western side of the highway bridge over Preak Piphot, this river port is the jumping-off point for an excursion upriver to Chi Phat (right). It may also be possible to hire a boat to explore the east coast of Botum Sakor National Park (p205).

SLEEPING
West of the bridge 250m, the extremely basic **Botum Sakor Guesthouse** (☎ 016 732731; r with/without bathroom 25,000r/15,000r) has six slightly musty rooms with bright pink mosquito nets and sinkless bathrooms. The bad news is that there's some dodgy electric wiring in the bathrooms; the good news is that you can get electrocuted only from 6pm to 10pm, when the town has electricity.

GETTING THERE & AWAY
Andoung Tuek is on NH48, 98km from Krong Koh Kong and 191km from Phnom Penh.

Buses travelling from Krong Koh Kong to Phnom Penh (US$6) and Sihanoukville

(US$5) pass by Andoung Tuek at about 9am or 9.30am; buses heading *towards* Krong Koh Kong can be picked up between 10am and 11am. In Chi Phat, the CBET office (below) can phone ahead for reservations. Share taxis passing by Andoung Tuek tend to be full.

For boats and motorbikes to Chi Phat, see p209.

Chi Phat
ជីផាត់
Once notorious for its loggers and poachers, the river village of Chi Phat (population 550 families) is now home to a pioneering **community-based ecotourism project** (CBET) offering travellers a unique opportunity to explore the Cardamoms ecosystems while contributing to their protection.

Silver langurs, long-tailed macaques, greater hornbills and other rainforest creatures can often be seen along the banks of **Stung Proat**, an unlogged tributary of the **Preak Piphot River** that's accessible from Chi Phat by boat. Gibbons are hard to spot, but can often be heard calling to each other through the forest canopy. According to a village elder, the last time a tiger was seen in these parts was 1975.

A variety of outdoor adventure activities, run by the local community, are on offer. Visitors can take **day treks** through the jungle, go **sunrise birdwatching** (per person for 2/3/4 people US$19/16/13) by rowboat, **mountain bike** to several sets of rapids, and shoot (with a camera) monkeys and hornbills with a former poacher as a guide (US$6 to US$10 per day).

Also on offer are one- to four-day **cycling trips** and **jungle treks** (per person per day all inclusive US$20-40) deep into the Cardamoms. Destinations include a **bat cave** tucked behind a waterfall; an area with mysterious, ancient **burial jars**; and – 45km away – the Areng Valley (p204). To really get away from it all, you can take a specialised **birdwatching tour** lasting five to seven days or the weeklong **Chi Phat Grand Tour**, which combines cycling, trekking and boating.

In the village, visitors can relax by playing volleyball, badminton or pool with the locals.

INFORMATION
In Chi Phat, the **CBET office** (☎ 092-720 925; www.eco adventurecambodia.com; ecotourism@wildlifealliance.org) – housed in Cambodia's first fully engineered bamboo structure – handles guesthouse,

CHI PHAT: AN ECOTOURISM CASE STUDY

Chi Phat's 550 families have long supplemented their meagre agricultural income with products from the nearby forests. Gathering nontimber forest products (known in development lingo as NTFPs) and small quantities of firewood can be ecologically sustainable, but around Chi Phat the wholesale forest destruction carried out during 'the logging time' – the anarchic 1990s – left the whole ecosystem, and the villagers' livelihoods, way out of whack. For many, poaching endangered animals became a way of life.

When the **Wildlife Alliance** (www.wildlifealliance.org) came on the scene in 2002 in a last-ditch effort to save the southern Cardamoms, local villagers and outsiders were encroaching on protected land, destroying the forest by illegal logging, and hunting endangered animals for local consumption and sale on the black market. The only way to prevent ecological catastrophe – and, among other things, to save macaques from being trapped, sold for US$60 and shipped to Vietnam to be eaten – was to send in teams of enforcement rangers to crack down on 'forestry and wildlife crimes'.

But enforcing the law impinged on local people's ability to earn money to feed their children (or buy motorbikes), generating a great deal of resentment. Many didn't see that environmental degradation – caused, in part, by their own unsustainable activities – would leave them far worse off in a few years' time, though most everyone noticed that animals were getting harder and harder to find.

The Wildlife Alliance realised that in order to save the Cardamoms forests, it needed the co-operation of locals, and that such cooperation would be forthcoming only if income-generating alternatives to poaching and logging were available. In such a remote area, one of the only resources is the forest itself, and one of the few ways to earn money from plants and animals without destroying them is ecotourism.

Thus the Wildlife Alliance launched what's known in NGO parlance as a community-based ecotourism (CBET) project. Coordinated by Oran Shapira, an Israeli former ranger experienced in collective endeavours from his kibbutz upbringing, the first step was empowering the local community. A committee of 14 elected representatives was established to assess positive and negative impacts (eg of contact with Western culture), set goals and manage the project. Many of those who joined as 'stakeholders' were former loggers and wildlife traders.

After three years of slow, steady work, the Chi Phat CBET project is up and running, and initially sceptical locals are warming to the idea and are beginning to see forest conservation in a different light. Ecotourists, drawn largely by word of mouth, have begun coming up to Chi Phat and the income generated – income that goes into both the villagers' pockets and a community development fund – is starting to make a real difference. Chi Phat is seen as a model for other CBET projects, and delegations from around Cambodia now come here to see how it's done.

Groups working to support sustainable, low-impact CBET projects like that in Chi Pat have banded together to form the **Cambodia Community-Based Ecotourism Network** (CCBEN; www.ccben.org) – its website has details on other such initiatives around the country.

homestay and activities reservations and can arrange for motorboat and motorbike transport from/to Andoung Tuek. A satellite internet connection is available for use in an emergency.

Some mobile phones (eg those with the prefixes 012, 016 and 081) now work in Chi Phat. Handsets can be recharged at the CBET office.

Bookings for Chi Phat can also be made via a consortium of ecofriendly travel agencies known as the **Friends of Chi Phat** – for details, see the CBET office websites.

DANGERS & ANNOYANCES

At the cargo-boat dock in Andoung Tuek (p209) and in nearby coffee shops, scammers sometimes accost travellers, purveying misinformation, offering bogus tourist services and demanding spurious payments. For reliable information, contact the ecotourism project's CBET office (opposite) in Chi Phat, or check out its website.

SLEEPING

Chi Phat's CBET project has eight family-run **guesthouses** (d US$5), many decorated with outrageously colourful plastic flowers (a trend started by one guesthouse owner with flamboyant tastes) and **homestay rooms** (s/d US$3/4), one inside each of 15 local houses. Some of these places are in town, others are out in the countryside, surrounded by orchards. At one homestay, the enterprising owners distil rice liqueur potent enough to be flammable. They're so proud of their product that you'll be offered a tumbler no matter when you visit – even if it's 8am, as it was when we dropped by.

Rooms – inspected monthly by the CBET committee – come with mosquito nets, cotton sheets, foam mattresses, free filtered water, a laminated sheet on local customs and 12V fans powered either by generator (from 6pm to 10pm) or rechargeable car battery. Toilets (Western or squat) and showers (a rainwater cistern with a plastic bucket) are outside, but are clean and commodious.

Chi Phat's first **forest shelter**, at the Damnak Kos Bird Watching Campsite, was inaugurated in December 2009 and as we go to press, three additional forest shelters, for use by hikers and cyclists on overnight treks, are being prepared. Most will be equipped with ecotoilets, solar-powered electric light and either hammocks or field beds.

MOEURK MEE *Daniel Robinson*

By inclination and predilection, Moeurk Mee is a pragmatist, but almost despite himself he's also an idealist – a perfect combination to have when your job is to convince poachers and loggers to work together in order to attract ecotourists.

Program officer for the community-based ecotourism (CBET) project in Chi Phat, the 25-year-old native of Kandal Province (near Phnom Penh) first became interested in ecotourism as a student of tourism management at the Royal University of Phnom Penh. The subject attracted him, he says, because it's 'in the middle between development and conservation', both of which involve hands-on work whose success, or failure, depends on one thing: results.

'The real situation now', Mee says, is that 'the people use the forest to earn a living. If the people continue to hunt the wildlife and to cut trees, this place is going to become a wilderness'. Sustainable development can provide less destructive ways for local people to support their families but, he explains, 'ecotourism is a new concept. In the beginning it was hard to explain to them why they should participate – they had no idea about ecotourism – but more and more villagers, they begin to see the visible results, especially after money started coming in. Then they saw that we were not just talking'.

Mee's job is 'to sit with the local people, teach them how to run this project, make a plan, decide what we are going to do, help them to implement the plan, follow up and monitor'. He sees his role as 'not to do for them, but to teach them, discuss what they should do and should not do, suggest tasks for them to carry out, with encouragement and comment'.

At the time of this writing, '123 families get direct benefit from this project – they are very happy. And about 15 families get indirect benefit', Mee explains. 'One hundred and 38 families – that's a good start. Through them we can prove to the community that this CBET project really helps them. Year by year, as the number of tourists increases, the job will be to extend this project to other families, help other families'.

Mee's long-term goal is 'to help the environment and the people in a sustainable way'. In a few years, he hopes that he won't be needed in Chi Phat because locals will 'do business with the tourists' on their own and 'understand and protect the unique natural and cultural resources in this area by themselves'. His vision for Chi Phat is both practical and attainable: 'I want this community to be a nice and beautiful place. Tourists – they come and enjoy, discover, have experiences, meet friendly people', and they 'spend money that the villagers benefit from directly and that will improve their livelihoods'.

When asked about his own plans for the future, Mee smiles and declares, 'Australia, that is my goal!' Down Under, he would like to study tourism management or rural development. 'I have a plan. From now until I am 40, I want to work for an NGO related to ecotourism. When I am more than 40, I want to work for the government', either with the Ministry of Tourism or the Ministry of the Environment.

GETTING THERE & AWAY
Chi Phat is on the Preak Piphot River 21km upriver from Andoung Tuek (for bus connections, see p206). In Andoung Tuek, all boats dock underneath the bridge, on the eastern (Phnom Penh) bank of the river.

The CBET office can arrange river transport to/from Chi Phat; options include a six-person wooden long-tail boat (US$20, 1½ to two hours), a 20-seat wooden motorboat (US$35, 1½ hours) or a six-person speedboat (US$50, 30 minutes). The ride is especially enchanting just after dawn, when the water is often smooth as glass.

Cargo boats (10,000r per person, two to 2½ hours) make daily merchandise runs between Andoung Tuek (departure at noon or 12.30pm) and Chi Phat (departure at 8am or 8.30am). Most buses from Phnom Penh, Sihanoukville and Krong Koh Kong arrive in Andoung Tuek an hour or two before the cargo boat sets sail for Chi Phat.

It's also possible to travel from Andoung Tuek to Chi Phat by *moto* (about US$5 from Andoung Tuek, US$7 from Chi Phat); bookings can be made through the CBET office in Chi Phat. The road was recently upgraded by a sugar-cane company, but parts are rough and, in the wet season, very muddy.

Stung Phong Roul Waterfall
Believed by locals to be inhabited by a powerful spirit, this is one of Cambodia's most spectacular waterfalls, with five big drops arrayed around a vertiginous curve in the river. Clambering around is tough but worth it, as there are some good swimming holes at the right time of year.

The uppermost waterfall is a dramatic 10m high. Flat rock ledges border clear and surprisingly cool pools, and are ideal for a romantic picnic. If you sit quietly with your feet in the water, little fish (goodness knows how they got up here) may nibble your toes.

The 18MW Kirirom III hydroelectric dam being built 2km upriver from the waterfall is likely to leave the falls almost completely dry, so visit soon or there may not be much to see.

GETTING THERE & AWAY
Stung Phong Roul (Steung Pongrul) Waterfall is about 20km northeast of Sre Ambel in the foothills of the Elephant Mountains. As the crow flies, Kirirom National Park (p127) is 20km further to the northeast.

In the dry season you can get to the falls by motorbike, though be warned: there are sinkholes big and deep enough to swallow an entire motorcycle, and getting around the rotted-out bridges can be a wet affair. From just northwest of the Sre Ambel bridge, turn northeast off NH48 and follow the dirt road to the Bailey bridge. From there, an arrow-straight one-time logging road heads east and then north-northeast to a cleft in the forested hills. A 20-minute walk up the slope takes you to the uppermost waterfall.

In Sre Ambel, you can hire a *moto* (US$15 return, one hour to the base of the mountain). In the wet season it's possible to go most of the way by boat. The falls are rarely visited even by locals so it may be hard to find someone who knows the way.

KOMPONG SOM PROVINCE
ខេត្តកំពង់សោម

Sandwiched between Kampot and Koh Kong Provinces, this diminutive province is dominated by its main city, the dynamic port city of Sihanoukville. Nearby islands, some with fine beaches, afford superb diving and snorkelling. Other natural sites include Ream National Park, 18km east of Sihanoukville, and the Kbal Chhay Cascades.

SIHANOUKVILLE
ក្រុងព្រះសីហនុ
☎ 034 / pop 155,000

Surrounded by white-sand beaches and undeveloped tropical islands, Sihanoukville (Krong Preah Sihanouk), also known as Kompong Som, is Cambodia's most happening beach destination. Visitor numbers have risen steadily in recent years – and are likely to skyrocket if flights to Siem Reap are resumed – but for the time being, despite the boomtown rents, the city and its sandy bits remain pretty laid-back.

Named in honour of the then-king, Sihanoukville was hacked out of the jungle in the late 1950s to create Cambodia's first and only deep-water port, strategically vital because it meant that the country's international trade no longer had to pass through Vietnam's Mekong Delta. During the 1960s the city experienced a tourism miniboom.

SOUTH COAST

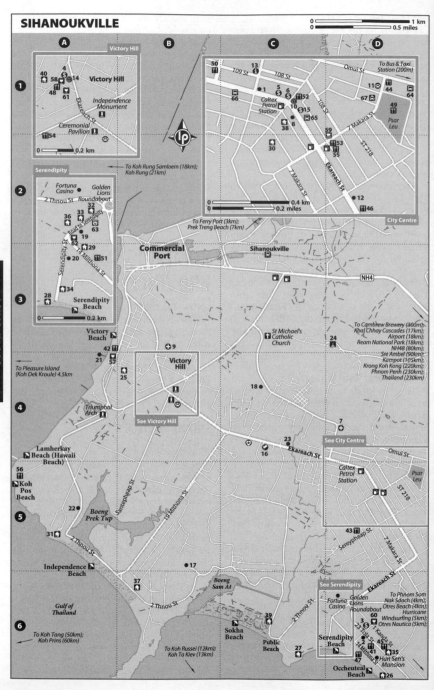

SIHANOUKVILLE

SOUTH COAST

INFORMATION		
Ana Travel	**1**	C1
Ana Travel	**2**	D6
ANZ Royal ATM	**3**	D6
ANZ Royal ATM	**4**	A1
ANZ Royal Bank	**5**	C1
Canadia Bank	**6**	C1
Casablanca Books	(see 32)	
CT Clinic	**7**	D4
Eco-Trek Tours	(see 32)	
F1 Laundry	**8**	C1
Hand of Help	**9**	B3
Internet Shops	**10**	C1
Mr Heinz Books	(see 5)	
Post Office	**11**	D1
Q&A	**12**	D2
Storage 4U	(see 23)	
Tourism Office	**13**	C1
TTS Internet Service	**14**	A1
Union Commerical Bank	**15**	C1
Utopia Information Centre	(see 62)	
Vietnamese Consulate	**16**	C4

SIGHTS & ACTIVITIES		
Airport	(see 57)	
Claude Diving Centre	**17**	B5
Coasters	(see 28)	
Dive Shop	(see 33)	
EcoSea Dive	(see 28)	
EcoSea Dive	(see 5)	
EcoSea Dive	(see 36)	
Fitness & Boxing Center	**18**	C4
Relax	**19**	A2
Scuba Nation Diving Center	**20**	A3
Seeing Hands Massage 3	(see 12)	
Starfish Bakery & Café	(see 55)	

Sun-Tours	**21**	A4
Tame Monkeys	**22**	A5
Traditional Khmer Cookery	**23**	C4
Wat Leu	**24**	D3

SLEEPING		
Bungalow Village	**25**	B4
Chiva's Shack	**26**	D6
Cloud 9 Bungalows	**27**	C6
Coasters	**28**	A3
Coolabah Resort	**29**	A3
Geckozy Guesthouse	**30**	C2
Green Mood	(see 48)	
Independence Hotel	**31**	A5
Mick & Craig's	**32**	A2
Monkey Republic	**33**	A2
New Sea View Villa	**34**	A3
Orchidée Guesthouse	**35**	D6
Reef Resort	**36**	A2
Sea Breeze Guesthouse	**37**	B6
Small Hotel	**38**	C1
Sokha Beach Resort	**39**	C6
Sunset Garden Guesthouse	**40**	A1
Utopia	(see 62)	

EATING		
Angelo's	**41**	D6
Brown's	**42**	A3
Chez Claude	(see 17)	
Chom Ka Spey	**43**	D5
Food Stalls	**44**	D1
Green Mood	(see 48)	
Happa	(see 36)	
Happy Herb Pizza	**45**	D6
Holy Cow	**46**	D2
K2	**47**	D6
Koh Lin	**48**	A1

Ku Kai	(see 36)	
New Sea View Villa	(see 34)	
Psar Leu	**49**	D1
Psar Pinechikam	**50**	B1
Rainy Season Pizza	**51**	A3
Restaurants	**52**	C1
Samudera Supermarket	**53**	D2
Snake House	**54**	A2
Starfish Bakery & Café	**55**	D2
Treasure Island	**56**	A5

DRINKING		
Airport	**57**	A4
Aquarium	(see 28)	
Corner Bar	**58**	A1
Gelato Italiano	**59**	D2
Golden Lion Plaza	**60**	D6
Monkey Republic	(see 33)	
Retox Bar	**61**	A1
Utopia	**62**	A2

ENTERTAINMENT		
Top Cat Cinema	**63**	A2

SHOPPING		
M'lop Tapang Gift Shop	(see 20)	
Rajana Crafts	(see 55)	

TRANSPORT		
Bus & Taxi Station	**64**	D1
Capitol Tour	**65**	C1
Mick & Craig's	(see 32)	
Mr Heinz Books	(see 5)	
Phnom Penh Sorya	**66**	C1
Q&A	(see 12)	
Taxis to Kampot	**67**	D1

The main attractions here, in addition to the islands, are the beaches ringing the headland. None of them qualify as Southeast Asia's finest, but on weekdays it's still possible to have stretches of casuarina- and coconut-palm-shaded sand to yourself. On weekends and holidays Sihanoukville is hugely popular with well-to-do Phnom Penhers.

Orientation

The shabby city centre, spread out along and north of Ekareach St, is where you'll find banks, businesses and the new bus station. It is roughly equidistant from the two main beach areas, the Serendipity-Occheuteal area, 2km to the south, and Victory Beach, 2.5km to the northwest.

Serendipity Beach – as the northwestern tip of Occheuteal Beach is known – is linked to the end of Ekareach St by Serendipity St (the rutted dirt access road down to Serendipity Beach) and the Rd to Serendipity (linking the corner of Serendipity St and 14 Milthona St

with the Golden Lions Roundabout). Victory Hill (Weather Station Hill, also known as 'The Hill'), once the main backpacker haven, is up the hill from Victory Beach.

Information

Sihanoukville is developing so fast it's hard to keep track of all the new establishments and activities sprouting up around town.

BOOKSHOPS

Casablanca Books (☎ 012 484051; Rd to Serendipity; 🕑 8am-10pm) Next to Mick & Craig's, this shop sells new and used English paperbacks.

Mister Heinz Books (☎ 097-894 7502; 219 Ekareach St, City Centre; 🕑 9am-6pm or later) Stocks 6500 books in over 10 languages, including lots of used English paperbacks. Most can be sold back for 50% of what you paid.

Q&A (☎ 012 598072; 95 Ekareach St, City Centre; 🕑 7.30am-7.30pm; 🛜) A pleasant secondhand bookshop with 8000 titles in over 20 languages. Doubles as a cafe, with hot drinks, shakes, salads and breakfast (mains US$3 to US$5.50). Also sells bus tickets and supplies travel tips.

SOUTH COAST

INTERNET ACCESS

The city centre's many **internet shops** (per hour 4000r) include places at Nos 173, 187, 189, 191 and 193 Ekareach St. In the Serendipity and Occheuteal areas, internet outfits are sprinkled along the Rd to Serendipity and can also be found at Coasters guesthouse and near K2 restaurant. In Victory Hill, try **TTS Internet Service** (Ekareach St, Victory Hill; per hr 4000r; 8am-11pm).

LAUNDRY

Lots of places around Serendipity Beach do laundry for 3000r per kilo – keep an eye out for roadside signs. In the city centre, laundries can be found along the same street as the Small Hotel, but their rates are per-piece and pricey.

F1 Laundry (012 849689; 152 Ekareach St; 7am-8pm) Laundry costs US$1 per kilo if you can wait 24 hours, US$2 per hour if you need it in three hours.

LEFT LUGGAGE

Storage 4U (092-738615; khmercookery@hotmail. com; 335 Ekareach St; per day/month US$1.50/20) Safe, secure storage for your backpack, suitcase or motorbike, eg while you're out on one of the islands. Free pick-up and delivery. Run by the same people as the Traditional Khmer Cookery.

MEDICAL SERVICES

CT Clinic (934222; ct_clinic@yahoo.com; 47 Boray Kamakor St, City Centre; 24hr for emergencies) Expats and NGO workers head here when they need care, including emergency trauma treatment and rabies shots. Has a reliable in-house pharmacy.

Hand of Help (934331; www.ngo-handofhelp.org; Victory Hill; 24hr for emergencies) *The* place to come for snake antivenin (the Snake House no longer handles snake-bite first aid). Next to the New Peak Hotel.

MONEY

Sihanoukville's banks – all with ATMs – are in the city centre, especially along the north side of Ekareach St facing the Caltex petrol station. ATMs can also be found around Serendipity (eg at the Reef Resort and the Golden Sand Hotel) and at Victory Hill.

ANZ Royal Bank (215 Ekareach St)
Canadia Bank (197 Ekareach St)
Union Commercial Bank (195 Ekareach St)

POST

Post office (19 7 Makara St, City Centre) Over the road from Psar Leu.

TOURIST INFORMATION

Guesthouses, pubs and the Q&A bookshop (p211) are generally the best sources of information and can equip you with two free booklets, the *Sihanouk Ville Visitors Guide* (www.canbypublications.com) and the *Sihanoukville Advertiser*. You might also try www.sihanoukville-cambodia.com.

Tourism office (933894; cnr Sopheakmongkol & 109 Sts, City Centre; 8-11.30am & 2-5pm Mon-Fri) In an old salmon-coloured villa. Friendly but pretty useless.

TRAVEL AGENCIES

Ana Travel (www.anainternet.com); City Centre (933729; 235 Ekareach St; 7.30am-10pm); Occheuteal Beach (934239; 23 Tola St; 9am-6pm or 7pm) Arranges tours, land transport and Cambodian visa extensions (for one/three/six/12 months US$50/85/155/290).

Eco-Trek Tours (012 987073; ecotrektourscambodia@ yahoo.com; Rd to Serendipity; 8am-10pm) Adjacent to Mick & Craig's, this agency runs snorkelling excursions to Koh Russei and Koh Preus (US$15, including lunch) and trips to Ream National Park (US$20), Kampot and Kep.

Utopia Information Centre (934319; (www. utopiacambodia.com; cnr Rd to Serendipity & 14 Milthona St; 8am-8pm) Offers island tours, snorkelling and all-day trips to Ream National Park (US$20).

VISAS

For help extending a Cambodian visa, contact Ana Travel (above) or Samudera Supermarket (p219).

Vietnamese consulate (933466; 310 Ekareach St; 8am-noon & 2-4pm Mon-Fri, 8am-noon Sat) Issues some of the world's speediest Vietnamese visas (for one month US$40), usually on the spot. A multiple-entry visa (US$50), also valid for a month, takes one day. Bring a passport photo.

Dangers & Annoyances

The most common problem is theft on the beaches while visitors are out swimming, often by drug addicts or children. Don't take anything valuable to the beach unless someone is keeping an eagle's eye on it.

Lone women – and lone men, too – should exercise caution when walking after dark on Occheuteal Beach (especially around Chiva's Shack and further southeast), on Otres Beach and along the poorly lit parts of Ekareach St (between the city centre and Victory Hill) as tourists have recently been the victims of muggings, one murder and at least one rape. Audacious daytime robberies and motorbike-jackings have been reported at the far end of Occheuteal Beach and on the Independence Beach road (2 Thnou St), between the Independence Hotel and the Sokha Beach Resort. A few violent incidents have also taken place along Victory Hill's main drag. The 'chicken farm' red-light district near the container port is notorious for drunken brawls, robberies and assaults.

As in Phnom Penh, drive-by bag snatchings occasionally happen and are especially dangerous when you're riding a *moto*. Shoulder bags are an attractive target, so on a *moto* or *remork* it's common sense to hold them tightly in front of you, especially at night. Never put a bag or purse in the front basket of a motorbike or bicycle. Motorcycle theft is also a popular criminal pastime in Sihanoukville, so if you rent wheels, make sure they come with a strong padlock.

The currents off Occheuteal can be deceptively strong, especially during the wet season.

One annoyance for locals is underdressed foreigners wandering about town. Cambodia is not Thailand; Khmers are generally more conservative than their neighbours. Just look at the Cambodians frolicking in the sea – most are fully dressed. Wearing bikinis on the beach is fine, but cover up elsewhere. Topless or nude bathing is a definite no-no.

Sights & Activities
BEACHES

Sihanoukville's sandy beaches are in a state of flux as developers move in and murky leases are signed to cash in on the tourism boom.

The best all-rounder is 4km-long **Occheuteal Beach**. In addition to sitting under parasols on rented chairs, you can get a foot massage, hire an inner tube (small/large 2000r/US$1), charter a banana boat (US$10 per circuit) or ruin everyone else's peace of mind with a jet ski (US$60 per hour). The ramshackle restaurant shacks, convenient for a drink (beers start at 2000r) or a grilled meal (Khmer mains cost US$2 to US$4), lack even short-term leases and may be removed by government bulldozers at any time. You might want to swim away from the rivulets of wastewater that flow from the shacks into the surf. Changing rooms (1000r) are available at Chiva's Shack.

Much of the southern section of the beach, about 1.5km of prime waterfront, has been walled off pending its transformation into another exclusive Sokha resort complex. If you see a low-flying helicopter, it's probably landing at the gargantuan beachfront **mansion** owned by Prime Minister Hun Sen.

A rocky strip at the northwestern end of Occheuteal has emerged as a happy,

THE LAST BATTLE OF THE VIETNAM WAR

The final bloody confrontation of the Vietnam War took place off the coast of Sihanoukville.

On 12 May 1975, two weeks after the fall of Saigon, Khmer Rouge forces, using captured US-made Swift boats, seized an American merchant ship, the SS *Mayagüez* (named after a city in Puerto Rico) while it was on a routine voyage from Hong Kong to Thailand. The vessel was anchored 50km southwest of Sihanoukville off **Koh Tang** – now a popular scuba-diving destination – while the 39 crew members were taken to Sihanoukville.

Determined to show resolve in the face of this 'act of piracy', President Gerald Ford ordered that the ship and its crew be freed. Naval planes from the US aircraft carrier *Coral Sea* bombed Sihanoukville's oil refinery and the Ream airbase, and Marines prepared for their first hostile boarding of a ship at sea since 1826.

On 15 May, Marines stormed aboard the *Mayagüez* like swashbuckling pirates but found it deserted. In parallel, airborne Marine units landed on Koh Tang. Thought to be lightly defended, the island turned out to have been fortified in anticipation of a Vietnamese attack (Vietnam also claimed the island). In the course of the assault, most of the US helicopters were destroyed or damaged and 15 Americans were killed.

Unbeknownst to the Americans, early on 15 May the Khmer Rouge had placed the crew of the *Mayagüez* aboard a Thai fishing boat and set it adrift – but the men weren't discovered by US ships until after the assault on Koh Tang had begun. In the chaotic withdrawal from the island, three Marines were accidentally left behind and, it is believed, later executed by the Khmer Rouge.

The Vietnam War Memorial in Washington DC, lists American war dead chronologically, which is why the names of the Marines who perished in the '*Mayagüez* Incident' appear at the bottom of the very last panel.

easy-going travellers' hang-out known as **Serendipity Beach**. At the atmospheric, mid-range bar-restaurants, waves lap just a few metres from the tables – very romantic, especially at sundown and in the evening.

At the southern end of Occheuteal Beach (the fishing village here was recently removed by the government), go up and over the small headland, **Phnom Som Nak Sdach** ('hill of the king's palace'), and you'll get to **Otres Beach**, a seemingly infinite strip of casuarinas and almost-empty sand that can just about give southern Thailand a run for its money. Sadly, Otres has been leased to the big boys, so much might change during the lifetime of this book. For now, the area is still pretty quiet, with a strip of mellow food shacks. **Otres Nautica** (☎ 092-230065; daylight hr year-round) is a laid-back, French-run outfit that rents sea kayaks (per hour/day US$3/15) and Hobie Cat sailing catamarans (US$10/50) that you can take out to nearby islands. They can also arrange snorkelling excursions on a fishing boat. **Hurricane Windsurfing** (☎ 017 471604) rents out kayaks and paddle boards.

To get to Otres Beach from Serendipity (about 5km), follow the road southeast along the beach and skirt the closed section; motorbikes can drive up and over the headland, but cars and *remorks* have to detour a bit inland. From the city centre, you can take Omui St from Psar Leu east out of town for about 7km; much of this route is strewn with boulders that make it impassable to *remorks* and a rough ride for passenger cars.

The hippy buzz is gone, but under Russian management, **Victory Beach** has found a new niche as a refuge for expats who aren't in the mood for Occheuteal's busy backpacker scene. Clean, hassle-free and family-friendly, the area and its midrange beach eateries get very quiet after sundown – despite the best efforts of **Airport** (p219), a flashy new nightspot which, unlike the real airport, actually has an airplane: a genuine **Antonov An-24 turboprop** whose grounding is a blessing to air travellers everywhere as no one will try to fly the contraption ever again. Visible offshore is a tiny, mysterious, Russian-owned **pleasure island** (www.miraxresort.com).

About 1.5km to the southwest, next to a shady grove, is **Lamherkay Beach**, also known as Hawaii Beach. It's hugely popular with car-owning Khmers on weekends and holidays but quiet on weekdays. Thatch-roofed restaurants serve seafood and other BBQ dishes. Changing rooms are available for 1000r. **Koh Pos** (Koh Puos; Snake Island), the island 800m offshore, has been leased by Russians with big resort plans, which is why it's being linked to the mainland by a 32m-high concrete bridge.

Further southwest, on the tip of the headland, is tiny **Koh Pos Beach**, nice and shady but with sometimes-rough waters.

Southeast of here, **Independence Beach** (7-Chann Beach), named after the hotel that has dominated the landscape for almost 50 years, is a good stretch of clean sand. At press time, it was mostly fenced off pending massive development by powerful people. The only open sections are below the Independence Hotel and opposite the Sea Breeze Guesthouse.

Midway between Independence and Serendipity lies 1.5km-long **Sokha Beach**, perhaps Sihanoukville's prettiest stretch. Except for a short public area at the eastern end, it is now part of the exclusive Sokha Beach Resort (p217). Tourists are welcome to enjoy the sand but are expected to buy something to drink or eat. Except on particularly crowded high-season days, nonguests can use the hotel's huge **swimming pool** – and, of course, the nearby beach – for US$4 (US$6 on holidays or when a cruise ship is in port; 50% off for children under 12). Privatising the beach may have been a colossal act of thievery perpetrated on the entire Cambodian public, but while you swim here your stuff will be safe – if there are any hoodlums skulking around here, they aren't the small-time kind.

About 7km northeast of the ferry port is casuarina-lined **Prek Treng Beach**, also known as Hun Sen Beach. Largely deserted (for now), it is marked by a number of Khmer-style open pavilions and is popular around sunset with Cambodian families and couples in the mood for romance.

ISLANDS

More than a dozen tropical islands, some with gorgeous, blissfully empty beaches, dot the waters off Sihanoukville. Word has it that they've all been leased to international developers with dreams of creating the next Ko Chang or Ko Samui, so hurry if you want to see them in their natural state.

Perhaps Sihanoukville's best getaway (though someone has called it 'paradise with insects'), **Koh Rung Samloem** (US$10 one-way, 2½ hours), 10km from end to end, boasts a

SOUTH COAST

large heart-shaped gulf, Saracen Bay, as well as good beaches on its northern and southwestern ends. The old French road network is overgrown, but you can fish, snorkel and take short treks. The island's amazing wildlife ranges from macaques, black squirrels and sea eagles to oversized salamanders, lizards and iguanas. You can stay at **Lazy Beach Bungalows** (☎ 016 214211; www.lazybeachcambodia.com; office on Serendipity St; bungalow US$25-30), on the southwest coast, whose 12 bungalows come with bathrooms, and balconies with hammocks. **EcoSea Dive** (☎ 934347, 012 606646; www.ecoseadive.com; offices at 225 Ekareach St, Rd to Serendipity & Serendipity Beach; d US$30) has five en-suite bungalows.

Just north of Koh Rung Samloem, 15km-long **Koh Rung** (Koh Rong; US$10 one-way, 2½ hours) has lots of deserted little beaches, a superb 5km beach on the southwestern coast, trekking trails and three hamlets. Island wildlife includes macaques, hornbills, kestrels, sea eagles and, offshore, a very rare kind of nudibranch (sea slug). The **Dive Shop** (☎ 933664; www.diveshopcambodia.com) has hillside **bungalows** (dm US$10, d US$15, 3-5 people US$35) with en-suite bathrooms and electricity from 6pm to 10.30pm. Another option is **Sok San Beach Bungalows** (horn socheata@yahoo.com; ☎ 099-605255, 097-6772424; r US$10, bungalow US$15), on a long, palm-fringed beach. Big changes are planned, with a ring road and airport on the drawing boards.

Off the coast of Ream National Park, **Koh Ta Kiev** is home to uber-rustic **Jonty's Jungle Camp** (☎ 092-502374; www.jontysjunglecamp.com), where visitors have the choice of hammocks (US$6) and tree houses (US$10 to US$22). Another option is **Koh Ta Kiev Beach Bungalow Resort** (☎ 011 708795, 012 495446).

In preparation for resort development, **Koh Russei** (Bamboo Island; one hour by boat) is set to be cleared of bungalows.

Trips to the islands can be arranged through various travel agencies (p212), dive shops (below) and guesthouses.

The day and overnight island cruises offered by **Sun-Tours** (☎ 016 396201; www.suntours-cambodia.com), with departures from Victory Beach, get rave reviews.

DIVING

The reefs around Sihanoukville are rich in corals, sponges and all sorts of sea life, including eels, anemones, stingrays and dolphins. Some of the finest diving – visibility is often phenomenal – is around the distant,

uninhabited islands of **Koh Tang** (see p213) and **Koh Prins**, which require an overnight trip, though there's also decent diving closer in around **Koh Rung** and **Koh Rung Samloem** (two hours one-way).

Marine Conservation Cambodia (www.marineconservationcambodia.org) is working to protect the area's reefs and coastal breeding grounds.

Reliable operators:

Claude Diving Centre (☎ 934100, 012 824870; www.bestcambodia.com; above 2 Thnou St) Claude has been exploring the waters off Sihanoukville for 15 years now and specialises in longer trips to distant reefs.

Coasters (☎ 933776; www.cambodia-beach.com; Serendipity St) Offers PowerSnorkel diving (US$10 per hour), great for beginners because you don't need dive certification, and boat trips to Koh Ta Kiev (US$10).

Dive Shop (☎ 933664; www.diveshopcambodia.com; Rd to Serendipity; ☷ 7am-8pm) Cambodia's 2nd PADI five-star dive centre is also a National Geographic Dive Center. Offers one-day and sleep-aboard diving trips and has bungalows on Koh Rung.

EcoSea Dive (☎ 934347; www.ecoseadive.com; 225 Ekareach St, City Centre; ☷ 10am-7pm) Offers PADI and SSI courses, one-/two-dive packages (US$45/65), snorkelling excursions (US$20) and two-day snorkelling trips (US$49) with an overnight on Koh Rung Samloem. Also has offices on the Rd to Serendipity and at Serendipity Beach.

Scuba Nation Diving Center (☎ 012 604680; www.divecambodia.com; Serendipity St) The 1st PADI five-star dive centre in Cambodia. Also offers National Geographic Diver certification. Highly professional instructors with first-class equipment offer classes in English, Swedish, French and Dutch.

MONKEY BUSINESS

On most days in the late afternoon, three troupes of **tame monkeys** gather on 2 Thnou St, behind and on the chain-link fence enclosing the grounds of the Independence Hotel, hoping to score peanuts and bananas from passing humans. Locals often stop by with their kids, generating a great deal of mirth and mutual interprimate admiration.

WAT LEU

Spectacular views of almost the entire city – and gorgeous sunset panoramas – await at Wat Leu (Wat Chhnothean), situated on a peaceful, forested hilltop 1.5km northwest of the city centre (next to three red-and-white radio telecom towers). The small museum opens for groups.

From the city centre, a *moto* ride due north up the hill costs US$1 to 6000r. *Remorks* have to take the long way around and so cost US$4.

MASSAGE
Sihanoukville has no shortage of dodgy places offering 'happy end' rubs, but there are also some genuine massage venues, some staffed by disabled locals:

Relax (☎ 011 686987; Rd to Serendipity; per hr US$8-18; ☽ 10am-9.30pm) English-owned and managed, this place's Khmer, lavender, jasmine oil and foot massages get great reviews. Will soon offer manicures and pedicures (US$5 to US$10). Absolutely no hanky-panky.

Seeing Hands Massage 3 (☎ 012 799016; 95 Ekareach St; per hr US$6; ☽ 8am-9pm; ☒) The two masseurs and four masseuses who work here, some of them English-speaking, are blind.

Starfish Bakery & Café (☎ 012 952011; behind 62 7 Makara St, City Centre; per hr US$6-10; ☽ 7am-6pm) Blind and disabled masseuses, trained by Western massage therapists, perform Khmer, Thai, oil, foot and Indian head massages. Profits go towards social projects.

From November to May, the **Fitness & Boxing Center** (below) offers one- to five-day massage courses with a professional masseur from France.

COOKING
Traditional Khmer Cookery (☎ 092-738615; khmercookery@hotmail.com; 335 Ekareach St; whole day per person US$25; ☽ 10am-5pm Mon-Sat) Teaches traditional culinary techniques (four courses) in classes with no more than eight participants. Special requests (eg veggie) are happily accommodated. Specialities include squid with Kampot pepper, whole steamed fish with sweet-and-sour sauce, and pomelo salad with prawns.

BREWERY VISIT
Every single can and bottle of Angkor Beer, Klang Beer, Bayon Beer, Angkor Extra Stout and Black Panther Premium Stout was brewed at the **Cambrew Brewery** (☎ 939618; www.cambodianbeer.com, www.angkorbeer.com.kh; NH4), which offers free **tasting sessions** (☽ 3-5pm Wed) and **tours**. At the time of research these activities were suspended due to swine flu (H1N1); guesthouses can provide updates and details.

FITNESS
The French-run **Fitness & Boxing Center** (Centre de Fitness et de Boxe Asiatique; ☎ 015 620534; Boray Kamakor St; per day incl aerobics US$3.50; ☽ Oct-Jun 5am-9pm, Jul-Sep 6am-8pm), in a villa 2km northwest of the bus station, is a fully outfitted fitness club with 165 machines, free weights, aerobics (most days at 5.15pm) and Khmer and Thai boxing classes (US$4).

Sleeping
Sihanoukville now has scores of guesthouses and hotels, only a fraction of which appear below. Prices quoted are for the high season (approximately November to March); rates drop during the rainy season and, at some establishments, skyrocket on Khmer holidays.

SERENDIPITY & OCCHEUTEAL
The area between Serendipity Beach and the Golden Lions Roundabout is Sihanoukville's main traveller hang-out. You pay a premium to stay right on the water. Two and three blocks inland from Occheuteal Beach, 23 Tola St and 1 Kanda St are home to a growing assortment of guesthouses and midrange hotels.

Utopia (☎ 934319; www.utopiacambodia.com; cnr Rd to Serendipity & 14 Milthona St; dm Nov-Jun US$2, Jul-Oct free, r US$10; ☐ ☎ ☒) Dorm beds – there are 26 – don't come any cheaper. Free lockers available.

Chiva's Shack (☎ 012 360911; www.chivasshack.com; Occheuteal Beach; r US$3-4) A shambolic, on-the-beach crash pad with an old-time hippy vibe. Promises 'lazy days, party nights'. Bathrooms are shared. The rough-hewn restaurant is open 24 hours.

our pick Monkey Republic (☎ 012 490290; www.monkey-republic.com; monkeyrepubliccambodia@yahoo.co.uk; Rd to Serendipity; r US$6-9; ☐) A favourite hang-out of the young backpacker crowd, this lively, British-run establishment has 26 bright blue bungalows set around two banana-tree-shaded courtyards. All come with simple furnishings, fans, mosquito nets and verandahs.

Mick & Craig's (☎ 012 727740; www.mickandcraigs.com; Rd to Serendipity; r US$7-10; ☎) Set behind its popular restaurant, Mick & Craig's 17 neat, pastel rooms are straightforward and practical. Excellent value.

Orchidée Guesthouse (☎ 933639; www.orchidee-guesthouse.com; 23 Tola St; d US$13-28, tr US$30-40; ☒ ☐ ☎ ☒) A delightful 10m pool surrounded by chairs and palms is the centrepiece of this restful place. Its 69 well-kept rooms – some poolside, others bungalow-style – have air-con, hot water, a fridge and well-designed bathrooms. Prices include breakfast (except for the US$13 rooms). Excellent value.

Coasters (☎ 933776; www.cambodia-beach.com; Serendipity St; r with fan US$15-25, with air-con from US$25; ❌ 🖥 🛜) The 17 solid rooms and bungalows, many with verandahs for some quality contemplation, are spread across the hillside above the beach, although the bar and restaurant run right to the water's edge. Has a magical atmosphere in the early evening.

New Sea View Villa (☎ 092-759753; www.sihanoukville-hotel.com; Serendipity St; d with fan/air-con from US$17/20; ❌ closed Sep; ❌ 🖥 🛜) Has 16 clean, spacious rooms with spring mattresses, all meticulously maintained. A favourite with in-the-know expats.

Cloud 9 Bungalows (☎ 012 479365; www.cloud9bungalows.com; r US$20-30) The last bungalow complex on Serendipity Beach has a cosy tropical bar and seven rustic, Khmer-style bungalows with fans, glassless windows, mosquito nets and ocean-view balconies. Prices drop by 25% to 50% in the low season. Access is also possible from 2 Thnou St.

our pick Coolabah Resort (☎ 017 678218; www.coolabah-hotel.com; 14 Milthona St; r US$45-70; ❌ 🖥 🛜) A fine new addition to Sihanoukville's accommodation scene, this friendly, Aussie-owned establishment offers four-star quality, including top-notch mattresses, linens and soundproofing. Among the amenities: a plunge pool and a lounge-style bar.

Reef Resort (☎ 934281; www.reefresort.com.kh; Rd to Serendipity; d US$42.50-47.50, q US$65-70; ❌ 🛜 🎬) The 14 good-sized rooms afford views of a 12.5m pool, surrounded by a patio and lots of luscious purple orchids. Prices include breakfast. Bus station pick-up is available.

VICTORY HILL & BEACH

Victory Hill (Weather Station Hill), the original backpackers' area, has lost its hippie vibe and today most of the lodgers here are middle-aged males. The places listed below, though, are isolated from the hullabaloo of the Hill's mildly sleazy main strip.

Green Mood (☎ 011 917251; r US$2-12) Run by three young Italians, this place has 10 simple, clean fan rooms; the cheapest come with shared bathrooms.

Sunset Garden Guesthouse (☎ 012 562004; d US$5-10; ❌) Run by an enthusiastic woman of a certain age, this spotless, family-run hostelry, in an Italianate house surrounded by a neatly tended garden, has 14 spacious, spotless rooms.

Bungalow Village (☎ 012 490293; bungalow village@hotmail.com; r US$6-15) Set in a hillside garden shaded by tropical trees, this classic backpacker hangout is just 200m from the beach and has an old-fashioned chill-out zone where you can lounge on boulders like a lizard. The eight basic bungalows have wood-plank walls, glassless windows, fans and hot water.

CITY CENTRE

The bustling city centre, preferred by many long-termers, is convenient if you're travelling by public transport and has lots of banks and businesses as well as the main market.

Geckozy Guesthouse (☎ 012 495825; www.geckozy-guesthouse.com; r US$5-8) Six basic rooms in an old wooden house on a quiet side street.

our pick Small Hotel (☎ 934330; www.thesmallhotel.info; r US$13-18; ❌ 🖥 🛜) Run by a cheerful Swedish-Khmer couple, this guesthouse is as cosy as sitting in front of a fireplace on a snowy Scandinavian night. The 11 spotless rooms have air-con, hot water and fridge. Often full from November to March, so book ahead.

INDEPENDENCE BEACH

Sea Breeze Guesthouse (☎ 934205, 077-970403; www.seabreezecambodia.com; 2 Thnou St; r US$20-40; ❌ 🖥 🛜) Equidistant (3.5km) from the city centre, Victory Beach and Serendipity Beach, this Aussie-run place offers peace, quiet and 16 spacious, simply furnished rooms. Offers free pick-up and free transport to/from anywhere in town.

Independence Hotel (☎ 934300; www.independencehotel.net; 2 Thnou St; r from US$140; ❌ 🖥 🛜 🎬) Opened in 1963, this striking seven-storey hotel still has the jet-set feel of Sihanouk's movie-star heyday. After years of abandonment and neglect, it was reopened in 2007 and now has 52 classic rooms with sea views, landscaped gardens and a private beach. Beach-adjacent bungalows are being added.

SOKHA BEACH

Sokha Beach Resort (☎ 935999; www.sokhahotels.com; 2 Thnou St; r US$200-220, ste US$250-1000; ❌ 🖥 🛜 🎬) This opulent Khmer-style complex has a 1.5km private beach, a huge pool with its own tiny tropical island, and a children's playground. Service is not up to true ultraluxury standards, but Phnom

Penh families with kids love the place. Has 210 rooms, suites and bungalows (200 more will be added in 2010). Promotional rates are available online.

Eating

Sihanoukville offers an impressive array of good-value dining; this chapter offers just a taste of what's available.

SERENDIPITY & OCCHEUTEAL

The beachfront tables right on Serendipity Beach, lit with candles in the evening, are hard to beat for atmosphere, especially around sunset. Cheaper fare, including lots of grilled options, is on offer in the beach shacks along Occheuteal Beach. Two blocks inland, 12 Tola St is developing into a restaurant zone, with a plethora of BBQ places in the evening.

The beach attracts vendors selling everything from pineapples to fried minilobsters served with salt, pepper and lemon juice. You may find it all a bit of a hard sell if you're just trying to relax on the sand, but provided you bargain, this can be an inexpensive way to snack your way through the day.

K2 (☎ 011 304447; Occheuteal Beach; mains US$2-4) Run by a fellow from Gujarat, this basic beachside eatery serves inexpensive Pakistani, Indian and Mogul cuisine, including veggie and halal meat options.

Happy Herb Pizza (☎ 012 632198; 23 Tola St; small/medium/large from US$3/5.50/8.50; ☽ 7am-11pm) Serves Khmer dishes (US$1.50 to US$3) and 23 kinds of pizza, all available 'happy' (ie ganja-fortified).

Rainy Season Pizza (☎ 092-583372; 14 Milthona St; ☽ 24hr) Recently relocated from Victory Hill, this French-owned place serves succulent pizzas (slice US$2, pizza US$5 to US$6). Free delivery.

our pick **New Sea View Villa** (☎ 092-759753; Serendipity St; mains US$4-7; ☽ 8am-4pm & 6-10pm) Renowned for serving up some of city's tastiest cuisine. Dinner specialities include wasabi prawns, baked scallops in wine sauce, *magret* of duck in raspberry sauce and, for dessert, carrot cake, tiramisu and crème brûlée. Has good veggie options such as lasagne.

our pick **Happa** (☎ 934380; Rd to Serendipity; mains US$4-7; ☽ 5pm-midnight) Authentic teppan-yaki with a variety of sauce options is tastefully served amid tropical decor with Japanese touches. Under the same roof, Ku Kai

(☎ 012 593339; open 5pm to 9pm Tuesday to Sunday) serves sashimi and tempura dishes (US$4.75).

Angelo's (☎ 011 309014; 23 Tola St; mains US$4-13.50; ☽ 4pm-midnight) Serves excellent grilled prawns, calamari, lobster, barracuda, Australian T-bone steak and the house speciality, Coca Cola ribs (pork ribs marinated in the famous fizzy drink, cooked and then barbecued).

VICTORY HILL & BEACH

Even if you're staying elsewhere in town, it's worth checking out this lively area (including adjacent bits of Ekareach St) for its wide range of tasty and inexpensive cuisines.

Koh Lin (☎ 012 588625; Victory Hill; mains 5000-26,000r; ☽ 9am-11pm) Serves good-value Cambodian, Vietnamese and French bistro classics at five candle-lit tables. Dessert options include profiteroles, crème caramel and crêpes. The name is a play on a play on the French word *colline* (hill).

Green Mood (☎ 011 917251; Victory Hill; mains US$3-4; ☽ 11.30am-3pm & 6-11pm) Serves 15 kinds of authentic Italian pasta – no surprise as the owners are from Bergamo.

Brown's (☎ 012 930526; Victory Beach; mains US$3.25-5; ☽ 9am-sunset) Right on the sand. Popular for its Asian dishes and burgers.

Snake House (☎ 012 673805; www.snake-house.com, in Russian; mains US$3.50-9.50; ☽ 7am-10pm or 11pm; ☏) At this truly unique establishment diners enjoy Russian cuisine and sushi at glass-topped tables with live serpents living inside (the snakes are kept here to produce antivenins). The complex includes a guesthouse, a bar with a small pool (US$1) for cavorting, caged birds and iguanas, and a crocodile farm (US$3; free for diners) – one false step and the toothy reptiles will eat as well as you did.

CITY CENTRE

In the evening, a row of informal restaurants appears on the east side of Sophamongkol St just north of Ekareach St. At the popular **food stalls** (cnr Omui & 7 Makara Sts; mains 3500r) – most numerous in the evening – a block north of blue-roofed Psar Leu (the main market), options include barbecue chicken, rice porridge or noodles with chicken, and a variety of Cambodian desserts.

our pick **Chom Ka Spey** (☎ 016 940171; mains small/large 8000r/15,000r; ☽ 10am or 11am-about 11pm) Known as Cabbage Farm Restaurant to in-the-know expats, this place gets rave reviews for its seafood and spicy seasonings. An authentic Khmer dining experience. Look for an Angkor Beer sign with writing in Khmer and Chinese.

Holy Cow (☎ 012 478510; 83 Ekareach St; mains US$2-4.50; 🕙 9.30am-11pm) At this chic-funky cafe-restaurant, options include bagels with cream cheese, pasta, sandwiches made with homemade bread (US$2.50 to US$3.50), and a good selection of veggie options, including two vegan desserts, both involving chocolate. The small upstairs shop sells M'lop Tapang products (p220).

Starfish Bakery & Café (☎ 012 952011; www.starfishcambodia.org; behind 62 7 Makara St; mains US$3.50-4.50; 🕙 7am-6pm) Tucked down a red-earth alley, this relaxing, NGO-run garden cafe serves filling Western breakfasts, light lunches (sandwiches, quiche, fajitas, salads) and teatime treats such as brownies and apple tarts. Veggie options are legion. Income goes to sustainable development projects.

OTHER AREAS
Treasure Island (☎ 016 876618; Koh Pos Beach; mains US$2-15; 🕙 10am-2pm & 4-9pm) Wealthy Chinese with a hankering for 'Hong Kong–style' fish and seafood love this isolated, hangarlike seafoodery. Most everything is fresh and housed in tanks – just point to what you want and the staff will pluck it out. Prices are reasonable, but read the fine print – some items are sold by weight (sea snails go for up to US$18 per kilo). Serves two dozen mostly French wines.

our pick **Chez Claude** (☎ 934100; www.bestcambodia.com; above 2 Thnou St; mains US$3.50-14; 🕙 7am-11pm or midnight) Reached by its own miniature cable car, this all-wood eyrie – perched high above Sokha Beach – has an outstanding reputation for French, Vietnamese and Cambodian cuisine, especially seafood. The wines are mainly French. Worth the trip out here.

SELF-CATERING
In the city centre, fruit and veggie stalls can be found at **Psar Leu** (7 Makara St) – the vendors across the street, next to the Kampot taxis, are open 24 hours – and at the smaller and slightly more expensive **Psar Pinechikam** (Boray Kamakor St cnr St 109). **Samudera Supermarket** (☎ 933441; 64 7 Makara St, City Centre; 🕙 7am-9pm) stocks Western edibles, including cheese and wine.

Drinking
There's no shortage of venues to quaff locally brewed Angkor Beer, available on draught for as little as US$0.50.

SERENDIPITY & OCCHEUTEAL
Some of the food shacks along Occheuteal Beach stay open very late (the bar at Chiva's Shack is open 24 hours). For something a bit more stylish, try the restaurant-bars along Serendipity Beach. **Golden Lion Plaza** (1 Kanda St), an artificial alley with 10 foreign-owned bars, makes it easy to bar-hop.

Monkey Republic (☎ 012 490290; www.monkey-republic.com; Rd to Serendipity) A great place to meet fellow travellers. Has a chill-out area upstairs.

Utopia (☎ 934319; www.utopiacambodia.com; cnr Rd to Serendipity & 14 Milthona St; 🕙 9.30am-2am or later; 🖵 🛜) A backpackers' party bar with a pool, a pole that spouts fire, and really big bashes. Happy hour is from 9pm to 10pm.

Aquarium (☎ 016 410806; www.cambodia-beach.com; Serendipity Beach; mains US$3-5.50; 🕙 7am-9.30pm, bar until late) A colourfully lit bar and BBQ restaurant with live blues and country music three times a week.

VICTORY BEACH
This area gets pretty quiet after sundown but **Airport** (🕙 until midnight), a Russian-owned bar-disco-diner (mains US$4.50 to US$7) that opened in late 2008, is trying to change all that. A hangarlike space with one side open to the sea, its most surprising feature is an Antonov An-24 turboprop whose cockpit you can visit. Don't bring cameras, knives, guns or hand grenades, all forbidden by a sign at the entrance.

VICTORY HILL
The Victory Hill nightlife scene has recently gone a bit sleazy, but the area still has some of the city's best pubs and bars.

Retox Bar (☎ 012 819451; 🕙 May-Nov 2pm-1am, Dec-Apr 10am-about 2am) A favourite of local expats, this poster-plastered pub often has live music (from 8.30pm) and jam sessions (instruments available). The food is 100% veggie.

Corner Bar (☎ 934461; 🕙 noon-2am Tue-Sun) A friendly, British-owned sports bar with pub food, including very fine pizzas. Screens rugby and football on four TVs and, weather permitting, organises beach cricket (4pm Monday) and football matches (4.30pm Tuesday).

SOUTH COAST

CITY CENTRE
Gelato Italiano (49 7 Makara St; ⏱ 8am-9pm) Run by students from Sihanoukville's Don Bosco Hotel School, this Italian-style cafe serves espresso, latte, ice coffee and banana splits (US$3), as well as its creamy namesake (2000r per scoop) and light meals (mains US$2.50 to US$5).

Entertainment
Top Cat Cinema (☎ 011 617799; Rd to Serendipity; tickets US$3; 🎬) is a very popular minicinema that shows films on an 8m hi-def screen. Has cosy satellite chairs and powerful air-con.

Shopping
M'lop Tapang Gift Shop (☎ 097-9427387; www.mlop tapang.org; Serendipity St) Run by a local NGO that works with at-risk children, this shop sells bags, scarves and gift items made by street kids (and their families) so that they can attend school instead of peddling on the beach. Several other handicrafts shops are right nearby.

Rajana Crafts (www.rajanacrafts.org; behind 62 7 Makara St; ⏱ 7am-6pm) A nonprofit shop on the grounds of the Starfish Bakery & Café that sells fair-trade jewellery, clothing, accessories and crafts. Profits are invested in teaching handicraft skills to young Cambodians.

Getting There & Away
National Highway 4 (NH4), which links Sihanoukville to Phnom Penh (230km), is in excellent condition thanks to an upgrade financed by the US government – which begs the question: if it was built with American aid money, why the tolls? Due to heavy lorry traffic and the prevalence of high-speed overtaking on blind corners, this is one of Cambodia's most dangerous highways, and it's doubly dicey around dusk and at night.

NH3 to Kampot (105km) and NH48 to Krong Koh Kong (220km) and the Thailand border (230km) are also in tip-top shape.

AIR
Temple-beach combo holidays will be an easy option when Sihanoukville International Airport (IATA code: KOS), 18km east of town, again has flights to/from Siem Reap. International flights to/from Vietnam's Phu Quoc Island, Korea and Malaysia may also be on the cards.

BOAT
Except in stormy weather, **ferries** (☎ 016 851934, 012 857735; Cambodians/foreigners US$12.50/15) to Koh Sdach (p205) depart from the ferry port, 3km north of the city centre, at 1pm on alternate days. Near the ferry pier you can see wooden fishing boats (US$8000, not including the motor) being built by hand.

At the time of research ferries were no longer going to Krong Koh Kong (see p199), but rumour has it there may be some sailings in the dry season.

BUS
Ten bus companies, with staff who speak basic English, have ticket offices at the shabby new **bus and taxi station** (Omui St), which is little more than a trash-strewn gravel parking lot. Some companies charge foreigners

---

SINS OF COMMISSION, SINS OF OMISSION
At Sihanoukville's new bus station, only members of the official 'motodup association' (read: cartel) are allowed to pick up arriving passengers (independent drivers sent to fetch someone must show their charge's name). As a result, you may be quoted inflated prices for onward local transport. Bargaining is likely to be futile – if you don't agree to the set price (usually 8000r to the beaches) no one else will take you. Walk out to the main street, though, and you should be able find a *moto* driver who'll accept the market rate (4000r), though first you may have to shake the possibly persistent driver the cartel have assigned you according to a rotation system. Confrontations between independents and cartel drivers sometime develop. The situation with *remorks* – ideal for travel with a big pack – is similar.

Many guesthouses pay US$2 to *moto* drivers who bring them customers, but some places pay drivers far higher sums – US$4 or even US$5 – to send custom their way, so if you've just arrived, getting your *moto* guy to take you where *you* want may turn into a battle of wills. If your chosen hostelry is one that won't ante up, don't be surprised to hear that it's closed, has contaminated water or is 'full of prostitutes'.

MOTORBIKES & THE POLICE

Foreigners are again being allowed to rent motorbikes in Sihanoukville, but a new difficulty has cropped up: the traffic police have taken up the enforcement of certain laws with uncharacteristic diligence inspired, say locals, by the lure of revenue from on-the-spot 'fines'.

At surprise roadblocks, police verify that motorbikes are equipped with two side mirrors and that drivers (though not riders) are wearing helmets. Foreigners are especially attractive targets, both because they can be assessed heftier fines (locals pay US$1 for minor infractions and 5000r for riding bare-headed) and because they can also be fined for lacking a valid Cambodian driving licence (international driving licences are not recognised). The confiscation of motorbikes from people who refuse to render unto Caesar is not unknown.

Favourite spots for surprise police roadblocks include the Golden Lions Roundabout and the intersection next to the Caltex petrol station on Ekareach St. Veteran expats have observed that roadblocks are rarely seen in rainy weather and multiply before major holidays, for which cops, like everyone else, need cash. Some rental outfits have 'agreements' with the police: in exchange for certain 'gifts', traffic cops refrain from demanding that tourists driving their particular motorbikes carry Cambodian drivers licences.

---

more than Khmers. Bookings made through guesthouses, hotels and travel agencies incur a commission.

The cheapest services to Phnom Penh (four to 4½ hours) are offered by **Capitol Tour** (☎ 934042; bus & taxi station), which charges 13,000r and has five departures from 7.30am to 1.30pm, and **Phnom Penh Sorya** (☎ 933888; www.ppsoryatransport.com; bus & taxi station), which charges US$4 and has seven buses from 7am to 2pm. Departures are limited between 9am and 12.15pm and nonexistent after 2.15pm. It is usually possible to board buses at these two companies' hassle-free city-centre offices, situated at 167 Ekareach St and 235 Ekareach St, respectively.

Virak-Buntham (☎ 016 754358; bus & taxi station) has an 8am bus to Krong Koh Kong (US$13, four hours) via the Koh Kong Conservation Corridor, Ko Chang (US$27, eight to 10 hours), Ko Samet (US$35, 11 hours) and Bangkok (US$35, 11 to 12 hours). **Bun Thou Express** (☎ 016 6077727; bus & taxi station) also goes to Krong Koh Kong and Thailand, but at the time of research was working with Virak-Buntham.

At 8pm, Virak-Buntham runs a red-eye special to Siem Reap (US$20, 10 hours, arrival time 6am), with a stop in Phnom Penh (US$7, four hours, arrival time midnight).

SHARE TAXI

Some share-taxi drivers seem to think they're Michael Schumacher, so if you don't like blind overtaking you may want to wait for a bus.

Share taxis to Phnom Penh (four hours) congregate next to the new bus station's triumphal gate. Few drivers speak any English. Expect to pay US$5 for a cramped seat or US$40 for a taxi to call your own. Cramped minibuses cost 15,000r. To get to Krong Koh Kong, you may have to change at Plauv Bombek Sre Ambel, the junction where NH4 meets NH48.

Share taxis (US$4) and crowded minibuses (US$2) to Kampot, most frequent in the morning, leave from an open lot across 7 Makara St from Psar Leu. A private taxi costs US$25 to Kampot and US$50 to the Vietnamese border. Travel agencies and guesthouses can provide details on shuttle services to Kampot (about US$7).

Getting Around

Some hotels and guesthouses offer free pick-up at the bus station if you book ahead.

BICYCLE

Cycling is a pleasant way to explore Sihanoukville. Basic city bikes can be rented at two bookshops, **Mister Heinz Books** (☎ 097-8947502; 219 Ekareach St, City Centre; per day US$1.50; ☯ 9am-6pm or later) and **Q&A** (☎ 012 598072; 95 Ekareach St, City Centre; per day US$1.50; ☯ 7.30am-7.30pm). Mick & Craig's (p216) is planning to rent proper mountain bikes for US$6 to US$8 a day; Craig is happy to provide information on cycle-touring.

MOTO & REMORK

Sihanoukville's *moto* drivers are notorious for aggressively touting passers-by and – more than anywhere else in Cambodia – shamelessly trying to overcharge, so haggle hard (with a smile) over the price before setting out. Expect to pay a bit more than in Phnom Penh.

From the city centre, a *moto* costs 3000r to US$1 to Victory Hill and Serendipity, Occheuteal and Victory Beaches, and US$1.50 to US$2 to the ferry dock. Travel from Occheuteal to Victory Hill costs 6000r to US$2. From Otres Beach, *motos* cost US$1.50 to US$2 to Serendipity and US$2 to US$3 to the city centre. Expect to pay a bit more (2000r or so) at night.

From Occheuteal, *remorks* cost US$2 to US$3 to the city centre (drivers sometimes ask for double that) and US$3 to US$4 to Victory Hill.

Hiring a *moto* (including the driver) for the day costs US$10 plus petrol; a *remork* is about US$20 a day.

Many guesthouses can arrange a simple motorbike for about US$5 a day. If you're driving yourself, be especially careful at intersections equipped with traffic lights (first seen here in 2008), through which locals are in the habit of driving even when the light is red. Actually stopping for a red light may so surprise locals that you risk getting hit from behind.

AROUND SIHANOUKVILLE
Ream National Park
ឧទ្យានជាតិរាម

Just 18km east of Sihanoukville, Ream National Park – also known as Preah Sihanouk National Park – comprises 150 sq km of primary forests (mostly lowland evergreen forest and mangrove swamps) and 60 sq km of marine habitats.

The park is home to breeding populations of a number of regionally and globally endangered birds of prey, including the Brahminy kite, grey-headed fish-eagle and white-bellied sea-eagle – look for them soaring over **Prek Toeuk Sap Estuary**, which is salty in the dry season and freshwater in the wet. Endangered birds that feed on the mudflats include the lesser adjutant, milky stork and painted stork. The park's more common feathered residents include the great egret, little egret, woolly-necked stork, black-capped kingfisher and stork-billed kingfisher.

Despite its protected status, Ream is gravely endangered by planned tourist development, especially along its coastline. By visiting, you can demonstrate that the park, in its natural state, is not only priceless to

humanity, but also a valuable economic resource for Sihanoukville.

SIGHTS, ACTIVITIES & SLEEPING

Invigorating **jungle walks** led by rangers – most, but not all, speak English – are easy to arrange (hiking unaccompanied is not allowed) at **park headquarters** (☎ 016 767686, 012 875096; ☉ 8am-6pm), facing the airport, which has a small display on local flora and fauna. A two- to three-hour walk from the **Keng Kong Recreation Site** (9.5km south of the park's HQ) to the **Andoung Tuek Cascades** costs US$6 per person; pond swimming is possible during the wet season. A hike into the park's mountainous interior, lasting up to five or six hours, costs US$4 per hour per participant. It's best (but not obligatory) to phone ahead. The income generated goes to help protect the park.

Ranger-led **boat trips** (1-5 people US$45, 6 or more people per person US$8) on the Prek Toeuk Sap Estuary and its mangrove channels, lasting at least five hours, are another option. You can often spot monkeys, dolphins and a variety of birds, in addition to sunbathing, swimming and snorkelling (equipment hire is US$2).

In the coconut-shaded fishing village of **Thmor Thom** (population 47 families), the national park has a ranger post known as **Dolphin Station** because, from November to May, you can often spot dolphins, especially in the morning. It's possible to overnight here in an overwater **bungalow** (per person US$5) with outside toilets and no electricity; meals are available from villagers. The village is a 25-minute walk from **Koh Sampoach Beach**, the park's finest.

Ream National Park's territory includes two islands with some fine snorkelling, **Koh Thmei** and – just off Vietnam's Phu Quoc Island – **Koh Seh**. In the dry season, if it's not too windy, you can get out there by wooden motorboat (US$55 return to Koh Thmei, US$65 return to Koh Seh for up to 15 people) from the Prek Toeuk Sap ranger station.

Several Sihanoukville travel agencies (p212) offer day trips to the park for about US$20, including a boat ride, a jungle walk and lunch.

GETTING THERE & AROUND

To get to Ream National Park, 18km east of Sihanoukville, take NH4 to Sihanoukville International Airport; the park headquarters is 700m south of NH4, right across the road from the green-roofed terminal building.

A return trip from Sihanoukville by *moto* should cost US$7 to US$15; the price depends on how well the driver speaks English and how long you stay. A private taxi costs US$25 to US$35 for the day. A coastal road linking the park with Otres Beach and Sihanoukville is planned.

Boats can be arranged either at park headquarters or at their departure point, the Prek Toeuk Sap Ranger Station, at the NH4 bridge that's situated about 3km past the airport.

Kbal Chhay Cascades

Thanks to their appearance in *Pos Keng Kong* (The Giant Snake; 2000), the most successful Cambodian film of the post-civil-war era, these **cascades** (admission US$1) on the Prek Toeuk Sap River draw huge numbers of domestic tourists. That's why there are so many **picnicking platforms** (per day 5000r, more on holidays).

From the parking area, a rough log **toll bridge** (for locals/tourists 300r/500r) – a miniature version of Cambodia's user-fee-based highway system – leads to several miniature sandy coves, more lounging areas and some perilous rapids. The best spot for a safe, refreshing dip, by children as well as adults, is across another bridge, on the far bank of a cool, crystal-clear tributary of the brown-tinted main river. Free changing booths are available. Not much water flows here in the dry season.

The cascades are about 17km from the centre of Sihanoukville. To get there, head east along NH4 for 9km and then, at the sign, north along a wide dirt road for 8km. By *moto/remork* a return trip should cost US$7/15.

KAMPOT PROVINCE

ខេត្តកំពត

Kampot Province has emerged as one of Cambodia's most alluring destinations for tourists both foreign and domestic thanks to a hard-to-beat combination of old colonial architecture, abundant natural attractions and easy intraregional transport. Highlights include Bokor National Park and its abandoned hill station, the caves around Kompong Trach and, in an adjacent mini-province of its own, the beguiling – and possibly haunted – seaside resort of Kep. Enchanted visitors often end up staying in the sleepy, atmospheric provincial capital of Kampot rather longer than planned.

Kampot Province is renowned for producing some of the world's finest pepper (see p225). Durian haters be warned: Kampot is Cambodia's main producer of this odoriferous fruit.

KAMPOT

កំពត

☎ 033 / pop 33,000

Ever more visitors are being seduced, gently, by the charming riverside town of Kampot, a sleepy place with a relaxed atmosphere and one of Cambodia's finest (though run-down) ensembles of French colonial architecture. Eclipsed as a port when Sihanoukville was founded in 1959, Kampot makes an excellent base for exploring Bokor National Park and the verdant coast east towards Vietnam, including Kep and a number of superb cave-temples. Not on offer here: a beach.

For details on the Prek Chak–Xa Xia border crossing to Vietnam, see p344.

Orientation

Commercial activity is concentrated on 7 Makara St, which stretches from the Obelisk Roundabout to River Rd, and around Psar Leu, the old market, which is being redeveloped. Psar Samaki, the main market, is 400m north of the Obelisk Roundabout. The main transport hub is right around the Total petrol station, linked to Psar Leu by a broad avenue.

Information

For information on local projects and Kampot-area volunteering, check out the free newsletter *Kampot Dar'laing* or contact Bodhi Villa guesthouse. The free *Kampot Survival Guide* takes a tongue-in-cheek look at local expat life.

Bokor Clinic & Maternity (☎ 932289; n_saroeun@ yahoo.com; consultation US$10; ☻ emergency 24hr, consultation 7am-noon & 2-6pm) The best medical clinic in town, with four English-speaking doctors and ultrasound, x-ray and ECG machines.

Canadia Bank One block northwest of Obelisk Roundabout. The ATM has turbo air-con.

Kampot Network (7 Makara St; per hr 3000r; ☻ 7am-10pm) One of several internet cafes along 7 Makara St.

Kepler's Kampot Books (☎ 012 306410; www. keplerbook.com; ☻ 8am-8pm) Secondhand books in English, French, German, Dutch, Swedish and Japanese and internet for 3000r per hour.

Sy Internet (7 Makara St; per hr 3000r; ☉ 6am-10pm) Internet access.

Tourist Information Centre (☉ 7.30-11.30am & 2-5pm) Supposed to open up in late 2010.

Sights & Activities

Kampot's most enjoyable activity is strolling along streets that evoke days long gone. Blocks lined with decrepit **French-era shophouses** can be found in the triangle delineated by the Obelisk

Roundabout, the post office and the **old French bridge**, which is quite a sight: destroyed during the Khmer Rouge's rise to power, it has been repaired in a mishmash of styles. The **old cinema** (7 Makara St), **Kampot Prison** and the **old governor's mansion** – the latter two are very French – are worth a look (from the outside). A **promenade** runs all along the river.

Visitors are welcome to drop by and observe the students of the **Kampot Traditional Music**

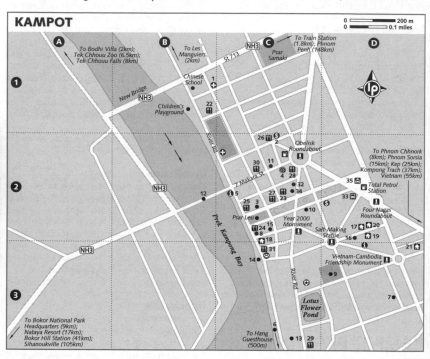

INFORMATION		
Bokor Clinic & Maternity	1	B1
Canadia Bank	2	C2
Kampot Network	(see 11)	
Kepler's Kampot Books	3	C2
Sy Internet	4	C2
Tourist Information Centre (Planned)	5	C2

SIGHTS & ACTIVITIES		
Aerobics	6	C3
FarmLink	7	D3
Kampot Massage by the Blind	8	C2
Kampot Prison	9	D3
Kampot Traditional Music School	10	C2
Old Cinema	11	C2
Old French Bridge	12	B2
Old Governor's Mansion	13	C3

Promenade	14	C3
Seeing Hands Massage V	15	C2
Sok Lim Tours	16	D2
Wild Orchid Adventure Tours	(see 19)	

SLEEPING		
Blissful Guesthouse	17	D2
Bokor Mountain Lodge	18	C2
Mea Culpa	(see 29)	
Orchid Guesthouse	19	D2
Pepper Guesthouse	20	D2
Rikitikitavi	(see 31)	
Ta Eng Guesthouse	21	D3

EATING		
Akashi Café	22	B1
Bakery 333	23	C2
Bamboo Light Café	24	C2
Blissful Guesthouse	(see 17)	

Bokor Mountain Lodge	(see 18)	
Coco House	25	C2
Eateries	26	C2
Epic Arts Café	27	C2
Fruit Stalls	(see 26)	
Heng Dy Grocery	28	C2
Jasmine	(see 25)	
Mea Culpa	29	C3
Night Market	30	C2
Rikitikitavi	31	C3
Rusty Keyhole	(see 18)	
Vimean Tip Bakery	(see 28)	

TRANSPORT		
Cheang Try	32	C2
Hua Lian	(see 33)	
Phnom Penh Sorya	33	D2
Sean Ly	34	C2
Share Taxis	35	D2

KAMPOT PEPPER

Before Cambodia's civil war, no Paris restaurant worth its salt would be without pepper from Kampot Province, but the country's pepper farms were all but destroyed by the Khmer Rouge, who believed in growing rice, not spice.

Today, thanks to a group of eco-entrepreneurs and foodies who are passionate about pepper, Kampot-grown peppercorns, delicate and aromatic but packing a powerful punch, are making a comeback.

Kampot pepper is grown on family farms that dot Phnom Voa and nearby valleys, northwest of Kompong Trach, where the unique climate and farmers' fidelity to labour-intensive growing techniques produce particularly pungent peppercorns. In fact, Kampot pepper is so extraordinary that it's about to become Cambodia's first-ever product to receive a 'geographical indication' (GI), just like French cheeses. Increased sales have made a huge difference for Kampot's pepper families and especially for the girls who were able to get married because their parents could finally afford the dowry.

Peppercorns are picked from February to May. Black pepper is plucked from the trees when the corns are starting to turn yellow and turns black during sun-drying; red pepper is picked when the fruit is completely mature; and mild white pepper is soaked in water to remove the husks. September to February is the season for green pepper, whose sprigs have to be eaten almost immediately after harvesting – the Crab Market restaurants of Kep (p234) are one of the best places to experience its gentle freshness.

A packet of pepper makes an excellent souvenir or gift: the corns are lightweight and unbreakable, and if stored properly – that is, *not* ground! – will stay fresh for years. In Kampot, you can purchase pouches of peerless pepper, and see pepper being dried and sorted, at **FarmLink** (☎ 012 365321; www.farmlink-cambodia.com; 8-11am & 2-5pm Mon-Fri), one of the pioneers of GI pepper production. Its website even lets you trace your pepper back to the farmer who grew it.

SOUTH COAST

School (☎ 011 435283; 8-11am & 6.30-7.30pm Mon-Fri), which trains children who are orphaned or who have disabilities in traditional music and dance. There's no charge, but donations are welcome. Guesthouses have details on performances, held about once a month.

Les Manguiers guesthouse, 2km north of town, rents out **river kayaks** for two hours/half-day/full day for US$3/5/8 (marginally more for two-person boats).

Along the riverfront, you can join the locals for **aerobics** (admission 1000r; about 5pm-sundown daily).

Blind masseurs and masseuses offer soothing bliss at **Kampot Massage by the Blind** (☎ 012 662114; River Rd; per hr US$4; 7am-10pm) and, for shiatsu and Japanese-style massage, **Seeing Hands Massage V** (☎ 012 697391; per hr US$4; 8am-11pm).

Tours

One of the best ways to explore Kampot Province is to take an organised day trip. Popular options (prices are per person) include:

- an all-day trip up to Bokor Hill Station (on foot when the road is closed; see p231).
- Kep, including Rabbit Island, Phnom Chhnork, Phnom Sorsia, a pepper plantation (see above) and, in the dry season, salt fields (US$10 to US$15, including lunch).
- a boat excursion (US$5), either to scenic areas upstream or – at around 5pm, when the fishing boats head out to sea – downstream.
- excursions that combine cycling with hiking, kayaking or a boat ride (US$15 to US$20, including lunch).
- excursions by bamboo train (see p252) from Kompong Trach and perhaps Kampot.

Reliable tour operators:
Sok Lim Tours (☎ 012 719872, 012 796919; www.soklimtours.com) Kampot's oldest and largest outfit, well regarded all around. Has trained pepper plantation guides.
Wild Orchid Adventure Tours (☎ 092-226996) Based at Orchid Guesthouse. Has plans for 250cc and 400cc dirt-bike tours.

Sleeping

After a chilly day atop Bokor, a hot shower might be a welcome treat.

SOUTH COAST

THE COST OF KEEPING COOL

Due to the underdeveloped state of Cambodia's electricity grid – many towns get their mains supply from antiquated diesel generators – Cambodians pay considerably more for electricity than do vastly wealthier people in the West. In Kampot, for example, 1kWh of electricity costs a whopping 1200r. That's seven times the price in the UK, 10 times what you'd pay in the USA and 14 times what consumers are charged in Australia or Canada. To put it another way, an Australian earning minimum wage has to work for 18 seconds to buy one kWh of electricity while your *average* Cambodian has to work 1½ hours – 300 times as long! That's why Cambodians adopted power-saving fluorescent light bulbs so much faster than most Westerners.

When you run your hotel room's air-con unit at these rates, just three hours of coolness costs about US$1 – what many Cambodians earn in a day. And it costs almost as much to keep a hot-water boiler on for an hour. That's why air-con rooms cost considerably more than ones with fans – no-one is getting rich except, perhaps, the well-connected owners of the local electricity company.

The expense of diesel electricity is one of the reasons that large-scale hydroelectric projects are being planned in and around the Cardamoms, some of them in environmentally sensitive areas.

BUDGET

our pick **Bodhi Villa** (☎ 012 728884; www.bodhivilla. com; dm US$3, r US$5-10; 🖥 🛜) Situated 2km towards Tek Chhouu Falls from town (500m upriver from the railway track), this happy hideaway – with five bungalows, two of them floating, and four rooms – is tucked away behind a luxuriant garden. Aussie-run, it has a fully equipped digital recording studio (free), a waterfront chill-out bar, live music every Friday from 7.30pm, and equipment for water sports. A *moto/remork* from town should cost 4000r/6000r.

Blissful Guesthouse (☎ 092-472914; www.blissful guesthouse.com; r US$5-7; 🛜) Surrounded by a tropical garden, this atmospheric old wooden house has 11 simple rooms, four with shared bathroom – the old-time backpacker vibe lives on. Has a popular bar-restaurant.

Ta Eng Guesthouse (☎ 012 330058; r US$5-10) On a street lined with 1960s row houses, Ta Eng – opened in 1992 – has expanded from a family homestay into a welcoming guesthouse with 10 well-kept rooms and rooftop views. The gracious, elderly owner speaks French and English.

Pepper Guesthouse (☎ 017 822626; pepperguest house@yahoo.com; r with fan/air-con from US$5/15; 🖥 🛜) Next to Blissful in a spacious, 15-room villa, Pepper is owned by a welcoming Khmer family. Guests get free bicycles.

Orchid Guesthouse (☎ 092-226996; orchidguest housekampot@yahoo.com; r with fan/air-con from US$5/15; 🕱 🖥 🛜) Set in a manicured garden full of (what else?) orchids, this hostelry has 11 comfortable, colourful rooms and a water-lily pond out back. Provides free bicycles.

Les Manguiers (☎ 092-330050; www.mangomango. byethost18.com; r US$10-18, bungalow US$22-40; 🖥 🛜) This idyllic, family-friendly complex, 2km north of the new bridge along a dirt road, is set in a grassy sugar-palm garden right on the river. It has seven rooms and nine simple but tasteful wooden bungalows, all with fan and cold water; badminton and *pétanque* courts; four over-water gazebos; canoes (per hour US$2); and basic bicycles (free). Meals are served table d'hôte-style. A *moto/remork* from town should cost US$1/3.

Hang Guesthouse (☎ 932170; www.hang.esmart web.com; r with fan/air-con US$10/25; 🕱 🖥) On the waterfront 700m downriver from the post office, this serene place is ideal if you want to get away from it all. The seven rooms face a quiet garden. Bicycles are free, so it's easy to get into town.

MIDRANGE

Mea Culpa (☎ 012 504769; www.meaculpakampot.com; r US$25; 🕱 🛜) Behind the governor's mansion in a palatial villa, the six spacious rooms come with big windows, a DVD library and free tea and coffee.

Rikitikitavi (☎ 012 235102; www.rikitikitavi-kam pot.com; River Rd; r US$35-45; 🕱 🖥 🛜) Has five of the classiest and most comfortable rooms in town.

Bokor Mountain Lodge (☎ 932314; www.bokorlodge. com; River Rd; r including breakfast US$35-50; 🕱 🖥 🛜) A majestic colonial building facing the river, built in 1904, has been turned into an evocative boutique hotel. The six spacious rooms have 3.5m ceilings and all the amenities; pricier ones come with a river view.

Nataya Resort (☎ 012 822863; www.natayaresort.com; r US$55; 🐕 🖵 🐾) Situated 17km west of Kampot, this brand-new resort is owned by the wife of the pre-1975 Cambodian ambassador to Malaysia. Amenities include a 2km-long coconut-shaded beach, a 25m swimming pool, a stylish restaurant with excellent Khmer, Thai, Chinese and Indian food, and 26 semicircular bungalows with four-poster beds and hardwood floors.

Eating & Drinking

Restaurants line River Rd south of the old French bridge. To eat like the locals, try the signless little **eateries** (🕑 6am-10pm), under canvas roofs just west of Canadia Bank, and the sidewalk stalls of the **night market** (7 Makara St; 🕑 4pm-midnight), where options include chicken rice soup (4000r). Both places have Khmer desserts (1000r) such as sticky-rice soup with jackfruit and sticky rice with coconut sauce.

Coco House (☎ 012 974198; River Rd; mains US$2-6.50; 🕑 7am-10pm) Asian and Western dishes, including delicious fish *amoc*, are served with flair and ceremony.

Bokor Mountain Lodge (☎ 932314; River Rd; mains US$2.25-12; 🛜) This atmospheric restaurant serves a good selection of European dishes. Specialities include BBQ seafood, Argentine steak and, on Sunday, lamb roast. Serves wine by the glass.

Epic Arts Café (☎ 932247; www.epicarts.org.uk; mains US$2.50-3; 🕑 7am-6pm; 🛜) A great place for breakfast or scrumptious cakes with tea or coffee. Staffed by deaf and disabled young people, this funky eatery can also pack a bagel lunch for a trip up to Bokor. Profits fund dance, music and art education for deaf and disabled Cambodians.

Blissful Guesthouse (☎ 092-472914; mains US$2.50-4; 🕑 7.30am-10pm) The English chef boldly fuses European and Khmer culinary traditions.

Rusty Keyhole (☎ 092-758536; River Rd) Serves widely praised food, including BBQ, and wine by the glass. A great place to talk sports.

Jasmine (☎ 012 927313; River Rd; lunch mains US$2.50-4.75; dinner mains US$3.50-9; 🕑 10am-10pm, closed Tue; 🛜) California meets Cambodia at this semiformal place. Wine by the glass costs US$3.50. Screens films every Monday night at 7.30pm.

Bamboo Light Café (☎ 089-476578; River Rd; curries US$3-6; 🕑 7am-11pm) Local expats appreciate the fine subcontinental (and especially Sri Lankan) flavours, including masala and biriani dishes and veggie options. The chapatti, puri and pappadam will make your mouth water.

Mea Culpa (☎ 012 504769; mains from US$3; 🛜) Baked in a wood-fired oven, the delicious pizza (US$5.50 to US$9) is served in a garden pavilion whose lawn is mowed by a cow. Sandwiches are US$3 to US$4.

our pick Akashi Café (☎ 092-775900; mains US$3.50-5.75; 🕑 11am-5pm except Wed) Run by an Anglo-Japanese couple, this homey place, in a purple villa, serves a nonmeat menu renowned for its freshness. Homemade specialities include breads, cakes, ice cream, sandwiches and quiches. Serves great coffee.

our pick Rikitikitavi (☎ 012 235102; River Rd; mains US$4.75-7.75; 🕑 7am-10pm; 🛜) Named after the mongoose in Rudyard Kipling's *The Jungle Book*, this stylish terrace restaurant is known for its Kampot pepper chicken (on salad or in a sandwich), *saraman* (Cambodian beef curry), burgers, burritos, salads, apple pie and veggie options. Serves wine by the glass.

SELF-CATERING

There are fruit stalls next to Canadia Bank. Fresh baguettes are available at **Bakery 333** (🕑 6am-6pm) – look for the piles of split wood (for the oven) out front. For Western edibles, including yoghurt and peanut butter, you can't beat **Heng Dy Grocery** (☎ 932925; Obelisk Roundabout; 🕑 7am-9pm). Next door at **Vimean Tip Bakery** (Obelisk Roundabout; 🕑 7am-8pm) you can buy doughnuts (1000r) and bean-paste pastries (1500r).

Getting There & Away

Kampot, on NH3, is 148km southwest of Phnom Penh, 105km east of Sihanoukville and 25km northwest of Kep.

Two bus companies, **Phnom Penh Sorya** (☎ 092-181801; www.ppsoryatransport.com; 🕑 7am-6pm) and **Hua Lian** (☎ 012 939917; 🕑 6am-7pm), have ticket stands next to Sokhoda Restaurant (facing the Total petrol station). Buses to Phnom Penh (US$5, four to five hours) that take the long way around – via Kep (US$2, 40 minutes), Kompong Trach and Angk Tasaom (gateway to Takeo) – depart at about 7am and 12.30pm. Across the street you can catch share taxis (US$5, 2½ hours via NH3), packed-to-the-gills minibuses (15,000r) and private taxis (US$45) to Phnom Penh.

Share taxis to Sihanoukville cost US$5 (15,000r for Khmers), minibuses are 15,000r and a private taxi is US$25. Guesthouses have details on comfortable minibus services (US$7) offering door-to-door service.

A moto/remork/private taxi to Kep should run to about US$5/8/15.

If you're going to the **Prek Chak–Xa Xia border crossing** (6am-5pm or 5.30pm) with Vietnam, tour agencies and guesthouses can arrange a direct moto (US$8 to US$10, one hour), remork (US$10 to US$20, 1½ hours), share taxi (US$5, one hour) or private taxi (US$20 to US$25). A moto all the way to Ha Tien, in Vietnam, costs US$15.

Getting Around

A moto ride in town costs 2000r (3000r in the evening); remorks cost about US$1.

Two excellent, adjacent shops rent out motorbikes (also available from some guesthouses) and dirt bikes:

Cheang Try (012 974698; 6.30am-7pm) Small bikes cost US$3 a day, new 125cc Hondas are US$5 and a car with a driver is US$40 a day. Guided all-day tours by motorbike or remork cost US$25. The owner speaks good English.

Sean Ly (012 944687; 7am-9pm) Rents 125cc bikes for US$3 a day (US$5 for a new one) and 250cc trail bikes for US$10. A 4WD pickup, without a driver, is US$35 a day.

For tips and information on 250cc dirt biking around Kampot, ask at Rusty Keyhole or Blissful Guesthouse.

Wild Orchid Adventure Tours rents out bicycles (US$1 a day).

AROUND KAMPOT

The limestone hills east towards Kep are honeycombed with caves, some of which can be explored with the help of local kids and a torch/flashlight. Phnom Chhnork, surrounded by blazingly green countryside, is a real gem and can easily be visited in an afternoon along with Phnom Sorsia.

Tek Chhouu Falls

ទឹកឈូវ

Hugely popular with locals, this **picnicking and bathing spot** (admission US$1) has a series of small rapids, lots of little eateries and – a prerequisite for any proper Khmer day out – plenty of picnicking platforms. Until floods knocked it down in late 2009, a bouncy pedestrian

suspension bridge led to an **island** whose far side has some tiny strips of sand (it's now served by small boats). Small/large inner tubes cost 2000r/3000r.

Half a kilometre upriver, the **Kamchay hydroelectric dam** is being built by a Chinese company. Vital stats: 115m high, 568m wide, 193.2MW. The US$280-million project, which will flood parts of Bokor National Park, is slated for completion in late 2011.

A moto to Tek Chhouu Falls from Kampot (8km), past durian fields, should cost about US$5 return (US$3 in the low season).

Tek Chhouu Zoo

This privately owned **zoo** (012 434272; locals/foreigners 4000r/US$4), 1.5km towards Kampot from the falls, has seen better days, but it lets you get *much* closer to the animals – including two elephants you can greet by shaking their trunks – than Western zoos. The animals, most of them rescued from the wildlife trade, appear healthy (some of the monkeys, of half-a-dozen species, have babies) but sad – and look like they'll appreciate the food your admission fee will buy. The entrance is marked by twin statues of roaring tigers.

Phnom Chhnork

ភ្នំឈ្នក

The base of **Phnom Chhnork** (Phnom Chngouk; admission US$1) is a short walk through the rice fields from Wat Ang Sdok, where a monk will collect the entry fee and a gaggle of friendly local kids, some with precociously fluent English, will offer their services as guides.

A well-tended staircase with 203 steps leads up the hillside and down into a cavern as graceful as a Gothic cathedral. There you'll be greeted by a **stalactite elephant**, with a second elephant outlined on the flat cliff face to the right. Nearby is a formation that looks like a **calf's head**. Tiny chirping bats live up near two natural chimneys that soar towards the blue sky, partly blocked by foliage of an impossibly green hue.

Inside the cave's main chamber stands a remarkable 7th-century (Funan-era) **brick temple**, dedicated to Shiva. The temple's brickwork is in superb condition thanks to the protection afforded by the cave. Poke your head inside and check out the ancient stalactite that serves as a *linga*. A slippery passage, flooded in the rainy season, leads through the hill.

Phnom Chhnork occupies a bucolic site surrounded by a quilt work of rice paddies and meticulously tended vegetable plots (tomato, cucumber, lettuce, cabbage, mint). The view from up top, and the walk to and from the wat, is especially magical in the late afternoon and around sunset.

Phnom Chhnork is about 8km from Kampot. A bit past the rhino statue in the middle of NH33 (5.5km from town), turn northeast; across the road from the Cham mosque, look for a sign reading 'Phnom Chhngok Resort'. A *moto/remork* from Kampot costs about US$5/8 return.

Phnom Sorsia
ភ្នំសូរស្យៃ

Not quiet as magical as Phnom Chhnork, **Phnom Sorsia** (Phnom Sia; admission free) has a gaudily painted modern temple and several natural caves.

From the parking area in front of the school, a stairway leads up the hillside to a colourful temple. From there, steps lead left up to **Rung Damrey Saa** (White Elephant Cave), named not for a failed megaproject but rather for a mineral formation situated to the right of the two Buddha statues. A bit past a slippery, sloping passage where one false step will send you into the abyss, a hand-sized hole leads to a **hidden pool** filled with refreshingly cool water. Nearby you can glimpse a peep show of tiny terraced paddy fields. Shine your flashlight up and you may spot bats.

From the colourful temple, steps angle up to the right to the **Bat Cave**. Inside, countless bats flutter and chirp overhead, flying out to the forest and back through a narrow natural chimney. Locals use bamboo poles to hunt the creatures by swatting them out of the air. The circuit ends near a hilltop **stupa** with impressive views.

The local kids who guide tourists – and insistently ask for huge tips – are not likely to keep much of what you pay them. As soon as visitors hand over the cash, adults swoop down and reapportion it to their advantage.

The turn-off to Phnom Sorsia is on NH33 13.5km southeast of Kampot and 2.5km northwest of the White Horse Roundabout 7km north of Kep. Look for a sign reading 'Phnom Sorsia Resort' – from there a dirt road leads about 1km northeast through the rice fields.

BOKOR NATIONAL PARK

This **park** (Preah Monivong National Park; 1581 sq km; admission US$5), at the southern tip of the Elephant Mountains, is famed for its abandoned French hill station, refreshingly cool climate and lush primary rainforest.

Bokor's moist evergreen forests – with dry dipterocarp and mixed deciduous forests in the north – shelter a wide variety of rare and threatened animals, including the Indian elephant, tiger (photographed not long ago with camera traps), leopard, Asiatic black bear, Malayan sun bear, pileated gibbon, pig-tailed macaque, slow loris, red muntjac deer, lesser mouse deer, pangolin (p204), yellow-throated martin, small Asian mongoose and various species of civet, porcupine, squirrel and bat. Over 300 species of bird, including several types of hornbill, also live here. Don't expect to see much wildlife, though – most of the animals survive by staying in more remote areas and, in addition, are nocturnal.

The park is threatened by poaching and illegal logging, especially in the north, as well as by squatters, a titanic mountaintop tourism project and, in the southeast, the Kamchay hydropower project. In the 1990s there was talk of making Bokor a World Heritage Forest but, sadly, the government's inability to protect the park put an end to the initiative.

Bokor, including the hill station, is believed to be free of land mines, but as always in Cambodia, do the sensible thing and stick to well-worn paths.

BOKOR HILL STATION
ស្ថានីយដ៍ភ្នំបូរគោ

In the early 1920s the French – ever eager to escape the lowland heat – established a hill station atop Phnom Bokor (1080m), known for its dramatic vistas of the coastal plain one vertical kilometre below – and for frequent pea-soup fogs.

The hill station was twice abandoned to the howling winds: first when Vietnamese and Khmer Issarak (Free Khmer) forces overran it in the late 1940s while fighting for independence from France, and again in 1972, when the Lon Nol regime left it to the Khmer Rouge forces that were steadily taking over the countryside. Because of its commanding position, the site was strategically important to all sides during the civil war and was one location the Vietnamese really had to fight for during their 1979 invasion. For several months, the

SOUTH COAST

Khmer Rouge held out in the Catholic church while the Vietnamese shot at them from the Bokor Palace, 500m away.

Today, Bokor Hill Station is a ghost town, its once-grand buildings turned into eerie, windowless shells. Over time they have become carpeted with bright-orange lichen that gives them an otherworldly cast. Mountain mists float through the rooms and stairwells, and the sea views are either breathtaking or a complete white-out. Appropriate, then, that the foggy showdown that ends the Matt Dillon crime thriller *City of Ghosts* (2002) was filmed here.

At the **Bokor Palace**, a grand, four-storey hotel that opened in 1925, you can wander up and down the corridors, around the kitchens and through the ballroom to the suites above, passing variegated ceramic floors, tiled bathrooms and a giant fireplace where cocksure colonial French and upper-crust Khmers could warm up on a nippy night. On cold, foggy days it can get pretty creepy up here as mists drop visibility to nothing and the wind keens through the ballroom.

The squat belfry of the Romanesque-style **Catholic church** still holds aloft its cross, and fragments of glass brick cling to the corners of the nave windows; one side window holds the barest outline of a rusty crucifix. It's easy to imagine a small crowd of French colonials in formal dress assembled here for Sunday Mass. The subdividing walls inside were built by the Khmer Rouge. A bit up the hill, a sheer drop overlooks virgin rainforest.

In 2008, Sok Kong, the exceptionally well-connected fellow who owns all those Sokimex petrol stations and holds the entry-fee concession for Angkor, secured title to a whopping 140 sq km of Bokor land, much of it atop Phnom Bokor, in order to create a 'world-class tourist city'. The centrepiece of his 15-year, US$1-billion megaproject, slated to include 1000 villas and two Arnold Palmer–designed golf courses, is the bombastically named 'Sokha Bokor 5 Star International Hotel & Casino Resort', with '650 deluxe rooms' and a 'grand ballroom' big enough for 2000 people. All of this inside a protected national park! Rumour has it that the Bokor Palace is going to be meticulously restored to its 1920s glory, but at the time of research, the entire project was on hold: the only evidence – other than the road upgrade – that the colossal undertaking had even been started was a forest of rusting rebar near the church.

OTHER SIGHTS

The first buildings you come to on the drive from Kampot comprise Sihanouk's villa complex, known as the **Black Palace**. Shaded by pine trees (not a tree you see along the coast), the villas have been thoroughly stripped, but one dining room retains sections of its elegant marble floor and the bathrooms are partly tiled in midcentury shades of pink and lemon yellow.

A few kilometres before you get to the hill station, to the left of the main road, is the aptly named **Emerald Valley**.

Lichen-caked **Wat Sampeau Bram Roi** (Five Boats Wat) owes its name to five oddly sculpted rocks that some people say resemble boats, although what they were smoking at the time is up for debate. From the wat's terrace, there are tremendous views over the jungle to the coastline below, including Vietnam's Phu Quoc Island. Sadly – and this wasn't the case even a couple of years ago – you can often hear the buzz of chainsaws in the jungle far below. The four cement supports once anchored a Khmer Rouge radar station. Wild monkeys like to hang out around the wat.

From the wat, an 11km trail – vehicle bridges are being built – leads to two-tiered **Popokvil Falls**, whose name translates as 'Swirling Clouds'. Stay alert: in these parts there's always the possibility of an unexpected encounter with a three-legged female tiger nicknamed Tripod who has been known to roam the ridge along here.

TREKKING

There's huge potential for day hikes and overnight treks in Bokor, but it's almost completely unrealised. However, travel agents in Kampot (p225) may be able to rustle something up. The Sam Veasna Center (p346) organises birding trips.

The national park charges US$20 a day for the services of an experienced but non-English-speaking **ranger** (☎ 012 923738; bokornp@camintel.com). You'll need to bring your own protection against mosquitos, leeches, snakes and rain.

Sleeping

Near the old hill station, the **Preah Monivong 'Bokor' National Park Training & Research Facility**

(☎ 012 923738; bokornp@camintel.com; dm US$5, r US$20), donated by USAID, has simple rooms with hot water and up to four beds. Kitchen facilities are available. Bring warm clothes as temperatures can plummet as low as 12°C (53°F) at night.

Getting There & Away

Park headquarters, at the bottom of the hill, is 9km west of Kampot. The 32km road from there up to the hill station was built from 1917 to 1921 by Cambodian forced labourers, hundreds of whom perished.

A Chinese company is building a new road for Sokimex but it's only sporadically open to the public (eg on major Khmer holidays). Until construction is finished, the only way to get up to Bokor Hill Station is to join a group – local conditions permitting, travel agents in Kampot (p225) can arrange an ascent on foot and/or by vehicle. At press time the road project was making very slow progress – depending on whom you ask, because of either landslides or cash flow problems.

When the road is open, Bokor offers some truly hardcore mountain biking.

KOMPONG TRACH
កំពង់ត្រាច

The sheer ugliness of Kompong Trach is made all the more glaring by the exceptional beauty of the surrounding countryside, especially around Wat Kiri Sela, the area's star attraction.

It may be possible to hire a **bamboo train** (see p252) behind Phnom Kompong Trach – the guides at Wat Kiri Sela know who to contact.

For details on the Prek Chak–Xa Xia border crossing to Vietnam, see p344.

Wat Kiri Sela
វត្តគីរីសេលា

For an enchanting mixture of dramatic natural beauty and Buddhist piety, it's hard to beat **Wat Kiri Sela** (Phnom Kompong Trach, Wat Kirisan; admission US$1), a Buddhist temple built at the foot of a karst formation – locals say it resembles a dragon – riddled with over 100 caverns and passageways. There's definitely **rock-climbing** (www.rockclimbingincambodia.com) potential here.

From the wat buildings (home to four monks and four nuns), an underground passage – 'the dragon's mouth' – leads past formations resembling the body of a turtle and the dangling tongue (or perhaps tonsil)

of a dragon to the centre of the hill, where the vine-draped cliffs of a **hidden valley** – 'the dragon's stomach' – unfold before you. This is the sort of place where you wouldn't be surprised to see a dinosaur munching on foliage or, *à la Jurassic Park,* chewing on a lawyer.

From here, hard-to-spot caves lead into – and all the way through – the hill, taking you to natural **stalactite formations** that look like the head of an eel, the head of a crocodile, a military boot and a hillside of miniature rice terraces. Friendly local high school students with torches/flashlights, eager to put their remarkably fluent English to use, are happy to serve as guides. The reclining Buddha was inaugurated in 1999 to replace one destroyed by the Khmer Rouge.

About 300m around the mountain from the wat, behind a lone treelike bush, a narrow path leads over loose stones and then up carved steps to a tiny triangular opening, where an old concrete ladder descends 5m into the darkness (warning: the second-to-top and bottom two rungs are missing). Two more wooden ladders lead ever deeper into the slimy, slippery depths of the **cave**, where a guide – essential here – can point out slumbering bats and surprising limestone formations, one of which looks like a jackfruit.

It takes about two hours to walk all the way around the mountain.

Sleeping

Kompong Trach's **Kiri Sela Guesthouse** (☎ 012 330201; r with fan/air-con US$7/12) has 22 very average rooms. The property's Corinthian colonnade is easy to spot on the town's main drag.

Getting There & Away

Kompong Trach is on NH33 37km east of Kampot, 23km northeast of Kep and 18km north of the Prek Chak–Xa Xia border crossing to Vietnam. To get to Wat Kiri Sela – a great day trip from Kep or Kampot – take the dirt road opposite the Acleda Bank for 2km.

Phnom Penh Sorya (www.ppsoryatransport.com) and Hua Lian buses on the Kampot–Phnom Penh run pass by here and cost about US$3 to Phnom Penh (via Angk Tasaom) and US$2 to Kep. Minibus prices are similar. A *moto/ remork* to Kep costs about US$3/5.

A *moto* to the **Prek Chak–Xa Xia border crossing** (☉ 6am-5pm or 5.30pm) costs US$4 or US$5. At the border, certain *motos* can take you from the Cambodian side to the Vietnamese border post (300m past the Cambodian one) and then all the way to the Vietnamese town of Ha Tien (9km) for US$3 (more for an English-speaking driver).

Coming to Prek Chak, *remorks* and taxis have been known to drop off passengers before the border in order to force them to overpay for an onward *moto* – make sure yours stops right at the Cambodian border barrier.

KRONG KEP

ក្រុងកែប

Krong Kep (also spelled Kaeb) is a province-level municipality that consists of little more than Kep Peninsula, whose west coast faces – across the water – Bokor National Park and Vietnam's Phu Quoc Island.

KEP

កែប

☎ 036 / pop 4000

The seaside resort of Kep-sur-Mer, famed for its spectacular sunsets and splendid seafood, was founded as a colonial retreat for the French elite in 1908. In the 1960s, Cambodian high rollers continued the tradition, but Khmer Rouge rule brought evacuation, followed, in the 1980s, by systematic looting. Today, scores of Kep's luxurious prewar villas remain blackened shells, relics of a once-great (or at least rich and flashy) civilisation that met a sudden and violent end.

After several false starts, Kep finally seems to be rising from (or among) the ruins, which still give parts of the town a postapocalyptic feel. Especially on weekends and holidays, the seashore is again popular with the Phnom Penh elite: drawn by the languid, Riviera-like atmosphere, they drive down in SUVs to picnic and frolic on the rather ordinary beaches (even before the war, white sand had to be shipped in from Sihanoukville to keep up appearances).

For details on the Prek Chak–Xa Xia border crossing to Vietnam, see p344.

Orientation

From the Northern Roundabout, heading north for 7km takes you past ruined villas to the White Horse Roundabout on NH33; turning east takes you up the slope to a cluster of hillside guesthouses; and turning west brings you to the Crab Market. From there, the coastal road leads 1.5km around the headland to Kep Beach, which is right below Kep Beach Roundabout. The boat dock is 2.5km further east, past Coconut Beach.

Information

A free local brochure, *The Kep Revival*, has ads, articles and maps. Kep does not have any banks or ATMs.

Green House (☎ 089-440161; per hr US$1) A travel agency with internet access.

Kep Tourism Office (Kep Beach Roundabout) Not much goes on inside this fine building, but a new information pavilion is being built outside.

Rith Travel (☎ 016 789994; Crab Market; per hr US$1; ☒ 6.30am-9pm) A travel agency that handles snorkelling and transport to Vietnam. Also has internet computers.

Sights & Activities

For details on Koh Tonsay (Rabbit Island), see p235.

BEACHES & WATER SPORTS

Despite having coarse sand, being rather narrow (especially at high tide) and facing south (ie no full-on sunsets), **Kep Beach** is hugely popular with Khmer families. Across the street are small eateries and dining platforms with hammocks. The eastern end of the shaded **promenade** is marked by a **Sela Cham P'dey**, a statue that depicts a nude fisher's wife waiting expectantly for her husband to return.

Coconut Beach (in Khmer, Chhne Derm Dont), with its dining platforms and eateries, begins a few hundred metres southeast of Kep Beach, just past the **giant crab statue** and across the NH33A from the Provincial Hall and two gilded statues that resemble oversized chickens.

At the **Knai Bang Chatt Sailing Club** (☎ 012 349742; ☒ 10am-11pm), you can play volleyball, table tennis or *pétanque*; hire a canoe or Hobie Cat (US$4/15 an hour); and dine (mains US$5 to US$15) or sip cocktails (US$4) in a New England–style pavilion with a generous waterside terrace and gorgeous sunsets.

The 10m **swimming pool** at Kep Lodge, with views west towards Phnom Bokor, costs US$5 for non-guests (free if you order US$5 worth of food).

VILLAS

From the Northern Roundabout, NH33A heads north past the mildewed shells of handsome **mid-20th-century villas** that speak of happier, carefree times – and of the terrible

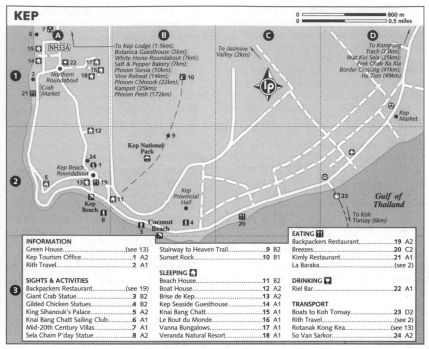

KEP

INFORMATION		
Green House	(see 13)	
Kep Tourism Office	1	A2
Rith Travel	2	A1

SIGHTS & ACTIVITIES		
Backpackers Restaurant	(see 19)	
Giant Crab Statue	3	B2
Gilded Chicken Statues	4	B2
King Sihanouk's Palace	5	A2
Knai Bang Chatt Sailing Club	6	A1
Mid-20th Century Villas	7	A1
Sela Cham P'day Statue	8	A2

Stairway to Heaven Trail	9	B2
Sunset Rock	10	B1

SLEEPING		
Beach House	11	B2
Boat House	12	A2
Brise de Kep	13	A2
Kep Seaside Guesthouse	14	A1
Knai Bang Chatt	15	A1
Le Bout du Monde	16	A1
Vanna Bungalows	17	A1
Veranda Natural Resort	18	A1

EATING		
Backpackers Restaurant	19	A2
Breezes	20	C2
Kimly Restaurant	21	A1
La Baraka	(see 2)	

DRINKING		
Riel Bar	22	A1

TRANSPORT		
Boats to Koh Tonsay	23	D2
Rith Travel	(see 2)	
Rotanak Kong Kea	(see 13)	
So Van Sarkor	24	A2

years of Khmer Rouge rule and civil war. Built according to the precepts of the modernist style, with clean lines, lots of horizontals and little adornment, they once played host to glittering jet-set parties and may do so again someday, though for the time being many shelter squatters (and, some say, ghosts). Don't even think of buying one – they were all snapped up for a song in the mid-1990s by well-connected speculators.

On top of the hill northwest of Kep Beach is a **palace** built by King Sihanouk in the early 1990s. Before his overthrow in 1970, Kep was one of his favourite spots, and he used to entertain visiting foreign dignitaries on an outlying island nicknamed Île des Ambassadeurs. The king may have harboured thoughts of retirement here, but his poor health and Cambodia's political instability meant that he never actually stayed at the palace, which remains unfurnished. At the time of research it was closed to visitors.

KEP NATIONAL PARK
The interior of Kep peninsula is occupied by **Kep National Park**, degraded in recent years by illegal logging, but finally guarded by a complement of rangers. Directly behind the Beach House guesthouse, the signposted **Stairway to Heaven** leads 800m up the hill to a pagoda, a nunnery and – 400m further on – **Sunset Rock**, with superb views. A track passable to cars goes as far as the nunnery. An 8km **circuit** around the park, signposted in yellow, passes behind the Beach House and the Veranda Natural Resort.

For details on visiting the park, drop by the **Backpackers Restaurant** (p234) and ask for Christian.

Sleeping
Kep Seaside Guesthouse (☎ 012 684241; sengbunly@bnckh.com; r with fan/air-con from US$7/15; ✦) Right on the water but beachless, this three-storey place – dormitory-like in appearance – has 25 no-frills rooms and a laid-back management style. Room 20 has a full-frontal sea view. Often fills up with domestic tourists on weekends and holidays. A new building with 26 more rooms is being built.

Botanica Guesthouse (☎ 016 562775; www.kep-botanica.com; r US$8-10; ▢ ⌂) A Belgian-owned place with five bungalows and a breezy 'world kitchen' restaurant set in a flowery garden. About 2km north of the Northern Roundabout (towards Kampot); a *moto* to the Crab Market costs 3000r to 4000r.

Brise de Kep (☎ 012 301017; Kep Beach; r with fan/air-con from US$8/15; 🖳 🛜) A new place with a great little balcony bar and five spacious rooms that come with high ceilings and foam mattresses.

Boat House (☎ 099-504820; www.theboathousekep. com; r US$8-20; 🖳 🛜) In a quiet villa between the two roundabouts, this new British- and Khmer-run place has an all-wood lounge area, five fan rooms (two with shared bathroom) and a bit of the vibe of old Indochine. Great for a quiet, romantic getaway. Bicycles are free.

Vanna Bungalows (☎ 012 755038; www.vannabun galows.com; r with fan/air-con from US$10/20; 🗷 🖳 🛜) Popular with in-the-know expats, this relaxed place has 17 solidly built bungalows – most with fridges and hot water – set in pleasant hillside gardens. The sunset sea views from the restaurant's verandah are gorgeous.

Jasmine Valley (☎ 097-7917636; www.jasminevalley. com; r US$19-44; 🛋) This new ecolodge, on a verdant hillside just below Kep National Park, has eight solar-powered bungalows; six are made of adobe and two are perched atop columns. Amenities include a sauna and a 'natural' swimming pool (under construction). To get there from the boat dock, turn northwest at the hospital and take the serpentine road for 2km; a *moto* from the Crab Market should cost US$1.50 to US$2.50, and a *remork* US$3 to US$5.

Le Bout du Monde (☎ 011 964181; http://leboutdu monde.new.fr; d incl breakfast US$20-85) The French-owned 'end of the earth' has six fan-equipped bungalows with wood-slat floors, wicker walls, brick bathrooms and safes. The bar-restaurant has superb sunset views of Bokor.

our pick **Vine Retreat** (☎ 011 706231; www. thevineretreat.com; near Chamcar Bei village; d US$23-35; 🖳 🛜 🛋) This new, socially responsible ecolodge is 14km northeast of Kep, inside the geographical indication zone for Kampot pepper (p225). The eight comfortable rooms, with solar hot water and decent mattresses, look out on an organic farm and a naturally filtered swimming pond; the top floor has a quiet chill-out area. To get there from the White Horse Roundabout, head east for 3km or 4km, turn left (north) between two pillars decorated with cement durians, and keep going for 4.5km.

Veranda Natural Resort (☎ 012 888619; www. veranda-resort.com; r with fan/air-con from US$30/48;

🗷 🛜 🛋) Spread across the hill above town, this 20-bungalow complex – built of wood, bamboo and stone – is a memorable spot for a romantic getaway. The restaurant (known for its pastries) and bar afford stunning sunset views. New for 2010: a 25m swimming pool.

Kep Lodge (☎ 092-435330; www.keplodge.com; r US$33-38; 🖳 🛜 🛋) The six hillside bungalows come with fans, hot water, mosquito nets and verandahs (more, with air-con, are planned). The restaurant (open from 7am to 10pm), overlooking the pool, has breathtaking sunset views and Phnom Penh prices. From the Northern Roundabout, go 1km north along NH33A and then 700m east. A *moto/remork* from the Crab Market costs US$1/3. Bicycles are free.

Beach House (☎ 012 240090; www.thebeachhousekep. com; r US$40-55; 🗷 🛜 🛋) Just above Kep Beach, this place has 16 two-star-level rooms with tile floors and sea-view verandahs. For cooling off there's a 6m-long pool with a mini-waterfall.

Knai Bang Chatt (☎ 012 349742; www.knaibang chatt.com; r US$150-350; 🖳 🛜 🛋) This ultrachic, ultraluxury 11-room boutique hotel, occupying three waterfront villas from the 1960s, has a spa, a beachside infinity pool (nonchlorine) and breathtaking sunset views.

Eating & Drinking

Dining in Kep is all about fresh seafood. For the best deals head to the Crab Market, a row of waterfront shacks where you can tuck into mouth-watering grilled, fried and steamed crab, prawns, squid and fish. The crabs (35,000r a kilo) are local – they're kept alive in pens tethered a few metres off the pebbly beach – but the prawns and fish are brought in from Kampot.

Botanica Guesthouse, Le Bout du Monde, Vanna Bungalows, Veranda Natural Resort and Knai Bang Chatt Sailing Club all have decent restaurants.

Backpackers Restaurant (☎ 089-763865; Kep Beach Roundabout; mains US$1-3) A French- and Khmer-run cafe with inexpensive veggie dishes. The best source of information on hiking in Kep National Park.

Salt & Pepper Bakery (☎ 099-219004; White Horse Roundabout; sourdough loaf US$2.50; 🕑 8am-5pm Mon-Fri, to noon Sat) A cheerful woman from Hamburg runs this airy cafe, where a hot drink can be enjoyed with delicious homemade bread (eg heavy German sourdough), cake (eg California chocolate), cookies or breakfast. Situated 50m north (towards Kampot) from the White Horse Roundabout.

our pick **Kimly Restaurant** (☎ 089-822866; Crab Market; mains from US$2.50; ⏱ 10am-10pm) The oldest and most famous of the Crab Market eateries. Specialities here include crabs (small/large US$6.50/8.75) and prawns (US$5/7.50) with sprigs of green Kampot pepper.

La Baraka (☎ 092-127548; Crab Market; mains US$4.50-5.50; ⏱ 7am-10pm or later) A French-run pizzeria; also has pasta.

Breezes (☎ 097-675 9072; mains US$5-8; ⏱ 9am-9pm) Just 10m from the water line, this new, Dutch-owned restaurant boasts sleek furnishings and fine views of Koh Tonsay. Dishes are Asian (not necessarily Khmer), Western and fusion.

Riel Bar (☎ 017 902771; www.kep-riel-bar.com; Northern Roundabout) Occupying a hangarlike space out-fitted with wicker chairs and a couple of ham-mocks, this unpretentious bar-restaurant is owned by a Dutch former sound engineer. Specialities include homemade ice cream con-fected without eggs (to avoid salmonella).

Getting There & Away

Kep is 25km from Kampot (from which Kep makes an easy day trip), 41km from the Prek Chak–Xa Xia border crossing to Vietnam and 172km from Phnom Penh.

Phnom Penh Sorya (www.ppsoryatransport.com) and Hua Lin buses link the town with Kampot (US$2, 45 minutes), Kompong Trach (5000r), Angk Tasaom (near Takeo) and Phnom Penh (US$4 or US$5). Buses heading towards Phnom Penh pass by at about 8am and 1pm. Stops are on-request (eg near your guesthouse) but usually include the Northern Roundabout and Kep Beach Roundabout. Guesthouses can make bookings.

A *moto/remork/*taxi to Kampot costs about US$7/10/20. Drivers hang out at the northern end of Kep Beach; guesthouses can make arrangements.

A *moto/remork/*taxi to the Prek Chat–Xa Xia crossing to Vietnam costs US$8/15/20 and takes about 1½ hours. **Rith Travel** (☎ 016 789994; Crab Market) can make arrangements.

A ferry service to Vietnam's Phu Quoc Island is being discussed.

Getting Around

Kep has almost no street lighting so a torch/flashlight is useful if you'll be walking around at night.

Moto drivers hang out at Kep Beach and the Crab Market. A *moto* ride from the Crab Market to Kep Beach or the boat dock costs

US$1; *remorks* charge US$1/6000r for one/two people. After about 9pm the only way to find a *moto* is by phoning.

Hiring a *moto* for the day costs about US$15, including a trip out to Wat Kiri Sela near Kompong Trach. Hiring a *remork* for a whole day, including a pepper-farm visit, is US$20.

Motorbikes can be rented from **So Van Sarkor** (Sovann Sakor, ☎ 012 608345; Kep Beach Roundabout; per day old/new $6/7; ⏱ 6am or 7am-10pm); **Rotanak Kong Kea** (☎ 017 818303; Kep Beach; per day old/new US$6/8; ⏱ 6am-10pm), next to Brise de Kep guesthouse; and Kep Lodge (US$8 a day).

Bicycles can be rented from Rith Travel (US$2 a day), Rotanak Kong Kea (US$2 a day), Knai Bang Chatt Sailing Club (US$4 a day) and Botanica Guesthouse.

AROUND KEP

Kep makes a good base for visiting several delightful cave-temples, including **Wat Kiri Sela** near Kompong Trach (p231), **Phnom Chhnork** (p228) and **Phnom Sorsia** (p229).

Koh Tonsay

កោះទន្សាយ

Koh Tonsay (Rabbit Island; population: 25 families), said to have the nicest beaches of any Kep-area island – except Phu Quoc, whose loss to Vietnam is still bitterly resented – is so named because locals say it resembles a rabbit, an example of what too much local brew can do to your imagination. If you like rusticity, come now before the island is changed forever by development.

At the 250m-long, tree-lined **main beach**, which faces west towards the setting sun, you can dine on seafood, lounge around on raised bamboo platforms and stay in thatched bunga-lows. North American travellers of a certain age may be tempted to hum the theme tune from *Gilligan's Island*. Many people say Koh Tonsay is a 'tropical paradise', but don't expect the sani-tised resort version – this one has shorefront flot-sam, flies, chickens, packs of dogs and wandering cows.

From the southern end of the main beach, a 10-minute walk takes you to a fishing hamlet and two more sand **beaches**, one on either side of the island's narrow southern tip. It's possible, though not necessarily easy, to walk all the way around Koh Tonsay.

The island's interior is forested and, except along the beaches, trees grow right up to the water's edge. On the **hilltop**, accessible in the dry season, you can see the remains of a one-time Khmer Rouge bunker.

Other Kep-area islands include **Koh Pos** (Snake Island; about 30 minutes past Koh Tonsay), which has a deserted beach and fine snorkelling, but no overnight accommodation (getting out there costs US$40 to US$50 for an all-day trip by 10-person boat); and small, beachless **Koh Svai** (Mango Island), whose summit offers nice views.

SLEEPING & EATING

Guesthouses along the main beach – family-run and with tiny open-air restaurants – include **Yeay Am** (☎ 012 343759) and **Yeay Meng** (☎ 012 893102), which charge US$5 for a rudimentary bungalow with a mosquito net and, across the yard, a sit-down toilet; en-suite bathroom bungalows are US$7. Meals cost US$3 to US$5 for fish, crab, squid, shrimp or free-range chicken. (The latter may wander under your table and one diner reports having his feet, well, henpecked!)

GETTING THERE & AWAY

Guesthouses and *moto* drivers are happy to arrange round-trip boat transport out to Koh Tonsay (6km, 20 minutes) for US$7 per person, including land transport to the dock. For groups, it's cheaper to go to Kep's boat dock yourself, where the fee is US$20 return for up to 10 people. On the ride, keep an eye out for schools of little silver fish jumping out of the water in unison.

If you'd like to overnight on Koh Tonsay and be picked up the next day, make this clear when you book or you may be charged US$5 per person to get back – as a general rule, travellers stranded on islands are in a pretty weak bargaining position.

TAKEO PROVINCE

ខេត្តតាកែវ

Often referred to as 'the cradle of Cambodian civilisation', Takeo Province was part of what Chinese annals called 'water Chenla', no doubt a reference to the extensive annual floods that still blanket much of the area. Today, this impoverished, rural province's main tourist draws are the same temples that, for centuries, brought the kings of Angkor here for elaborate ceremonies: Tonlé Bati (p125) and Phnom Chisor (p126), near Phnom Penh; and, accessible from the provincial capital of Takeo, Angkor Borei and Phnom Da.

TAKEO

តាកែវ

☎ 032 / pop 39,000

Takeo town, the quiet, lakeside provincial capital, is an excellent base from which to take a zippy motorboat ride to several pre-Angkorian temples (p238).

Cycling groups en route from the Mekong Delta to Phnom Penh, via the Phnom Den–Tinh Bien border crossing, often stop off here because NH2 has luxuriously wide, paved verges/shoulders. For details of the border crossing to Vietnam, see p344.

Orientation

Laid out on a grid, Takeo is hemmed in by a large *boeng* (lake) to the north and a huge flood zone to the east. The old town centre is around Psar Nat (Meeting Market). The main commercial strip stretches along NH2 (St 20) from Independence Monument to the bustling main market, Psar Thmei (New Market), which is next to the bus and taxi station.

Information

Acleda Bank (NH2) Takeo's only bank has a 24-hour ATM that handles Visa cash advances.
Takeo Tourism (☎ /fax 931323; 🕑 7.30-11am & 2-5pm Mon-Fri, also open Sat & Sun) May be able to arrange a guide (US$15 to US$20) to Angkor Borei and Phnom Da. A new information pavilion is being built out the front.
VTC Internet (per hr 1500r; 🕑 6am-8pm) Internet access.
Xpress Internet Café (NH2; per hr 2000r; 🕑 6am-9pm)

Sights

The best area for a stroll is around **Psar Nat**, a concrete monstrosity built after the overthrow of the Khmer Rouge that's now a lively food court. It's surrounded by streets lined with arcaded, **French-era shophouses**.

Along the northern edge of town, the **lakefront promenade** is a popular late-afternoon hang-out for local youth. At its western end, a cement **pier** (St 3 btwn St 15 & St 17) that's seen better days attracts young couples in the mood to commune with lily pads and frogs – and each other. In the late afternoon there's Western-style **aerobics** (cnr St 3 & St 12; 🕑 5-6pm) for women.

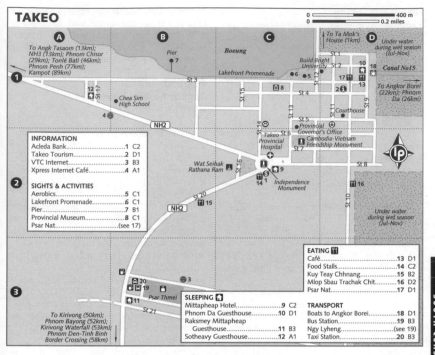

The one-room **Provincial Museum** (☎ 017 458280; St 4; admission US$2; ◷ 7-11am & 2-5pm), built in the flamboyant style of a Khmer temple, exhibits ancient Hindu and Buddhist carvings, including several *linga* and two Sanskrit stelas, found in Takeo Province. If it's locked, look around for the caretaker.

Takeo Province's most notorious native son, Ta Mok – aka 'The Butcher' – served as the Khmer Rouge's chief of staff in the 1960s and was later commander of the Southwestern Zone, where he presided over horrific atrocities. Paranoid about his personal security, in 1976 'Uncle Mok' had a three-storey headquarters built 1km north of town in the middle of the lake (he also had two residences near Anlong Veng – see p268 and p271). Used as an administrative centre by the high-ranking cadres who implemented Cambodia's genocide (and by experts from China), **Ta Mok's House** is now occupied by a police training facility, but you can wander around the grounds; access is via a 150m-long railings-free bridge.

For details on Angkor Borei and Phnom Da, see p238.

Sleeping

Phnom Da Guesthouse (☎ 016 826083; St 9; r with fan/air-con US$5/10; ✿) Facing the lake, this nicely situated, family-run hostelry has 10 rooms with high ceilings and fake flowers, and a grille-enclosed balcony with watery views. Make sure to ask specifically for a room with a window.

Sotheavy Guesthouse (☎ 016 869482, 012 935133; NH2 cnr St 17; d with fan/air-con from US$5/10; ✿) This yellow, four-storey establishment, wrapped in balconies, has 32 midsized rooms with low moulded ceilings, compact bathrooms and air-con you can really crank up.

Mittapheap Hotel (☎ 931205, 012 341744; St 20; d with fan/air-con from US$5/10; ✿) Facing Independence Monument, this place has 33 clean, well-kept rooms in four buildings arrayed around a coconut-shaded cement yard. Staff speak some English. Pricier rooms have hot water.

Raksmey Mittapheap Guesthouse (☎ 016 882362; NH2; r with fan/air-con US$5/10) Facing Psar Thmei, this well-maintained, 18-room place is convenient to public transport but can get noisy in the morning.

Eating & Drinking

There are food stalls around Independence Monument. In the evening, this is the place to snack on Cambodian desserts or enjoy a *tukalok* (fruit shake).

Café (St 9; 🕒 6am-5pm) This unpretentious place, run by a tall lad, serves Takeo's best iced coffee (1500r) – but no food – under a tin roof.

our pick **Psar Nat** (St 10; 🕒 6am-about 8pm) The food court here has a dozen food stalls that are great for coffee, breakfast soup (2000r), *num kong* (delectably chewy Khmer doughnuts; 200r) and *num kroch* (fried dumplings filled with beans and palm sugar). Also has vegetable sellers.

Kuy Teay Chhnang (NH2; 🕒 6am-7pm or later) This popular eatery, whose name means 'delicious noodles', specialises in early morning Chinese soups (4000r), a lip-smacking way to begin the day. Also serves rice-based Khmer dishes. There's no English sign – look for a fake brick facade.

Mlop Sbau Trachak Chit (☎ 011 974040; St 10; mains 5000r; 🕒 10am-9pm) Delicious, good-value Khmer dishes are served in over-the-lake pavilions. Specialities include *sach ko ang* (grilled beef). Look for the Anchor Beer sign.

Getting There & Around

Takeo is on NH2 77km south of Phnom Penh, 50km north of Kirivong and 58km north of the Phnom Den–Tinh Bien border crossing to Vietnam.

To Phnom Penh, **Ngy Lyheng** (☎ 023-351101) runs four buses (US$2.50) a day from the **bus station** (NH2), but share taxis (US$3) and minibuses, which stop at the adjacent taxi station, are more popular; a private taxi costs US$20.

If you're heading south along NH2 to Kirivong and/or the Phnom Den–Tinh Bien border crossing to Vietnam (see also opposite), a minibus is US$3, a share taxi US$5 and a private taxi US$35. To get to the border, you may have to change modes of transport in Kirivong.

The four daily buses that link Phnom Penh with Kampot (p227), via Kompong Trach and Kep, pass by Angk Tasaom, the chaotic transport junction 13km west of Takeo on NH3. At Angk Tasaom you can also pick up share taxis and minibuses that go direct to Kampot. To get from Takeo to Angk Tasaom, hop on a trailer pulled by a motorbike (2000r) from Psar Thmei, a *remork* (US$5) from Psar

Thmei or the hospital, or a *moto* (US$2) wherever you spot one.

Within Takeo, a *moto* from Psar Thmei to Psar Nat costs 2000r. Boats to Angkor Borei leave from the dock on quayside St 9.

AROUND TAKEO
Angkor Borei & Phnom Da
អង្គរបុរី និង ភ្នំដា

The highlight of a visit to Takeo is the 20km **boat ride** to **Angkor Borei**. Strategically situated on the margins of the Mekong Delta, this riverine townlet, today an impoverished backwater, was known as Vyadhapura when it served as the capital of 'water Chenla' in the 8th century.

Angkor Borei was also an important centre during the earlier Funan period (1st to 6th centuries), when Indian religion and culture were carried to the Mekong Delta by traders, artisans and priests from India (the great maritime trade route between India and China passed by the Mekong Delta). The earliest datable Khmer inscription (AD 611) was discovered at Angkor Borei, which is surrounded by a 5.7km moated wall that hints at its past greatness. The town was bombed during the Vietnam War.

Angkor Borei is home to a small **archaeological museum** (☎ 012 201638; admission US$1; 🕒 all day) featuring locally discovered Funan- and Chenla-era artefacts, including human bones, pottery, jewellery and stone carvings. Research on the town and its surrounds is being carried out by the **Lower Mekong Archaeological Project** (www.anthropology.hawaii.edu/Projects/LOMAP), affiliated with the University of Hawaii.

Angkor Borei has two very basic guesthouses.

The twin hills of **Phnom Da** (admission US$2), 3km south of Angkor Borei, are spectacularly isolated, Mont St-Michel–style, by the annual floods. The rocky slopes shelter five artificial **caves**, used for centuries as Hindu and Buddhist shrines and, during the Vietnam War, as hideouts by the Viet Cong. On top, 142 steps up, is a **temple** whose foundations were laid in the 6th century; the 18m-high structure itself dates from the 11th century. Exceptionally, the entrance faces due north; the other three sides have blind doors decorated with bas-relief *nagas*. The finest carvings have been taken to museums in Angkor Borei, Phnom Penh and Paris.

About 50m northeast of the temple, a huge **floating boulder** sits balanced on just three points. Vietnam can be seen 8km to the southeast.

Nearby, on a second hillock, is 8m-high **Wat Asram Moha Russei**, a restored Hindu sanctuary that probably dates from around the year AD 700. It's known as the 'Indian temple' because of its similarity to contemporary temples in South India.

GETTING THERE & AWAY

Angkor Borei and Phnom Da are about 20km east of Takeo town along Canal No 15, built in the 1880s to connect Takeo with the Tonlé Bassac river and the Mekong Delta. Clearly delineated in the dry season, the waterway is surrounded by flooded rice fields the rest of the year.

For great, bracing, open-air fun, zip along the canal in a fibreglass motorboat (US$30 return, 35 minutes to Angkor Borei, 10 to 15 minutes more to Phnom Da), available for hire at Takeo's boat dock. All but a small part of what you pay will be spent on fuel. In the rainy season the water can get rough in the afternoon, so it's a good idea to head out early. Bring a hat and, in the wet, rain gear. Many of the heavily laden boats you pass are bringing terracotta tiles and smuggled fuel from Vietnam.

Larger boats (3000r per person, two hours) link Takeo's boat dock with Angkor Borei, departing from Takeo at about 2pm and from Angkor Borei at about 9am. Another option is to wait around for enough locals to fill a share-motorboat (US$2.50 one way) to overflowing.

A *moto* from Takeo to Phnom Da costs US$2 return.

Phnom Bayong & Environs

ភ្នំបាយ័ង្គ

Affording breathtaking views of Vietnam's pancake-flat Mekong Delta, the cliff-ringed summit of Phnom Bayong (313m) is graced by a 7th-century **Chenla temple** built to celebrate a victory over Funan. The *linga* originally in the inner chamber is now in Paris' Musée Guimet, but a number of flora- and fauna-themed **bas-relief panels** can still be seen, eg on the lintels of the three false doorways and carved into

the brickwork. The site, once surrounded by two concentric walls (remnants are still visible), still attracts pilgrims and is tended by Buddhist nuns who live nearby in basic huts.

The steep walk up to the temple takes about 2½ hours return. The trail is not clearly marked, so it's a good idea to hire a local kid (or five) with a machete. Along the way you're likely to see locals out collecting leaves and roots for the preparation of traditional medicines. Bring plenty of water and thick eyebrows (or at least a handkerchief to wipe the sweat from your forehead). The descent over smooth rocky inclines will help prepare your leg muscles for the next ski season.

Kirivong town has three guesthouses, including **Tran Hout Guesthouse** (☎ 016 500033; NH2; r US$5-8), whose 17 tiny rooms are lightless and have poor ventilation.

About 28km west along the Phnom Bayong access road (highway 113) is **Phnom Tchea Tapech**, whose summit is marked by a 14m-high standing Buddha inaugurated in 2006. It is reached by a monumental staircase.

Kirivong Waterfall (Phar Ouk Waterfall), 2.5km west of the southern edge of Kirivong town, is popular with locals, especially on warm weekends. Toilets were recently installed as part of a clean-up campaign that is slated to include a trail upgrade. Market stalls sell the area's most famous products: topaz and quartz, either cut like gems or carved into tiny Buddhas and *nagas*.

GETTING THERE & AWAY

Kirivong (Kiri Vong) town is on NH2 50km south of Takeo and 8km north of the Phnom Den–Tinh Bien border crossing. Phnom Bayong is about 3km west of the northern edge of Kirivong town; the turn-off is marked by a painted panel depicting the temple.

From Takeo, a *moto* to Phnom Bayong costs about US$10 (US$15 return). It's cheaper to take a share taxi or a minibus to Kirivong town and then hop on a *moto* at the turn-off.

From the Phnom Den–Tinh Bien border crossing, it may be possible to catch a *remork* or *moto* to Kirivong's Ton Lop Market, from where minibuses go to Takeo and Phnom Penh. Catching a taxi at the border may involve phoning to have one sent from Kirivong town.

SOUTH COAST

Northwestern Cambodia

Mixing easy-to-get-to towns and temples with back-of-the-beyond adventure, Northwestern Cambodia extends from the now-paved Poipet border crossing with Thailand eastward to the wilds of Kompong Thom Province; and from the Dangkrek Mountains, on Cambodia's northern border with Thailand, southward into the untamed Cardamom Mountains. In the centre lies the miraculous body of water known as the Tonlé Sap Lake (p67).

Of the region's urban areas, Battambang – Cambodia's third-largest city – attracts the most visitors thanks to an alluring blend of general mellowness, French-era architecture and excellent day-trip options. Other towns serve mainly as gateways: Kompong Thom is near the pre-Angkorian temples of Sambor Prei Kuk; Pursat makes a good jumping-off point for the wilds of the northern Cardamoms; and Anlong Veng is a short *moto* ride from a string of eerie Khmer Rouge sites.

Northwestern Cambodia's remote plains and jungles conceal some of the country's most inspired temples. The once-notorious roads to spectacular Prasat Preah Vihear, declared a World Heritage site in 2008, and Koh Ker are slowly improving, while Banteay Chhmar, a top candidate for World Heritage site status, has a pioneering community-based homestay project. The roads to sprawling Preah Khan, shrouded in mystery, still spend the wet season under water.

The Northwest has some of Cambodia's most important wilderness areas, most of them well off the beaten track. The Cardamom Mountains, in the far southwest, are home to pristine jungle and rare wildlife, while the forests and marshes of Preah Vihear and Kompong Thom Provinces provide ideal habitat for endangered birds such as the giant ibis, Cambodia's national bird.

HIGHLIGHTS

- Soak up colonial-era charm in the riverside town of **Battambang** (p249), surrounded by lush countryside and hilltop temples
- Sail out to the colourful floating villages at **Kompong Luong** (p247) and near **Kompong Chhnang** (p242)
- Make an adventurous overland pilgrimage to the majestic mountain-top temple of **Prasat Preah Vihear** (p279)
- Journey to the 10th-century capital of **Koh Ker** (p274), its massive temples forgotten in the forests for a thousand years
- Explore Southeast Asia's first temple city, the impressive pre-Angkorian ruins of **Sambor Prei Kuk** (p284)

★ ELEVATION: 5-1500M	★ POPULATION: 3.6 MILLION	★ AREA: 71,157 SQ KM

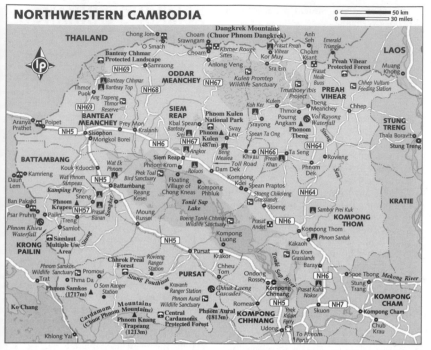

NORTHWESTERN CAMBODIA

Getting There & Away

Northwestern Cambodia has five international border crossings with Thailand:

- Poipet–Aranya Prathet (p261), 48km west of Sisophon and 153km west of Siem Reap. At the western terminus of NH5 – paved at long last! – this is Cambodia's most popular crossing with Thailand.
- Psar Pruhm–Ban Pakard (p260), 22km west of Pailin and 102km southwest of Battambang. The access road, NH57, is pretty churned up.
- Choam–Choam Srawngam (p271), 16km north of Anlong Veng and 134km north of Siem Reap. Linked to Siem Reap by the excellent NH67.
- O Smach–Chong Jom (p267), a punishing 40km northeast of Samraong and 120km north of Kralanh.
- Kamrieng–Daun Lem, 90km west-north-west of Battambang and 50km north-northwest of Pailin. Really just an outpost, and almost never used by foreigners.

Within Cambodia, the obvious gateways to the region are Siem Reap and Phnom Penh.

In the dry season, the fabled forest trail from Koh Kong Province (p201), on the Gulf of Thailand, north through the Cardamoms to Pursat is not quite as daunting it was as a few years back. The jungle track linking Thala Boravit (across the Mekong from Stung Treng; see p303) with Tbeng Meanchey is supposed to be turned into a road at some point.

A memorable, if slow, boat service links Siem Reap with Battambang. It should be possible to disembark from the Siem Reap–Phnom Penh fast boats at Kompong Chhnang.

Getting Around

South of the lake, NH5 connects Phnom Penh with Kompong Chhnang, Kompong Luong, Pursat, Battambang, Sisophon and the Poipet–Aranya Prathet border crossing to Thailand. North of the lake, NH6 links Phnom Penh with Kompong Thom, Siem Reap and Sisophon.

Roads that head north from NH6 include (from east to west):

- NH64 from Kompong Thom to Tbeng Meanchey, which at the time of research was degraded despite annual gradings and repeated government promises of a major overhaul.

■ A generally decent toll road from Dam Dek via Beng Mealea and Koh Ker to Tbeng Meanchey; the section within Siem Reap Province is paved. North of there the roads are in bad shape, especially in the wet season, but are being improved because of Prasat Preah Vihear's newfound strategic and symbolic importance.

■ The recently upgraded NH67 from Siem Reap to Anlong Veng (1½ hours) and the Choam–Choam Srawngam border crossing to Thailand.

■ NH68 from Kralanh to Samraong, cut by flooding in late 2009, but likely to be in fine form by the time you read this as it is due to be upgraded in 2010. The road from Samraong northeast to the O Smach–Chong Jom border crossing with Thailand is in a rather hellacious state.

■ NH69 from Sisophon via Banteay Chhmar to Samraong was, at the time of research, undergoing a major upgrade.

Doing a loop north of Angkor along Cambodia's northern border with Thailand – from Sisophon (on NH5 and NH6) to Banteay Chhmar, Samraong, Anlong Veng, Sra Em (near Prasat Preah Vihear), Tbeng Meanchey and Kompong Thom (on NH6), or vice versa – is getting easier by the year, though it's still a challenge in the wet, when the trip could be dubbed 'the Churning of the Ocean of Mud'. This route passes minefields and goes through areas so remote they're still being homesteaded, but if you're keen on outback jungle adventure you'd better hurry – in a few years, major ribbons of asphalt will connect the major sights.

Commercial and passenger traffic serving all these towns is oriented south towards NH6 (and, often, Siem Reap) rather than east or west, the result being that there's only light vehicular traffic – and virtually no public transport – from Banteay Chhmar northeast to Samraong, and from there east to Anlong Veng. Because of the ongoing tensions with Thailand in the Prasat Preah Vihear sector, share taxis now link Siem Reap and Anlong Veng with Sra Em.

KOMPONG CHHNANG PROVINCE

ខេត្តកំពង់ឆ្នាំង

Kompong Chhnang is a relatively wealthy province thanks to its proximity to the capital and its fishing and agricultural industries, supported by abundant water resources.

KOMPONG CHHNANG

កំពង់ឆ្នាំង

☎ 026 / pop 42,000

Kompong Chhnang (Clay Pot Port), on the Tonlé Sap River, is a tale of two cities: the generally sleepy centre, arrayed around a huge, grassy park; and the bustling dockside. Nearby sights include two floating villages, a hamlet famous for its distinctive pottery and some drop-dead gorgeous countryside, typically Cambodian in its union of verdant rice fields and towering sugar palms.

Orientation

The city centre is anchored by Psar Leu (Central Market), which is two blocks northeast of the Acleda Bank and the bus and taxi station. Independence Monument, in a grassy park, is 500m south.

Kompong Chhnang has a second commercial strip about 3km northeast of the centre, around Psar Krom (Lower Market) and the waterfront.

Information

Acleda Bank (NH5) Has an ATM that handles Visa cash advances.
Canadia Bank (NH5) Has an ATM.
Photo Service (per hr US$2; ⊙ 6am-8pm) Facing the triangular Naga Roundabout, this is a photo shop with internet access.
Sovannphum Hotel (☎ 989333; NH5; per hr US$1) Has an internet computer in the lobby.

Sights & Activities

The **monkeys** that live in and around the **Provincial Hall** sometimes wander out to Prison St at midday and in the afternoon.

FLOATING VILLAGES

A short sail from Kompong Chhnang's **waterfront**, on the Tonlé Sap River, takes you to two colourful floating villages: **Phoum Kandal**, which has neighbourhoods to the east and northwest; and **Chong Kos**, beyond

NORTHWESTERN CAMBODIA

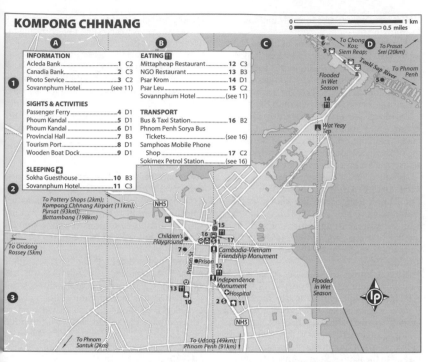

KOMPONG CHHNANG

INFORMATION	
Acleda Bank	**1** C2
Canadia Bank	**2** C3
Photo Service	**3** C2
Sovannphum Hotel	(see 11)

SIGHTS & ACTIVITIES	
Passenger Ferry	**4** D1
Phoum Kandal	**5** D1
Phoum Kandal	**6** D1
Provincial Hall	**7** B3
Tourism Port	**8** D1
Wooden Boat Dock	**9** D1

SLEEPING	
Sokha Guesthouse	**10** B3
Sovannphum Hotel	**11** C3

EATING	
Mittapheap Restaurant	**12** C3
NGO Restaurant	**13** B3
Psar Krom	**14** D1
Psar Leu	**15** C2
Sovannphum Hotel	(see 11)

TRANSPORT	
Bus & Taxi Station	**16** B2
Phnom Penh Sorya Bus Tickets	(see 16)
Samphoas Mobile Phone Shop	**17** C2
Sokimex Petrol Station	(see 16)

Phoum Kandal. Much less commercial than Kompong Luong (p247), they have all the amenities of a mainland village – houses, machine-tool shops, veggie vendors, a mosque, a petrol station – except that almost everything floats. Many of the residents are ethnic Vietnamese.

To get a waterborne look at the floating villages, you can take a **one-hour excursion** (☎ 012 878331; for foreigners/Khmers per person US$2.50/1.50, minimum 10 people) from the Tourism Port, docking point for life-vest-equipped motor launches with either 15 or 35 seats. Chartering an entire vessel is US$20 per hour.

A cheaper, quieter and more ecological option, available about 300m to the northwest, is to get around like the floating villagers do: on a **wooden boat** (per hr US$5) of the sort that's rowed standing up.

For a discount river cruise, you can hop on a **passenger ferry** (1000r, 30 minutes, departures at 8.30am, 11am, 1.30pm and 4pm) to Kompong Lang District, about 6km away on the other side of the Tonlé Sap River. The vessels, with space for several dozen people, dock 100m northwest of the Tourism Port.

Also across the Tonlé Sap River are several rather dilapidated brick-built **temples** dating from the Chenla period, including **Prasat Srei**.

ONDONG ROSSEY & PHNOM SANTUK
The quiet village of **Ondong Rossey**, where the area's famous red pottery is made under every house, is a delightful 7km ride west of town through serene rice fields dotted with sugar palms, many with bamboo ladders running up the trunk. The unpainted pots, decorated with etched or appliqué designs, are either turned with a foot-spun wheel (for small pieces) or banged into shape with a heavy wooden spatula (for large ones). Artisans are happy to show you how they do it.

The golden-hued mud piled up in the yards is quarried at nearby **Phnom Krang Dai Meas** and pounded into fine clay before being shaped and fired; only at the last stage does it acquire a pinkish hue. Pieces (from 1000r), including piggy banks, can be purchased at the **Pottery Development Center**.

In Kompong Chhnang, shops selling Ondong Rossey **pottery** can be found along

NORTHWESTERN CAMBODIA

NH5 several kilometres towards Battambang from town.

A visit to Ondong Rossey can be combined with **Phnom Santuk**, a rocky hillock behind Wat Santuk, which is a few kilometres southwest of Kompong Chhnang. The boulder-strewn summit affords fine views of the countryside, including the Tonlé Sap, 20km to the north.

By bicycle or *moto*, combining Ondong Rossey and Phnom Santuk makes for a truly magical circuit, especially early in the morning or late in the afternoon. There are no road signs, so it's a good idea to go with a local.

KOMPONG CHHNANG AIRPORT

The Khmer Rouge were not known as great builders, but in 1977 and 1978, slave labourers built an airfield using cement of such high quality that even today the 2440m runway and access roads look like they were paved just last week.

No one knows for sure, but it seems that Kompong Chhnang Airport (IATA code KZC), never operational under the Khmer Rouge, was intended to serve as a base for launching air attacks against Vietnam. Chinese engineers oversaw the work of tens of thousands of Cambodians suspected of disloyalty to the Khmer Rouge. Anyone unable to work was killed, often with a blow to the head delivered with a bamboo rod. In early 1979, as Vietnamese forces approached, almost the entire workforce was executed. Estimates of the number of victims, buried nearby in mass graves, range from 10,000 to 50,000.

In the late 1990s, a plan to turn the airport into a cargo hub for air-courier companies came to nought. These days, local teenagers come out here to tool around on their motorbikes, do doughnuts and drag race, while cows graze between the taxiway and the runway. On sunny days the sun creates convincing mirages.

On an anonymous slope a few kilometres away, the Khmer Rouge dug a **cave** – said to be 3km deep – apparently for the purpose of storing weapons flown in from China. Now home to swirling bats, it can be explored with a torch/flashlight but, lacking ventilation, gets very hot and humid. You may have to bushwhack your way up the hillside.

On a hillside near a cluster of bullet-pocked cement **barracks**, stripped of anything of value, is a massive cement **water tank**. Inside it's a remarkable echo chamber: stand in the middle and clap and thunder will come back at you from every direction, reverberating for a full 10 seconds.

Getting There & Away

The airport is about 12km west of town. Take NH5 towards Battambang for 7km and then turn left onto a concrete road that looks like a 1930s German autobahn. Some of the *moto* and *remork-moto (tuk tuk)* drivers in Kompong Chhnang know the way.

Sleeping

Sokha Guesthouse (☎ 988622; Prison St; r with fan/aircon from US$5/12; ✂) Set in a shady garden, this 31-room place offers the most charming accommodation in town, with rooms that are simple but spotless. Internet connectivity is planned. The walk out here can be a tad dark at night.

Sovannphum Hotel (☎ /fax 989333; sovannphum kpchotel@yahoo.com; NH5; r with fan/air-con from US$7/13; ✂ 🖳 🤶) Clean, well-run and well-kept, this is now the hostelry of choice for the NGO crowd. Has 30 good-sized rooms with modern bathrooms, a restaurant and wi-fi reception in the lobby.

Eating

There are plenty of food stalls at the two markets, Psar Leu and Psar Krom but, at the latter, not on the abandoned upper level, which sellers have considered haunted ever since a German tourist shot himself there – or maybe he was murdered – about 10 years ago. The port has snack stalls. Aid workers often eat at the unmarked **NGO restaurant** (meal US$1.50) around the corner from the Sokha Guesthouse.

Sovannphum Hotel (☎ 989333; NH5; mains from 4500r; ☺ 6am-9pm) The restaurant serves a decent selection of Khmer classics.

Mittapheap Restaurant (☎ 012 949297; NH5; mains 8000-20,000r; ☺ 5am-9pm) Facing Independence Monument. The service is as indifferent as the selection of Khmer dishes is uninspired.

Getting There & Away

Kompong Chhnang is 91km north of Phnom Penh, 93km southeast of Pursat and 198km southeast of Battambang.

BOAT

The fast ferries linking Phnom Penh with Siem Reap pass right by Kompong Chhnang.

If you'd like to get off here, inform the boat company in advance. Sokha Guesthouse can book you a boat seat to Siem Reap.

BUS

On NH5 you can try to flag down a bus heading to Phnom Penh, but buses going in the other direction, ie towards Pursat and Battambang, are often full.

Phnom Penh Sorya (☎ 016 400031; www.ppsoryat ransport.com; ⏰ 6.30am-5.30pm) has a ticket stall at the bus and taxi station; staff can call ahead to see if seats are available. To Phnom Penh (15,000r, 1½ to two hours), buses leave hourly from about 9.30am to 5.30pm; to Battambang (20,000r, two hours) and Poipet (30,000r, five hours), there are hourly departures from 8am to about 2pm.

Across the street, **Samphoas Mobile Phone Shop** (☎ 012 900190) sells westbound seats on Neak Kror Horm buses; destinations include Battambang (19,000r) and Poipet (28,000r).

TAXI

The easiest and fastest way to get to Phnom Penh is by share taxi (12,000r, 1½ to two hours), which wait both at the bus and taxi station, and on the waterfront, near the ferry to Kompong Lang District. Share taxis do not serve destinations to the northwest (eg Battambang).

Getting Around

Moto drivers hang out at the bus and taxi station and, in the morning, outside the Sokha Guesthouse. They charge 2000r for short hops around town, US$5 to US$8 for a half-day trip and US$10 for an all-day (7am to 5pm) excursion. The Sovannphum Hotel has *remorks* (US$10 return to the old airport).

Sokha Guesthouse rents bicycles (US$1 a day) and motorbikes (US$6 a day).

PURSAT PROVINCE

ខេត្តពោធិ៍សាត់

Famed for its oranges, Cambodia's fourth-largest province stretches from the remote forests of Phnom Samkos, on the Thai border, eastwards to the fishing villages and marshes of Tonlé Sap Lake. It encompasses the northern reaches of the Cardamom Mountains, linked by dodgy roads with the town of Pursat.

PURSAT

ពោធិ៍សាត់

☎ 052 / pop 57,000

The provincial capital, known for its marble carvers, is no beauty spot, but makes a good base for a day trip to the floating village of Kompong Luong (p247) or an expedition into the wilds of the Central Cardamoms Protected Forest (p248).

Orientation

Pursat's main commercial street, north–south St 3, is two blocks west of St 1, which runs along the river. Both streets are perpendicular to NH5.

Information

Acleda Bank (NH5) Has an ATM that handles Visa cash advances.

Canadia Bank (NH5) Has an ATM.

Department of Tourism (☎ 012 838854; ⏰ 7-11am & 2-5pm Mon-Fri) Has displays on province highlights on the walls and a few handouts.

Pheng Ky Computer (St 1; per hr US$1; ⏰ 6am-8pm) Internet access.

Sights & Activities

A pleasant few hours can be spent strolling north along St 1 and then south along the east bank of the river.

When you first see **Koh Sampov Meas** (Golden Ship Island), the town's very modest answer to Singapore's Sentosa, it's hard to believe your eyes: what's an ocean-going supertanker doing in the Pursat River?! In fact, the island's singular appearance reflects a local legend about a boat that ran aground and turned into an island. In the late afternoon, the manicured lawns and Khmer-style pavilions are *the* place to see and be seen as locals – especially young people – drop by for **aerobics** (⏰ classes from 5pm), a snack, or a game of badminton. Eastward across the river is a yellow, onion-domed **Cham mosque**, topped with a star and crescent.

A long block north, you can take a vertiginous walk across a crumbling **Khmer Rouge–era dam**, part of a grandiose project intended to make it possible to grow rice in the dry season (the scheme never worked). On the rural east bank, walk south along the river road and you'll come upon a number of **marble-carving shops**, where artisans make – and sell – everything from tiny tchotchkes to huge smiling Buddhas (also on sale in shops along NH5, including **Chea Phally Marble Carving**). You may also see groups

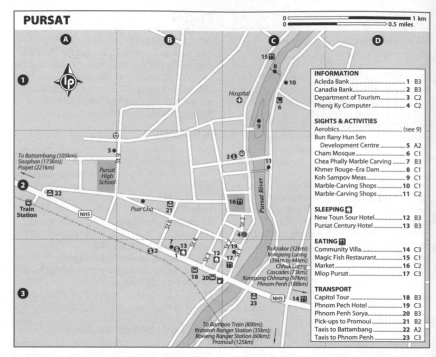

PURSAT

INFORMATION	
Acleda Bank	1 B3
Canadia Bank	2 B3
Department of Tourism	3 C2
Pheng Ky Computer	4 C2

SIGHTS & ACTIVITIES	
Aerobics	(see 9)
Bun Rany Hun Sen Development Centre	5 A2
Cham Mosque	6 C1
Chea Phally Marble Carving	7 B3
Khmer Rouge–Era Dam	8 C1
Koh Sampov Meas	9 C1
Marble-Carving Shops	10 C1
Marble-Carving Shops	11 C2

SLEEPING	
New Toun Sour Hotel	12 B3
Pursat Century Hotel	13 B3

EATING	
Community Villa	14 C3
Magic Fish Restaurant	15 C1
Market	16 C2
Mlop Pursat	17 C3

TRANSPORT	
Capitol Tour	18 B3
Phnom Pech Hotel	19 C3
Phnom Penh Sorya	20 B3
Pick-ups to Promoui	21 B2
Taxis to Battambang	22 A2
Taxis to Phnom Penh	23 C3

of women making *naom banchok* (thick rice noodles) that they sell fresh in the market.

The **Bun Rany Hun Sen Development Centre** (☎ 951606; St 9; ⏰ 7-11am & 2-5pm Mon-Fri & Sat morning) teaches cloth and mat weaving, sewing, marble carving and other artisanal skills to young people, and markets the items they make. Travellers are welcome to visit classes.

Bamboo trains (*norry* or *lorry*; p252) *sometimes* pass by the train station and the train crossing 800m south of NH5 on the road to Kravanh. A three- or four-hour private excursion costs about US$10 plus petrol, or you can hop on with the locals. Ask locals for help in flagging one down – success is most likely in the early morning. (Illegal cargos, such as wood, are generally moved at night.) For the best scenery, head towards Phnom Penh. One option is to get off at the village of **Chheu Tom** and catch a *moto* to **Chhuk Laeng Cascades** (Chroek Laeng or Chrok La Eing; one hour), situated 73km southeast of Pursat and 41km south of Krakor.

Sleeping

New Toun Sour Hotel (Hotel Than Sour Thmey, Hotel Thmey Thansour; ☎ 951506; St 2; r with fan/air-con US$6/13;

⌗ ▢ 🛜) Its lobby chock full of carved wooden doodads, this welcoming place has 43 large, clean rooms with hot water and fridges.

Pursat Century Hotel (☎ 951446; pursatcentury hotel@yahoo.com; NH5; r with fan/air-con from US$7/15; ⌗ 🛜) Opened in 2009, this multistorey establishment has set new standards for Pursat. The 110 rooms offer two-star comfort and a sprig of fake cherry blossoms by each bed.

Eating

At the new **market** (St 1) you'll find both daytime eateries and a night market, as well as the usual fruit and veggie stalls. The New Toun Sour Hotel has a restaurant.

Mlop Pursat (☎ 012 928586; St 1; ⏰ 6-11am) This shady garden is *the* place to go for breakfast – specialities include chicken rice (6000r) and the best soups (3500r) in town.

Community Villa (☎ 012 178 9050; www.knkscam bodia.org; NH5; mains 4000-10,000r; ⏰ 6am-7pm) Run by a Cambodian NGO that teaches job skills to at-risk young people, Community Villa – on NH5 500m east of the bridge – serves tasty Khmer dishes, including ginger fish, and *tukalok* (fruit shake) drinks. A small gift

Chipping Ongar [ongkiosk2]

Thank you for visiting
CHIPPING ONGAR LIBRARY
Renewals/Enquiries:
Tel 0345 603 7628
You can also renew online at
www.essex.gov.uk/libraries

Borrowed Items 09/10/2019 13:43
XXXXXXXXXX4109

Item Title	Due Date
* Vietnam.	30/10/2019
* Cambodia.	30/10/2019
* The Hairy Bikers' perfect	30/10/2019
* Micro	30/10/2019
* Night after night	30/10/2019
* In a house of lies	30/10/2019
* Hush hush	30/10/2019

* Indicates items borrowed today
Thank you for using Essex Libraries

shop sells *krama*, wallets and purses made by rural women.

Magic Fish Restaurant (Tep Machha Restaurant; ☎ 951537; St 1; mains 5000-15,000r; ۞ 10am-9pm or later) Just north of the Khmer Rouge–era dam, this riverside place has tasty Khmer dishes and great river views.

Getting There & Around

Pursat is 105km southeast of Battambang and 188km northwest of Phnom Penh along NH5.

Buses pass through Pursat virtually all day long, shuttling between Poipet and Battambang (10,000r, 1½ hours) to the northwest, and Kompong Chhnang and Phnom Penh (18,000r, four hours) to the southeast. A few direct services head to Siem Reap (25,000r, five hours) and Kompong Cham (35,000r). Bus companies with Pursat offices include **Capitol Tour** (☎ 951650; NH5 cnr St 3; ۞ 6.30am-7.15pm) and **Phnom Penh Sorya** (☎ 012 687565; www.ppsorya transport.com; NH5; ۞ 6am-7pm).

Share taxis to Phnom Penh (20,000r, 3½ hours) and Kompong Chhnang (20,000r) can be found on NH5 just east of the bridge, while those to Battambang (15,000r, 1½ hours) stop across NH5 from the old train station (near the small Sokimex petrol station). To Battambang there are also pick-ups (outside/inside 7000r/10,000r).

Pick-ups (outside/inside 10,000r/15,000r) and share taxis (20,000r, four hours) to the remote Cardamoms town of Promoui (Veal Veng) leave from next to the old market, Psar Cha. During the dry season, it *may* be possible to find a pick-up from Promoui south through the Cardamoms to Krong Koh Kong.

The **Phnom Pech Hotel** (☎ 951515; St 1) rents out bicycles (US$2.50 a day) and motorbikes (US$8) and can arrange a round-trip *moto/ taxi* trip to Kompong Luong for US$10/30.

KOMPONG LUONG
កំពង់លួង

pop 10,000

Kompong Luong has all the amenities you'd expect to find in an oversized fishing village – except that here everything floats! The result is a partly ethnic-Vietnamese Venice without the dry land. The cafes, shops, chicken coops, fish ponds, ice-making factory, crocodile farm and karaoke bars are kept from sinking by boat hulls, barrels or bunches of bamboo, as are the Vietnamese pagoda (with bougain-villeas on the front porch), the blue-roofed

church and the colourful houses, some with flower pots on their verandas – similar, perhaps, to terrestrial homes with aquariums. The cool teenagers zip around in boats with oversized motors, while little old ladies paddle rhythmically the old-fashioned way. The only thing you can't do in Kompong Luong, it seems, is play pool properly – for obvious reasons, the nearest decent pool halls are on dry land.

In the dry season, when water levels drop and the Tonlé Sap shrinks, the entire aquapolis is towed, boat by boat, a few kilometres north. That's why there used to be a sign on NH5 indicating that the distance to Kompong Luong is a maximum of 7km, a minimum of 2km. Not much fun for the postman!

The population of this fascinating and picturesque village is partly Vietnamese, so – reflecting their ambiguous status in Cambodian society – you may find the welcome here slightly more subdued than in most rural Cambodian towns, at least from adults. Khmer Rouge massacres of Vietnamese villagers living around Tonlé Sap Lake were commonplace during the first half of the 1990s, and even as late as 1998 over 20 Vietnamese were killed in a pogrom near Kompong Chhnang.

Sleeping

About 800m north of Krakor junction along the road to Kompong Luong, **Hotel 59** (☎ 012 384009; r with fan/air-con from US$5/13; ⌘), opened in late 2009, has 30 bare-bones rooms, ridiculously broad hallways and, out the back, a fish pond.

Getting There & Around

Kompong Luong is between 39km and 44km east of Pursat, depending on the time of year. From Pursat, round-trip transport options include *moto* (US$10, 45 minutes) and private taxi (US$30). The turn-off from NH5 is in Krakor next to the Sokimex petrol station.

The government-set rate for a spin around Kompong Luong in a life-vest-equipped four-passenger wooden **motorboat** (☎ 092-240286) is US$3 per person *per hour* (keep an eye on your watch) for two to four people.

Taxis to Phnom Penh leave from Krakor's Sokimex petrol station early in the morning.

NORTHERN CARDAMOM MOUNTAINS

As the Central Cardamoms Protected Forest (CCPF) and adjacent wildlife sanctuaries slowly open up to ecotourism, Pursat is emerging as the Cardamoms' northern gateway.

For details on the southern reaches of the Cardamom Mountains, which stretch all the way to the Gulf of Thailand, see p200.

Roads in the area are heavily rutted and some bridges have holes big enough for a car tyre to fall through. From Pursat, it's possible to find a taxi to Kravanh, Rovieng or Promoui – ask around at Psar Cha in Pursat or enquire at your guesthouse.

Central Cardamoms Protected Forest

For information on the CCPF and road access to its southern sections, see p204.

The CCPF's enforcement ranger teams get technical and financial support from **Conservation International** (CI; www.conservation.org). To coordinate a visit, arrange a guide, or stay at a **ranger station** (eg Kravanh, Rovieng or O Som), contact Conservation International's **La Peng Ly** (☎ 012 908560; lly@conservation.org).

Areas in and near the CCPF are still being de-mined, so stay on roads and well-trodden trails.

KRAVANH RANGER STATION

The Forest Administration rangers (in tan uniforms) and armed military policemen (in dark green uniforms) based at this CCPF ranger station, deep in the Cardamoms jungle in the Tang Rang area south of Pursat, play an unending game of cat and mouse with loggers, poachers and encroachers – a game with life-and-death consequences for the rainforest, its fauna and Cambodia's biodiversity. Teams based here often go out on long-range foot patrols, sleeping rough under tarps for a week or more.

For information on trans-CCPF treks to/from Kravanh, see p204. It may be possible to stay in a dorm bed (and, in the near future, a proper room) at Kravanh, where life has the pace and feel of a remote military outpost.

ROVIENG RANGER STATION

An impressive collection of seatless cars and ox carts loaded with illegal wood fills the yard at this frontline ranger station, but the most valuable contraband here is aromatic *moras preuv* (sassafras, or safrole) oil, extracted from the roots of the endangered *Dysoxylum loureiri* tree. One tonne of wood produces just 30L of the oil, which has a delightful, sandalwoodlike scent. Local people use it in traditional medicine and it keeps away both mossies and rats, but the liquid interests smugglers because it can be used to make the drug Ecstasy. Other impounded objects stored here include chainsaws, snares (including some specially designed to catch pangolins; see p204) and guns.

Bulletin-board photos show clandestine sawmills, stills for extracting *moras preuv* oil, confiscated bush meat and animals observed by rangers while on patrol, including leopards, foxes, crocodiles, monkeys, pangolins, deer, manchettes and wild pigs.

A few kilometres from Rovieng (and 53km southwest of Pursat) are the **L'Bak Kamronh Rapids**, which attract Khmers on holidays. About 25km west of Rovieng, in Promoui Commune, the old-growth **Chhrok Preal Forest** can be visited with a guide.

The land on either side of the road to Rovieng was deforested by the Vietnamese to prevent ambushes and later settled by destitute homesteaders, in some cases before anyone checked for mines. In many areas clear-cut a few years ago, but now protected, the forest is growing back – a hopeful sign of regeneration.

By car, Rovieng is two hours from Pursat.

Phnom Aural Wildlife Sanctuary

Sadly, Phnom Aural Wildlife Sanctuary (2538 sq km), just east of the CCPF, is rapidly being destroyed from the south and the east by corrupt land speculation and rampant illegal logging.

Hiking up **Phnom Aural** (1813m), Cambodia's highest peak, takes a day and a half; getting down takes a day. About halfway up is the site of a **crashed aircraft** that may have been bringing arms from China to the Khmer Rouge in the spring of 1975. A guide who knows the way, and where to find water, can be hired in the village of Sra Ken.

Cambodia's only hot springs, **Te Teuk Pus**, are situated in the southern part of Phnom Aural Wildlife Sanctuary in Kompong Speu Province, about 75km west-northwest of the provincial capital, Kompong Speu.

Phnom Samkos Wildlife Sanctuary

Sandwiched between the CCPF and the Thai frontier, the Phnom Samkos Wildlife Sanctuary (3338 sq km) is well and truly out in the sticks. It is threatened by a copper-mining concession and the Chinese-built Atai hydroelectric dam, which will flood 52 sq km – now being clear-cut – starting in 2011.

Boasting Cambodia's second-highest peak, **Phnom Samkos** (1717m), the sanctuary's main town is **Promoui** (Veal Veng), 125km and four hours from Pursat over a pretty rough road (see p247) that passes by Rovieng. This remote little burg has three **guesthouses** (r US$5). A local guide can take you by motorbike to hill-tribe villages.

A ruinous track heads south via **O Som** (where there's a CCPF ranger station) to Krong Koh Kong and the Koh Kong Conservation Corridor (see p200). In the dry season, it *may* be possible to hire a pick-up to the coast in Promoui.

BATTAMBANG PROVINCE

ខេត្តបាត់ដំបង

Battambang (Bat Dambang), said by proud locals to produce Cambodia's finest rice, sweetest coconuts and tastiest oranges (don't bring this up in Pursat), has a long border with Thailand and a short stretch of the Tonlé Sap shoreline. The region has an enduring tradition of producing many of Cambodia's best-loved singers and actors.

Battambang has passed from Cambodia to Thailand and back again several times over the past few centuries. Thailand ruled the area from 1795 to 1907 and again during WWII (1941 to 1946), when the Thais cut a deal with the Japanese and the Vichy French.

BATTAMBANG

បាត់ដំបង

☎ 053 / pop 140,000

Battambang has a charm and urban sophistication all its own. Cambodia's fourth tourist destination (after Siem Reap, Phnom Penh and Sihanoukville), it brings together the resources of a modern city with some of Cambodia's best-preserved colonial architecture and small-town friendliness. Timeless hilltop temples and bucolic villages can be seen on leisurely day trips by bicycle, *moto* or the fabled bamboo train. The most scenic river trip in the country links Battambang with Siem Reap.

Battambang has more Hindu representations (eg roundabout statues) than you find in most parts of Cambodia and has long had Christian communities.

Orientation

Battambang's city centre is on the west bank of Stung Sangker; its focal point is Psar Nat (Meeting Market). St 1 runs along the riverfront, St 2 is one block inland and St 3 serves as the main commercial thoroughfare; in between are St 1½ and St 2½.

The liveliest street on the up-and-coming East Bank is Old NH5.

Information

ANZ Royal Bank (St 1) Has ATMs here and at the East Bank's Golden Palace Hotel.

Canadia Bank (☎ 952267) Has ATMs.

Centre Culturel Français (☎ 952897; www.ccf-cambodge.org) Valiantly trying to keep French culture alive in the age of English, the French Cultural Centre has an upstairs *médiathèque* (open 9am to noon and 3.30pm to 7pm Monday to Saturday) with books and DVDs; puts on art exhibitions, dance performances and concerts; and screens films from France (some with English subtitles) at 7pm on Friday.

Clinic Yi Kuok (formerly Stung Sangker Clinique; ☎ 953163; yikuokbtb@yahoo.com; ⏰ 24hr) The best medical clinic in Battambang, with English-speaking doctors trained in France and Vietnam, modern facilities, and the city's only CT scanner. Can handle rabies shots and snake bites.

Emergency (☎ 952822; emergency@online.com.kh; ⏰ 24hr for emergencies) This 70-bed, Italian-run 'surgical centre for war victims' (www.emergency.it) *cannot* help with tropical diseases or routine illness, but may be able to save your life if you need emergency surgery, eg because of a traffic accident or a life-threatening abdominal condition. Has two ambulances.

Green Net (St 1; ⏰ 7am-7pm or later) One of three internet shops on the same block.

KCT Internet (⏰ 6am-8pm; per hr 1500r) Next to White Rose restaurant.

Pulp (☎ 012 178 3584; 83 St 2½) Sells books and serves drinks and edibles.

Smiling Sky Bookshop (☎ 012 298005; 113 St 2; ⏰ 8am-7.30pm or 8pm) Sells used books in English, French and German.

Star Net (per hr 1500r; ⏰ 7am-8pm) Internet access just off St 3.

Tok Song Sour Internet (St 3; per hr 1500r; ⏰ 7am-8pm) Many locals' preferred internet shop.

Tourist Information Office (☎ 730217; www.battambang-town.gov.kh; St 1; 8am-6pm) Has brochures and maps of Battambang, Siem Reap and Phnom Penh.

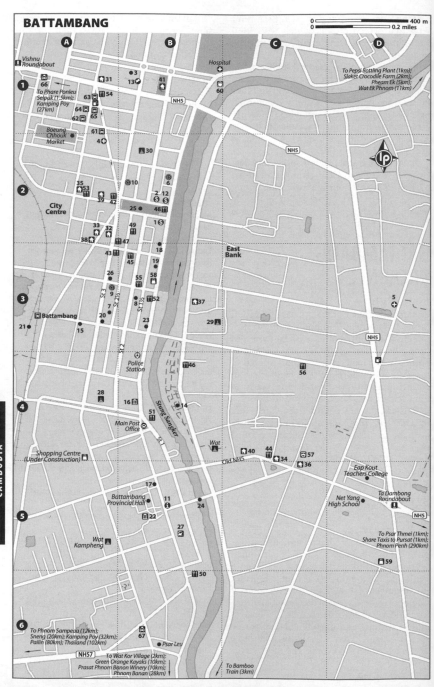

BATTAMBANG

0 — 400 m
0 — 0.2 miles

INFORMATION
ANZ Royal Bank.............................**1** B2
Canadia Bank..................................**2** B2
Centre Culturel Français..............**3** B1
Clinic Yi Kuok................................**4** A2
Emergency......................................**5** D3
Green Net..**6** B2
KCT Internet.............................(see 55)
Pulp...**7** A3
Smiling Sky Bookshop..................**8** B3
Star Net..**9** A3
Tok Song Sour Internet..............**10** B2
Tourist Information Office..........**11** B5
Union Commercial Bank...............**12** B2
Vietnamese Consulate..................**13** B1

SIGHTS & ACTIVITIES
Aerobics...**14** B4
Australian Centres for
  Development..............................**15** A3
Battambang Museum....................**16** B4
Battambang Provincial
  Hall Guardhouse.......................**17** B5
Colonial Buildings.......................**18** B3
Colonial Buildings.......................**19** B3
French Shophouses.......................**20** A3
French-Era Train Repair
  Sheds..**21** A3
Governor's Residence...................**22** B5
Nikon Photo Studio......................**23** B3
Old French Bridge........................**24** B5
Psar Nat..**25** B2

Seeing Hands Massage.................**26** A3
Smokin' Pot Cooking
  Classes.....................................(see 52)
Victory Club...................................**27** B5
Wat Damrey Sar.............................**28** A4
Wat Kandal.....................................**29** B3
Wat Phiphétaram..........................**30** B2

SLEEPING 🏠
Banan Hotel...................................**31** A1
Chhaya Hotel.................................**32** A2
Chhaya II Hotel.............................**33** A2
Golden Palace Hotel.....................**34** C4
Holiday Hotel................................**35** A2
Khemara Battambang
  Hotel..**36** C5
La Villa..**37** B3
Lux Hotel..**38** A2
Royal Hotel....................................**39** A2
Spring Park Hotel.........................**40** C4
Stung Sangke Hotel......................**41** B1

EATING 🍴
Chea Neang.....................................**42** A2
Fresh Eats Café.........................(see 49)
Gecko Café......................................**43** A3
Green House Café..........................**44** C4
International Bakery...................(see 60)
Khmer Delight...............................**45** B3
Korean Steam Boat.......................**46** B4
La Villa.......................................(see 37)
Lux-Tang Bakery...........................**47** B2

Night Market.................................**48** B2
Pomme d'Amour............................**49** B2
Psar Nat.....................................(see 25)
Riverside Balcony
  Bar...**50** B6
Riverside Night
  Market...**51** B4
Smokin' Pot....................................**52** B3
Sunrise Coffee House...................**53** A2
Vegetarian Foods
  Restaurant..................................**54** A1
White Rose.....................................**55** B3
X-Gold Beer Garden......................**56** C4

ENTERTAINMENT 🎭
Sky Disco..**57** C4

SHOPPING 🛍
Fresh Eats Café.........................(see 49)
Hat Bunthoeun..............................**58** B3
Rachana Handicrafts....................**59** D5

TRANSPORT
Boat to Siem Reap........................**60** B1
Capitol Tour...................................**61** A1
Neak Kror Horm............................**62** A1
Paramount Angkor
  Express..**63** A1
Phom Penh Sorya.........................**64** A1
Ponleu Angkor Khmer..................**65** A1
Taxi Station....................................**66** A1
Taxis to Pailin..............................**67** B6

Union Commercial Bank (St 1) Has an ATM.

Vietnamese Consulate (☎ 952894; ⏱ 8-11am & 2-4pm Mon-Fri) If you've visited Vietnam before, a one-month visa (US$35) takes just a few hours; if not, you may have to leave your passport for two or three days.

Sights

Some of Battambang's finest **colonial buildings** are on the waterfront, especially along the two blocks of St 1 south of **Psar Nat** (Meeting Market), itself an architectural monument, albeit a modernist one. The four-faced clock tower is worth a glance – but not to find out the time. There are more old **French shophouses** along St 3, just east of the train station, for example.

The mustard yellow **Governor's Residence**, recently renovated, is another handsome legacy of very early 1900s. Designed by an Italian architect for the last Thai governor, who departed in 1907, it has imposing balconies and a grand reception room with 5m ceilings. The interior is closed, but you can stroll the grounds – provided you manage to talk your way past the guard at the entrance to the adjacent Battambang Provincial Hall. Except for the neo-Khmer laterite gate, the intersection out front looks much as it did in the 1930s:

check out the French-only milestone, the neat lawns and the **old French bridge**, now reserved for pedestrians and motorbikes.

Two elegant, though as yet nameless, east–west **avenues**, with parkland down the middle, grace the city centre. One passes by the Centre Culturel Français (one block north of NH5), while the other stretches west from the worthwhile **Battambang Museum** (☎ 092-214688; St 1; admission US$1; ⏱ 8-11am & 2-5pm), now open seven days a week. Highlights include fine Angkorian lintels and statuary from all over Battambang Province, including Phnom Banan and Sneng. Signs are in Khmer, English and French.

Battambang's Buddhist temples survived the Khmer Rouge period relatively unscathed thanks to a local commander who ignored orders from on high. They include **Wat Phiphétaram**, a long block north of Psar Nat, built in 1888; **Wat Damrey Sar**, west of the Battambang Museum; and **Wat Kandal** on the East Bank, once famed for its library. A number of the monks at all three wats speak English and are glad for a chance to practise; they're often around in the late afternoon.

In the area around the old train station – where the time is always 8.02, according to the clock – and along the tracks just south of there, you can explore a treasure trove of crumbling, **French-era train repair sheds**, warehouses and stripped rolling stock, evocative of times long gone. Some of the wagons' constructor's plates read '1930 Köln' (Cologne, Germany). German reparations from WWI, perhaps? Or were the wagons confiscated after WWII and shipped out here in the last days of French Indochina?

Activities

Day trips out of town are one of the highlights here – see p256.

COURSES

Always wanted to learn how to prepare authentic family-style Khmer dishes? Daily from 9.30am to 12.30pm, **Smokin' Pot** (☎ 012 821400; vannaksmokingpot@yahoo.com; St 1½) offers **cooking classes** (US$8) that start with a trip to Psar Nat and culminate in a three-course lunch (you eat what you cook). Reserve a day ahead.

Contact the Royal Hotel for details on the cooking classes offered by **Ch'ngainh! Ch'ngainh!** (☎ 012 639360; sambath_9@hotmail.com; US$10), 2km from the centre.

The **Australian Centres for Development** (☎ 952370; acd@online.com.kh; per hr US$5), near

the old train station, offers 10-week Khmer language courses.

FITNESS & SWIMMING

In New York or London they may be achieving inner harmony with t'ai chi, but on Battambang's East Bank they're burning off the rice carbs doing Western **aerobics** (1000r), held every day (unless it's raining) from about 6am to 7am and 5pm to 7pm. Led by a local hunk with a portable sound system, just five minutes of working out should be enough to teach you how to count in Khmer – at least up to four.

The **Victory Club** (☎ 017 530168; per day incl towel & locker US$2.50; ☉ 6am-8pm) has a 25m pool and, upstairs, about two dozen fitness machines.

Nonguests can use the **pool** (adult/child incl towel & locker US$5/3; ☉ 7am-9pm) and fitness room of the Stung Sangke Hotel.

KAYAKING

One- to three-person kayaks can be rented from **Green Orange Kayaks** (☎ 085-506910; feda@online.com.kh; ☉ 7am-5pm Mon-Fri), run by an NGO (www.fedacambodia.org) that offers free English classes. The half-day trip from its grassy campus, 10km south of Battambang towards Phnom Banan, downriver to the city

---

ALL ABOARD, EVERYONE OFF, ALL ABOARD, EVERYONE OFF!

Battambang's **bamboo train** is one of the world's all-time classic rail journeys. From O Dambong, on the east bank 3.7km south of Battambang's old French bridge, the train clicks and clacks southeast to O Sra Lav along warped, misaligned rails and vertiginous bridges left by the French.

Each bamboo train – known in Khmer as a *norry* (*nori*) or *lorry* – consists of a 3m-long wooden frame, covered lengthwise with slats made of ultralight bamboo, that rests on two barbell-like bogies, the aft one connected by fan belts to a 6HP gasoline engine. Pile on 10 or 15 people or up to three tonnes of rice, crank it up and you can cruise along at about 15km/h.

The genius of the system is that it offers a brilliant solution to the most ineluctable problem faced on any single-track line: what to do when two trains going in opposite directions meet. In the case of bamboo trains, the answer is simple: one car is quickly disassembled and set on the ground beside the tracks so the other can pass. The rule is that the car with the fewest passengers has to cede priority. Motorbikes pull rank, though, so if you bring one along you'll get VIP treatment.

What happens, you may ask, when a bamboo train meets a real train barrelling down the track? First, Cambodian trains don't barrel, they crawl. Second, bamboo-train conductors know the real train's schedule. And third, the real train can be heard tooting its horn from a great distance, providing more than enough time to dismount and disassemble.

Hiring a private bamboo train from O Dambong to O Sra Lav (12km return, 1¼ hours) costs US$10, though it's much cheaper to take a share-*norry* with locals transporting veggies, charcoal or wood to market.

Sadly, bamboo trains are likely to be banned when the Phnom Penh–Poipet rail line is upgraded.

costs US$12 per person (including life jackets); an optional guide is US$3. To rent on Saturday or Sunday, make contact on a weekday.

MASSAGE

At **Seeing Hands Massage** (☎ 092-379903; per hr US$6; ⏰ 7am-10pm), trained blind masseurs and masseuses offer soothing, Japanese-style work-overs.

PORTRAITURE

For as little as US$2, you can pose in traditional Khmer costume and have your photo taken at **Nikon Photo Studio** (☎ 012 864884; 23 St 1; ⏰ 6am-5pm). Prices include make-up and a suitably kitschy background.

TEACHING

Volunteer English teachers are welcomed by the **Cambodian Education Center** (p258) in Pheam Ek and the **Khmer New Generation Organization** (☎ 092-790597; www.kngo-home.org).

Sleeping

Battambang offers excellent accommodation value, particularly in the midrange category.

CITY CENTRE

Most of the city's hotels are within a few bustling blocks of Psar Nat. Very cheap guesthouses can be found around the taxi park. The rival Royal and Chhaya Hotels can help arrange guides and transport.

Chhaya Hotel (☎ 952170; chhaya.best@yahoo.com; 118 St 3; r with fan US$3-7, with air-con US$10; ☒ ▣ 🕸) This sprawling, shambolic establishment, a veteran address for budget backpackers, has 84 uninspiring rooms. Behind it, the new Chhaya II Hotel will have about 50 air-con rooms and family suites for US$12 to US$25.

Royal Hotel (☎ /fax 952522; royalasiahotelbb@yahoo. com; r with fan/air-con from US$6/10; ☒ ▣ 🕸) Long hugely popular with independent travellers, the 45-room Royal doesn't have any bells and whistles, just clean, comfortable, spacious lodgings with fridge and TV.

Lux Hotel (☎ 092-335767; r with fan/air-con from US$7/13; ☒) Opened in mid-2009 in a supercentral spot, the five-storey Lux has cheesy lobby murals and 24 modern, comfortable rooms with top-quality furnishings. Great value all around. Internet and wi-fi are planned.

Banan Hotel (☎ /fax 953242; NH5; r with air-con from US$13; ☒ ▣) Combines modern, three-star

comfort with Khmer-style wooden furnishings. The 30 rooms come with all the mod-cons and there's plenty of parking out back. More rooms and a swimming pool are being added.

Holiday Hotel (☎ 081-999006; www.holidayhotel -bb.com; r US$14-50; ☒ ▣ 🕸) Three-star comfort, huge picture windows and glass-enclosed shower stalls are the order of the day at this 71-room, seven-storey hotel, opened in 2009. Also boasts a stainless-steel lift and, in the lobby, a crystal chandelier.

Stung Sangke Hotel (☎ 953495/6/7; www.stung sangkehotel.com; NH5; d from US$45; ☒ ▣ 🕸 📺) This seven-storey hotel, opened in 2008, has 130 international-standard rooms, a 14m swimming pool and fitness and business centres.

EAST BANK

Spring Park Hotel (☎ /fax 730999; Old NH5; r with fan/air-con from US$6/11; ☒ ▣) Has 93 comfortable, modern rooms with internet connections and underground parking. Excellent value.

Golden Palace Hotel (☎ 953901; www.goldenpalace hotels.com; Old NH5; r with air-con US$11-20; ☒ ▣ 🕸) Businesslike in the best sense of the word, this modern hotel has 50 spotless, practical rooms with internet connections. Offers solid value and free pick-up from bus stops or the ferry landing.

Khemara Battambang Hotel (☎ 732727; www. khemarahotel.com; Old NH5; r from US$15; ☒ ▣) An attractive, apricot-coloured establishment with a terracotta roof and sandstone-floored hallways. The 32 three-star rooms tastefully mix Khmer and modern design and come with Western-standard bathrooms and internet connections.

our pick **La Villa** (☎ 730151; www.lavilla-battam bang.com; d incl US$60-85; ☒ ▣ 🕸 📺) One of Cambodia's most romantic and evocative boutique hotels, this delightful seven-room hostelry, in a French-era villa built by a rich Sino-Khmer merchant, was totally renovated in vintage 1930s style. Room prices include breakfast. Has a 12m pool. Often full, so reserve ahead.

Eating

CITY CENTRE

At Psar Nat, you can dine cheaply in the area between the two buildings. A **night market** (⏰ 4-9pm) with BBQ chicken, frog and beef can be found in the market's northeast corner, facing Canadia Bank. The neon-lit **riverside**

night market (St 1; ◷ approx 3pm-midnight) is across from the Battambang Museum.

ourpick Vegetarian Foods Restaurant (☎ 012 642234; mains 1500-3500r; ◷ 6.30am-11am & 2-7pm, often also open 11am-2pm) Serves some of the most delicious vegetarian food in Cambodia, including Chinese, Vietnamese and Khmer soups, spring rolls, 'meatball' dumplings and homemade soy milk (2500r). Tofu, soybeans, mushrooms and vegetables serve as stand-ins for meat. Run by an ideologically vegetarian ethnic-Chinese family. Unbeatable value.

Fresh Eats Café (☎ 089-473370; St 2½; mains US$1.50-3; ◷ 6am-9pm) Run by an NGO that helps children whose families have been affected by HIV/AIDS, this little place serves cheap, tasty food, including Western breakfasts, bagels, fried spring rolls and Khmer curry. Half a block south of Psar Nat.

White Rose (☎ 012 693855; St 2; mains 7000-12000r; ◷ 6.30am-10pm) Has a mammoth menu of good-value Khmer, Chinese, Vietnamese and Thai dishes, including soups, veggie options and marvellous *tukalok* (fruit shakes).

Sunrise Coffee House (☎ 953426; mains 8000r-13,000r; ◷ 6.30am-8pm Mon-Sat) The closest thing in Battambang to an American college-town cafe, this is a great place for coffee, fresh-baked banana bread, California-style wraps, veggie or chicken quesadillas, homemade tortillas, tuna melts and breakfast (served all day).

Smokin' Pot (☎ 012 821400; St 1½; mains US$2-3.50; ◷ 7am-about 11pm) Cheery and laid-back, the Pot serves good Khmer, Thai and Western food; roast chicken with coconut, beef *loklak* (stir-fried marinated beef served with pepper-and-lemon sauce) and 'happy' chicken soup are favourites. Doubles as a cooking school (see p252).

Khmer Delight (☎ 953195; mains US$2.25-4; ◷ 7am-11pm; 🛜) A mellow place with ceiling fans and coloured wall lamps that serves a pleasing mix of Khmer, Western and fusion dishes, including breakfast, sandwiches, tuna wraps and veggie options.

Gecko Café (☎ 017 712428; www.geckocafecambodia. com; St 3; mains US$3-5.50; ◷ 8am-10pm or later; 🛜) An atmospheric, American-owned cafe that occupies the corner balcony of an old French shop-house. Serves Western and Mexican dishes, including burritos, pizza and pasta. Hand and foot massages cost US$4/6 for 30/60 minutes.

Riverside Balcony Bar (☎ 730313; St 1; mains US$3.50-7.50; ◷ 4pm-11pm or midnight except Mon) On the all-wood verandah of a gorgeous old house high above the riverbank, this breezy hideaway is renowned for its burgers, but also serves pasta and pizza.

Pomme d'Amour (☎ 012 415513; 63 St 2½; mains US$5-8.50; ◷ 11am-10pm) The French-run 'Apple of Love', half a block south of Psar Nat, serves fine French cuisine at elegantly set tables. Specialities include locally sourced beef, grilled chicken with creamy mustard, blue cheese and black Kampot pepper, and authentic crêpes.

EAST BANK

A lively restaurant scene has been developing on the East Bank, especially along the edges of the triangle defined by Old NH5 and the old French bridge.

Green House Café (☎ 012 883187; Old NH5; mains US$1.50-3; ◷ 6.30am-9pm or 9.30pm) Serves coffee, fresh shakes, Khmer rice and noodle favourites, salads and Western dishes (eg burgers). Popular with students from the nearby high school and colleges.

X-Gold Beer Garden (☎ 012 977337; mains 8000r-25,000r; ◷ 6.30am-11pm) Perhaps the best of the East Bank beer gardens, X-Gold has great food, a delightful terrace and live Khmer music (from 6pm to 11pm) that isn't too loud for a conversation.

Korean Steam Boat (☎ 012 228457; mains 10,000r-25,000r; ◷ 3-10pm) Seated on bright red plastic chairs at stainless steel tables in an outdoor pavilion, diners BBQ their own beef, pork, chicken, fish or seafood – in Khmer this is known as *phnom pleung* (hill of fire).

La Villa (☎ 730151; mains US$6-15; ◷ noon-2.30pm & 6-9pm; 🕮) An island of civilised charm, Battambang's finest restaurant – attached to its most atmospheric hostelry – serves Khmer, Vietnamese, French and Italian dishes, and wines from around the world. Specialities include fish *amoc*, a tender fish fillet in lemon sauce, French onion soup and locally raised beef steak. It also has a Hemingwayesque bar (open from noon to 9.30pm) that serves locally made Banon brandy (see p257).

SELF-CATERING

Fruit and veg are available around the perimeter of the western half of Psar Nat.

Chea Neang (St 3; ◷ 7am-8pm) This grocery stocks Western products, including cheese, wine, yoghurt and Wall's ice cream.

Lux-Tang Bakery (St 3; ☾ 5am-8pm) For dough-nuts, muffins, pastries and excellent ba-guettes (500r).

International Bakery (St 1; ☾ 6am-midnight) Next to the ferry dock, 'Strong Man' bakery (check out the cut-out) sells baguettes, cakes and pastries.

Entertainment

Phare Ponleu Selpak (☎ 952424; www.phareps.org), a multiarts centre for disadvantaged children, regularly sends circus (*cirque nouveau)* performers to Europe, Japan and Australia. In Battambang, performances (adult/child US$8/4), often followed by dinner (US$6; book a day ahead), are held every Thursday at 7pm; for other dates, see the website or check the sheets posted in hotels and cafes. During the day, it's often possible to **observe** (☾ 8-11am & 2-5pm Mon-Fri) circus, dance, music, drawing and graphic arts classes. To get there from the Vishnu Roundabout on NH5, head west for 900m, turn right (north) and con-tinue for 600m.

Sky Disco (☎ 092-751535; admission usually free, on holidays US$1; ☾ 8pm-1am) Battambang's hottest dance venue, with a mixture of Khmer love ballads, disco, hip-hop and rock for the 18-to-25 demographic.

Shopping

Fresh Eats Café (☎ 089-473370; St 2½; ☾ 6am-9pm) Sells colourful purses, *kramas,* stuffed animals and other handicrafts made by vulnerable women.

Rachana Handicrafts (☎ 952506; ☾ 7.30am-5.30pm) A tiny NGO-run sewing workshop on the outskirts of town that trains disadvan-taged women and sells purses, stuffed toys, *kramas,* and cotton and silk accessories.

Hat Bunthoeun (☎ 012 476104; 88 St 1; ☾ 7am-7pm) One of several shops along St 1 south of Psar Nat that sells wood and stone carvings, silver jewellery, drums and kitschy oil paint-ings for the domestic souvenir market.

Getting There & Away

Battambang is 290km northwest of Phnom Penh along NH5 and 80km northeast of Pailin along NH57 (formerly NH10).

BOAT

The riverboat to Siem Reap (US$18 at the dock, US$20 through guesthouses; departure

at 7am) squeezes through narrow waterways and passes by protected wetlands, taking be-tween 5½ hours (in October) and nine or more hours (February to April). Cambodia's most enchanting boat trip, it's operated on alternate days by **Angkor Express** (☎ 012 601287) and **Chann Na** (☎ 012 354344). In the dry season, passengers are driven to a navigable section of the river. The best seats are away from the noisy motor.

BUS

Battambang does not have a central bus sta-tion. Rather, bus companies have offices and stops on or near NH5 – these include **Capitol Tour** (☎ 953040; ☾ 6am-7.30pm), **Neak Kror Horm** (☎ 953838; ☾ 5am-8pm), **Phnom Penh Sorya** (☎ 092-181804; ☾ 5.30am-9pm), **Paramount Angkor Express** (☎ 092-575572; ☾ 6am-7pm) and **Ponleu Angkor Khmer** (☎ 092-517792; ☾ 6am-8.30pm).

All send buses southeast to Phnom Penh (US$4 to US$5 depending on the company, five hours), Pursat (US$2.50 to US$3, two hours) and Kompong Chhnang (same prices as Phnom Penh, 3½ hours), with frequent departures from 6am to 2.30pm; northwest to Sisophon (US$2 to US$2.50, one hour), Poipet (US$3 to US$4, two hours) and Bangkok (US$13, eight hours), with early afternoon departures; and around the Tonlé Sap to Siem Reap (US$3.75 to US$5, three to four hours), with departures until mid-morning. Phnom Penh Sorya has a morn-ing service to Kompong Cham (35,000r, seven hours). Above-quoted prices are valid at company offices; guesthouses charge a commission.

TAXI

At the **taxi station** (NH5), share taxis to Poipet (US$5) via Sisophon (15,000r) leave from the northwest corner; taxis to Siem Reap (25,000r, two hours) congregate in the north-east corner; and taxis to Phnom Penh (US$8, 3½ hours) leave from the southeast corner. Across NH5 there are pick-ups to Sisophon (outside/inside 7000r/10,000r) and Poipet (10,000r/15,000r). A private taxi costs about US$40 to Siem Reap and US$40 to US$50 to Phnom Penh. Bargain hard. Reservations can be made through the Chhaya and Royal Hotels.

Share taxis to Pursat leave from **Psar Thmei** (NH5), 1km east of Ta Dambong Roundabout. For details on getting to Pailin, see p260.

Getting Around

A *moto* ride in town costs 2000r, while a *remork* – lots hang out around the western end of Psar Nat – is US$1 (US$2 for several passengers).

Hiring a *moto* driver who speaks English or French costs US$6 to US$8 for a half-day in and around town and US$12 for a day trip out of the city. Many of the *moto* drivers who hang out at the Royal Hotel, and their bitter rivals at the Chhaya Hotel, speak decent English.

Gecko Moto (☎ 089-924260; www.geckocafecambodia. com; St 3; ☺ 8am-7pm) rents out 100cc motorbikes for US$8 a day and has road maps; the Chhaya and Royal Hotels charge US$6 to US$8.

Bicycles are a great way to get around and can be ridden along either bank of the river in either direction. They are available for US$1.50 or US$2 a day at Gecko Moto, Sunrise Coffee House and the Royal and Chhaya Hotels.

AROUND BATTAMBANG

Before setting out, try to link up with an English-speaking *moto* driver, as it really adds to the experience. Possible itineraries include a loop via Phnom Sampeau to Phnom Banan, with either a winery visit or a bamboo train ride (p252) on the way back. If you've got your own wheels, Wat Phnom Sampeau and Sneng (Sneung) can be visited on the way to Pailin.

Admission to Phnom Sampeau, Phnom Banan and Wat Ek Phnom costs US$2. If you purchase a ticket – sold by the Tourist Police – at one site, it's valid all day long at the other two.

A round trip to Phnom Sampeau, Phnom Banan or Wat Ek Phnom costs US$5 to US$7 by *moto* and US$12 to US$15 by *remork* (for one passenger). For a full-day trip to several sights, count on paying US$12 to US$15 by *moto* and US$30 by *remork*.

For details on sites not mentioned below, check out the guidebook *Around Battambang* (US$10 for the 2006 edition) by Ray Zepp, which has details on temples, wats and excursions in the Battambang and Pailin areas. Proceeds go to monks and nuns working to raise HIV/AIDS awareness and to help AIDS orphans.

Phnom Sampeau

ភ្នំសំពៅ

At the summit of this fabled limestone outcrop, 12km southwest of Battambang along NH57 (towards Pailin), a complex of **temples** (admission US$2) affords gorgeous views. Beware the macaques that live around the summit, dining on bananas left as offerings, as some can be bad-tempered and aggressive. Access is via a steep staircase or, past the eateries, a cement road.

As you descend from the golden stupa at the summit, turn left under the gate decorated with a bas-relief of Eiy Sei (an elderly Buddha). A **deep canyon**, its vertical sides cloaked in greenery, descends steeply through a natural arch to a 'lost world' of stalactites, creeping vines and bats; two Angkorian warriors stand guard.

In the area between the two sets of antennas, two government **artillery pieces**, one with markings in Russian, the other in German, are still deployed. They point westwards towards **Phnom Krapeu** (Crocodile Mountain), a one-time Khmer Rouge stronghold.

About half-way up the hill, a road leads under a gate and 250m up to the **Killing Caves of Phnom Sampeau**, now a place of pilgrimage. An enchanted staircase, flanked by greenery, leads into a cavern where a golden reclining Buddha lies peacefully next to a glass-walled memorial filled with the bones and skulls of some of the people bludgeoned to death by Khmer Rouge cadres before being thrown through the overhead skylight. Next to the base of the stairway is the **old memorial**, a rusty cage made of chicken wire and cyclone fencing and partly filled with human bones.

At the base of the hill, a 30m-high **Buddha** is being carved out of the cliff face. Due to a lack of funds, only the top of the Buddha's head has been liberated from the natural rock outcrop.

Phnom Banan

វត្តប្ដាណន់

Exactly 358 stone steps lead up shaded Phnom Banan, 28km south of Battambang, to **Prasat Banan** (admission US$2), whose five towers are reminiscent of the layout of Angkor Wat. Indeed, locals claim it was the inspiration for Angkor Wat!

Udayadityavarman II, son of Suryavarman I, built Prasat Banan in the 11th century, and its hillside location offers incredible views across the surrounding countryside. There are impressive carved lintels above the doorways to each tower and bas-reliefs on the upper parts of the central tower. Many of this temple's best carvings are now in the Battambang Museum (p251).

CAMBODIA'S WINE COUNTRY

Midway between Battambang and Phnom Banan, in an area best known for its production of hot chilli peppers (harvested from October to January), one of the world's most exclusive wines is grown on 4 hectares of vines and aged to...well, something.

Prasat Phnom Banon Winery (☎ 012 665238; Bot Sala Village; ☯ 6am-6pm), Cambodia's only winemaking enterprise, grows Shiraz and Cabernet Sauvignon grapes to make reds (US$15 a bottle), and tropics-resistant Black Queen and Black Opal grapes to make rosés (US$6) – liquids it's hard to describe without resorting to superlatives. Let's just say that both have a bouquet unlike anything you've ever encountered in a bottle with the word 'wine' on the label, and a taste as surprising as the aftertaste. Officially recognised by Cambodia's Ministry of Industry, Mines & Energy, Banon wines belong to that exclusive club of wineries whose vintages improve significantly with the addition of ice cubes. Also made here is Banon brandy (US$12 for 0.7L), which has a heavenly bouquet and a taste that has been compared favourably to turpentine. Sampling takes place in an attractive garden pavilion, and you can visit the vineyards and production facilities.

The winery is 10km south of Battambang and 8km north of Phnom Banan.

From the temple, a narrow stone staircase leads south down the hill to three **caves**, two of which are not mined and can thus be visited with a torch-/flashlight-equipped local guide.

Wat Kor Village

About 2km south of Battambang's Riverside Balcony Bar, on the road to Phnom Banan, is Wat Kor Village, known for its 21 **Khmer heritage houses**. Built of now-rare hardwoods almost a century ago and surrounded by orchard gardens, they have wide verandahs and exude the ambience of another era.

One of the most interesting is **Khor Sang House** (☎ 017 529552; serey07@yahoo.com; admission US$1), its floors worn lustrous by a century of bare feet. Decorated with old furniture, family photos and old school certificates, it was built in 1907 by the French-speaking owner's grandfather, who served as a secretary to the province's last Thai governor. The holes in the wood plank floor allowed people who were ill to bathe without going outside. The back section dates from 1890. You can organise to stay here for US$6 a night.

Battambang's Tourist Information Office (p249) has details on accommodation in Wat Kor.

Wat Ek Phnom

វត្តឯកភ្នំ

An atmospheric, partly collapsed, 11th-century temple, **Wat Ek Phnom** (Aek Phnum; admission US$2) is surrounded by the remains of a laterite wall and an ancient *baray* (reservoir). A lintel

showing the **Churning of the Ocean of Milk** can be seen above the eastern portal to the central temple. This is a very popular picnic and pilgrimage destination for Khmers, especially at festival times, and for women hoping to have children.

On the way from Battambang by bicycle or *moto*, it's possible to make a number of interesting stops. About 1.2km north of Battambang's ferry landing is a 1960s **Pepsi bottling plant**, its logo faded but otherwise virtually unchanged since production ceased abruptly in 1975. You can still see the remains of the old production line (down an alley behind the cement water tanks) and, at the far end of the warehouse out back, thousands of dusty empties – bearing Pepsi's old script logo – whose contents quenched someone's thirst back when Nixon was in the White House.

Drive 700m further and, at the sign for the Islamic Local Development Organisation, turn left (west). After 250m you'll get to a signless house, behind which is the **Slaket crocodile farm**. It's open all day, including mealtimes – the crocs are always happy to have tourists for lunch.

Return to the main road and drive another 3.5km, past several wats, to the village of **Pheam Ek**, whose speciality is making rice paper for spring rolls. All along the road, in family workshops, you'll see rice paste being steamed and then placed on a bamboo frame for drying in the sun. This is not an easy way to make a living – 100 rice sheets sell for 3500r. The coconuts grown in this area are said to be especially sweet. Wat Ek Phnom is 5.5km further on.

The nonprofit **Cambodian Education Center** in Pheam Ek, 13km from Battambang, provides free English instruction to local kids and is always looking for volunteer teachers (the Khmer staff are all volunteers, too). For details contact **Racky Thy** (☎ 092-301697; rith_gentleman@yahoo.com).

Wat Ek Phnom is 11km from Battambang's ferry landing by the shortest route and 21km if you go via the Pepsi plant and Pheam Ek. Combining both makes for a nice 32km circuit.

Kamping Poy
កំពីងពួយ

Also known as the Killing Dam, Kamping Poy (Poi or Puoy), 27km west of Battambang (if you go via NH5 and then follow the irrigation canal), was one of the many grandiose Khmer Rouge projects intended to recreate the sophisticated irrigation networks that helped Cambodia wax mighty under the kings of Angkor. As many as 10,000 Cambodians are thought to have perished during its construction, worked to death under the shadow of executions, malnutrition and disease. These days, thanks to the dam, the Kamping Poy area is one of the few parts of Cambodia to produce two rice crops a year.

Despite the lake's grim history – and the fact that there's little to see except the dam and its sluice gates – the area's eateries, dining platforms and row boats (US$2.50 for two or three hours) are a popular destination for Battambangers on weekends and holidays. It's easy to combine a visit here with a stop at Phnom Sampeau.

Sneng
ស្នឹង

This town, on NH57 20km southwest of Battambang towards Pailin, is home to two small yet interesting temples. **Prasat Yeay Ten**, dedicated to Shiva, dates from the end of the 10th century and, although in a ruinous state, has above its doorways three delicately carved lintels that somehow survived the ravages of time and war; the eastern one depicts the Churning of the Ocean of Milk. The temple is situated on the east side of the highway, so close to the road that you can't miss it.

Behind Prasat Yeay Ten, 200m to the east, is a contemporary wat; tucked away at the back of the wat compound are three **brick sanctuaries** that have some beautifully preserved carvings around the entrances. The sanctuaries look like pre-Angkorian Chenla temples, but given the limited Chenla presence in western Cambodia, it is possible that they date from the same period as Prasat Kravan (p182) at Angkor, ie the early 10th century.

KRONG PAILIN

The province-level municipality of Krong Pailin is best known for its gem mines, now pretty much exhausted; land mines, which still claim limbs and lives; and as a refuge for Khmer Rouge retirees.

During the civil war, the Pailin area's gem and timber resources – sold on international markets with help from Thai army generals – served as the economic crutch that kept the Khmer Rouge war machine going. In the mid-1990s, it was a staging area for regular dry-season offensives that overran government positions as far east as Phnom Sampeau.

In 1996, the Khmer Rouge supremo in these parts, Ieng Sary (Brother Number Three), defected to the government side, bringing with him 3000 fighters and their dependants. His reward: amnesty and free reign in Krong Pailin, a miniprovince carved out of Battambang Province to serve as a Khmer Rouge fiefdom. Only in late 2007 were Ieng and his wife arrested for war crimes and crimes against humanity. Around the same time, two other Khmer Rouge retirees were taken into custody from their homes in Pailin: Khieu Samphan, the Khmer Rouge's one-time head of state, and Nuon Chea (Brother Number Two), the group's chief ideologue. Ieng's son, Ieng Vuth, currently serves as deputy governor of Pailin.

If you're cycling to Cambodia from Thailand, you're much less likely to get run over if you cross at the Psar Pruhm–Ban Pakard border crossing (see p343), 22km northwest of town, than at Poipet, on the terrifyingly busy NH5.

PAILIN
ប៉ៃលិន
☎ 055 / pop 22,000

The fly-blown, Wild West town of Pailin has little to recommend it except a particularly colourful hilltop temple – unless you're an ex–Khmer Rouge commander, in which case it's an ideal place to retire among friends.

Information

Acleda Bank (NH57) Has an ATM that handles Visa cash advances.

Boyada Phone Shop (per hr US$1; ☺ 7am-8pm) Has four internet computers.

Canadia Bank (NH57) Has an ATM.

Pailin Border Market (Psar Pruhm, Thai border) About 200m up the hill from the crossing. Has money-changers.

Victoria Supermarket (Psar Pruhm, Thai border; per hr 5000r; ☺ 7am-midnight) Internet access at the frontier.

Sights & Activities

From NH57, stairs lead through a garish gate – the faded *nagas* (mythical serpents) were once bubblegum pink, spearmint green and sunflower yellow – up to **Wat Phnom Yat**, a psychedelic temple centred on an ancient *po* tree. A life-sized cement **tableau** shows butt-naked sinners (about the only nudity you'll see in Cambodia) being heaved into a cauldron (for the impious), de-tongued (for liars) and forced to climb a spiny tree (for adulterers). Medieval European triptychs never made hell seem so uninviting. Nearby, the repentant pray for forgiveness, a highly pertinent message given who lives around here. Next to the upper sanctuary, look for the three-headed elephants and a sinner, painted green, having his entrails devoured by two ravenous birds. The sunrises and sunsets up here are usually nice enough to take your mind off the fire and brimstone.

At the base of the hill, an impressive gate from 1968 leads to **Wat Khaong Kang**, an important centre for Buddhist teaching before the Khmer Rouge madness. The exterior wall is decorated with an especially long bas-relief of the Churning of the Ocean of Milk.

Te Meng Suor (☎ 016 533356; ☺ 7am-5pm), one of the few gem shops left in Pailin, has a good

selection of cut and uncut sapphires and rubies. At a few tiny shops around the eastern end of **Psar Samaki** (Psar Pailin), you can still see gems being cut by hand. Many of the stones on sale in Pailin are of inferior quality. After a hard rain, you often see local people hunting for gems – but rarely finding them – along the verges/shoulders of roads.

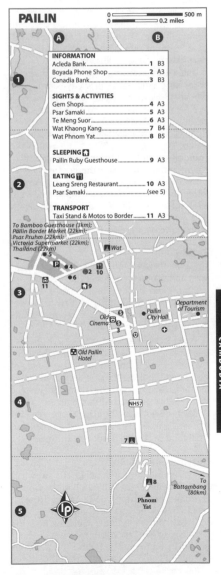

Moto drivers can take you to several **waterfalls** outside town. The problem is that they're at their most impressive during the rainy season, when the roads are often impassable.

Sleeping

At the Psar Pruhm–Ban Pakard border crossing, options include the 150-room **Diamond Crown** (☎ 012 400657, in Thailand 082-219 7227; hoteldia mondcrown@yahoo.com; r with fan US$8, with air-con US$15-35; 🖭), one of three casino-hotels set up to milk cash from Thai gamblers, and the brand-new, 76-room **Victoria Hotel** (☎ 011 550001; victoria. hotel@gmail.com; r from US$30 or 1000B; 🖭).

Pailin Ruby Guesthouse (☎ 636 3603; r with fan/air-con from US$5/10; 🖭) A new city-centre place whose 48 clean, spacious rooms come with spring mattresses. It's worth paying US$2 extra for an exterior window.

ourpick **Bamboo Guesthouse** (☎ 012 405818, from Thailand 081-279 9725; r US$12-25; 🖭) An island of tranquillity on the northwestern outskirts of town, about 3km from the centre. The 27 bungalows come with air-con, hot water, fridge and cable TV. Pricier units, made entirely of rare, reddish and no longer available *beng* wood, have a forest-lodge feel. Run with verve by a family from Kampot.

Eating

In Pailin, there are food stalls along the northwest and southeast edges of Psar Samaki.

The Psar Pruhm–Ban Pakard border crossing has food stalls at Pailin Border Market, or you can self-cater at **Victoria Supermarket** (🕑 7am-midnight).

Leang Sreng Restaurant (☎ 016 842115; breakfast soup 4000r; 🕑 6am-11pm) This informal, open-fronted eatery is known for its big bowls of beef soup – look for the sign decorated with a laughing cow. Several other restaurants can be found between here and Psar Samaki.

Bamboo Guesthouse (☎ 012 405818; mains 35-150B; 🕑 6am-10pm) Serves Pailin's best Khmer and Thai food in shaded outdoor pavilions.

Getting There & Away

NH57 (sometimes still called Highway 10) from Battambang to Pailin (80km, 2½ hours) is finally being upgraded. At the time of research, new bridges were going up.

In Battambang, taxis to Pailin leave from the west side of **Psar Leu** (southern end of St 3). A share taxi to Pailin town (2½ hours) costs 25,000r (20,000r if you're travelling in the other direc-

tion); pick-ups are 10,000r/15,000r outside/inside. A private taxi from Battambang direct to the border (one-way/return US$35/65) will give you the option of stopping off at Phnom Sampeau and Sneng.

The 22km road from Pailin to the Psar Pruhm–Ban Pakard border crossing is in pretty good shape. At the border, share taxis (25,000r to Battambang, 5000r or 50B to Pailin) stop near Victoria Supermarket. Khmers pay 15,000r or 150B for a *moto* from the border to Pailin. In Pailin, taxis and *motos* stop along NH57 just south of Psar Samaki.

Paramount Angkor Express (☎ 012 320737; www. paramountangkorexpress.com) links the border with Pailin (5000r) and Battambang (13,000r, three to 3½ hours). Departures are at 7.30am from Psar Pruhm (the office is 100m towards the border from the Diamond Crown Hotel) and sometime between 1pm and 3pm from the company's Battambang office.

A rough track goes from Treng District, about 25km east of Pailin, southward through the Cardamom Mountains to Krong Koh Kong (see p201).

SAMLAUT

The northernmost tip of the Cardamom Mountains – home to elephants, gibbons, pangolins, hornbills and many other endangered creatures – covers the southern half of Krong Pailin (pretty much everything south of NH57). Known as the **Samlaut Multiple Use Area** (600 sq km; highest point 1164m), this expanse of forested mountains is contiguous with two Thai parks, including Namtok Klong Kaew National Park, with which it may soon be joined in a cross-border **Peace Park**. Since mid-2008, rogue Cambodian law enforcement elements have taken advantage of the Prasat Preah Vihear crisis with Thailand to take over parts of Samlaut for the purpose of illegal logging. Countless land mines make the area too dangerous for ecotrekking.

Samlaut is administered and patrolled with help from the **Maddox Jolie-Pitt Foundation** (MJP; www.mjpasia.org), named after the adopted Cambodian-born son of its founder and president, the American actress Angelina Jolie. In 2006, the Samlaut administration signed a five-year sister-park agreement with Sequoia and Kings Canyon National Park (www.nps.gov/seki) in California.

BANTEAY MEANCHEY PROVINCE

ខេត្តបន្ទាយមានជ័យ

Sandwiched between the casinos of Poipet, Cambodia's most important border crossing with Thailand, and the glories of Angkor, agricultural Banteay Meanchey (Fortress of Victory) often gets overlooked by travellers rushing on to Siem Reap or Battambang. Highlights include the Angkorian temples of Banteay Chhmar and the rare birds of Ang Trapeng Thmor Reserve (p151).

POIPET

ប៉ោយប៉ែត

☎ 054 / pop 45,000

Long the armpit of Cambodia, notorious for its squalor, scams and sleaze, Poipet (pronounced 'poi-*peh*' in Khmer) has recently applied some thick make-up and deodorant, at least in the border-adjacent casino zone. Based mainly on the custom of Thais, whose own country bans gambling, its nine casino resorts with names like Tropicana and Grand Diamond City are helping turn the town into the Las Vegas of Cambodia, though outside the border zone it's still a chaotic, trash-strewn strip mall sprinkled with dodgy massage parlours. The Khmers' gentle side is little in evidence, but don't worry – the rest of the country does not carry on like this.

The faster you get used to making quick conversions between Cambodian riel, US dollars and Thai baht, all of which are in use here, the easier: a good approximate rule of thumb is 4000r = US$1 = 33B, so 100B = US$3 = 12,000r.

Orientation & Information

Poipet stretches from the border (the filthy O Chrou stream) and the clean, modern casino zone eastwards along NH5 for a few kilometres. Cambodian visas (see p342) are issued at the Visa Service, next to the ceremonial Kingdom of Cambodia gate – do not buy a visa anywhere else, no matter what the touts say, or you'll pay 1000B to 1300B instead of the official fee of US$20 (660B)! Passports are stamped 200m further on, just beyond the big hotels and right before the 'big roundabout' that marks the eastern edge of the casino zone and, effectively, the western terminus of

NH5. Poipet's market is about 1km east of the roundabout and a block north of NH5.

Don't change money at the places suggested by touts, no matter how official they look. In fact, there's no need to change money at all – baht work just fine here.

In a medical emergency, evacuation across the border to Thailand is possible 24 hours a day.

ANZ Bank (NH5, 1.5km east of big roundabout) Has ATMs here and in the casino zone.

Canadia Bank (NH5, 1km east of big roundabout) Has a 24-hour ATM.

Internet & Email (big roundabout, south side; per hr 3000r; ☽ 24hr) A rudimentary internet shop just outside the casino zone.

Internet shops (casino zone) One block north of NH5, around the night market.

Sights & Activities

The **casino zone**, with its air-conditioned hotel-casinos, is basically an island of Thailand on Cambodian territory. It's a lot more family-oriented than you might expect, and better-off Khmer families come here to enjoy the feeling of being 'abroad'.

A few hundred metres north of the Visa Service, a mixed Thai-Khmer pop group performs free outdoor **concerts** (☽ 7.30pm-1am) every night. The **Star Vegas**, a block north of the Visa Service, has a clean, modern **swimming pool** (150B).

The upscale **Jiwa Spa** (casino zone; ☽ 24hr), inside the Poipet Holiday Palace (just south of the Visa Service), has a wide range of massages (from 350B), a sauna (350B) and a small fitness room (200B).

Sleeping

The modern megahotels in the casino zone offer three-star rooms, including breakfast and 500B in casino chips, starting at 1000B (plus a 1000B deposit – nothing like staying at a place that doesn't quite trust you!). Cheap hotels and guesthouses, some of them brothels, are strung out along NH5 and around the bus station.

Huy Kea Hotel (☎ 012 346333, from Thailand 085-280 7228; NH5, 600m east of big roundabout; r with fan/air-con US$6/11 or 250B/350B; ✄) A friendly, efficient place with clean, decent rooms; fan rooms are on the upper floors. Convenient to the border, the bus station and the market.

Viroch Hotel (☎ 967315; viroch.hotel@yahoo.com; big roundabout, north side; r 500B; ✄) Graced with a neo-classical lobby (sort of) and a permanently out-of-order lift, this place has 24 spacious rooms with shiny white tile floors. Clean and very convenient to the casino zone.

Eating

The cheapest eats are around the market and along NH5. The casino zone's night market,

a block north of NH5, has clean, well-lit restaurants and pubs.

Some of the casino-zone hotels offer all-you-can-eat buffets – the Poipet Holiday Palace has a Thai and Chinese buffet for 150B, while the nearby Holiday Poipet's **Aiko Japanese Buffet** (11am-11pm) charges

---

POIPET TRANSPORT SCAMS

The moment you enter Cambodia at Poipet, whether you know it or not, you are the duly purchased client of a monopoly that has paid – not, one can safely assume, entirely into state coffers – for the exclusive right to provide you with onward land transport. Poipet is famous for its audacious scams, but the ingenious thing about this arrangement is that it's actually an official provincial government concession, designed both to raise the standard of service for tourists and to enrich certain well-connected worthies.

At the time of research, Poipet had two rival bus stations. The **Poipet Tourist Passenger International Terminal** (PTPIT, pronounced pit-pit), situated 8km east of town in the middle of nowhere, had just been officially opened. The complex, which includes a proper exchange bureau and places selling bottled water for five times the street price, belongs to the same South Korean company that runs the Chong Kneas dock near Siem Reap.

The other station, the **International Tourist Terminal** (ITT, aka the bus station), has been operating as a monopoly for years. Situated 1.5km east of the casino zone, it is clean and orderly, with English-speaking staff, currency exchange, a minimarket and posted fares that are higher than the prices locals pay by up to 250%. Staff have been known to demand even higher rates when they think they can get away with it, eg in the late afternoon.

As you exit the immigration police office (where passports are stamped), fencing herds you into the 'Free Shuttle Bus Station', departure point for OSP buses to the ITT (agents wear yellow shirts), and VCD buses to the PTPIT (agents wear black polo shirts).

At the ITT, transport out of Poipet is orchestrated by three 'associations' (well-connected for-profit companies, not cooperatives) that work on a rotational basis: each handles bus and taxi bookings for tourists on every third day. All charge the same fares, offering buses/four-passenger share taxis to Sisophon (US$5/5), Siem Reap (US$9/12), Battambang (US$10/10) and Phnom Penh (US$15/25). The taxis here all carry an official 'tourism licence', a photo ID that's posted in the windshield. Posted fares at the PTPIT are slightly cheaper.

Here's where the big profits come in: when four tourists pay US$12 each for a share taxi from the ITT to Siem Reap, only US$30 of the US$48 goes to the taxi driver. Much of the rest, except for US$1 paid to OSP for the 'free' shuttle, finds its way into various and sundry pockets.

For the cash-strapped traveller, the obvious solution is to mosey out to NH5 and find a taxi the way Cambodians do (see opposite). The problem is that 'association' enforcers, with police backing (it's an official monopoly, after all), often intervene to prevent independent taxi drivers from accepting foreign custom. Readers report that when they declined OSP's shuttle offer, an 'association' agent followed them for blocks and intimidated any taxi driver they came upon. Drivers who are caught 'poaching' tourists are 'fined' by the 'association'. The trick, therefore, is to give the agent the slip, perhaps by saying you'll be overnighting in Poipet.

Remember, though, that once you've escaped the monopoly, you're on your own in dealing with the petty scams the monopolies were designed to end. Taxi drivers (especially at the big roundabout) may demand exorbitant sums to get you to Siem Reap, or a local tout may offer to help you find a taxi to Siem Reap and then overcharge, demanding, say, US$40 and then paying just US$20 to the driver.

The main result of these arrangements, other than the transfer of lucre into unseen pockets, is a lot of angry tourists. Some take out their frustrations on the taxi drivers, but these fellows have no choice but to accept work from the 'associations'. They're certainly not the ones getting rich from the whole scheme.

359B. The **Poipet Casino Resort** (🕑 11am-11pm) has an up-the-stairs restaurant with 'Italian-American cuisine', including pizza (small/large 189B/259B). The Tropicana is known for its outdoor, cook-it-yourself BBQ.

The best coffee in town is brewed at the Poipet Holiday Palace's **Palais Coffee Shop** (casino zone; 🕑 8am-11pm Sun-Thu, to 1am Fri & Sat), a Starbuck's knock-off whose products you can sip with something sweet from the adjacent Holiday Cake Shop.

Cheayden Chobmeth Restaurant (☎ 017 949939; NH5, 1.6km east of big roundabout; small/large mains 60B/100B; 🕑 7am-2am; 🖳) Directly across NH5 from Acleda Bank, this cheery establishment serves Khmer and Thai dishes under coloured fairy lights.

Getting There & Away

For details on the Poipet–Aranya Prathet border crossing with Thailand, see p341.

Poipet is 48km west of Sisophon and 153km west of Siem Reap. The heavily trafficked NH5 has *finally* been paved! Most tourists coming from Thailand arrive in the late morning or early afternoon in order to leave enough time for onward travel.

The long-defunct railway line from Sisophon to Poipet is being resurrected.

BUS

To get to the **bus station** (International Tourist Terminal) from the big roundabout, go 1.3km east along NH5, turn left under the rusty gate and continue north for 200m. Some buses also pick up passengers at company offices, situated along NH5 near the turn-off to the bus station.

The many bus companies here include **Capital Tours** (☎ 967350; NH5, north side, 150m west of bus station turn-off), preferred by many NGO workers; **Phnom Penh Sorya** (☎ 092-181802; www.ppsoryatransport.com; NH5, south side, facing bus station turn-off), a respected company with great prices; and **GST** (☎ 012727771; NH5, south side, 50m west of bus station turn-off). Destinations include Sisophon (US$2 to US$3, 40 minutes), Siem Reap (US$5, 2½ hours to four hours), Battambang (US$3.75, two hours) and Phnom Penh (US$7.50, seven hours). Getting to Siem Reap may involve changing buses at Sisophon. Phnom Penh Sorya has a direct service to Kompong Cham. Almost all departures are between 6.15am and 10.30am, though the bus station monopoly (opposite) has pricey afternoon buses to Siem Reap (US$9).

Several companies, including Capitol, offer midafternoon services to Bangkok (300B).

TAXI

Nonmonopoly share taxis – some of them Thai right-hand-drive Camrys that provide front-seat passengers the thrill of seeing oncoming traffic before the driver can – are available during daylight hours, both in the parking lot of the **post office** (big roundabout, south side) and – this is where most of them are – along NH5 about 1.3km east of the roundabout (near the bus station turn-off).

Destinations include Sisophon (US$2.50, 40 minutes), Siem Reap (US$5, 2½ hours) and Battambang (US$5, two hours). The usual fee for a private taxi is six times the single-seat fare (Cambodian share taxis pack two and sometimes three passengers in front and four in back). Be prepared for a cheerfully chaotic rugby scrum of taxi touts and negotiate hard (smiling helps).

Packed-to-the-gills pick-ups, which stop along NH5, are a bit cheaper, in part because riding in the back is so dangerous (even in a minor accident everyone goes flying).

Getting Around

Inside the casino zone, free casino-run shuttles whisk guests to and fro. *Moto* drivers wait at the big roundabout; a ride from the border to the bus station costs 2000r (US$1 at night).

SISOPHON

ស៊ីសុផុន

☎ 054 / pop 98,000

Strategically situated at northwest Cambodia's great crossroads, the intersection of NH5 and NH6, Sisophon (also known as Svay, Svay Sisophon, Srei Sophon and Banteay Meanchey) makes a convenient first stop if you're coming from Poipet, and is a good base for exploring the Angkorian temples of Banteay Chhmar.

Orientation & Information

NH6 (from Siem Reap and Phnom Penh) intersects NH5 (from Battambang and Phnom Penh) at the western tip of the triangular town centre.

Acleda Bank Has a 24-hour ATM that handles Visa cash advances.

Bayon Web (per hr 2000r; 🕑 7am-about 8pm) Internet access facing the Golden Crown Guesthouse.

Canadia Bank Has an ATM.

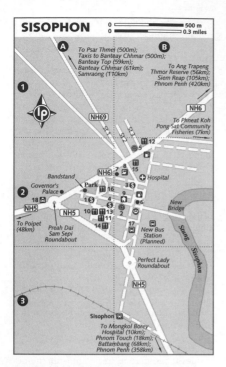

SISOPHON

0 _____ 500 m
0 _____ 0.3 miles

To Psar Thmei (500m);
Taxis to Banteay Chhmar (500m);
Banteay Top (59km);
Banteay Chhmar (61km);
Samraong (110km)

To Ang Trapeng
Thmor Reserve (56km);
Siem Reap (105km);
Phnom Penh (420km)

NH69

NH6

To Phneat Koh
Pong Sat Community
Fisheries (7km)

Bandstand

Park

Hospital

Governor's
Palace

NH5

New
Bridge

To Poipet
(48km)

Preah Dai
Sam Sepi
Roundabout

New Bus
Station
(Planned)

Stung Sisophon

Perfect Lady
Roundabout

NH5

Sisophon

To Mongkol Borey
Hospital (10km);
Phnom Touch (18km);
Battambang (68km);
Phnom Penh (358km)

INFORMATION	
Acleda Bank	1 A2
Bayon Web	2 B2
Canadia Bank	3 B2
Lao Puoy Kheang Exchange	4 A2
Pacific Internet	5 B2

SIGHTS & ACTIVITIES	
École d'Art et de Culture Khmers	6 B2
Pyramid Spa	7 B2
Swimming Pool	8 B2

SLEEPING	
Golden Crown Guesthouse	9 B2

EATING	
Dy & Phong Restaurant	10 A2
Food Stalls	11 A2
Golden Crown Restaurant	(see 9)
Kem Heng Restaurant	12 B2
Phay Kik	(see 11)
Psar Sisophon	13 A2
Sok Yi Grocery	14 A2
Sorm Rethy Bakery	15 B2
Suon Kamsan Restaurant	16 A2

TRANSPORT	
Bus & Taxi Station	17 B2
Share Taxis to Poipet	18 A2

NORTHWESTERN CAMBODIA

Lao Puoy Kheang Exchange (☎ 012 837239; 🕑 5am-5pm) A reliable exchange place that accepts a wide variety of currencies.
Pacific Internet (NH6 cnr St 3; per hr 2000r; 🕑 7am-7pm) Internet access facing the Sokimex petrol station.

Sights

The **École d'Art et de Culture Khmers** (School of Khmer Art & Culture; ☎ 017 449277; 🕑 7-11am & 2-5pm Mon-Fri, 7-11am Sat), housed in a brownish Khmer-style building, teaches children traditional music, *apsara* dancing, painting, sculpture and shadow puppetry. It's often possible to observe a class or see students practising.

At the **Phneat Koh Pong Sat Community Fisheries**, a fish sanctuary run by monks 8km east of town, you can feed schools of fat, frisky fish from a peaceful riverside pavilion on the grounds of a wat. Monks sell food pellets and dry bread (500r). It makes a delightful excursion by bicycle, *moto* or car, especially in the late afternoon.

For a massage, try the new **Pyramid Spa** (☎ 017 565262; per hr from US$5; 🕑 9am-midnight). Behind it is a 25m **swimming pool** (admission 3000r; 🕑 4-9pm Sat & Sun) with changing rooms that's open to tourists even when officially closed.

Phnom Touch (small mountain), 18km towards Battambang on the west side of NH5, has several temples on and around it, and affords gorgeous views.

Sleeping

Golden Crown Guesthouse (☎ 958444; fax 710578; r US$5-15; ❄) The NGO crowd's lodging of choice, with 72 clean, well-designed rooms that come with hot water and fridges.

Eating

At Psar Sisophon, the city centre's main market, there are food stalls with good breakfast soups (3000r) on the southern side; the best ice coffee (2000r) is served by **Phay Kik** (🕑 6am-7pm), an older guy you can identify because he always wears a flat cap.

Kem Heng Restaurant (☎ 012 502091; NH6 cnr St 3; mains 5000r-7000r; 🕑 5am-8.30pm or later) Easy to spot thanks to its yellow-and-orange walls and red plastic chairs, this eatery has good sweet-and-sour dishes and reasonable prices. Across from the Sokimex petrol station.

Dy & Phong Restaurant (☎ 958874; mains 6000r-8000r; 🕑 7am-11pm) With wind chimes and birds' nests hanging from the ceiling, this mellow cafe-restaurant serves Khmer and some Western dishes. The upstairs dining area has air-con. There's often live acoustic guitar from about 7pm to 8pm.

Golden Crown Restaurant (☎ 958444; mains US$2-5; ⏱ 6am-8pm) A new and very popular eatery featuring Khmer dishes, including 'hill of fire' BBQ (US$5).

Suon Kamsan Restaurant (☎ 012 829006; mains 10,000-20,000r; ⏱ 6am-10pm) A popular corner place with Western and Khmer breakfasts, reliable Khmer mains and some Thai dishes. Khmer crooners perform at full volume nightly from 6pm to 10.30pm.

SELF-CATERING

Sorm Rethy Bakery (NH6 facing St 2; ⏱ 4am-8pm) Has bread and super sponge cake (1000r per slice).

Sok Yi Grocery (⏱ 6am-6pm) Stocks Western edibles, including fresh milk and yoghurt from Thailand, wine and ice cream.

Getting There & Away

Sisophon is 48km (40 minutes by car) east of Poipet, 105km west of Siem Reap, 61km south of Banteay Chhmar and 68km northwest of Battambang.

Long-haul buses and most share taxis stop at the bus and taxi station, about 400m south of NH6. Eight bus companies, including **Capitol Tour** (☎ 012 525782), which often has the best prices, **Rith Mony** (☎ 012 444427) and **Phnom Penh Sorya** (www.ppsoryatransport.com) serve Poipet (5000r to 10,000r depending on the company, 40 minutes), Siem Reap (15,000r to 20,000r, 1½ hours), Battambang (7000r to 10,000r, 1½ hours), Phnom Penh (US$5 or US$6, seven hours) and Bangkok (US$10). Most eastbound buses depart between 6.30am and 11.45am; buses to Poipet and Bangkok leave midmorning and throughout the afternoon.

Share taxis to Phnom Penh (US$10, five hours) congregate in the bus station's southwest corner, taxis to Siem Reap (US$5, 1½ hours) in the northeast corner, and taxis to Battambang (15,000r, one hour) can be found in the southeast corner. A private taxi to Siem Reap costs US$25 or US$30. In the northwest corner you'll find pick-ups to Poipet (outside/inside 50B/70B).

Share taxis to Poipet (10,000r, 40 minutes) stop on NH5 a bit west of its intersection with NH6.

For details on transport to Banteay Chhmar, see p266.

BANTEAY CHHMAR
បន្ទាយឆ្មារ

The temple complex of **Banteay Chhmar** (admission US$5) was constructed by Cambodia's most prolific builder, Jayavarman VII (r 1181–1219), on the site of a 9th-century temple. Originally enclosed by a 9km-long wall, it housed one of the largest and most impressive Buddhist monasteries of the Angkorian period and, today, is one of the few temples to feature the enigmatic, Bayon-style **visages of Avalokiteshvara**, with their mysterious – and world-famous – smiles. Being conserved with help from the **Global Heritage Fund** (www.global heritagefund.org), it's a top candidate for Unesco World Heritage site status.

Banteay Chhmar is renowned for its 2000 sq m of intricate carvings, including scenes of daily life. On the temple's east side, a huge **bas-relief** on a partly toppled wall dramatically depicts naval warfare between the Khmers (on the left) and the Chams (on the right), with the dead – some being devoured by crocodiles – at the bottom. Further south (to the left) are scenes of land warfare with infantry and elephants. There are more martial bas-reliefs along the exterior of the temple's south walls.

The once-grand entry gallery is now a jumble of fallen sandstone blocks, though elsewhere a few intersecting galleries have withstood the ravages of time, as have some almost-hidden 12th-century inscriptions. Sadly, all the *apsaras* (nymphs) have been decapitated by looters.

Unique to Banteay Chhmar was a sequence of eight **multiarmed Avalokiteshvaras** on the exterior of the southern section of the temple's western ramparts, but several of these were dismantled and trucked into Thailand in a brazen act of looting in 1998. The segments intercepted by the Thais are now on display in Phnom Penh's National Museum (p93); the two figures that remain in situ – one with 22 arms, the other with 32 – are truly spectacular.

Orientation & Information

The main road through town runs east–west south of the *baray* (the reservoir surrounding the temple) and then takes a 90-degree turn, heading north just east of the *baray*. The market and taxi park are at the turn; a few hundred metres north is the temple's main (eastern) entrance. Across the road and a bit south is the **community-based tourism office** (☎ 012 237605), which arranges homestays and ox-cart rides, and rents bicycles.

Other Temples

Banteay Top (Fortress of the Army), set among rice paddies southeast of Banteay Chhmar, may only be a small temple, but there's something special about the atmosphere here. Constructed around the same time as Banteay Chhmar, it may be a tribute to the army of Jayavarman VII, which confirmed Khmer dominance over the region by conclusively defeating the Chams. One of the damaged towers looks decidedly precarious, like a bony finger pointing skyward. To get there from Banteay Chhmar, go south (towards Sisophon) along NH69 for 7km and then head east for 5km.

There are nine fascinating **satellite temples** in the vicinity of Banteay Chhmar, all in a ruinous state and some accessible only if you chop through the jungle. These include Prasat Mebon, Prasat Ta Prohm, Prasat Prom Muk Buon, Prasat Yeay Choun, Prasat Pranang Ta Sok and Prasat Chiem Trey.

Activities

You can see **silk** being woven and buy top-quality silk products destined for the French market at **Soieries du Mékong** (Mekong Silk Mill; www.soieriesdumekong.com, in French; ⏰ 7.30am-noon & 1.30-5pm Mon-Fri), 150m south of where NH69 from Sisophon meets the *baray*. It's affiliated with the French NGO **Enfants du Mékong** (☎ 012 307069; www.enfantsdumekong.com). The temple's planned **visitors centre** will sell locally made silks.

To meet one of the half-dozen local **beekeepers**, ask at the market for *tuek kmom* (honey).

At the headquarters of the **Banteay Chhmar Protected Landscape** (☎ 012 197 1225), 2km towards Sisophon from town, it may be possible to hire a guide (non-English speaking) for a nature walk.

Sleeping & Eating

Thanks to a pioneering community-based **homestay project** (☎ 012 237605; cbtbanteaychhmar@ yahoo.com; r US$7), it's possible to stay in Banteay Chhmar and three nearby hamlets. Rooms are inside private homes and come with mosquito nets, fans that run when there's electricity (6pm to 10pm) and downstairs bathrooms.

Part of the income goes into a community development fund.

Near the temple's eastern entrance, rustic **Banteay Chhmar Restaurant** (☎ 077-743136) – the only place you can have dinner without pre-ordering – serves really tasty Khmer food.

Getting There & Away

Banteay Chhmar is 61km north of Sisophon and about 50km southwest of Samraong along NH69, which is supposed to be paved in 2010 – at least, that's what the provincial governor has promised. The temple can be visited on a day trip from Siem Reap.

From Sisophon's Psar Thmei (1km north of NH6), most northbound share taxis go only as far as Thmor Puok, though early in the morning and at lunchtime a few continue on to Banteay Chhmar (northbound/southbound 10,000r/15,000r, 1¼ hours). From Sisophon, Rith Mony has a very slow early afternoon bus to Thmor Puok (US$2.50). The very few pick-ups that link Sisophon's Psar Thmei with Samraong pass by Banteay Chhmar.

ODDAR MEANCHEY PROVINCE

ខេត្តឧត្ដរមានជ័យ

The remote, dirt-poor province of Oddar Meanchey (Otdar Mean Chey) produces very little apart from opportunities for aid organisations. Khmer Rouge sites around Anlong Veng are starting to attract visitors, both foreign and Cambodian.

The province has two seldom-used international border crossings with Thailand, Choam–Choam Srawngam and O Smach–Chong Jom.

SAMRAONG

សំរោង

☎ 065 / pop 22,000

There are towns called Samraong throughout Cambodia – the name means 'dense jungle', sadly a rarity in this area today. Very few travellers pass by this Samraong, the provincial-backwater capital of Oddar Meanchey, unless they're on the way to the border crossing at O Smach, 40km north.

Orientation & Information

The centre of town, to the degree that there is one, runs northward from the scruffy

---

> ### LAND MINE ALERT!
>
> Banteay Meanchey and Oddar Meanchey are among the most heavily mined provinces in Cambodia. Do not, under any circumstances, stray from previously trodden paths. If you've got your own wheels, travel only on roads or trails regularly used by locals.

---

little market, where you'll find an Acleda Bank whose 24-hour ATM does Visa cash advances. Internet access is available at the **M-Fone shop** (per hr US$1; ☺ 6am-about 8pm), on the east side of the main drag about 200m north of Acleda Bank.

Thai baht are in wide use here. Samraong has 24-hour electricity.

Sleeping & Eating

Heng Meanchey Hotel (☎ 012 275256; r with fan/air-con US$5/12) Clean, serviceable rooms about 100m north of Acleda Bank. There are several small eateries nearby.

Chhoeun Prak Kap Hotel (☎ 391777, 085-383868; r with fan/air-con from US$7/13; ☒ 🖵 �🛜) Samraong's nicest surprise: a proper tourist-class hotel. The 35 rooms come with plenty of space, lots of light, hot water, a useable desk and a minifridge. To get there from Acleda Bank, go 500m north and then 500m east (ie turn right).

Pkay Proeuk Restaurant (Phkay Preuk; ☎ 391888; mains 5000r-15,000r; ☺ 6am-10pm) An airy, hangar-like place with overhead fans, the usual Khmer favourites and the best breakfast in town. Some say the grass shack next door has even tastier food. Situated 300m east of the Chhoeun Prak Kap Hotel.

Getting There & Away

The road from Samraong to Kralanh (75km due south), NH68, is supposed to get some asphalt sometime soon. In the wet season, the road to Banteay Chhmar (about 50km) – also slated for an upgrade – is such a mess that passenger cars may not be able to get through. As for Anlong Veng, about 70km to the east: while some sections of the road are now, unbelievably, paved, others are a throwback to the bad old days.

Share taxis (25,000r, 2½ hours) to Siem Reap, via NH68, depart from the market. In the dry season there *may* be a bus to Siem

Reap and pick-ups or taxis via Banteay Chhmar to Sisophon. There's no public transport east to Anlong Veng.

For details on getting to/from O Smach, see below.

O SMACH

អូរស្មាច់

Only a trickle of foreign visitors use the O Smach–Chong Jom border crossing (see p342), which is really in the boonies on the Cambodian side. The glitzy frontier zone features two big casino-hotels, a paved dual carriageway a few hundred metres long (Thais drive on the left while Cambodians drive both ways on both sides – chaos!) and an orderly, modern market, **New O Smach Market**. This is what much of Cambodia may look like in 20 years.

South of the triumphal arch next to the market, you're in outback Cambodia. The road to Samraong meanders between minefields and at one point, during the wet, you have the choice of paying US$1 for the privilege of using a dodgy log bridge jerry-built by enterprising villagers, or driving through a muddy stream of indeterminate depth. Along the way, you pass motorbikes so overloaded with fruit, cheap household items and petrol smuggled in from Thailand that they often topple over.

O Smach shot to fame in July 1997 as Funcinpec forces regrouped here after the coup, holding out against superior Cambodian People's Party (CPP) forces until a peace agreement was brokered that allowed the 1998 elections to go ahead. With the advent of peace, the military moved in and cleared locals off safe land to sell it to a casino developer. Meanwhile, the people who'd been evicted were forced to relocate to mined land that the military claimed to have cleared. As happens all too often in Cambodia, the strong exploited the weak, but this episode was particularly heartless and brought to international attention the issue of military land grabs in 'peacetime' Cambodia.

Information

New O Smach Market has moneychangers. **K-I-M School** (New O Smach Market, shop A-30; ☺ 8am-11pm) should offer internet by the time you read this.

Sleeping & Eating

A bit over 1km from the frontier, **TD Na Guesthouse** (☎ 016 312549; r with fan/air-con from

25,000r/45,000r; ⓧ) sports a style that can only be described as half neoclassical, half Spanish and half Khmer. The 18 rooms (10 more are being added) are big, but are somewhat short of spotless.

For something fancier, you can stay up at the border at the Royal Hill Hotel, grandly lit up with fairy lights at night. More family oriented than you might expect (Mum and the kids need something to do while Dad gambles), it offers a generous lunch and dinner **buffet** (100B; ⓨ 11am-4pm & 5-10pm). Across the parking lot, the outdoor cafe-diner has free **concerts** (ⓨ 8pm-1am nightly) of Thai pop music.

Getting There & Away

O Smach – a good place to buy cheap petrol – is easily accessible from Thailand, but getting there from Samraong (40km) requires an arduous, serpentine journey over slippery inclines and around gaping potholes.

Just past Cambodian immigration, tens of *motos* and a few taxis await passengers or freight. To Samraong (1½ to two hours), a *moto* should cost 250B, a share taxi 15,000r and a private taxi US$25 – these are the prices in Samraong; at the border drivers try to charge almost double that. And once you get to Samraong, where are you? Nowhere.

To Siem Reap (2½ hours), a share taxi is 30,000r and a private taxi 1500B.

There is no public transport east to Anlong Veng or southwest to Banteay Chhmar.

ANLONG VENG
អន្លង់វែង

For almost a decade this was the ultimate Khmer Rouge stronghold: home to Pol Pot, Nuon Chea, Khieu Samphan and Ta Mok, among the most notorious leaders of Democratic Kampuchea. Anlong Veng fell to government forces in April 1998 and about the same time Pol Pot died mysteriously nearby. Soon after, Prime Minister Hun Sen ordered that NH67 be bulldozed through the jungle to ensure that the population didn't have second thoughts about ending the war.

Today Anlong Veng is a poor, dusty town with little going for it except the nearby Choam–Choam Srawngam border crossing, which takes you to a pretty isolated part of Thailand. For those with an interest in contemporary Cambodian history and/or human beings' capacity for evil, the area's Khmer Rouge sites are an important – if troubling

and enigmatic – part of the picture. In this area, most of the residents, and virtually the entire political leadership and upper class, are ex–Khmer Rouge or their descendents.

Thanks in part to improved road connections to Siem Reap, the local economy is developing fast.

Orientation & Information

The town's focal point is the Dove of Peace Roundabout, its monument a gift of Hun Sen. From here, roads lead north to the Choam border crossing, east to Sra Em and Prasat Preah Vihear, and south to Siem Reap (along NH67).

Acleda Bank (ⓨ 7.30am-2pm Mon-Fri, to noon Sat) The only bank in town. No ATM just yet.

VTC Computer (per hr US$1; ⓨ 6am-9pm) Anlong Veng's only internet shop.

Sights & Activities

A **museum** on the Khmer Rouge era is being built by Anlong Veng district deputy governor Nhem En, best known for having been the official photographer at Tuol Sleng Prison (S-21) in Phnom Penh.

TA MOK'S HOUSE & GRAVE

To his former supporters, many of whom still live in Anlong Veng, Ta Mok (Uncle Mok, AKA Brother Number Five) was harsh but fair, a benevolent builder of orphanages and schools, and a leader who kept order, in stark contrast to the anarchic atmosphere that prevailed once the government took over. But to most Cambodians, Pol Pot's military enforcer, responsible for thousands of deaths in successive purges during the terrible years of Democratic Kampuchea, was best known as 'the Butcher'. Arrested in 1999, he died in July 2006 in a Phnom Penh hospital, awaiting trial for genocide and crimes against humanity.

Ta Mok's house (admission US$2), on a peaceful lakeside site, is a Spartan structure with a bunker in the basement, five childish wall murals downstairs (one of Angkor Wat, four of Prasat Preah Vihear) and three more murals upstairs, including an idyllic wildlife scene. About the only furnishings that weren't looted are the **floor tiles** – on these very bits of ceramic, the men who killed 1.7 million Cambodians planned offensives, passed death sentences and joked with friends. The trees around the house have been growing quietly since Khmer

LAND MINES: DEADLY LEGACY OF WAR

Although fighting ended over a decade ago, Cambodia's civil war is still claiming new victims: civilians who have stepped on a mine or been injured by unexploded ordnance (UXO), also known as explosive remnants of war (ERW).

The first massive use of mines came in the mid-1980s, when Vietnamese forces – using forced local labour – constructed a 700km-long minefield along the entire Cambodian–Thai border. After the Vietnamese withdrawal, more mines were laid by the Cambodian government to prevent towns, villages, military positions, bridges, border crossings and supply routes from being overrun, and by Khmer Rouge forces to protect areas they still held. Lots more government mines were laid in the mid-1990s in offensives against Khmer Rouge positions around Anlong Veng and Pailin.

Today, Cambodia has one of the world's worst land-mine problems and the highest number of amputees per capita of any country – over 25,000 Cambodians have lost limbs due to mines and other military explosives. Despite extensive mine-risk-education (MRE) campaigns, an average of 20 Cambodians are injured or killed every month. This is a vast improvement on the mid-1990s, when the monthly figure was more like 300, and as recently as 2006 casualty rates were almost twice as high, but it's still wartime carnage in a country officially at peace.

To make matters more complicated, areas that seem safe in the dry season can become dangerous in the wet season as the earth softens. It's not uncommon for Cambodian farmers to settle on land during the dry season, only to have their dreams of a new life shattered a few months later when a family member has a leg blown off.

A number of groups are working to clear mines, whacking through the undergrowth square metre after laborious square metre. Between 1992 and 2008, 820,000 antipersonnel mines, 20,000 antitank mines and 1.77 million UXOs were removed from 486 sq km, but another 4000 sq km still need to be cleared. If you travel in the more remote parts of provinces such as (listed, in descending order, according to the number of mine incidents in 2008–09) Battambang, Banteay Meanchey, Krong Pailin, Oddar Meanchey, Preah Vihear and Pursat, you're likely to see de-mining teams run by the **Cambodian Mine Action Centre** (CMAC; www.cmac.org.kh), the **HALO Trust** (www.halotrust.org) and the **Mines Advisory Group** (MAG; www.maginternational.org) in action.

Some sage advice about mines:

- In remote areas, never leave well-trodden paths.
- Never touch anything that looks remotely like a mine or munitions.
- If you find yourself accidentally in a mined area, retrace your steps only if you can clearly see your footprints. If not, stay where you are and call for help – as advisory groups put it, 'better to spend a day stuck in a minefield than a lifetime as an amputee'.
- If someone is injured in a minefield, do *not* rush in to assist even if they are crying out for help – find someone who knows how to safely enter a mined area.
- Do not leave the roadside in remote areas, even for the call of nature. Your limbs are more important than your modesty.

For details on the Cambodian Land Mine Museum near Siem Reap, see p133.

Rouge times, oblivious to the horrific human events swirling around them.

Swampy **Ta Mok's Lake** was created on Brother Number Five's orders, but the water killed all the trees, their skeletons a fitting monument to the devastation he and his movement left behind. In the middle of the lake, due east from the house, is a small brick structure – an outhouse, all that remains of **Pol Pot's residence** in Anlong Veng.

The **cages** in the parking garage were used to hold Khmer Rouge prisoners.

To get to Ta Mok's house, head north from the Dove of Peace Roundabout for about 2km, turn right and continue 200m past the so-called Tourism Information hut.

From the turn-off to Ta Mok's house, driving a further 7km north takes you to Tumnup Leu, where a right turn and 400m brings you to **Ta Mok's grave**. Situated next to a very modest pagoda, filthy and overrun by ants, and the concrete foundations of **Ta Mok's sawmill**, it is now marked by an elaborate, Angkorian-style mausoleum built by his rich grandson in 2009.

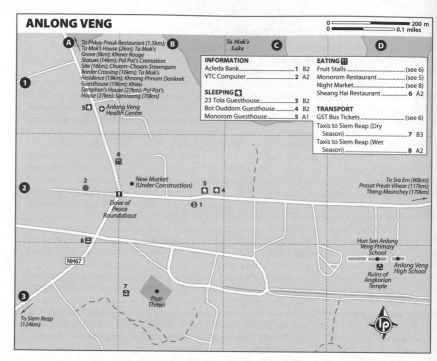

ANLONG VENG

INFORMATION
Acleda Bank......................................**1** B2
VTC Computer...................................**2** A2

SLEEPING
23 Tola Guesthouse...........................**3** B2
Bot Ouddom Guesthouse..................**4** B2
Monorom Guesthouse.......................**5** A1

EATING
Fruit Stalls..(see 6)
Monorom Restaurant.....................(see 5)
Night Market...................................(see 8)
Sheang Hai Restaurant...................**6** A2

TRANSPORT
GST Bus Tickets..............................(see 6)
Taxis to Siem Reap (Dry
  Season)...**7** B3
Taxis to Siem Reap (Wet
  Season)...**8** A2

The cement tomb bears no name or inscription, but this doesn't seem to bother the locals who stop by to light incense – and, in a bizarre local tradition, hope his ghost grants them a winning lottery number.

ALONG THE THAI FRONTIER

Further north, atop the Dangkrek Mountains, are a number of other key Khmer Rouge sites, each marked with a light blue Ministry of Tourism sign. For years the world wondered where Pol Pot and his cronies were hiding out – the answer was right here, close enough to Thailand that they could flee across the border if government forces drew nigh.

About 2km before the frontier, where the road splits to avoid a house-sized boulder, look out for a group of **statues** – hewn entirely from the surrounding rock by the Khmer Rouge – depicting a woman carrying bundles of bamboo sticks on her head and two uniformed Khmer Rouge soldiers (the latter were decapitated by government forces). Now a macabre place of popular pilgrimage, local people come here to leave offerings of fruit and incense in order to honour the souls of dead Khmer Rouge soldiers.

At the pass (a few hundred metres before the frontier), turn right (east) next to a newish, cream-coloured, three-storey building and then, after 50m, hang a left and hop across the rivulet of sewerage. In front of you, under a rusted corrugated iron roof and surrounded by rows of partly buried glass bottles, is the **cremation site of Pol Pot**, who was hastily burned in 1998 on a pile of rubbish and old tyres – a fittingly inglorious end, some say, given the suffering he inflicted on millions of Cambodians.

Bizarre as it may sound, Pol Pot is remembered with affection by some locals, and people sometimes stop by to light incense. According to neighbours, every last bone fragment has been snatched from the ashes by visitors in search of good-luck charms – Pol Pot, too, is said to give out winning lottery numbers.

In 1997, Pol Pot ordered that former Khmer Rouge defence minister Son Sen – who was trying to reach an accommodation with the government – and his family be murdered and then had their bodies run over by trucks.

This incident led to Pol Pot's overthrow and arrest by Ta Mok, followed by his Khmer Rouge show trial (held near the cremation site) and his mysterious death, ostensibly due to a heart attack.

A few hundred metres north, next to a ramshackle **smugglers' market**, is the old **Choam–Choam Srawngam border crossing** (for more nformation see p343). A bit to the west, on the nicely paved main road, the Thais have constructed a spiffy new crossing, but the Cambodians say it's on Cambodian territory – yet another Thai land grab. So for now, with no end to the dispute in sight, the old facilities will have to do.

From the smugglers' market, a dirt road with potholes the size of parachutes – navigable only by 4WD vehicles and motorbikes – heads east, parallel to the escarpment. After about 3km you come to the overgrown brick walls and cement floor of another **Ta Mok residence**, hidden by mango, jackfruit and tamarind trees. Nearby, next to the radio tower, is the cement shell of the Khmer Rouge's **radio station**. Domestic tourists come to **Peuy Ta Mok** (Ta Mok's Cliff) to enjoy spectacular views of Cambodia's northern plains, and some stay at the **Khnong Phnom Dankrek Guesthouse** (☎ 012 444067; r US$7.50), whose six rooms have mosquito nets and windows with shutters instead of glass. A path leads a few hundred metres east, through the cliff-side jungle, to a **waterfall** (dry except during rains).

From here the road continues northeast past minefields (still being cleared by the Halo Trust in late 2009), slash-and-burn homesteads and army bases. After about 8km you come to **Khieu Samphan's house**, buried in the jungle on the bank of a stream, from where it's a few hundred metres along an overgrown road to **Pol Pot's house**. Surrounded by a cinderblock wall, the jungle hideout was comprehensively looted, though you can still see a low brick building whose courtyard hides an underground bunker. Many of the courtyard's tiles have been carted off, revealing the frozen-in-cement footprints of the trusted Khmer Rouge cadres who built the place. Visitors might find this a good spot to read David Chandler's biography of Pol Pot, *Brother Number One*.

The Choam border crossing is a good place to find a *moto* driver who knows the serpentine route all the way to Pol Pot's house (30,000r).

Sleeping

23 Tola Guesthouse (☎ 017 358868; r with fan/air-con from US$6/15; ❀) Features hallways tiled in Delft blue and 27 rooms with light yellow walls.

Bot Ouddom Guesthouse (☎ 011 500507; r with fan/air-con from 25,000r/US$15; ❀) Owned by the family of the deputy governor, this establishment has 40 spacious, spotless rooms, some with massive hardwood beds. The new annexe looks out on Ta Mok's Lake.

Monorom Guesthouse (☎ 011 293046; r US$10-15; ❀) A proper tourist-class hotel whose 20 spacious, comfortable rooms come with air-con and hot water. An annexe with 50 rooms is being added out back. Internet access is planned.

Eating

South of the roundabout there are a few all-day eateries and a lively night market whose blazing braziers barbecue chicken, fish and eggs on skewers. There are **fruit stalls** (❀ 7am-8pm or later) next to Sheang Hai Restaurant.

Phkay Preuk Restaurant (☎ 012 884823; NH67; mains 5000r-20,000r; ❀ 6am-10pm) Situated about 2km north of town and a few buildings south of the turn-off to Ta Mok's house, this popular eatery serves tasty, great-value Khmer dishes in private pavilions.

Sheang Hai Restaurant (☎ 012 786878; mains US$2-6; ❀ 5am-9pm or 10pm) Named after the Chinese city of Shanghai (the Chinese-Cambodian owner's nickname), this mess-hall-like place serves Chinese and Khmer dishes, including fried rice and *tom yam* soup, on massive wooden tables. Make sure not to order bush meat from endangered species.

Monorom Restaurant (☎ 011 907791; mains US$2-6; ❀ 6am-10pm) A brightly lit place that's about as swish as it gets in Anlong Veng.

Getting There & Around

Anlong Veng is 124km north of Siem Reap (along the excellent NH67), 16km south of the Choam–Choam Srawngam border crossing (along a gloriously paved road), 70km northeast of Samraong and about 90km west of Sra Em (turn-off for Prasat Preah Vihear).

To Siem Reap, share taxis (20,000r, 1½ hours) and pick-ups (outside/inside 10,000r/15,000r) are most frequent in the morning, which is also when share taxis go east to Sra Em (20,000r, two hours); some continue on to Kor Muy (25,000r, 2½

NORTHWESTERN CAMBODIA

hours). In the dry season, taxis depart from Psar Thmei; in the wet season they congregate along NH67 near the access road to Psar Thmei. In Siem Reap, taxis leave from in front of the Prohm Meas Guesthouse, on NH6 3.5km east of the Royal Palace, 100m east of the ANZ Royal Bank and 800m west of the main taxi station.

Sheang Hai Restaurant sell tickets for GST buses to Siem Reap (15,000r, two hours, departure at 7.30am).

There is no public transport to Samraong.

To get from Anlong Veng to the Choam–Choam Srawngam border crossing, you can take either a *moto* (10,000r to 15,000r one-way) or a private taxi (US$15). At the border there aren't any taxi touts but English-speaking Visa Service officials are happy to summon a taxi. One recent traveller was taken to Anlong Veng, by *moto*, by the officer who issued him his visa!

To get to Ta Mok's house, locals pay 2000r for a *moto*. A *moto* circuit to the border, via Ta Mok's house and grave, costs 30,000r (60,000r including a tour of Pol Pot's house).

PREAH VIHEAR PROVINCE

ខេត្តព្រះវិហារ

Bordering Thailand and Laos to the north, vast Preah Vihear Province – much of it heavily forested and extremely remote – is home to three of Cambodia's most impressive Angkorian legacies. Prasat Preah Vihear, stunningly perched on a promontory high in the Dangkrek Mountains, became Cambodia's second Unesco World Heritage site in 2008, sparking an armed stand-off with Thailand. The mighty Preah Khan isn't as far north, but is reachable only in the dry season. Fortunately, there's good news regarding the 10th-century capital of Koh Ker, now a fairly straightforward toll-road drive from Siem Reap (via Beng Mealea).

Preah Vihear Province – true 'outback' Cambodia – remains desperately poor, in part because many areas were under Khmer Rouge control until 1998, and in part because of the catastrophic state of the transport infrastructure: until very recently, there wasn't a single paved road in the entire province! The needs of the Cambodian

army in its confrontation with Thailand and the patriotic fervour unleashed by the Prasat Preah Vihear crisis, seem to have had a salutary effect on the implementation of long-promised road upgrades.

Much of Preah Vihear has very little light pollution, so on clear nights the Milky Way spectacularly lives up to its name.

Hidden Cambodia (www.hiddencambodia.com) operates dirt-bike tours to the Angkorian temples during the dry season. For something more upmarket, try the temple safari offered by **Hanuman Tourism** (www.hanumantourism.com).

Getting There & Around

For now, travel around Preah Vihear is neither quick nor comfortable, and in the rainy season most roads are only marginally passable to ordinary passenger cars.

The province's main transport artery, the north–south NH64 from Kompong Thom to Tbeng Meanchey (157km), occasionally gets graded, but the rains speedily turn it back into a quagmire. Consequently, most people with their own wheels get to Koh Ker and Tbeng Meanchey by taking the toll road (10,000r for a car) from Dam Dek, on NH6 115km northwest of Kompong Thom and 30km southeast of Siem Reap. At the time of research, it was paved until the Preah Vihear Province border, but new bridges were being put in north of there, and paving is planned – so they say – for 2011.

North of Tbeng Meanchey, sections of the roads to Prasat Preah Vihear and Choam Ksant turn into a morass of potholes and ruts in the wet season. Thanks to Chinese engineers and the Cambodian defence budget, an upgrade is slowly being effected. The area is still being homesteaded, so along the road you often see the tiny wooden shacks that shelter the poorest of the poor.

The government intends to upgrade roads all over the province, including NH64 and the route to Prasat Preah Vihear, so by the time you read this the situation may have improved – but we all know what the road to hell is paved with.

PREAH KHAN

ព្រះខ័ន

Covering almost 5 sq km, **Preah Khan** (admission US$5) – not to be confused with a temple of the same name at Angkor – is the largest temple enclosure constructed during the

Angkorian period, quite a feat when you consider the competition. Thanks to its back-of-beyond location, the site is astonishingly quiet and peaceful.

Preah Khan's history is shrouded in mystery, but it was long an important religious site and some of the structures here date back to the 9th century. Both Suryavarman II, builder of Angkor Wat, and Jayavarman VII lived here at various times during their lives, suggesting that Preah Khan was something of a second city in the Angkorian empire. Originally dedicated to Hindu deities, it was reconsecrated to Mahayana Buddhist worship during a monumental reconstruction undertaken by Jayavarman VII in the late 12th and early 13th centuries.

At the eastern end of the 3km-long *baray* (reservoir) is a small pyramid temple called **Prasat Damrei** (Elephant Temple). At the summit of the hill, two of the original exquisitely carved elephants can still be seen; two others are at Phnom Penh's National Museum (p93) and Paris' Musée Guimet.

In the centre of the *baray* is **Prasat Preah Thkol** (known by locals as Mebon), an island temple similar in style to the Western Mebon at Angkor. At the *baray's* western end stands **Prasat Preah Stung** (known to locals as Prasat Muk Buon or Temple of the Four Faces), perhaps the most memorable structure here because its central tower is adorned with four enigmatic Bayon-style faces.

It's a further 400m southwest to the walls of Preah Khan itself, which are surrounded by a moat similar to the one around Angkor Thom. Near the eastern *gopura* (entrance pavilion) there's a **dharmasala** (pilgrims' rest house). Much of this central area is overgrown by forest.

As recently as the mid-1990s, the central structure was thought to be in reasonable shape, but some time in the second half of the decade thieves arrived seeking buried statues under each *prang* (temple tower). Assaulted with pneumatic drills and mechanical diggers, the ancient temple never stood a chance and many of the towers simply collapsed in on themselves, leaving the depressing mess we see today. Once again, a temple that had survived so much couldn't stand the onslaught of the 20th century and its all-consuming appetites.

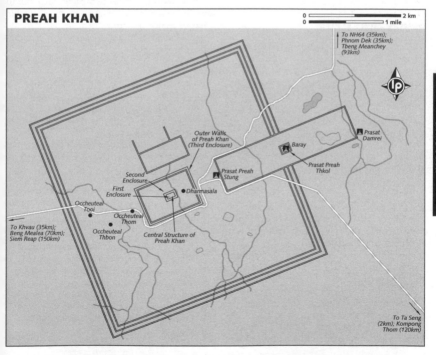

PREAH KHAN

0 — 2 km
0 — 1 mile

To NH64 (35km);
Phnom Dek (35km);
Tbeng Meanchey
(93km)

Outer Walls
of Preah Khan
(Third Enclosure)

Baray

Prasat
Damrei

Second
Enclosure

Prasat Preah
Stung

Prasat Preah
Thkol

First
Enclosure

Dharmasala

Occheuteal
Tool

Occheuteal
Thom

To Khvau (35km);
Beng Mealea (70km);
Siem Reap (150km)

Occheuteal
Thbon

Central Structure of
Preah Khan

To Ta Seng
(2km); Kompong
Thom (120km)

NORTHWESTERN
CAMBODIA

Among the carvings found at Preah Khan was the bust of Jayavarman now in Phnom Penh's National Museum and widely copied as a souvenir for tourists. The body of the statue was discovered a few years ago by locals who alerted authorities, making it possible for a joyous reunion of head and body in 2000.

Most locals refer to this temple as Prasat Bakan; scholars officially refer to it as Bakan Svay Rolay, combining the local name for the temple and the district name. Khmers in Siem Reap often refer to it as Preah Khan, Kompong Svay.

Locals say there are no land mines in the vicinity of Preah Khan, but stick to marked paths just to be on the safe side.

Sleeping & Eating

Getting the most out of a visit to Preah Khan really requires an overnight stay. With a hammock and mosquito net, it's possible to camp within the Preah Khan complex (coordinate your location with the tourist police, who will appreciate a small tip for keeping an eye on you), or you can overnight in a **homestay** (r US$3) in Ta Seng, 3km from the temple.

Getting There & Away

Unless you don't mind travelling by ox cart, it's virtually impossible to get to Preah Khan during the wet season (roughly May to November). The best time to visit is from February to April, as the trails are reasonably dry then.

There's no public transport to Preah Khan, so your best bet is to hire a *moto,* a jacked-up Camry or pick-up truck in Stoeng (on NH6), Kompong Thom (120km, five hours) or Tbeng Meanchey (four or five hours). If you've got the cash, you might consider chartering a 4WD.

Only experienced bikers should attempt to get to Preah Khan on rental motorcycles, as conditions range from difficult to extremely tough from every side. Take a wrong turn in this neck of the woods and you'll end up in the middle of nowhere, so consider bringing along a knowledgeable *moto* driver (US$15 a day plus petrol).

Coming from Siem Reap there are several options. If you've got four wheels, the most straightforward route is to take NH6 to Stoeng and then head north. By motorcycle, you can take NH6 to Kompong Kdei,

head north to Khvau and then ride east. An amazing alternative is to approach from Beng Mealea along the ancient Angkor road (Cambodia's own Route 66 – NH66). You'll cross about 10 splendid Angkorian *naga* bridges, including the remarkable 77m-long **Spean Ta Ong**, 7km west of Khvau. The road from Beng Mealea to Khvau is now in fine condition and may well be turned into a Koh Ker–style toll road during the lifetime of this book. The approach from the east, via Phnom Dek (on NH64 between Kompong Thom and Tbeng Meanchey), is pretty degraded these days though it lets you visit Sambor Prei Kuk on the way.

KOH KER

កោះកេរ្ដិ៍

Abandoned for centuries to the forests of the north, **Koh Ker** (admission US$10), capital of the Angkorian empire from AD 928 to AD 944, was long one of Cambodia's most remote and inaccessible temple complexes. Now, however, thanks to recent de-mining and the opening of a toll road from Dam Dek (via Beng Mealea), Koh Ker (pronounced ko-*kaye* or ko-*kye*) is within day-trip distance of Siem Reap. But to really appreciate the temples – the ensemble has 42 major structures in an area that measures 9km by 4km – it's necessary to spend at least one night.

Several of the most impressive sculptures in the National Museum (p93) in Phnom Penh come from Koh Ker, including the huge *garuda* (mythical half-man, half-bird creature) that greets visitors in the entrance hall and a unique carving depicting a pair of wrestling monkey-kings.

Most visitors start at **Prasat Krahom** (Red Temple), the second-largest structure at Koh Ker, named for the red bricks from which

---

LAND-MINE ALERT!

Many of the Koh Ker temples were mined during the war, but by 2008 most had been cleared: de-mining teams reported removing from the area a total of 1382 mines and 1,447,212 pieces of exploded and unexploded ordnance. However, considering what's at stake, it's best to err on the side of caution, so do not stray from previously trodden paths or wander off into the forest.

THE IRON KUY OF CAMBODIA

The Kuy are an ethnic minority found in northern Cambodia, Southern Laos and Northeastern Thailand. In Cambodia, the Kuy have long been renowned as smelters and smiths. It is thought that the Kuy may have produced iron – used for weaponry, tools and construction supports – since the Angkorian period.

The Kuy stopped smelting iron around 1950, but high-quality smithing continues to be practised in some communities. When travelling along NH64 between Kompong Thom and Tbeng Meanchey, it is possible to stop at Rumchek, about 2km south of the iron mines of Phnom Dek. Kuy smith Mr Ma Thean lives in Rumcheck and can produce a traditional Kuy jungle knife in just one hour. The experience includes a chance to work the bellows and is a good way to support a dying art.

---

it is constructed. Sadly, none of the carved lions for which this temple was once known remain, though there's still plenty to see – stone archways and galleries lean hither and thither and impressive stone carvings grace lintels and doorposts. A *naga*-flanked causeway and a series of sanctuaries, libraries and gates lead past trees and vegetation-covered ponds. Just west of Prasat Krahom, at the far western end of a half-fallen colonnade, are the remains (most of the head) of a statue of Nandin.

The principal monument at Koh Ker is **Prasat Thom** (Prasat Kompeng), a 55m-wide, 40m-high sandstone-faced pyramid with seven tiers. This striking structure, just west of Prasat Krahom, looks like it could almost be a Mayan site somewhere on the Yucatan Peninsula. At press time, the staircase to the top was closed for safety reasons. Some 40 inscriptions, dating from 932 to 1010, have been found here.

South of this central group is a 1185m-by-548m *baray* (reservoir) known as the **Rahal**. It is fed by Stung Sen, which supplied water to irrigate the land in this arid area.

Some of the largest Shiva *linga* (phallic symbols) in Cambodia can still be seen in four temples about 1km northeast of Prasat Thom. The largest is in **Prasat Thneng**, while **Prasat Leung** (Prasat Balang) is similarly well endowed.

Sleeping & Eating

If you bring a mosquito net (there's malaria out here) and a hammock (there are also snakes), it's possible to sleep near Prasat Krahom – ask a police official for a good spot. Nearby are a few small **eateries** (open during daylight) run by the wives of the policemen stationed here.

About 200m south of the Koh Ker toll plaza, which is 8km south of Prasat Krahom, the quiet **Mom Morokod Koh Ker Guesthouse** (☎ 011 935114, 092-317713; r from US$10) has 11 clean, spacious rooms with fancy carved-wood doors, painted wood-plank walls, and bathrooms.

From the toll plaza, if you go 1km south and then 1km east you come to the village of Srayong, whose residents enjoy electricity from 6pm to 10pm. The friendly, family-run **Ponloeu Preah Chan Guesthouse** (☎ 012 489058; r US$5) has 14 rooms with bare plank walls, glassless windows, mosquito nets and just enough space for a double bed. Toilets and showers are out back, across a small covered courtyard. One room has a bathroom with a squat toilet.

Srayong has a few eateries at both the old and the new markets, Psar Cha and Psar Thmei.

Getting There & Away

Koh Ker is 127km northeast of Siem Reap (2½ hours by car) and 72km west of Tbeng Meanchey (two hours). The toll road from Dam Dek, paved only as far as the Preah Vihear Province line, passes by Beng Mealea (p191), 61km southwest of Koh Ker; one-day excursions from Siem Reap often visit both temple complexes. Admission fees may be collected at the toll barrier near Beng Mealea; make sure you get a proper printed receipt.

From Siem Reap, hiring a private car for a day trip to Koh Ker costs about US$80.

There's no public transport to Koh Ker, though a few pick-ups link Srayong, 10km south of Prasat Krahom, with Siem Reap. It might also be possible to take one of the share taxis that link Siem Reap with Tbeng Meanchey and get off at Srayong.

NORTHWESTERN CAMBODIA

TBENG MEANCHEY
ត្បូងមានជ័យ

☎ 064 / pop 22,000

Tbeng Meanchey (pronounced tbai man-*chey*), often referred to by locals as Preah Vihear (not to be confused with Prasat Preah Vihear), is one of Cambodia's sleepier provincial capitals. Sprawling and dusty red (or muddy red, depending on the season), it has the grid layout of a large city but, in fact, consists of little more than two parallel main roads, running north to south, on which dogs lounge in the middle of the day. There's very little to see or do here, but the town makes a good staging post for the bone-jarring haul to the mountain-top temple of Prasat Preah Vihear, 110 punishing kilometres further north.

Until 1999, because of Khmer Rouge activity, the only way in or out of Tbeng Meanchey was by air.

Orientation & Information

The centre of town, insofar as there is one, is around the taxi park and the market, a mass of low shacks on Koh Ker St known as Psar Kompong Pranak. A long block east, NH64 is known in town as Mlou Prey St.

Acleda Bank (Koh Ker St) Has a 24-hour ATM that does Visa cash advances.

MSN Computer (Koh Ker St; per hr US$1; ◷ 7am-6pm) Internet access.

Tourist office (☎ 012 496154; Mlou Prey St; ◷ 7.30-11.30am & 2-5pm Mon-Fri) A new tourist information pavilion is set to open in 2010.

Sights

Established by the Vietnam Veterans of America Foundation (www.veteransforamerica.org), **Weaves of Cambodia** (☎ 092-346415), known locally as Chum Ka Mo, is a silk-weaving centre that provides work and rehabilitation for land-mine and polio victims, widows and orphans. Its artisans, at their hand looms from 7am to 11am and 1pm to 5pm Monday to Friday and Saturday morning, produce silk scarves (US$25 to US$40) and sarongs (US$70) for export. To get there from the hospital on NH64, head half-a-block south and four anonymous blocks east.

Provincial tourism authorities have plans to develop a small-scale ecotourism project 13km west of Tbeng Meanchey (towards Koh Ker) near **Wat Bak Kam** (Wat Sang Virak Seila). Nestled at the base of 45km-long **Phnom Tbeng**,

the village of **Thmor Pourng Angkam** is the edge of the rainforest. With a guide (eg a monk), it's possible to **climb** the mountain's steep flanks to two ponds (swimmable from about June to December), an ethnic-minority village and the summit (1½ to two hours). Homestays are planned for 2010 – the tourism office in Tbeng Meanchey has details.

A few kilometres east, also at the base of the mountain, is **Peng Oreah Kor Pagoda**, whose attractions include a **slab of rock** with two tiny temples on top and a forest **cave** where monks meditate and spend the night.

Vol Rayong Waterfall, 19km south of town, has water in the wet season. The turn-off is 16km south of town; the last 1km must be covered on foot.

Sleeping

Prom Tep Guesthouse (☎ 012 964645; Koh Ker St; r with fan/air-con from US$6/16; ✷ 💻) Large enough to be a hotel, this three-storey place – on a broad avenue that may one day be fashionable – has 25 big, impersonal rooms, all with cable TV and Western toilets, some with fridge. In the dry season, south-facing rooms can get hot.

Monyroit Guesthouse (☎ 012 789955; St A10; r with fan/air-con US$8/16; ✷) A three-storey place whose 12 spacious rooms, accessed via a steep staircase, have lots of windows, high ceilings, solid wooden beds and cold water. New rooms with hot water are under construction next door. The owner drives a Hummer.

Heng Heng Guesthouse (☎ 012 900992; Mlou Prey St; r with fan/air-con US$8/16; ✷) This 35-room place offers the best rooms in town. Top-floor rooms have soaring ceilings.

Eating

Cattle are raised in these parts, so beef is a tasty, if tough, dining option.

Food stalls can be found along the northern side of **Psar Kompong Pranak** (Koh Ker St). There are several eateries facing the taxi park and around the corner on Koh Ker St. **Choeum Piseth Bakery** (Koh Ker St; ⏰ 5.30am-8pm) sells cakes, baguettes (500r) and pastries (1000r).

Mlop Dong Restaurant (☎ 011 709011; St A10; mains 7000r; ⏰ 6am-7.30pm) This timber-shed eatery serves up the standard Khmer staples, including fried veggies. In the morning locals drop by for a quick noodle soup.

Dara Raksmey Restaurant (☎ 012 556146; Mlou Prey St; mains 8000r-20,000r; ⏰ 6.30am-9pm or 10pm) Tbeng Meanchey's finest and fanciest, with

mirror-clad columns, massive wooden tables and the usual selection of popular Khmer dishes.

Getting There & Around

Tbeng Meanchey is 157km north of Kompong Thom along the unpaved NH64, which often deteriorates into a pathetic, potholes-pocked fiasco despite repeated government promises of an upgrade. In other directions, Tbeng Meanchey is 110km south of Prasat Preah Vihear along rough roads, 72km east of Koh Ker, 150km northeast of Dam Dek (three hours) via a mostly unpaved toll road, and 185km northeast of Siem Reap.

Both **GST** (☎ 012 200128; Koh Ker St) and **Thong Ly** (☎ 012 503016; Koh Ker St) send 7am buses to Kompong Thom (20,000r, five hours) and Phnom Penh (25,000r, eight hours).

Share taxis, which leave from the **bus and taxi station** (St A10), go to Kompong Thom (25,000r, three hours) and, much less frequently, to Siem Reap (30,000r, departure at 7am), Choam Ksant (20,000r, two to 2½ hours) and Prasat Preah Vihear (30,000r, 2½ hours). Private taxis can be hired to Siem Reap (US$50 one-way), Kompong Thom (US$45 one-way) and Prasat Preah Vihear (one-way/return US$50/70).

For more information on getting to Prasat Preah Vihear and Koh Ker, see p280 and p275 respectively.

A forest track that can be waterlogged year-round links Tbeng Meanchey with Thala Boravit, across the Mekong from Stung Treng (see p303). In the dry season, it can be traversed over the course of a very long day by pick-ups, 4WD vehicles and motorbikes. An all-season road is planned.

TMATBOEY IBIS PROJECT

Cambodia's remote northern plains – the largest remaining block of deciduous dipterocarp

NORTHWESTERN
CAMBODIA

forest, seasonal wetlands and grasslands in Southeast Asia – have been described as the region's answer to Africa's savannahs. Covering much of northwestern Preah Vihear Province, they are one of the last places on earth where you can see Cambodia's national bird, the critically endangered **giant ibis** (nests from July to November). Other rare species that can be spotted here include the woolly-necked stork, white-rumped falcon, green peafowl, Alexandrine parakeet, grey-headed fish eagle and no less than 16 species of woodpecker, as well as owls and raptors. Birds are easiest to see from December to March.

In a last-ditch effort to ensure the survival of the giant ibis, protect the only confirmed breeding sites of the **white-shouldered ibis** (nests from December to March), and save the habitat of other globally endangered species, including the sarus crane (breeds June to October) and greater adjutant, the **Wildlife Conservation Society** (www.wcs.org) set up a pioneering community ecotourism project. Situated in the isolated village of Tmatboey (Thmat Baeuy; population 223 families) inside the **Kulen Promtep Wildlife Sanctuary**, the initiative – a 2007 winner of Wild Asia's **Responsible Tourism Award** (www.wildasia.net) – provides local villagers with education, income and a concrete incentive to do everything possible to protect the ibis. Visitors agree in advance to make a donation to a village conservation fund – but only if they actually *see* one or more of the birds.

Tmatboey is about four to five hours from Siem Reap (via Beng Mealea and Koh Ker) and one hour north of Tbeng Meanchey. The site is accessible year-round, though at the height of the wet season the only way to get there may be by *moto*. To arrange a three-day, two-night visit (US$450 per person for a group of four, including accommodation, guides and food), contact the Siem Reap–based **Sam Veasna Center** (Map p134; ☎ 063-963710; www.samveasna.org). Visitors sleep in wooden bungalows with bathrooms and solar hot water.

CHHEP VULTURE-FEEDING STATION

In order to save the three critically endangered species, the white-rumped, slender-billed and red-headed vultures, the **Wildlife Conservation Society** (WCS; www.wcs.org) set up a 'vulture restaurant' at Chhep, on the edge of the ultra-remote **Preah Vihear Protected Forest** (right).

With at least a week's advance coordination, visitors can observe these almost-extinct carrion eaters dining on the carcass of a domestic cow – and, through fees, contribute to the project's funding.

The feeding station, accessible only in the dry season and even then only by 4WD, is about 50km northeast of Tbeng Meanchey (80km in the wet season). For details, contact the Siem Reap–based **Sam Veasna Center** (Map p134; ☎ 063-963710; www.samveasna.org). Accommodation is at a forest camp maintained by the WCS. In 2008, only about 30 tourists visited Chhep.

CHOAM KSANT
ជោំក្សាន្ត

Choam Ksant, an overgrown village with an end-of-the-line feel, survives in part thanks to petty trade with Thailand via **Anh Seh**, 26km and then a two-hour walk north into the Dangkrek Mountains. The crossing is closed to foreigners but the area affords panoramic views and lets you get close to untamed nature. The Cambodian army is upgrading the access road.

The area east of Choam Ksant is truly the back of the beyond. Historically important **Prasat Neak Buos** is visitable by *moto*, pick-up or 4WD in the dry season; the tourism office in Tbeng Meanchey may be able to provide a guide (US$30 a day). **Preah Vihear Protected Forest** hugs the Thai and Laotian frontiers in the so-called **Emerald Triangle** (in Khmer, Dompon Trey Kon Morokot), where the Cambodian, Thai and Laotian borders meet. Plans are afoot for cross-border conservation (www.itto.int) of the area's deciduous dipterocarp forest, home to about 50 threatened species, including the Asian elephant, gaur, banteng and pileated gibbon. Stay on the paths – frontier areas are heavily mined.

As far as accommodation is concerned, the best of a sorry lot is Sok San Guesthouse, across the street from the health centre, which has about a dozen very basic, all-wood rooms with shared bathroom. There's electricity from 6pm to 10pm.

The market, with food stalls, is one block north of Acleda Bank.

Roads from Choam Ksant south to Tbeng Meanchey (20,000r by share taxi, two to 2½ hours) and west to Sra Em (no public transport) are slowly being improved, though wet-season conditions are still wretched.

PRASAT PREAH VIHEAR
ប្រាសាទព្រះវិហារ

The most dramatically situated of all the Angkorian monuments, 800m-long **Prasat Preah Vihear** (www.preahvihearauthority.org; admission temporarily free) is perched high atop an escarpment in the Dangkrek Mountains (elevation 625m). The views are breathtaking: lowland Cambodia, 550m below, stretches as far as the eye can see, with the holy mountain of Phnom Kulen (p190) looming in the distance.

Prasat Preah Vihear, an important place of pilgrimage during the Angkorian period, was built by a succession of seven Khmer monarchs, beginning with Yasovarman I (r 889–910) and ending with Suryavarman II (r 1112–1152), builder of Angkor Wat. Like other temple-mountains from this period, it was designed to represent Mt Meru and was dedicated to the Hindu deity Shiva, though, unlike Angkor Wat, it's laid out along a north-to-south processional axis.

The best place to start a visit is at the bottom of the grey-sandstone **Monumental Stairway**. As you walk southward up the slope, you come to five cruciform *gopura* (pavilions), decorated with exquisite carvings and separated by esplanades up to 275m long. Delicate **Gopura V**, the first you come to, appears on the 1995-series 50,000r banknote and the 2008-series 2000r banknote. On the pediment above the southern door to **Gopura IV**, look for an early rendition of the Churning of the Ocean of Milk, a theme later depicted awesomely at Angkor Wat. The galleries around **Gopura I**, with their inward-looking windows, are in a remarkably good state of repair, but the Central Sanctuary is just a pile of rubble. Did it collapse or was it dismantled? Archaeologists don't know. Nearby, the cliff affords **stupendous views** of Cambodia's northern plains – this is a fantastic spot for a picnic.

At the time of research, the long-closed, 1800m **Eastern Stairway**, used for centuries by pilgrims climbing up from Cambodia's northern plains, was being de-mined in preparation for reopening. To get there, turn north off the Sra Em–Kor Muy highway onto a paved road at a point 5km east of Kor Muy and 200m west of the big tree at the bend in the road.

It may be possible to visit **no-man's-land** between the Cambodian and Thai front lines – ask your *moto* driver-guide from Kor Muy to take you to **Sambok Kmom** (literally, 'beehive'), a few hundred metres west of the

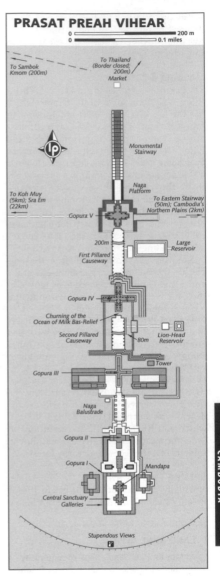

PRASAT PREAH VIHEAR

0 — 200 m
0 — 0.1 miles

To Thailand (Border closed; 200m); Market

To Sambok Kmom (200m)

Monumental Stairway

Naga Platform

To Eastern Stairway (50m); Cambodia's Northern Plains (2km)

To Koh Muy (5km); Sra Em (22km)

Gopura V

Large Reservoir

200m

First Pillared Causeway

Gopura IV

Churning of the Ocean of Milk Bas-Relief

Second Pillared Causeway

80m

Lion-Head Reservoir

Tower

Gopura III

Naga Balustrade

Gopura II

Gopura I

Mandapa

Central Sanctuary Galleries

Stupendous Views

bottom of the Monumental Stairway. Nearby is a **Buddhist temple** inside Cambodia that, by agreement, is visited every day by 10 unarmed Thai soldiers.

A **museum** is being built 7km south of Sra Em, on the road to the temple.

The best guidebook to Prasat Preah Vihear's architecture and carvings is *Preah*

Vihear by Vittorio Roveda. These days it may be hard to find in Cambodia, though, as it was published in Thailand and the text is in English and Thai.

Sleeping & Eating

The best base for a visit to Prasat Preah Vihear is Sra Em, 27km south of the temple, which has the feel of a Wild West boomtown. All four guesthouses are, shall we say, rudimentary, and some are both uncomfortable and filthy. The best of the lot is the **Tuol Monysophon Guesthouse** (☎ 099-620757; r with/without bathroom US$10/7.50), 500m west (towards Anlong Veng) from the central, three-way crossroads. Opened in 2009, it has 25 rooms with mosquito nets and wood-plank floors. You might also try the new **Sraem Srey Nat Guesthouse** (☎ 012 644745; r with/without bathroom 30,000/20,000r), a few buildings north of the crossroads.

Kor Muy, 5km down the hill from the temple, has five rudimentary guesthouses, but the entire population is supposed to be moved in the near future to Hun Sen Environmental Village, 4km north of Sra Em.

Perhaps because Cambodia's army officers like to eat well (the foot soldiers stationed around the temple, many of them ex–Khmer Rouge, complain of not having enough to eat), Sra Em has surprisingly good dining. At **Pkay Prek Restaurant** (Phkay Proek Srorem Restaurant; ☎ 012 636-617; mains 4000-15,000r; ⏰ 6am-10pm), the speciality – served in open-air pavilions – is delicious *phnom pleung* (hill of fire; US$3.75), which you BBQ yourself. Be careful not to order the meat of endangered animals shot by soldiers bivouacked in the nearby forests.

Getting There & Away

Normally, the easiest way to get to Prasat Preah Vihear – known as Khao Phra Wiharn

(Sacred Monastery) to the Thais – is from Thailand, as there are paved roads from Kantharalak almost up to the Monumental Stairway. But these are not normal times: because of the armed stand-off between Thailand and Cambodia (see the boxed text, opposite), the border – open until mid-2008 for visa-free day trips (US$10) – is now sealed with concertina wire and looks unlikely to reopen any time soon.

The poor state of the roads, especially in the wet season, turns any trip up to Prasat Preah Vihear into something of trek. That said, the roads up here are improving, as are the public-transport options. Share taxis now link the junction town of Sra Em, 27km from the temple, with Siem Reap (30,000r from Sra Em, US$10 from Siem Reap, three hours), Anlong Veng (20,000r, 1½ hours) and Tbeng Meanchey (25,000r, two hours). A private taxi from Siem Reap costs US$70 one-way. Some taxis also serve Kor Muy, at the base of the mountain. There's no regular service to Choam Ksant. In Siem Reap, taxis depart from in front of the Prohm Meas Guesthouse, on NH6 3.5km east of the Royal Palace, 100m east of the ANZ Royal Bank and 800m west of the main taxi station.

For travel from Sra Em to Kor Muy (22km), a share taxi costs 10,000r per person, while a *moto* is 15,000r. From there, the return trip up to the temple (5km each way), past sandbagged machine-gun positions, costs US$5 by *moto* or US$20 to US$25 by jacked-up pick-up truck (the cement road is too steep for normal motorcars). Some *moto* drivers – many are off-duty army officers – are happy to act as guides.

KOMPONG THOM PROVINCE

ខេត្តកំពង់ធំ

An easy stopover if you're travelling overland between Phnom Penh and Siem Reap, Kompong Thom is starting to draw more visitors thanks to several unique sites near the provincial capital, Kompong Thom, including the pre-Angkorian temples of Sambor Prei Kuk and the extraordinary hilltop shrines of Phnom Santuk. The most noteworthy geographical feature in the province – Cambodia's second largest –

LAND-MINE ALERT!

As late as 1998, land mines were used by the Khmer Rouge to defend Prasat Preah Vihear against government forces. Cambodia denies having laid new landmines during the armed stand-off with Thailand in 2008 and 2009, but rumours persist. In December 2009, a Cambodian soldier was killed by a mine not far from the temple's Monumental Stairway so do not, under any circumstances, stray from marked paths.

ARMED STAND-OFF AT PRASAT PREAH VIHEAR

For generations, Prasat Preah Vihear has been a source of tension between Cambodia and Thailand. This area was ruled by Thailand for several centuries, but retroceded to Cambodia during the French protectorate, under the treaty of 1907. In 1959, the Thai military seized the temple from Cambodia and then–Prime Minister Sihanouk took the dispute to the International Court of Justice in the Hague, gaining worldwide recognition of Cambodian sovereignty in a 1962 ruling.

The next time Prasat Preah Vihear made international news was in 1979, when the Thai military pushed more than 40,000 Cambodian refugees across the border in what was then the worst case of forced repatriation in UN history. The area was mined and many – perhaps several hundred – refugees died from injuries, starvation and disease before the occupying Vietnamese army could cut a safe passage and escort them on the long walk south to Kompong Thom.

Prasat Preah Vihear hit the headlines again in May 1998 because the Khmer Rouge regrouped here after the fall of Anlong Veng and staged a last stand that soon turned into a final surrender.

In July 2008, Prasat Preah Vihear was declared Cambodia's second Unesco World Heritage site. The Thai government, which claims 4.6 sq km of territory right around the temple (some Thai nationalists even claim the temple itself), initially supported the bid, but the temple soon became a pawn in Thailand's chaotic domestic politics. Within a week, Thai troops crossed into Cambodian territory, sparking an armed confrontation that has taken the lives of at least seven soldiers on both sides. The lively Cambodian market at the bottom of the Monumental Stairway, which used to have a guesthouse, burned down during an exchange of fire in April 2009.

At the time of research, the stand-off was continuing, helping various Thai politicians and Hun Sen burnish their nationalist credentials, but the border was quiet and the temple was open to tourists and pilgrims (though, on average, just five foreigners a day were visiting). Before making the trek up here, ask around to make sure that the situation isn't again nearing the boiling point.

---

is Stung Sen, a serpentine river that eventually joins the Tonlé Sap River.

Kompong Thom came under US bombardment in the early 1970s in an effort to reopen the Phnom Penh–Siem Reap road severed by the Khmer Rouge.

Almost all the sights in Kompong Thom Province are along or near NH6.

KOMPONG THOM

កំពង់ធំ

☎ 062 / pop 66,000

A bustling commercial centre, Kompong Thom is on NH6 midway between Phnom Penh and Siem Reap. It's an ideal base from which to explore Sambor Prei Kuk (p284) and Phnom Santuk (p286).

Orientation

NH6 is oriented north-to-south as it passes through Kompong Thom. The town's focal point is the main market, Psar Kompong Thom. Other landmarks include the Arunras Hotel, which is 300m north of the Elephants and Tigers Statue and 300m south of the two bridges over Stung Sen.

Information

Acleda Bank (NH6) The bank's new building, 1km south of the Elephant and Tigers Statue, has a 24hr ATM that takes Visa cards.

American Restaurant (Prachea Thepatay St; per hr 3000r; ☺ 7am-about 9pm) Internet access.

Chamroeun Rith Pharmacy (NH6; per hr 3000r; ☺ 6.30am-7.30pm or 8pm) Internet access as well as medications.

Department of Tourism (Prachea Thepatay St; ☺ 8-11am & 2-5pm Mon-Fri) Upstairs in an old wooden building. May have handouts.

Im Sokhom Travel Agency (☎ 012 691527; guideim sokhom@yahoo.com) Runs guided tours, including cycling trips to Sambor Prei Kuk.

Po Sothea Internet (NH6 cnr St 5; per hr 4000r; ☺ 7am-8pm) Another pharmacy with internet access.

Sights & Activities

On the river's south bank about 500m west of the bridge, next to the old **French governor's residence**, is the most extraordinary sight: hundreds of large **bats** (in Khmer, *chreoun*), with 40cm wingspans, live in three old mahogany trees. They spend their days suspended upside down like winged fruit, fanning themselves

NORTHWESTERN CAMBODIA

with their wings to keep cool. Around dusk (from about 5.30pm or 6pm) they fly off in search of food. This species of bat, although protected, is considered quite edible in Cambodia – that so many can nest here safely may have something to do with the presence of the Ministry of the Environment right across the street.

The **old French bridge** over Stung Sen is similar to the one in Kampot except that here the spans were never blown up. The parallel **new steel bridge**, opened in 1997, was built with Australian assistance, which is why it's decorated with hopping kangaroos at each end.

Just west of the bridges, the **riverfront park** is *the* place to see and be seen after about 4pm on weekdays and on weekend evenings; it's especially popular with young people. Under the big tree nearest the bridges, there's **aerobics** (☯ 5.45-6.15pm) for women.

Boats can sometimes be hired on the north bank of the river, a bit west of the bridges.

Moto drivers can help you head upstream to **Wat Sampeau Meas Sampeau Prak** (Gold and Silver Boat Temple), a complex of three temples in the most surprising shapes. Getting there may require a river crossing.

Sleeping

There are bargain-basement guesthouses on Dekchau Meas St, but some do most of their business as brothels and all are opposite the taxi park, which means early morning horn action.

Ponleu Thmey Guesthouse (☎ 012 910896; NH6; r with fan US$3-7, with air-con US$12; 🖭) A family-run, Khmer-style guesthouse with 20 rooms that are well above average in comfort, cleanliness and maintenance. Has private parking.

Arunras Hotel (☎ /fax 961294; 39 Sereipheap Blvd; r with fan/air-con from US$6/15; 🖭) The town's most prominent landmark, this seven-storey establishment is known for having Kompong Thom's only lift, serving mediocre food to bus passengers, hosting a racy 'karaoke' parlour on the 5th floor, and offering 26 good-value, tourist-class rooms with crisp red blankets. Runs the cheaper, 57-room Arunras Guesthouse next door.

Stung Sen Royal Garden Hotel (☎ /fax 961228; Stung Sen St; d/tr US$20/30; 🖭) In an attractive riverside location, this is Kompong Thom's nicest hostelry. The 32 rooms offer two-star comfort, picture windows and roomy bath-

rooms; the triples are huge, with enough space for callisthenics.

Sambor Village (☎ 961391; www.samborvillage.com; Prachea Thepatay St; r US$50-85; 🖳 🛜 🖭) Opened in early 2009, this garden guesthouse has 19 spacious bungalow rooms arrayed around a 15m swimming pool. Situated 700m east of NH6.

Eating

The best selection of fruit and vegetable stalls is at the back (on the western side) of the market, **Psar Kompong Thom** (Sereipheap Blvd). The fruit stalls on NH6, near the Arunras Hotel, have an unfortunate propensity to overcharge foreigners.

our pick **Elephant and Tigers Statue Night Market** (NH6; ☯ 4pm-2am). You can dine on dishes such as noodle soup with curry chicken (3500r) and chicken-rice porridge (3000r), but the specialities here are Khmer desserts (1000r) involving sticky-rice powder, scraped ice, coconut milk, sweetened condensed milk, bananas, taros, beans, corn and sesame seeds.

Psar Kompong Thom Night Market (NH6; ☯ 4pm-2am) Sit on a plastic chair at a neon-lit table and dig into chicken rice soup (3000r), chicken curry noodles (3500r), yummy processed meat sandwiches (3000r) or a *tukalok* (shake; 2500r).

Angkor Restaurant (Prachea Thepatay St; mains 4000r-5000r; ☯ 7am-9.30pm or 10pm) Serves delicious fish, chicken and beef dishes to an almost exclusively local clientele. Located next to Bayon (where else would Angkor be?).

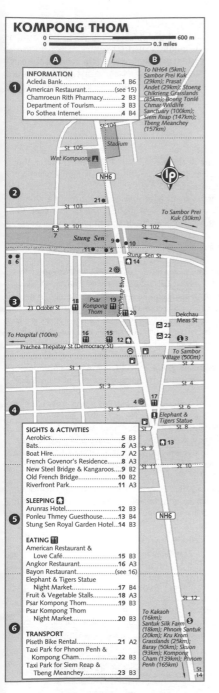

KOMPONG THOM

INFORMATION
Acleda Bank...................................1 B6
American Restaurant...............(see 15)
Chamroeun Rith Pharmacy.........2 B3
Department of Tourism................3 B3
Po Sothea Internet.......................4 B4

To NH64 (5km);
Sambor Prei Kuk
(29km); Prasat
Andet (29km); Stoeng
Chikreng Grasslands
(85km); Boeng Tonlé
Chmar Wildlife
Sanctuary (100km);
Siem Reap (147km);
Tbeng Meanchey
(157km)

To Sambor Prei
Kuk (30km)

To Hospital (100km)

To Sambor
Village (500km)

SIGHTS & ACTIVITIES
Aerobics..5 B3
Bats...6 A3
Boat Hire.......................................7 A2
French Govenor's Residence.........8 A3
New Steel Bridge & Kangaroos.....9 B2
Old French Bridge.......................10 B2
Riverfront Park...........................11 A3

SLEEPING
Arunras Hotel..............................12 B3
Ponleu Thmey Guesthouse.........13 B4
Stung Sen Royal Garden Hotel....14 B3

EATING
American Restaurant &
　Love Café.................................15 B3
Angkor Restaurant.....................16 A3
Bayon Restaurant...................(see 16)
Elephant & Tigers Statue
　Night Market...........................17 B4
Fruit & Vegetable Stalls..............18 A3
Psar Kompong Thom...................19 B3
Psar Kompong Thom
　Night Market...........................20 B3

TRANSPORT
Piseth Bike Rental......................21 A2
Taxi Park for Phnom Penh &
　Kompong Cham.......................22 B3
Taxi Park for Siem Reap &
　Tbeng Meanchey.....................23 B3

To Kakaoh
(16km);
Santuk Silk Farm
(18km); Phnom Santuk
(20km); Kru Krom
Grasslands (25km);
Baray (50km); Skuon
(93km); Kompong
Cham (139km); Phnom
Penh (165km)

Bayon Restaurant (☎ 012 419202; Prachea Thepatay St; mains incl rice 5000r-6000r; ☯ 7am-9pm) Lacking English signs or even a printed menu, this corner restaurant is where locals come for flavourful Khmer cooking. Look for a sign decorated with Bayon faces.

American Restaurant (☎ 092-599810; Prachea Thepatay St; mains US$3-7.50; ☯ 7am-about 9pm) Run by a former Peace Corps volunteer and his Khmer wife, this outpost of culinary Americana specialises in thin-crust Neapolitan pizzas, spaghetti, sandwiches, burgers and hand-made ice cream, as well as Khmer dishes and freshly brewed Vietnamese coffee (US$1). Next door, the affiliated Love Café, with less expensive cuisine, is a trendy place for local teenagers to meet for a date.

Getting There & Around

Kompong Thom is on NH6 165km north of Phnom Penh, 147km southeast of Siem Reap and about 157km south of Tbeng Meanchey.

Dozens of buses travelling between Phnom Penh (US$5, four hours) and Siem Reap (US$5, two hours) pass through Kompong Thom and can easily be flagged down outside the Arunras Hotel. The Arunras Restaurant, on the ground floor of the Arunras Hotel, sells Mekong Express tickets to Phnom Penh but charges a commission.

Share taxis are the fastest way to Phnom Penh (US$5) and Siem Reap (US$4) and also go to Kompong Cham (US$5); minibuses to Phnom Penh and Siem Reap cost US$3. Heading north to Tbeng Meanchey (often referred to as Preah Vihear), pick-ups (outside/inside US$3/5, four to six hours) are the most common form of transport, though when NH64 is in reasonable condition share taxis (25,000r) also do the run. All depart from the taxi park, one block east of NH6 – vehicles to Siem Reap and Tbeng Meanchey congregate in the northern section, while those to Phnom Penh and Kompong Cham depart from the southern section.

Moto drivers can be found across NH6 from the Arunras Hotel.

Bicycles can be rented at **Piseth Bike Rental** (☎ 012 835726; 295 St 103; 1/2/3 days US$2/2/3; ☯ 6am-5pm). For mountain bikes (US$5 a day), try the **American Restaurant** (☎ 092-599810; Prachea Thepatay St). **Im Sokhom Travel Agency** (☎ 012 691527) rents bicycles (US$1 a day) and motorbikes (US$5 a day).

NORTHWESTERN
CAMBODIA

AROUND KOMPONG THOM
Sambor Prei Kuk
សំបូរព្រៃគុក

Cambodia's most impressive group of pre-Angkorian monuments, **Sambor Prei Kuk** (admission collected at bridge US$3; car parking 2000r) encompasses more than 100 mainly brick temples scattered through the forest, among them some of the oldest structures in the country. Originally called Isanapura, it served as the capital of Chenla during the reign of the early 7th-century King Isanavarman and continued to serve as an important learning centre during the Angkorian era.

KEO KINAL *Daniel Robinson*

Apsaras danced and seven-headed *nagas* stood guard when the archaeologist Keo Kinal was born, inside the Angkor Conservation compound in Siem Reap. The year was 1973 and his father, the eminent archaeologist Pich Keo, was in charge of Angkor Conservation and its huge collection of Angkorian statuary, the last director before darkness descended.

Mr Pich was one of only three Cambodian archaeologists to emerge alive from the Khmer Rouge terror. 'He survived', says his son, 'because he didn't wear glasses', and he managed to keep secret his identity as an intellectual and a speaker of French – both tantamount to a death sentence under the Khmer Rouge – while he worked 'like a coolie…to transport fish from the lake to provide for the community. My mother, as other ladies, worked in the rice fields'. Kinal's elder brother died of malnutrition and illness in 1976.

When I spoke with Kinal at Sambor Prei Kuk (above), where he was overseeing an excavation 3m under the floor of a pre-Angkorian brick temple, he was, as usual, accessorised with a dashing *krama*. His team had just uncovered a delicately carved stone block and he was helping two men in hard hats clean it off. As damp earth was brushed away, the outline of an elegant deity emerged.

Despite being born with a silver archaeologist's trowel in his mouth, Kinal did not grow up dreaming of following in his father's muddy footsteps. 'In reality', he says, 'I was not interested in archaeology at all. I wanted to study in the Faculty of Medicine but I failed the [admissions] exam. Then I took the exam for literature – but failed. The next exam was for the Faculty of Economics. But still I fail! The fourth one was engineering. But again I fail – because of money: I cannot pay' – under the table – 'to "pass" the exam. So my father suggested that I apply for archaeology. That exam I could pass!'

From 1991 to 1996 Kinal studied in the Faculty of Archaeology at the Royal University of Fine Arts and after graduation spent three months in Nara, Japan, at the National Research Institute for Cultural Properties. 'That was my first winter because in Cambodia, no winter!' he laughs. 'It was my first time seeing snow! Before, I saw snow on the TV, finally I have a chance to play in snow. We rode snow saucers and excavated under the snow' – just what you'd expect an archaeologist to do. In 2003, Kinal returned to Japan to do a master's degree at the prestigious Tokyo National University of the Arts.

Back in Cambodia, Kinal found himself lecturing on Western art history at the Faculty of Archaeology. 'While I was a lecturer, I had the chance, with the sponsorship of Unesco, to visit Rome for one month. I visited many, many temples, including the Colosseum and, of course, the Pantheon. But the most interesting for me were the catacombs.' He still can't get over the sheer size of the Pantheon, noting that its dome is 43m in diameter and 'the hole in the top' – the oculus – is '9m in diameter – that is fantastic!'

Surprisingly, perhaps, there seem to have been points of contact between Pantheon-era Rome and Funan-era Cambodia. 'From the 2nd century AD we have the maritime trade from the Roman Empire, crossing the [Mekong Delta] port of Oc Eo, to China', Kinal explains. As for the Roman coins unearthed at Oc Eo, which is in the Mekong Delta about 70km south of Angkor Borei (p238): 'When merchants stopped there probably they used [Roman] coins to do the exchange'. In ancient Cambodia all the roads most certainly did not lead to Rome but, it seems, at least one did. Kinal hopes to follow it someday soon back to Italy: 'I wish to visit other places, especially Pompeii and Venice'.

Keo Kinal lives with his wife on the grounds of Angkor Conservation in Siem Reap and works for the Ministry of Culture and Fine Arts.

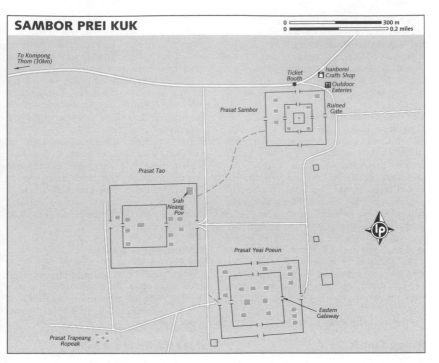

SAMBOR PREI KUK

The main temple area consists of three complexes, each enclosed by the remains of two concentric walls. Their basic layout – a central tower surrounded by shrines, ponds and gates – may have served as an inspiration for the architects of Angkor five centuries later. Many of the original statues are now in the National Museum (p93) in Phnom Penh. The area's last mines were cleared in 2008.

For a **digital reconstruction** of Sambor Prei Kuk created by the Architecture Department of the University of California at Berkeley, check out http://steel.ced.berkeley.edu /research/sambor.

Forested and shady, Sambor Prei Kuk has a serene and soothing atmosphere, and the sandy paths make for a pleasant stroll. Past the ticket booth, the **Isanborei Crafts Shop** (closed in wet season) sells a worthwhile English brochure (2000r), high-quality, hand-crafted baskets and wood items, and T-shirts with original designs. Nearby, outdoor eateries sell drinks and chicken or beef with rice.

The principle temple group, **Prasat Sambor** (7th and 10th centuries) is dedicated to Gambhireshvara, one of Shiva's many incarnations (the other groups are dedicated to Shiva himself). Several of Prasat Sambor's towers retain brick carvings in fairly good condition, and there is a series of large *yonis* (female fertility symbols) around the central tower that appear to date from a later period, demonstrating the continuity between pre-Angkorian and Angkorian culture.

Prasat Yeai Poeun (Prasat Yeay Peau) is arguably the most atmospheric ensemble, as it feels lost in the forest. The eastern gateway is being both held up and torn asunder by an ancient tree, the bricks interwoven with the tree's extensive, probing roots. A truly massive tree shades the western gate.

Prasat Tao (Lion Temple), the largest of the Sambor Prei Kuk complexes, boasts excellent examples of Chenla carving in the form of two large, elaborately coiffed stone lions. It also has a fine, rectangular pond, **Srah Neang Pov.**

In the early 1970s, Sambor Prei Kuk was bombed by US aircraft in support of the Lon Nol government's doomed fight against the Khmer Rouge. Some of the craters, ominously close to the temples, can still be seen.

Visitors to Sambor Prei Kuk often find themselves accompanied by a gaggle of sweet but persistent local children selling colourful scarves (US$1). Some travellers find them a distraction, but others, after warming to their smiles, have been known to leave with a pile of cheap textiles.

GETTING THERE & AWAY

If you're interested in the chronological evolution of Cambodian temple architecture, you might want to see Sambor Prei Kuk before heading to Angkor.

To get here from Kompong Thom, follow NH6 north for 5km before continuing straight on NH64 towards Tbeng Meanchey (the paved road to Siem Reap veers left). After 11km (look for an elaborate laterite sign) turn right and continue for 14km. Another option is to head east out of Kompong Thom on St 102 – some *moto* drivers prefer this quiet, circuitous route through the countryside.

From Kompong Thom, a round-trip *moto* ride out here (under an hour) should cost US$10 (US$15 including Phnom Santuk). By car the trip takes about an hour.

Phnom Santuk

ភ្នំសន្ទុក

Its forested slopes adorned with Buddha images and a series of pagodas, **Phnom Santuk** (Phnom Sontuk; admission US$2) is the most important holy mountain (207m) in this region and a hugely popular site of Buddhist pilgrimage.

Santuk's extraordinary ensemble of wats and stupas is set high above the surrounding countryside, which means there are lots of stairs to climb – 809, in fact. You can wimp out and take the recently paved, 2.5km road, but if you do, you'll miss the troupes of monkeys that await visitors along the stairway and the experience of winding up through the forest and emerging at a grouping of *prasat*-style wats (some of them still being built) with more *nagas* and dragons that you can count. Around the main structures, polychrome figures – some pinned down like Gulliver by the roots of ancient trees – are carved into the huge boulders. Just beneath the southern summit, there are a number of **reclining Buddhas**; several are modern incarnations cast in cement, others were carved into the living rock in centuries past. A multitiered **Chinese pagoda** is decorated with porcelain figurines.

Adding a note of mischievousness and comedy, monkeys hop from tree to tree, raid pilgrims' offerings and treat the old radio towers like vertical jungle gyms, apparently thoroughly enjoying the view.

Phnom Santuk has an active wat and the seven local monks are always interested in receiving foreign tourists. Boulders a bit below the summit afford **panoramic views** south towards the Tonlé Sap.

For travellers spending the night in Kompong Thom, Phnom Santuk is a good place from which to catch a magnificent **sunset** over the rice fields, though this means coming down in the dark (bring a torch/flashlight).

There are clean squat toilets (500r) near the eateries and dining platforms at the base of the staircase.

GETTING THERE & AWAY

The 2km paved road to Phnom Santuk intersects NH6 18km towards Phnom Penh from Kompong Thom; look for a sign reading 'Santuk Mountain Site'. From Kompong Thom, a round-trip by *moto* costs about US$5.

Stone Masons of Kakaoh

The village of Kakaoh, along NH6 16km towards Phnom Penh from Kompong Thom (about 2km northwest of the turn-off to Phnom Santuk), is famous for its stonemasons, who fashion Buddha statues, decorative lions and other traditional Khmer figures with hand tools and a practised eye. It's fascinating to watch the figures, which range in height from 15cm to over 5m, slowly emerge from slabs of stone in five different hues: white, grey, red, yellow and green. A 2.5m-high Buddha carved from a single block of stone will set you back US$1800 to US$3500 depending on the quality of the materials, not including airline overweight fees. Statues produced here are often donated by well-off Khmers to wats.

Santuk Silk Farm

Situated 300m towards Kompong Thom from the paved access road to Phnom Santuk and 100m off NH6, the **Santuk Silk Farm** (☎ 012 906604; budgibb@yahoo.com; admission free; ☼ during daylight) is one of the few places in Cambodia where you can see the entire process of silk production, starting with the seven-week lifecycle of the silkworm, a delicate creature that feeds only on mulberry leaves and has to be protected from predators such as geckos, ants and mosquitoes. Although most of the raw silk used here comes from China and Vietnam, the local worms produce 'Khmer golden silk', so-called because of its lush golden hue. You can watch artisans – the farm has a staff of 16 – weaving scarves (US$20 to US$25) and other items by hand from 7am to 11am and 1pm to 5pm Monday to Friday and from 7am to 11am Saturday. The peaceful garden site has clean, top-quality Western toilets; complimentary coffee, tea and cold water are on offer.

The farm is run by Budd Gibbons, an American Vietnam War veteran who's lived in Cambodia since 1996, and his Cambodian wife. If possible, call ahead a couple of hours before your visit.

Prasat Kuha Nokor
ប្រាសាទគុហានរគរ

This 11th-century temple, constructed during the reign of Suryavarman I, is in extremely good condition thanks to a lengthy renovation before the civil war. It is on the grounds of a modern wat and is an easy enough stop for those with their own transport. The temple is signposted from NH6 about 60km southeast of Kompong Thom and 22km north of Skuon and is 2km from the main road. From NH6, you can get a *moto* to the temple.

Prasat Andet
ប្រាសាទអណ្ដែត

Dating from the same period as Sambor Prei Kuk (7th century), this small brick temple, sporting some ominous cracks, stands right next to a gaudily painted modern wat. Prasat Andet would have been the focal point of an important commercial centre trading on the Tonlé Sap (it's near the wet-season shore of the lake), and some researchers believe it continued to play such a role during the time of Angkor. Worth a detour only for dedicated temple-trackers with time on their hands, it's supposed to be undergoing restoration in 2010.

To get there from Kompong Thom, drive along NH6 towards Siem Reap for 26km and turn south (left) in the village of Sampeau Meas, just past Ksan Ko market, and continue on the signless roads for about 3km.

Eastern Cambodia

Eastern Cambodia is home to a diversity of landscapes and peoples, shattering the illusion that the country is all paddy fields and sugar palms. There *are* plenty of those in the lowland provinces, but in the northeast they yield to the forested mountains of Mondulkiri and Ratanakiri, both up-and-coming ecotourism areas. This is a vast region, stretching from the dragon's tail, where the borders of Cambodia, Laos and Vietnam meet, to the dragon's mouth, where the mighty Mekong continues its journey into the delta and on to the South China Sea. The river and its tributaries snake through the land, breathing life into the fields, blanketing the landscape in dazzling greens and providing a livelihood for millions of people.

If it's a walk on the wild side that fires your imagination, then the northeast is calling. Peppering the area are thundering waterfalls, crater lakes and meandering rivers. Trekking, biking, kayaking and elephant adventures are all activities beginning to take off. The rolling hills and lush forests provide a home to many ethnic minority groups, known collectively as Khmer Leu (Upper Khmer) or *chunchiet* (ethnic minorities). With different dialects, lifestyles and looks, these people are a world away from their lowland Khmer neighbours.

The 'Wild East' atmosphere doesn't stop there. This is also home to rare wildlife such as tigers, leopards and elephants, although the chances of seeing some of these are about as likely as seeing the kouprey – the country's national symbol, now believed to be extinct. The Mekong is home to dwindling numbers of the rare freshwater Irrawaddy dolphin, which can be viewed year-round near Kratie. Do the maths: it all adds up to an amazing experience.

HIGHLIGHTS

- Disappear for a day – or a week – in the forests of **Ratanakiri** (p305) or **Mondulkiri** (p312)
- Catch a glimpse of the rare freshwater Mekong Irrawaddy dolphin near **Kratie** (p300) or **O'Svay** (p304)
- Dive into the crystal-clear waters of the crater lake of **Boeng Yeak Lom** (p306) in Ratanakiri
- Soak up the charms of relaxing **Kompong Cham** (p292), gateway to historic temples, lush countryside and friendly locals
- Observe elephants in their element at the **Elephant Valley Project** (p316) in Mondulkiri
- Experience the 'real Cambodia' on bike, foot or kayak along the **Mekong Discovery Trail** (p300) around Kratie and Stung Treng

ELEVATION: 5-1500M	POPULATION: 6 MILLION	AREA: 68,472 SQ KM

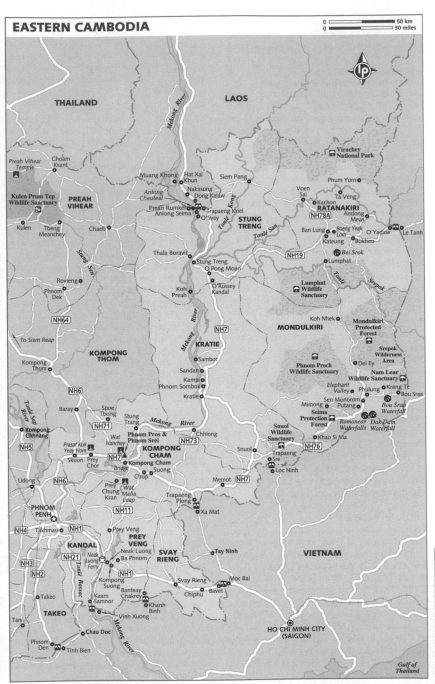

EASTERN CAMBODIA

0 — 50 km
0 — 30 miles

THAILAND

LAOS

Preah Vihear Temple

Cholam Ksant

Kulen Prum Tep Wildlife Sanctuary

PREAH VIHEAR

Kulen Tbeng Meanchey Chaeb

Muang Khong Hat Xai Khun Siem Pang

Anlong Cheuteal Nakasong Dong Kalaw

Preah Rumkel Trapaeng Kriel O'Svay

Anlong Seima

Thala Boravit

STUNG TRENG

Stung Treng O Pong Moan

Koh Preah O'Russey Kandal

NH7

Virachey National Park

Voen Sai Phum Yorn

Kachon Ta Veng Andong Meas

RATANAKIRI
NH78A

Ban Lung Boeng Yeak Lom

Kateung Bokheo O'Yadaw Le Tanh

NH19

Bei Srok

Lumphat

Lumphat Wildlife Sanctuary

Rovieng

Phnom Dek

NH64

To Siem Reap

KOMPONG THOM

Kompong Thom

NH6

Koh Nhek

MONDULKIRI

Mondulkiri Protected Forest

Srepok Wilderness Area

Nam Lear Wildlife Sanctuary

KRATIE

Sambor

Sandan Kampi

Phnom Sombok

Kratie

Phnom Prech Wildlife Sanctuary

Dei Ey

Elephant Valley

Sen Monorom Phulung Krang Te Bou Sraa

Mimong Putang

Seima Protection Forest

Bou Sraa Waterfall

Romanear Waterfalls Dak Dam Waterfall

Baray

Spoe/ Tbong

Stung Trang

NH71

Wat Hanchey

Mekong River

Chhlong

NH73

Kompong Chhnang

Prasat Kuk Yeay Hom

Skuon Prey Chor

NH7

Phnom Pros & Phnom Srei

KOMPONG CHAM

Kompong Cham Suong

Bridge

Chup

Snuol Wildlife Sanctuary

Snuol

Trapaeng Sre

Loc Ninh

Khao Si Ma

NH76

NH5

Udong

NH6

Prey Chung Kran

Wat Maha Leap

Trapaeng Plong

Memot NH7

PHNOM PENH

NH4 Takhmau NH1

Prey Veng

PREY VENG

Neak Luong Ba Phnom

Xa Mat

Tay Ninh

VIETNAM

KANDAL

NH21

Neak Luong Ferry

NH1

SVAY RIENG

Kompong Suong

Banteay Chakrey

Svay Rieng

Moc Bai

Chiphu Bavet

NH3

NH2

Kaam Samnor

Khanh Binh

Vinh Xuong

Takeo

TAKEO

Tani

Phnom Den Tinh Bien

Chau Doc

Mekong River

HO CHI MINH CITY (SAIGON)

Gulf of Thailand

EASTERN CAMBODIA

History

In the 1960s Vietnamese communist forces sought sanctuary in eastern Cambodia to escape the fire power and might of the US army, and much of the area was heavily under the influence of the Vietnamese. Prince Sihanouk became increasingly anti-American as the '60s progressed, and cut a deal to tacitly supply the Vietnamese communists with weapons from the Chinese, via the port of Sihanoukville. By the end of the decade, as the USA began its bombing raids and incursions, the Vietnamese communists had moved deep into the country. Following the overthrow of Sihanouk, Lon Nol demanded that all Vietnamese communist forces withdraw from Cambodia within one week, an ultimatum they could not possibly meet, and open war erupted. In just a few months, much of eastern Cambodia fell to the Vietnamese communists and their Khmer Rouge allies.

During much of the rule of the Khmer Rouge, the eastern zones were known to be more moderate than other parts of the country and it wasn't until 1977 that Pol Pot and the central government tried to impose their will on the east. Militarily, eastern Cambodia was independent and strong, and the crackdown provoked what amounted to a civil war between Khmer Rouge factions. This tussle lingered until December 1978, when the Vietnamese invasion forced the Khmer Rouge leadership to flee to the Thai border. The east became one of the safest areas of the country during much of the 1980s, as the Khmer Rouge kept well away from areas that were close to the Vietnamese border.

These days the region is experiencing an economic renaissance, as new roads are built and the rubber industry bounces back.

Getting There & Away

Eastern Cambodia is home to several important international border crossings between Cambodia and its neighbours. The Mekong River border at Voen Kham–Trapaeng Kriel (formerly Dom Kralor), shared with Laos to the north, is an ever-more-popular route for travellers. East of Phnom Penh are plenty of border crossings with Vietnam, including the old favourite Bavet–Moc Bai crossing on the road to Ho Chi Minh City, and the evocative Mekong River crossing at Kaam Samnor–Vinh Xuong. See p339 for more on border crossings in this region.

For those already in Cambodia, Phnom Penh is the usual gateway to the region, with a host of reliable roads fanning out to the major cities. The region's main north–south artery, National Highway 7 (NH7), is in great shape all the way to the Lao border. By the time you read this, both Ban Lung (Ratanakiri) and Sen Monorom (Mondulkiri) should be connected to NH7 by newly sealed roads. These roads will put Sen Monorom within six hours' drive of Phnom Penh, and Ban Lung within eight hours' drive.

At the time of writing there were no commercial flights to the region, although airports exist in Ban Lung and Sen Monorom.

Getting Around

Eastern Cambodia is one of the more remote parts of the country and conditions vary widely between wet and dry seasons. Getting around the lowlands is easy enough, with buses, minibuses and taxis plying the routes between major towns.

Getting to more off-the-beaten track locales is a different matter, as the punishing rains of the wet season leave rural roads in a sorry state of disrepair. A good road can turn bad in a matter of weeks and journey times become hit and miss. Some 'roads', such as the infamous track linking Mondulkiri and Ratanakiri provinces via Koh Nhek, are passable only by motorbike, which makes the region prime territory for off-road enthusiasts.

SVAY RIENG PROVINCE

ខេត្តស្វាយរៀង

This small province occupies a jut of land sticking into Vietnam, an area known as the parrot's beak. During the Vietnam War, American forces were convinced that this was where the Vietnamese communists' version of the Pentagon was situated. While there were undoubtedly a lot of Vietnamese communists hiding in Cambodia during much of the war, there was no such thing as a 'Vietnamese Pentagon'. In 1969 the Americans began unauthorised bombing in this area and in 1970 joined forces with the South Vietnamese for a ground assault. There is really nothing to attract visitors to the province, which is why 99.99% zoom through it on their way to Vietnam.

SVAY RIENG
ស្វាយរៀង
☎ 044 / pop 21,000

Svay Rieng is a blink-and-you'll-miss-it provincial capital that many travellers whistle past when making the journey between Phnom Penh and Ho Chi Minh City. There is quite literally nothing to do here. Winding its way through town is Tonlé Wayko, a tributary of the Mekong.

If you happen to need a place to bunk for the night, there are a bunch of guesthouses clustered around the central junction. **Tonlay Waikor Hotel** (☎ 945718; NH1; r US$10; ❄) is the only real hotel in town. The rooms are basic but comfortable and include cable TV (but no hot water).

For sustenance, try stilted **Boeng Meas Restaurant** (NH1; mains US$1; ☀ 6.30am-9.30pm) near the riverside, a popular option with Khmers passing through town.

It's easy enough to get here on one of the frequent buses linking Phnom Penh with Ho Chi Minh City. Get off at the NH1 junction and take a *moto* into town for 1000r to 2000r. *Motos* hanging out around the Vietnamese border at Bavet ask for US$5 to take you to Svay Rieng.

PREY VENG PROVINCE
ខេត្តព្រៃវែង

Prey Veng is a small but heavily populated agricultural region nestled on the east bank of the Mekong. There is little of significance to be seen in the province today, but it may have played a significant role in Cambodian history, as one of the earliest pre-Angkorian kingdoms was located in the area around Ba Phnom. It is a province that has experienced few visitors; the provincial capital is a sleepy place on NH11, a lightly trafficked road linking NH1 and NH7.

PREY VENG
ព្រៃវែង
☎ 043 / pop 55,000

Few travellers make it to Prey Veng, a sleepy backwater between Neak Luong and Kompong Cham. Not a lot happens here and most of the population is tucked up in bed by 9pm. But for those who want to escape their fellow tourists, it offers an alternative route between Phnom Penh and Kompong Cham.

There are a few decaying colonial structures around town, attesting to a once-important centre. During most of the year, a vast lake marks the western edge of town, but from March to August this evaporates and the local farmers cultivate rice.

Sleeping & Eating
Both of the following include hot-water showers and cable TV.

Mittapheap Hotel & Restaurant (☎ 012 997757; r US$4-10; ❄) There are two versions of this hotel: the run-down original on the southwest corner of the town's central crossroads, and a spiffy new edition across the street on the southeast corner. Lean towards the latter, which has immaculate rooms, friendly English-speaking service, and a great open-air restaurant packed with inexpensive Khmer, Chinese and Vietnamese dishes.

Angkor Thom Hotel (☎ 011 272201; r US$5-10; ❄) This bright orange high-rise just south of Mittapheap features 27 spotless rooms.

Getting There & Away
Prey Veng is 90km east of Phnom Penh and 78km south of Kompong Cham. Share taxis and minibuses depart when full to Phnom Penh (8000r to 10,000r, two hours) and Kompong Cham (8000r to 12,000r, 1½ hours). Rides in both directions fizzle out after about 9am. A *moto* to Neak Luong costs 15,000r.

NEAK LUONG
អ្នកលើង
☎ 043 / pop 22,000

Neak Luong is the point at which travellers speeding between Phnom Penh and the Vietnamese border have to slow to a stop to cross the mighty Mekong River. The **car ferry** (passengers/cars 100r/5800r; ☀ 5.30am-midnight) chugs back and forth, giving kids ample time to try to sell you strange-looking insects and other unidentifiable food on sticks.

This is all about to change, however, as a new bridge spanning the Mekong near Neak Luong is under construction and may even be completed by the time you read this. It will be the second bridge to span the Mekong's girth in Cambodia – the first is in Kompong Cham.

The only reason to stop here would be to catch a boat down to Kaam Samnor (45km), gateway to Vietnam and the Mekong Delta (see p343 for information on how to do this), or to hire a *moto* to go to Ba Phnom (US$5).

THE BOMBING OF NEAK LUONG　Nick Ray

Neak Luong is depicted in the opening sequences of *The Killing Fields* (1984), the definitive film about Cambodia's civil war and genocide. In August 1973, American B-52s mistakenly razed the town to the ground in an attempt to halt a Khmer Rouge advance on Phnom Penh. The intensive bombardment killed 137 civilians and wounded 268. The US government tried to cover it up by keeping the media out, but Sydney Schanberg, played by Sam Waterstone in the film, managed to travel to the city by river and publicise the true scale of the tragedy. The US ambassador offered compensation of US$100 per family and the navigator of the B-52 was fined US$700, which pretty much summed up the American attitude to the price of Cambodian lives in this most miserable of sideshows.

Buses to Neak Luong from Phnom Penh leave from Psar Thmei (6000r to 10,000r).

BA PHNOM
បាភ្នំ

Ba Phnom is one of the earliest religious and cultural sites in Cambodia, dating back to the 5th century AD and the time of the mysterious Funan. Some scholars consider it the birthplace of the Cambodian nation, in the same way that Phnom Kulen is revered as the first capital of Angkor. It remained an important place of pilgrimage for kings of the subsequent empires of Chenla and Angkor and continued to be a place of spiritual significance into the 19th century, but its past conceals a darker side: according to French records, human sacrifices were carried out here and were only finally stamped out in 1872.

Today there is little left to see considering the site's extensive history. At the eastern extremity of the small group of hills lie the kitsch ruins of an 11th-century temple known as **Preah Vihear Chann**. The temple was evidently destroyed by the ravages of time, but has been rebuilt by the local monastery using a few original blocks and a whole lot of cement, all set under a corrugated roof.

There is a modern **wat** at the base of the hill and a steep set of concrete steps lead up the slope to some brightly painted **pagodas** on the summit, from where there are great views of the surrounding plains.

To get to Ba Phnom turn north off NH1 at Kompong Suong, about 9km east of Neak Luong. Follow this dirt road for 3km before turning right and bearing east along the base of the hill. After another 7km, turn left under a wat-style arch and head to the bottom of the hill. A *moto* from Neak Luong costs about US$7 return. *Motodups* (*moto* drivers) in Prey Veng (about 30km) ask US$12 for the ride.

KOMPONG CHAM PROVINCE
ខេត្តកំពង់ចាម

Kompong Cham draws a growing number of visitors thanks to its role as a gateway to the northeast. Attractions include several pre-Angkorian and Angkorian temples, as well as some pleasant riverbank rides for bicyclists and motorcyclists. The provincial capital offers an accessible slice of the real Cambodia, a land of picturesque villages, pretty wats and fishing communities.

The most heavily populated province in Cambodia, Kompong Cham has supplied a steady stream of Cambodia's current political heavyweights, including Prime Minister Hun Sen and senate head Chea Sim. Most Kompong Cham residents enjoy quieter lives, living off the land or fishing along the Mekong River. Rubber was the major prewar industry and there are huge plantations stretching eastwards from the Mekong. Some of Cambodia's finest silk is also produced in this province and most of the country's *kramas* (scarves) originate here.

KOMPONG CHAM
កំពង់ចាម
☎ 042 / pop 46,000

More a quiet town than a bustling city, Kompong Cham is a peaceful provincial capital spread along the banks of the Mekong. It was an important trading post during the French period, whose legacy is evident as you wander through the streets of chastened yet classic buildings.

Long considered Cambodia's third city after Phnom Penh and Battambang, Kompong Cham has lately been somewhat left in the dust by the fast-growing tourist towns of Siem Reap

---

INCY WINCY SPIDER *Nick Ray*

Locals in the small Cambodian town of Skuon (otherwise known affectionately as Spiderville) eat eight-legged furry friends for breakfast, lunch and dinner. Most tourists travelling between Siem Reap and Phnom Penh pass through Skuon without ever realising they have been there. This is hardly surprising, as it has nothing much to attract visitors, but it is the centre of one of Cambodia's more exotic culinary delights – the deep-fried spider.

Buses usually make a bathroom stop in Spiderville, so take a careful look at the eight-legged goodies the food sellers are offering. The creatures, decidedly dead, are piled high on platters, but don't get too complacent as there are usually live samples lurking nearby.

The spiders are hunted in holes in the hills to the north of Skuon and are quite an interesting dining experience. They are best treated like a crab and eaten by cracking the body open and pulling the legs off one by one, bringing the juiciest flesh out with them – a cathartic experience indeed for arachnophobes. They taste a bit like…um, chicken. Alternatively, for a memorable photo, just bite the thing in half and hope for the best. Watch out for the abdomen, which seems to be filled with some pretty nasty-tasting brown sludge, which could be anything from eggs to excrement; spider truffles, perhaps?

No one seems to know exactly how this microindustry developed around Skuon, although some have suggested that the population may have developed a taste for these creatures during the years of Khmer Rouge rule, when food was in short supply.

---

and Sihanoukville. Kompong Cham remains an important travel hub and acts as the gateway to eastern and northeastern Cambodia. This role has grown thanks to the first bridge to span the Mekong's width in Cambodia, dramatically cutting journey times to popular destinations like Kratie and Mondulkiri.

Orientation & Information

Kompong Cham may be one of Cambodia's larger cities, but that doesn't make it very big. Arriving from Phnom Penh, you'll find all roads east end up at the Mekong, near many of the guesthouses and hotels. The market (Psar Thmei) is a few blocks west of the river.

ANZ Royal Bank (Preah Monivong Blvd; ⏰ 8.30am-4pm Mon-Fri) International banking in Kompong Cham (the times they are a changin'), plus a working ATM.

Sophary Internet Service (Vithei Pasteur; per hr 2500r) Internet access.

Sights & Activities

There's still a fair-sized population of Cham Muslims around (hence the name 'Kompong Cham'). One Cham village is on the left bank of the Mekong north of the French lighthouse. Its big, silver-domed mosque is clearly visible from the right bank. Another one is south of the bridge just beyond **Wat Day Doh**, which is worth a wander en route.

Line dancing takes place on the riverfront near the bridge at dusk if you want to get down with the locals.

WAT NOKOR
វត្តនគរ

The original fusion temple, **Wat Nokor** (entry US$2) is a modern Theravada Buddhist pagoda squeezed into the walls of an 11th-century Mahayana Buddhist shrine of sandstone and laterite. It is a kitsch kind of place and many of the older building's archways have been incorporated into the new building as shrines for worship. On weekdays there are only a few monks in the complex and it is peaceful to wander among the many alcoves and their hidden shrines. The entry price includes admission to Phnom Pros and Phnom Srei just outside of town.

To get here, head out of town on the road to Phnom Penh, and take the left fork at the large roundabout about 1km from town. The temple is at the end of this pretty dirt road.

KOH PAEN
កោះប៉ែន

For a supremely relaxing bicycle ride, it's hard to beat Koh Paen, a rural island in the Mekong River, connected to the southern reaches of Kompong Cham town by an elaborate bamboo bridge (500r to 1000r) in the dry season or a local ferry (with/without bicycle 1500/1000r) in the wet season (the ferry terminal is opposite Wat Day Doh). The bamboo bridge is an attraction in itself, totally built by hand each year and looking like it is made of matchsticks from afar. During the dry season,

EASTERN CAMBODIA

several sandbars, the closest thing to a beach in this part of Cambodia, appear around the island. In the driest months you can ride to the island across one of these sandbars, about 3km beyond (east of) the bamboo bridge.

OLD FRENCH LIGHTHOUSE
ចម្បៀរាំងចាស់

Looming over the Mekong River opposite town is an old French lighthouse. For years it was an abandoned shell, but has recently been renovated, including an incredibly steep metal staircase, more like a series of ladders. Don't attempt the climb if you are scared of heights. There are great views across the Mekong from the summit, especially at sunset.

Tours
Frank from Lazy Mekong Daze (opposite) runs sunset cruises on the Mekong in a traditional boat. These sometimes stop off at an interesting rural village on an island about 30 minutes upstream. The tours cost US$5 to US$7 per person, depending on the length of the cruise and how many people are on board (capacity is about 14 passengers).

Sleeping
Many visitors prefer to stay on the riverfront, with a view over the Mekong, but keep in mind that there is a lot of noise as soon as the sun comes up – including the muezzin's call from the Cham mosque across the river.

Bopere Guesthouse (☎ 092-510365; Vithei Pasteur; r with/without bathroom US$5/3) It's bare bones, but then what do you expect for this kind of budget? The rooms upstairs are in infinitely better shape than the grubby ones below, albeit with little escape from the street noise.

Phnomprak Trochakcheth Guesthouse (☎ 099-559418; Riverside St; s/d US$5/6) Free toothbrushes and other toiletries in a five-buck riverfront room? Consider our interest piqued. Service is indifferent and rooms are a tad small, but they are clean and even have TVs.

Phnom Pros Hotel (☎ 941444; Kosamak Neary Roth St; phnomproshotel@yahoo.com; r US$6-12; 🖭) A large hotel in the centre of town, this place is owned by a nephew of Samdech Hun Sen, Cambodia's prime minister, so security should not be a worry. The rooms include all the trimmings, such as satellite TV, fridge and hot water.

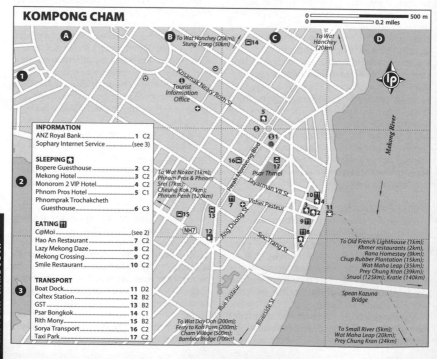

KOMPONG CHAM

0 _____ 500 m
0 _____ 0.2 miles

To Wat Hanchey (20km); Stung Trang (50km);

To Wat Hanchey (20km)

Kosamak Neary Roth St

Tourist Information Office

Mekong River

INFORMATION
ANZ Royal Bank..............................1 C2
Sophary Internet Service............(see 3)

SLEEPING
Bopere Guesthouse........................2 C2
Mekong Hotel..................................3 C2
Monorom 2 VIP Hotel....................4 C2
Phnom Pros Hotel..........................5 C1
Phnomprak Trochakcheth
    Guesthouse...............................6 C3

EATING
C@Moi..(see 2)
Hao An Restaurant.........................7 C2
Lazy Mekong Daze.........................8 C2
Mekong Crossing...........................9 C2
Smile Restaurant..........................10 C2

TRANSPORT
Boat Dock.....................................11 D2
Caltex Station...............................12 B2
GST...13 B2
Psar Bongkok................................14 C1
Rith Mony.....................................15 B2
Sorya Transport............................16 C2
Taxi Park......................................17 C2

Preah Monivong Blvd

Psar Thmei

Jayarman VII St

Vithei Pasteur

To Wat Nokor (1km); Phnom Pros & Phnom Srei (7km); Cheung Kok (7km); Phnom Penh (120km)

Ang Duong St

Soc Trang St

Rue Pasteur

Riverside St

To Wat Day Doh (200m); Ferry to Koh Paen (200m); Cham Village (500m); Bamboo Bridge (700m)

To Old French Lighthouse (1km); Khmer restaurants (2km); Rana Homestay (9km); Chup Rubber Plantation (15km); Wat Maha Leap (35km); Prey Chung Kran (39km); Snuol (125km); Kratie (140km)

Spean Kazuna Bridge

To Small River (5km); Wat Maha Leap (20km); Prey Chung Kran (24km)

EASTERN CAMBODIA

Mekong Hotel (☎ 941536; Riverside St; r with fan/air-con US$7/15) This riverfront property, popular with tour groups, is beginning to show its age. No attempt at decoration is made in the stark white rooms, although they do include satellite TV and hot water. Ask for a Mekong view. The corridors are so vast, they are begging for a futsal tournament.

Monorom 2 VIP Hotel (☎ 092-777102; www.monoromviphotel.com; Riverside St; r US$15-25; ✻ ▢ ☎) This flashy new riverfront property is superb value. The lavish top-whack rooms have private balconies peering at the Mekong and large bathrooms loaded with toiletries. All rooms boast hot water and an eyebrow-raising painting of a half-nude Khmer princess. The US$15 rooms are windowless.

Rana Homestay (☎ 012 686240; www.rana-cambodia.blogspot.com; per person US$22-25) Located in the countryside beyond Kompong Cham, this homestay offers an insight into life in rural Cambodia. The price includes all meals and tours of the local area. There's a two-night minimum stay.

Eating

There are several good restaurants in town, including a couple of Western places, and a lot of cheaper hole-in-the-wall dives dotted around the market. Stalls line the newly refurbished waterfront selling snacks and cold beers until late in the evening. Across the bridge over the Mekong on NH17 is a rash of Khmer restaurants, many of which have live bands or karaoke if you are in the mood for a little entertainment.

Mekong Crossing (☎ 012 432427; Riverside St; mains US$2-4) Occupying a prime corner on the riverfront, this old favourite serves an enticing mix of Khmer curries and Western favourites, like big burgers and tasty sandwiches. Owner and long-time resident Joe is a fountain of information on the area.

C@Moi (Vithei Pasteur; mains US$2-4.50) A French couple has retired here to cook a few modest but delicious French dishes such as *steak à cheval* (steak and egg) in a Khmer townhouse.

Hao An Restaurant (Preah Monivong Blvd; mains US$2-7) The original Kompong Cham diner draws a legion of Khmers criss-crossing the country. The picture menu of Khmer and Chinese favourites sets the record for the most images on a menu – including an adorable one of a cuddly baby goat on the raw-meat menu.

Lazy Mekong Daze (☎ 099-569781; Riverside St; mains US$2.50-4.50) This Western spot on the riverfront has lost none of its relaxing ambience under new owner Frank, a Frenchman. With a pool table and a range of Khmer, Thai and Western food (try the pizza baguettes), it has become the go-to place to assemble after dark.

Smile Restaurant (Riverside St; www.bsda-cambodia.org; mains US$2.50-4.50) This new nonprofit restaurant run by the Buddhism and Society Development Association is a big hit with the NGO crowd for its big breakfasts, healthy menu and free wi-fi.

Getting There & Away

Sorya Transport (Preah Monivong Blvd) has 10 daily air-con buses between Kompong Cham and the capital (13,000r, 2½ hours). **Rith Mony** (NH7) and **GST** (Preah Monivong Blvd) run less frequent trips. Share taxis (US$3.50) make the trip in under two hours from the taxi park near the New Market (Psar Thmei), and overcrowded minibuses also do the run (10,000r).

Rith Mony and/or Paramount Angkor buses from Phnom Penh to Sen Monorom (US$7.50), Ban Lung (US$10) and Stung Treng (US$7, six hours) pass through here, as do Sorya's buses to Stung Treng and Pakse in Laos. Most buses come through around 10am. Most buses bound for Stung Treng and Ban Lung take the long road via Snuol and stop in Kratie (US$4, 3½ hours). Morning share taxis and minibuses get to Kratie in two hours via Chhlong, departing when full from the Caltex station at the main roundabout. In the rainy season, you may have to take a pick-up or share taxi to Sen Monorom from the Psar Bongkok (Old Market).

Rith Mony has one daily direct trip to Siem Reap, departing at 7am (US$5, five hours). Sorya does this route with a bus transfer in Skuon. GST has a daily trip to Battambang (30,000r, 6½ hours).

For motorcyclists, there is a scenic dry-season route to Kratie that follows the Mekong River. Take the river road north out of Kompong Cham as far as Stung Trang (pronounced Trong) district and cross the Mekong on a small ferry before continuing up the east bank of the Mekong through Chhlong to Kratie. This is a very beautiful ride through small rural villages and takes about four hours on a trail bike.

There are no longer any passenger boats running on the Mekong.

EASTERN CAMBODIA

Getting Around

Kompong Cham has a surplus of *moto* and *remork-moto (tuk tuk)* drivers who speak great English and can guide you around the sites. If you sip a drink overlooking the Mekong, one of them will find you before too long. **Mr Vannat** (☎ 012 995890; vannat_kompongcham@yahoo.com) is the veteran of the group and has a 4WD for hire (he also speaks French), but all of these guys are pretty good and rates are extremely reasonable. Figure on US$10/15 or less per day for a *moto/remork* including gas (slightly more if including Wat Maha Leap in your plans).

Moto journeys around town are only 1000r or so; a little more at night. Most guesthouses or hotels can arrange motorbike rental. Bopere Guesthouse rents bicycles for US$2 per day.

AROUND KOMPONG CHAM

Phnom Pros & Phnom Srei
ភ្នំប្រុសភ្នំស្រី

'Man Hill' and 'Woman Hill' are the subjects of local legends with many variations, one of which describes a child taken away at infancy only to return a powerful man who falls in love with his own mother. Disbelieving her protestations, he demanded her hand in marriage. Desperate to avoid this disaster, the mother cunningly devised a deal; a competition between her team of women and his team of men to build the highest hill by dawn. If the women won, she would not give her hand. As they toiled into the night, the women built a fire with the flames reaching high into the sky. The men, mistaking this for sunrise, lay down their tools and the impending marriage was foiled. Locals love to relay this tale, each adding their own herbs and spices as the story unfolds. Admission is US$2 and includes entry to Wat Nokor.

Phnom Srei has fine views of the countryside during the wet season and a very strokeable statue of Nandin (sacred bull that was Shiva's mount). Phnom Pros is a good place for a cold drink, among the inquisitive monkeys that populate the trees. The area between the two hills was once a killing field. A small, gilded brick stupa on the right as you walk from Man Hill to Woman Hill houses a pile of skulls.

The hills are about 7km out of town on the road to Phnom Penh. Opposite the entrance to Phnom Pros lies **Cheung Kok** village, home to a local ecotourism initiative aimed at introducing visitors to rural life in Kompong Cham.

Run by the NGO **Amica** (www.amica-cambodge.org, in French), villagers can teach visitors about harvesting rice, sugar palm and other crops. There is also a small shop in the village selling local handicraft products.

Wat Maha Leap
វត្តមហាលាភ

Sacred Wat Maha Leap is one of the last remaining wooden pagodas left in the country. More than a century old, it was only spared devastation by the Khmer Rouge because they converted it into a hospital. Many of the Khmers who were put to work in the surrounding fields perished here; 500 bodies were thrown into graves on site, now camouflaged by a tranquil garden.

The pagoda itself is beautiful. The wide black columns supporting the structure are complete tree trunks, resplendent in gilded patterns. The Khmer Rouge painted over the designs to match their austere philosophies, but the monks have since stripped it back to its original glory.

The journey to Wat Maha Leap is best done by boat from Kompong Cham. You follow the Mekong downstream for a short distance before peeling off on a sublime tributary known as 'Small River', which affords awesome glimpses of rural Cambodian life. A 40HP outboard (US$40 per round-trip including stops in nearby weaving villages) gets there in less than an hour each way, while slower long boats (US$30) take about 90 minutes. Hire boats on the river opposite Mekong Hotel.

Small River is only navigable from about July to late December. At other times you'll have to go overland. It's pretty difficult to find on your own without some knowledge of Khmer, as there are lots of small turns along the way, so hire a *moto* (US$10 per round-trip including a stop in Prey Chung Kran, one hour each way). It's 20km by river and almost twice that by road.

Prey Chung Kran
ព្រៃចង្រ្កាន

Kompong Cham is famous for its high-quality silk. The tiny village of Prey Chung Kran is set on the banks of the river and nearly every household has a weaving loom. Under the cool shade provided by their stilted homes, they work deftly to produce *kramas* of fashion and tradition. The most interesting thing to watch is the dyeing process as the typical diamond and dot tessellations are formed at this stage. Prey Chung Kran is about 4km from Wat Maha Leap. There are additional weavers all along the road between Wat Maha Leap and Prey Chung Kran.

Wat Hanchey
វត្តហាន់ជ័យ

Wat Hanchey is a hilltop pagoda that was an important centre of worship during the Chenla period, and today offers some of the best Mekong views in Cambodia. During the time of the Chenla empire, this may have been an important transit stop on journeys between the ancient cities of Thala Boravit (near Stung Treng to the north) and Angkor Borei (near Takeo to the south), and Sambor Prei Kuk (near Kompong Thom to the west) and Banteay Prei Nokor (near Memot to the east).

Sitting in front of a large, contemporary wat is a remarkable brick sanctuary dating from the 8th century. The well-preserved writing on the walls of the entryway is in an unidentified script. A hole in the roof lets in a lone shaft of light. The foundations of several other 8th-century structures, some of them destroyed by American bombs, are scattered around the compound along with a clutch of bizarre fruit and animal statues.

Moto drivers charge about US$7 return for the trip, which takes about 40 minutes each way from Kompong Cham. In the dry season, cycling here through the pretty riverbank villages is a good way to pass a day.

Rubber Plantations
ចំការកៅស៊ូ

Kompong Cham was the heartland of the Cambodian rubber industry and rubber plantations still stretch across the province. Many of them are back in business and some of the largest plantations can be visited. Using an extended scraping instrument, workers graze the trunks until the sap appears, dripping into the open coconut shells on the ground. At **Chup Rubber Plantation**, about 15km east of Kompong Cham, you can observe harvesting in action and wander at will around the **factory** (admission US$1) where they process the rubber.

KRATIE PROVINCE
ខេត្តក្រចេះ

In a pretty province spanning the Mekong, much of Kratie's population makes its living from the mother river's waters. Beyond the river, it's a remote and wild land that sees few outsiders. Most visitors are drawn to the rare freshwater Irrawaddy dolphins found in Kampi, about 15km north of the provincial capital. The town of Kratie is a little charmer and makes a good base from which to explore the surrounding countryside.

The provincial capital was one of the first towns to be 'liberated' by the Khmer Rouge (actually it was the North Vietnamese, but the Khmer Rouge later took the credit) in the summer of 1970. It was also one of the first provincial capitals to fall to the liberating Vietnamese forces in the overthrow of the Khmer Rouge on 30 December 1978.

In the past, getting about was easier by boat than by road, as most roads in the province were pretty nasty. However, Kratie is now connected by NH7 to Kompong Cham and Phnom Penh to the south and Stung Treng

---

KRAMA CHAMELEON Nick Ray

The colourful checked scarf known as the *krama* is almost universally worn by rural Khmers and is still pretty popular in the cities. The scarves are made from cotton or silk and the most famous silk *kramas* come from Kompong Cham and Takeo Provinces.

Kramas have a multitude of uses. They are primarily used to protect Cambodians from the sun, the dust and the wind, and it is for this reason many tourists end up investing in one during a visit. However, they are also slung around the waist as mini-sarongs, used as towels for drying the body, knotted at the neck as decorations, tied across the shoulders as baby carriers, placed upon chairs or beds as pillow covers, used to tow broken-down motorbikes and stuffed inside motorbike tyres in the advent of remote punctures – the list is endless.

Kramas are sold in markets throughout Cambodia and are an essential purchase for travellers using pick-up trucks or taking boat services. They have become very much a symbol of Cambodia and, for many Khmers, wearing one is an affirmation of their identity.

and the Lao border to the north, making it a major cultural crossroads.

KRATIE

ក្រចេះ

☎ 072 / pop 79,000

Kratie is a thriving travel hub and the natural place to break the journey when travelling overland between Phnom Penh and Champasak in southern Laos. It is *the* place in the country to see Irrawaddy dolphins, which live in the Mekong River in ever-diminishing numbers. A lively riverside town, Kratie (pronounced kra-*cheh*) has an expansive riverfront and some of the best Mekong sunsets in Cambodia. There is a rich legacy of French-era architecture, as it was spared the wartime bombing that destroyed so many other provincial centres.

Information

Phone services are available at kiosks around the market. You Hong Guesthouses I and II (opposite) have lively internet cafes and big walls o' travel info. Most other recommended guesthouses are also pretty switched on to travellers' needs. A Canadia Bank with a MasterCard/Cirrus ATM machine is due to open sometime in 2010 on the riverfront just north of Balcony Guesthouse.

Acleda Bank (⏰ 7.30am-4pm Mon-Fri) Has an ATM that accepts Visa cards and can change travellers cheques (US dollars and euros).

Tourist office (Rue Preah Suramarit) By the river, it was expanding when we visited. Plans are to have brochures and maps available, plus information on the Mekong Discovery Trail.

Sights & Activities

The main activity that draws visitors to Kratie is the chance to spot the elusive Irrawaddy river dolphin (see the boxed text, p300).

Lying just across the water from Kratie is the island of **Koh Trong**, an almighty sandbar in the middle of the river. Cross to the island by boat and enjoy a slice of rural island life. This could be the Don Khong of Cambodia in years to come and attractions include an old stupa and a small floating village, as well as the chance to encounter one of the rare Mekong mud turtles who inhabit the western shore. Catch the little ferry from the port (with/without bicycle 1000r/500r). Bicycle rental is available on the island for US$1.

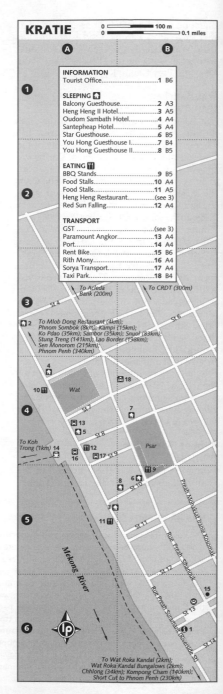

KRATIE

0 — 100 m
0 — 0.1 miles

INFORMATION
Tourist Office...................1 B6

SLEEPING 🏠
Balcony Guesthouse.............2 A3
Heng Heng II Hotel.............3 A5
Oudom Sambath Hotel...........4 A4
Santepheap Hotel..............5 A4
Star Guesthouse...............6 B5
You Hong Guesthouse I.........7 B4
You Hong Guesthouse II........8 B5

EATING 🍴
BBQ Stands....................9 B5
Food Stalls..................10 A4
Food Stalls..................11 A5
Heng Heng Restaurant......(see 3)
Red Sun Falling..............12 A4

TRANSPORT
GST........................(see 3)
Paramount Angkor.............13 A4
Port.........................14 A4
Rent Bike....................15 B6
Rith Mony....................16 A4
Sorya Transport..............17 A4
Taxi Park....................18 B4

To Acleda Bank (200m)
To CRDT (300m)

To Mlob Dong Restaurant (4km);
Phnom Sombok (8km); Kampi (15km);
Ko Pdao (35km); Sambor (35km); Snuol (83km);
Stung Treng (141km); Lao Border (198km);
Sen Monorom (215km);
Phnom Penh (340km)

Wat

To Koh Trong (1km)

Psar

Mekong River

Preah Monivong

Rue Preah Shanouk

Rue Preah Suramarit (Riverside St)

To Wat Roka Kandal (2km);
Wat Roka-Kandal Bungalows (2km);
Chhlong (34km); Kompong Cham (140km);
Short Cut to Phnom Penh (230km)

EASTERN CAMBODIA

Wat Roka Kandal (www.cambodian-craft.com; admission 2000r), about 2km south of Kratie on the road to Chhlong, is a beautiful little temple dating from the early 19th century, one of the oldest in the region. To see the beautifully restored interior, which serves as showroom for local wicker handicrafts, ask around for someone with the key.

Sleeping

Most accommodation is on or near enough to the riverfront. Exceptions to the rule of bulky, rock-hard pillows are practically nonexistent – perhaps the town pillow maker is being paid off by the town chiropractor.

Balcony Guesthouse (☎ 016 604036; www.balcony guesthouse.net; Rue Preah Suramarit; r with/without bathroom from US$6/4; ✗ ⓢ) This relaxing new place sets the standard for budget accommodation in Kratie. Book ahead, however, as its six rooms fill up fast. Highlights are the delicious restaurant, cosy balcony and (paid) wi-fi. Even the shared bathroom has hot water.

You Hong Guesthouse II (☎ 012 957003; youhong _kratie@yahoo.com; 91 St 10; r with fan/air-con US$5/13) Newly opened near the riverfront, its lively little restaurant-bar, plastered wall-to-wall with travel info, is a prime gathering point for backpackers. There are only four rooms – if they are full you might try its more established sister, You Hong Guesthouse I, overlooking the market. Rooms at both places are uninspiring, however.

Santepheap Hotel (☎ 971537; santepheaphotel@ yahoo.com; Rue Preah Suramarit; r US$5-20; ✗) The don of hotels in Kratie, this expansive place has large fan rooms at the back for just US$5 with TV and bathroom. Air-con rooms come in various shapes and sizes, some with plush wood trim and hot water. Popular with tour groups.

Oudom Sambath Hotel (☎ 012 965944; 439 Rue Preah Suramarit; r with fan/air-con from US$7/15) A smart hotel on the riverfront, it has tidy, well-appointed rooms with air-con, hot water and cable TV for those with the cash. Pay a bit extra for riverfront views.

Also recommended:

Star Guesthouse (kratiestar@hotmail.com; r US$4) Reliable peddler of information, with a bustling street-side restaurant and noisy, leaky rooms.

Heng Heng II Hotel (☎ 011 282821; hengheng2 hotel@yahoo.com; Rue Preah Suramarit; r with fan/ air-con US$7/15) Standard Khmer high-rise hotel with no major problems.

Wat Roka Kandal Bungalows (Rue Preah Suramarit; r US$10) Big bungalows with wraparound verandahs overlooking the Mekong entice, but had fallen into disrepair when we visited.

Eating & Drinking

The food stalls that set up shop overlooking the Mekong are a fine spot for a cheap meal or a sunset drink. You'll find two famous Kratie specialities here: *krolan* (sticky rice, beans and coconut milk steamed inside a bamboo tube) and *nehm* (tangy, raw, spiced river fish wrapped in banana leaves). Both keep for a couple of days without refrigeration. The south end of the *psar* (market) turns into a carnival of BBQ stands hawking meat-on-a-stick by night.

Red Sun Falling (☎ 012 476528; Rue Preah Suramarit; mains 6000-12,000r) One of the liveliest little spots in town, this place kicks off when owner Joe puts on his party hat to play. With a relaxed ambience, subtle tunes and a small bookshop by day, the kitchen turns out a solid selection of Asian and Western meals, including a homemade cake of the day.

Mlob Dong Restaurant (NH7; mains 9000-18,000r) It's a bit out of the way for riverfront aficionados, but if you have bolted down from the Lao border, this may be your first chance for a Khmer-style night out, complete with a local band and *rom vong*, the closest thing to line dancing in Cambodia.

Several guesthouses and hotels also have decent restaurants attached. One of the most popular local restaurants is **Heng Heng Restaurant** (mains 8000-15,000r), attached to the Heng Heng II Hotel (left), with all the leading dishes from the world of Cambodian and Chinese cooking.

Getting There & Away

As the time of writing, buses were still travelling the long way to Phnom Penh (340km) via Snuol, but that will likely change once the road to Chhlong is sealed, probably by early 2011 (the road south from Chhlong to Suong district is already sealed). Travelling via Chhlong trims 100km and two hours off the journey time. Taxis, minibuses and express minivans already take this route.

Express minivans, which pick you up from your guesthouse at 6am, are the fastest and most comfortable way to get to Phnom Penh (US$8, four hours). Sor at You Hong Guesthouse II (left) can sort this out, and make reservations for the early-morning return trips from Phnom Penh as well. Share taxis (US$9) and overcrowded minibuses (US$5) also head to Phnom Penh, usually between 6am and 8am. Additional rides depart after lunch.

Sorya Transport, Rith Mony, Paramount Angkor, and GST send buses to Phnom Penh (US$5, 6½ hours) via Snuol (US$2, one hour) and Kompong Cham (US$4, three hours). Trips are fairly frequent until about 1pm, when the last buses (originating at the Lao border) come through. Transfer in Skuon for Siem Reap (US$9).

Heading in the other direction, buses bound for Stung Treng (US$5, 2½ hours), Ban Lung (US$10, six hours), the Lao border (US$8, 3½ hours) and Pakse (in Laos; US$17, six hours) pass through between noon and 2pm. Morning minibuses (30,000r) also make the run to Ban Lung, and there's a 7am minivan to the Lao border via Stung Treng.

Several direct minibuses service Sen Monorom, leaving in the morning when full (30,000r, 4½ hours). The other option is to take a Phnom Penh–bound bus as far as Snuol and transfer, but be sure to get to Snuol by noon or you may be stranded.

Getting Around

Most guesthouses can arrange motorbike hire (US$5). An English-speaking *motodup* will set you back US$15 per day. **Rent Bike** (Rue Preah Sihanouk) has bicycles available for US$1 per day.

AROUND KRATIE
Mekong Discovery Trail

It's well worth sticking around Kratie for a few days to explore the various bike rides and activities on offer along the **Mekong Discovery Trail** (www.mekongdiscoverytrail.com), a new initiative to open up stretches of the Mekong River around Stung Treng and Kratie to community-based tourism. The project is still in its infancy, but deserves support, as it intends to provide fishing communities an alternative income in order to protect the Irrawaddy dolphin and other rare species on this stretch of river.

An excellent booklet outlining half-day to several-day excursions around Kratie is available at Red Sun Falling (p299) and most guesthouses in Kratie. Bicycling is the recommended method for navigating the 190km of existing roads and ferry crossings that encompass the 'trail', although a motorbike also works just fine. Routes criss-cross the Mekong frequently by ferry and traverse several Mekong islands, including Koh Trong (p298).

Homestays are another integral part of the project. Several options are outlined in the project booklet, including an enticing program managed by **Cambodian Rural Development**

DOLPHIN-WATCHING AROUND KRATIE

The freshwater Irrawaddy dolphin *(trey pisaut)* is an endangered species throughout Asia, with shrinking numbers inhabiting stretches of the Mekong in Cambodia and Laos, and isolated pockets in Bangladesh and Myanmar. The dark blue to grey cetaceans grow to 2.75m long and are recognisable by their bulging foreheads and small dorsal fins. They can live in fresh or salt water, although they are seldom seen in the sea. For more on this rare creature, see www.panda.org/greatermekong.

Before the civil war, locals say, Cambodia was home to as many as 1000 dolphins. However, during the Pol Pot regime, many were hunted for their oils, and their numbers continue to plummet even as drastic protection measures have been put in place, including a ban on fishing and motorised boat traffic on much of the Mekong between Kratie and Stung Treng. The dolphins continue to die off at an alarming rate, and experts now estimate that there are fewer than 70 Irrawaddy dolphins left in the Mekong between Kratie and the Lao border.

The place to see them is at Kampi, about 15km north of Kratie, on the road to Sambor. A *moto/remork* should be around US$5/10 return depending on how long the driver has to wait. Motorboats shuttle visitors out to the middle of the river to view the dolphins at close quarters. It costs US$9 per person for one to two persons and US$7 per person for groups of three or more. Encourage the boat driver to use the engine as little as possible once near the dolphins, as the noise is sure to disturb them. It is also possible to see them near the Lao border in Stung Treng province (see p304).

Team (CRDT; ☎ 023-357230; www.crdt.org.kh; 695 St 2, Kratie) on Koh Pdao, an island 35km north of Kratie. Participants do some serious interacting with locals and even get their hands dirty on volunteer building or farming projects. Diversions include cycling and dolphin spotting from the shore. It costs US$35/50 for one/two nights including all meals and transport.

Phnom Sombok
ភ្នំសំបុក

Phnom Sombok is a small hill with an active wat, located on the road from Kratie to Kampi. The hill offers the best views across the Mekong on this stretch of the river and a visit here can easily be combined with a trip to see the dolphins for an extra dollar or so.

Sambor
សំបូរ

Sambor was the site of a thriving pre-Angkorian city during the time of Sambor Prei Kuk and the Chenla empire. Not a stone remains in the modern town of Sambor, which is locally famous for having the largest **wat** in Cambodia, complete with 108 columns. Known locally as Wat Moi Roi (Wat Sorsor Moi Roi; 100 Columns Temple), it was constructed on the site of a 19th-century wooden temple, a few pillars of which are still located at the back of the compound. This temple is a minor place of pilgrimage for residents of Kratie Province. To get to Sambor, follow the Kampi road north to Sandan, before veering left along a reasonable 10km stretch of road – it's about 35km in total.

CHHLONG
ឆ្លូង

Chhlong is a pleasant riverside port town that stands to become a major travel crossroads once they finish paving the road north to Kratie. The town's main attraction is the old governor's residence, a gorgeous, yellow-and-white French colonial mansion near the river that has been converted into high-end boutique hotel **Le Relais de Chhlong** (☎ 012 991801). The hotel is under new management and was closed for extensive renovations when we visited. It should reopen by early 2011, with a swimming pool and rooms in the US$80 to US$100 range.

Not much else happens in Chhlong. A few decrepit French colonial buildings line the river. Architecture buffs might drop in at the **house of a hundred pillars** (1884), about 500m north of Le Relais. According to the house's owner, the Khmer Rouge removed many of the pillars so that today only 56 remain.

Chhlong is worth a wander if you are driving through with your own transport, but is probably not worth a special trip from Kratie.

SNUOL
ស្នួល

☎ 072 / pop 19,000

This sorry little town is little more than a stopping/transfer point for transport bound for Mondulkiri. If you are unfortunate enough to need to sleep here, there's a nice new hotel, **Chompa Pich** (☎ 399014; r with fan/air-con US$7/13), just out of town on the road to Sen Monorom.

If you are looking to transfer in Snuol for Mondulkiri, be sure to arrive well before noon as public transport options dry up after lunch. Buses from Phnom Penh to Sen Monorom come through between 11am and noon. Wait for these southeast of the centre on the road to Sen Monorom.

From the market, a few morning pickups head to Sen Monorom (inside/on the back US$5/3) and Kratie (inside/on the back US$2/1.25). Two or three morning minibuses that originate in Kratie also swing through. Minibuses to Kratie come through between 3pm and 4pm. A private taxi to Kratie (83km) costs US$20.

Snuol is only about 15km north of the Trapaeng Sre–Loc Ninh border crossing, which is open to foreigners (see p344).

STUNG TRENG PROVINCE
ខេត្តស្ទឹងត្រែង

Poor old Stung Treng has long been the neglected middle child, sandwiched between the luminary siblings of Ratanakiri Province and Champasak in southern Laos. But with a spiffy new border station and a network of recently upgraded roads now plugging Stung Treng into the rest of the country, the province may be about to cash in on its significant tourism potential.

Much of that potential lies near the northern village of O'Svay, where several ecotourism initiatives have recently been launched on a sublime stretch of the Mekong. Here you can kayak out to a pod of rare Irrawaddy dolphins near the Laos border, passing islands, waterfalls, and bird-infested wetlands on the way.

The stretch of the Mekong between O'Svay and Stung Treng town can be explored by bicycle, boat or motorbike. From Stung Treng you can proceed by motorbike or boat to remote Siem Pang on the border of Virachey National Park, an area rich in birds and other wildlife.

More travellers than ever are crossing the Laos border at Trapaeng Kriel (formerly Dom Kralor), but few stop for long in Stung Treng. Those who do take a few days to explore will be well ahead of the tourist pack.

STUNG TRENG
ស្ទឹងត្រែង
☎ 074 / pop 24,500

While new roads have helped to put Stung Treng back on the map, they have also made it easier to pass through and many travellers are no longer overnighting here. It is located on the banks of Tonlé San, which flows into the mighty Mekong on the western outskirts of the city. Some locals call Tonlé San the 'Tonlé Sekong', as it merges with the Tonlé Kong 10km east of town. There is a major new bridge across the San, which is a key link in the new road between Kratie and the Lao border.

Information

Acleda Bank (☎ 973684), near the *psar* (market), changes travellers cheques and has a 24-hour ATM that accepts Visa cards only. If coming from Laos, have a backup plan in case the ATM is down.

For telephone services, try the mobile-phone kiosks sprinkled around the market.
Internet Service (per hr 4000r), near the market, has internet access.

Near the southeast corner of the market is a bike shop hiring out 250cc trail bikes (US$20 per day) and old mountain bikes (US$2 per day).

TOURIST INFORMATION
Mlup Baitong (☎ 012 425172; www.mlup.org; pon sambo@yahoo.com) NGO that organises dolphin-watching trips and manages homestay programs along the Mekong Discovery Trail.
Riverside Guesthouse (right) Specialises in getting people to/from Laos, Siem Reap or just about anywhere

else. Also runs boat tours, including trips to Kratie (four hours) and to the Lao border via the resident dolphin pod. English-speaking guides here can take you places on motorbikes, including to Tbeng Meanchey.
Tourist Information Center (☎ 099-709677; ☯ 8-11am & 2.30-4pm) Inconveniently located near the new bridge, it's run by the helpful Theany, who also works at Xplore-Asia.
Xplore-Asia (☎ 6388867; www.xplore-cambodia.com) Doles out brochures, booklets and advice, and tailors one-to several-day cycling-and-kayak combo tours along the Mekong Discovery Trail. Rents out kayaks (US$30 per day), motorbikes (US$7 per day) and sturdy Trek mountain bikes (US$5 per day). One-way mountain bike rental to southern Laos and Phnom Penh is available.

Sights & Activities
THALA BORAVIT
ថាឡាបុរវិត

Thala Boravit was an important Chenla-period trading town on the river route connecting the ancient city of Champasak and the sacred temple of Wat Phu with the southern reaches of the Chenla empire, including the ancient cities of Sambor Prei Kuk (Isanapura) and Angkor Borei. For all its past glories, there is very little to see today. It is hardly worth the effort for the casual visitor, but temple fiends may feel the urge to tick it off. Thala Boravit is on the west bank of the Mekong River and boats cross from Stung Treng roughly every 30 minutes throughout the day (3500/1500r with/without a motorbike).

MEKONG BLUE
មេគង្គប្លូ

A silk-weaving centre on the outskirts of Stung Treng, **Mekong Blue** (☎ 012 622096; www.mekongblue.com; ☯ 7.30-11.30am & 2-5pm Mon-Sat) is part of the Stung Treng Women's Development Centre. Mekong Blue specialises in exquisite silk products for sale and export. It is possible to see the dyers and weavers in action at this centre, most of whom come from vulnerable or impoverished backgrounds. There is a small showroom on site with a selection of silk on sale, plus a cafe. The centre is located about 4km east of the centre.

Sleeping
Riverside Guesthouse (☎ 012 439454; r US$5-10; ☯ 🖥 🛜) This popular traveller crossroads relocated to a spruced-up new building shortly after we visited. Owned by fixing legend Mr T of Tree Top Ecolodge (p307) in Ban Lung,

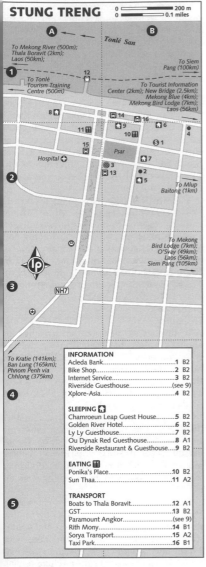

STUNG TRENG

INFORMATION
Acleda Bank..............................1 B2
Bike Shop.................................2 B2
Internet Service........................3 B2
Riverside Guesthouse..............(see 9)
Xplore-Asia.............................4 B2

SLEEPING
Chamroeun Leap Guest House..........5 B2
Golden River Hotel....................6 B2
Ly Ly Guesthouse.......................7 B2
Ou Dynak Red Guesthouse............8 A1
Riverside Restaurant & Guesthouse..9 B2

EATING
Ponika's Place.........................10 B2
Sun Thaa................................11 A2

TRANSPORT
Boats to Thala Boravit...............12 A1
GST.......................................13 B2
Paramount Angkor....................(see 9)
Rith Mony..............................14 B1
Sorya Transport.......................15 A2
Taxi Park...............................16 B1

it has a lively little restaurant (mains US$1.50 to US$3) downstairs.

our pick Tonlé Tourism Training Centre (☎ 973638; fieldco@tourismforhelp.org; s/d from US$6/8) Located in a shady spot on the riverfront about 500m west of the ferry dock, this small guesthouse doubles as a training centre to give underprivileged locals a helping hand into the tourism

industry. Rooms are tastefully furnished (no TVs) and simple but big enough. The four rooms share an immaculate bathroom and a comfy balcony with views of the Tonlé San.

Mekong Bird Lodge (☎ 099-709677; cottage US$6-10) This ecolodge is situated on a bluff over a peaceful eddy of the Mekong, about 4km north of town. Pricier cottages have private balconies with hammocks and sunset views. Power cuts out at 8pm. Kayaks are available for rent and the birdwatching is said to be great.

Golden River Hotel (☎ 012 980678; r US$15-35; ✖ ▢) This brand-new hotel on the riverfront qualifies as fancy in Stung Treng. Quarters are clean and have a few business-class amenities, but could use more (and more comfortable) furniture.

The market area is surrounded by generic, family-owned, high-rise guesthouses catering to Khmer businessmen. They come with a fair range of amenities, like toiletries and cable TV, but English is limited and many rooms tend to be windowless. The best rooms are at **Ly Ly Guesthouse** (☎ 012 937859; r with fan/air-con US$6/12). Other safe choices are **Chamroeun Leap Guest House** (☎ 973616; s/d from $5/7; ✖), where one son speaks English; and **Ou Dynak Red Guesthouse** (☎ 011 963676; r with fan/air-con US$7/15).

Eating

On the riverside promenade west of the ferry dock, a handful of street-side vendors peddle cold beer (3000r) and noodle soup until late in the evening. The southwest corner of the market has cheap-and-quick eateries with pots for your perusal.

Ponika's Palace (mains US$2-4) If you're hankering for Western fare, look no further. Burgers, pizza and English breakfasts grace the menu, along with Indian food and wonderful Khmer curries. The affable Ponika speaks English.

Mekong Blue (☎ 973977; mains US$2-4) This relaxing cafe offers traditional Khmer flavours and is set in the countryside outside town. It is best to call ahead and make a booking for lunch and dinner, as it doesn't get that many drop-in diners.

Sunn Tha (mains US$2.50-4) The food here is only so-so, but it's about the only restaurant in town open past 9pm.

Getting There & Away

NH7 south to Kratie (141km) and north to the Lao border is in great shape these days. Sorya Transport (three daily), Paramount Angkor (three daily), Rith Mony (two daily) and GST (one daily) operate morning buses to Phnom Penh (US$8, nine hours) that pass through Kratie (US$5) and Snuol. A few express mini-buses do the trip to Phnom Penh via Chhlong, picking you up from your guesthouse around 4am (US$10, seven hours). These return to Stung Treng the next morning; call Riverside Guesthouse (p302) in Stung Treng to arrange rides from Phnom Penh. A 1pm van heads to Kratie (US$5) from the taxi park. Share taxis and crowded minibuses also do morning runs to Kratie and Phnom Penh.

For the inside story on the border crossing with Laos, see p340. For getting to/from Ban Lung in Ratanakiri, see p308.

There is also a trail that leads across northern Cambodia from Stung Treng to either Tbeng Meanchey or Kompong Thom. It is unwise for the average traveller to take this route, but, for adventure addicts who don't mind a very long and bumpy bike ride, it is an option. First, cross the Mekong to Thala Boravit, from where a jungle trail leads west to the large village of Chaeb. If trail conditions are bad you may need to overnight in Chaeb in the wat or with some locals. From Chaeb, there is an old logging road west that joins with the main road from Kompong Thom to Tbeng Meanchey. A few *moto* drivers in Stung Treng brave this route, but it's pricey – at least US$60 to Tbeng Meanchey (more for an English-speaking guide/driver). This route should not be attempted in the wet season.

AROUND STUNG TRENG
O'Svay & Anlong Seima
អូរស្វាយ

These small villages are emerging as hotbeds of ecotourism thanks to their proximity to the Anlong Cheuteal Irrawaddy dolphin pool near the Lao border. Sightings of dolphins are practically guaranteed here, while sightings of other tourists are rare. With Ramsar-recognised wetlands, dozens of islands, a rich array of bird life and various rapids and waterfalls cascading down from Laos, this is one of the Mekong River's wildest and most beautiful stretches.

You can easily hire long-tailed boats in both O'Svay and Anlong Seima (Voen Khao) to explore the area and view the dolphins at Anlong Cheuteal. O'Svay is closer to Stung Treng but further from the dolphins. It's the better choice for those who want to observe a bit more of the river on their way out to the dolphins. Anlong Seima is only 5km from the main Lao overland border crossing. Travellers coming in from Laos could get here in about 10 minutes on the back of a *moto*, spend a day on the river, and proceed to Stung Treng in the late afternoon.

Three-passenger boats cost US$13 from Anlong Seima and US$15 from O'Svay. There's an additional US$1 per person charge to see the dolphins. You can usually just show up and find a boat, or organise in advance through Mlup Baitong or Xplore-Asia in Stung Treng (see p302). Another option is to hire kayaks through Xplore-Asia and paddle out to the dolphins.

These trips all take place along the Mekong Discovery Trail (see p300). Mlup Baitong can also organise homestays in two villages: Preah Rumkel, located near the dolphin pod at Anlong Cheuteal; and O'Russey Kandal, about 28km south of Stung Treng. CRDT in Kratie (p301) runs a homestay project in Koh Preah, about 15km south of Stung Treng.

Siem Pang
សៀមប៉ាង

A relatively well-off town that stretches for about 6km along the Tonlé Kong, Siem Pang is a good place to observe rural life or just relax by the riverside. This remote outpost in the far north of Stung Treng Province is now a little bit closer to civilisation thanks to a new road connecting it to the NH7 highway.

A ferry takes passengers (1000r) and motorbikes (2500r) across the river, where the scenic trail to Voen Sai in Ratanakiri starts. **Theany Guesthouse** (☎ 012 675413; r US$5) offers one-way motorbike rentals for this ride (US$25), along with simple rooms in an appealing wooden house.

Siem Pang acts as the western gateway to Virachey National Park and is renowned for its rich wildlife. Rare giant ibises and white-shouldered ibises roost around here, and **BirdLife International** (☎ 092-994002, in Phnom Penh 023-993631; www.birdlife.org) runs a **vulture-feeding station** that attracts all three species of critically endangered vultures found in Cambodia. It's set up for research rather than tourism, but if you time your visit for the monthly 'feed', which involves killing a water buffalo or cow and leaving it in a field near an observation hideout, you may get a chance to observe the vultures. Or you can ante up US$150 and they'll organise a feed for your viewing enjoyment.

A relaxing way to get to Siem Pang is on the slow boat from Stung Treng (US$5, eight hours), which departs daily at 7am in both directions. Otherwise, regular morning and occasional afternoon vans do the trip (US$5, 2½ hours). The trip from Stung Treng takes about 2½ hours on a motorbike. From Stung Treng, drive 55km north on NH7, turn right, and proceed another 52km on a rather sandy unsealed road.

RATANAKIRI PROVINCE

ខេត្តរតនគិរី

Up-and-coming Ratanakiri is making a name for itself as a diverse region of outstanding natural beauty that provides a remote home for a mosaic of minority peoples. The Jarai, Tompuon, Brau and Kreung are the Khmer Leu (Upper Khmer) people, with their own languages, traditions and customs. There is also a large Lao population throughout the province and multiple languages will be heard in villages such as Voen Sai.

Adrenaline-producing activities are plentiful. Swim in clear volcanic lakes, shower under waterfalls, or trek in the vast Virachey National Park – it's all here. Tourism is set to take off, but that is if the lowland politicians and generals don't plunder the place first. Ratanakiri is the frontline in the battle for land, and the slash-and-burn minorities are losing out thanks to their tradition of collective ownership. The forest is disappearing at an alarming rate, being replaced by rubber plantations and cashew-nut farms. Hopefully someone wakes up and smells the coffee – there's plenty of that as well – before it's too late.

Gem mining is big business in Ratanakiri, hardly surprising given the name actually translates as 'hill of the precious stones'. There is good-quality zircon mined in several parts of the province, as well as other semi-precious stones. The prices are low compared with the West, but don't get suckered into a dream deal, as gem scams are as old as the hills themselves.

Ratanakiri Province played its part in the country's contemporary tragedy, by serving as a base for the Khmer Rouge leadership during much of the 1960s. Pol Pot and Ieng Sary fled here in 1963 and established headquarters in Ta Veng in the north of the province.

Roads in Ratanakiri are not as impressive as the sights. In the dry season, prepare to do battle with the dust of 'red-earth Ratanakiri', which will leave you with orange skin and hair. The roads look like carrot soup during the wet season. The ideal time to explore is November after the rains have stopped and before the dust madness begins.

BAN LUNG

 បានលុង

☎ 075 / pop 25,000

Affectionately known as 'dey krahorm' (red earth) after its rust-coloured affliction, Ban Lung provides a popular base for a range of Ratanakiri romps. It may look like autumn all year round, but it's just that the leaves, like everything else, are cloaked in a blanket of dust. Fortunately the dust is becoming less of a problem within town limits as more and more streets are sealed.

The town itself is busy and lacks the backwater charm of Sen Monorom in Mondulkiri, but with attractions such as Boeng Yeak Lom (p306) just a short hop away, there is little room for complaint. Many of the minorities from the surrounding villages come to Ban Lung to buy and sell at the market. The town was originally known as Labansiek before the civil war, but the district name of Ban Lung has gradually slipped into use among locals.

Information

Acleda Bank (☎ 974220) has an ATM that accepts Visa cards only, changes travellers cheques and handles Western Union money transfers.

The post office on the road to Bokheo has international phone services, but the mobile-phone kiosks around the market are cheaper. Try **Redland Internet** (per hr 4000r) or **Srey Mom** (per hr 6000r) for internet access.

Visitors will find their guesthouse or the recommended tour companies (see p307) to be most useful in the quest for local knowledge. Check out www.yaklom.com for more ideas on what to do in Ratanakiri.

Sights & Activities

There are no real sights in the centre of town. The big draw is Boeng Yeak Lom, while multiday treks around Ban Lung are picking up steam. See p307 for advice on choosing a guide.

EASTERN CAMBODIA

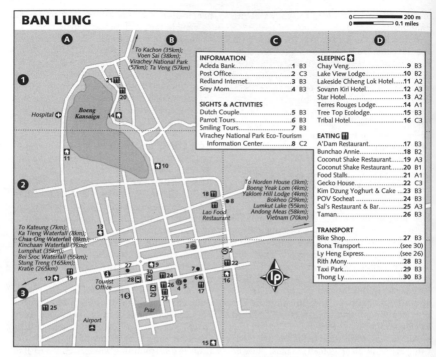

BAN LUNG

INFORMATION	
Acleda Bank	1 B3
Post Office	2 C3
Redland Internet	3 B3
Srey Mom	4 B3

SIGHTS & ACTIVITIES	
Dutch Couple	5 B3
Parrot Tours	6 B3
Smiling Tours	7 B3
Virachey National Park Eco-Tourism Information Centre	8 C2

SLEEPING	
Chay Veng	9 B3
Lake View Lodge	10 B2
Lakeside Chheng Lok Hotel	11 A2
Sovann Kiri Hotel	12 A3
Star Hotel	13 A2
Terres Rouges Lodge	14 A1
Tree Top Ecolodge	15 B3
Tribal Hotel	16 C3

EATING	
A'Dam Restaurant	17 B3
Bunchao Annie	18 B2
Coconut Shake Restaurant	19 A3
Coconut Shake Restaurant	20 B1
Food Stalls	21 A1
Gecko House	22 C3
Kim Dzung Yoghurt & Cake	23 B3
POV Socheat	24 B3
Sal's Restaurant & Bar	25 A3
Taman	26 B3

TRANSPORT	
Bike Shop	27 B3
Bona Transport	(see 30)
Ly Heng Express	(see 28)
Rith Mony	28 B3
Taxi Park	29 B3
Thong Ly	30 B3

BOENG YEAK LOM
 បឹងយក្សទ្លោម

At the heart of the protected area of **Yeak Lom** (admission US$1) is a beautiful blue crater lake set amid the vivid greens of the towering jungle. The lake is believed to have been formed 700,000 years ago and some people swear it must have been formed by a meteor strike as the circle is so perfect. The indigenous minority people in the area have long considered Yeak Lom a sacred place and their legends talk of mysterious creatures that inhabit the waters of the lake. It is one of the most peaceful, beautiful locations Cambodia has to offer and the water is extremely clear. Several wooden piers are dotted around the perimeter, making it perfect for swimming.

A small **Cultural & Environmental Centre** has information on ethnic minorities in the province, local handicrafts on display, suggested walks around the lake and **inner tubes** (per hr 4000r) for rent. The local Tompuon minority has a 25-year lease to manage the lake through to 2021, and proceeds from the entry fee go towards improving life in the nearby villages. However, developers, backed by local

politicians, are actively trying to have the lease annulled and build hotels and a road around the lake, and a casino on a sacred mountain near the lake.

Boeng Yeak Lom is 5km east of Ban Lung's central roundabout. Turn right off the road to Bokheo at the statue of the minority family. *Motos* are available for around US$3 return, but expect to pay more if the driver has to wait around. It takes almost an hour to get to on foot from Ban Lung.

TREKKING

Overnight treks are all the rage in Ratanakiri these days. Diehard trampers spend up to eight days sleeping in replica US Army hammocks and checking out some of the country's last virgin forest in and around Virachey National Park. Shorter trips are possible, as are several-day kayaking excursions on the Tonlé San and overnight stays in ethnic-minority villages.

Keep in mind that trekking in Virachey National Park is the exclusive domain of **Virachey National Park Eco-Tourism Information Center** (☎ weekdays 075-974013, weekends 077-965196;

http://viracheyecotourism.blogspot.com; soukhon07@yahoo.com; Department of Environment Compound; ☒ 8am–noon & 2-5.30pm Mon-Fri). Private tour operators also offer multiday treks, but these only go as far as the park's buffer zone. There's little forest left standing outside the park boundary, so be careful that you're not being taken for a loop – literally – around and around in the same small patch of forest.

Despite being shut out from the park, private operators can still design creative treks that take in minority villages and scenic spots around the province. Just be sure to make clear arrangements with your guide to ensure you get what is expected out of a trip.

Tours

We strongly recommend using indigenous guides for organised treks and other excursions around Ban Lung (see the boxed text, p313). Unfortunately, the level of English among indigenous guides tends to be only fair. If you need a more fluent English guide, we suggest hiring both an English-speaking Khmer guide and a minority guide, if it's in your budget.

A newly formed association of **Tompuon guides** (www.yeakloam.com; yeak.loam@yahoo.com) is a good place to look for an indigenous guide. The association also runs an exclusive tour of several Tompuon villages around Boeng Yeak Lom. You can observe weavers and basket makers in action, learn about animist traditions, and eat a traditional indigenous meal of bamboo-steamed fish, fresh vegetables, 'minority' rice and, of course, rice wine. The association also has English-teaching and other volunteer opportunities available.

Among private tour companies, only Yaklom Hill Lodge (p308) employs a full-time indigenous (Tompuon) guide, but you'll need to request him. Virachey National Park (opposite) also employs some indigenous guides and uses minority porters.

The following private tour companies run a mix of tours and claim to benefit local communities by supporting relevant NGOs and/or engaging in minority livelihood projects. However, they do not employ indigenous guides (although they do engage minority porters on request). Cost depends on the route, but figure on US$15 a day for an English-speaking guide and more for transport, food and lodging along the way.

Dutch Couple (☎ 017 571682; www.ecotourism.cambodia.info) Excursions include kayak trips around Ta Veng.

Parrot Tours (☎ 012 764714; sitha_guide@yahoo.com)
Smiling Tours (☎ 012 247713; smeyadventure@gmail.com)

ELEPHANT TOURS

Most guesthouses and hotels can arrange short elephant rides from nearby villages to local waterfalls. One of the most popular rides is from the village of Kateung to the spectacular waterfall of Ka Tieng. The ride takes about one hour, passing through beautiful rubber plantations. The usual charge is US$8 per person per hour (US$10 if you book in Ban Lung). For longer elephant rides, Mondulkiri Province (p314) remains the more popular option.

Sleeping

If the following are full, the area around the roundabout in the centre of town is awash in generic three-storey hotels catering to Cambodian travellers and offering fan rooms (many windowless) for $5 to $10.

Tribal Hotel (☎ 974074; r US$3-20; ☒) There are rooms to suit all budgets at this popular old standby, albeit none are great value. The leaky $3 rooms (without mosquito nets) are for the desperate only. Pricier rooms look smart but suffer from a lack of TLC.

Chay Veng (☎ 012 686954; r with fan/air-con US$5/10; ▣) This new kid on the block is run by an energetic pair of young English-speaking brothers. Rooms are fairly standard Khmer fare, only cleaner and brighter than most. Each floor has a comfortable common seating area overlooking Ban Lung's main drag.

Lake View Lodge (☎ 092-785259; r with fan/air-con US$5/15; ☒) This backpacker pad has eight large rooms with wood floors and high ceilings in a converted old villa. It sits near the shores of Boeng Kansaign, and the dilapidated 2nd-floor balcony has partial lake views. Owner Sophat also runs a tour company.

our pick Tree Top Ecolodge (☎ 012 490333; www.treetop-ecolodge.com; s/d/cottage incl breakfast US$8/10/15; ☏) Recent Stung Treng transplant 'Mr T' has set the standard for budget accommodation in Cambodia with this gem. Standard rooms have hot water, solid-wood bed frames draped in mozzie nets, and private porches. Or 'splurge' for a private bungalow hidden in the trees beyond the restaurant. Like the bungalows, the restaurant is fashioned from hardwood and dangles over a lush ravine, affording great views of the hillside beyond.

Up-to-date travel advice is plentiful, especially for those aiming for Laos.

Yaklom Hill Lodge (☎ 011 725881; www.yaklom. com; s/d/tr incl breakfast US$10/15/20) The rustic wooden bungalows at Ratanakiri's only true ecolodge are set amid lush forest near Boeng Yeak Lom, 5km east of Ban Lung's central roundabout. Hiking trails lead to the lake and beyond. A generator enables hot showers from 6pm to 9pm, while solar power provides enough juice for lights (but not fans) at other times. Pick-up in town is included in the room prices.

Norden House (☎ 6900640; www.nordenhouseyaklom. com; r US$20; 🖳) This bungalow resort sits in a peaceful location on the road to Boeng Yeak Lom. Rooms are stylish and include a TV and DVD player (but no cable), hot water and free internet access. The fine restaurants serves Swedish specialities.

Terres Rouges Lodge (☎ 974051, 012 959115; www. ratanakiri-lodge.com; r/bungalow US$35/85; ❄ 🖳 🛜 🏊) Ban Lung's lone upmarket option is undoubtedly one of the most atmospheric places to stay in provincial Cambodia. The standard rooms in the main house are done up in classy colonial style, with beautiful Cambodian furniture, tribal artefacts and a long common verandah. Set in the gorgeous garden near the 14m pool is a series of exquisite, generously sized bungalows.

Other good options:

Star Hotel (☎ 012 958322; r US$5-10; ❄) The capacious rooms in this converted villa have hot water but are beginning to show their age. Has a well-regarded restaurant.

Sovann Kiri Hotel (☎ 974001; r with fan/air-con from US$5/10) A sprawling, well-appointed business hotel on the way into town.

Lakeside Chheng Lok Hotel (☎ 390063; lakeside -chhenglokhotel@yahoo.com; r US$5-20; ❄) Good all-rounder in a prime spot overlooking Boeng Kansaign.

Eating & Drinking

Among hotel restaurants, Terres Rouges' stands out. To get down with the locals, head to the lakefront near Coconut Shake Restaurant around sunset, plop down on a mat, and order cheap beer and snacks from waterfront shacks.

Bunchao Annie (bunchao 2500r; 🕙 11am-8pm) The proprietress here specialises in *bunchao* – meat, baby shrimps, sprouts, a few veggies and spices wrapped inside a thin egg pancake wrapped inside a piece of cabbage, and dipped

in a tangy orange sauce. It's in an unmarked shack opposite Lao Food Restaurant.

Coconut Shake Restaurant (Boeng Kansaign; mains 6000-12,000r). The best coconut shakes in the northeast are found here. Dare to try the 'fish and ship' or the 'friend toes' (French toast?). A second location recently opened on the main drag.

Gecko House (mains 7000-14,000r; 🕙 10am-11pm) A charming little restaurant-bar, with inviting sofas, soft lighting and famously frosty beer mugs, this is a great place by day or night.

Sal's Restaurant & Bar (☎ 012 284377; mains US$1.75-5) This welcoming restaurant-bar, popular with Ban Lung's small expat community, is the place to come for comfort food from home, including Indian curries, spicy Mexican and great burgers. Some dishes take awhile to prepare, so call ahead if you don't want to wait.

A'Dam Restaurant (mains US$2-4) This open-air restaurant features Thai tastes, Khmer classics and some Western dishes, all depicted on a voluminous picture menu. A pool table and dart board tempt barflies.

In the market area, try **Kim Dzung Yoghurt & Cake** (mains 4000r; 🕙 breakfast) for fried eggs, yoghurt and quality coffee; **Taman** (mains 5000r) for noodle soup; and **POV Socheat** (mains 8000r) for an English menu of cheap Cambodian faves.

Getting There & Away

At the time of writing, Ratanakiri's airport had been closed to commercial flights for almost three years.

Meanwhile, it's getting easier and easier to get to Ban Lung by road. Highway NH19 between Ban Lung and O Pong Moan (the junction 19km south of Stung Treng) was being rebuilt at the time of writing and should be fully sealed by 2011. Until then, portions of this could be rough going, especially in the wet season.

Buses to Phnom Penh (US$10, 11 hours) operate only in the dry season for now. Thong Ly, Rith Mony and Ly Heng Express make the trip, with early morning departures in either direction via Kratie, Snuol and Kompong Cham.

Speedy express minibus services pick you up at your guesthouse at 6am and take the shortcut to Phnom Penh via Chhlong (US$12, nine hours). Organise these through your guesthouse, or alternatively through Ly Heng Express or **Bona Transport** (☎ 012 567161). Call Tree Top Ecolodge (p307) to arrange a pick-up if coming from Phnom Penh. Share taxis to Phnom Penh are losing popularity as the roads improve, while pick-up trucks are mainly a wet-season option.

Private minibus services offering guesthouse pick-ups also go to Stung Treng (US$6, 2½ hours). Otherwise take a share taxi (30,000r) or slower pick-up truck (inside/on the back 20,000/16,000r) from the taxi park.

There is no real road linking Ratanakiri to Mondulkiri, contrary to what older maps may show. There is a road as far south as Lumphat, but after crossing the Tonlé Srepok by ferry, it descends into a series of sandy ox-cart tracks until Koh Nhek in northern Mondulkiri Province. Hardcore bikers love this route, but only attempt it if you have years of biking experience or are an extremely hardy soul with an iron backside. Anyone seriously considering this option should link up with a local who knows the route, as there are lots of opportunities to get lost. A range of motorbike spares, copious amounts of water and a compass should make for a smoother journey. It is almost impossible in the wet season.

Believe it or not, a few intrepid *moto* drivers in both Ban Lung and Sen Monorom ply this route. The journey takes about nine hours, with a few long breaks along the way, and costs $50 to $70. This is one case where it's worth paying more for an experienced, English-speaking driver. The difficult stretch between Koh Nhek and Lumphat took us four hours on the back of a Honda Dream.

Getting Around

Motorbikes (US$5 to US$7), cars (from US$30) and 4WDs (from US$40) are available for hire from most guesthouses in town.

Norden House has well-maintained 250cc bikes for rent at US$25 per day. Local guides with motorbikes offer their services around the province and rates range from US$15 to US$20 per day for a good English-speaking driver-guide (less for a Khmer speaker).

For something cheaper and more environmentally friendly, consider a bicycle (US$1 to US$3 per day), available from some hotels and the cycle shops on the main drag.

AROUND BAN LUNG
Waterfalls

There are numerous waterfalls in the province, but many are difficult to reach in the wet season and lack water in the dry season. The three most commonly visited are **Chaa Ong**, **Ka Tieng** and **Kinchaan** (Kachang), all within 10km from town and attracting a 2000r admission fee. Directions are signposted 3km west of town on the road to Stung Treng.

The most spectacular of the three is Chaa Ong, as it is set in a jungle gorge and you can clamber behind the waterfall or venture underneath for a power shower. Ka Tieng is the most enjoyable, as it drops over a rock shelf allowing you to clamber all the way behind. There are some vines on the far side that are strong enough to swing on for some Tarzan action.

Voen Sai
វិនសៃ
pop 3000

Located on the banks of the Tonlé San, Voen Sai is a cluster of Chinese, Lao and *chunchiet* villages. Originally, the town was located on the north bank of the river and known as Virachey, but these days the main settlement is on the south bank.

From the south side, cross the river on a small ferry (500/3000r without/with a motorbike) and walk west for a couple of kilometres, passing through the Khmer village, a Lao community and a small *chunchiet* area, before finally emerging in a wealthy Chinese village complete with large wooden houses and inhabitants who still speak Chinese. Check out how neat and tidy it is compared with the surrounding communities.

Kachon is a 40-minute boat ride east of Voen Sai and has an impressive **Tompuon cemetery** (admission US$1). When a lengthy period of mourning is complete, villagers hold a big celebration and add two carved wooden likenesses of elephant tusks to the structures. Some of these tombs date back many years and have been abandoned to the jungle. Newer tombs of wealthy individuals have been cast in concrete and show some modern touches like shades and mobile phones. Remember that this is a sacred site for local Tompuon people – see the boxed text, p310, for advice on visiting *chunchiet* cemeteries responsibly.

The cemetery is in the old settlement of Kachon on the north bank of the Tonlé San. The cemetery in new Kachon on the south bank is off limits to outsiders. Expect to pay around US$15 for the boat trip from Voen

Sai to Kachon, including a jaunt to the Chinese and Lao villages opposite Voen Sai. Alternatively, travel to new Kachon by road from Voen Sai and pay a local a few thousand riel to take you across the river.

Voen Sai is 39km northwest of Ban Lung on an average-to-poor road. It is easy enough to get to under your own steam on a motorbike or with a vehicle. English-speaking guides ask US$10 to US$15 to take you out here on a *moto*.

Skilled motorbike and mountain-bike riders can ride from Voen Sai to Siem Pang in Stung Treng along a scenic trail that begins on the north side of the river. One-way motorbike rentals for the reverse trip are available in Siem Pang (see p304).

Ta Veng
តាវែង

Ta Veng is an insignificant village on the southern bank of Tonlé San, but acts as the main gateway to Virachey National Park and the base for many treks run by private operators in the park's buffer zone. It was in the Ta Veng district that Pol Pot, Ieng Sary and other leaders of the Khmer Rouge established their guerrilla base in the 1960s. Locals say nothing today remains of the remote base although, in a dismal sign of decline, they

point out that Ta Veng had electricity before the war.

Ta Veng is about 57km north of Ban Lung on a roller-coaster road through the mountains that affords some of the province's better views. The road passes through several **minority villages**, where it is possible to break the journey. There are some very steep climbs in sections and, for this reason, it wouldn't be much fun in the rain. Travel by motorbike or charter a vehicle.

It is possible to hire small boats in Ta Veng for river jaunts (US$10 to US$15 in the local area or US$70 to US$80 for the five-hour trip to Voen Sai).

Andong Meas
អណ្ដូងមាស
pop 1500

Andong Meas district is growing in popularity thanks to a combination of minority villages, **Jarai cemeteries** and a short river trip, although the cemeteries were badly damaged by the ravages of typhoon Ketsana in 2009. There is a walkable trail from Andong Meas to a Jarai village and cemetery on the banks of the Tonlé San. It's two hours walking one-way or 30 minutes in a fast long-tailed boat (US$15 return). Do not enter any Jarai cemetery without permission and a Jarai escort. Expect to pay US$1 to US$3 for the privilege.

A visit here can be combined with a visit to the current hot spot for **gem mining** in Bokheo, 29km east of Ban Lung. Locals dig a large pit in the ground and then tunnel horizontally in their search for amethyst and zircon. When we visited, the mines were about 1km out of town on the road to Andong Meas, but they tend to move around.

Andong Meas lies 58km northeast of Ban Lung. Turn left off the sealed highway just before you enter Bokheo. From here, it's a straight shot on a reasonable dirt road. One-way from Ban Lung should take about 1½ hours.

Lumkut Lake
បឹងលំគុត

Lumkut is a large crater lake hemmed in by dense forest on all sides – similar to Boeng Yeak Lom. If you want to have a dip, walk clockwise about a quarter of the way around the lake to a pier that allows easy access to the water. The lake is about 55km southeast of

---

RESPECT THE DEAD

The *chunchiet* of Ratanakiri bury their dead amidst the jungle, carving effigies of the deceased to stand guard over the graves. There are many cemeteries scattered throughout the forests of Ratanakiri, but most of them are strictly off limits to visitors. Enter *chunchiet* cemeteries only with permission from the village chief and preferably in the company of a local. If you are lucky enough to be allowed into a cemetery, touch nothing, act respectfully and ask permission before taking photos.

Unfortunately, there have been many reports of tourists ignoring clearly marked signs (in English) urging outsiders to abstain from entering *chunchiet* cemeteries. Worse, unscrupulous art collectors and amateur anthropologists from Europe have reportedly been buying up the old effigies from poor villagers, something tantamount to cultural rape.

Ban Lung. Turn right off the road to O'Yadaw about 4km east of Bokheo.

Virachey National Park
ឧទ្យានជាតិវិរៈជ័យ

This **park** (admission US$5) is one of the largest protected areas in Cambodia, stretching for 3325 sq km east to Vietnam, north to Laos and west to Stung Treng Province. The park has never been fully explored and is home to a number of rare mammals, including elephants, clouded leopards, tigers and sun bears, although your chances of seeing any of these beasts are extremely slim. However, you'll likely hear endangered gibbons and might spot great hornbills, giant ibises, Germain's peacock-pheasants and other rare birds. Optimists speculate that there may even be isolated rhinoceroses or kouprey (wild oxen) in the park, but this is unlikely. So important is the park to the Mekong region that it was designated an Asean Heritage Park in 2003.

Virachey has the most organised ecotourism program in Cambodia, focusing on small-scale culture, nature and adventure trekking. The program aims to involve and benefit local minority communities. All treks into the park must be arranged through the Virachey National Park Eco-Tourism Information Center (p306). The park offers two- to eight-day treks led by English-speaking, park-employed rangers. Private tour operators are forbidden from taking tourists into the park, but can make arrangements for you through the park office.

A section of the park is accessible from Siem Pang in Stung Treng district (p304). However, to legally enter the park in Siem Pang, you must still secure permits in Ban Lung.

Lumphat
លុមផាត់
pop 2000

The former provincial capital of Lumphat, on the banks of the Tonlé Srepok, is something of a ghost town these days thanks to sustained US bombing raids in the early 1970s. This is also the last gasp of civilisation, if it can even be called that, for hardcore bikers heading south on the tough trails to Mondulkiri Province.

The Tonlé Srepok is believed to be the river depicted in the seminal antiwar film *Apocalypse Now*, in which Martin Sheen's Captain Benjamin Willard goes upriver into Cambodia in search of renegade Colonel Kurtz, played by Marlon Brando.

Bei Srok (Tuk Chrouu Bram-pul; admission 2000r) is a popular waterfall with seven gentle tiers. It's about 20km east of Lumphat. Many Ban Lung tour companies offer it as a day tour (US$15 to US$20) combined with some abandoned gem mines nearby and bomb-crater spotting around Lumphat.

To get to Lumphat from Ban Lung, take the road to Stung Treng for about 15km before heading south. The 35km journey takes around an hour. Pick-ups leave early in the morning from Lumphat and return in the afternoon on most days.

TREKS IN VIRACHEY NATIONAL PARK

There are three treks available in Virachey. Prices listed are per person for a group of two and include transport by *moto* to the trail head, park admission, food, guides, porters, hammocks and boat transport where necessary. Prices drop the larger the group.

Kalang Chhouy Sacred Mountain Trek (2 days US$59) This shorter trek starts from near Koklak village and includes a night by the Chai Chanang Waterfall. On the second day, continue to Phnom Gong, a sacred mountain for the Brau people, and swim at the Tju Preah rapids.

O'Lapeung River Valley Trek (3/4 days US$115/138) This trek starts from Ta Veng with a boat ride on the Tonlé San and O Tabok Rivers to the Brau village of Phum Yorn, where trekkers experience a homestay. The trek continues to the summit of Phnom Meive and into the O'Lapeung valley to a campsite. On the third day, the route passes along a section of the Ho Chi Minh Trail and it may be possible to see some war relics. After a second night in the Brau village, you return to Ta Veng by inflatable kayak.

Phnom Veal Thom Wilderness Trek (7/8 days US$258/286) The longest trek into Virachey starts from Ta Veng with an overnight homestay in a Brau village. The trek goes deep into the heart of the Phnom Veal Thom grasslands, an area rich in wildlife such as sambar deer, gibbon, langur, wild pig, bear and hornbill. Trekkers return via a different route and pass through beautiful areas of evergreen forest.

MONDULKIRI PROVINCE

ខេត្តមណ្ឌលគិរី

A world apart from lowland Cambodia, Mondulkiri is the original Wild East of the country. Climatically and culturally, it's also another world, which comes as a relief after the heat of the plains. Home to the hardy Bunong (Pnong) people and their noble elephants, it is possible to visit traditional villages and learn the art of the mahout. The landscape is a seductive mix of pine clumps, grassy hills and windswept valleys that fade beguilingly into forests of jade green and hidden waterfalls. Wild animals, such as bears, tigers and especially elephants, are more numerous here than elsewhere, although sightings are usually limited to birds, monkeys and the occasional wild pig.

Mondulkiri means 'Meeting of the Hills', an apt sobriquet for a land of rolling hills. In the dry season it is a little like Wales with sunshine; in the wet season, like Tasmania with more rain. At an average elevation of 800m, it can get quite chilly at night, so carry something warm.

Mondulkiri is the most sparsely populated province in the country, with just two people per square kilometre. Almost half the inhabitants come from the Bunong minority group, with other minorities making up much of the rest of the population. There has been an influx of migrants in recent years, drawn to the abundant land and benign climate. Fruit and vegetable plantations are popping up, but hunting remains the profession of choice for many minorities. Conservationists have grand plans for the province, creating wildlife sanctuaries and initiating sustainable tourism activities, but are facing off against speculators and industrialists queuing up for natural resources.

Roads are pretty poor throughout the province, but the main highway to Phnom Penh should be fully paved by 2011, bringing journey times down to six hours. The road to Koh Nhek is unrecognisable from the mess of bygone years. Improved access has fuelled an explosion of domestic tourists, so book ahead at weekends.

SEN MONOROM

សែនមនោរម្យ

☎ 073 / pop 7000

The provincial capital of Mondulkiri, Sen Monorom is little more than an overgrown village. A charming community set in the spot where the famous hills meet, the centre of town has two lakes, leading some dreamers to call it 'The Switzerland of Cambodia'. The area around Sen Monorom is peppered with minority villages and picturesque waterfalls, making it the ideal place to spend some time. Many of the Bunong people from nearby villages come to Sen Monorom to trade, and the distinctive baskets they carry on their backs make them easy to distinguish from the immigrant lowlanders. Set at more than 800m, when the winds billow it's notably cooler than the rest of Cambodia, so bring some warm clothing.

Information

The leading guesthouses in town are also good sources of information.

Acleda Bank (NH76) Changes major currencies and has a Visa-only ATM.

Green House (☎ 017 905659) Affable restaurant owner Sam Nang is the best source of information in town. He organises the standard treks and excursions to sights around Sen Monorom, plus tailored mountain-bike tours. Quality mountain bikes (per day US$5), motorbikes (US$6 to US$8) and a 250cc trail bike (US$15) are available for hire. He also arranges transport by *moto* to Ban Lung (US$60). Internet access costs 4000r per hour, and laptop users can plug in a LAN cable.

Middle of Somewhere (☎ 012 474879; www.bunong center.org; ☺ 6am-6pm) This NGO-run 'drop-in centre' for Bunong people is a champion of sustainable tourism in the region. It organises various half- to full-day tours led by indigenous guides. Also sells authentic Bunong baskets, beads, musical instruments and cotton textiles.

WWF (☎ 012 466343; www.panda.org) Involved in a host of ecotourism initiatives around Sen Monorom.

Sights & Activities

Not much happens in Sen Monorom itself but there's plenty to see and do nearby, including trips out to Bunong villages, elephant riding and an array of overnight treks.

There are a few worthwhile sights within a short motorbike ride or a long walk from town. **Monorom Falls** (admission free) is the closest thing to a public swimming pool for Sen Monorom. It has an attractive location in the forest, about 3km northwest of town. *Motos* can take people out here for about US$2 or so for the return trip.

Looming over the northeast corner of the air strip, **Wat Phnom Doh Kromom** has Mondulkiri's best sunset vista.

TREAD LIGHTLY IN THE HILLS

Tourism can bring many benefits to highland communities: cross-cultural understanding, improved infrastructure, cheaper market goods, employment opportunities and tourist dollars supporting handicraft industries. However, there are also negatives, such as increased litter and pollutants, dependency on tourist dollars, and the erosion of local values and practices.

As tourism proliferates in the northeast, the negatives are beginning to outweigh the positives. Most of the benefits of increased tourism in Ratanakiri and Mondulkiri are not going to the ethnic-minority highlanders, but to the lowland Khmers who dominate the tourism industry. Khmer tour operators often pay lip service to responsible tourism, but ultimately their motivations are financial; they rarely encourage their clients to visit in a way that avoids corrupting indigenous communities.

That is why we recommend hiring indigenous guides directly. Not only does this ensure that your tourist dollars go directly to indigenous communities, it will also enrich your own visit. Indigenous guides can greatly improve your access to the residents of highland communities, who are animists and rarely speak Khmer. They also understand taboos and traditions that might be lost on Khmer guides. Their intimate knowledge of the forests is another major asset.

More tips on visiting indigenous communities responsibly:

Interaction
- Be polite and respectful – doubly so with elderly people.
- Dress modestly.
- Taste traditional wine if you are offered it, especially during a ceremony. Refusal will cause offence.
- Honour signs discouraging outsiders from entering a village, for instance during a spiritual ceremony. A good local guide will be able to detect these signs.
- Learn something about the community's culture and language and demonstrate something good about yours.

Gifts
- Individual gifts create jealousy and expectations. Instead, consider making donations to the local school, medical centre or community fund.
- If you do give individual gifts, keep them modest (such as matches).
- Do not give children sweets or money.
- Do not give clothes – communities are self-sufficient.

Shopping
- Haggle politely and always pay the agreed (and fair) price.
- Do not ask to buy a villager's personal household items, tools or the jewellery or clothes they are wearing.
- Don't buy village treasures, such as altar pieces or totems.

Photographs
- Do not photograph without asking permission first – this includes children. Some hill tribes believe the camera will capture their spirit.
- Don't photograph altars.
- Don't use a flash.
- Don't show up for 15 minutes and expect to be granted permission to take photos. Invest some time in getting to know the villagers first (see below).

Travel
- Make a point to travel in small, less disruptive groups.
- Try to spend some real time in minority villages – at least several hours if not an overnight. If you don't have a few hours to invest, don't go.

EASTERN CAMBODIA

Check out the observation deck of **Phnom Bai Chuw** (Raw Rice Mountain), about 5km north of Wat Phnom Doh Kromom, for a jaw-dropping view of the emerald forest. It looks as though you are seeing a vast sea of treetops, hence the locals have named it Samot Cheur (Ocean of Trees).

Tours

As in Ratanakiri, multiday forest treks are becoming immensely popular in Mondulkiri. Again, we recommend securing indigenous Bunong guides for these trips. They know the forests intimately and can break the ice with the locals in any Bunong villages you visit.

Middle of Somewhere (p312) employs several Bunong guides who can take you into Bunong villages and/or lead any of the popular day excursions. Other tour operators, such as Nature Lodge (right) and Green House (p312), usually employ Bunong people as porters on longer excursions, but you should request this service.

Most of the guesthouses listed under Sleeping (below) run the full gamut of treks and tours around Sen Monorom. Figure on about US$35 per person, per day for overnight trips, including all meals, transfer to the trail head by *moto*, and an English-speaking guide. Per-person prices go down for larger groups. The WWF runs its own set of tours north of Sen Monorom in the Mondulkiri Protected Forest (see p317).

ELEPHANT TOURS

The villages of Phulung, 7km northeast of Sen Monorom, and Putang, 9km southwest of town, are the most popular places to arrange an elephant trek. Treks cost US$20 to US$25 per person, including lunch and transport to and from the village. It can get pretty uncomfortable up on top of an elephant after a couple of hours; carry a pillow to ease the strain.

It is also possible to negotiate a longer trek with an overnight stay in a Bunong village, costing US$40 to US$50 per person.

For the most humane and ecofriendly elephant experience in the area, head out of town to the Elephant Valley Project (see the boxed text, p316).

Sleeping

Hot water is a nice bonus in chilly Mondulkiri, but you'll typically pay an extra US$5 for it.

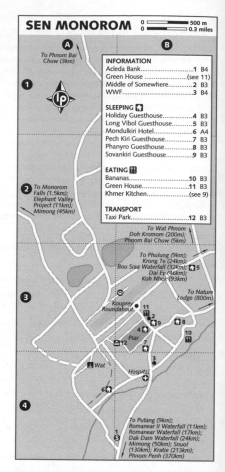

Places without hot-water showers can usually provide flasks of boiling water for bathing. There is rarely need for air-conditioning in this neck of the woods. The Elephant Valley Project (see the boxed text, p316) offers an alternative lodging experience.

Sovankiri Guesthouse (☎ 017 472769; r with/without bathroom from US$5/3) Sovankiri is a favourite among backpackers for its cheap rooms and ideal central location behind the delectable Khmer Kitchen restaurant (opposite). The budget rooms are leaky and share a rather grim bathroom. The US$7 rooms are a substantial upgrade.

our pick Nature Lodge (☎ 230272; www.nature lodgecambodia.com; cottage with/without bathroom US$10/5) Located on a windswept hilltop near town, this quirky ecoresort has basic bungalow accommodation with hot showers and an incredible Swiss Family Robinson–style chalet with sunken beds and hidden rooms. The inviting restaurant is decorated with abandoned tree trunks and roots and has a good range of traveller fare and a pool table. Also on the menu is a range of multiday excursions. Punters gather around the bar by evening to trade tips on area trips and find trekking companions.

Holiday Guesthouse (☎ 011 580060; r with cold/hot water US$5/10) Occupying a typically gaudy concrete Khmer high-rise, it is generally cleaner and more user-friendly than its centrally located brethren along main street. Excursions can be arranged.

Long Vibol Guesthouse (☎ 012 944647; longvibol 12@yahoo.com; r US$5-15) Vibol's is an attractive wooden resort with a variety of rooms set amid a lush garden 900m northeast of the kouprey statue. Although he doesn't personally guide treks any more, Vibol is the elder statesman among the tour guides of Mondulkiri, making this a top spot for information.

Pech Kiri Guesthouse (☎ 012 932102; r US$5-30) Once upon a time, this was the only guesthouse in town and it is still going strong under the lively direction of Madame Deu. The cheap original rooms near reception are showing their age as management diverts attention to building flashier, pricier digs at the back.

Phanyro Guesthouse (☎ 017 770867; r with cold/hot water US$6/8) This formidable newcomer, already a Mondulkiri favourite, comprises a clutch of cottages perched on a ridge overlooking the river valley about 500m east of the centre. The rooms fail to exploit the views but are big, sturdy, and about the cleanest in town.

Mondulkiri Hotel (☎ 390139; r US$15-30;) It looks out of place in this pristine land of rolling hills, but the hulking concrete exterior conceals the most modern and comfortable rooms in town. All are equipped with air-con, smart bathrooms, cable TV and fridge.

Eating & Drinking

Green House (mains US$1.50-3.50) The food here may not rival Khmer Kitchen, but its bamboo- and reggae-infused ambience is second to none, making it *the* place for a cocktail after a long day of trekking.

Khmer Kitchen (mains US$2-4) You wouldn't expect much from this unassuming streetside eatery, but it whips up some of the most flavoursome Khmer food in the land. The *kari saik trey* (fish coconut curry) and other curries are particularly toothsome.

Bananas (☎ 092-412680; mains US$5-8; 9am-2pm & 5-10pm) Garrulous Sihanoukville transplant Tania serves Western European comfort food, like Flemish stew and coq au vin, with a dose of expat insight on life in Cambodia. There's a Sunday roast – arrive early for a drink on the riverside terrace.

Getting There & Away

Sen Monorom's airstrip has been closed to commercial flights for some time, so visitors who want to get to this unique region have to come overland, which these days is pretty straightforward. From Phnom Penh there are surfaced roads all the way to Snuol. The newly widened road (NH76) from Snuol to Sen Monorom remained unsealed at the time of writing, but was gradually being upgraded to bitumen. Hardcore dirt bikers may still prefer the old French road heading east from Khao Si Ma, which runs roughly parallel to the NH76.

Rith Mony and Thong Ly run morning buses to/from Phnom Penh (US$7.50, eight hours) via Snuol (US$3.75, three hours) and Kompong Cham (US$6.25, five hours). For now buses run in the dry season only, but they should operate year-round once the road from Snuol is sealed. Faster morning share taxis (US$12.50) and minivans (US$10) to Phnom Penh are best reserved a day in advance through your guesthouse or at the taxi park.

Minivans are the way forward to Kratie (30,000r, 4½ hours). Count on at least one early morning departure and two or three departures around 12.30pm. It's wise to reserve the morning van in advance. A few pick-ups do early morning runs to Snuol (inside/on the back US$5/3).

To get to Ratanakiri, you must either backtrack to Snuol or Kratie and pick up transportation there, or brave the harsh trail north to Ban Lung; see p308 for more details on this hardcore route.

Getting Around

English-speaking *moto* drivers cost US$15 to US$20 per day. Sample round-trip *moto* prices for destinations around Sen Monorom are US$10 to Bou Sraa, US$8 to Dak Dam Waterfall and US$4 to Phnom Bai Chuw.

Most guesthouses rent out motorbikes for US$5 to US$8. Pick-up trucks and 4WDs can

EASTERN CAMBODIA

be chartered for the day. It costs about US$40 or so around Sen Monorom in the dry season, and more again in the wet season.

AROUND SEN MONOROM

If you're looking to escape the tourist trail, worthwhile DIY adventures include Nam Lear Wildlife Sanctuary, about an hour's *moto* ride beyond Bou Sraa Village; oodles of hidden waterfalls; and heaps of stuff both on and off the rugged road from Dei Ey to Mimong.

Bou Sraa Waterfall

ទឹកជ្រោះប៊ូស្រា

Plunging into the dense Cambodian jungle below, this is one of the country's most impressive **falls** (admission 5000r). Famous throughout the country, this double-drop waterfall has an upper tier of some 10m and a spectacular lower tier with a thundering 25m drop. To get to the bottom of the lower falls, cross the bridge over the river and follow a path to a precipitous staircase that continues to the bottom; it takes about 15 minutes to get down.

Bou Sraa is a 33km, one-hour journey east of Sen Monorom on a half-completed toll road. Prices are 3000r for a small motorbike, 5000r for a large motorbike and 15,000r for a car or 4WD. Hire a *moto* driver for the day or charter a car in a group. Basic snacks and drinks are available at the falls, but pack a picnic if you want something more sophisticated.

Other Waterfalls

Other popular waterfalls in Mondulkiri include **Romanear Waterfall**, 18km southeast of

---

THE ELEPHANT VALLEY PROJECT

For an original elephant experience, visit the **Elephant Valley Project** (☎ 099-696041; jackhighwood@ yahoo.co.uk). Part of the **Elephants Livelihood Initiative Environment** (www.elie-cambodia.org), the project entices local mahouts to bring their often overworked and wounded elephants to this sanctuary, where, in the words of project coordinator Jack Highwood, 'they can learn how to act like elephants again'.

A young Briton with a contagious passion for elephants, Highwood is on a mission to improve the lot of Mondulkiri's working elephants. While Bunong tradition calls for giving elephants a certain amount of down time, Highwood says that economic incentives to overwork elephants prove too great for the impoverished mahouts of Mondulkiri. In addition to toting tourists around on their backs, elephants are hired to haul around anything and everything – including illegally cut timber. 'In Mondulkiri, the elephant is basically seen as a cheap tractor', he says.

Most tour companies in Mondulkiri make a point to stress that their tours employ only humanely treated elephants. Highwood commends this, but wonders whether it's possible to know the truth. 'Most elephants in Mondulkiri are in a highly abused state,' he says. 'They are beaten on the head and made to do things they aren't meant to be doing.'

Enter the Elephant Valley Project. Mahouts who bring their elephants here (there were five at the time of writing) are paid a competitive working wage to retire their elephants full time to ecotourism. Mahouts continue to work with their elephants, feeding and caring for them and making sure they don't escape into the wild. The elephants, for their part, can spend their days blasting through the forest in search of food, uprooting saplings to get to their yummy roots and hanging out by the river spraying mud on one another.

Highwood no longer allows visitors to ride the elephants here. Instead, you simply walk through the forest with them and observe them in their element. In the process you learn a lot about not only elephant behaviour but also Bunong culture and forest ecology.

If you do opt for an elephant-riding tour elsewhere, Highwood recommends inspecting the elephant closely for signs of abuse. Signs of malnourishment, such as protruding ribs, a protracted spine or abscesses on the back under the basket are clear signs that an elephant is being mistreated.

A two-day stay, including all meals, transport to the site and a night's accommodation in exquisite bungalows tucked into the jungle on a ridge overlooking the valley, costs US$100 per person. A day trip costs US$50, but don't show up unannounced. Middle of Somewhere (p312) can handle bookings. Short- and long-term volunteers who want to help the project while learning mahout skills are welcome, although volunteers must pay extra to cover training costs.

Sen Monorom, and **Dak Dam Waterfall**, 25km southeast of Sen Monorom. Both are very difficult to find without assistance, so it's best to take a *moto* driver or local guide. Romanear is a low, wide waterfall with some convenient swimming holes. There is also a second Romanear Waterfall, known rather originally as **Romanear II**, which is near the main road between Sen Monorom and Snuol. Dak Dam is similar to the Monorom Falls (p312), albeit with a greater volume of water. The waterfall is several kilometres beyond the Bunong village of Dak Dam and locals are able to lead the way if you can make yourself understood.

Bunong Villages

Several Bunong villages around Sen Monorom make for popular excursions, although the frequently visited villages that appear on tourist maps have assimilated into modern society. In general, the further out you go, the less exposed the village. Trips to Bunong villages can often be combined with waterfalls or elephant treks. Each guesthouse has a preferred village to send travellers to, which is a great way to spread the wealth.

WWF has recently helped two villages launch projects geared towards giving tourists a glimpse into traditional Bunong lifestyles. In **Krang Te**, about 25km east of Sen Monorom, you can ride elephants, view traditional dancing, learn to weave baskets and buy locally produced honey, fruit and Bunong handicrafts. About

46km north of Sen Monorom on the road to Koh Nhek, the village of **Dei Ey** offers homestays, traditional meals, elephant rides and trekking in surrounding Mondulkiri Protected Forest. Portions of the proceeds from these initiatives go into a community fund designed to improve local livelihoods and protect the forest.

SEIMA PROTECTION FOREST
តំបន់ការពារព្រៃឈើតែវរសីម៉ា

This 3000-sq-km protected area may host the country's greatest treasure trove of mammalian wildlife. A recent World Conservation Society (WCS) study counted over 42,000 black-shanked doucs in Seima, along with 2500 yellow-cheeked crested gibbons – unprecedented concentrations of both of these endangered species of primate. An estimated 150 wild elephants – accounting for more than half of the total population in Cambodia – prowl the park, along with bears and seven species of cat. The bird life is also impressive, and the jungle, which is lusher and denser than the dry forest in western Mondulkiri, has been relatively well preserved.

The park remains difficult to visit, however. The only way in is with WCS partner and birdwatching specialist **Sam Veasna Center** (☎ 063-963710 www.samveasna.org). Its bird guides are highly trained but expensive at US$100 per day, on top of a flat US$30-per-person conservation fee. Accommodation is in facilities run by the Forestry Administration.

MONDULKIRI PROTECTED FOREST: THE AFRICAN EXPERIENCE IN CAMBODIA

Before the civil war, the vast grasslands of northern Mondulkiri were home to huge herds of gaur, banteng and wild buffalo. Visitors lucky enough to witness their annual migrations compared the experience to the Serengeti and the annual wildebeest migrations. Sadly, the long civil war took its toll and, like Uganda and other African countries, thousands of animals were killed for bush meat.

WWF has been working hard to return this area to its former glory through ecotourism initiatives in the Mondulkiri Protected Forest, one of the largest protected areas in Cambodia, which provides a home to tigers, leopards, bears, langurs, gibbons, wild cow and rare bird life. Results have been mixed so far – ambitious plans for a high-end ecolodge in the heart of the protected area were scrapped, replaced by a plan to build an 'eco-tent camp' on an extremely remote stretch of the Tonlé Srepok in the northeast of the province. Access will be via an old French road that branches off the main road between Dei Ey and Koh Nhek.

One potential problem is that the cats, bears and other exotic prowlers that patrol the area are extremely difficult to spot. WWF hopes to increase the chance of sightings through night drives and strategically located hides. But it notes that attractions are not limited to those of a mammalian ilk. There is also primary-growth forest, river tours on the Srepok, and plenty of bird life. Check with the WWF's Sen Monorom office (p312) or **Phnom Penh office** (☎ 023-218034) to find out the latest on the camp.

The WCS helps the Forestry Administration manage the park and maintains an office at the park headquarters, 5km east of Khao Si Ma. The elephants and other high-profile animals that dwell in Seima are shy and elusive; without guaranteed sightings, it's proving difficult to develop ecotourism in a way that will benefit the forest, the animals and the local Bunong community. 'We're still trying to find ways to crack the ecotourism nut,' says Edward Pollard, a WCS technical advisor who works on site.

The road to Sen Monorom passes right through Seima Protection Forest – look out for monkeys above!

MIMONG
 មីមុង

Welcome to the Wild East, where the gold rush lives on. Mimong district is famous for its **gold mines** and this has drawn speculators from as far away as Vietnam and China on the trail of wealth. Miners descend into the pits on ancient mine carts that are connected to dodgy-looking winches, sometimes going to a depth of 100m or more. It's not for the faint-hearted and several miners die in accidents each year.

The main problem is getting here, as the road is so bad that it takes about four hours to cover the 47km from Sen Monorom, and few *moto* drivers make the trip (ask for Mony at Middle of Somewhere, p312). The road improves slightly on the other side of Mimong and it is possible to link up with NH7 to Kratie to the west (taking another four hours).

KOH NHEK
កោះញែក
pop 6000

The final frontier as far as Mondulkiri goes, this village in the far north of the province is a strategic place on the challenging overland route between Sen Monorom and Ratanakiri Province (see p308 for the skinny on this route). Thanks to a new (unsealed) road covering the 93km from Sen Monorom, Koh Nhek is not quite the remote outpost it once was. A newly opened Acleda Bank is a sign of changing times.

There is a pair of unnamed guesthouses in town. One is 500m west of the main intersection, opposite a public well, the other is three houses before the main intersection, on the right as you enter town from the south. Both charge 20,000r for a room. The store on the northeast corner of the main intersection has food and some basic supplies, including coldish beer – well earned once you get here.

Directory

CONTENTS

Accommodation	319
Activities	320
Business Hours	321
Children	322
Climate Charts	323
Courses	323
Customs Regulations	323
Dangers & Annoyances	323
Discount Cards	326
Embassies & Consulates	326
Festivals & Events	326
Food	326
Gay & Lesbian Travellers	327
Holidays	327
Insurance	327
Internet Access	327
Legal Matters	328
Maps	328
Money	328
Photography & Video	330
Post	331
Shopping	331
Telephone & Fax	332
Time	333
Toilets	333
Tourist Information	334
Travellers with Disabilities	334
Visas	334
Volunteering	335
Women Travellers	336
Work	336

ACCOMMODATION

Accommodation in Cambodia has improved immensely during the past decade and everything is available, from the classic budget crash pad to the plush palace. Most hotels quote in US dollars, but some places in the provinces quote in riel, while those near the Thai border quote in baht. We provide prices based on the currency quoted to us at the time of research. In Phnom Penh, Siem Reap, Sihanoukville and Kep there are options to suit all wallets. Elsewhere around Cambodia, the choice is limited to budget and midrange options, but these places provide great value for money. Even some of the provincial capitals like Ban Lung, Battambang and Kompong Thom now have midrange boutique hotels.

In this guide, budget accommodation refers to guesthouses where the majority of rooms are within the US$2 to US$20 range, midrange generally runs from US$20 up to US$80 and top end is considered US$80 and up, up, up.

Budget guesthouses used to be restricted to Phnom Penh, Siem Reap and Sihanoukville, but as tourism takes off in the provinces, they are turning up in most of the other provincial capitals. Costs hover around US$2 to US$5 for a bed. In many rural parts of Cambodia, the standard rate for cheap hotels is US$5, usually with bathroom and satellite TV. There may be a few places starting at 10,000r, but they tend to make more by the hour than they do by the night, so don't count on much sleep.

In Phnom Penh, Siem Reap and the South Coast, which see a steady flow of tourist traffic, hotels improve significantly once you start spending more than US$10 a night. For US$15 it is usually possible to find an air-con room with satellite TV and attached bathroom. If you spend between US$20 and US$50 it is possible to arrange something very comfortable with the possible lure of a swimming pool. Most smaller provincial cities also offer air-conditioned comfort in the US$10 to US$20 range.

There are now a host of international-standard hotels in Siem Reap, several in Phnom Penh and a couple on the coast in Sihanoukville and Kep. Some are operated by familiar international brands such as Orient Express and Raffles. Most quote hefty walk-in rates and whack 10% tax and 10% service on as well. Book through a travel agent for a lower rate including taxes and service.

Some guesthouses in Cambodia do not have hot water, but most places have at least a few more expensive rooms where it is available. Smaller places in remote areas may have bathrooms where a large jar or cement trough is filled with water for bathing purposes. Don't climb into it – just sluice the water with the plastic scoop or metal bowl.

While many of the swish new hotels have lifts, older hotels often don't and the cheapest rooms are at the top of several flights of stairs. It's a win-win-win situation: cheaper rooms, a bit of exercise and better views.

There is often confusion over the terms 'single', 'double', 'double occupancy' and 'twin'. A single has one bed, even if two people sleep in it. If there are two beds in the room, that is a twin, even if only one person occupies it. Two people staying in the same room is double occupancy. In some hotels 'double' means twin beds, in others it means double occupancy.

Homestays

Homestays are popping up in the provinces and offer a good way to meet the local people and learn about the Cambodian lifestyle. There are several organised homestays around the country in provinces like Kompong Cham and Kompong Thom, as well as lots of informal homestays in out-of-the-way places such as Preah Vihear. In the minority areas of Mondulkiri and Ratanakiri, it is often possible to stay with tribal villagers. The Mekong Discovery Trail (p300) includes several homestays between Kratie and the Lao border.

ACTIVITIES

Tourism in Cambodia is catching up fast and there are now more activities than ever to get that adrenaline buzz. Phnom Penh and Siem Reap remain the places with most of the action, but Sihanoukville and Kep are making a name for themselves for fun in the sun with water sports.

Birdwatching

Birdwatching is a big draw, as Cambodia is home to some of the region's rarest large waterbirds including adjutants, storks and pelicans. For more on the birds of Cambodia see p67, and for the low-down on bird sanctuaries and birding opportunities around Siem Reap, see p151.

Boat Trips

With so much water around the country, it is hardly surprising that boat trips are popular with tourists. Some of these are functional, such as travelling up the Tonlé Sap River from Phnom Penh to Siem Reap (p120), or along the Sangker River from Siem Reap to Battambang (p255). Others are the traditional tourist trips, such as those available in Phnom Penh (p98), Siem Reap (p151) and Sihanoukville (p222), or check out dolphin-spotting in Kratie (p300).

Cycling

As Cambodia's roads continue to improve, cycling tourists are an increasingly common sight. It's a real adventure and brings visitors that much closer to the uberfriendly locals. Local kids will race you at any opportunity and families will beckon cyclists in for some

---

PRACTICALITIES

■ The usual voltage is 220V, 50 cycles, but power surges and power cuts are common, particularly in the provinces. Electrical sockets are usually two-prong, flat or round pin.

■ Most guesthouses and hotels have cheap laundry services, but check they have a dryer if it's the wet season. There are laundry shops in every town.

■ The *Phnom Penh Post* is now daily and offers the best balance of Cambodian and international news, including business and sport. The *Cambodia Daily* is a long-running English-language newspaper. *AsiaLife* is a free monthly listings magazine (a sort of *Time Out: Phnom Penh*).

■ BBC World Service broadcasts on 100.00FM in Phnom Penh. Cambodian radio and TV stations are mainly government-controlled and specialise in karaoke videos and soap operas.

■ Cambodians use the metric system for everything except precious metals and gems, where they prefer Chinese units of measurement.

fruit or hot tea. Some of the main roads are getting busier and others remain dusty, but there are some great routes for those willing to put in the effort. The south coast of Cambodia remains a rewarding region for cyclists, while the northeast holds future promise for serious mountain-bikers. The most popular place for cycling is around the majestic temples of Angkor where the roads are paved and the forest thick. Bikes are available for hire in most towns in Cambodia for US$2 a day for a basic bike to around US$7 a day for a good imported mountain bike, but serious tourers should bring their own wheels or purchase something in Bangkok or Phnom Penh.

Dirt Biking

For experienced riders, Cambodia is one of the most rewarding off-road biking destinations in the world. The roads are generally considered some of the worst in Asia (or best in Asia for die-hard biking enthusiasts). There are incredible rides all over the country, particularly in the north and northeast, but it is best to stay away from the main highways as traffic and dust make them a choking experience. For more on dirt biking, see p348, including recommended motorcycle touring companies.

Diving & Snorkelling

Snorkelling and diving are available off the coast of Sihanoukville. The jury is still out about the dive sites, as much is still to be explored, but while it may not be as spectacular as Indonesia or the Philippines, there is plenty in the deep blue yonder. It is best to venture further afield to dive sites such as Koh Tang and Koh Prins (p215), staying overnight on a boat. There are many unexplored areas off the coast between Koh Kong and Sihanoukville that could one day put Cambodia on the dive map of Asia.

Golf

Cambodia is an up-and-coming golfing destination thanks to several new courses in Siem Reap (p136), one of which now hosts an annual PGA event on the Asian tour. There are also a couple of courses in Phnom Penh (p99).

Rock Climbing

There is not really any organised commercial rock climbing in Cambodia, but there is plenty of karst in the southeast of the country around Kampot and Kep. See the website www.rockclimbingincambodia.com if you are serious about tackling some ascents.

Trekking

Trekking is not the first thing you associate with Cambodia due to the presence of land mines, but there are several relatively safe areas of the country, including the nascent national parks. The northeastern provinces of Mondulkiri and Ratanakiri were never mined, and with their wild, natural scenery, abundant waterfalls and ethnic minority populations, they are emerging as the country's leading trekking destinations. Always take a guide, however, as there are some unexploded bombs in these areas from the American bombing campaign of the early 1970s. Elephant treks are also possible in these northeastern provinces.

Cambodia is steadily establishing a network of national parks with visitor facilities; Bokor National Park (p229), Kirirom National Park (p127) and Ream National Park (p222) all promise trekking potential, while Virachey National Park (p311) in Ratanakiri has multi-day treks.

Angkor is emerging as a good place for gentle walks between the temples – one way to experience peace and solitude as visitor numbers skyrocket.

Watersports

As the Cambodian coast takes off, there are more adrenaline buzzes available including boating, windsurfing and kite surfing off the beaches of Sihanoukville (p209).

BUSINESS HOURS

Most Cambodians get up very early and it is not unusual to see people out and about exercising at 5.30am if you are heading home – ahem, sorry, getting up – at that time. Government offices, which are open from Monday to Friday and Saturday mornings, theoretically begin the working day at 7.30am, break for a siesta from 11.30am to 2pm, and end the day at 5pm. However, it is a safe bet that few people will be around early in the morning or after 4pm, as their real income is often earned elsewhere.

Banking hours vary slightly according to the bank, but most keep core hours of 8am to 3.30pm Monday to Friday, plus Saturday morning. Attractions such as museums are normally open seven days a week, and these days staff have had their arms twisted to stay open through lunch.

Local restaurants are generally open from about 6.30am until 9pm and international restaurants until a little later. Local restaurants may stay open throughout, while international restaurants sometimes close between sittings. Many bars are open all day, but some open only for the night shift, especially if they don't serve food.

Local markets operate seven days a week and usually open and close with the sun, running from 6.30am to 5.30pm. Markets shut up shop for a few days during the major holidays of Chaul Chnam Khmer (Khmer New Year), P'chum Ben (Festival of the Dead) and Chaul Chnam Chen (Chinese New Year). Shops tend to open from about 8am until 6pm, sometimes later.

CHILDREN

Children can live it up in Cambodia as they are always the centre of attention and almost everybody wants to play with them. For the full picture on surviving and thriving on the road with kids, check out Lonely Planet's *Travel with Children* for a rundown on health precautions for kids and advice on travel during pregnancy.

Practicalities

When it comes to feeding and caring for babies, pretty much everything you'll need is available in Phnom Penh and Siem Reap, but supplies dry up quickly elsewhere. Cot beds are available in international-standard midrange and top-end hotels, but not elsewhere. Consider investing in a sturdy hammock or two if travelling to lesser-known destinations. There are no safety seats in rented cars or taxis, unless you book in advance for a reputable travel company. Some restaurants can supply a high chair when it comes to eating.

Breastfeeding in public is very common in Cambodia, so there is no need to worry about crossing a cultural boundary. But there are few facilities for changing babies other than the usual bathrooms, so take a baby bag everywhere you go. For kiddies too young to handle chopsticks, most restaurants also have cutlery.

The main worry throughout Cambodia is keeping an eye on what strange things infants are putting in their mouths. Their natural curiosity can be a lot more costly in a country where dysentery, typhoid and hepatitis are commonplace. Keeping their hydration levels up and insisting they use sunscreen is also important.

Phnom Penh, Siem Reap and other urban areas of Cambodia are pretty straightforward these days, although be very aware of the chaotic traffic conditions in the capital – better to restrict your child's movements than have them wander into danger. Remote Cambodia is not a good travel destination for children as there are still many land mines littering the countryside. No matter how many warnings a child is given, can you be certain they won't stray from the path?

Sights & Activities

There is plenty to keep kids happy in Phnom Penh, Siem Reap and the South Coast, but in the smaller provincial towns the boredom factor might creep in. Phnom Penh has a good selection of swimming pools (p100) and even a go-kart track (p99). Boat trips on the river should be a hit, but best of all is the Phnom Tamao Wildlife Rescue Centre (p126), about 45km south of the city, with tigers, sun bears and elephants.

At Angkor, the temples may be too much for younger children, but will be appreciated by inquisitive older children. Younger ones might prefer crumbling ruins like Ta Prohm (p181) or Beng Mealea (p191) to the more museumlike renovated temples. *Remork-motos* (aka *tuk tuks*; motorbikes with a cute little hooded trailer hitched to the back) are a fun way for families to get around the Angkor area. Cambodian Cultural Village (p133) may be kitsch, but it is the right tonic after the temples. Hot-air balloons and helicopter rides round off some action-packed options in Siem Reap.

The national parks don't have enough visible wildlife to deliver, but some have waterfalls, including Kirirom National Park (p127) and Bokor National Park (p229). Another area for attractive waterfalls is the northeast and the provinces of Mondulkiri and Ratanakiri, where kids can also ride elephants. The air is clean, at least when cars aren't kicking up red dust, and there are wide-open spaces.

Cambodia has a long coastline, and Sihanoukville (p209) is the number-one beach spot. There are plenty of local children hanging out on the beach, many of them trying to make a living, and this can be an interesting bonding experience for kids. Pay close to attention to any playtime in the sea, as there are some deceptively strong currents in the wet season.

CLIMATE CHARTS

Life in Cambodia is fairly steamy in the lowlands, with a classic tropical climate. It gets a little cooler up in the hills of the northeast, but even there it rarely gets cold.

Average daily temperatures range from the high 20s in the 'cool' season of December and January, to the high 30s and beyond in the hot months of April and May. The rain kicks in around June and falls thick and fast throughout August and September, bringing the landscape back to life ready for a new harvest.

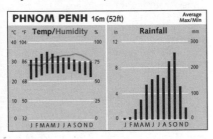

COURSES
Cooking

For the full story on cooking courses in Cambodia, see p63.

Language

The only language courses available in Cambodia at present are in Khmer and are aimed at expat residents of Phnom Penh rather than travellers. If you are going to be based in Phnom Penh for some time, however, it would be well worth learning basic Khmer. Try the Institute of Foreign Languages at the **Royal University of Phnom Penh** (Map pp84–5; ☎ 012 866826; Russian Blvd). Also check out the noticeboards at popular guesthouses, restaurants and bars, where one-hour lessons are often advertised by private tutors. There are also regular listings under the Classifieds in the *Phnom Penh Post* and *Cambodia Daily*.

CUSTOMS REGULATIONS

If Cambodia has customs allowances, it is close-lipped about them. A 'reasonable amount' of duty-free items is allowed into the country. Travellers arriving by air might bear in mind that alcohol and cigarettes are on sale at prices well below duty-free prices on the streets of Phnom Penh – a branded box of 200 cigarettes costs just US$9 and international spirits start as low as US$7 a litre.

Like any other country, Cambodia does not allow travellers to import weapons, explosives or narcotics – there are enough in the country already. It is illegal to take ancient stone sculptures from the Angkor period out of the country.

DANGERS & ANNOYANCES

As memories of war grow ever more distant, Cambodia has become a much safer country in which to travel. Remembering the golden rule – stick to the marked paths in remote areas – means you'd be very unlucky to have any problems. But it doesn't hurt to check on the latest situation before making a trip few other travellers undertake, particularly if travelling by motorcycle.

The **Cambodia Daily** (www.cambodiadaily.com) and the **Phnom Penh Post** (www.phnompenhpost.com) newspapers are both good sources for breaking news on Cambodia – check out their websites before you hit the road.

Begging

Begging is common throughout Cambodia, although much more evident in Phnom Penh and Siem Reap than elsewhere. There are many reasons for begging in a society as poor as Cambodia, some more visually evident than others, such as amputees who have lost their limbs to land mines. It is entirely up to individual visitors whether to give or not, and to decide how much to offer, but remember that it is common practice for Buddhists to give to those more needy than themselves.

Big brown eyes, runny noses and grubby hands…the sight of children begging is familiar throughout the developing world, and Cambodia is no exception. There are many child beggars around Phnom Penh and the temples of Angkor, and with their angelic faces it is often difficult to resist giving them some money. However, there are a number of issues to consider: giving to child beggars may create a cycle of dependency that can continue into adulthood; the children may not benefit directly from the money, as they are often made to beg by a 'pimp' or their family; and some child beggars, particularly around central Phnom Penh, may use the money to buy glue to feed their sniffing habit. One way to help these impoverished children is to buy them some food or drink, or give them some of your time and attention – it is amazing how quickly they will forget about begging once they are being taught something simple like a whistle, a trick or a game.

The most common beggars around the country are land-mine victims. Many of them sustained their injuries fighting, while others have had their legs blown off while working or playing innocently in the fields. You may tire of their attention after a few days in Cambodia, but try to remember that in a country with no social security-network, begging is often all they can do to survive.

When giving to beggars, try to offer smaller denominations to avoid making foreigners more of a target than they already are.

Checkpoints

During the long years of civil war there were checkpoints on roads throughout the country, but these days they are a rare sight. Where there are checkpoints on major roads, spot checks may be carried out to make sure drivers have paid their road tax or are not carrying illegal guns.

If you are travelling in a taxi or pick-up truck in remote areas of Cambodia and come across a checkpoint, the driver should take care of the payment. If you are on a motorbike, you are unlikely to be stopped. However, should you ever find money being demanded of you, try to negotiate the sum to an acceptable level. Do not under any circumstances attempt to take photos of the individuals concerned, as things could turn nasty.

Scams

Most current scams are fairly harmless, involving a bit of commission here and there for taxi or *moto* drivers, particularly in Siem Reap. More annoying are the 'cheap' buses from Bangkok to Siem Reap, deservedly nicknamed the 'Scam Buses' for using the wrong border crossings, driving slowly and selling passengers to guesthouses, but thankfully these are a dying breed.

There have been one or two reports of police set-ups in Phnom Penh, involving planted drugs. This seems to be very rare, but if you fall victim to the ploy, it will require patience and persistence to sort out, inevitably involving

embassies and the like. It may be best to pay them off before more police get involved at the local station, as the price will only rise when there are more people to pay off.

Cambodia is renowned for its precious stones, particularly the rubies and sapphires that are mined around the Pailin area in western Cambodia. There are, however, lots of chemically treated copies around, as much of the high-quality stuff is snapped up by international buyers. The long and short of it is: don't buy unless you really know your stones.

On the subject of fakes, there is quite a lot of fake medication floating about the region. Safeguard yourself by only buying prescription drugs from reliable pharmacies or clinics. Similarly, there are a lot of dodgy recreational drugs around, some of which could seriously damage your health: see the boxed text, p328, for more on this.

Security

Cambodia is a pretty safe country in which to travel these days – it is now possible to travel throughout Cambodia with no more difficulty than in neighbouring Thailand or Vietnam. Once again though, remember the golden rule – *stick to marked paths in remote areas*. Politically, Cambodia has proven an unpredictable country and this makes it hard to guarantee safety of travel at any given time. Suffice to say that you are no longer a target just because you are a tourist.

Cambodia is something of a lawless society in which arms are often preferred to eloquence when settling a dispute. This 'Wild East' atmosphere rarely affects tourists, but it is worth knowing about as you can expect to hear gunshots from time to time (usually someone firing into the air when drunk). Phnom Penh is arguably one of the more dangerous places; it

> ### PLANET OF THE FAKES
>
> Cambodia is awash with pirated books and poor photocopies, including Lonely Planet titles. We know you wouldn't dream of buying a photocopied Lonely Planet guide, and that's very sensible given that old editions are sometimes wrapped in new covers, pages are bound in the wrong order and the type is so faded as to be almost unreadable. Be warned, if this is a photocopy, it may self-destruct in five seconds.

is here that the most guns are concentrated and the most robberies take place. This is closely followed by Sihanoukville, which has sadly developed a reputation for robbery and sneak theft. Elsewhere in the provinces you would be very unlucky to have any incident befall you, as the vast majority of Khmers are immensely hospitable, honest and helpful. More importantly, perhaps, the majority of Khmers are experiencing peace for the first time in more than 30 years and don't want it disturbed.

Trying to pinpoint any lingering areas of concern around the country is always difficult as circumstances change quickly. Pailin and large parts of Oddar Meanchey and Preah Vihear Provinces were Khmer Rouge controlled until just a few years ago, but are now considered safe. As the trial for surviving Khmer Rouge leaders continues, it could be a different story – just because the former rebels now wear baseball caps instead of Mao caps doesn't mean they have forgotten the fight. However, since the trial began, there have been no problems in these areas.

Should anyone be unlucky enough to be robbed, it is important to note that the Cambodian police are the best that money can buy! Any help, such as a police report, is going to cost you. The going rate depends on the size of the claim, but US$5 to US$20 is a common charge. Some tourist police, however, will now provide this service for free.

Snakes

Visitors to Ta Prohm at Angkor and other overgrown archaeological sites should beware of snakes. They are very well camouflaged so keep your eyes peeled. For details of what to do in case of snake bite, see p361.

Theft & Street Crime

Given the number of guns in Cambodia, there is less armed theft than one might expect. Still, hold-ups and motorcycle theft are a potential danger in Phnom Penh and Sihanoukville. There is no need to be paranoid, just cautious. Walking or riding alone late at night is not ideal, certainly not in rural areas.

Pickpocketing and theft by stealth is more a problem in Vietnam than in Cambodia, but it pays to be careful. The current hot spots are crowded vehicles on popular tourist routes such as Siem Reap to Poipet or Phnom Penh, and in the markets of Phnom Penh. Don't make it any easier for thieves by putting your passport and wads of cash in your back pocket. As a precaution, keep a 'secret' stash of cash separate from the bulk of your funds. There has been bag snatching in Phnom Penh in the last few years and the motorbike thieves don't let go, dragging passengers off *motos* and endangering lives.

Traffic Accidents

Traffic conditions in Cambodia are chaotic, although no worse than in many other developing countries. If you are riding a bike in Phnom Penh, stay very alert and take nothing for granted. Traffic moves in all directions on both sides of the road, so don't be surprised to see vehicles bearing down on you. The horn is used to alert other drivers to a vehicle's

FESTIVAL WARNING

In the run-up to major festivals such as P'chum Ben or Chaul Chnam Khmer, there is a palpable increase in the number of robberies, particularly in Phnom Penh. Cambodians need money to buy gifts for relatives or to pay off debts, and for some individuals theft is the quick way to get this money. Be more vigilant at night at these times and don't take valuables out with you unnecessarily.

presence – get out of the way if you hear a car or truck behind you.

Moto drivers in Cambodia are now required to wear helmets by law, but this doesn't yet apply to passengers so they do not provide safety helmets. Fortunately most of them drive at sensible speeds. If you encounter a reckless driver, ask them to slow down or pay them off and find another *moto*.

Having a major traffic accident in Phnom Penh would be bad enough, but if you have one in rural Cambodia, you are in big trouble. Somehow you will have to get to Phnom Penh, Siem Reap or Battambang for medical treatment.

The basic rule is to drive carefully. See p348 for safety tips.

Undetonated Mines, Mortars & Bombs

Never touch any rockets, artillery shells, mortars, mines, bombs or other war material you may come across. A tactic of the Khmer Rouge was to lay mines along roads and in rice fields in an effort to maim and kill civilians. The only concrete results of this policy are the many limbless people you see all over Cambodia.

The most heavily mined part of the country is along the Thai border area, but mines are a problem all over Cambodia. In short: *do not stray from well-marked paths under any circumstances*. If you are planning any walks, even in safer areas such as the remote northeast, it is imperative you take a guide as there may still be unexploded ordnance (UXO) from the American bombing campaign of the early 1970s.

Violence

Violence against foreigners is extremely rare and is not something you should waste much time worrying about, but it pays to take care in crowded bars or nightclubs in Phnom Penh. If you get into a stand-off with rich young Khmers in a bar or club, swallow your pride and back down. Still think you can 'ave 'em? Many carry guns and have an entourage of bodyguards: enough said.

DISCOUNT CARDS

Senior travellers and students are not eligible for discounts in Cambodia – all foreigners who are rich enough to make it to Cambodia are rich enough to pay as far as Cambodians are concerned.

EMBASSIES & CONSULATES

Quite a few countries have embassies in Phnom Penh, though some travellers will find that their nearest embassy is in Bangkok. It's important to realise what your country's embassy can and can't do to help if you get into trouble. Generally speaking, it won't be much help if the trouble you're in is remotely your own fault. Remember that you are bound by the laws of the country you are in. Your embassy won't be sympathetic if you end up in jail after committing a crime, even if such actions are legal in your own country.

In genuine emergencies you might get some assistance, but only if all other channels have been exhausted. If you have all your money and documents stolen, your embassy might assist with getting a new passport, but a loan for onward travel is out of the question.

Those intending to visit Laos should note that Lao visas are available in Phnom Penh for US$30 to US$45, depending on nationality, and take two working days. For Vietnam, one-month single-entry visas cost US$30 to US$35 and take just one day, faster still at the Vietnamese consulate in Sihanoukville.

Embassies in Phnom Penh (☎ 023):

Australia (Map pp84-5; ☎ 213413; 16 National Assembly St)
China (Map pp84-5; ☎ 720920; 256 Mao Tse Toung Blvd)
France (Map pp84-5; ☎ 430020; 1 Monivong Blvd)
Germany (Map p87; ☎ 216381; 76-78 St 214)
India (Map pp84-5; ☎ 210912; 777 Monivong Blvd)
Indonesia (Map p87; ☎ 216148; 90 Norodom Blvd)
Japan (Map pp84-5; ☎ 217161; 194 Norodom Blvd)
Laos (Map pp84-5; ☎ 982632; 15-17 Mao Tse Toung Blvd)
Malaysia (Map p87; ☎ 216177; 5 St 242)
Myanmar (Map pp84-5; ☎ 223761; 181 Norodom Blvd)
Philippines (Map p87; ☎ 222303; 33 St 294)
Singapore (Map p87; ☎ 221875; 92 Norodom Blvd)
Thailand (Map pp84-5; ☎ 726306; 196 Norodom Blvd)
UK (Map pp84-5; ☎ 427124; 27-29 St 75)
USA (Map p87; ☎ 728000; 1 St 96)
Vietnam Phnom Penh (Map pp84-5; ☎ 362531; 436 Monivong Blvd); Sihanoukville (Map p210; ☎ 012 340495; Ekareach St)

FESTIVALS & EVENTS

For the inside story on festivals and events in Cambodia, see the Events Calendar (p19).

FOOD

Cambodian cuisine may be less well known than that of its popular neighbours Thailand and Vietnam, but it is no less tasty. See p57 for the full story on Cambodian cuisine.

GAY & LESBIAN TRAVELLERS

While Cambodian culture is tolerant of homosexuality, the gay and lesbian scene here is certainly nothing like that in Thailand. The former King Norodom Sihanouk was a keen supporter of equal rights for same-sex partners and this seems to have encouraged a more open attitude among younger Cambodians. Both Phnom Penh and Siem Reap have a few gay-friendly bars, but it is a low-key scene compared with some parts of Asia.

With the vast number of same-sex travel partners – gay or otherwise – checking into hotels across Cambodia, there is little consideration over how travelling foreigners are related. However, it is prudent not to flaunt your sexuality. As with heterosexual couples, passionate public displays of affection are considered a basic no-no.

Utopia (www.utopia-asia.com) features gay travel information and contacts, including detailed sections on the legality of homosexuality in Cambodia (it is legal, but gay marriage isn't) and some local gay terminology.

HOLIDAYS

Public Holidays

During public holidays and festivals, banks, ministries and embassies close down, so plan ahead if visiting Cambodia during these times. Cambodians also roll over holidays if they fall on a weekend and take a day or two extra during major festivals. Add to this the fact that they take a holiday for international days here and there and it soon becomes apparent that Cambodia has more public holidays than any other nation on earth!

International New Year's Day 1 January
Victory over the Genocide 7 January
International Women's Day 8 March
International Workers' Day 1 May
International Children's Day 8 May
King's Birthday 13–15 May
King Mother's Birthday 18 June
Constitution Day 24 September
King Father's Birthday 31 October
Independence Day 9 November
International Human Rights Day 10 December

INSURANCE

A travel-insurance policy that covers theft, property loss and medical expenses is more essential for Cambodia than for most other parts of Southeast Asia. There is a wide variety

---

INSURANCE ALERT!

Do not visit Cambodia without medical insurance. Hospitals are extremely basic in the provinces and even in Phnom Penh the facilities are generally not up to the standards to which you may be accustomed. Anyone who has a serious injury or illness while in Cambodia may require emergency evacuation to Bangkok. With an insurance policy costing no more than the equivalent of a bottle of beer a day, this evacuation is free. Without an insurance policy, it will cost between US$10,000 and US$20,000 – somewhat more than a six-pack. Don't gamble with your health in Cambodia or you may end up another statistic.

---

of insurance policies available, and it's wise to check with a reliable agent as to which is most suitable for Cambodia. Worldwide travel insurance is available at www.lonelyplanet.com/travel_services. You can buy, extend and claim online anytime – even if you're already on the road.

When buying your travel insurance *always* check the small print:

- Some policies specifically exclude 'dangerous activities' such as scuba diving and riding a motorcycle. If you are going to be motorbiking in Cambodia, check that you will be covered.
- Check whether the medical coverage is on a pay first, claim later basis; if this is the case, keep all documents relating to any medical treatment.
- In the case of Cambodia, it is essential to check that medical coverage includes the cost of emergency evacuation (see the boxed text, above).

INTERNET ACCESS

Internet access is available in most towns throughout the country. In Phnom Penh prices just keep dropping, thankfully, and now average US$0.50 or less per hour. Siem Reap is a little more expensive at US$0.50 to US$1 per hour, while in other provinces it can range from US$1 an hour to as much as US$3 an hour. Most internet cafes also supply headsets to allow cheap phone calls via Skype or similar software. Expensive hotels often charge exorbitant prices for internet access, so check the conditions before you surf.

If travelling with a laptop, remember that Cambodia's power-supply voltage will vary from that at home, risking damage to your equipment. The best investment is a universal AC adapter, which enables you to plug it in anywhere without frying its innards.

Visitors carrying a laptop who are looking for a direct connection to a server have several choices. The most convenient option is usually via wi-fi networks, which are increasingly common in Phnom Penh and Siem Reap. Many cafes and restaurants offer free wi-fi for customers, while hotels sometimes levy a charge.

Those still working on fixed-line connections can pick up one of the prepaid internet cards available from shops, hotels, petrol stations and some restaurants. They come in a range of values from US$10 to US$50.

LEGAL MATTERS

Marijuana is not legal in Cambodia and police are beginning to take a harder line on it. There have been several busts (and a few set-ups, too) of foreigner-owned bars and restaurants where ganja was smoked – the days of free bowls in guesthouses are definitely history. Marijuana is traditionally used in some Khmer food, so it will continue to be around for a long time, but if you are a smoker, be discreet. It's probably only a matter of time before the Cambodian police turn the regular busting of foreigners into a lucrative sideline.

This advice applies equally to other narcotic substances, which are also illegal. And think twice about scoring from an unfamiliar *moto* driver, as it may end with you getting robbed after passing out.

Travellers should note that they can be prosecuted under the law of their home country regarding age of consent, even when abroad.

MAPS

The best all-rounder for Cambodia is the Gecko *Cambodia Road Map*. At 1:750,000 scale, it has lots of detail and accurate place names. Other popular foldout maps include Nelles *Cambodia, Laos and Vietnam Map* at 1:1,500,000, although the detail is limited, and the Periplus *Cambodia Travel Map* at 1:1,000,000, with city maps of Phnom Penh and Siem Reap.

There are lots of free maps, subsidised by advertising, that are available in Phnom Penh and Siem Reap at leading hotels, guesthouses, restaurants and bars.

For serious map buffs or cartographers, Psar Thmei (Central Market) in Phnom Penh is well stocked with Vietnamese and Khmer-produced maps of towns and provinces, as well as US military maps from the 1970s at a scale of 1:50,000.

MONEY

Cambodia's currency is the riel, abbreviated in this guide by a lower-case 'r' written after the sum. Cambodia's second currency (some would say its first) is the US dollar, which is accepted everywhere and by everyone, though change may arrive in riel. Dollar bills with a small tear are unlikely to be accepted by Cambodians, so it's worth scrutinising the change you are given to make sure you don't have bad bills. In the west of the country, the Thai baht (B) is also commonplace. If three currencies seems a little excessive, perhaps it's because the Cambodians are making up for

---

YABA DABA DO? YABA DABA DON'T!

Watch out for *yaba*, the 'crazy' drug from Thailand, known rather ominously in Cambodia as *yama* (the Hindu god of death). Known as ice or crystal meth back home, it's not just any old diet pill from the pharmacist, but homemade meta-amphetamines produced in labs in Cambodia and the regions beyond. The pills are often laced with toxic substances, such as mercury, lithium or whatever else the maker can find. *Yama* is a dirty drug and more addictive than users would like to admit, provoking powerful hallucinations, sleep deprivation and psychosis. Steer clear of the stuff unless you plan on an indefinite extension to your trip.

Also be very careful about buying 'cocaine'. One look at the map and the distance between Colombia and Cambodia should be enough to make you dubious, but it's much worse than that. Most of what is sold as coke, particularly in Phnom Penh, is actually pure heroin and far stronger than any smack found on the streets back home. Bang this up your hooter and you are in serious trouble – several backpackers die each year in the lakeside guesthouse ghetto of Boeng Kak in Phnom Penh.

lost time: during the Pol Pot era, the country had *no* currency. The Khmer Rouge abolished money and blew up the National Bank building in Phnom Penh.

The Cambodian riel comes in notes of the following denominations: 50r, 100r, 200r, 500r, 1000r, 2000r, 5000r, 10,000r, 20,000r, 50,000r and 100,000r.

Throughout this book, prices are in the currency quoted to the average punter. This is usually US dollars or riel, but in the west it is sometimes baht. While this may seem inconsistent, this is the way it's done in Cambodia and the sooner you get used to thinking comparatively in riel, dollars or baht, the easier your travels will be.

In parts of the country that use Thai baht, paying in riel or US dollars is often significantly (up to 25%) cheaper than paying in baht. The standard conversion rate used by businesses is 4000r = US$1 = 40b, but in reality both 4000r and US$1 are worth just 33b at current rates.

For a listing of exchange rates at the time of going to print, see the Quick Reference section on the inside front cover of this book.

ATMs
There are now credit-card-compatible ATMs (Visa, MasterCard, JCB, Cirrus) in most major cities including Phnom Penh, Siem Reap, Sihanoukville, Battambang and Kompong Cham. There are also ATMs at the Cham Yeam and Poipet borders if arriving from Thailand. Machines dispense US dollars. Large withdrawals of up to US$2000 are possible, providing your account can handle it. Stay alert when using them late at night. ANZ Royal Bank has the most extensive network, including ATMs at petrol stations and popular hotels, restaurants and shops, closely followed by Canadia Bank. However, ANZ Royal charges US$4 per transaction, while Canadia Bank is free for now. Acleda Bank has the widest network of branches in the country, including all provincial capitals, and has been upgrading ATMs to accept international cards, making far-flung travel that much easier to plan.

Bargaining
It is important to haggle over purchases made in local markets in Phnom Penh and Siem Reap, otherwise the stallholder may 'shave your head' (local vernacular for 'rip you off'). Bargaining is the rule in markets, when

arranging share taxis and pick-ups, and in some guesthouses. The Khmers are not ruthless hagglers, so a persuasive smile and a little friendly quibbling is usually enough to get a fair price. Try to remember that the aim is not to get the lowest possible price, but a price that is acceptable to both you and the seller. Remember back home, we pay astronomical sums for items, especially clothes, that have been made in poorer countries for next to nothing, and we don't even get the chance to bargain for them, just the opportunity to contribute to a corporate director's retirement fund. At least there is room for discussion in Cambodia, so try not to become obsessed by the price. And also remember that in many cases a few hundred riel is more important to a Cambodian with a family to support than to a traveller on an extended vacation. After all, no one bargains over a beer in a busy backpacker bar, so why bargain so hard over a cheap bottle of water?

Black Market
The black market no longer exists in Cambodia when it comes to changing money. Exchange rates on the street are the same as those offered by the banks; you just get to avoid the queues and paperwork.

Cash
The US dollar remains king in Cambodia. Armed with enough cash, you won't need to visit a bank at all because it is possible to change small amounts of dollars for riel at hotels, restaurants and markets. Hardened travellers argue that your trip ends up being slightly more expensive if you rely on US dollars rather than riel, but in reality there's very little in it. However, it never hurts to support the local currency against the greenback. It is always handy to have about US$10 worth of riel kicking around, as it is good for *motos, remork-motos* and markets. Pay for something cheap in US dollars and the change comes in riel. In remote areas of the north and northeast, locals only deal in riel or small dollar denominations.

The only other currency that can be useful is Thai baht, mainly in the west of the country. Prices in towns such as Krong Koh Kong, Poipet and Sisophon are often quoted in baht, and even in Battambang it is as common as the dollar.

In the interests of making life as simple as possible when travelling overland, organise a supply of US dollars before arriving in Cambodia. Cash in other major currencies can be changed at banks or markets in Phnom Penh or Siem Reap. However, most banks tend to offer a poor rate for any nondollar transaction so it can be better to use moneychangers, which are found in and around every major market.

Western Union and MoneyGram are both represented in Cambodia for fast, if more expensive, money transfers. Western Union is represented by SBC and Acleda Bank, and MoneyGram is represented by Canadia Bank.

Credit Cards

Top-end hotels, airline offices and upmarket boutiques and restaurants generally accept most major credit cards (Visa, MasterCard, JCB and sometimes American Express), but many pass the charges straight on to the customer, meaning an extra 3% on the bill.

Cash advances on credit cards are available in Phnom Penh, Siem Reap, Sihanoukville, Kampot, Battambang, Kompong Cham and other major towns. Canadia Bank and Union Commercial Bank offer free cash advances, but most other banks advertise a minimum charge of US$5.

Several travel agents and hotels in Phnom Penh and Siem Reap can arrange cash advances for about 5% commission; this can be particularly useful if you get caught short at the weekend.

Tipping

Tipping is not traditionally expected here, but in a country as poor as Cambodia, tips can go a long way. Salaries remain extremely low and service is often superb thanks to a Khmer commitment to hospitality. Hence a tip of just US$1 might be half a day's wages for some. Many of the upmarket hotels levy a 10% service charge, but this doesn't always make it to the staff. If you stay a couple of nights in the same hotel, try to remember to tip the staff

---

TIPPING TIP

In many Cambodian restaurants, change will be returned in some sort of bill holder. If you leave the change there it will often be taken by the restaurant proprietor. If you want to make sure the tip goes to the staff who have served you, then leave the tip on the table or give it to the individuals directly.

---

that clean your room. Consider tipping drivers and guides, as the time they spend on the road means time away from home and family.

It is considered proper to make a small donation at the end of a visit to a wat, especially if a monk has shown you around; most wats have contribution boxes for this purpose.

Travellers Cheques

Acleda Bank now offers travellers cheque encashment at most branches, bringing financial freedom to far-flung provinces like Ratanakiri and Mondulkiri. It is best to have cheques in US dollars, though it is also possible to change euros at Acleda Bank and most major currencies at branches of Canadia Bank. Generally, you pay about 2% commission to change travellers cheques.

PHOTOGRAPHY & VIDEO

Many internet cafes in Phnom Penh, Siem Reap, Battambang and Sihanoukville will burn CDs or DVDs from digital images using card readers or USB connections. The price is about US$2.50 if you need a CD or US$1.50 if you don't. Digital memory sticks are widely available in Cambodia and are pretty cheap. Digital cameras are a real bargain in Cambodia thanks to low tax and duty, so consider picking up a new model in Phnom Penh rather than Bangkok or Saigon.

Print film and processing is relatively inexpensive in Cambodia, with most labs charging about US$4 for a roll. Slide film is also available at competitive prices in Phnom Penh.

If you carry a video camera, make sure you have the necessary charger, plugs and transformer for Cambodia. Take care with some of the electrical wiring in guesthouses around the country, as it can be pretty amateurish. In Phnom Penh and Siem Reap, it is possible to obtain video tapes for most formats, but elsewhere around the country you are unlikely to find much of use. If you are shooting on HD, then pick up the tapes before arriving in Cambodia, as it's still not widely available.

Photographing People

The usual rules apply. Be polite about photographing people, don't push cameras into their faces, and have some respect for monks and people at prayer. In general, the Khmers are remarkably courteous people and if you ask nicely, they'll agree to have their photograph taken. The same goes for filming, although in rural areas you will often find children desperate to get in front of the lens and astonished at seeing themselves played back on an LCD screen. It is the closest most of them will get to being on TV. Some people will expect money in return for their photo being snapped: be sure to establish this before clicking away.

Technical Tips

The best light conditions in Cambodia begin around 20 minutes after sunrise and last for just one to two hours, roughly corresponding to 6am to 8am. The same applies for the late-afternoon light, which begins to assume a radiant warm quality around an hour before sunset. From 10am to around 4pm you can expect the light to be harsh and bleaching – there's not much you can do with it unless you have a polariser. For endless tips on better travel photography, pick up a copy of Lonely Planet's *Travel Photography*.

POST

The postal service is hit and miss from Cambodia; send anything valuable by courier or from another country. Make sure postcards and letters are franked before they vanish from your sight.

Postal rates are listed in post offices in the major towns and cities. Postcards cost 1800r to 3000r to send internationally. Letters and parcels sent further afield than Asia can take up to two or three weeks to reach their destination. Use a courier to speed things up: **DHL** (Map p87; ☎ 023-427726; www.dhl.com; 353 St 110), **FedEx** (Map pp84-5; ☎ 023-216712; www.fedex.com; 701D Monivong Blvd) or **TNT** (Map p87; ☎ 023-430922; www.tnt.com; 28 Monivong Blvd). All have offices in Phnom Penh and some have branch offices in Siem Reap. A slightly cheaper courier option is **EMS** (Map p87; ☎ 023-723511; Main Post Office, St 13), with offices at every major post office in the country.

Phnom Penh's main post office has a poste restante box at the far-left end of the post counter, but long-term travellers are better off getting their stuff sent to Bangkok.

SHOPPING

There is excellent shopping to be had in Cambodia, particularly in Phnom Penh and Siem Reap. As well as the inevitable range of souvenirs, there are many high-quality handicrafts made to support disadvantaged groups in Cambodia.

For tips on how to haggle, see p329.

Antiques

Cambodia has a reasonable range of antiques, although a lot disappeared or was destroyed during the war years. Popular items include textiles, silver, swords, coins, ceramics and furniture, but when buying antiques be very careful of fakes – they are extremely common in this part of the world. If the prices seem too good to be true, then they usually are and you'll end up with a well-aged, modern copy. This is particularly the case with 'old' bronzes from 'the time of Angkor' and a lot of 'ancient' Chinese pieces. Remember that ancient sandstone carvings from the Angkorian or pre-Angkorian periods cannot legally be taken out of the country.

For those settling in Cambodia for any length of time, there are some very nice pieces of antique furniture available in markets and shops in Phnom Penh, with Chinese, French and Khmer influences all evident.

Artwork

The choice of art was, until recently, limited to the poor-quality Angkor paintings seen throughout the country. However, the selection is improving in Phnom Penh and Siem Reap. Psar Chaa (p148) in Siem Reap and the art shops on St 178 (p117) in Phnom Penh are good hunting grounds, and there are a number of upmarket galleries in the capital. Cambodia has a budding art scene and local luminaries hold regular exhibitions at hotels, restaurants and cafes.

Clothing

Many international brands are made in factories around Phnom Penh, including Colombia, Gant, Gap, Levis and Nautica; there is a lot of 'leakage', with items turning up in Psar Tuol Tom Pong (p119) in Phnom Penh at very low prices.

Sculpture

The beauty and intricacy of Cambodian sculpture is evident for all to see around the temples of Angkor and in the National Museum in Phnom Penh. There are many skilled stone carvers in Cambodia today, and replica sculpture is widely available in Phnom Penh and Siem Reap. Popular items include busts of Jayavarman VII and statues of Hindu deities such as Shiva, Vishnu and Harihara. Do not attempt to buy ancient stone sculptures in Cambodia: looting is a huge problem in remote parts of the country and it would be grossly irresponsible for any visitor to add to the problem.

Silk & Textiles

Cambodia is world renowned for its exquisite silk. Much of the country's silk is still traditionally hand-woven, and dyed using natural colours from plants and minerals. The best silk comes from Kompong Cham and Takeo Provinces, but not all the silk sold in Cambodia originates from here (some silk is imported from China and Vietnam). Concerted efforts are underway to reintroduce mulberry trees and locally cultivated silk across the country. There are silk farms in Siem Reap and some of the other provincial centres renowned for silk. Some of the best places to buy silk include Artisans d'Angkor (p132) in Siem Reap, which also operates branches at the international airports; at recommended shops in Phnom Penh (see the boxed text, p118) and Siem Reap (see the boxed text, p148) that support disabled and impoverished Cambodians; and at Psar Tuol Tom Pong (p119) in Phnom Penh. In the provinces, there are several high-quality silk operations, including Mekong Blue (p302) in Stung Treng and Weaves of Cambodia (p276) in Tbeng Meanchey.

Silver

Cambodian silver is valued overseas for the detail of hand-carving on most of the pieces. However, not all silver has that much silver content, so it is important to be careful what you buy. Cambodian silver ranges from copies with no silver, to 50% silver alloy, right up to pure silver. Reputable establishments will often tell you the purity of their silver, but market sellers might try to pull a fast one. The easiest way for novices to determine the quality is to feel the weight. Pure silver should be heavier than alloys or plate.

Woodcarving

Woodcarving is a rich tradition in Cambodia and there are many wooden items that make nice decorative pieces. Reproduction Buddhas are very popular with visitors and there is no restriction on taking Buddha images out of the country. There are also wooden copies available of most of the principal Angkorian sculptures, as well as finely carved animals. Weaving wheels are quite popular and are often elaborately decorated, making nice wall mounts. Betel-nut boxes are plentiful, as are

jewellery boxes inlaid with mother of pearl, lacquer or metalwork.

TELEPHONE & FAX

Cambodia's landline system was totally devastated by the long civil war, leaving the country with a poor communications infrastructure. The advent of mobile phones has allowed Cambodia to catch up with its regional neighbours by jumping headlong into the technology revolution. Mobile phones are everywhere in Cambodia, but landline access in major towns is also improving, connecting more of the country to the outside world than ever before.

Domestic Calls

Local calls are usually pretty cheap, even from hotel rooms. Calling from province to province is considerably more expensive by fixed lines. The easiest way to call in most urban areas is to head to one of the many small private booths on the kerbside, usually plastered with numbers like 012 and 016 and with prices around 300r. Operators have a selection of mobile phones and leased lines to ensure that any domestic number you want to call is cheap. Local phone calls can also be made on the MPTC and Camintel public payphones,

DOMESTIC TELEPHONE AREA CODES

Banteay Meanchey Province	☎ 054
Battambang Province	☎ 053
Kampot Province	☎ 033
Kandal Province	☎ 024
Kep Province	☎ 036
Koh Kong Province	☎ 035
Kompong Cham Province	☎ 042
Kompong Chhnang Province	☎ 026
Kompong Speu Province	☎ 025
Kompong Thom Province	☎ 062
Kratie Province	☎ 072
Mondulkiri Province	☎ 073
Oddar Meanchey Province	☎ 065
Phnom Penh	☎ 023
Preah Vihear Province	☎ 064
Prey Veng Province	☎ 043
Pursat Province	☎ 052
Ratanakiri Province	☎ 075
Siem Reap Province	☎ 063
Sihanoukville Province	☎ 034
Stung Treng Province	☎ 074
Svay Rieng Province	☎ 044
Takeo Province	☎ 032

which are sometimes still seen in places like Phnom Penh, Siem Reap and Sihanoukville. It can sometimes be difficult to get through to numbers outside Phnom Penh, and there is no directory-inquiries service. Some hotels have telephone directories for the capital if you need to track down a number. Check the **Yellow Pages** (www.yp.com.kh), which has a pretty comprehensive coverage of businesses, services and government offices.

Fax

Sending faxes is getting cheaper as telephone charges drop. The cheapest fax services are those via the internet; these can be arranged at internet cafes for around US$1 to US$2 a page. Some of the more popular midrange hotels have reliable business centres, but be aware that faxing from Cambodia's top-end hotels is expensive, costing three times the price charged elsewhere.

International Calls

When it comes to calling overseas, there is now a whole lot more choice than in the bad old days of calls going via Moscow. There are several telephone cards available for card phones, several prepaid calling cards for use from any telephone, private booths offering calls via mobile phones and the growing world of internet phone calls. Calling from hotels attracts a surcharge and the more expensive the hotel, the heftier the hit.

The cheapest way to call internationally is via internet phone. Most of the shops and cafes around the country providing internet services also offer internet calls. Calls usually cost between 200r and 2000r per minute, depending on the destination. Calling the USA and Europe is generally the cheapest, but there is a hefty surcharge for connecting to mobile numbers. While the price is undoubtedly right, the major drawback is that there is often a significant delay on the phone, making for a conversation of many 'hello?'s and 'pardon?'s. Using services such as Skype makes these calls a little clearer and slightly cheaper or you can hook up with a fellow Skype user for free. Most internet cafes also provide webcams, so you can see family and friends while catching up on the gossip.

M Fone offers a handy tourist SIM card. This costs US$10 and can be inserted into any unlocked phone. Calls are cheap at just US$0.25 per minute and the line is usually clear. The card lasts for seven days from activation.

If dialling from a mobile or using card phones, instead of using the original international access code of ☎ 001, try ☎ 007, which works out cheaper. The name is not Bond, but Tele2.

Mobile Phones

When travelling with a mobile phone on international roaming, just select a network upon arrival, dial away and await a hefty phone bill once you return home. Note: Cambodian roaming charges are extraordinarily high.

Those who are planning on spending longer in Cambodia will want to hook up with a local network. Those with their own phone need only purchase a SIM card for one of the local service providers, but if you are travelling with a locked phone linked to your network back home, then you can't switch SIM cards. Local phone shops can usually unlock your phone for a small charge. Mobile phones are very cheap in Cambodia and secondhand ones are widely available. Most of the local companies offer fixed-contract deals with monthly bills, or pay-as-you-go cards for those who want flexibility. All offer regular promotions, so it is worth shopping around. Note that most mobile companies now offer cheap internet-based phone calls accessed through a gateway number. Make sure you use the cheap prefix, as calls will be just US$0.25 or less per minute.

TIME

Cambodia, like Laos, Vietnam and Thailand, is seven hours ahead of Greenwich Mean Time or Universal Time Coordinated (GMT/UTC). When it is midday in Cambodia it is 10pm the previous evening in San Francisco, 1am in New York, 5am in London, 6am in Paris and 3pm in Sydney.

TOILETS

Cambodian toilets are mostly of the sit-down variety. The occasional squat toilet turns up here and there, particularly in the most budget of budget guesthouses in the provinces. If you end up in the sticks, you will find that hygiene conditions deteriorate somewhat, but rural Cambodian bathrooms are often in a better state than those in rural China or India.

The issue of toilets and what to do with used toilet paper is a cause for concern. Generally, if there's a wastepaper basket next to the toilet, that is where the toilet paper goes, as many sewerage systems cannot handle toilet paper. Toilet paper is seldom provided in the toilets at bus and train stations or in other public buildings, so keep a stash with you at all times.

Many Western toilets also have a hose spray in the bathroom, aptly named the 'bum gun' by some. Think of this as a flexible bidet, used for cleaning and ablutions as well as hosing down the loo.

Public toilets are rare, the only ones in the country being along Phnom Penh's riverfront and some beautiful wooden structures dotted about the temples of Angkor. The charge is usually 500r for a public toilet, although they are free at Angkor. Most local restaurants have some sort of toilet; pay 500r if you are not eating or drinking anything.

Should you find nature calling in rural areas, don't let modesty drive you into the bushes: *there may be land mines not far from the road or track*. Stay on the roadside and do the deed, or grin and bear it until the next town.

TOURIST INFORMATION

Cambodia has only a handful of tourist offices, and those encountered by the independent traveller in Phnom Penh and Siem Reap are generally of limited help. However, in the provinces it is a different story, as the staff are often shocked and excited to see visitors. They may have to drag the director out of a nearby karaoke bar, even at 10am, but once it is made clear that you are a genuine tourist, they will usually tell you everything there is to know about places of interest. More and more towns are ambitiously opening tourist offices, but they generally have little in the way of brochures or handouts. You'll find some tourist offices listed in the relevant destination sections in this book, but lower your expectations compared with regional powerhouses like Malaysia and Singapore. Generally, fellow travellers, guesthouses, hotels and free local magazines are more useful than tourist offices.

Cambodia has no official tourist offices abroad and it is unlikely that Cambodian embassies will be of much assistance in planning a trip, besides issuing visas, which are available on arrival anyhow.

TRAVELLERS WITH DISABILITIES

Broken pavements, potholed roads and stairs as steep as ladders at Angkor ensure that for most people with mobility impairments, Cambodia is not going to be an easy country in which to travel. Few buildings in Cambodia have been designed with the disabled in mind, although new projects, such as the international airports at Phnom Penh and Siem Reap, and top-end hotels, include ramps for wheelchair access. Transport in the provinces is usually very overcrowded, but taxi hire from point to point is an affordable option.

On the positive side, the Cambodian people are usually very helpful towards all foreigners, and local labour is cheap if you need someone to accompany you at all times. Most guesthouses and small hotels have ground-floor rooms that are reasonably easy to access.

The biggest headache also happens to be the main attraction – the temples of Angkor. Causeways are uneven, obstacles common and staircases daunting, even for able-bodied people. It is likely to be some years before things improve, although some ramping is now being introduced at major temples.

Wheelchair travellers will need to undertake a lot of research before visiting Cambodia. There is now a growing network of information sources that can put you in touch with others who have wheeled through Cambodia before. Try contacting the following:

Mobility International USA (☎ 54-1343 1284; www.miusa.org)

Royal Association for Disability and Rehabilitation (Radar; ☎ 020-7250 3222; www.radar.org.uk)

Society for Accessible Travel & Hospitality (SATH; ☎ 212-447 7284; www.sath.org)

Lonelyplanet.com has a travel forum called Thorn Tree, which is a good place to seek advice from other travellers.

VISAS

Most visitors to Cambodia require a one-month tourist visa (US$20), although some visitors enter on a one-month business visa (US$25). Most nationalities receive a one-month visa on arrival at Phnom Penh and Siem Reap airports, and at land borders, but do check if you are carrying an African, Asian or Middle Eastern passport, as there are some restrictions and conditions for citizens of some countries in these regions. One passport-sized photo is required and you'll be 'fined' US$1 if you don't have one. It is also possible to arrange a visa through Cambodian embassies overseas or an online e-visa (US$20, plus a US$5 processing fee) through the **Ministry of Foreign Affairs** (www.mfaic.gov.kh). Arranging a visa ahead of time can help prevent potential overcharging at some land crossings. However, be aware that there are some fake visa sites that have been operating out of China, so only use the official site listed here.

Those seeking work in Cambodia should opt for the business visa as, officially, it is easily extended for long periods and, unofficially, can be extended indefinitely, including multiple entries and exits. A tourist visa can be extended only once and only for one month, and does not allow for re-entry.

Travellers are sometimes overcharged when crossing at land borders with Thailand, as immigration officials demand payment in baht and round up the figure considerably. Arranging a visa in advance avoids this potential problem. Before the current border flare-up between Cambodia and Thailand, travellers making the day trip to Prasat Preah Vihear from Thailand did not require visas, but were sometimes asked to leave their passport on the Thai side of the border.

Overstaying the visa currently costs US$5 a day.

Visa Extensions

Visa extensions are issued by the large immigration office located directly across the road from Phnom Penh International Airport.

There are two ways of getting an extension (one official and one unofficial) and, unsurprisingly, the time and money involved differ greatly. Officially, a one-month extension costs US$35, three months US$65, six months US$125, and one year US$200 (note that three-, six- and 12-month extensions are only available to those with a business visa); your passport will be held for 25 days and there will be more paperwork than a communist bureaucrat could dream up. This is fine for expats with an employer to make the arrangements, but those on their own really need to go unofficial. They don't call it corruption in Cambodia but 'under the table', and you can have your passport back the next day for the inflated prices of US$45 for one month, US$80 for three months, US$165 for six months and US$265 for one year. Once you are one of the 'unofficials', it is pretty straightforward to extend the visa ad infinitum. Travel agencies and some motorbike-rental shops in Phnom Penh can help with arrangements, sometimes at a discounted price.

VOLUNTEERING

There are fewer opportunities for volunteering than one might imagine in a country as impoverished as Cambodia. This is partly due to the sheer number of professional development workers based here, and development is a pretty lucrative industry these days.

Cambodia hosts a huge number of NGOs, some of whom do require volunteers from time to time. The best way to find out who is represented in the country is to drop in on the **Cooperation Committee for Cambodia** (CCC; Map p87; ☎ 023-214152; 35 St 178) in Phnom Penh. This organisation has a handy list of all NGOs, both Cambodian and international, and is extremely helpful.

There are a couple of professional Siem Reap–based organisations helping to place volunteers. **ConCERT** (Map p134; ☎ 063-963511; www.concertcambodia.org) has a 'responsible volunteering' section on its website that offers some sound advice on preparing for a stint as a volunteer. **Globalteer** (☎ 063-761802; www.globalteer.org) coordinates the Cambodia Kids Project and offers volunteer placements with local orphanages and day centres, but this does involve a weekly charge.

Grass-roots organisations are appreciative of volunteers. Try the Lazy Gecko Café (p107) in Phnom Penh, which supports Jeannie's Orphanage, and the Starfish Bakery & Café (p219) in Sihanoukville, which helps to raise funds for local projects. Other places that can readily benefit from volunteers are certain orphanages in Phnom Penh, Siem Reap and other towns in Cambodia, as some of these are in a very rundown condition.

The other avenue is professional volunteering through an organisation back home that offers one- or two-year placements in Cambodia. One of the largest organisations is **Voluntary Service Overseas** (VSO; www.vso.org.uk) in the UK, but other countries also have their own organisations, including **Australian Volunteers International** (AVI; www.australianvolunteers.com) and New Zealand's **Volunteer Service Abroad** (VSA; www.vsa.org.nz). The UN also operates its own volunteer program; details are available at www.unv.org. Other general volunteer sites with links all over the place include www.worldvolunteerweb.com and www.volunteerabroad.com.

For general tips on voluntourism in Cambodia, visit www.voluntourism101.org.

SHOULD WE BE VISITING ORPHANAGES?

In recent years, visiting orphanages in the developing world – and Cambodia in particular – has become a popular activity, but is it always good for the children and the country in the longer run? Tough question. 'Orphan tourism' and all the connotations that come with it could be considered a scary development that is bringing unscrupulous elements into the world of caring for Cambodian children. There have already been reports of new orphanages opening up with a business model to bring in a certain number of visitors per month. In other cases, the children are not orphans at all, but are 'borrowed' from the local school for a fee.

In a report released in November 2009, Save the Children stated that most children living in orphanages throughout the developing world have at least one parent still alive. More than eight million children are living in institutions, with most sent there by their families because of poverty rather than the death of a parent. Many are in danger of abuse and neglect from carers, as well as exploitation and international trafficking, with children aged under three most at risk.

'One of the biggest myths is that children in orphanages are there because they have no parents. This is not the case,' the report said. 'Most are there because their parents simply can't afford to feed, clothe and educate them.'

Many orphanages in Cambodia are doing a good job in tough circumstances. Some are world class, enjoy funding and support from wealthy benefactors, and don't need visitors; others are desperate places that need all the help they can get. However, if a place is promoting orphan tourism, then proceed with caution, as the adults may not always have the best interests of the children at heart. Cambodia is a confusing and confounding place and it's not for us to play judge and jury, but we do believe travellers should be informed before they make a decision.

WOMEN TRAVELLERS

Women will generally find Cambodia a hassle-free place to travel, although some of the guys in the guesthouse industry will try their luck from time to time. Foreign women are unlikely to be targeted by local men, but at the same time it pays to be careful. As is the case anywhere in the world, walking or riding a bike alone late at night is risky, and if you're planning a trip off the beaten trail it would be best to find a travel companion.

Despite the prevalence of sex workers and women's employment as 'beer girls', dancing companions and the like, foreign women will probably find Khmer men to be courteous and polite. It's best to keep things this way by being restrained in your dress; flaunting a pierced belly button is likely to get the blood racing among Khmer males. Khmer women dress fairly conservatively, and it's best to follow suit, particularly when visiting wats. In general, long-sleeved shirts and long trousers or skirts are preferred. It is also worth having trousers for heading out at night on *motos*, as short skirts aren't too practical.

Tampons and sanitary napkins are widely available in the major cities and provincial capitals, but if you are heading into very remote areas for a few days, it is worth having your own supply.

WORK

Jobs are available throughout Cambodia, but apart from teaching English or helping out in guesthouses, bars or restaurants, most are for professionals and are arranged in advance. There is a lot of teaching work available for English-language speakers; salary is directly linked to experience. Anyone with an English-language teaching certificate can earn considerably more than those with no qualifications.

For information about work opportunities with NGOs call into the CCC (p335), which has a noticeboard for positions vacant and may also be able to give advice on where to look. If you are thinking of applying for work with NGOs, you should bring copies of your education certificates and work references. However, most of the jobs available are likely to be on a voluntary basis, as most recruiting for specialised positions is done in home countries or through international organisations.

Other places to look for work include the classifieds sections of the *Phnom Penh Post* and the *Cambodia Daily*, and on the noticeboards at guesthouses and restaurants in Phnom Penh.

Do not expect to make a lot of money working in Cambodia, but if you want to learn more about the country and help the locals improve their standard of living, it can be a very worthwhile experience.

Transport

CONTENTS

GETTING THERE & AWAY	**337**
Entering the Country	337
Air	337
Land	339
River	345
Tours	345
GETTING AROUND	**346**
Air	346
Bicycle	346
Boat	347
Bus	347
Car & Motorcycle	348
Hitching	350
Local Transport	350
Share Taxi & Pick-Up Trucks	352
Train	352

GETTING THERE & AWAY

ENTERING THE COUNTRY

Cambodia has two international gateways for arrival by air, Phnom Penh and Siem Reap, and a healthy selection of land borders with neighbouring Thailand, Vietnam and Laos. Formalities at Cambodia's international airports are traditionally smoother than at land borders, as the volume of traffic is greater. Crossing at land borders is relatively easy, but immigration officers may try to wangle some extra cash, either for your visa or via some other scam. Stand your ground. Anyone without a photo for their visa form will be charged about US$1 at the airport, and as much as 100B at land borders with Thailand.

Arrival by air is popular for those on a short holiday in Cambodia, as travelling overland to or from Cambodia puts a dent in your time in the country. Travellers on longer trips usually enter and exit by land, as road and river transport is very reasonably priced in Cambodia.

Passport

Not only is a passport essential, but you also need to make sure that it's valid for at least six months beyond the *end* of your trip – Cambodian immigration will not issue a visa if you have less than six months' validity left on your passport.

It's also important to make sure that there is plenty of space left in your passport. Do not set off on a six-month trek across Asia with only two blank pages left – a Cambodian visa alone takes up one page. It is sometimes possible to have extra pages added to your passport, but most people will be required to get a new passport. This is possible for most foreign nationals in Cambodia, but it can be time consuming and costly, as many embassies only process new passports in Bangkok.

Losing a passport is not the end of the world, but it is a serious inconvenience. To expedite the issuing of a new passport, keep a photocopy of your passport details somewhere separate from your passport.

For the story on visas, see p334.

AIR

Airports & Airlines

Phnom Penh International Airport (PNH; ☎ 023-890520; www.cambodia-airports.com) is the gateway to the Cambodian capital, while **Siem Reap International Airport** (REP; ☎ 063-380283; www.cambodia-airports.com) serves visitors to the temples of Angkor. Both airports have a good range of services, including restaurants, bars, shops and ATMs. **Sihanoukville International Airport** (KOS) is likely to welcome its first international flights during the lifetime of this book.

Flights to Cambodia are expanding, but most connect only as far as regional capitals.

THINGS CHANGE...

The information in this chapter is particularly vulnerable to change. Check directly with the airline or a travel agent to make sure you understand how a fare (and ticket you may buy) works and be aware of the security requirements for international travel. Shop carefully. The details given in this chapter should be regarded as pointers and are not a substitute for your own careful, up-to-date research.

CLIMATE CHANGE & TRAVEL

Climate change is a serious threat to the ecosystems that humans rely upon, and air travel is the fastest-growing contributor to the problem. Lonely Planet regards travel, overall, as a global benefit, but believes we all have a responsibility to limit our personal impact on global warming.

Flying & Climate Change

Pretty much every form of motor travel generates CO_2 (the main cause of human-induced climate change) but planes are far and away the worst offenders, not just because of the sheer distances they allow us to travel, but because they release greenhouse gases high into the atmosphere. The statistics are frightening: two people taking a return flight between Europe and the US will contribute as much to climate change as an average household's gas and electricity consumption over a whole year.

Carbon Offset Schemes

Climatecare.org and other websites use 'carbon calculators' that allow jetsetters to offset the greenhouse gases they are responsible for with contributions to energy-saving projects and other climate-friendly initiatives in the developing world – including projects in India, Honduras, Kazakhstan and Uganda.

Lonely Planet, together with Rough Guides and other concerned partners in the travel industry, supports the carbon-offset scheme run by climatecare.org. Lonely Planet offsets all of its staff and author travel.

For more information check out our website: lonelyplanet.com.

However, budget airlines have taken off in recent years and are steadily driving down prices. Bangkok offers the most connections to Cambodia, and it is usually possible to get on a flight with any of the airlines at short notice, although flying Bangkok Airways to Siem Reap can get very busy from November to March.

If you are heading to Cambodia for a short holiday and want a minimum of fuss, Thai Airways offers the easiest connections from major cities in Europe, the USA and Australia. Singapore Airlines' regional wing, Silk Air, and budget airline Jetstar offer at least one flight a day connecting Cambodia to Singapore. Other regional centres with flights to Cambodia are Ho Chi Minh City (Saigon), Hanoi, Vientiane, Luang Prabang, Pakse, Kuala Lumpur, Seoul, Taipei, Hong Kong, Guangzhou and Shanghai.

Domestic airlines in Cambodia tend to open up and close down regularly. If you have the choice, enter the country on an international carrier rather than a local outfit.

Some airlines offer open-jaw tickets into Phnom Penh and out of Siem Reap, which can save some time and money. The majority of the following telephone numbers are for Phnom Penh offices (☎ 023). See the Siem Reap section for airline offices there (p149).

AIRLINES FLYING TO/FROM CAMBODIA

Air Asia (AK; ☎ 356011; www.airasia.com) Daily budget flights connecting Phnom Penh and Siem Reap to Kuala Lumpur and Bangkok.

Asiana Airlines (OZ; ☎ 890440; www.asiana.co.kr) Regular connections between Phnom Penh and Seoul.

Bangkok Airways (PG; ☎ 722545; www.bangkokair.com) Daily connections from Phnom Penh and Siem Reap to Bangkok.

Cambodia Angkor Airways (K6; ☎ 6666786; www.cambodiaangkorair.com) Daily connections from Phnom Penh and Siem Reap to Ho Chi Minh City (Saigon).

China Eastern Airlines (MU; ☎ 063-965229; www.ce-air.com) Regular flights from Siem Reap to Kunming.

China Southern Airlines (CZ; ☎ 430877; www.cs-air.com) Regular flights from Phnom Penh to Guangzhou.

Dragon Air (KA; ☎ 424300; www.dragonair.com) Daily flights between Phnom Penh and Hong Kong.

Eva Air (BR; ☎ 219911; www.evaair.com) Daily flights between Phnom Penh and Taipei.

Jetstar (3K; ☎ 220909; www.jetstar.com) Daily budget flights from both Phnom Penh and Siem Reap to Singapore.

Korean Air (KE; ☎ 224047; www.koreanair.com) Regular flights connecting Phnom Penh and Siem Reap with Seoul and Incheon.

Lao Airlines (QV; ☎ 216563; www.laoairlines.com) Regular flights from Phnom Penh and Siem Reap to both Pakse and Vientiane.

Malaysia Airlines (MY; ☎ 426688; www.malaysiaair lines.com) Daily connections from Phnom Penh and Siem Reap to Kuala Lumpur.

Shanghai Airlines (FM; ☎ 723999; www.shang hai-air.com) Regular flights linking Phnom Penh with Shanghai.

Siem Reap Airways (FT; ☎ 720022; www.siemreap airways.com) Services were suspended for much of 2009 and into early 2010, but usually connects Siem Reap and Phnom Penh to Hong Kong.

Silk Air (MI; ☎ 426807; www.silkair.com) Daily flights linking Phnom Penh and Siem Reap with Singapore, plus some flights between Siem Reap and Danang.

Thai Airways (TG; ☎ 214359; www.thaiair.com) Daily flights connecting Phnom Penh and Bangkok.

Vietnam Airlines (VN; ☎ 363396; www.vietnamair.com. vn) Daily flights linking both Phnom Penh and Siem Reap with both Hanoi and Ho Chi Minh City, as well as Phnom Penh and Vientiane, and Siem Reap with Luang Prabang.

Tickets

When buying airline tickets, it is always worth shopping around. Buying direct from the airline is usually more expensive, unless the airline has a special promotion or you are flying with a budget carrier offering online deals. As a rule, it is better to book as early as possible, as prices only get higher as the seats fill up.

The time of year has a major impact on flight prices. Starting out from Europe, North America or Australia, figure on prices rising dramatically over Christmas and during July and August, and dropping significantly during lax periods of business like February, June and October.

Thailand – political problems aside – is the most convenient gateway to Cambodia when travelling from outside the region. In Bangkok, the Banglamphu area, especially Khao San Rd, is a good place to buy tickets to Cambodia. Those who are travelling into Cambodia by air through Vietnam can easily pick up tickets in Ho Chi Minh City.

When buying tickets in Cambodia, the main agents are in Phnom Penh, although

many now operate branch offices in Siem Reap. Agents can normally save you a few dollars on the airline price, much more for long-haul flights or business-class seats.

To research and buy a ticket on the internet, try these services:

Cheapflights (www.cheapflights.com) No-frills website with a number of destinations.

Kayak (www.kayak.com) Reliable fare-comparison website.

Lonely Planet (www.lonelyplanet.com) Use the Trip Planner service to book multistop trips.

Lowest Fare (www.lowestfare.com) They promise…'the lowest fares'.

STA Travel (www.statravel.com) Leading student-travel agency with cheap fares, plus separate websites for the UK, Australia and New Zealand.

Trailfinders (www.trailfinders.co.uk) Popular UK flight specialist.

Travel.com (www.travel.com) This website also has numerous destinations.

Travelocity (www.travelocity.com) Popular US website for flights.

LAND

For years, overland travellers were restricted to entering or exiting Cambodia at the Bavet–Moc Bai border crossing with Vietnam. However, lots of new land crossings between Cambodia and its neighbours have opened, offering overland connections with Laos, Thailand and Vietnam. However, many of the newly opened borders are in relatively off-the-beaten-path destinations and are aimed at promoting trade more than serving tourists. For the latest on Cambodian border crossings, check out the Immigration Department website at http://cambodia -immigration.com.

Border Crossings

Cambodia shares one border crossing with Laos, six crossings with Thailand and eight with Vietnam. Cambodian visas are now available at all the land crossings with Laos, Thailand and Vietnam. There are some crossings that remain closed to foreigners due to ongoing tensions between Cambodia and Thailand, including the border at Prasat Preah Vihear (p280). There are also many more locals-only crossings that foreigners are not currently permitted to use.

ATMs offering cash advances are found near the Cham Yeam and Poipet borders with Thailand. However, at the rest of the borders, there are very few moneychanging facilities

---

INTERNATIONAL DEPARTURE TAX

There is a departure tax of US$25, payable by cash or credit card, on all international flights out of both Phnom Penh International Airport and Siem Reap International Airport.

TRANSPORT

on the Cambodian side, so be sure to have some small-denomination US dollars handy or baht if crossing from Thailand. Market stalls are an option for changing local currencies – Vietnamese dong, Lao kip and Thai baht. Remember that black marketeers have a well-deserved reputation for short-changing or outright theft.

Cambodian immigration officers at the land border crossings – especially with Thailand – have a bad reputation for petty extortion. Travellers are occasionally asked for a small 'immigration fee' of some kind, particularly when entering via the Lao or Thai borders. More serious scams include overcharging for visas by demanding payment in Thai baht (anywhere between 1000B and 1300B instead of 700B) and forcing tourists to change US dollars into riel at a poor rate. Hold your breath, stand your ground, don't start a fight and remember that not all Cambodians are as mercenary as the boys in blue.

Senior government officials in Phnom Penh are trying to crack down on overcharging for visas and general petty extortion at the borders, as it gives Cambodia a bad image. In order to help bring an end to this, we suggest you covertly take the name of any official demanding extra money at the border and pass it on to the Tourist Police in Phnom Penh or Siem Reap.

LAOS

Cambodia and Laos share a remote frontier that includes some of the wildest areas of both countries. There is only one border crossing open to foreigners.

Trapaeng Kriel–Dong Kalaw

The border between Cambodia and Laos is officially open from 8am to 4pm daily. It is very popular as an adventurous and cheap way to combine travel to northeastern Cambodia and southern Laos. It has traditionally been a confusing border due to two possible entry and exit points and the border recently (late 2009) moved 4km further north to Trapaeng Kriel (formerly Dom Kralor), about 65km north of Stung Treng.

To enter Cambodia using this route, visas are available on arrival at Trapaeng Kriel. The great news is that with the new border post, Lao visas are also finally available on arrival, ranging from US$30 to US$42 depending on nationality. Both sides of the border seem to charge a processing fee for those crossing, ranging from US$1 at any time (US$3 to US$4 after hours). Probably a hardship allowance for working the beat on this remote border.

To leave Cambodia, travel to the remote town of Stung Treng (p302). From Stung Treng there are minibuses (US$5) heading north to the border at around 7am or so and again just after lunch, but as onward transport is almost nonexistent on the Lao side it may be best to book a transfer on to Ban Nakasong (US$2) in Laos, which guesthouses can help arrange. Otherwise try and arrange a *moto* for about US$4. There are also a couple of buses during the day, including Rith Mony at about

CAMBODIA BORDER CROSSINGS AT A GLANCE

Country	Border Crossing	Connecting
Cambodia/Laos	Trapaeng Kriel/Dong Kalaw	Stung Treng/Si Phan Done
Cambodia/Thailand	Poipet/Aranya Prathet	Siem Reap/Bangkok
	Cham Yeam/Hat Lek	Krong Koh Kong/Trat
	O Smach/Chong Jom	Samraong/Surin
	Choam/Choam Srawngam	Anlong Veng/Sangkha
	Psar Pruhm/Ban Pakard	Pailin/Chantaburi
	Kamrieng/Daun Lem	Battambang/Chanthaburi
Cambodia/Vietnam	Bavet/Moc Bai	Phnom Penh/Ho Chi Minh City
	Kaam Samnor/Vinh Xuong	Phnom Penh/Chau Doc
	Prek Chak/Xa Xia	Kampot/Ha Tien
	Phnom Den/Tinh Bien	Takeo/Chau Doc
	O'Yadaw/Le Tanh	Ban Lung/Pleiku
	Trapaeng Plong/Xa Mat	Kompong Cham/Tay Ninh
	Trapaeng Sre/Loc Ninh	Snuol/Loc Ninh
	Banteay Chakrey/Khanh Binh	Neak Luong/An Phu

8am and Phnom Penh Sorya Transport (from Phnom Penh) after 3pm, the latter continuing to Pakse.

Riverside Guesthouse (p302) in Stung Treng has boats (from US$50 for the boat, two hours) that can be chartered up the Mekong from Stung Treng. They take up to six people, but drop you in Anlong Seima (formerly known as Voen Khao), a Cambodian village near the old Lao border crossing of Voen Kham. Confused? We know the feeling. However, the boat trip can incorporate dolphin viewing, making it better value than a straight transfer.

Heading south, most of the above can be done in reverse. The minibuses head back to Stung Treng any time after 8.30am and the buses both depart the border around 10am or so. If you are stuck, it might be possible to charter a minibus for about US$30 and a *moto* for around US$10 if you bargain hard.

Another option is to take one of the dirt-cheap boat trips advertised on Don Khone and Don Khong, costing just a few dollars, which include the waterfalls and dolphin viewing. Once you get to Voen Kham and the dolphin viewing, jump ship and arrange a motorbike to take you to the immigration post on the main highway.

A word of warning about 'through buses' from southern Laos to Siem Reap: a number of travellers have reported being made to change bus in Kompong Cham and being charged another US$5 for the privilege of continuing to Siem Reap.

THAILAND

Cambodia and Thailand share an 805km border and there are now six legal international border crossings, and many more options for locals. Land borders with Thailand are open from 7am to 8pm daily. Tourist visas are available at all crossings for US$20. There are now clear signs displaying the US$20 charge, but many people are still charged 1000B or more. For the latest sagas on land crossings between Thailand and Cambodia, visit www.talesofasia.com.

Poipet–Aranya Prathet

The original land border crossing between Cambodia and Thailand has earned itself a bad reputation in recent years, with scams galore to help tourists part with their money. See the boxed text, p342, for more details.

There are two slow trains a day from Hualamphong train station in Bangkok to the Thai border town of Aranya Prathet (48B, six hours); take the 5.55am service unless you want to spend the night in a border town. There are also regular bus services from Bangkok's Mo Chit northern terminal to Aranya Prathet (1st/2nd class 215/125B, four to five hours). From Aranya Prathet, take a *tuk tuk* (motorised three-wheeled pedicab, 80b) or local bus (15b) for the final six kilometres to the border.

Once across the border, try not to get roped into the 'free' tourist shuttle to the 'International Tourist Terminal' (p262), which arranges transport to major cities, but at inflated prices: Phnom Penh (US$15, seven hours); Siem Reap (US$9, two hours); or Battambang (US$10, two hours). Stay solo and walk to the bus company offices for cheaper fares. The vast majority of the buses depart very early in the morning (before 8am). It is also possible to negotiate taxis if you can avoid the International Tourist Terminal. Aim to pay no more than US$30 to Siem Reap or Battambang.

The road to Siem Reap (153km) is now in superb condition, making the onward journey to Siem Reap less than two hours in a good vehicle.

Leaving Cambodia, it is easy enough to get to Poipet from Siem Reap, Battambang or even Phnom Penh. By land there is no departure tax to leave Cambodia. From Poipet, take a *tuk tuk* to Aranya Prathet, from where there are regular buses to Bangkok between 4am and 10pm or the slow train at 1.55pm.

Cham Yeam–Hat Lek

The Cham Yeam–Hat Lek border crossing, between Cambodia's Krong Koh Kong and Trat in Thailand, is popular with travellers linking the beaches of Cambodia and Thailand. It offers connections from Bangkok, Ko Samet and Ko Chang to the Cardamom Mountains, Sihanoukville and Phnom Penh. It gets very busy – and slow – on Fridays, when lots of Cambodians cross into Thailand for a weekly market.

Coming from Bangkok, take a bus to Trat (from 223B, five to six hours) from the city's Eastern or North & Northeastern bus stations. Buses depart regularly from 6am until 11.30pm. Another convenient option for travellers staying in the Khao San Rd area is

TRANSPORT

WELCOME TO SCAMBODIA

Poipet is a Wild West kind of place and has attracted a lot of unsavoury characters clinging to the coat-tails of the economic boom. Unfortunately, many of these are involved in the travel business and carry on like some sort of mafia, giving Cambodia a bad name. The Cham Yeam border, near Koh Kong, is not much better and notorious for overcharging for visas. Below are some tips to navigate the maze, but rest assured that not everyone in Cambodia is out to scam you.

To avoid any visa overcharging at Bavet, Cham Yeam and Poipet, it may be worth arranging an **e-visa** (www.mfaic.gov.kh; US$20 plus a processing fee of US$5) in advance. It takes three days to issue and you can exit at any land border crossing.

Poipet–Aranya Prathet

Right after you cross the stinky stream that marks the border, you come to 'Cambodian Visa Service', where the price of a tourist visa is posted as US$20. However, before you make it this far, plenty of enterprising people will have expended lots of creative energy in trying to make you part with up to double the dollars for the visa.

A Cambodian 'consulate' has been set up inside Thailand, but there are no marked prices and 'officials' try to charge anywhere between 1000B and 1300B (US$30 to US$39) for the visa. Various techniques are employed, including the line that visas are no longer available at Poipet or that the visa will take two or three days to issue at the border. The trick is to survive the Thai side and make it to the 'Cambodian Visa Service' counter. Pay for the visa in US dollars only, as if you pay in Thai baht, then the charge will immediately jump up to 800B to 1000B.

For more details on the Poipet shenanigans, see p262.

Cham Yeam–Hat Lek

At the time of writing, immigration officials at the Cham Yeam border are demanding 1200B (US$36) for a tourist visa that should cost US$20. Government employees in Cambodia are notoriously underpaid and many 'buy' their jobs from senior officials. This involves a 'monthly fee' to keep the position and it seems tourists are being made to foot the bill.

We have heard reports of polite and persistent travellers who have managed to pay just US$25 or even US$20 (by claiming they only have US dollars, asking for a receipt or threatening to complain to the Ministry of Foreign Affairs or Interior in Phnom Penh), but these visas tend to be processed *very* slowly. Others have been told that if they don't pay the 1200B fee, then they can go back to Thailand.

---

to take one of the minibuses bound for Koh Chang, getting off at Trat.

From Trat, take a minibus straight to the Thai border at Hat Lek (120B). Once on the Cambodian side of the border you can take a *moto* (motorcycle with driver; 100B plus 11B toll) or taxi (200B plus 44B toll) to Krong Koh Kong.

It is now quick and easy to travel by road from Krong Koh Kong to Phnom Penh or Sihanoukville. The road is surfaced with four major bridges, bringing journey times down dramatically. See p199 for details.

The fast boat services that used to connect Krong Koh Kong with Sihanoukville have been suspended for some time, although they could resume during the lifetime of this book.

Leaving Cambodia, take a taxi or *moto* from Krong Koh Kong across the toll bridge to the border. Once in Thailand, catch a minibus to Trat from where there are regular buses to Bangkok. Alternatively, stay the night in Trat and then head to Ko Chang or the surrounding islands the following day.

Other Crossings

Several more out-of-the-way crossings are open for international traffic. The **O Smach–Chong Jom** (see p267) crossing connects Cambodia's Oddar Meanchey Province and Thailand's Surin Province, but it is very remote. Share taxis link Siem Reap (30,000r, four hours) with Samraong via NH68. From Samraong, take a *moto* (250B) or a charter taxi (US$25) for the punishing drive to O Smach (40km, nearly two hours) and its frontier casino zone. On the Thai side, it's easy, as *sawngthaew* (pick-ups) and *motos* take arrivals to the bus stop for Surin (70km, 1½hr). Cambodian visas are available for US$20 plus a US$2 'processing fee'. Sometimes 1000B is requested.

The **Choam–Choam Srawngam** crossing, a short distance from the site of Pol Pot's cremation, is 16km north of Anlong Veng or 134km north of Siem Reap. From Anlong Veng, a sealed road heads up to the border (10,000r to 15,000r by *moto*). The swanky Thai border complex is mothballed, as the Cambodians argue it is on their territory. Instead, head to the old crossing a few hundred metres east, next to the old smugglers market. Visa fees seem to be US$22, but service is fast and with a smile. On the Thai side, you are in a pretty remote area, but there are some *sawngthaew* to Phusing, which has bus connections to Kantharalak or Si Saket. It may be possible to charter a vehicle direct to Si Saket. For transport options from Anlong Veng to Siem Reap (on a great new road) and Sra Em (near Prasat Preah Vihear), see p271.

The border at **Psar Pruhm–Ban Pakard** is 102km southwest of Battambang and 22km northwest of Pailin via rapidly improving roads. To travel this way independently, take a bus from Bangkok to Chanthaburi (160B, four hours) and then a minibus from there to Ban Pakard (150B, 1½ hours). A private taxi from Chanthaburi to Ban Pakard is about 1000B. On the Cambodian side, visas cost US$20 or 800B and the crossing is hassle-free. Cross the Cambodian border into the casino area and then arrange transport to Pailin (p260).

There is another remote border at **Kamrieng–Daun Lem** in Battambang Province, but it is really just an outpost with a casino catering to Thai gamblers and not very accessible from the Cambodian side.

There is also a crossing for visa-less day trips at **Prasat Preah Vihear** (p279), the stunning Cambodian temple perched atop the Dangkrek mountains. It is currently closed due to an armed confrontation between Cambodia and Thailand over border demarcation in the area. We are hoping that it may, however, reopen during the lifetime of this book.

VIETNAM
Cambodia and Vietnam share a long frontier with a bevy of border crossings. Foreigners are currently permitted to cross at eight places and there are new crossings opening every year. Cambodian visas are now available at all crossings. Vietnamese visas should be arranged in advance, as they are not available on arrival. Luckily, Cambodia is the easiest place in the world to pick up Vietnamese visas. It is no longer necessary to stipulate your exact point of entry and exit on the Vietnam visa, or the exact date of arrival, making for the sort of carefree travel overlanders prefer.

Bavet–Moc Bai
The original land crossing between Vietnam and Cambodia has seen steady traffic for nearly two decades. The trip by bus between Phnom Penh and Ho Chi Minh City takes about five to seven hours, including the border crossing, although it can take a lot longer before and after festivals. There are now lots of companies offering direct services with no need to change buses. Choose from Capitol Tour, GST, Mai Linh, Mekong Express, Phnom Penh Sorya, Sapaco and more. All charge between US$9 and US$12; see p120 for contact details. Some frequent travellers suggest it is best to take a Vietnamese bus company when travelling to Ho Chi Minh City (Mai Linh or Sapaco) and a Cambodian bus company when travelling to Phnom Penh.

Kaam Samnor–Vinh Xuong
Cambodia and Vietnam opened their border on the Mekong back in 2000 and it is now very popular with independent travellers. It is a far more interesting trip than taking the road, as it involves a fast boat on the Mekong in Cambodia and travel along some very picturesque areas of the Mekong Delta in Vietnam. Coming from Ho Chi Minh City, it is possible to book a cheap Mekong Delta tour through to Chau Doc and then make your own way from there.

There are several boat companies offering direct services between Phnom Penh and Chau Doc. **Capitol Tour** (☎ 023 217627; slow/fast boat US$10/17) is the cheapest option offering a combination of road to Neak Luong and river to Chau Doc. Departing at 7.30am daily, the fast boat option takes five hours, the slow boat eight hours. **Hang Chau** (Map p87; ☎ 012-883542; slow/fast boat US$15/24) pulls out from Chau Doc at 9am and departs Phnom Penh at noon.

TRANSPORT

The more upmarket **Blue Cruiser** (Map p87; ☎ 016-824343; 93 Sisowath Quay; US$35) departs Chau Doc at 8.30am and Phnom Penh at 1.30pm. Both take about three hours or so. **Victoria Hotels** (www.victoriahotels-asia.com; US$80) also has a boat making several runs a week between Phnom Penh and its Victoria Chau Doc Hotel. All of these boats depart from the Tourist Boat Dock (Map p87) in Phnom Penh.

Adventurous travellers can plot their own course. From the west bank of the Mekong in Neak Luong (p291), ask around for outboards to Kaam Samnor – they leave from a small pier 300m south of the ferry. There is also a slow boat (US$4) operated by **Ly Kim Hong** (☎ 011-806606 in Neak Luong), which leaves around 9am and takes more than two hours. Or charter a speedboat for about US$50 (one hour). There are separate offices for immigration and customs on both sides of the border, so it can end up taking as much as an hour to navigate. Luggage has to be x-rayed on the Vietnamese side of the border. Once officially in Vietnam at the village of Vinh Xuong, catch a minibus to Chau Doc (US$2, one hour) or negotiate for a *xe om (moto)* for around US$5. Those entering Cambodia via Vinh Xuong can just run the aforementioned route in reverse.

Lastly, there are several companies offering luxury cruises between Ho Chi Minh City and Siem Reap via the Kaam Samnor–Vinh Xuong border crossing. International player **Pandaw Cruises** (www.pandaw.com) is an expensive option favoured by high-end tour companies. Cambodian company **Toum Teav Cruises** (www.cf-mekong.com) is smaller and is well regarded for its personal service and excellent food. Newcomers **Indochina Sails** (www.indochina-sails.com), operating *RV La Marguerite*, and **Heritage Line** (www.heritage-line.com), with the *Jayavarman VII*, look to be taking the competition to a new level on this route. However, the full seven-day cruises mean a lot of time on the water with similar scenery as company. It's arguably better just to opt for a shorter sector such as Ho Chi Minh City to Phnom Penh or Phnom Penh to Siem Reap.

Prek Chak–Xa Xia

The Prek Chak–Xa Xia crossing (open from 6am to 5.30pm) connects Kep and Kampot with the Mekong Delta town of Ha Tien. This crossing offers the prospect of linking the Cambodian coast with the beautiful Vietnamese island of Phu Quoc, formerly the Cambodian island of Koh Tral. There is still little in the way of regular transport, but expect bus services to start at some stage. For now, it is possible to take a *moto* from Kompong Trach (US$3), Kep (US$8) or Kampot (US$10) to the border, cross into Vietnam and take a *xe om (moto)* to Ha Tien (US$2). It is also possible to charter a taxi from Kampot (US$25) or pay for a seat in a share taxi (US$5) to the border.

There are also well-founded rumours that a ferry may soon link Kep with Vietnam's Phu Quoc island, as evidenced by the international boat terminal that has been built near Kep harbour.

Other Crossings

It's open season when it comes to border crossings between Cambodia and Vietnam, but many are a little out of the way for the average traveller.

The **Phnom Den–Tinh Bien** crossing (7am to 5pm) has been open for some time now, but is rarely used, as most travellers prefer the Mekong crossing at Kaam Samnor or the newer Prek Chak crossing to the south. It lies about 60km southeast of Takeo town in Cambodia and offers connections to Chau Doc. A seat in a minibus will cost about 5000r from Takeo to the border if you get going early enough. Otherwise a *moto* will cost about US$8.

There is a border crossing in Ratanakiri province at **O'Yadaw–Le Tanh** (open from 7am to 5pm), offering connections between Ban Lung and Pleiku, in Vietnam's central highlands. NH19 from Ban Lung to the O'Yadaw border is in good shape and traffic is picking up. Pick-ups (inside/outside 15,000/10,000r) or share taxis (US$5) run to the O'Yadaw town, about 25km from the border. From there it's a charter or a hitch to the border. Easier is the through minibus to O'Yadaw (40,000r, 7.30am). Tarmac beckons on the Vietnamese side, with a *xe om* ride to Duc Co and then bus connections to Pleiku. In reverse, the minibus heads back to Ban Lung around noon or you can charter a taxi for US$40.

There is a cluster of border crossings in the east of Cambodia that connect obscure towns and are not really on the radar. The **Trapaeng Plong–Xa Mat** (open from 7am to 5pm) and

Trapaeng Sre–Loc Ninh (7am to 5pm) crossings are both off NH7 and the Xa Mat crossing could be useful for those planning to visit the Cao Dai temple travelling to or from Ho Chi Minh City. Travelling from Cambodia to Vietnam, hop off a bus at Krek and take a *moto* to Trapaeng Plong (US$2, 12km). Cross over and then take a bus to Tan Bien for connections to Tay Ninh or a *xe om (moto)* to Tay Ninh (about US$10, 40km).

The **Banteay Chakrey–Khanh Binh** crossing is really out of the way and sees almost no foreign travellers.

Bus

It is possible to use buses to cross into Cambodia from Laos, Thailand or Vietnam. The most popular way to or from Vietnam is a cheap bus via Bavet on the Cambodian side and Moc Bai in Vietnam. From Thailand, many travellers make the overland trip from Bangkok to Siem Reap via the Poipet–Aranya Prathet border crossing, or from Bangkok or Trat to Krong Koh Kong or Sihanoukville via the Cham Yeam–Hat Lek crossing. There are now several companies offering cross-border buses between Phnom Penh or Stung Treng and Pakse in southern Laos.

Car & Motorcycle

Car drivers and motorcycle riders will need registration papers, insurance documents and an International Driving Licence (although not officially recognised) to bring vehicles into Cambodia. It is complicated to bring in a car, but relatively straightforward to bring in a motorcycle, as long as you have a *carnet de passage* (vehicle passport). This acts as a temporary import-duty waiver and should save a lot of hassles when dealing with Cambodian customs. Increasing numbers of international bikers are crossing into Cambodia, while most of the foreign cars that tend to make it are Thai-registered.

RIVER

There is a river border crossing between Cambodia and Vietnam on the banks of the Mekong. There are regular fast passenger boats plying the route between Phnom Penh and Chau Doc in Vietnam, via the Kaam Samnor–Vinh Xuong border crossing. There are also several luxurious riverboats running between Ho Chi Minh City and the temples of Angkor.

TOURS

In the early days of tourism in Cambodia, organised tours were a near necessity. The situation has changed dramatically and it is now much easier to organise your own trip. Budget and midrange travellers in particular can go it alone, as arrangements are cheap and easy on the ground. If you are on a tight schedule, it can pay to book a domestic flight in advance if planning to link the temples of Angkor and Siem Reap with Cambodia's capital, Phnom Penh. Once at Angkor, guides and all forms of transport under the sun are plentiful.

Shop around before booking a tour, as there is lots of competition and some companies, such as those listed here, offer more interesting itineraries than others. There are also several good companies based in Cambodia that are trying to put a little something back into the country.

Australia

Adventure World (☎ 02-8913 0755; www.adventure world.com.au) Offers adventure tours of Cambodia, as well as neighbouring Vietnam and Laos.

Intrepid Travel (☎ 1300 360 667; www.intrepidtravel. com.au) Small group tours for all budgets with an environmental, social and cultural edge.

Peregrine (☎ 02-9290 2770; www.peregrineadven tures.com) Small group and private tours supporting responsible tourism.

Cambodia

About Asia (☎ 855-92 121059; www.asiatravel-cam bodia.com) Small bespoke travel company specialising in Siem Reap and Cambodia with a growing reputation. Profits help build schools in Cambodia.

Cambodia Expeditions (☎ 855-12 583759; www. cambodiaexpeditions.com) Adventurous outfit promoting motorbike tours, expeditions and trekking tours.

Hanuman Tourism (☎ 855-23 218396; www. hanumantourism.com) Long-running locally owned, locally operated company with innovative tours like Temple Safari.

Journeys Within (☎ 855-63 964748; www.journeys -within.com) A boutique tourism company offering trips to Cambodia and the Mekong region. Operates a small boutique hotel in Siem Reap and has a charitable arm (see www.journeyswithinourcommunity.org for more information) helping schools and communities.

Local Adventures (☎ 855-23 990460; www. cambodia.nl) Cambodian-based company specialising in off-the-beaten-path tours to the less-visited regions of the country. Assists Cambodian children through the Cambodian Organisation for Learning and Training (www. colt-cambodia.org).

TRANSPORT

PEPY Ride (☎ 855-23 222804; www.pepyride.org) Specialist cycling company that runs adventurous bike rides through Cambodia to raise funds to build schools and improve education. Also offers noncycling trips.

Sam Veasna Center (☎ 855-63 761597; www. samveasna.org) Established ecotourism operator specialising in birdwatching tours around Cambodia, including Ang Trapeang Thmor and Ttamboey. Supports conservation and education.

France

Compagnie des Indes & Orients (☎ 01-5363-3340; www.compagniesdumonde.com) Offers organised tours covering more of Cambodia than most.

Intermedes (☎ 01-4561-9090; www.intermedes.com) Offers specialised private tours.

La Route des Indes (☎ 01-4260-6090; www.laroute desindes.com) High-end tours with an academic edge.

UK

Audley Travel (☎ 01604-234855; www.audleytravel. com) Popular tailor-made specialist covering Cambodia.

Bamboo Travel (☎ 020-7720 9285; www.bamboo travel.co.uk) Offers innovative and off-the-beaten-track itineraries around Cambodia and Indochina.

Carpe Diem (☎ 0845-2262198; www.carpe-diem -travel.com) Not-for-profit travel company specialising in original adventures in Cambodia and Laos.

Hands Up Holidays (☎ 0776-501 3631; www.hands upholidays.com) A popular company bringing guests closer to the people of Cambodia through its responsible holidays with a spot of volunteering.

Mekong Travel (☎ 01494-674456; www.mekong -travel.com) A name to inspire confidence in the Mekong region.

Symbiosis (☎ 020-7924 5906; www.symbiosis-travel. com) Small bespoke travel company with an emphasis on cycling and diving.

Wild Frontiers (☎ 020-7376 3968; www.wildfrontiers. co.uk) Adventure specialist with themed tours and innovative adventures.

USA

Asia Transpacific Journeys (☎ 800-642 2742, www. asiatranspacific.com) Group tours and tailor-made trips across the Asia-Pacific region.

Distant Horizons (☎ 800-333 1240; www.distanthori zons.com) Educational tours for discerning travellers.

Geographic Expeditions (☎ 800-777 8183; www. geoex.com) Well-established high-end adventure-travel company.

Myths & Mountains (☎ 800-670 6984; www.myths andmountains.com) Voted one of Nat Geo Adventure's Top Ten Best Travel Companies.

GETTING AROUND

AIR
Airlines in Cambodia

Domestic flights offer a quick way to travel around the country. The problem is that the airlines themselves seem to come and go pretty quickly. There is currently only one domestic airline fully operational in Cambodia, **Cambodia Angkor Airways** (K6; ☎ 023-424496; www. cambodiaangkorair.com; hub Phnom Penh), and that operates almost as an offshoot of Vietnam Airlines. It serves the Phnom Penh to Siem Reap route with modern ATRs from France. There should finally be flights between Sihanoukville and Siem Reap sometime during the lifetime of this book. There are currently no flights to Ratanakiri.

There are up to four flights a day between Phnom Penh and Siem Reap (from US$75/120 one way/return) and it is usually possible to get on a flight at short notice. Book ahead in peak season.

The baggage allowance for domestic flights is only 10kg for each passenger, but unless you are way over the limit it is unlikely you will have to pay for excess baggage.

Helicopter

Helicopters Cambodia (☎ 023-213706; www.helicopters cambodia.com) has offices in Phnom Penh and Siem Reap and operates reliable choppers that are available for hire. It mostly operates scenic flights around Angkor, but can be chartered for any journey. Newcomer Helistar has also moved into this business.

BICYCLE

Cambodia is a great country for adventurous cyclists to explore. Needless to say, given the country's legendary potholes, a mountain bike is the best bet. Basic cycling safety equipment and authentic spare parts are also in short supply, so bring all this from home. A bell is essential – the louder the better – as are bright lights (front and rear). Many roads

---

DOMESTIC DEPARTURE TAX

The airport tax for domestic flights is US$6 from Phnom Penh and Siem Reap airports, but is usually included in the ticket price these days.

remain in bad condition, but there is usually a flat unpaved trail along the side. Travelling at such a gentle speed allows for much more interaction with the locals. Although bicycles are common in Cambodian villages, cycling tourists are still very much a novelty and will be wildly welcomed in most small villages. In many parts of the country there are new dirt tracks being laid down for motorcycles and bicycles, and these are a wonderful way to travel into remote parts of Cambodia.

Much of Cambodia is pancake flat or only moderately hilly. Safety, however, is a considerable concern on the newer surfaced roads, as local traffic travels at high speed. Bicycles can be transported around the country in the back of pick-ups or on the roof of minibuses.

Cycling around Angkor is an awesome experience as it really helps to get a measure of the size and scale of the temple complex. Mountain biking is likely to take off in Mondulkiri and Ratanakiri Provinces over the coming years, as there are some great trails off the beaten track. It is already a reality around Chi Phat (p206) in the Cardamom Mountains. Guesthouses and hotels throughout Cambodia rent out bicycles for around US$2 per day, or US$7 to US$10 for an imported named brand like Trek. Repair stalls are never far away.

For the full story on cycle touring in Cambodia, see Lonely Planet's *Cycling Vietnam, Laos & Cambodia,* which has the lowdown on planning a major ride.

PEPY Ride (☎ 023-222-804; www.pepyride.org) is a bicycle and volunteer tour company offering adventures throughout Cambodia. PEPY promotes 'adventurous living, responsible giving' and uses proceeds to help build schools in rural Cambodia and fund education programs.

BOAT

Cambodia's 1900km of navigable waterways are not as important as they once were for the average tourist, given major road improvements. North of Phnom Penh, the Mekong is easily navigable as far as Kratie, but there are no longer regular passenger services on these routes, as the roads have taken all the business. There are scenic boat services between Siem Reap and Battambang, and the Tonlé Sap Lake is also navigable year-round, although only by smaller boats between March and July.

Traditionally the most popular boat services with foreigners are those that run between Phnom Penh and Siem Reap (p120). The express services do the trip in as little as five hours, but it is not the most interesting boat journey in Cambodia, as the Tonlé Sap Lake is like a vast sea, offering little scenery. It's much smarter (and much cheaper) to take a bus on the paved road instead. If you end up on the roof of the boat, remember to use sunblock and wear a head covering.

The small boat between Siem Reap and Battambang (p255) is more rewarding, as the river scenery is truly memorable, but it can take forever.

BUS

The range of road transport is extensive in Cambodia. On sealed roads, the large air-conditioned buses are the best choice. Elsewhere in the country, a share taxi or minibus is the way to go.

Bus services have come on in leaps and bounds in the last few years and the situation is getting even better as more roads are upgraded. Bus travel is arguably the safest way to get around the country these days. The services used most regularly by foreigners are those from Phnom Penh to Siem Reap, Battambang, Sihanoukville, Kompong Cham and Kratie, and the tourist buses from Siem Reap to Poipet.

There is a clean and comfortable bus service to towns and villages in the vicinity of Phnom Penh, such as Udong and Phnom Chisor. Operated by **Phnom Penh Sorya Transport** (Map p87; www.ppsoryatransport.com; ☎ 210359; Psar Thmei), these services are cheap and English-speaking staff can direct you onto the right bus.

WARNING

Many more people are now killed and injured each month in traffic accidents than by land mines. While this is partly down to land-mine awareness efforts and ongoing clearance programs, it is also down to a huge rise in the number of vehicles on the roads and drivers travelling at dangerous speeds. Be extremely vigilant when travelling under your own steam and take care crossing the roads on the high-speed national highways. It is best not to travel on the roads at night due to a higher prevalence of accidents at this time. This especially applies to bikers, as several foreigners are killed each year in motorbike accidents.

TRANSPORT

ROAD DISTANCES (KM)

	Phnom Penh	Siem Reap	Sihanoukville	Ban Lung	Battambang	Bavet (Vietnam)	Kampot	Koh Kong	Kompong Cham	Kompong Thom	Kratie	Poipet (Thailand)	Sen Monorom	Stung Treng	Takeo	Tbeng Meanchey
Phnom Penh	-															
Siem Reap	316	-														
Sihanoukville	230	546	-													
Ban Lung	545	715	775	-												
Battambang	293	171	523	838	-											
Bavet (Vietnam)	169	485	399	634	462	-										
Kampot	148	464	105	693	441	317	-									
Koh Kong	280	596	230	825	573	449	235	-								
Kompong Cham	120	290	350	425	413	214	268	300	-							
Kompong Thom	165	151	395	564	322	334	313	445	140	-						
Kratie	258	574	488	287	551	342	406	538	138	277	-					
Poipet (Thailand)	410	152	640	867	117	579	558	690	442	303	580	-				
Sen Monorom	370	540	600	155	663	410	518	650	250	389	215	692	-			
Stung Treng	399	569	629	165	692	439	547	679	279	418	141	721	356	-		
Takeo	75	391	190	620	368	244	85	355	195	240	333	485	445	474	-	
Tbeng Meanchey	302	288	532	701	459	501	450	582	276	137	414	440	526	555	377	-

Minibuses serve most provincial routes, but are not widely used by Western visitors. They are very cheap, but often uncomfortably overcrowded and sometimes driven by maniacs. Only really consider them if there is no alternative. 'Express minibuses' now connect Phnom Penh and northeastern destinations such as Stung Treng and Ban Lung. Usually Hyundai Starex people carriers, these can be a faster and more comfortable way to travel than old minibuses.

CAR & MOTORCYCLE

Car and motorcycle rental are comparatively cheap in Cambodia and many visitors rent a car or bike for greater flexibility to visit out-of-the-way places and to stop when they choose. Almost all car rental in Cambodia includes a driver, which is good news given the abysmal state of many roads, the lack of road signs and the prominence of the psychopathic driver gene among many Cambodian road users.

Driving Licence

A standard driving licence is not much use in Cambodia. In theory, to drive a car you need an International Driving Licence, usually issued through your automobile association back home, but Cambodia is not currently a recognised country. It is very unlikely that a driving licence will be of any use to most travellers to Cambodia, save for those coming to work with one of the many foreign organisations in Cambodia.

When it comes to renting motorcycles, it's a case of no licence required. If you can drive the bike out of the shop, you can drive it anywhere, or so the logic goes. Police in Sihanoukville have a reputation for demanding a licence and levying a fine for those not holding the relevant paperwork.

Fuel & Spare Parts

Fuel is relatively expensive in Cambodia compared with other staples, at around 4000r (US$1) a litre. Fuel is readily available throughout the country, but prices generally rise in rural areas. Even the most isolated communities usually have someone selling petrol out of Fanta or Johnnie Walker bottles. Some sellers mix this fuel with kerosene to make a quick profit – use it sparingly, in emergencies only.

When it comes to spare parts, Cambodia is flooded with Chinese, Japanese and Korean motorcycles, so it is easy to get parts for Hondas, Yamahas or Suzukis, but finding a part for a Harley or a Ducati is another matter. The same goes for cars – spares for Japanese cars are easy to come by, but if you are driving something obscure, bring substantial spares.

Hire
CAR
Car hire is generally only available with a driver and is most useful for sightseeing around Phnom Penh and Angkor. Some tourists with a healthy budget also arrange cars or 4WDs with drivers for touring the provinces. Hiring a car with a driver is about US$30 to US$35 for a day in and around Cambodia's towns. Heading into the provinces it rises to US$50 or more, plus petrol, depending on the destination, and for those staying overnight, the driver will also need looking after. Hiring 4WDs will cost around US$60 to US$120 a day, depending on the model and the distance travelled. Driving yourself is just about possible, but also inadvisable due to chaotic road conditions, personal liability in the case of an accident and higher charges.

MOTORCYCLE
Motorcycles are available for hire in Phnom Penh and some other popular tourist destinations. In Siem Reap (and at times in Sihanoukville), motorcycle rental is forbidden, so anyone planning any rides around Siem Reap needs to arrange a bike elsewhere. In other provincial towns, it is usually possible to rent a small motorcycle after a bit of negotiation. Costs are US$3 to US$7 per day for a 100cc motorcycle and around US$10 to US$25 for a 250cc dirt bike.

Drive with due care and attention, as medical facilities and ambulances are less than adequate outside of Phnom Penh, Siem Reap and Battambang. If you have never ridden a motorcycle before, Cambodia is not the best place to start, but once out of the city it does get easier. If you're jumping in at the deep end, make sure you are under the supervision of someone who knows how to ride.

The advantage of motorcycle travel is that it allows for complete freedom of movement and you can stop in small villages that Westerners rarely visit. It is possible to take motorcycles upcountry for tours, but only experienced off-road bikers should take to these roads with a dirt bike. Even riders with more experience should take care if intending to ride into remote regions of Cambodia, as roads in this country are not the same as roads at home. Anyone planning a longer ride should try out the bike around Phnom Penh for a day or so first to make sure it is in good health.

For those with experience, Cambodia has some of the best roads in the world for dirt biking, particularly in the provinces of Preah Vihear, Mondulkiri, Ratanakiri and the Cardamom Mountains.

There are several specialised dirt-bike touring companies:

Dancing Roads (www.dancingroads.com) Offers motorbike tours around the capital and gentle tours further afield to the South Coast. Based in Phnom Penh, the driver-guides are fun and friendly.

Hidden Cambodia (www.hiddencambodia.com) A Siem Reap–based company specialising in motorcycle trips throughout Cambodia, including the remote temples of northern Cambodia and beyond.

Red Raid Cambodia (www.motorcycletourscambodia .com) More expensive but experienced French-run outfit running trips throughout Cambodia, including the Cardamoms.

Siem Reap Dirt Bikes (www.siemreapdirtbikes.com) Siem Reap–based, as you might guess, they offer everything from day trips to six-day remote temple adventures.

Insurance
If you are travelling in a tourist vehicle with a driver, then it is usually insured. When it comes to motorcycles, many rental bikes are not insured and you will have to sign a contract agreeing to a valuation for the bike if it is stolen. Make sure you have a strong lock and always leave it in guarded parking where available.

Do not even consider hiring a motorcycle if you are daft enough to be travelling in Cambodia without medical insurance. The cost of treating serious injuries, especially if you require an evacuation, is bankrupting for budget travellers.

Road Conditions & Hazards
Whether travelling or living in Cambodia, it is easy to lull yourself into a false sense of security and assume that down every rural road is yet another friendly village. However, even with the demise of the Khmer Rouge, odd incidents of banditry and robbery do occur in rural areas. There have also been some nasty bike-jackings in Sihanoukville.

TRANSPORT

When travelling in your own vehicle, and particularly by motorcycle in rural areas, make certain you check the latest security information in communities along the way.

Expatriates working in Phnom Penh may end up driving a 4WD or car, but will certainly need to drive with more care than at home. In Phnom Penh traffic is a law unto itself and in the provinces roads can resemble roller coasters. Be particularly careful about children on the road – you'll sometimes find kids hanging out in the middle of a major highway. Livestock on the road is also a menace; hit a cow and you'll both be pizza (especially if you are only on a motorbike). The risks increase after dark.

Other general security suggestions for those travelling by motorcycle:

- Try to get hold of a good-quality helmet for long journeys or high-speed riding.
- Carry a basic repair kit, including some tyre levers, a puncture-repair kit and a pump.
- Always carry a rope for towing on longer journeys in case you break down.
- In remote areas always carry several litres of water, as you never know when you will run out.
- Travel in small groups, not alone.
- When in a group, stay close together in case of any incident or accident.
- Don't be cheap with the petrol – running out of fuel in a rural area could jeopardise your health, especially if water runs out, too.
- Do not smoke marijuana or drink alcohol and drive.
- Keep your eyes firmly fixed on the road; Cambodian potholes eat people for fun.

Road Rules

If there are road rules in Cambodia it is doubtful that anyone is following them. Size matters and the biggest vehicle wins by default. The best advice if you drive a car or ride a motorcycle in Cambodia is to take nothing for granted and assume that your fellow motorists are visually challenged psychopaths. Seriously though, in Cambodia traffic drives on the right. There are some traffic lights at junctions in Phnom Penh, Siem Reap and Sihanoukville, but where there are no lights, most traffic turns left into the oncoming traffic, edging along the wrong side of the road until a gap becomes apparent. For the

uninitiated it looks like a disaster waiting to happen, but Cambodians are quite used to the system. Foreigners should stop at crossings and develop a habit of constant vigilance. Never assume that other drivers will stop at red lights: these are considered optional by most Cambodians, especially at night.

Phnom Penh is the one place where, amid all the chaos, traffic police take issue with Westerners breaking even the most trivial road rules. Make sure you don't turn left at a 'no left turn' sign or travel with your headlights on during the day (although strangely, it doesn't seem to be illegal for Cambodians to travel without headlights at night). New laws require that bikes have mirrors, and that drivers (not passengers, even children) wear helmets, are being enforced around the country by traffic police eager to levy fines. Foreigners are considered popular targets.

HITCHING

Hitching is never entirely safe in any country, and we don't recommend it. Travellers who decide to hitch should understand that they are taking a small but potentially serious risk. People who do choose to hitch will be safer if they travel in pairs and let someone know where they are planning to go. Hitching with truck drivers is a possibility, but it is very uncomfortable and should be considered extremely unsafe for lone women. Expect to pay for the ride.

LOCAL TRANSPORT

Bus

There are currently no local bus networks in Cambodia, even in the capital, Phnom Penh.

Cyclo

As in Vietnam and Laos, the *cyclo* (pedicab) is a cheap way to get around urban areas. In Phnom Penh *cyclo* drivers can either be flagged down on main roads or found loitering around markets and major hotels. It is necessary to bargain the fare if taking a *cyclo* from outside an expensive hotel or popular restaurant or bar. Fares range from 1000r to US$1 (about 4000r). There are few *cyclos* in the provinces, and in Phnom Penh the *cyclo* is fast losing ground to the *moto*.

Lorry

No, not a big truck, but the Cambodian name for a local train made from wood and

---

THE MOTO BURN

Be careful not to put your leg near the exhaust pipe of a *moto* after long journeys; many travellers have received nasty burns, which can take a long time to heal in the sticky weather and often require antibiotics.

---

bamboo, and powered by a small petrol engine. In the Battambang area, it is known as a *norry* or a 'bamboo train' (p252). Great fun until you meet another train coming the other way – aaaaargh!

Moto

Motos, also known as *motodups* (meaning *moto* driver), are small motorcycle taxis. They are a quick way of making short hops around towns and cities. Prices range from 1000r to US$1 or more, depending on the distance and the town; expect to pay more at night. It used to be that prices were rarely agreed in advance, but with the increase in visitor numbers, a lot of drivers have got into the habit of overcharging. It's probably best to negotiate up front, particularly in the major tourist centres, outside fancy hotels or at night. Some travellers carry lightweight bicycle helmets to wear when riding pillion.

Outboards

Outboards (pronounced 'out-boor') are the equivalent of Venice's *vaporetto*, a sort of local river-bus or taxi. Found all over the country, they are small fibreglass boats with 15HP or 40HP engines, and can carry up to six people for local or longer trips. They rarely run to schedules, but locals wait patiently for them to fill up. Those with time on their hands can join the wait; those in a hurry can charter the whole boat and take off. Another variation is the longtail rocket boats imported from Thailand that connect small villages on the upper stretches of the Mekong. Rocket is the definitive word and their safety is questionable.

Remork-kang

The *remork-kang* is a trailer pulled by a bicycle, effectively a kind of *cyclo* with the passenger travelling behind. The coming of the *moto* has led to a dwindling in numbers, but they are still sometimes seen in Battambang

or Kampot. Fares are about the same as *moto* rides.

Remork-moto

The *remork-moto* is a large trailer hitched to a motorcycle and pretty much operates as a low-tech local bus with oh-so-natural air-conditioning. They are used throughout rural Cambodia to transport people and goods, and are often seen on the edge of towns ready to ferry farmers back to the countryside.

Most popular tourist destinations, including Phnom Penh, Siem Reap and the South Coast, have their very own tourist versions of the *remork-moto (remork)*, with a cute little canopied trailer hitched to the back of the motorbike for two people in comfort or as many as you can pile on at night. These make a great way to explore the temples, as you get the breeze of the bike but some protection from the elements. These are usually referred to as *tuk tuks* by foreigners travelling in Cambodia.

Rotei Ses

Rotei means 'cart' or 'carriage' and *ses* is 'horse', but the term is used for any cart pulled by an animal. Cambodia's original 4WD, ox carts are a common form of transport in remote parts of the country, as they are the only things that can get through thick mud in the height of the wet season. They are usually pulled by water buffalo or cows. Horse-and-carts are commonly seen in rural Cambodia, although very few tourists like the idea of being pulled along by one of these pitiful horses. Some local community tourism initiatives now include cart rides.

REMORK VS TUK TUK

So just what are those motorbikes with the cute little carriages pulled behind? *Remork-motos? Remorks? Tuk tuks?* The debate rumbles on. Officially, Cambodians call them *remork-motos*, which is often shortened to *remork*. In Thailand, the high-octane three-wheeled taxis in Bangkok are known as *tuk tuks* and this moniker has hopped across the border into common usage in Cambodia. However, some Cambodians take offence at the use of the name *tuk tuk*, so for the time being we are opting for *remork*. Remarkable.

> **WARNING**
>
> *Moto* drivers and *cyclo* riders with little or no English may not understand where you want them to go even though they nod vigorously. This is a particular headache in a big city like Phnom Penh – see the boxed text, p122.

Taxi

Taxi hire in towns and cities is getting easier in Cambodia, but there are still very few metered taxis, with just a couple of operators in Phnom Penh. Guesthouses, hotels and travel agents can arrange cars for sightseeing in and around towns.

SHARE TAXI & PICK-UP TRUCKS

In these days of improving roads, pick-up trucks are losing ground to 'express minibuses' or pumped-up Toyota Camrys that have their suspension jacked up like monster trucks. When using share taxis or pick-ups, it is an advantage to travel in numbers, as you can buy spare seats to make the journey more comfortable. Double the price for the front seat and quadruple it for the entire back row. It is important to remember that there aren't necessarily fixed prices on every route, so you have to negotiate and prices do fluctuate with the price of petrol.

Share taxis and pick-ups take on the bad roads that buses would break down on as well as some of the busier roads that buses serve. Share taxis are widely available for hire and for major destinations they can be hired individually or you can pay for a seat and wait for other passengers to turn up. Guesthouses are also very helpful when it comes to arranging share taxis – at a price, of course.

When it comes to pick-ups, passengers can sit in the cab or, if money is short and comfort an alien concept, out on the back; trucks depart when seriously full. Passengers sitting out back should carry a scarf to protect against the dust and sunscreen to protect against the sun. In the wet season a raincoat is as good as compulsory. Arranging a pick-up directly is less expensive than getting a guesthouse to organise it, but involves considerable aggravation. Haggle patiently to ensure a fair price.

In very remote areas, particularly in the wet season, when the roads are even more abysmal than usual, huge six-wheel-drive Russian military trucks serve as periodic transport. These are known as *lan damrei* (elephant trucks).

TRAIN

Cambodia's rail system is, like the old road network, one of the most notorious in Asia. There are no longer passenger services, but it may be possible to negotiate a ride on a freight train if you are feeling really masochistic. The prettiest sections of the network are between Takeo and Kampot and from there to Sihanoukville. Trains travel at an average speed of 20km/h, bridges are not always maintained and the ride is often as bumpy as on some of the roads, as the old rails are so warped.

The railway will soon be completely rehabilitated to bring speeds up to 50km/h. Eventually, the Cambodian network will be plugged into the Trans-Asian Railway which will eventually link Singapore and China, but connecting Phnom Penh with Ho Chi Minh City via a Mekong bridge will take a few years yet. In the meantime, ardent trainspotters should be able to pay their way onto a cargo train, but bear in mind it takes more than 12 hours to Battambang, and that's if the train doesn't derail. It's more fun to take to the rails on the bamboo train (p252) around Battambang.

The rail network consists of about 645km of single-track metre-gauge lines. The 385km northwestern line, built before WWII, links Phnom Penh with Pursat and Battambang. The final stretch from Sisophon to Poipet was pulled up by the Khmer Rouge in the 1970s. The 254km southwestern line, which was completed in 1969, connects Phnom Penh with Takeo, Kampot and Sihanoukville.

Health Dr Trish Batchelor

CONTENTS

BEFORE YOU GO	**353**
Insurance	353
Recommended Vaccinations	353
Further Reading	353
Other Preparations	353
IN TRANSIT	**355**
Deep Vein Thrombosis (DVT)	355
Jet Lag & Motion Sickness	355
IN CAMBODIA	**356**
Availability & Cost of Health Care	356
Infectious Diseases	356
Traveller's Diarrhoea	359
Environmental Hazards	360
Women's Health	362

Your health is more of a concern in Cambodia than most other parts of Southeast Asia, due to poor sanitation and a lack of effective medical-treatment facilities. Once you venture into rural areas you are very much on your own, although most towns have a reasonable clinic these days.

If you feel particularly unwell, try to see a doctor rather than visit a hospital; hospitals in rural areas are pretty primitive and diagnosis can be hit and miss. If you fall seriously ill in Cambodia you should head to major centres Phnom Penh or Siem Reap (or Bangkok if this is going to be closer), as these are the only places in the country with decent emergency treatment. Pharmacies in the larger towns are remarkably well stocked and you don't need a prescription to get your hands on anything from antibiotics to anti-malarials. Prices are also very reasonable, but do check the expiry date, as some medicine may have been on the shelves for quite a long time.

Don't let these warnings make you paranoid. Travel health really depends on your level of predeparture preparation, your daily health care while travelling and also how you handle any medical problems that may develop. While the potential dangers can seem quite frightening, in reality few travellers experience anything more than an upset stomach.

BEFORE YOU GO

INSURANCE

Make sure that you have adequate health insurance. See p327 for details.

RECOMMENDED VACCINATIONS

Plan ahead for getting your vaccinations (see the boxed text, p354): some of them require more than one injection over a period of time, while others should not be given together. Note that some vaccinations should not be given during pregnancy or to people with allergies.

It is recommended that you seek medical advice at least six weeks before travel. Be aware that there is often a greater risk of disease during pregnancy and among children.

Record all vaccinations on an International Certificate of Vaccination, available from your doctor. It is a good idea to carry this as proof of your vaccinations when travelling in Cambodia.

FURTHER READING

If you are planning on travelling in remote areas for a long period of time, you may consider taking a more detailed health guide, such as Lonely Planet's *Healthy Travel: Asia & India,* which is a handy pocket-sized guide packed with useful information including pre-trip planning, emergency first aid, immunisation and disease information, and what to do if you get sick on the road. *Where There Is No Doctor,* by David Werner, is a very detailed guide intended for those going to work in an underdeveloped country.

Lonely Planet's *Travel with Children* includes advice on travel health for younger children.

OTHER PREPARATIONS

Make sure you're healthy before you start travelling. If you're going on a long trip, make a visit to a dentist before you depart. If you wear glasses, take a spare pair and your prescription.

HEALTH

If you require a particular medication, try to ensure that you take an adequate supply, as it may not be available locally. Take part of the packaging that shows the generic name rather than the brand only, as this will make getting replacements easier. To avoid any problems, it is also a good idea to have a legible prescription or letter from a doctor to show that you use the medication regularly.

Medical Kit Checklist

Following is a list of items you should consider including in your medical kit – consult your pharmacist for brands available in your country.

- aspirin or paracetamol (acetaminophen in the USA) – for pain or fever
- antihistamine – for allergies, eg hay fever; to ease the itch from insect bites or stings; and to prevent motion sickness

---

REQUIRED & RECOMMENDED VACCINATIONS

Vaccinations you may want to consider for a trip to Cambodia are listed here, but it is imperative that you discuss your needs with your doctor. For more details about the diseases themselves, see the individual entries later in this section.

- **Diphtheria and tetanus** – vaccinations for these two diseases are usually combined. After an initial course of three injections (usually given in childhood), boosters are necessary every 10 years.

- **Hepatitis A** – this vaccine provides long-term immunity after an initial injection and a booster at six to 12 months. Alternatively, an injection of gamma globulin can provide short-term protection against hepatitis A – two to six months, depending on the dose. It is reasonably effective and, unlike the vaccine, is protective immediately but, because it is a blood product, there are current concerns about its long-term safety. The hepatitis A vaccine is also available in a combined form with the hepatitis B vaccine – three injections over a six-month period are required.

- **Hepatitis B** – travellers who should consider vaccination against hepatitis B include those on a long trip, as well as those visiting countries where there are high levels of hepatitis B infection (such as Cambodia); where blood transfusions may not be adequately screened; or where sexual contact or needle sharing is a possibility. Vaccination involves three injections, with a booster at 12 months. More rapid courses are available if necessary.

- **Japanese B Encephalitis** – consider vaccination against this disease if spending a month or longer in Cambodia, when making repeated trips, or if visiting during an epidemic. It involves three injections over 30 days.

- **Polio** – everyone should keep up-to-date with this vaccination, normally given in childhood. A booster every 10 years maintains immunity.

- **Rabies** – vaccination should be considered by those spending a month or longer in Cambodia, especially if they are cycling, handling animals, caving or travelling to remote areas. It's also recommended for children, as they may not report a bite. Vaccination involves having three injections over 21 to 28 days. Vaccinated people who are bitten or scratched by an animal will require two booster injections of vaccine; those not vaccinated require more.

- **Tuberculosis** – the risk of travellers contracting TB is usually very low, unless you will be living with, or closely associated with, local people. Vaccination against TB (BCG vaccine) is recommended for children and young adults who will be living in high-risk areas, including Cambodia, for three months or more.

- **Typhoid** – vaccination against typhoid may be required if you are travelling for more than a couple of weeks in Cambodia.

- **Yellow Fever** – a yellow-fever vaccine is now the only vaccine that is a legal requirement for entry into Cambodia when coming from an infected area. This refers to a direct flight from an infected area, but there are no direct flights from Africa or South America, the most likely places of infection.

- cold and flu tablets, throat lozenges and nasal decongestant
- multivitamins – consider for long trips, when dietary vitamin intake may be inadequate
- antibiotics – consider including these if you're travelling well off the beaten track; see your doctor before you go, as they must be prescribed, and carry the prescription with you
- loperamide or diphenoxylate – 'blockers' for diarrhoea
- prochlorperazine or metaclopramide – for nausea and vomiting
- rehydration mixture – to prevent dehydration, which may occur, for example, during bouts of diarrhoea; rehydration mixture is particularly important when travelling with children
- insect repellent, sunscreen, lip balm and eye drops
- calamine lotion, sting relief spray or aloe vera – to ease irritation from sunburn and insect bites or stings
- antifungal cream or powder – for fungal skin infections and thrush
- antiseptic (such as povidone-iodine) – for cuts and grazes
- bandages, Band-Aids (plasters) and other wound dressings
- water purification tablets or iodine
- scissors, tweezers and a thermometer – note that mercury thermometers are prohibited by airlines
- sterile kit (sealed medical kit containing syringes and needles) – highly recommended, as Cambodia has medical hygiene problems

IN TRANSIT

DEEP VEIN THROMBOSIS (DVT)

Deep vein thrombosis (DVT) occurs when blood clots form in the legs during plane flights, chiefly because of prolonged immobility. The longer the flight, the greater the risk. Though most blood clots are reabsorbed uneventfully, some may break off and travel through the blood vessels to the lungs, where they may cause life-threatening complications.

The chief symptom of DVT is swelling or pain of the foot, ankle, or calf, usually on just one side. When a blood clot travels to the lungs, it may cause chest pain and difficulty in breathing. Travellers with any of these symptoms should immediately seek medical attention.

To prevent the development of DVT on long flights, walk about the cabin, contract the leg muscles while sitting, drink plenty of fluids and avoid alcohol.

JET LAG & MOTION SICKNESS

Jet lag is experienced when a person travels by air across more than three time zones. It occurs because many of the functions of the human body (such as temperature, pulse rate and emptying of the bladder and bowels) are regulated by internal 24-hour cycles. When we travel long distances rapidly, our bodies take time to adjust to the 'new time' of our destination, and we may experience fatigue, disorientation, insomnia, anxiety, impaired concentration and loss of appetite. These effects will usually be gone within three days of arrival, but to minimise the impact of jet lag:

- rest for a couple of days prior to date of departure.
- try to select flight schedules that minimise sleep deprivation; arriving late in the day means you can go to sleep soon after you arrive. For very long flights, try to organise a stopover.
- avoid excessive eating (which bloats the stomach) and alcohol intake (which causes dehydration) during the flight. Instead, drink plenty of noncarbonated, nonalcoholic drinks such as fruit juice or water.
- make yourself comfortable by wearing loose-fitting clothes and perhaps bringing an eye mask and earplugs to help you sleep.
- on the flight, try to sleep at the appropriate time for the time zone to which you are travelling.

Eating lightly before and during a trip will reduce the chances of motion sickness. If you are prone to motion sickness, try to find a place that minimises movement – near the wing on aircraft, close to midships on boats, near the centre on buses. Fresh air usually helps; reading and cigarette smoke don't. Ginger (available in capsule form) and peppermint (including mint-flavoured sweets) are natural preventatives of motion sickness.

HEALTH

IN CAMBODIA

AVAILABILITY & COST OF HEALTH CARE

Self-diagnosis and treatment of health problems can be risky, so you should always seek professional medical help. Although we do give drug dosages in this section, they are for emergency use only. Correct diagnosis is vital.

An embassy, consulate or hotel can usually recommend a local doctor or clinic. Antibiotics should ideally be administered only under medical supervision. Take only the recommended dose at the prescribed intervals and use the whole course, even if the illness seems to be cured earlier. Stop immediately if there are any serious reactions and don't use the antibiotic at all if you are unsure that you have the correct one. Some people are allergic to commonly prescribed antibiotics such as penicillin or sulpha drugs; carry this information (eg on a bracelet) when travelling.

The best clinics and hospitals in Cambodia are found in Phnom Penh (p86) and Siem Reap (p131). A consultation usually costs in the region of US$20 to US$40, plus medicine. Elsewhere, facilities are more basic, although a private clinic is usually preferable to a government hospital. For serious injuries or illnesses, seek treatment in Bangkok.

INFECTIOUS DISEASES

Dengue

This viral disease is transmitted by mosquitoes and occurs mainly in tropical and subtropical areas of the world. There is only a small risk to travellers, except during epidemics, which usually occur during and just after the wet season in Cambodia.

Unlike the malaria mosquito, the *Aedes aegypti* mosquito, which transmits the dengue virus, is most active during the day and is found mainly in urban areas.

Signs and symptoms of dengue fever include a sudden onset of high fever, headache, joint and muscle pains (hence its old name, 'breakbone fever'), plus nausea and vomiting. A rash of small red spots appears three to four days after the onset of fever. Dengue is commonly mistaken for other infectious diseases, including influenza.

TRADITIONAL MEDICINE IN CAMBODIA

Traditional medicine or *thnam boran* is very popular in rural Cambodia. There are *kru Khmer* or traditional medicine men in most districts of the country and some locals trust them more than modern doctors and hospitals. Working with tree barks, roots, herbs and plants, they boil up brews to supposedly cure all ills. However, when it comes to serious conditions like snake bites, their treatments can be counterproductive and infectious. Other popular traditional remedies, even in the city, include *kor kchoal,* a vigorous coin massage to take away the bad wind, and *chup kchoal,* a massage using heated vacuum cups. The first leaves red streaks on the torso like the patient has been flayed, the second large round circles like a contagious disease.

Seek medical attention if you think you may be infected. A blood test can diagnose infection, but there is no specific treatment for the disease. Aspirin should be avoided, as it increases the risk of haemorrhaging, but plenty of rest is advised. Recovery may be prolonged, with tiredness lasting for several weeks. Severe complications are rare in travellers, but include dengue haemorrhagic fever (DHF), which can be fatal without prompt medical treatment. DHF is thought to be a result of secondary infection due to a different strain (there are four major strains) and usually affects residents of the country rather than travellers.

There is no vaccine against dengue fever. The best prevention is to avoid mosquito bites at all times – see Malaria, opposite, for more details.

Fungal Infections

Fungal infections occur more commonly in hot weather and are usually on the scalp, between the toes (athlete's foot) or fingers, in the groin and on the body (ringworm). Ringworm, a fungal infection, not a worm, is contracted from infected animals or other people. Moisture encourages these infections.

To prevent fungal infections wear loose, comfortable clothes, avoid artificial fibres, wash frequently and dry yourself carefully. If you do get an infection, wash the infected area at least daily with a disinfectant or medicated soap and water, and rinse and dry well. Apply an antifungal cream or powder like tolnaftate (Tinaderm). Try to expose the infected area to air or sunlight as much as possible. Wash all towels and underwear in hot water, change them often and let them dry in the sun.

Hepatitis

Hepatitis is a general term for inflammation of the liver. It is a common disease worldwide. There are several different viruses that cause hepatitis, and they differ in the way that they are transmitted. The symptoms are similar in all forms of the illness, and include fever, chills, headache, fatigue, feelings of weakness, and aches and pains, followed by loss of appetite, nausea, vomiting, abdominal pain, dark urine, light-coloured faeces, jaundiced (yellow) skin and yellowing of the whites of the eyes. People who have had hepatitis should avoid alcohol for some time after the illness, as the liver needs time to recover.

Hepatitis A is transmitted by ingesting contaminated food or water. You should seek medical advice, but there is not much you can do apart from resting, drinking lots of fluids, eating lightly and avoiding fatty foods. Hepatitis E is transmitted in the same way as hepatitis A; it can be particularly serious in pregnant women.

There are almost 300 million chronic carriers of hepatitis B in the world. It is spread through contact with infected blood, blood products or body fluids; for example, through sexual contact, unsterilised needles, blood transfusions or contact with blood via small breaks in the skin. Other risk situations include shaving, tattooing or body piercing with contaminated equipment. The symptoms of hepatitis B may be more severe than type A and the disease can lead to long-term problems such as chronic liver damage, liver cancer or a long-term carrier state. Hepatitis C and D are spread in the same way as hepatitis B and can also lead to long-term complications.

There are vaccines against hepatitis A and B, but there are currently no vaccines against the other types of hepatitis. Following the basic rules about food and water (hepatitis A and E) and avoiding risk situations (hepatitis B, C and D) are important preventative measures.

HIV/AIDS

Infection with the human immunodeficiency virus (HIV) may lead to acquired immune deficiency syndrome (AIDS), which is a fatal disease. Any exposure to blood, blood products or body fluids may put the individual at risk.

The disease is often transmitted through sexual contact or dirty needles, so vaccinations, acupuncture, tattooing and body piercing can be potentially as dangerous as intravenous drug use. HIV/AIDS can also be spread through infected-blood transfusions; although the blood centre in Phnom Penh does screen blood used for transfusions, it is unlikely to be done in many of the provinces.

If you do need an injection, ask to see the syringe unwrapped in front of you, or take a needle-and-syringe pack with you. Fear of HIV infection should never preclude any treatment for serious medical conditions.

According to WHO figures, Cambodian rates of infection are highest among sex workers. However, due to a concerted awareness campaign, HIV/AIDS infection rates have been steadily declining in the past decade from a high of around 5% of the population in the 1990s to less than 1% today.

Intestinal Worms

These parasites are most common in rural Cambodia. The various worms have different ways of infecting people. Some may be ingested in food such as undercooked meat (eg tapeworms) and some enter through your skin (eg hookworms). Infestations may not show up for some time, and although they are generally not serious, if left untreated they may cause severe health problems later. Consider having a stool test when you return home to check for worms to determine the appropriate treatment.

Japanese B Encephalitis

This viral infection of the brain is transmitted by mosquitoes. Most cases occur among locals living in rural areas, as the virus exists in pigs and wading birds. Symptoms include fever, headache and alteration in consciousness. Hospitalisation is needed for correct diagnosis and treatment. There is a high mortality rate among those who have symptoms; of those who survive many are intellectually disabled.

Malaria

This serious and potentially fatal disease is spread by mosquitoes. If you are travelling in endemic areas it is extremely important to avoid mosquito bites and to take tablets to prevent the disease developing if you become infected. There is no malaria in Phnom Penh, Siem Reap and most other major urban areas in Cambodia, so visitors on short trips to the most popular places do not need to take medication. Malaria self-test kits are widely available in Cambodia, but are not that reliable.

Symptoms of malaria include fever, chills and sweating, headache, aching joints, diarrhoea and stomach pains, usually preceded by a vague feeling of ill health. Seek medical help immediately if malaria is suspected, as, without treatment, the disease can rapidly become more serious or even fatal.

If medical care is not available, malaria tablets can be used for treatment. You need to use a different malaria tablet to the one you were taking when you contracted the disease, as obviously the first type didn't work. If travelling widely in rural areas of Cambodia, it is worth visiting a pharmacy to purchase a treatment dose – this will save you from complications in the event of an emergency. Antimalarials are available cheaply throughout Cambodia; try to buy them from a reputable clinic and always check the expiry date.

Travellers are advised to prevent mosquito bites at all times. The main messages:

- wear light-coloured clothing.
- wear long trousers and long-sleeved shirts.
- use mosquito repellents containing the compound DEET on exposed areas (prolonged overuse of DEET may be harmful, especially to children, but its use is considered preferable to being bitten by disease-transmitting mosquitoes).
- avoid perfumes or aftershave.
- use a mosquito net impregnated with mosquito repellent (permethrin) – it may be worth taking your own.
- impregnate clothes with permethrin to effectively deter mosquitoes and other insects.

MALARIA MEDICATION

Antimalarial drugs do not prevent you from being infected, but they kill the malaria parasites during their developmental stage, significantly reducing the risk of becoming very ill or dying. Expert advice on medication should be sought, as there are many factors to consider, including the area to be visited, the risk of exposure to malaria-carrying mosquitoes,

the side effects of medication, your medical history and whether you are a child or an adult, and whether you're pregnant. Travellers heading to isolated areas in Cambodia should carry a treatment dose of medication for use if symptoms occur. A drug called Malarine, supplied and subsidised by the European Union (EU) and WHO, is cheaply available in pharmacies throughout Cambodia. A combination of artesunate and mefloquinine, it is undoubtedly the most effective malaria killer available in Cambodia today. See the English instructions for advice about the appropriate dosage.

Schistosomiasis

Also known as bilharzia, this disease is transmitted by minute worms. They infect certain varieties of freshwater snails found in rivers, streams, lakes and, in particular, dams. The worms multiply and are eventually discharged into the water.

The worm enters through the skin and attaches itself to the intestines or bladder. The first symptom may be feeling generally unwell, or a tingling and sometimes a light rash around the area where the worm entered. Weeks later a high fever may develop. Once the disease is established, abdominal pain and blood in the urine are other signs. The infection often causes no symptoms until the disease is well established (several months to years after exposure), when damage to internal organs is irreversible.

The main method of preventing the disease is to avoid swimming or bathing in fresh water where bilharzia is present. Even deep water can be infected. If you do get wet, dry off quickly and dry your clothes as well.

A blood test is the most reliable way to diagnose the disease, but the test will not show positive until a number of weeks after exposure.

Sexually Transmitted Infections (STIs)

Gonorrhoea, herpes and syphilis are among these infections. Sores, blisters or a rash around the genitals and discharges or pain when urinating are common symptoms. With some STIs, such as wart virus or chlamydia, symptoms may be less marked or not observed at all, especially in women. Syphilis symptoms eventually disappear completely, but the disease continues and can cause severe problems in later years. While

EVERYDAY HEALTH

Normal body temperature is up to 37°C (98.6°F); more than 2°C (4°F) higher indicates a high fever. The normal adult pulse rate is 60 to 100 beats per minute (children 80 to 100, babies 100 to 140). As a general rule, the pulse increases about 20 beats per minute for each 1°C (2°F) rise in fever.

Respiration (breathing) rate is also an indicator of illness. Count the number of breaths per minute: between 12 and 20 is normal for adults and older children (up to 30 for younger children, 40 for babies). People with a high fever or serious respiratory illness breathe more quickly than normal. More than 40 shallow breaths a minute may indicate pneumonia.

abstinence from sexual contact is the only 100% effective prevention, using condoms is also effective. Reliable condoms are widely available throughout urban areas of Cambodia. Different STIs each require specific antibiotics. The treatment of gonorrhoea and syphilis is with antibiotics. There is no cure for herpes or HIV/AIDS (see p357).

Typhoid

Typhoid fever is a dangerous gut infection caused by contaminated water and food. Medical help must be sought.

In its initial stages sufferers may feel they have a bad cold or flu on the way, as early symptoms are a headache, body aches and a fever that rises a little each day until it is around 40°C (104°F) or higher. The victim's pulse is often slow relative to the degree of fever present – unlike a normal fever where the pulse increases. There may also be vomiting, abdominal pain, diarrhoea or constipation.

In the second week, the high fever and slow pulse continue, and a few pink spots may appear on the body; trembling, delirium, weakness, weight loss and dehydration may occur. Complications such as pneumonia, perforated bowel or meningitis may also present themselves.

TRAVELLER'S DIARRHOEA

Simple things like a change of water, food or climate can all cause a mild bout of diarrhoea, but a few rushed toilet trips with no other symptoms are not indicative of a major problem. Almost everyone gets a mild bout of the runs on a longer visit to Cambodia.

Dehydration is the main danger with diarrhoea, particularly in children or the elderly as dehydration can occur quite quickly. Under all circumstances *fluid replacement* is the most important thing to remember. Weak black tea with a little sugar, soda water, or soft drinks allowed to go flat and diluted 50% with clean water are all good. You need to drink at least the same volume of fluid that you are losing in bowel movements and vomiting. Urine is the best guide to the adequacy of replacement: if you have small amounts of concentrated urine, you need to drink more. Keep drinking small amounts often. Stick to a bland diet as you recover.

With severe diarrhoea, a rehydrating solution is preferable to replace lost minerals and salts. Commercially available oral rehydration salts are very useful; add them to boiled or bottled water. In an emergency you can make up a solution of six teaspoons of sugar and a half-teaspoon of salt to a litre of boiled or bottled water.

Gut-paralysing drugs such as Lomotil or Imodium can be used to bring relief from the symptoms of diarrhoea, although they do not actually cure the problem. Only use these drugs if you do not have access to toilets and *must* travel. For children under 12 years the use of Lomotil and Imodium is not recommended. Do not use these drugs if the person has a high fever or is severely dehydrated.

In certain situations antibiotics may be required: diarrhoea with blood or mucus (dysentery), any diarrhoea with fever, profuse watery diarrhoea, persistent diarrhoea not improving after 48 hours and severe diarrhoea. These suggest a more serious cause of diarrhoea, and gut-paralysing drugs should be avoided.

In these situations, a stool test may be necessary to diagnose what bug is causing the diarrhoea, so seek medical help urgently. Where this is not possible, the recommended drugs for bacterial diarrhoea – the most likely cause of severe diarrhoea in travellers – are norfloxacin (400mg twice daily for three days) or ciprofloxacin (500mg twice daily for five days). These are not recommended for children or pregnant women. The drug of choice for children would be co-trimoxazole (Bactrim, Septrin or Resprim) with dosage dependent on weight. A five-day course of the drug is given. Ampicillin or amoxycillin may be given in pregnancy, but medical care is necessary.

Amoebic Dysentery & Giardiasis

Two other causes of persistent diarrhoea in travellers are amoebic dysentery and giardiasis.

Amoebic dysentery, caused by the protozoan *Entamoeba histolytica,* is characterised by a gradual onset of low-grade diarrhoea, often with blood and mucus. Cramping abdominal pain and vomiting are less likely than in other types of diarrhoea, and fever may not be present. Amoebic dysentery will persist until treated and can recur and cause other health problems.

Giardiasis is caused by a common parasite, *Giardia lamblia.* Symptoms include stomach cramps, nausea, a bloated stomach, watery, foul-smelling diarrhoea and frequent gas. Giardiasis can appear several weeks after you have been exposed to the parasite. The symptoms may disappear for a few days and then return; this can go on for several weeks.

Seek medical advice if you think you have giardiasis or amoebic dysentery, but where this is not possible, tinidazole (Fasigyn) or metronidazole (Flagyl) are the recommended drugs to take, although the side effects of Flagyl are severe. Treatment is a 2g single dose of Fasigyn, or 250mg of Flagyl three times daily for five to 10 days.

ENVIRONMENTAL HAZARDS
Food

There is an old adage that says, 'If you can cook it, boil it or peel it you can eat it…otherwise forget it'. This is slightly extreme, but many travellers have found it is better to be safe than sorry. Vegetables and fruit should be washed with purified water or peeled where possible. Beware of ice cream that is sold in the street or anywhere it might have been melted and refrozen. Shellfish such as mussels, oysters and clams should be avoided as should undercooked meat, particularly in the form of mince. Steaming does not make shellfish safe for eating.

If a place looks clean and well run, and the vendor also looks clean and healthy, then the food is probably safe. In general, places that are packed with travellers or locals will be fine, while empty restaurants might be empty for a reason. The food in busy restaurants is cooked and eaten quite quickly with little standing around and is probably not reheated.

Heat Exhaustion

Dehydration and salt deficiency can cause heat exhaustion. Take time to acclimatise to high temperatures, drink sufficient liquids and do not do anything too physically demanding.

Salt deficiency is characterised by fatigue, lethargy, headaches, giddiness and muscle cramps; salt tablets may help, but adding extra salt to your food is better.

Anhidrotic heat exhaustion is a rare form of heat exhaustion that is caused by an inability to sweat. It tends to affect people who have been in a hot climate for some time, rather than newcomers. It can progress to heatstroke. Treatment involves removal to a

---

A BANANA A DAY…

If your diet is poor or limited in variety, if you're travelling hard and fast and therefore missing meals, or if you simply lose your appetite, you can soon start to lose weight and place your health at risk.

Make sure your diet is well balanced. Cooked eggs, tofu, beans, lentils and nuts are all safe ways to get protein. Fruit you can peel (bananas, oranges or mandarins, for example) is usually safe and a good source of vitamins. Melons can harbour bacteria in their flesh and are best avoided. Try to eat plenty of grains (including rice) and bread. Remember that although food is generally safer if it is well cooked, overcooked food loses much of its nutritional value. If your diet isn't well balanced or if your food intake is insufficient, it's a good idea to take vitamin and iron pills.

Make sure you drink enough – don't rely on feeling thirsty to indicate when you should drink. Not needing to urinate or voiding small amounts of very dark yellow urine is a danger sign. Always carry a water bottle with you on long trips. See above for information on heat exhaustion.

cooler climate or immediate cold showers and wet sheets.

Heatstroke

This serious and occasionally fatal condition can occur if the body's heat-regulating mechanism breaks down, causing the body temperature to rise to dangerous levels. Long, continuous periods of exposure to high temperatures and insufficient fluids can leave you vulnerable to heatstroke.

The symptoms: feeling unwell, not sweating very much (or at all) and a high body temperature (39°C to 41°C, or 102°F to 106°F). Where sweating has ceased, the skin becomes flushed and red. Severe, throbbing headaches and lack of coordination will also occur, and the sufferer may be confused or aggressive. Eventually the victim will become delirious or convulse. Hospitalisation is essential, but in the interim get victims out of the sun, remove their clothing, cover them with a wet sheet or towel and then fan continually. Give fluids if they are conscious.

Insect Bites & Stings

Bedbugs live in various places, but particularly in dirty mattresses and bedding, and are evidenced by spots of blood on bedclothes or on the wall. Bedbugs leave itchy bites in neat rows. Calamine lotion or Stingose spray may help.

All lice cause itching and discomfort. They make themselves at home in your hair (head lice), your clothing (body lice) or in your pubic hair (crabs). You catch lice through direct contact with infected people or by sharing combs, clothing and the like. Powder or shampoo treatment will kill the lice, and infected clothing should be washed in very hot, soapy water and left to dry in the sun.

Bee and wasp stings are usually painful rather than dangerous. However, in people who are allergic to them, severe breathing difficulties may occur and urgent medical care is then required. Calamine lotion or Stingose spray will relieve itching, and ice packs will reduce the pain and swelling.

Avoid contact with jellyfish, which have stinging tentacles – seek local advice on the safest swimming waters. Dousing in vinegar will deactivate any stingers that have not 'fired'. Calamine lotion, antihistamines and analgesics may reduce the reaction and relieve the pain.

Leeches may be present in damp rainforest conditions; they attach themselves to your skin to suck your blood. Trekkers often get them on their legs or in their boots. Salt or a lighted cigarette end will make them fall off. Do not pull them off, as the bite is then more likely to become infected. Clean and apply pressure if the point of attachment is bleeding. An insect repellent may keep them away, and walkers in leech-infested areas should consider having their boots and trousers impregnated with benzyl benzoate and dibutylphthalate (available from pharmacies in Cambodia).

Always check all over your body if you have been walking through a potentially tick-infested area, as ticks can cause skin infections and other more serious diseases. If a tick is found attached, press down around the tick's head with tweezers, grab the head and gently pull upwards. Try to avoid pulling the rear of the body as this may squeeze the tick's gut contents through the attached mouth parts into the skin, increasing the risk of infection and disease. Smearing chemicals on the tick will not make it let go and this is not recommended.

To minimise your chances of being bitten by a snake, always wear boots, socks and long trousers when walking through undergrowth where snakes may be present. Don't put your hands into holes and crevices, and be careful if collecting firewood.

Snake bites in Cambodia do not cause instantaneous death, but unfortunately antivenenes are not widely available in the country. Immediately wrap the victim's bitten limb tightly, as you would for a sprained ankle, and then attach a splint to immobilise the limb. Keep the victim still and seek medical attention, if possible with the dead snake for identification. However, do not attempt to catch the snake if there is any possibility of being bitten. Tourniquets and sucking out the poison are now comprehensively discredited.

Prickly Heat

Prickly heat is an itchy rash caused by excessive perspiration trapped under the skin. It usually strikes people who have just arrived in a hot climate. Keeping cool, bathing often, drying the skin and using a mild talcum or prickly heat powder, or resorting to the use of air-conditioning, may help.

HEALTH

NOT A GOOD PLACE FOR CONTACTS

People wearing contact lenses should be aware that Cambodia is an extremely dusty country and this can cause much irritation when travelling. It is generally bearable in cars, but when travelling by motorcycle or pick-up, it is most definitely not. Pack a pair of glasses.

Sunburn

You can get sunburnt surprisingly quickly, even through cloud. Use sunscreen, a hat, and a barrier cream for your nose and lips. Calamine lotion or Stingose are good for mild sunburn. Protect your eyes with good-quality sunglasses. Sunscreen is easily available in Phnom Penh, Siem Reap and Sihanoukville, but not elsewhere.

Water

The number-one rule is *be careful of the water and ice,* even though both are almost always factory-produced, a legacy of the French. If you don't know for certain that the water is safe, assume the worst. Reputable brands of bottled water or soft drinks are generally fine, but you can't safely drink tap water. Only use water from containers with a serrated seal. Tea and coffee are generally fine, as the water will have been boiled.

The simplest way of purifying water is to boil it thoroughly. Vigorous boiling should be satisfactory; however, at high altitude water boils at a lower temperature, so germs are less likely to be killed. Make sure you boil it for longer in these environments.

Consider purchasing a water filter for a long trip. Total filters take out all parasites, bacteria and viruses and make water safe to drink. They are often expensive, but can be more cost effective than buying bottled water. Chlorine tablets (Puritabs, Steritabs or other brands) will kill many pathogens, but not some parasites like giardia and amoebic cysts. Iodine is more effective in purifying water and is available in tablet form (such as Potable Aqua).

WOMEN'S HEALTH
Gynaecological Problems

Antibiotic use, synthetic underwear, sweating and contraceptive pills can lead to fungal vaginal infections, especially when travelling in hot climates. Thrush (yeast infection or vaginal candidiasis) is characterised by a rash, itching and discharge. Nystatin, miconazole or clotrimazole pessaries or vaginal cream are the usual treatment. Maintaining good personal hygiene and wearing loose-fitting clothes and cotton underwear may help prevent these infections.

STIs are a major cause of vaginal problems. Symptoms include a smelly discharge, painful intercourse and sometimes a burning sensation when urinating. Medical attention should be sought and male sexual partners must also be treated. For more details see p358. Besides abstinence, the best thing is to practise safe sex using condoms.

Pregnancy

Most miscarriages occur during the first three months of pregnancy. Miscarriage is common and can occasionally lead to severe bleeding. The last three months of pregnancy should also be spent within reasonable distance of good medical care. A baby born as early as 24 weeks stands a chance of survival, but only in a good modern hospital such as Calmette (p86) in Phnom Penh. Pregnant women should avoid all unnecessary medication, although vaccinations and malarial prophylactics should still be taken where needed. Additional care should be taken to prevent illness and particular attention should be paid to diet and nutrition.

HEALTH

Language

CONTENTS

Pronunciation	364
Accommodation	364
Conversation & Essentials	365
Directions	366
Eating Out	366
Emergencies	367
Health	367
Language Difficulties	368
Numbers & Amounts	368
Shopping & Services	368
Time & Days	369
Transport	369

The Khmer (or Cambodian) language is spoken by approximately nine million people in Cambodia, and is understood by many in bordering countries. Written Khmer is based on the ancient Brahmi script of southern India. It's arguably one of the oldest languages in Southeast Asia, as Khmer inscriptions have been dated back to the 7th century AD. Although separate and distinct from neighbouring Burmese, Lao and Thai languages, Khmer shares with them the common roots of Sanskrit and Pali – a heritage of centuries of linguistic and cultural interaction and of their shared faith in Theravada Buddhism. More recently, many French words (especially medical and technical terms) have entered the Khmer language during the colonial period.

Unlike the languages of neighbouring countries (Lao, Thai and Vietnamese), Khmer is nontonal, meaning that there are no special intonations within words that alter their meaning – which may be a relief for travellers in the region. Khmer grammar is also very simple. There are no verb conjugations nor endings for number or gender. Adding a few words changes sentence tense to past, present or future.

A bit of Khmer will go a long way, no matter how rough it is. The Khmers sincerely appreciate any effort to learn their language and are very supportive of visitors who give it a try. You'll find that as your skill and vocabulary increase, so does your social standing: people go out of their way to compliment you, *moto* fares and prices at markets drop, and you may even win a few friends.

Though English is fast becoming Cambodia's second language, the Khmer still cling to the Francophone pronunciation of the Roman alphabet and most foreign words. This is helpful to remember when spelling Western words and names aloud; thus 'ay-bee-see' becomes 'ah-bey-sey' and so on. French speakers will definitely have an advantage when addressing the older generation, as most educated Khmers studied French at some point during their schooling. Many household items retain their French names as well, especially those which were introduced to Cambodia by the French, such as *robinet* (tap, faucet) and *ampoule* (light bulb).

Recommended reading for those interested in further study of spoken and written Khmer are *Cambodian System of Writing and Beginning Reader*, *Modern Spoken Cambodian* and any other books by Frank Huffman. For a more in-depth guide to the language, check out Lonely Planet's *Southeast Asia* phrasebook. For a food and drink glossary, see p63.

Dialects

Although the Khmer language as spoken in Phnom Penh is generally intelligible to Khmers nationwide, there are several distinct dialects in other parts of the country. Most notably, the Khmers of Takeo Province tend to modify or slur hard consonant/vowel combinations, especially those that contain 'r'; thus *bram* (five) becomes *pe-am*, *sraa* (alcohol) becomes *se-aa*, and *baraang* (French or foreigner) becomes *be-ang*. In Siem Reap, sharp-eared travellers will notice a very Lao-sounding lilt to the local speech. Here, certain vowels are modified, such as *poan* (thousand), which becomes *peuan*, and *kh'sia* (pipe), which becomes *kh'seua*.

PRONUNCIATION

The haphazard transliteration system left over from the days of French rule does not reflect accurate pronunciation of Khmer words by English speakers. The pronunciation guide used in this chapter has been designed for basic communication rather than linguistic perfection. It uses the Roman alphabet to give the closest equivalents for the sounds of the Khmer language. Several Khmer vowels, however, have no English equivalent, thus they can only be approximated by English spellings.

Khmer place names in this book written in the Roman alphabet will follow their common or standard spellings.

Vowels

Vowels and diphthongs (vowel combinations) with an **h** at the end should be pronounced hard and aspirated (with a puff of air).

a, ah	shorter and harder than **aa**
aa	as the 'a' in 'father'
aa-œ	like a combination of **aa** and **œ**; when placed between consonants it's often pronounced like 'ao'
ae	as the 'a' in 'cat'
ai	as in 'aisle'
am	as the 'um' in 'glum'
ao	as the 'ow' in 'cow'
av	like a very nasal **ao**; the final 'v' is not pronounced
aw	as the 'aw' in 'jaw'
awh	as **aw** pronounced short and hard
ay	as **ai** but slightly more nasal
e	as in 'they'
eah	combination of 'e' and 'ah'; pronounced short and hard
eh	as the 'a' in 'date'; pronounced short and hard
ei	as **uh** followed by **ii**
eu	like saying 'oo' with the lips spread flat rather than rounded
eua	combination of **eu** and **a**
euh	as **eu** pronounced short and hard
euv	sounds like a very nasal **eu**; the final 'v' is not pronounced
ey	as in 'prey'
i	as in 'kit'
ia	like the 'ee' in 'beer' without the 'r'
ii	as the 'ee' in 'feet'
ih	as **ii**; pronounced short and hard

oah	a combination of 'o' and 'ah'; pronounced short and hard
oam	a combination of 'o' and 'am'
œ	as the 'er' in 'her', but more open
oh	as the 'o' in 'hose'; pronounced short and hard
ohm	as the 'ome' in 'home'
ow	as in 'glow'
u	as the 'u' in 'flute'; pronounced short and hard
ua	as the 'ou' in 'tour'
uah	as **ua**; pronounced short and hard
uh	as the 'u' in 'but'
uu	as the 'oo' in 'zoo'

Consonants

Khmer has some consonant combinations that may be unusual for English speakers, eg 'j-r' in *j'rook* (pig) and 'ch-ng' in *ch'ngain* (delicious). For ease of pronunciation, in this guide these types of consonant clusters are separated with an apostrophe.

ch	as in 'cheese'
j	as in 'jump'
k	as the 'g' in 'go'
kh	as the 'k' in 'kind'
ng	as the 'ng' in 'sing'; practise by repeating 'singing-nging-nging' until you can say 'nging' clearly
ny	as in the final syllable of 'onion', ie 'nyun'
p	a hard 'p' sound, as the final 'p' in 'puppy'
ph	as the 'p' in 'pond' (never as the 'ph' in 'phone')
r	as in 'rum', but hard and rolling, with the tongue flapping against the palate; in rapid conversation it is often omitted entirely
t	a hard 't' sound, similar to the 't' in 'stand'
th	as the 't' in 'two' (never as the 'th' in 'thanks')
w	as in 'would'; there is no equivalent to the English 'v' sound in Khmer

ACCOMMODATION

I've already found a hotel.
ខ្ញុំមានអូតែលហើយ
kh'nyohm mian ohtail hao-y

I'm staying at ...
ខ្ញុំស្នាក់នៅ ...
kh'nyohm snahk neuv ...

Where is a (cheap) hotel?
សណ្ឋាគារ/អូតែល(ថោក)នៅឯណា?
sahnthaakia/ohtail (thaok) neuv ai naa?

Could you write down the address, please?
សូមសរសេរអាស័យដ្ឋានឱ្យខ្ញុំ?
sohm sawse aasayathaan ao-y kh'nyohm?

Do you have a room?
អ្នកមានបន្ទប់ទំនេទេ?
niak mian bantohp tohmne te?

How much is it per day?
តំលៃមួយថ្ងៃប៉ុន្មាន?
damlay muy th'ngay pohnmaan?

Does the price include breakfast?
តំលៃបន្ទប់គិតទាំងម្ហូបពេលព្រឹកឬ?
damlay bantohp khuht teang m'hohp pel pruhk reu?

Can I see the room?
ខ្ញុំអាចមើលបន្ទប់បានទេ?
kh'nyohm aa-it mœl bantohp baan te?

I don't like this room.
ខ្ញុំមិនចូលចិត្តបន្ទប់នេះទេ
kh'nyohm muhn johl juht bantohp nih te

Do you have a better room?
អ្នកមានបន្ទប់ល្អជាងនេះទេ?
niak mian bantohp l'aw jiang nih te?

I'll take this room.
ខ្ញុំយកបន្ទប់នេះ
kh'nyohm yohk bantohp nih

I'd like a room ...
ខ្ញុំសុំបន្ទប់ ...   *kh'nyohm sohm bantohp ...*

  for one person
  សំរាប់មួយនាក់   *samruhp muy niak*
  for two people
  សំរាប់ពីរនាក់   *samruhp pii niak*
  with a bathroom
  ដែលមានបន្ទប់ទឹក   *dail mian bantohp tuhk*
  with a fan
  ដែលមានកង្ហារ   *dail mian dawnghahl*
  with a window
  ដែលមានបង្អួច   *dail mian bawng-uit*

I'm going to stay for ...
ខ្ញុំនឹងស្នាក់ទីនេះ ...   *kh'nyohm nuhng snahk tii nih ...*
  one day
  មួយថ្ងៃ   *muy th'ngay*
  one week
  មួយអាទិត្យ   *muy aatuht*

Can I leave my things here until ...?
ខ្ញុំអាចធ្វើអីវ៉ាន់របស់ខ្ញុំនៅទីនេះដល់ ... បានទេ?
kh'nyohm aa-it ph'nyaa-œ tohk eiwuhn r'bawh kh'nyohm neuv tii nih dawl ... baan te?

  this afternoon
  ល្ងាចនេះ   *l'ngiak nih*
  this evening
  យប់នេះ   *yohp nih*

CONVERSATION & ESSENTIALS
Forms of Address
The Khmer language reflects the social standing of the speaker and the subject through various personal pronouns and 'politeness words'. These range from the simple *baat* for men and *jaa* for women, placed at the end of a sentence and meaning 'yes' or 'I agree', to the very formal and archaic *Reachasahp* or 'royal language', a separate vocabulary reserved for addressing the king and very high officials. Many of the pronouns are determined on the basis of the subject's age and gender in relation to the speaker.

Foreigners are not expected to know all of these forms. The easiest and most general personal pronoun is *niak* (you), which may be used in most situations, for either gender. Men of your age or older may be called *lowk* (Mister). Women of your age or older can be called *bawng srei* (older sister) or, for more formal situations, *lowk srei* (Madam). *Bawng* is a good informal, neutral pronoun for men or women who are (or appear to be) older than you. For third person, male or female, singular or plural, the respectful form is *koat* and the common form is *ke*.

Hello.
  ជំរាបសួរ/   *johm riab sua/*
  សួស្តី   *sua s'dei*
Goodbye.
  លាសិនហើយ   *lia suhn hao-y*
See you later.
  ជួបគ្នាថ្ងៃក្រោយ   *juab kh'nia th'ngay krao-y*
Yes.
  បាទ   *baat* (said by a man)
  ចាស   *jaa* (said by a woman)
No.
  ទេ   *te*
Please.
  សូម   *sohm*

LANGUAGE

Thank you.
អរគុណ   *aw kohn*
You're welcome.
អត់អីទេ/សូមអញ្ជើញ   *awt ei te/sohm anjœ-in*
Excuse me/I'm sorry.
សុំទោស   *sohm toh*
Pardon? (What did you say?)
អ្នកនិយាយថាម៉េច?   *niak niyey thaa mait?*
Hi. How are you?
អ្នកសុខសប្បាយទេ?   *niak sohk sabaay te?*
I'm fine.
ខ្ញុំសុខសប្បាយ   *kh'nyohm sohk sabaay*
Where are you going?
អ្នកទៅណា?   *niak teuv naa?*
(Note that this is a very common question
used when meeting people, even strangers;
an exact answer is not necessary.)

What's your name?
អ្នកឈ្មោះអ្វី?   *niak ch'muah ei?*
My name is ...
ខ្ញុំឈ្មោះ ...   *kh'nyohm ch'muah ...*
Where are you from?
អ្នកមកពីប្រទេសណា?   *niak mao pii prateh naa?*
I'm from ...
ខ្ញុំមកពី ...   *kh'nyohm mao pii ...*
I'm staying at ...
ខ្ញុំស្នាក់នៅ ...   *kh'nyohm snahk neuv ...*
May I take your photo?
ខ្ញុំអាចថតរូបអ្នកបានទេ? *kh'nyohm aa-it thawt ruup*
                              niak baan te?

DIRECTIONS
How can I get to ...?
ផ្លូវណាទៅ ...?   *phleuv naa teuv ...?*
Is it far?
វានៅឆ្ងាយទេ?   *wia neuv ch'ngaay te?*
Is it near?
វានៅជិតទេ?   *wia neuv juht te?*
Is it near here?
វានៅជិតនេះទេ?   *wia neuv juht nih te?*
Go straight ahead.
ទៅត្រង់   *teuv trawng*
Turn left.
បត់ឆ្វេង   *bawt ch'weng*
Turn right.
បត់ស្តាំ   *bawt s'dam*

at the corner
នៅកាច់ជ្រុង   *neuv kait j'rohng*
behind
នៅខាងក្រោយ   *neuv khaang krao-y*
in front of
នៅខាងមុខ   *neuv khaang mohk*
next to
នៅជាប់   *neuv joab*
opposite
នៅទល់មុខ   *neuv tohl mohk*

north
ខាងជើង   *khaang jœng*
south
ខាងត្បូង   *khaang d'bowng*
east
ខាងកើត   *khaang kaot*
west
ខាងលិច   *khaang leit*

EATING OUT
Where is a ...?
...នៅឯណា?   *... neuv ai naa?*
   cheap restaurant
   ហាងបាយ,   *haang baay,*
   រេស្ទួរង់ថោក   *resturawn thaok*
   food stall
   កន្លែងលក់ម្ហូប   *kuhnlaing loak m'howp*
   market
   ផ្សារ   *psar*
   restaurant
   រេស្ទួរង់,   *resturawn,*
   ភោជនីយដ្ឋាន   *phowjaniyahtnaan*

Can you please bring me a ...?
សូមយក...មក   *sohm yohk ... mao*
   fork
   សម   *sawm*
   knife
   កាំបិត   *kambuht*
   plate
   ចាន   *jaan*
   spoon
   ស្លាបព្រា   *slaapria*

Do you have a menu in English?
មានម៉ឺនុយជាភាសា   *mien menui jea*
អង់គ្លេសទេ?   *piasaa awnglay te?*

EMERGENCIES

Help!
ជួយខ្ញុំផង!   juay kh'nyohm phawng!
Stop!
ឈប់!   chohp!
Watch out!
ប្រយ័ត្ន!   prawyaht!
It's an emergency!
នេះជារឿងបន្ទាន់!   nih jia reuang bawntoan!
Call a doctor!
ជួយហៅគ្រូពេទ្យមក!   juay hav kruu paet mao!
Call the police!
ជួយហៅប៉ូលីសមក!   juay hav polih mao!
I've been robbed.
ខ្ញុំត្រូវចោរប្លន់   kh'nyohm treuv jao plawn
Where are the toilets?
បង្គន់នៅឯណា?   bawngkohn neuv ai naa?

Can you help me, please?
អ្នកអាចជួយខ្ញុំបានទេ?
niak aa-it juay kh'nyohm baan te?
Can I please use the telephone?
ខ្ញុំប្រើទូរស័ព្ទបានទេ?
kh'nyohm braa-œ turasahp baan te?
I'd like to contact my embassy/consulate.
ខ្ញុំចង់ហៅស្ថានទូត/កុងស៊ុលរបស់ប្រទេសខ្ញុំ
kh'nyohm jawng hav s'thaantuut/kohngsuhl r'bawh
prawteh kh'nyohm

I'm vegetarian. (I can't eat meat.)
ខ្ញុំតមសាច   kh'nyohm tawm sait
Can I get this without the meat?
សូមកុំដាក់សាច?   sohm kohm dak sait?
I'm allergic to (peanuts).
កុំដាក់ (សណ្តែកដី)   kohm dak (sandaik dei)
Not too spicy, please.
សូមកុំធ្វើហឺរពេក   sohm kohm twœ huhl pek
This is delicious.
អានេះឆ្ងាញ់ណាស   nih ch'ngain nah
The bill, please.
សូមគិតលុយ   sohm kuht lui

HEALTH

I'm ill.
ខ្ញុំឈឺ   kh'nyohm cheu
My ... hurts.
... របស់ខ្ញុំឈឺ   ... r'bawh kh'nyohm cheu

I feel weak.
ខ្ញុំអស់កំលាំង   kh'nyohm awh kamlahng
I feel dizzy.
ខ្ញុំវិលមុខ   kh'nyohm wuhl mohk
I feel nauseous.
ខ្ញុំចង់ក្អួត   kh'nyohm jawng k'uat
I keep vomiting.
ខ្ញុំក្អួតច្រើន   kh'nyohm k'uat j'raa-œn

Where is a ...?
... នៅឯណា?   ... neuv ai naa?
  dentist
  ពេទ្យធ្មេញ   paet th'mein
  doctor
  គ្រូពេទ្យ   kruu paet
  hospital
  មន្ទីរពេទ្យ   mohntrii paet
  pharmacy
  កន្លែងលក់ថ្នាំ/   kuhnlaing luak th'nam/
  ឱសថស្ថាន   ohsawt s'thaan

I'm allergic to ...
ខ្ញុំមិនត្រូវធាតុ ...   kh'nyohm muhn treuv thiat ...
  antibiotics
  អង់ទីប៊ីយោទិក   awntiibiowtik
  penicillin
  ប៉េនីស៊ីលីន   penicillin

I need medicine for ...
ខ្ញុំត្រូវការថ្នាំសំរាប់ ...   kh'nyohm treuv kaa th'nam
                              samruhp ...
  diarrhoea
  រោគចុះរាក   rowk joh riak
  dysentery
  រោគមូល   rowk mual
  fever
  គ្រុន/ក្តៅខ្លួន   krohn/k'dav kh'luan
  pain
  ឈឺ   cheu

antiseptic
ថ្នាំសំលាប់មេរោគ   th'nam samlahp me rowk
aspirin
ប៉ារ៉ាសេតាម៉ុល   parasetamol
codeine
ខូឌីន   codiin
condoms
ស្រោមអនាម័យ   sraom ahnaamai

mosquito repellent

ថ្នាំការពារមូស   *th'nam kaa pia muh*

quinine

គីនីន   *kiiniin*

razor blade

កាំបិតការពុកកមាត់   *kambuht kao pohk moat*

sanitary napkins

សំឡីអនាម័យ   *samlei ahnaamai*

shampoo

សាប៊ូកក់សក់   *sabuu kawk sawk*

sunblock cream

ក្រែមការពារពន្លឺថ្ងៃ   *kraim kaa pia pohnleu th'ngay*

toilet paper

ក្រដាស់អនាម័យ   *krawdah ahnaamai*

LANGUAGE DIFFICULTIES

Does anyone here speak English?

ទីនេះមានអ្នកចេះភាសាអង់គ្លេសទេ?
tii nih mian niak jeh phiasaa awngle te?

Do you understand?

អ្នកយល់ទេ/អ្នកស្ដាប់បានទេ?
niak yuhl te/niak s'dap baan te?

I understand.

ខ្ញុំយល់/ខ្ញុំស្ដាប់បាន
kh'nyohm yuhl/kh'nyohm s'dap baan

I don't understand.

ខ្ញុំមិនយល់ទេ/ខ្ញុំស្ដាប់មិនបានទេ
kh'nyohm muhn yuhl te/kh'nyohm s'dap muhn baan te

What does this mean?

នេះមានន័យថាម៉េច?
nih mian nuh-y thaa mait?

What is this called?

នេះគេហៅថាម៉េច?
nih ke hav thaa mait?

Please speak slowly.

សូមនិយាយយឺតៗ
sohm niyay yeut yeut

Please write that word down for me.

សូមសរសេរពាក្យនោះឱ្យខ្ញុំ
sohm sawse piak nu ao-y kh'nyohm

Please translate for me.

សូមបកប្រែឱ្យខ្ញុំ
sohm bawk brai ao-y kh'nyohm

NUMBERS & AMOUNTS

Khmers count in increments of five – after reaching the number five *(bram)*, the cycle begins again with the addition of one, ie 'five-one' *(bram muy)*, 'five-two' *(bram pii)* and so on to 10, which begins a new cycle.

For example, 18 has three parts: 10, five and three.

There's also a colloquial form of counting that reverses the word order for numbers between 10 and 20 and separates the two words with *duh: pii duhn dawp* for 12, *bei duhn dawp* for 13 and so on. This form is often used in markets, so listen keenly.

1	មួយ	*muy*
2	ពីរ	*pii*
3	បី	*bei*
4	បួន	*buan*
5	ប្រាំ	*bram*
6	ប្រាំមួយ	*bram muy*
7	ប្រាំពីរ	*bram pii/puhl*
8	ប្រាំបី	*bram bei*
9	ប្រាំបួន	*bram buan*
10	ដប់	*dawp*
11	ដប់មួយ	*dawp muy*
12	ដប់ពីរ	*dawp pii*
16	ដប់ប្រាំមួយ	*dawp bram muy*
20	ម្ភៃ	*m'phei*
21	ម្ភៃមួយ	*m'phei muy*
30	សាមសិប	*saamsuhp*
40	សែសិប	*saisuhp*
100	មួយរយ	*muy roy*
1000	មួយពាន់	*muy poan*
1,000,000	មួយលាន	*muy lian*

SHOPPING & SERVICES

How far is the ...?

... ឆ្ងាយប៉ុន្មាន?   *... ch'ngaay pohnmaan?*

I want to see the ...

ខ្ញុំចង់ទៅមើល ...   *kh'nyohm jawng teuv mœl ...*

I'm looking for the ...

ខ្ញុំរក ...   *kh'nyohm rohk ...*

How much is it?

នេះថ្លៃប៉ុន្មាន?   *nih th'lay pohnmaan?*

That's too much.

ថ្លៃពេក   *th'lay pek*

I'll give you ...

ខ្ញុំឱ្យ ...   *kh'nyohm ao-y ...*

No more than ...

មិនលើសពី ...   *muhn lœh pii ...*

What's your best price?

អ្នកដាច់ប៉ុន្មាន?   *niak dait pohnmaan?*

What time does it open?
វាបើកម៉ោងប៉ុន្មាន? *wia baok maong pohnmaan?*
What time does it close?
វាបិទម៉ោងប៉ុន្មាន? *wia buht maong pohnmaan?*

Where is a/the ...?
... នៅឯណា? *... neuv ai naa?*
  bank
  ធនាគារ *th'niakia*
  cinema
  រោងកុន *rowng kohn*
  embassy
  ស្ថានទូត *s'thaantuut*
  museum
  សារមន្ទី *saramohntii*
  park
  សួន *suan*
  police station
  ប៉ុស្តប៉ូលិស/ *poh polih/*
  ស្ថានីយនគរបាល *s'thaanii nohkohbaal*
  post office
  ប្រៃសណីយ *praisuhnii*
  public telephone
  ទូរស័ព្ទសាធារណៈ *turasahp saathiaranah*
  temple
  វត្ត *wawt*

I want to change US dollars.
ខ្ញុំចង់ដូរដុល្លាអាមេរិក
kh'nyohm jawng dow dolaa amerik
What is the exchange rate for US dollars?
មួយដុល្លាដូរបានប៉ុន្មាន?
muy dolaa dow baan pohnmaan?

TIME & DAYS
What time is it?
ត៏ឡូវនេះម៉ោងប៉ុន្មាន?
eileuv nih maong pohnmaan?

in the morning	ពេលព្រឹក	*pel pruhk*
in the afternoon	ពេលរសៀល	*pel r'sial*
in the evening	ពេលល្ងាច	*pel l'ngiat*
at night	ពេលយប់	*pel yohp*
yesterday	ម្សិលមិញ	*m'suhl mein*
today	ថ្ងៃនេះ	*th'ngay nih*
tomorrow	ថ្ងៃស្អែក	*th'ngay s'aik*

Monday	ថ្ងៃចន្ទ	*th'ngay jahn*
Tuesday	ថ្ងៃអង្គារ	*th'ngay ahngkia*
Wednesday	ថ្ងៃពុធ	*th'ngay poht*
Thursday	ថ្ងៃព្រហស្បតិ៍	*th'ngay prohoah*
Friday	ថ្ងៃសុក្រ	*th'ngay sohk*
Saturday	ថ្ងៃសៅរ៍	*th'ngay sav*
Sunday	ថ្ងៃអាទិត្យ	*th'ngay aatuht*

TRANSPORT
Where is the ...?
... នៅឯណា? *... neuv ai naa?*
  airport
  វាលយន្តហោះ *wial yohn hawh*
  bus stop
  ចំណតឡានឈ្នួល *jamnawt laan ch'nual*
  train station
  ស្ថានីយរថភ្លើង *s'thaanii roht plœng*

What time does the ... leave?
... ចេញម៉ោងប៉ុន្មាន? *... jein maong pohnmaan?*
  bus
  ឡានឈ្នួល *laan ch'nual*
  train
  រថភ្លើង *roht plœng*
  plane
  យន្តហោះ/ *yohn hawh/*
  កប៉ាលហោះ *k'pal hawh*

I want to get off (here).
ខ្ញុំចង់ចុះ (ទីនេះ) *kh'nyohm jawng joh (tii nih)*
How much is it to ...?
ទៅ ... ថ្លៃប៉ុន្មាន? *teuv ... th'lay pohnmaan?*
Please take me to ...
សូមជូនខ្ញុំទៅ ... *sohm juun kh' nyohm teuv ...*
Here is fine, thank you.
ឈប់នៅទីនេះក5បាន *chohp neuv tii nih kaw baan*

Also available from
Lonely Planet:
Southeast Asia Phrasebook

Glossary

apsara – heavenly nymph or angelic dancer, often represented in Khmer sculpture
Asean – Association of Southeast Asian Nations
Avalokiteshvara – the Bodhisattva of Compassion and the inspiration for Jayavarman VII's Angkor Thom

baray – reservoir
boeng – lake

Chenla – pre-Angkorian period, 1st to 6th centuries
chunchiet – ethnic minorities
CPP – Cambodian People's Party
cyclo – pedicab; bicycle rickshaw

devaraja – cult of the god-king, established by Jayavarman II, in which the monarch has universal power
devadas – goddesses

EFEO – École Française d'Extrême Orient
essai – wise man or traditional medicine man

Funan – pre-Angkorian period, 6th to 8th centuries
Funcinpec – National United Front for an Independent, Neutral, Peaceful and Cooperative Cambodia; royalist political party

garuda – mythical half-man, half-bird creature
gopura – entrance pavilion in traditional Hindu architecture

Hun Sen – Cambodia's prime minister (1998–present)

Jayavarman II – the king (r 802–50) who established the cult of the god-king, kicking off a period of amazing architectural productivity that resulted in the extraordinary temples of Angkor
Jayavarman VII – the king (r 1181–1219) who drove the Chams out of Cambodia before embarking on an ambitious construction program, including the walled city of Angkor Thom

Kampuchea – the name Cambodians use for their country; to non-Khmers, it is associated with the bloody rule of the Khmer Rouge, which insisted that the outside world adopt the name Democratic Kampuchea from 1975 to 1979
Khmer – a person of Cambodian descent; the language of Cambodia
Khmer Krom – ethnic Khmers living in Vietnam

Khmer Loeu – Upper Khmer or ethnic minorities in northeastern Cambodia
Khmer Rouge – a revolutionary organisation that seized power in 1975 and implemented a brutal social restructuring, resulting in the suffering and death of millions of Cambodians in the following four years
kouprey – extremely rare wild ox of Southeast Asia, probably extinct
krama – scarf

linga – phallic symbols

Mahayana – literally, 'Great Vehicle'; a school of Buddhism (also known as the Northern School) that built upon and extended the early Buddhist teachings; see also *Theravada*
moto – small motorcycle with driver; a common form of transport in Cambodia
Mt Meru – the mythical dwelling of the Hindu god Shiva

naga – mythical serpent, often multiheaded; a symbol used extensively in Angkorian architecture
nandi – sacred ox, vehicle of Shiva
NGO – nongovernmental organisation
NH – national highway
Norodom Ranariddh, Prince – son of King Sihanouk and former leader of Funcinpec
Norodom Sihanouk, King – former king of Cambodia, film director and a towering figure in modern-day Cambodia

Pali – ancient Indian language that, along with Sanskrit, is the root of modern *Khmer*
phlauv – street; abbreviated to Ph
phnom – mountain or hill
Pol Pot – the former leader of the Khmer Rouge who is roundly blamed for the suffering and deaths of millions of Cambodians; also known as Saloth Sar
prasat – stone or brick hall with religious or royal significance
preah – sacred
psar – market

Ramayana – an epic Sanskrit poem composed around 300 BC featuring the mythical Ramachandra, the incarnation of the god Vishnu
remork-kang – trailer pulled by a bicycle
remork-moto – trailer pulled by a motorcycle; often shortened to *remork*
rom vong – Cambodian circle dancing

Sangkum Reastr Niyum – People's Socialist Community; a national movement, led by King Sihanouk, that ruled the country during the 1950s and 1960s

Sanskrit – ancient Hindu language that, along with Pali, is the root of modern Khmer language

stung – river

Suryavarman II – the king (r 1112–52) responsible for building Angkor Wat and for expanding and unifying the Khmer empire

Theravada – a school of Buddhism (also known as the Southern School or Hinayana) found in Myanmar (Burma), Thailand, Laos and Cambodia; this school confined itself to the early Buddhist teachings; see also *Mahayana*

tonlé – large river

UNDP – UN Development Programme
Unesco – UN Educational Scientific and Cultural Organization
Untac – UN Transitional Authority in Cambodia

vihara – temple sanctuary

WHO – World Health Organization

Year Zero – 1975; the year the Khmer Rouge seized power
yoni – female fertility symbol

The Authors

NICK RAY
Coordinating Author

A Londoner of sorts, Nick comes from Watford, the sort of town that makes you want to travel. He lives in Phnom Penh with his wife Kulikar and his young children, Julian and Belle. He has written for several guidebooks on Cambodia including Lonely Planet's *Southeast Asia on a Shoestring* and *Cycling Vietnam, Laos & Cambodia*. He also writes articles for newspapers and magazines, including *The Sunday Times* and *Wanderlust* in the UK. When not writing, he is often out exploring the remote parts of Cambodia as a location scout for the world of TV and film, including the movies *Tomb Raider* and *Two Brothers*. Motorbikes are a part-time passion (riding them a passion, maintaining them part-time) and he has travelled through all of Cambodia's provinces on two wheels.

DANIEL ROBINSON
Environment, South Coast, Northwestern Cambodia

Daniel Robinson researched the award-winning first edition of Lonely Planet's *Cambodia* guidebook back in 1989, when Phnom Penh–Siem Reap flights stayed over the middle of the Tonlé Sap to avoid ground fire and, for three days, he was the only guest at Siem Reap's only hotel; the story of his misadventures in a mined temple appears in *Lonely Planet Unpacked Again*. These days his favourite spots for chilling are the (for now) pristine west coast of Koh Kong Island, the foggy ruins of Bokor Hill Station and the rocky promontory at Prasat Preah Vihear, where breathtaking views stretch almost to Angkor. Daniel is based in Tel Aviv and Los Angeles.

GREG BLOOM
Eastern Cambodia

Greg has had the enviable task of following his wife around to Southeast Asian postings for the last seven years. After five years in Manila, he landed in 'small town' Phnom Penh in 2008 and immediately took a liking to the city and its residents. A mountain man at heart, he jumped at the opportunity to cover Cambodia's 'Wild East' for this title. When not writing about Southeast Asia, Greg might be found snouting around the former Soviet Union (he once called Kyiv home) or running around Asia's ultimate Frisbee fields. His blogs about this and other research trips are at www.mytripjournal.com/bloomblogs.

LONELY PLANET AUTHORS

Why is our travel information the best in the world? It's simple: our authors are passionate, dedicated travellers. They don't take freebies in exchange for positive coverage so you can be sure the advice you're given is impartial. They travel widely to all the popular spots, and off the beaten track. They don't research using just the internet or phone. They discover new places not included in any other guidebook. They personally visit thousands of hotels, restaurants, palaces, trails, galleries, temples and more. They speak with dozens of locals every day to make sure you get the kind of insider knowledge only a local could tell you. They take pride in getting all the details right, and in telling it how it is. Think you can do it? Find out how at **lonelyplanet.com**.

CONTRIBUTING AUTHOR

Dr Trish Batchelor wrote the Health chapter. Trish is a general practitioner and travel medicine specialist who works at the CIWEC Clinic in Kathmandu, Nepal, as well as being a medical advisor to the Travel Doctor New Zealand clinics. Trish teaches travel medicine through the University of Otago, and is interested in underwater and high-altitude medicine, and in the impact of tourism on host countries. She has travelled extensively through Southeast and East Asia and particularly loves high-altitude trekking in the Himalayas.

Behind the Scenes

THIS BOOK

This 7th edition of Cambodia was updated by Nick Ray, Daniel Robinson and Greg Bloom. Nick updated the previous four editions, and Daniel co-authored the original guide with Tony Wheeler in 1992. This guidebook was commissioned in Lonely Planet's Melbourne office, and produced by the following:

Commissioning Editor Shawn Low, Tashi Wheeler
Coordinating Editor Saralinda Turner
Coordinating Cartographer Andras Bogdanovits
Coordinating Layout Designer Margaret Jung
Managing Editors Melanie Dankel, Bruce Evans
Managing Cartographer David Connolly
Managing Layout Designer Sally Darmody
Assisting Editors Susie Ashworth, Jackey Coyle, Robyn Loughnane
Assisting Cartographers Birgit Jordan, Alex Leung, Peter Shields
Cover Research Naomi Parker, lonelyplanetimages.com
Internal Image Research Aude Vauconsant, lonelyplanetimages.com
Project Manager Chris Girdler
Language Content Branislava Vladisavljevic

Thanks to Lucy Birchley, Chris Love, Annelies Mertens, Trent Paton, John Taufa, Brian Turnbull, Celia Wood

THANKS
NICK RAY

As always a huge and heartfelt thanks to the people of Cambodia, whose warmth and humour, stoicism and spirit make it a happy yet humbling place to be. Biggest thanks are reserved for my lovely wife Kulikar Sotho, as without her support and encouragement the adventures would not be possible. And to our young children Julian and Belle for enlivening our lives immeasurably and bringing a new perspective to the 'For Children' sections.

Many thanks to my Mum and Dad, for all their support and encouragement, and their many visits to this part of the world. And thank you to my Cambodian family for welcoming me warmly and understanding my not so traditional lifestyle. Thanks to fellow travellers and residents, friends and contacts in Cambodia who have helped shaped my knowledge and experience in this country. There is no room to thank everyone, but you all know who you are, as we meet for beers regularly enough.

Thanks also to my co-author Daniel Robinson who put the groundwork in on this book back in 1989, when travel was a lot harder. Plus co-author and fellow resident Greg Bloom with whom I have enjoyed many a beer to iron out the border crossings.

THE LONELY PLANET STORY

Fresh from an epic journey across Europe, Asia and Australia in 1972, Tony and Maureen Wheeler sat at their kitchen table stapling together notes. The first Lonely Planet guidebook, *Across Asia on the Cheap,* was born.

Travellers snapped up the guides. Inspired by their success, the Wheelers began publishing books to Southeast Asia, India and beyond. Demand was prodigious, and the Wheelers expanded the business rapidly to keep up. Over the years, Lonely Planet extended its coverage to every country and into the virtual world via lonelyplanet.com and the Thorn Tree message board.

As Lonely Planet became a globally loved brand, Tony and Maureen received several offers for the company. But it wasn't until 2007 that they found a partner whom they trusted to remain true to the company's principles of travelling widely, treading lightly and giving sustainably. In October of that year, BBC Worldwide acquired a 75% share in the company, pledging to uphold Lonely Planet's commitment to independent travel, trustworthy advice and editorial independence.

Today, Lonely Planet has offices in Melbourne, London and Oakland, with over 500 staff members and 300 authors. Tony and Maureen are still actively involved with Lonely Planet. They're travelling more often than ever, and they're devoting their spare time to charitable projects. And the company is still driven by the philosophy of *Across Asia on the Cheap*: 'All you've got to do is decide to go and the hardest part is over. So go!'

Finally, thanks to the Lonely Planet team who have worked on this edition. The author may be the public face, but a huge amount of work goes into making this a better book behind the scenes and I thank you for your help.

DANIEL ROBINSON

NGO staff who generously shared their time and expertise include Janet Gracey, Elise Vermeulen and Emma Blackmore of VSO; Greg Bauer, Kelsey Hedrick, Tyler Jellison and Mitch Widener of the Peace Corps; Seng Bunra and La Peng Ly of Conservation International; Adam Starr of Fauna & Flora International; Nick Butler of the Sam Veasna Center; Xavier Gobin of Phare Ponleu Selpak; Oum Daraneth of the Centre for Khmer Studies; Magali and Noah Courtial of Enfants du Mékong; and Oran Shapira, Lesley Perlman, Dany Goldshtein, Moeurk Mee, Gil Chen and Amy Van Nice of Chi Phat and the Wildlife Alliance.

Also hugely helpful were Loumi Martin, Janet Newman and Jason Webb of Koh Kong; Chris Beaven, Antonia (Toni) Curman, Jean-François Dupuy, Duncan Garner, Lim Seng Hong, Erika Hilmersson, David Husbands, Scott McKenzee-Lee, Henrik Olsson and Nut Mom, Lee Verlander and Craig Warren of Sihanoukville; Sok Lim, Som Sovan and Angela Vestergaard of Kampot; Karen Schroeder-Ames and Yenng Phary of Kep; Jean James of Takeo; Chhan Chamroeun, Yang Chantha and Keo Kinal of Siem Reap; Kong Vibol, Pol Sinheng and You Sokha of Tbeng Meanchey; Chourn Bunnath, Kosei Fujimoto, Pheng Sam Oeun, Uk Topbotra, Vong Thadira and Prof Tsuneaki Yoshida, whom I met at Prasat Preah Vihear; Pa Song Heng of Poipet; Stephan Bognar, Thai Choeung Chan, Yves Deguin, Xavier Gobin and Pierrot Sem of Battambang; and Alysha Beyer, Brad Gordon and his wife Rattana, and Nora Lindström of Phnom Penh.

It was, as usual, a real pleasure working with my friends (and guides) Hang Vuthy of Sihanoukville and Racky Thy (Rith Vanna) of Battambang; my co-authors Nick Ray and Greg Bloom; LP editors Shawn Low, Chris Girdler and Saralinda Turner; and Tashi Wheeler, Commissioning Editor emeritus, who belongs to the second generation of Wheelers to dispatch me to Cambodia for Lonely Planet.

Finally, I'd like to thank my wife Rachel Safman for her backstopping, forbearance and overall good humour.

GREG BLOOM

A big thanks to my wife, Karin, for bringing us here and making it possible. And to my daughter, Anna, for being a constant source of comic relief. Thanks to Howie Nielson and the SVC folks for bringing me into their bird-watching world in Seima. I met various characters along the way who gave me some great tips. A special nod to Tania in Ban Lung, to Jean James and Theany in Stung Treng, and to both Kratie Joe and Kompong Cham Joe. Thanks to co-authors Nick and Daniel for the info swapping. And thanks to Nick and Tashi for making it happen.

OUR READERS

Many thanks to the travellers who used the last edition and wrote to us with helpful hints, useful advice and interesting anecdotes:

A Carla Andersen, Jules Atkins, Sandra Atkins, **B** Caroline Baize, Antony Barton, Kerri Bastin, Chloe Baylis, Magnus Bengtsson, Kate Bennett, Karin Blokziel, Sarah Booth, Peter Bramwell, Gary Brehm, Stacey Brennan, Andrea Briedé, Jurgen Bruyninx, Luella Buckley, Thomas Buechler, Simon Burdon, Georgina Burman, Lee Burrows, **C** Paul Chin, Anita Chopra, Jean-Philippe Claude, Jon Clements, Ally Collier, Clare Copley, Daniel Crowther, Jerry Czarnecki, **D** Devan Darby, Jane Dearden, Anja Dijkema, Yvonne Duijst, Dorn Duk, **E** Mark Eckenrode, Kevin Eperjesy, **F** Charles Failmezger, Marry Fermont, Emma Figueirado, Daniel Ford, **G** Gal Gafni, Allan Gathercoal, Lia Genovese, Dianna Graham and Pierre Gallant, Lacy Grotheer, **H** Sofie Hagens, Bernard Hanna, Nicole Hansen, John Hayward, Jamie Henderson, Peter Hendriks, Gary Hirson, James Hirst, Belinda Hoffer, Amber

SEND US YOUR FEEDBACK

We love to hear from travellers – your comments keep us on our toes and help make our books better. Our well-travelled team reads every word on what you loved or loathed about this book. Although we cannot reply individually to postal submissions, we always guarantee that your feedback goes straight to the appropriate authors, in time for the next edition. Each person who sends us information is thanked in the next edition and the most useful submissions are rewarded with a free book.

To send us your updates – and find out about Lonely Planet events, newsletters and travel news – visit our award-winning website: **lonelyplanet.com/contact**.

Note: we may edit, reproduce and incorporate your comments in Lonely Planet products such as guidebooks, websites and digital products, so let us know if you don't want your comments reproduced or your name acknowledged. For a copy of our privacy policy visit lonelyplanet.com/privacy.

Hoffman, Frank Höppener, **J** Esther Janssen, Mark Jarecki, Tim Jomartz-Knowles, **K** Kelly Knowles, Brian Kuhl, **L** Silke Lassen, Joel Lasser, Mark Lindley, Cloe Lowery, **M** John Maginness, Adam Martin, Julie Martinez, Grant McMillan, Ampay Medina, Lior Meirzon, Thavy Meng Jones, Sofie Merck, Krishnendu Mondal, **N** Hannele Nystrom, **O** Mary O'Neill, Rita Owen, **P** Souvik Paul, Claude Payen, Jayne Pearson, Elin Persson, Richard Petrie, Cick Pouw, Frances Prince, **R** Kerry Raymond, Frances Rein, Simon Robert, **S** Paul Sampson, Matilda Sandén, Rainer Schulze, Shawny Scott, Andrew Senderak, John Sidgwick, Anna Spruce, Kate Steer, Beth Stevenson, Anupma Sud, Malgorzata Szramkowska, Istvan Szucs, **T** John Tattersall, Dan Taylor, Inka Tetzlaff, Gees and Jan Tinholt, Benjamin Tipton, Ep Tissing, Richard Tucker, **V** Jan Willem Van Hofwegen, Marc Van Lierop, Kim Van Oudheusden, Huub Van Rooij, Katerina Vlady, Alexandra Von Muralt, Marianne Vrouwenvelder, **W** Jamie Waterhouse, Holly Webb, Sajith Weerasinghe, Joey Weiss, Alexandra Wells, Katelin Westwood, Elsbeth Wissink, Danielle Wolbers, Edgar Wyss, **Z** Natasha Zheltov, Rachel Zuercher

ACKNOWLEDGMENTS
Many thanks to the following for the use of their content:

Globe on title page ©Mountain High Maps 1993 Digital Wisdom, Inc.

Index

A

accommodation 319-20, *see also individual locations*

activities 320-1, *see also individual activities*

aid organisations, *see* nongovernmental organisations (NGOs)

AIDS 357

air travel 337-9, 346

American War, *see* Vietnam War

amoc 57, 61

amoebic dysentery 360

Andong Meas 310

Andoung Tuek 206

Ang Trapeng Thmor Reserve 151

Angkar 36, 45

Angkor region 153-93, **160-1**, *see also individual temples, temples*

  archaeology 157

  architecture 157-9

  books 27, 28, 158, 167, 168

  conservation 159

  food 163, 188

  hiking 179

  history 27-9, 153-6

  internet resources 158, 162, 165, 179

  itineraries 162-4, 179

  kings 155

  maps 159

  miniature temple replicas 133

  symbols 168

  tourist information 159, 162, 164, 175

  tours 165

  travel to/from 159, 165-6

Angkor Borei 238-9

Angkor Butterfly Centre 136

Angkor National Museum 132

Angkor Thom 172-8, **173**

Angkor Wat 167-72, **169**, **170**, 74

animals 67-8, *see also individual species*

animism 51-2

Anlong Seima 304

Anlong Veng 268-72, **270**

antiques 331

archaeology 157, 284

architecture 54, 157-9

area codes, *see inside front cover*

arts 53-6, *see also individual arts*

artwork 331

ATMs 329

B

Ba Phnom 292

bag snatching 91, 213, 325

Bakong 187-8

Baksei Chamkrong 179

ballet 53

ballooning 166

bamboo train *(norry)* 231, 246, 252, 350-1, **8**

Ban Lung 305-9, **306**

Banteay Chhmar 265-6

Banteay Kdei 182

Banteay Meanchey Province 261-6

Banteay Samré 186

Banteay Srei 189

Banteay Top 266

Baphuon 176-7

bargaining 329

bas-reliefs

  Angkor Wat 169-72

  Banteay Chhmar 265

  Bayon 174-6

  Phnom Bayong 239

bathrooms 333-4

Battambang 249-56, **250**, 7

Battambang Province 249-58

Bayon 172-6, **174**, 5

beaches

  Botum Sakor National Park 205

  Kep 232

  Koh Kong Island 203

  Koh Rung 215

  Koh Rung Samloem 215

  Koh Sdach 205-6

  Koh Tonsay 235

  Peam Krasaop Wildlife Sanctuary 203

  Ream National Park 222

  Sihanoukville 213-14

beer 58-9, 146, 216

begging 323-4

Beng Mealea 191-3, **192**, 75

Bengal florican 282

bicycle travel, *see* cycling

bilharzia 358

birds 67, *see also individual species*

birdwatching 67, 151, 206, 222, 277-8, 282, 304, 317, 320

boat travel 120, 149, 255, 345, 347, 351

boat trips 98, 152, 200, 201, 222, 238-9, 294, 304, 320

Boeng Tonlé Chhmar Wildlife Sanctuary 282

Boeng Yeak Lom 306

Bokor Hill Station 229-30, 7

Bokor National Park 229-31

Bokor Palace 230

bombing 33, 292, 326, *see also* land mines, unexploded ordnance (UXO)

Bon Om Tuk 19

books

  Angkor 27, 28, 158, 167, 168

  cooking 57

  health 353

  history 17, 25, 27, 30, 37

  Khmer Rouge 17, 34, 36, 37

  travel literature 16

border crossings 339-45

  Laos 340-1

  Thailand 341-3

  Vietnam 343-5

Botum Sakor National Park 205

Bou Sraa 316

bridges

  Chruoy Changvar Bridge (Japanese Friendship Bridge) 97

  Spean Ta Ong 274

  Spean Thmor 180-1

Buddha Day 19

Buddhism 51, 96-7

Bunong villages 317

bus travel 345, 347-8

business hours 321-2, *see also inside front cover*

butterflies 136

C

Cambodia Landmine Museum 133

Cambodian Cultural Village 133

Cambodian People's Party (CPP) 39-40, 41-2, 43, 51

Cambodia-Vietnam Friendship Monument 97

car travel 345, 348-50

Cardamom Mountains 200-1, 204, 206, 247-9
caves
  Killing Caves of Phnom Sampeau 256
  Phnom Chhnork 228
  Phnom Da 238
  Phnom Sorsia 229, 78
  Wat Kiri Sela 231
cell phones 333
Central Cardamoms Protected Forest 204, 248
ceramics 133
Cham people 50, 293
Chat Preah Nengkal 19
Chau Say Tevoda 180
Chau Srei Vibol 189
Chaul Chnam Chen 19
Chaul Chnam Khmer 19
checkpoints 324
Cheung Kok 296
Chhep Vulture-Feeding Station 278
Chhlong 301
child labour 115
child prostitution 90
children, travel with 322-3
  food 62
  Phnom Penh 101-2
  Siem Reap 137
Chinese New Year 19
Chinese people 50
Chi Phat 206-9
Choam Ksant 278
Choeung Ek 95-6
Chong Kneas 151-2
Chong Kos 242-3
Christianity 52
Chruoy Changvar Bridge 97
chunchiet 50-1, 305, 309, 310
chunchiet cemeteries 310
cinema 55-6, *see also* films
climate 14, 323
clothing 46, 47, 331
conservation 68, 72, 126, 159, 190, 207, 316
consulates 326
cooking courses 63, 98, 136, 216, 252
corruption 48
costs 14-15, *see also inside front cover*

000 Map pages
000 Photograph pages

courses 323
  cooking 63, 98, 136, 216, 252
  language 252, 323
CPP (Cambodian People's Party) 39-40, 41-2, 43, 51
credit cards 330
crocodiles 205, 257
culture 44-56
currencies 328-9
customs, *see* etiquette
customs regulations 323
cycling 98-9, 206, 225, 300, 312, 320-1, 346-7
cyclos 350

D
damming 71-2
dance 53, 117, 73
dangers 323-6, *see also* land mines, unexploded ordnance (UXO)
  bag snatching 91, 213, 325
  monkeys 96
  Phnom Penh 91
  Siem Reap 131-2
  Sihanoukville 212-13
deep vein thrombosis (DVT) 355
deforestation 70-1
dehydration 359, 360
Dei Ey 317
dengue 356
diarrhoea 359-60
dirt biking 22, 122, 201, 228, 321
disabilities, travellers with 334
diving 99, 198, 206, 215, 321
Documentation Center of Cambodia 94
dolphins 68, 203, 222, 300, 304
drinks 58-60, 362, *see also* beer, wine
  customs 59
driving, *see* car travel
drugs 328
DVT (deep vein thrombosis) 355
dysentery 360

E
Eastern Baray 185-6
Eastern Mebon 185-6
economy 47-9
electricity 226, 320
elephant rides 96, 166, 180, 307, 314, 317
elephants 68, 316, 79
embassies 326
emergencies, *see inside front cover*
environmental issues 70-2, *see also* conservation, *individual entries*

ethnic groups 49-51
etiquette 45-7, 59, 62-3, 313, 330-1
events 19
exchange rates, *see inside front cover*

F
fax services 333
Festival of the Dead 19
festivals 19
films 55-6
  Apocalypse Now 33
  Bophana 56, 94
  Lord Jim 56
  Pos Keng Kong 223
  The Killing Fields 33, 97, 292
  Tomb Raider 167, 172, 176, 182
  Two Brothers 67, 191, 192
floating villages
  Chong Kneas 151-2
  Chong Kos 242-3
  Koh Trong 298
  Kompong Khleang 152
  Kompong Luong 247
  Kompong Pluk 152
  Me Chrey 152
  Phoum Kandal 242-3
Flooded Forest of Kompong Pluk 152
food 57-8
  amoc 57, 61
  cooking courses 63, 98, 136, 216, 252
  customs 62-3
  environmental hazards 360
  for children 62
  internet resources 59, 60
  markets 61
  restaurants 60
  special occasions 60
  spiders 293
  street stalls 60-1
  vegetarian travellers 61-2
  vocabulary 63-5
French Embassy 97
Funcinpec 37-8, 39, 41, 42
fungal infections 356-7

G
gay travellers 327
gem cutting 259
gem mining 305, 310
geography 66
geology 66
giant ibis 277-8
giardiasis 360

gold mines 318
golf 99, 136, 321
gymnasiums 99, 216

H
handicrafts 55
health 353-62
heatstroke 360-1
helicopter travel 166, 346
hepatitis 357
hiking 321
　Angkor 179
　Kampot Province 230
　Kirirom National Park 127
　Koh Kong Province 201, 204, 206
　Kompong Som Province 222
　Mondulkiri Province 314
　Ratanakiri Province 306-7, 311
hill tribes 50-1, 305, 309, 310
Hinduism 51
history 25-43, *see also* Khmer
　Rouge
　Angkor 27-9, 153-6
　books 17, 25, 27, 30, 37
　Chams in Cambodia 27-8
　Chenla period 26
　famine 37
　French rule 29-32
　Funan period 26
　internet resources 29
　Phnom Penh 82-3
　prehistoric period 25
　recent history 42-3
　Thais in Cambodia 29
　UN in Cambodia 38-40
　Vietnam War 30-4
　Vietnamese in Cambodia 29,
　　36-8
　WWII 30
hitching 350
HIV 357
holidays 19, 327
homestays 320
　Angkor 192
　Banteay Chhmar 266
　Chi Phat 207, 208
　Dei Ey 317
　Kirirom National Park 127
　Kompong Cham 295
　Mekong Discovery Trail 300-1
　Ta Seng 274
horse riding 136
hot springs 248
hot-air ballooning 166
Hun Sen 40, 41, 43

I
ibis 277-8
leng Sary 33, 40-1, 258
immigration 49-51, 337
Independence Monument 97
Indravarman I 27, 154, 155
insect bites 361
insurance 327, 349
internet access 327-8
internet resources 16-18, 40
　Angkor 158, 162, 165, 179
　food 59, 60
　history 29
　Khmer Rouge 39, 43
　Phnom Penh 85
intestinal worms 357
Irrawaddy dolphins 68, 203, 300, 304
Islam 52
islands
　Koh Kong 203-4
　Koh Paen 293-4
　Koh Pos 236
　Koh Prins 215
　Koh Rung 215
　Koh Rung Samloem 214-15
　Koh Russei 215
　Koh Sdach 205-6
　Koh Seh 222
　Koh Svai 236
　Koh Ta Kiev 215
　Koh Tang 215
　Koh Thmei 222
　Koh Tonsay 235-6, *79*
　Koh Trong 298
itineraries 20-4
　Angkor 162-4, 179
　Phnom Penh 86

J
Japanese B Encephalitis 357
Japanese Friendship Bridge 97
Jarai cemeteries 310
Jayavarman II 27, 154, 155
Jayavarman IV 155
Jayavarman V 154, 155
Jayavarman VII 28, 155-6
jet lag 355

K
Kachon 309
Kakaoh 286
Kamping Poy (Killing Dam) 258
Kampot 223-8, **224**
Kampot pepper 225
Kampot Province 223-32

Kampuchea 39
Kbal Spean 190
Keo Kinal 284
Kep 232-5, **233**, *8*
Kep National Park 233
Khieu Samphan 41-2, 258, 271
Khmer Ceramics Centre 133
Khmer Krom people 50
Khmer language 363-9
Khmer Leu people 50-1, 305, 309, 310
Khmer New Year 19
Khmer people 49
Khmer Rouge
　books 17, 34, 36, 37
　history 32, 33-42, 213, 290
　in Phnom Penh 82, 94-6
　internet resources 39, 43
　sites 94-6, 244, 268-71
　trials 42-3
kickboxing 49, 99
Kien Svay 123-4
Killing Caves of Phnom Sampeau 256
Killing Dam (Kamping Poy) 258
Killing Fields of Choeung Ek 95-6
kings of Angkor 155, *see also*
　individual monarchs
Kirirom National Park 127
Kirivong 239
Knong Krapeur 204
Koh Kapi 203
Koh Ker 274-5
Koh Kong Conservation Corridor 200-9
Koh Kong Island 203-4
Koh Kong Province 196-209
Koh Kong Safari World 199
Koh Nhek 318
Koh Paen 293-4
Koh Pos 236
Koh Prins 215
Koh Rung 215
Koh Rung Samloem 214-15
Koh Russei 215
Koh Sdach 205-6
Koh Ta Kiev 215
Koh Tang 215
Koh Thmei 222
Koh Tonsay 235-6, *79*
Koh Trong 298
Kompong Cham 292-6, **294**
Kompong Cham Province 292-7
Kompong Chhnang 242-5, **243**
Kompong Chhnang Airport 244
Kompong Chhnang Province 242-5
Kompong Khleang 152
Kompong Luong 247

Kompong Pluk 152
Kompong Som Province 209-23
Kompong Thom 281-3, **283**
Kompong Thom Province 280-7
Kompong Trach 231-2
koupreys 68
kramas 187, 297
Krang Te 317
Kratie 298-300, **298**
Kratie Province 297-301
Kravanh Ranger Station 248
Krong Kep 232-6
Krong Koh Kong 196-200, **197**
Krong Pailin 258-60
Kru Krom grasslands 282
Kulen Promtep Wildlife Sanctuary 278
Kuy peôple 275

L
land mines 38, 70, 269, 326
   museum 133
   warnings 190, 259, 267, 274, 277, 280
language 363-9
   courses 252, 323
   food 63-5
laundry 320
legal matters 328
Les Chantiers Écoles 132-3
lesbian travellers 327
lingas 187
literature 16, 54, *see also* books
logging 70-1
Lolei 188
Lon Nol 32, 33-4
lorry, *see norry*
Lumkut Lake 310-11
Lumphat 311
Luu Meng 61

M
mail services 331
malaria 357-8
maps 159, 328
markets 61
   Phnom Penh 107, 113, 119-20
   Siem Reap 145-6, 148
massage 99-100, 136-7, 216, 253
Me Chrey 152
measures 320, *see also inside front cover*

medical insurance 327
medical services 356, *see also* health
meditation 124-5
Mekong Blue 302
Mekong Discovery Trail 300-1
Mekong River 66, 67, 71-2, 300, 80
metric conversions, *see inside front cover*
Mimong 318
mines, *see* land mines
miniature Angkor replicas 133
mobile phones 333
Moeurk Mee 208
Mondulkiri Protected Forest 317
Mondulkiri Province 312-18
money 14-15, 328-30, *see also inside front cover*
monkeys 96
motion sickness 355
motorcycle travel 221, 345, 348-50, *see also* dirt biking
motos 351
Mouhot, Henri 156
mountain biking, *see* cycling, tours
museums
   Angkor National Museum 132
   Battambang Museum 251
   Cambodia Landmine Museum 133
   Cambodian Cultural Village 133
   National Museum of Cambodia 93-4
   Tuol Sleng Museum 94-5
music 53-4

N
National Library 98
National Museum of Cambodia 93-4
national parks & wildlife reserves 69, 70
   Ang Trapeng Thmor Reserve 151
   Boeng Tonlé Chhmar Wildlife Sanctuary 282
   Bokor National Park 229-31
   Botum Sakor National Park 205
   Central Cardamoms Protected Forest 204, 248
   Kep National Park 233
   Kirirom National Park 127
   Kulen Promtep Wildlife Sanctuary 278
   Mondulkiri Protected Forest 317
   Peam Krasaop Wildlife Sanctuary 202-3
   Phnom Aural Wildlife Sanctuary 248
   Phnom Samkos Wildlife Sanctuary 248-9

Phnom Tamao Wildlife Rescue Centre 126
   Preah Vihear Protected Forest 278
   Prek Toal Bird Sanctuary 151
   Ream National Park 222
   Seima Protection Forest 317-18
   Southern Cardamoms Protected Forest 206
   Virachey National Park 304, 311
Neak Luong 291-2
newspapers 51, 320
Nhiem Chun 183
nongovernmental organisations (NGOs)
   environmental groups 68
   restaurants 60, 107, 144
   shops 118, 148
Norodom I 29-30
Norodom Ranariddh 40
Norodom Sihanouk 30-3, 37-8, 56
norry 231, 246, 252, 350-1, 8
Northern Cardamom Mountains 247-9
Nuon Chea 41-2

O
O Smach 267-8
Oddar Meanchey Province 266-72
Old French Lighthouse 294
Olympic Stadium 97
Ondong Rossey 243-4
orphanages 192, 336
O'Svay 304
outboards 351
ox-cart rides 351

P
Pailin 258-60, **259**
painting 55
pangolins 204
passports 337
P'chum Ben 19
Peam Krasaop Wildlife Sanctuary 202-3
pepper 225
Pheam Ek 257
Phimeanakas 177
Phnom Aural Wildlife Sanctuary 248
Phnom Bakheng 179-80, **180**
Phnom Banan 256-7
Phnom Bayong 239
Phnom Bok 188
Phnom Chhnork 228-9
Phnom Chisor 126-7
Phnom Da 238-9
Phnom Krom 188

000 Map pages
000 Photograph pages

Phnom Kulen 190-1
Phnom Penh 81-123, **84-5**, **87**
  accommodation 102-6
  activities 98-100
  banks 89-90
  dangers 91
  drinking 114-16
  emergency services 85
  entertainment 116-17
  food 106-14
  for children 101-2
  history 82-3
  internet access 85-6
  itineraries 86
  Khmer Rouge sites 94-6
  medical services 86-9
  shopping 117-20
  sights 92-8
  tourist information 91
  tours 102
  travel to/from 120-1
  travel within 121-3
  walking tour 100-1, **101**
Phnom Pros 296
Phnom Samkos Wildlife Sanctuary
  248-9
Phnom Sampeau 256
Phnom Santuk (Kompong Chhnang)
  244
Phnom Santuk (Kompong Thom) 286
Phnom Sombok 301
Phnom Sorsia 229, 78
Phnom Srei 296
Phnom Tamao Wildlife Rescue Centre
  126
phone cards 333
photography 330-1
Phoum Kandal 242-3
pick-up trucks 352
planning 14-18, see also itineraries
plants 68-9
Poipet 261-3
Pol Pot 33, 34-5, 36, 41, 269, 270-1
pollution 71
population 49
postal services 331
pradal serey 49, 99
Prasat Andet 287
Prasat Krau Romeas 191
Prasat Kravan 182-3
Prasat Kuha Nokor 287
Prasat Preah Vihear 279-80, 281, **279**
Prasat Rong Chen 191
Prasat Suor Prat 178
Prayuvong Buddha factories 98

Pre Rup 186
Preah Khan (Angkor) 184-5, **184**, 75
Preah Khan (Preah Vihear) 272-4, **273**
Preah Ko 187
Preah Neak Poan 185
Preah Palilay 177
Preah Pithu 177
Preah Vihear Protected Forest 278
Preah Vihear Province 272-80
pregnant travellers 362
Prek Toal Bird Sanctuary 151
Prey Chung Kran 296-7
Prey Veng 291
Prey Veng Province 291-2
prickly heat 361
public holidays 327
Pursat 245-7, **246**
Pursat Province 245-9

Q
quad biking 100, 137

R
radio 320
Rajendravarman II 154, 155
Ranariddh, Norodom 40
Ratanakiri Province 305-11
Ream National Park 222
religion 51-2, see also individual religions
remork-kangs 351
remork-motos 351
reptiles 67-8
responsible travel 15-16, 72, 313, 338,
  see also GreenDex
road distances 348
road safety 325-6
rock climbing 231, 321
Roluos Temples 187-8
rotei ses 351
Rovieng Ranger Station 248
royal ballet 53
Royal Enclosure 177
Royal Palace 92-3, 7
Royal Ploughing Ceremony 19
rubber plantations 297

S
safety, see dangers
Sam Rainsy Party 41, 42, 43
Sambor 301
Sambor Prei Kuk 284-6, **285**
Samlaut 260
Samraong 266-7
sand extraction 72
Santuk Silk Farm 286-7

scams 220, 262, 324, 342
schistosomiasis 358
sculpture 54-5, 331-2
Seima Protection Forest 317-18
Sen Monorom 312-16, **314**
sexually transmitted infections (STIs)
  358-9
shadow puppets 117, 133, 77
share taxis 352
shooting ranges 98
shopping 331-2
Siem Pang 304-5
Siem Reap 128-50, **130**, **134**
  accommodation 137-42
  activities 136-7
  banks 131
  dangers 131-2
  drinking 146-7
  emergency services 129
  entertainment 147
  food 142-6
  for children 137
  history 129
  medical services 131
  shopping 147-9
  sights 132-6
  tourist information 131
  tours 137
  travel to/from 149-50
  travel within 150
Sihamoni, King 43
Sihanouk, Norodom 30-3, 37-8, 56
Sihanoukville 209-22, **210**
  accommodation 216-18
  activities 213-16
  banks 212
  beaches 213-14
  dangers 212-13
  drinking 219-20
  entertainment 220
  food 218-19
  medical services 212
  shopping 220
  sights 213-16
  tourist information 212
  travel to/from 220-1
  travel within 221-2
silk 133, 286-7, 296-7, 302, 332
silver 332
Silver Pagoda 92-3
Sisophon 263-5, **264**
Skuon 293
snake bites 361
snakes 67-8, 325
SNC (Supreme National Council) 39

Sneng 258
snorkelling 198, 206, 215, 222, 321
Snuol 301
Southern Cardamoms Protected Forest 206
Spean Thmor 180-1
spiders 293
sports 49
Sra Damrei 191
Sra Srang 182
STIs (sexually transmitted infections) 358-9
Stoeng Chikrieng grasslands 282
Stung Treng 302-4, **303**
Stung Treng Province 301-5
sunburn 362
Supreme National Council (SNC) 39
Suryavarman I 27, 154-5
Suryavarman II 27-8, 155
sustainable travel 15-16, 72, 313, 338, see also GreenDex
Svay Rieng 291
Svay Rieng Province 290-1
swimming pools 100, 102, 137, 186, 252

T
Ta Keo 181
Ta Mok 35, 41, 237, 268-70, 271
Ta Nei 181
Ta Prohm (Angkor) 181-2, **182**, 6, 74
Ta Prohm (Tonlé Bati) 125
Ta Som 185
Ta Veng 310
Takeo 236-8, **237**
Takeo Province 236-9
tarantulas 293
taxis 352
Tbeng Meanchey 276-7, **276**
Te Teuk Pus 248
telephone services 332-3
temples 17, see also Angkor, wats
  Angkor Thom 172-8, **173**
  Angkor Wat 167-72, **169**, **170**, 74
  Ba Phnom 292
  Bakong 187-8
  Baksei Chamkrong 179
  Banteay Chhmar 265-6
  Banteay Kdei 182
  Banteay Samré 186
  Banteay Srei 189

Banteay Top 266
Baphuon 176-7
Bayon 172-6, **174**, 5
Beng Mealea 191-3, **192**, 75
Chau Say Tevoda 180
Chau Srei Vibol 189
Eastern Mebon 185-6
itineraries 22
Kbal Spean 190
Koh Ker 274-5
Lolei 188
Phimeanakas 177
Phnom Bakheng 179-80, **180**
Phnom Banan 256-7
Phnom Bayong 239
Phnom Bok 188
Phnom Chhnork 228-9
Phnom Chisor 126-7
Phnom Krom 188
Phnom Sampeau 256
Phnom Santuk 286
Phnom Sombok 301
Phnom Sorsia 229, 78
Prasat Andet 287
Prasat Krau Romeas 191
Prasat Kravan 182-3
Prasat Kuha Nokor 287
Prasat Preah Vihear 279-80, 281, **279**
Prasat Rong Chen 191
Prasat Suor Prat 178
Prasat Yeay Ten 258
Pre Rup 186
Preah Khan (Angkor) 184-5, **184**, 75
Preah Khan (Preah Vihear) 272-4, **273**
Preah Ko 187
Preah Neak Poan 185
Preah Palilay 177
Preah Pithu 177
Roluos 187-8
Sambor Prei Kuk 284-6, **285**
Silver Pagoda 92-3
Ta Keo 181
Ta Nei 181
Ta Prohm (Angkor) 181-2, **182**, 6, 74
Ta Prohm (Tonlé Bati) 125
Ta Som 185
Tep Pranam 177
Thala Boravit 302
Thommanon 180
Western Mebon 186
Yeay Peau 125

Tep Pranam 177
Terrace of Elephants 178
Terrace of the Leper King 177-8
Thala Boravit 302
theft 325, see also bag snatching
Thommanon 180
tigers 69
time 333
tipping 330
Tmatboey Ibis Project 277-8
toilets 333-4
Tomb Raider 167, 172, 176, 182
Tompuon cemeteries 309
Tonlé Bati 125-6
Tonlé Sap Lake 66, 67, 152, 78
Tonlé Sap River 19, 66, 67
tourist information 334, see also individual locations
tours 345-6
  Angkor 165
  birdwatching 151, 206, 278, 317
  cycling 206, 225, 300, 312
  Koh Kong Conservation Corridor 201
  Mondulkiri Province 314
  Phnom Penh 102
  Ratanakiri Province 307
traditional medicine 356
traffic accidents 325-6
trains 352, see also bamboo train (norry)
Trapaeng Rung 204
travel to/from Cambodia 337-46
travel within Cambodia 346-52
travellers cheques 330
trekking, see hiking
tuk tuks, see remork-motos
Tuol Sleng Museum 94-5
TV 51, 320
typhoid 359

U
Udayadityavarman II 155
Udong 124-5
unexploded ordnance (UXO) 326, see also land mines
UN Transitional Authority in Cambodia (Untac) 39-40
United Nations (UN) 38-40
Upper Khmer people, see Khmer Leu people

V
vacations 19, 327
vaccinations 353, 354
Vann Nath 95

INDEX

vegetarian travellers 61-2
video 330
Vietnamese people 49
Vietnam War 30-4, 213, 290
Virachey National Park 304, 311
Visakha Puja 19
visas 334-5, *see also* passports
Voen Sai 309-10
volunteering 192, 253, 258, 335
vultures 278, 304

W
walking, *see* hiking
Wat Kor Village 257
water 59, 362
Water Festival 19
waterfalls
    Bei Srok 311
    Bou Sraa Waterfall 316
    Chaa Ong 309
    Dak Dam Waterfall 317
    Ka Tieng 309
    Kbal Chhay Cascades 223
    Kinchaan 309
    Kirirom National Park 127
    Kirivong Waterfall 239
    Koh Por 202
    Phnom Kulen 190-1

Romanear II 317
Romanear Waterfall 316-17
Stung Phong Roul 209
Tatai Waterfall 202
Tek Chhouu 228
wats
    Sambor 301
    Wat Asram Moha Russei 239
    Wat Athvea 132
    Wat Bo 132
    Wat Dam Nak 132
    Wat Ek Phnom 257
    Wat Hanchey 297
    Wat Kiri Sela 231
    Wat Leu 215
    Wat Maha Leap 296
    Wat Moha Montrei 97
    Wat Nokor 293
    Wat Ounalom 96-7
    Wat Phnom 96
    Wat Preah Inkosei 132
    Wat Preah Keo 92-3
    Wat Roka Kandal 299
    Wat Sampeau Bram Roi 230
    Wat Thmei 132
weather 14, 323
websites, *see* internet resources
weights 320, *see also inside front cover*

Western Baray 186
Western Mebon 186
wildlife conservation 68, 126, 190,
    207, 316
wildlife reserves, *see* national parks &
    wildlife reserves
wine 257
women in Cambodia 52-3
women travellers 336
women's health 362
woodcarving 332
work 336, *see also* volunteering
worms, intestinal 357
WWII 30

Y
Yasovarman I 154, 155
Yeak Lom Protected Area 306
Year Zero 34
Yeay Peau 125
yoga 137

Z
zoos & animal sanctuaries
    Koh Kong Safari World 199
    Phnom Tamao Wildlife Rescue
        Centre 126
    Tek Chhouu Zoo 228

GreenDex

It's not only ecotourism that is starting to take off in Cambodia, but also community-based tourism in remote areas and a whole host of restaurants and shops dedicated to helping the disadvantaged or disabled. The following attractions, tours and properties have all been selected by Lonely Planet authors because they demonstrate an active sustainable-tourism policy; some are involved in conservation or environmental protection, others in training and development for the disadvantaged, and some to raise funds to support social projects in healthcare or education.

We want to keep developing our sustainable-tourism content. If you think we've omitted someone who should be listed here, or if you disagree with our choices, email us at talk2us@lonelyplanet.com.au and set us straight for next time. For more information about sustainable tourism and Lonely Planet, see www.lonelyplanet.com/responsibletravel.

EASTERN CAMBODIA

accommodation
Cambodian Rural Development Team 301
Elephant Valley Project 316
Mekong Bird Lodge 303
Tonlé Tourism Training Centre 302
Yaklom Hill Lodge 308

activities
dolphin-watching near Kratie 300
Mekong Discovery Trail 300

attractions
Boeng Yeak Lom 306
Bunong Villages 317
Cheung Kok 296
Elephant Valley Project 316
Mekong Blue 302
Mekong Discovery Trail 300
Mondulkiri Protected Forest 317
O'Svay & Anlong Seima 304
Seima Protection Forest 317
Virachey National Park 311

information
Mlup Baitong 302
WWF 312

shopping
Mekong Blue 302
Middle of Somewhere 312

tours
Middle of Somewhere 312
Mlup Baitong 302
Tompuon Guides 307
WWF 312

volunteering
Cambodian Rural Development Team 301
Elephant Valley Project 316

NORTHWESTERN CAMBODIA

accommodation
Banteay Chhmar Homestay Project 266

activities
Seeing Hands Massage 253

attractions
Banteay Chhmar Protected Landscape 266
Boeng Tonlé Chhmar Wildlife Sanctuary 282
Central Cardamoms Protected Forest 248
Chhep Vulture-Feeding Station 278
École d'Art et de Culture Khmers 264
Khmer Heritage Houses 257
Kravanh Ranger Station 248
Kru Krom Grasslands 282
Northern Cardamom Mountains 247
Ondong Rossey 243
Phare Ponleu Selpak 255
Phneat Koh Pong Sat Community Fisheries 264
Phnom Aural Wildlife Sanctuary 248
Phnom Samkos Wildlife Sanctuary 248
Preah Vihear Protected Forest 278
Rovieng Ranger Station 248
Samlaut Multiple Use Area 260
Santuk Silk Farm 286
Soieries du Mékong 266
Stoeng Chikrieng grasslands 282
Thmor Pourng Angkam 277
Tmatboey Ibis Project 277
Weaves of Cambodia 276

eating & drinking
Community Villa 246
Fresh Eats Café 254

information
Banteay Chhmar Community-Based Tourism Office 266
Maddox Jolie-Pitt Foundation 260

shopping
Fresh Eats Café 255
Isanborei Crafts Shop 285
Pottery Development Center 243
Rachana Handicrafts 255
Santuk Silk Farm 286
Soieries du Mékong 266
Weaves of Cambodia 276

volunteering
Cambodian Education Center 258
Khmer New Generation Organization 253

PHNOM PENH & AROUND

accommodation
Cambodia Vipassana Dhura Buddhist Meditation Centre 124
Quay 106

activities
Cambodia Vipassana Dhura Buddhist Meditation Centre 124
Nail Bar 99
Seeing Hands Massage 99

attractions
Apsara Arts Association 117
Chambok Community-Based Ecotourism 127
Kirirom National Park 127
Phnom Tamao Wildlife Rescue Centre 126
Sovanna Phum Arts Association 117

ating & drinking
Café Yejj 107
Ebony Apsara Café 107
Friends 107
Hagar 107
Lazy Gecko Café 107
Le Lotus Blanc 107
Le Rit's 107
Romdeng 107
Veijo Tonle 107

nformation
Cambodia Community-Based
Ecotourism Network 91
ChildSafe 91

hopping
Aw-kun Shop 118
Cambodian Handicraft
Association 118
Colours of Cambodia 118
Friends & Stuff 118
Java Café 118
Mekong Blue 118
Mekong Quilts 118
Meta House 118
NCDP Handicrafts 118
Nyemo 118
Rajana 118
Reyum 119
Sobbhana 118
Tabitha 118
Villageworks 118
Wat Than Artisans 118

ours
Cambodia Community-Based
Ecotourism Network 91

ansport
Cyclo Centre 123

oluntering
Free the Bears 126

**IEM REAP &
TEMPLES OF ANGKOR**
ccommodation
Paul Dubrule Hotel & Tourism
School 140
Sala Bai Hotel & Restaurant
School 138
Seven Candles Guesthouse
139
Shinta Mani 141
Soria Moria Hotel 140

ctivities
Khmer Ceramics Centre 133
Krousar Thmey Massage 136
Raja Yoga 137

Sanctuary Spa 137
Seeing Hands Massage 4 136

attractions
Ang Trapeng Thmor Reserve 151
Angkor Butterfly Centre 136
Cambodia Landmine Museum 133
Gecko Centre 152
Khmer Ceramics Centre 133
Les Chantiers Écoles 132
Prek Toal Bird Sanctuary 151

courses
Le Tigre de Papier 136

eating & drinking
Bakong Tea Garden 188
Butterflies Garden Restaurant 144
Common Grounds 144
Joe-to-Go 145
Le Café 145
Les Jardins des Delices 144
n.y.d.c. 145
Sala Bai Hotel & Restaurant
School 144
Singing Tree Café 144

entertainment
Acodo Orphanage 147
Beatocello 147

information
Angkor Centre for Conservation of
Biodiversity 190
German Apsara Conservation
Project 167

shopping
Artisans d'Angkor 148
Bloom 148
Hagar Design 148
IKTT 148
Krousar Thmey 148
Nyemo 148
Prolung Khmer 187
Rajana 148
Rehab Craft 148
Samatoa 149
Senteurs d'Angkor 148
Tabitha Cambodia 148

tours
Sam Veasna Center 151
Osmose 151

transport
White Bicycles 165

volunteering
ConCERT 131
Globalteer 335
Harmony Farm 192

SOUTH COAST
accommodation
Four Rivers Floating Ecolodge 202
Jasmine Valley 234
Jonty's Jungle Camp 215
Preah Monivong 'Bokor' National
Park Training & Research
Facility 230
Rainbow Lodge 202
Thma Bang Ranger Station 204
Vine Retreat 234

activities
Kampot Massage by the Blind 225
mangrove walk (Peam Krasaop
Wildlife Sanctuary) 202
Seeing Hands Massage 3 216
Starfish Bakery & Café Massage
216
trekking (Bokor National Park)
230

attractions
Areng Valley 204
Bokor National Park 229
Botum Sakor National Park 205
Central Cardamoms Protected
Forest 204
Chi Phat Community-Based
Ecotourism Project 206
Kep National Park 233
Koh Kong Conservation Corridor
200
Koh Kong Island 203
Peam Krasaop Wildlife
Sanctuary 202
Phnom Chhnork 228
Phnom Sorsia 229
Ream National Park 222
Southern Cardamoms Protected
Forest 206
Trapaeng Rung 204
Wat Kiri Sela 231

eating & drinking
Epic Arts Café 227
Gelato Italiano 220

information
Marine Conservation Cambodia
215

shopping
Kampot Pepper 225

tours
Blue Marlin 201
Blue Moon Guesthouse 201
Jungle Cross 201
Koh Kong Eco Tours 201
Neptune Guesthouse 201

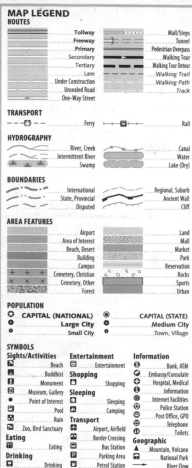

MAP LEGEND

ROUTES

- Tollway
- Freeway
- Primary
- Secondary
- Tertiary
- Lane
- Under Construction
- Unsealed Road
- One-Way Street
- Mall/Steps
- Tunnel
- Pedestrian Overpass
- Walking Tour
- Walking Tour Detour
- Walking Trail
- Walking Path
- Track

TRANSPORT

- Ferry
- Rail

HYDROGRAPHY

- River, Creek
- Intermittent River
- Swamp
- Canal
- Water
- Lake (Dry)

BOUNDARIES

- International
- State, Provincial
- Disputed
- Regional, Suburb
- Ancient Wall
- Cliff

AREA FEATURES

- Airport
- Area of Interest
- Beach, Desert
- Building
- Campus
- Cemetery, Christian
- Cemetery, Other
- Forest
- Land
- Mall
- Market
- Park
- Reservation
- Rocks
- Sports
- Urban

POPULATION

- CAPITAL (NATIONAL)
- Large City
- Small City
- CAPITAL (STATE)
- Medium City
- Town, Village

SYMBOLS

Sights/Activities
- Beach
- Buddhist
- Monument
- Museum, Gallery
- Point of Interest
- Pool
- Ruin
- Zoo, Bird Sanctuary

Eating
- Eating

Drinking
- Drinking
- Café

Entertainment
- Entertainment

Shopping
- Shopping

Sleeping
- Sleeping
- Camping

Transport
- Airport, Airfield
- Border Crossing
- Bus Station
- Parking Area
- Petrol Station
- Taxi Rank

Information
- Bank, ATM
- Embassy/Consulate
- Hospital, Medical
- Information
- Internet Facilities
- Police Station
- Post Office, GPO
- Telephone
- Toilets

Geographic
- Mountain, Volcano
- National Park
- River Flow
- Waterfall

LONELY PLANET OFFICES

Australia (Head Office)
Locked Bag 1, Footscray, Victoria 3011
☎ 03 8379 8000, fax 03 8379 8111
talk2us@lonelyplanet.com.au

USA
150 Linden St, Oakland, CA 94607
☎ 510 250 6400, toll free 800 275 8555
fax 510.893 8572
info@lonelyplanet.com

UK
2nd fl, 186 City Rd,
London EC1V 2NT
☎ 020 7106 2100, fax 020 7106 2101
go@lonelyplanet.co.uk

Published by Lonely Planet
ABN 36 005 607 983

© Lonely Planet 2010

© photographers as indicated 2010

Cover photograph: Smiling face of Avalokiteshvara, Bayon, Frank Carter/Lonely Planet Images. Many of the images in this guide are available for licensing from Lonely Planet Images: lonelyplanetimages.com.

Printed by Toppan Security Printing Pte. Ltd.
Printed in Singapore

Mixed Sources
Product group from well-managed forests and other controlled sources
www.fsc.org Cert no. SGS-COC-005002
© 1996 Forest Stewardship Council
FSC